T0235385

Lecture Notes in Computer Science 12184

More information about this series at http://www.springer.com/series/7409

Sakae Yamamoto · Hirohiko Mori (Eds.)

Human Interface and the Management of Information

Designing Information

Thematic Area, HIMI 2020
Held as Part of the 22nd International Conference, HCII 2020
Copenhagen, Denmark, July 19–24, 2020
Proceedings, Part I

 Springer

Editors
Sakae Yamamoto
Tokyo University of Science
Tokyo, Japan

Hirohiko Mori
Tokyo City University
Tokyo, Japan

ISSN 0302-9743 ISSN 1611-3349 (electronic)
Lecture Notes in Computer Science
ISBN 978-3-030-50019-1 ISBN 978-3-030-50020-7 (eBook)
https://doi.org/10.1007/978-3-030-50020-7

LNCS Sublibrary: SL3 – Information Systems and Applications, incl. Internet/Web, and HCI

This Springer imprint is published by the registered company Springer Nature Switzerland AG
The registered company address is: Gewerbestrasse 11, 6330 Cham, Switzerland

Foreword

The 22nd International Conference on Human-Computer Interaction, HCI International 2020 (HCII 2020), was planned to be held at the AC Bella Sky Hotel and Bella Center, Copenhagen, Denmark, during July 19–24, 2020. Due to the COVID-19 coronavirus pandemic and the resolution of the Danish government not to allow events larger than 500 people to be hosted until September 1, 2020, HCII 2020 had to be held virtually. It incorporated the 21 thematic areas and affiliated conferences listed on the following page.

A total of 6,326 individuals from academia, research institutes, industry, and governmental agencies from 97 countries submitted contributions, and 1,439 papers and 238 posters were included in the conference proceedings. These contributions address the latest research and development efforts and highlight the human aspects of design and use of computing systems. The contributions thoroughly cover the entire field of human-computer interaction, addressing major advances in knowledge and effective use of computers in a variety of application areas. The volumes constituting the full set of the conference proceedings are listed in the following pages.

The HCI International (HCII) conference also offers the option of "late-breaking work" which applies both for papers and posters and the corresponding volume(s) of the proceedings will be published just after the conference. Full papers will be included in the "HCII 2020 - Late Breaking Papers" volume of the proceedings to be published in the Springer LNCS series, while poster extended abstracts will be included as short papers in the "HCII 2020 - Late Breaking Posters" volume to be published in the Springer CCIS series.

I would like to thank the program board chairs and the members of the program boards of all thematic areas and affiliated conferences for their contribution to the highest scientific quality and the overall success of the HCI International 2020 conference.

This conference would not have been possible without the continuous and unwavering support and advice of the founder, Conference General Chair Emeritus and Conference Scientific Advisor Prof. Gavriel Salvendy. For his outstanding efforts, I would like to express my appreciation to the communications chair and editor of HCI International News, Dr. Abbas Moallem.

July 2020   Constantine Stephanidis

HCI International 2020 Thematic Areas and Affiliated Conferences

Thematic areas:

- HCI 2020: Human-Computer Interaction
- HIMI 2020: Human Interface and the Management of Information

Affiliated conferences:

- EPCE: 17th International Conference on Engineering Psychology and Cognitive Ergonomics
- UAHCI: 14th International Conference on Universal Access in Human-Computer Interaction
- VAMR: 12th International Conference on Virtual, Augmented and Mixed Reality
- CCD: 12th International Conference on Cross-Cultural Design
- SCSM: 12th International Conference on Social Computing and Social Media
- AC: 14th International Conference on Augmented Cognition
- DHM: 11th International Conference on Digital Human Modeling and Applications in Health, Safety, Ergonomics and Risk Management
- DUXU: 9th International Conference on Design, User Experience and Usability
- DAPI: 8th International Conference on Distributed, Ambient and Pervasive Interactions
- HCIBGO: 7th International Conference on HCI in Business, Government and Organizations
- LCT: 7th International Conference on Learning and Collaboration Technologies
- ITAP: 6th International Conference on Human Aspects of IT for the Aged Population
- HCI-CPT: Second International Conference on HCI for Cybersecurity, Privacy and Trust
- HCI-Games: Second International Conference on HCI in Games
- MobiTAS: Second International Conference on HCI in Mobility, Transport and Automotive Systems
- AIS: Second International Conference on Adaptive Instructional Systems
- C&C: 8th International Conference on Culture and Computing
- MOBILE: First International Conference on Design, Operation and Evaluation of Mobile Communications
- AI-HCI: First International Conference on Artificial Intelligence in HCI

Conference Proceedings Volumes Full List

1. LNCS 12181, Human-Computer Interaction: Design and User Experience (Part I), edited by Masaaki Kurosu
2. LNCS 12182, Human-Computer Interaction: Multimodal and Natural Interaction (Part II), edited by Masaaki Kurosu
3. LNCS 12183, Human-Computer Interaction: Human Values and Quality of Life (Part III), edited by Masaaki Kurosu
4. LNCS 12184, Human Interface and the Management of Information: Designing Information (Part I), edited by Sakae Yamamoto and Hirohiko Mori
5. LNCS 12185, Human Interface and the Management of Information: Interacting with Information (Part II), edited by Sakae Yamamoto and Hirohiko Mori
6. LNAI 12186, Engineering Psychology and Cognitive Ergonomics: Mental Workload, Human Physiology, and Human Energy (Part I), edited by Don Harris and Wen-Chin Li
7. LNAI 12187, Engineering Psychology and Cognitive Ergonomics: Cognition and Design (Part II), edited by Don Harris and Wen-Chin Li
8. LNCS 12188, Universal Access in Human-Computer Interaction: Design Approaches and Supporting Technologies (Part I), edited by Margherita Antona and Constantine Stephanidis
9. LNCS 12189, Universal Access in Human-Computer Interaction: Applications and Practice (Part II), edited by Margherita Antona and Constantine Stephanidis
10. LNCS 12190, Virtual, Augmented and Mixed Reality: Design and Interaction (Part I), edited by Jessie Y. C. Chen and Gino Fragomeni
11. LNCS 12191, Virtual, Augmented and Mixed Reality: Industrial and Everyday Life Applications (Part II), edited by Jessie Y. C. Chen and Gino Fragomeni
12. LNCS 12192, Cross-Cultural Design: User Experience of Products, Services, and Intelligent Environments (Part I), edited by P. L. Patrick Rau
13. LNCS 12193, Cross-Cultural Design: Applications in Health, Learning, Communication, and Creativity (Part II), edited by P. L. Patrick Rau
14. LNCS 12194, Social Computing and Social Media: Design, Ethics, User Behavior, and Social Network Analysis (Part I), edited by Gabriele Meiselwitz
15. LNCS 12195, Social Computing and Social Media: Participation, User Experience, Consumer Experience, and Applications of Social Computing (Part II), edited by Gabriele Meiselwitz
16. LNAI 12196, Augmented Cognition: Theoretical and Technological Approaches (Part I), edited by Dylan D. Schmorrow and Cali M. Fidopiastis
17. LNAI 12197, Augmented Cognition: Human Cognition and Behaviour (Part II), edited by Dylan D. Schmorrow and Cali M. Fidopiastis

18. LNCS 12198, Digital Human Modeling and Applications in Health, Safety, Ergonomics and Risk Management: Posture, Motion and Health (Part I), edited by Vincent G. Duffy
19. LNCS 12199, Digital Human Modeling and Applications in Health, Safety, Ergonomics and Risk Management: Human Communication, Organization and Work (Part II), edited by Vincent G. Duffy
20. LNCS 12200, Design, User Experience, and Usability: Interaction Design (Part I), edited by Aaron Marcus and Elizabeth Rosenzweig
21. LNCS 12201, Design, User Experience, and Usability: Design for Contemporary Interactive Environments (Part II), edited by Aaron Marcus and Elizabeth Rosenzweig
22. LNCS 12202, Design, User Experience, and Usability: Case Studies in Public and Personal Interactive Systems (Part III), edited by Aaron Marcus and Elizabeth Rosenzweig
23. LNCS 12203, Distributed, Ambient and Pervasive Interactions, edited by Norbert Streitz and Shin'ichi Konomi
24. LNCS 12204, HCI in Business, Government and Organizations, edited by Fiona Fui-Hoon Nah and Keng Siau
25. LNCS 12205, Learning and Collaboration Technologies: Designing, Developing and Deploying Learning Experiences (Part I), edited by Panayiotis Zaphiris and Andri Ioannou
26. LNCS 12206, Learning and Collaboration Technologies: Human and Technology Ecosystems (Part II), edited by Panayiotis Zaphiris and Andri Ioannou
27. LNCS 12207, Human Aspects of IT for the Aged Population: Technologies, Design and User Experience (Part I), edited by Qin Gao and Jia Zhou
28. LNCS 12208, Human Aspects of IT for the Aged Population: Healthy and Active Aging (Part II), edited by Qin Gao and Jia Zhou
29. LNCS 12209, Human Aspects of IT for the Aged Population: Technology and Society (Part III), edited by Qin Gao and Jia Zhou
30. LNCS 12210, HCI for Cybersecurity, Privacy and Trust, edited by Abbas Moallem
31. LNCS 12211, HCI in Games, edited by Xiaowen Fang
32. LNCS 12212, HCI in Mobility, Transport and Automotive Systems: Automated Driving and In-Vehicle Experience Design (Part I), edited by Heidi Krömker
33. LNCS 12213, HCI in Mobility, Transport and Automotive Systems: Driving Behavior, Urban and Smart Mobility (Part II), edited by Heidi Krömker
34. LNCS 12214, Adaptive Instructional Systems, edited by Robert A. Sottilare and Jessica Schwarz
35. LNCS 12215, Culture and Computing, edited by Matthias Rauterberg
36. LNCS 12216, Design, Operation and Evaluation of Mobile Communications, edited by Gavriel Salvendy and June Wei
37. LNCS 12217, Artificial Intelligence in HCI, edited by Helmut Degen and Lauren Reinerman-Jones

38. CCIS 1224, HCI International 2020 Posters - Part I, edited by Constantine Stephanidis and Margherita Antona
39. CCIS 1225, HCI International 2020 Posters - Part II, edited by Constantine Stephanidis and Margherita Antona
40. CCIS 1226, HCI International 2020 Posters - Part III, edited by Constantine Stephanidis and Margherita Antona

http://2020.hci.international/proceedings

Human Interface and the Management of Information Thematic Area (HIMI 2020)

Program Board Chairs: **Sakae Yamamoto, Tokyo University of Science, Japan, and Hirohiko Mori, Tokyo City University, Japan**

- Yumi Asahi, Japan
- Shin'ichi Fukuzumi, Japan
- Michitaka Hirose, Japan
- Yen-Yu Kang, Taiwan
- Keiko Kasamatsu, Japan
- Daiji Kobayashi, Japan
- Kentaro Kotani, Japan
- Hiroyuki Miki, Japan
- Ryosuke Saga, Japan
- Katsunori Shimohara, Japan
- Takahito Tomoto, Japan
- Kim-Phuong Vu, USA
- Marcelo M. Wanderley, Canada
- Tomio Watanabe, Japan
- Takehiko Yamaguchi, Japan

The full list with the Program Board Chairs and the members of the Program Boards of all thematic areas and affiliated conferences is available online at:

http://www.hci.international/board-members-2020.php

HCI International 2021

The 23rd International Conference on Human-Computer Interaction, HCI International 2021 (HCII 2021), will be held jointly with the affiliated conferences in Washington DC, USA, at the Washington Hilton Hotel, July 24–29, 2021. It will cover a broad spectrum of themes related to Human-Computer Interaction (HCI), including theoretical issues, methods, tools, processes, and case studies in HCI design, as well as novel interaction techniques, interfaces, and applications. The proceedings will be published by Springer. More information will be available on the conference website: http://2021.hci.international/.

General Chair
Prof. Constantine Stephanidis
University of Crete and ICS-FORTH
Heraklion, Crete, Greece
Email: general_chair@hcii2021.org

http://2021.hci.international/

Contents – Part I

Information Presentation and Visualization

Rethinking the Usage and Experience of Clustering in Web Mapping 3
  Loïc Fürhoff

Environmental Control Units for Inpatient Care at Veterans Affairs Spinal
Cord Injury Centers: Heuristic Evaluation and Design Recommendations 23
  Gabriella M. Hancock, Sam Anvari, Matthew T. Nare, Nicole B. Mok,
  Aram Ayvazyan, Kelsey M. McCoy, Xiaolu Bai, Gregory P. Mather,
  Amanda S. McBride, and Natalia Morales

A Generalized User Interface Concept to Enable Retrospective System
Analysis in Monitoring Systems 39
  Viviane Herdel, Bertram Wortelen, Mathias Lanezki,
  and Andreas Lüdtke

Utilizing Geographical Maps for Social Visualization to Foster Awareness
in Online Communities of Practice 58
  Markus Jelonek

SeeMe2BPMN: Extending the Socio-Technical Walkthrough with BPMN . . . 72
  Ufuk Kacmaz, Thomas Herrmann, and Markus Jelonek

Designing a Dashboard Visualization Tool for Urban Planners to Assess
the Completeness of Streets 85
  Greice C. Mariano, Veda Adnani, Iman Kewalramani, Bo Wang,
  Matthew J. Roorda, Jeremy Bowes, and Sara Diamond

Exploring Ontology-Based Information Through the Progressive Disclosure
of Visual Answers to Related Queries 104
  Dalai S. Ribeiro, Alysson Gomes de Sousa, Rodrigo B. de Almeida,
  Pedro Henrique Thompson Furtado, Hélio Côrtes Vieira Lopes,
  and Simone Diniz Junqueira Barbosa

A Template for Data-Driven Personas: Analyzing 31 Quantitatively
Oriented Persona Profiles 125
  Joni Salminen, Kathleen Guan, Lene Nielsen, Soon-gyo Jung,
  and Bernard J. Jansen

Does Visualization of Health Data Using an Accelerometer Be Associated
with Promoting Exercise Among Elderly People?   145
    Yurika Shiozu, Shoki Muramatsu, Ryo Shioya, Katsuhiko Yonezaki,
    Mizuki Tanaka, and Katsunori Shimohara

A Visualization Tool for the CIRMMT Distinguished Lecture Series   156
    Marcelo M. Wanderley, Mathias Bredholt, and Christian Frisson

Gender Difference in Preference for Apple Watch Dial Interface   170
    Jian Wang and Yen Hsu

A Detailed Examination of User Interactions with Two Different
Data Interfaces   183
    Rui Wang and Tamara Babaian

Service Design and Management

Feature Analysis of Customers Purchasing Cars in Japan   201
    Kenta Hara and Yumi Asahi

Waiting Time Analysis at University Hospitals Based
on Visitor Psychology   212
    Shigeyoshi Iizuka, Shozo Nishii, Eriko Tanimoto, Hiro Nakazawa,
    Asuka Kodaka, and Takanori Takebe

Creating New Strategies for the Changing Sports Business
~ The Case of Nippon Professional Baseball ~   222
    Masaru Kondo and Yumi Asahi

Consumer Analysis of High Sensitivity Layer   236
    Yoshio Matsuyama and Yumi Asahi

Comprehensive Evaluation of an Educational Information Management
Solution for Parents: MyStudentScope   250
    Theresa Matthews, Jinjuan Heidi Feng, Ying Zheng, and Zhijiang Chen

Ontology Construction for Annotating Skill and Situation
of Airline Services to Multi-modal Data   265
    Satoshi Nishimura, Yuichi Oota, and Ken Fukuda

Proposal for the Tablet-Based Disaster Response Evacuation Drill
for Elementary School Children   279
    Makoto Oka, Chiharu Terui, Sakae Yamamoto, and Hirohiko Mori

Hearing Method for User Requirement Extract in Participatory
Design -Designing for Service Involving Local Residents-   290
    Fuko Oura, Takeo Ainoya, and Keiko Kasamatsu

Effective Disaster Prevention Map Creation Using Road Network Analysis   301
Kaname Takenouchi and Ikuro Choh

Analysis of Mental Model of Users with Network Malfunction   312
Haruka Yoshida, Kenta Tsukatsune, and Sumaru Niida

Information in VR and AR

Virtual Reality Applications Using Pseudo-attraction Force
by Asymmetric Oscillation   331
Tomohiro Amemiya

Galvanic Taste Stimulation Method for Virtual Reality
and Augmented Reality   341
Kazuma Aoyama

Development of VR Learning Spaces Considering Lecture Format
in Asynchronous E-learning   350
Takumi Baba, Toru Tokunaga, Toru Kano, and Takako Akakura

Augmented Reality Shopping System Through Image Search
and Virtual Shop Generation   363
*Zhinan Li, Ruichen Ma, Kohei Obuchi, Boyang Liu, Kelvin Cheng,
Soh Masuko, and Jiro Tanaka*

Multimodal Inspection of Product Surfaces Using Mobile
Consumer Devices   377
Christopher Martin and Annerose Braune

One-Handed Character Input Method for Smart Glasses   393
Toshimitsu Tanaka, Yuri Shibata, and Yuji Sagawa

Health Education VR   407
Sachiyo Ueda, Satoshi Fujisawa, Yasushi Ikei, and Michiteru Kitazaki

Feedback Control of Middle Finger MP Joint Using Functional Electrical
Stimulation Based on the Electrical Stimulus Intensity-Joint Torque
Relation Model   417
Kyosuke Watanabe, Makoto Oka, and Hirohiko Mori

Augmented Reality Fashion Show Using Personalized 3D Human Models . . .   435
*Shihui Xu, Jingyi Yuan, Xitong Sun, Yuhan Liu, Yuzhao Liu,
Kelvin Cheng, Soh Masuko, and Jiro Tanaka*

Author Index   451

Contents – Part II

Recommender and Decision Support Systems

Enhancing Peoples' Training Experience: A Gym Workout Planner Based
on Soft Ontologies 3
    Rita de Cássia Catini, Paulo Cesar de Macedo, Julio Cesar dos Reis,
    and Rodrigo Bonacin

Music Interpretation Support System - Integration Support Interface
of Impressions from Listening to Music and Reading Its Score 22
    Tomoko Kojiri and Akio Sugikami

A Model of Decision Makings with Predictions 39
    Tetsuya Maeshiro, Yuri Ozawa, and Midori Maeshiro

Decision Support System with Institutional Research: A Student-Centered
Enrollment Advising System 55
    Takeshi Matsuda, Yuki Watanabe, Katsusuke Shigeta, Nobuhiko Kondo,
    and Hiroshi Kato

Early Findings from a Large-Scale User Study of CHESTNUT:
Validations and Implications. 65
    Xiangjun Peng, Zhentao Huang, Chen Yang, Zilin Song, and Xu Sun

CHESTNUT: Improve Serendipity in Movie Recommendation
by an Information Theory-Based Collaborative Filtering Approach 78
    Xiangjun Peng, Hongzhi Zhang, Xiaosong Zhou, Shuolei Wang, Xu Sun,
    and Qingfeng Wang

Is This the Right Time to Post My Task? An Empirical Analysis on a Task
Similarity Arrival in TopCoder 96
    Razieh Saremi, Mostaan Lotfalian Saremi, Prasad Desai,
    and Robert Anzalone

User-Centred Design of a Process-Recommender System
for Fibre-Reinforced Polymer Production 111
    Thomas Schemmer, Philipp Brauner, Anne Kathrin Schaar,
    Martina Ziefle, and Florian Brillowski

Information, Communication, Relationality and Learning

A Long-Term Evaluation of Social Robot Impression 131
    Saizo Aoyagi, Satoshi Fukumori, and Michiya Yamamoto

Services Task Model Based Dialogue Scenarios Design Towards L2 WTC
Support Oriented Dialogues Authoring Tool   145
  Emmanuel Ayedoun, Yuki Hayashi, and Kazuhisa Seta

Educational Environment of Video System Using Superimposing
Symbols to Support for Skill Training   164
  Naka Gotoda, Yusuke Kometani, Rihito Yaegashi,
  and Toshihiro Hayashi

Appeal of Inconspicuous Body Movements During Spatial Invasion:
Frequency Analysis of Movements   175
  Yosuke Kinoe and Yuna Akimori

How to Emote for Consensus Building in Virtual Communication   194
  Yoshimiki Maekawa, Fumito Uwano, Eiki Kitajima,
  and Keiki Takadama

Learning Support for Historical Interpretation Using Semantically
Enhanced Historical Cartoons   206
  Daiki Muroya, Kazuhisa Seta, and Yuki Hayashi

"Two Way or Go Away": Development of DPP (Digital Presentation
Platform) Which Supports to Make a College Teachers Get Two-Way
Communication Classroom as a Facilitators   219
  Keizo Nagaoka and Ryoji Kubota

A Comparison of Cartoon Portrait Generators Based on Generative
Adversarial Networks   231
  Yusuke Nakashima and Yuichi Bannai

A Proposal of Estimating Method for Agreement
in Face-to-Face Communication   245
  Masashi Okubo and Yuki Fujimoto

System Design of Community Toward Wellbeing   254
  Katsunori Shimohara

Multimodal Interaction-Aware Integrated Platform for CSCL   264
  Aoi Sugimoto, Yuki Hayashi, and Kazuhisa Seta

The Influence of Human-Computer Sagittal Interaction
in Peripersonal Space on Affective Valence Appraisals   278
  Xinyan Wang and Yen Hsu

A Validation of Textual Expression About Disaster Information
to Induce Evacuation   289
  Tomonori Yasui, Takayoshi Kitamura, Tomoko Izumi,
  and Yoshio Nakatani

Supporting Work, Collaboration and Creativity

Assessing Current HMI Designs and Exploring AI Potential
for Future Air-Defence System Development   305
  Zara Gibson, Joseph Butterfield, Robin Stuart Ferguson, Karen Rafferty,
  Wai Yu, and Alf Casement

How to Design a Research Data Management Platform? Technical,
Organizational and Individual Perspectives and Their Relations.   324
  Lennart Hofeditz, Björn Ross, Konstantin Wilms, Marius Rother,
  Stephanie Rehwald, Bela Brenger, Ania López, Raimund Vogl,
  and Dominik Rudolph

Interaction by Taking a Picture for Smartphone Generation   338
  Keita Kaida, Hirohiko Mori, and Makoto Oka

Proposal and Evaluation of Contribution Value Model for Creation
Support System.   350
  Yoshiharu Kato, Tomonori Hashiyama, and Shun'ichi Tano

Analysis of Human Factor in Air Traffic Control Unsafe Events
Based on Improved DECIDE Model   365
  Jun-jie Liu, Rui-rui Zhang, Yin-lan Du, and Qian-yu Bao

Expanding and Embedding a High-Level Gesture Vocabulary for Digital
and Augmented Musical Instruments   375
  Eduardo A. L. Meneses, Takuto Fukuda, and Marcelo M. Wanderley

Visual Compiler: Towards Translating Digital UI Design Draft
to Front-End Code Automatically   385
  Jiemao Pan, Xiang Chen, Ting Chen, Bin Tang, Junbiao Yang,
  Yuhong Chen, Yixiong Lin, Chao Xiao, and Jian Meng

Research on Design of Tai-Chong and Yong-Quan Acupoints
Physiotherapy Apparatus Based on Traditional Chinese Medicine Theory. . . .   395
  Huabin Wang, Baoping Xu, and Yu-Chi Lee

Developing an AR Remote Collaboration System with Semantic Virtual
Labels and a 3D Pointer   407
  Tzu-Yang Wang, Yuji Sato, Mai Otsuki, Hideaki Kuzuoka,
  and Yusuke Suzuki

Will the Process of Creation Impact the Viewer's Appraisal
of the Creativeness of Artificial Intelligence Artworks?   418
  Rui Xu and Yen Hsu

Information in Intelligent Systems and Environments

Experimental Study on Improvement of Sign Language Motion
Classification Performance Using Pre-trained Network Models   433
  Kaito Kawaguchi, Zhizhong Wang, Tomoki Kuniwa,
  Paporn Daraseneeyakul, Phaphimon Veerakiatikit, Eiji Ohta,
  Hiromitsu Nishimura, and Hiroshi Tanaka

An Intermediate Mapping Layer for Interactive Sequencing   447
  Mathias Kirkegaard, Mathias Bredholt, and Marcelo M. Wanderley

Drowsy Bather Detection Using a Triaxial Accelerometer   457
  Hisashi Kojima, Chika Oshima, and Koichi Nakayama

Development of a Prototyping Support Tool for a Data Utilization
Skill-Development Program: Development and Evaluation of a Camera
Sensor Pod with an AI-Based People-Counting Function   469
  Yusuke Kometani, Koichiro Yonemaru, Naoto Hikawa,
  Kyosuke Takahashi, Naka Gotoda, Takayuki Kunieda,
  and Rihito Yaegashi

Data Paradigm Shift in Cross-Media IoT System.   479
  Shih-Ta Liu, Su-Chu Hsu, and Yu-Hsiung Huang

Optimizing Combinations of Teaching Image Data for Detecting
Objects in Images   491
  Keisuke Nakamura, Ryodai Hamasaki, Chika Oshima,
  and Koichi Nakayama

Optimal Route Search Based on Multi-objective Genetic Algorithm
for Maritime Navigation Vessels.   506
  Ryosuke Saga, Zhipeng Liang, Naoyuki Hara, and Yasunori Nihei

The Integration of Web-Based and Mobile-Based Participatory Sensing
Interfaces Apply to the Identification and Assessment of Contextual
Features in the City.   519
  Yang Ting Shen, Pei Wen Lu, and Feng Cheng Lin

Home Care System for Supporting Caregivers and Elderly Care Receivers. . .   529
  Madoka Takahara, Kakiha Gosho, Fanwei Huang, Ivan Tanev,
  and Katsunori Shimohara

Development of Multi-DoF Robot Arm with Expansion and Contraction
Mechanism for Portability   539
  Taiga Yokota and Naoyuki Takesue

Author Index   551

Information Presentation and Visualization

Rethinking the Usage and Experience of Clustering in Web Mapping

Loïc Fürhoff[(⊠)] [iD]

School of Management and Engineering Vaud (HEIG-VD), Media Engineering
Institute (MEI), University of Applied Sciences Western Switzerland (HES-SO),
Yverdon-les-Bains, Switzerland
loic.furhoff@heig-vd.ch
https://mei.heig-vd.ch/

Abstract. Although the notion of 'too many markers' have been mentioned in several research, in practice, displaying hundreds of Points of Interests (POI) on a web map in two dimensions with an acceptable usability remains a real challenge nowadays. Web practitioners often make excessive use of clustering aggregation to overcome performance bottlenecks without effectively resolving issues of perceived performance. This paper tries to bring a broad awareness by identifying a sample of experience issues which describe a general reality of clustering, and provide a pragmatic survey of potential technologies optimisations. At the end, we discuss the usage of technologies and the lack of documented client-server workflows, along with the need to enlarge our vision of the various clutter reduction methods.

Keywords: Clustering · Geographic visualisation · Geographic Information System · Web-based interaction · Icons aggregations · Perceived performance

1 Introduction

Assuredly, Big Data is the key word for the 21st century. Few people realise that a substantial part of these massive quantities of data are categorised as geospatial. Nowadays, satellite-based radionavigation systems are omnipresent on all types of new digital devices. New trends have appeared in the last five years – highlighting each time an original way to consume location data.

Nonetheless even today, the simplest case of displaying hundreds of Points of Interests (POI) on a web map in two dimensions with an acceptable usability can be a real challenge. Especially with the perspective of the user, the navigation experience can be utterly painful. Unquestionably, the choice of technology and their performance has a strong impact on the interactive experience as much as the choice of data visualisation. Furthermore, practitioners often only have a unique point of view due to their education limited to a single or a few number of fields. On the contrary, the discipline of geovisualisation embraces and requires knowledge in many fields: Mathematics, Geoinformatics, Geospatial, Web Development, Accessibility, Information Architecture, Data-visualisation, etc.

© Springer Nature Switzerland AG 2020
S. Yamamoto and H. Mori (Eds.): HCII 2020, LNCS 12184, pp. 3–22, 2020.
https://doi.org/10.1007/978-3-030-50020-7_1

The present paper tries to bring about a general awareness by presenting and discussing the use of different technologies and their effects on common performance bottlenecks. The ambition is to provide a modest and pragmatic survey of the approaches to enhance web map user experience with a focus on the perceived performance and question practices of today.

2   The Practice of Aggregation

The modern web map history certainly began with the launch of Google Maps in 2005. Even though MapQuest and Yahoo companies made an appearance a few months before, the public paid attention to this new kind of medium only a bit later [17]. Arranging a large quantity of markers on a web map rapidly land on the issue list. Therefore basic aggregation libraries using clustering methods were published during the same year ([43] is one of the pioneers).

The usage of aggregation originated from the necessity to overcome mainly two points. At that time, the iconic Google maps Pin made its way along with the map technology which certainly contributes to the popularity of the service. The unique shape of this icon allows the user to locate a precise place without obscuring the area. Regardless this peculiar design, some characteristics like the vertical shape and the drop shadow also emphasised a classic problematic – the cluttering of icons. The visualisation system is confronted by the limitation of preserving markers with a reasonable and accessible size which allow the user to see them and click on them, meanwhile letting the user to interact with the zoom property of the map. Markers, even with few of them, can overlap themselves at the minimum zoom level. A large number of points reduce proportionally the potential usable minimum zoom level. A lot of research has been made on finding algorithms for automatic symbol placement such as Point-Feature Label Placement(PFLP) or for instance the conflict graph algorithm. However markers have specific attributes which render these mechanisms inoperative [9]. Unlike labels, POIs cannot simply be removed from the map without clearing away important information when the available space is insufficient. Quite the contrary, the existence of markers on a map in most cases is to highlight information. Markers also differentiate from labels by using a fixed location without conceding flexibility.

The second point of using aggregation is the proportional degradation of performance for each marker appended to a map. In web application, performance covers a large range of topics explained by the inherent complexity of the client-server model at the core of the World Wide Web. Displaying markers inside a Geographic Information System (GIS) software, as it was before web map or today to prepare and review a data set, bypass this complexity. The main one being that the data and the GIS software are on the same computer. Whereas on the web, vulnerabilities or weak points can arise at multiple layers of the network model.

2.1 Visualise Aggregation

In practice for visualising an abundance of markers and in the field of interactive web map, only a couple of visualisations are suitable: Heatmaps, Tiled Heatmaps (grid of rectangles, hexagons, etc.) and Markers Clustering.

[34] presented, compared and discussed these methods. [13] tried to use Voronoi visualisation as another alternative. Other representations exist, nonetheless they are generally adopted in the field of statistics which allow the system to have a limited interactivity of the zoom feature and allow the marker to be striped of its intrinsic attributes like the fixed position.

Without being able to quantify it, developers intuitively seem to choose clustering methods more often when they need a visualisation to be understood by many. Also according to the survey of [34] and in terms of user comprehension, the clustering of markers is a method better understood for density of precise spatial location or point data like the location of a restaurant or a hotel whereas (tiled) heatmaps would be more suited to areal data like the population density of a country. The aim of this paper is to concentrate on the depiction of precise and fixed geographical point data, therefore we will focus on clustering methods.

3 Perceived Performance Issues

Paradoxically since a few years, performance as a topic is making a huge comeback in web development. Each year, mobile devices receive superior processors and faster electronics, but Web-giant company like Google are still pushing for better performance [41]. In the meantime, several studies showed the relation between the Time to Interactive (TTI) measure, in other words, the time that a user is waiting before being able to use a web page, and the percentage of users quitting a web page or on the contrary the increase of conversion when a low TTI is measured [6].

Around four years after the launch of Google Maps, multiple JavaScript libraries were present on the market to defeat overlapping issues with aggregation. [47] established one of the first comparisons of these algorithms to focus on performance. He tries to measure the total load time of each library towards the main popular web browsers. This kind of TTI analysis (with the tool of the time), like many others, considers only a subset of the performance issue – by examining the time for markers to be transmitted and rendered by the clustering algorithms. However many other human factors step in which are sometimes not easy to evaluate and compare with numbers and metrics. In this section, we'll try to list some of the common current and perceived issues with too many markers and clustering, impacting user experience beyond the aspect of loading times or classic lags.

3.1 Zoom Latency

In the example Fig. 1, the process, which happens after each interaction, is blocking all the layers (the markers and the base layer) and the navigation. This process affects the navigation and is generally caused by the loading of markers or the calculation of clusters.

3.2   Scattering Latency

It happens that when a cluster is decomposed the script has too high latency on recalculation which impacts the underlying animation (Fig. 2). Markers translate to their respective position to show their affiliations to the cluster. The experience is perceived as a non-necessary waiting time.

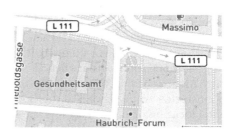

Fig. 1. Video example of Zoom Latency https://doi.org/10.6084/m9. figshare.9332690 https://wheelmap. org, Solzialhelden—ⓒ Mapbox— ⓒ OpenStreetMap

Fig. 2. Video example of Scattering Latency https://doi.org/10.6084/m9. figshare.9332543 https://wheelmap. org, Solzialhelden—ⓒ Mapbox— ⓒ OpenStreetMap

3.3   Markers Flashing

When the user interacts with the zoom, markers or clusters are disappearing by flashing or flickering (Fig. 3). Sometimes artefacts of old markers are appearing as well on the map.

3.4   Rendering Latency

Markers size has a delay and does not follow the zoom interaction (Fig. 4). Besides the loss of comparison across zoom, the result is disturbing and specially not enjoyable.

3.5   Inadequate Gap Distance

Chosen parameters or clustering method create too much distance between markers inside a cluster. Sometimes, developers choose to have a greater number of clusters to improve client-side latency (Fig. 5. However it also impacts the user experience. The user loses to some extent the perception of density.

3.6   Triggering Delay

Having too many markers on a map sometimes constrain developers to make design choice. In Fig. 6, the library is loading new markers only when the users release the click which creates a delay and reduce the smoothness of the experience.

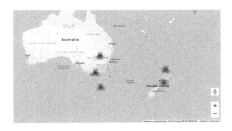

Fig. 3. Video example of Markers Flashing with Google MarkerClusterer library https://doi.org/10.6084/m9.figshare.9332237 https://developers.google.com/maps/documentation/javascript/marker-clustering, Map data—© 2019 Google

Fig. 4. Video example of Markers Flashing with Google MarkerClusterer library https://doi.org/10.6084/m9.figshare.9332480 https://query.wikidata.org, Leaflet—Wikimedia—© OpenStreetMap contributors

Fig. 5. Video example of Inadequate Gap Distance https://doi.org/10.6084/m9.figshare.9332105 https://bl.skywatch.ch/map, Leaflet—© OpenStreetMap

Fig. 6. Video example of Triggering Delay https://doi.org/10.6084/m9.figshare.9332588 https://github.com/mapbox/supercluster, Leaflet—© OpenStreetMap contributors

4   Specific Points to Consider

Before entering the main part of this paper, the readers should be aware that the results need to be only considered for a general usage. The following points are describing two situations where further observations are necessary.

4.1   Markers at the Same Exact Position

In some situation, it can happen that markers are positioned at the exact same place or within a too small distance. Such a distance is dependent on the maximum zoom level that a map allows or, in other words, the minimum scale of the map.

 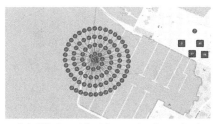

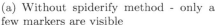

(a) Without spiderify method - only a few markers are visible

(b) With spiderify method applied

Fig. 7. 92 overlapping markers at the exact same position https://bl.skywatch.ch/map, Leaflet—© OpenStreetMap

In Fig. 7, the map was made to display points in time recorded from a mobile device which provide weather information. In Fig. 7(a), the screenshot show and edge case. The owner of a Skywatch BL device recorded points in a boat still attached to the dock.

To overhaul this problem, the unique practical way to do it nowadays is to the spiderify method (Fig. 7(b)) which consist to grab all the markers placed in the same position and arrange them in a spiral. A straight line connects each marker to their real position. In practice, this method can be easily combined with clustering libraries.

4.2   Spatiotemporal Data

Points which change overtime can create particular issues on performance. Generally in those kinds of situations, the markers position is often fixed through time and has a shape which can fluctuate to reflect an indication of a state. The performance could be altered due to the update of markers. Standard library will handle the update simply by clearing and renewing all the markers each time they are adjusted [50].

5   Multiple Levels of Optimisations

For a long time, web mapping was restrained to the server with technology such as WMS. However year over year, JavaScript which has been for a long time mocked became a compelling language and opened an era of pure client-side calculations and rendering. Today, we are moving towards a perspective of efficiently combine and reunite server and client.

In this section we will examine the anatomy of a web map and try to identify the mainsprings to enhance each level or layer. The objective is to get a simple and accessible overview of current and future web technology without deep and too technical knowledge.

The first approach to battle with an abundance of points on a map is to try to diminish them based on their attributes. Either the markers are filtered in pre-processing stage or within the user interface. Chapter 3 of [23] based on the classification of Recommender Systems (RSs) is already entirely devoted to this technique. The aim of this present paper is to examine purely technical methods therefore it is assumed that readers have taken cognisance of content-based optimisations like [23] to filter markers which should be the first consideration in a 'too many markers' problem.

5.1   File Size and Decoding Time

This subsection aims at improving principally loading time and transmission issues that [47] early alluded.

Without doubt, GeoJSON, the standardised extension of the JSON, has become de facto standard format in web mapping. This versatile format supports multiple types of geometries and every common library is supporting it. One of the major reasons behind the adoption of GeoJSON is the tidy and human-readable appearance of the data opposed to the verbosity of the venerable XML format. The notion of human readable is generally in opposition to the consideration of transmission over a network. Consequently many advise and attempts to optimise have been enunciated and described for a long time in the geospatial community [45, 49] including removing unused properties, reducing precision of coordinates, 'minifying' (removing all unnecessary characters for instance whitespaces or new line characters), applying Delta and zigzag encoding on coordinates.

The common belief and potential error for novices is to shrink the file size as far as possible, howbeit optimising file size may impact decoding time and can be counterproductive. In that perspective, proposed extensions of GeoJSON made some waves recently: GeoJSONL, Newline Delimited JSON (ndjson), JSON Lines (jsonl), and GeoJSON Text Sequences. All share the same objective to improve parsing by merely reorganising the structure of the GeoJSON. The file size stays the same as the original file which has been optimised with other techniques or not, but the memory usage to decode the file is slightly decreased which results in lower latency.

Binary File Format. Despite all the research, file size and parsing optimisation have their limits. Considering the display of thousands of markers in a web map, it's not rare to have to serve a GeoJSON of several tens of megabytes even after optimisation or using techniques like lossless server compression with GZIP, Zopfli or Brotli algorithms.

GeoJSON was principally made as an interchange file format and not designed for transmission. The general suggested alternative is the use of a binary encoding format which in theory should be lighter and faster at parsing. Protocol Buffers (Protobuf) developed by Google is the most widespread serialisation library and by extension format. Two major organisations have adopted this library for their own usage. The Openstreetmap association and the company Mapbox are using it for storing and serving vector data whilst having totally different specification. In practice, Protobuf seems to deliver mixed results [8,26,27,54], though it has a clear advantage in compressing numbers and hence feature like multi-polygon which probably explains the choice of Mapbox to use it in their vector tile specification. In fact, lossless server compression like GZIP as a great impact on GeoJSON and compare favourably with Protobuf. It's not certain that JSON and GeoJSON will be replaced in the future with such a solution. Although Protobuf is largely supported by Google on multiple programming language and stacks, it requires a complete switch of infrastructure and paradigm. In fact, the first intention of Google is to package Protobuf within their gRPC communication architecture. Saw by many an alternative to REST and GraphQL, gRPC is not principally directed at back-ends for communication between a server and a web browser but rather for native applications or low-powered appliances which require high-speed transmission or persistent connection e.g. Internet of things (IoT) devices.

5.2   Computation

Algorithms and calculations are playing a large part in issues like zoom (Fig. 1) and scattering latency (Fig. 2). In those situations, markers are generally already loaded and cached which means that the calculation of clusters should be accounted for these issues. Some optimised systems are requesting only markers present inside the browser viewport and in that case, each zoom needs another network request. However even for those systems, the interaction should be smoother with caching strategies at least when the zoom level is reached a second time, but it is often not the case. In this section, we'll first examine how we can alleviate the calculation of clusters and try to get an elementary view on clustering algorithms.

Asynchronous Interaction Events. Throttling and debouncing are the most commonly applied technique by developers for interaction optimisations since the invention of the terms in 2009 [11]. When the user move or zoom the map for example, the browser trigger a huge number of events per second following pixel-by-pixel any change made by the user. Computing or drawing at that rate can block the UI Thread and is often largely superfluous. Throttling and deboucing act as intermediates to control the right amount of needed changes. In their basic implementation, both execute after a certain delay. The main difference is that throttling limit and guarantee a maximum number of times a function can be called over time. These techniques might be considerate as workarounds and it can be difficult to find the right compromise between performance and interaction with latency perception (e.g. in Fig. 6).

Relieve the UI Thread. Some libraries are implementing loading solutions to soften the perception of latency. One noticeable technique is chunk loading.

With a basic algorithm, the data are cut according to the time of loading. This workaround allows the browser to alternate between the loading of the markers data and other elements or layers of the web map. Lags should be shorter and the perception of speed slightly improved, but it does not completely solve the problem.

An alternative would be to push all or the main computing operations in parallel, in a background thread, with the Web Workers API. A part of frustrations are assuredly eliminated with just this method since the navigation will not be blocked, but the user will be disoriented as the loading will appear asynchronous. Additionally Web Workers are not able to render DOM elements, so combined with the technique of rendering markers with DOM elements, it will not have an extensive impact.

Just as well as a binary format are invading the browser, the development of compiled programming language is slowly appearing on the browser side. WebAssembly (Wasm) is an open standard promoted by the World Wide Web Consortium (W3C). It allows to use low-level language like C/C++, D or Rust and have near-native performance which means lower time of calculation. Wasm was designed to work alongside JavaScript. However it's hard to tell how both will cohabit in the future. Although the technology is shipped in all the major browsers since November 2017 [32], Wasm is still considered as experimental in the community and as far as we know, no tangible experience was done in web mapping as of today's date. This technology will need time to be propagated first, but mainly to take down some essential limitations like the weakness of intermediate communications between Wasm and the JavaScript APIs which are essential, but affect the theoretical advantage of performance.

Clustering Algorithms. The notion of clustering is used in multiple scientific disciplines and has a long history of at least ninety years. Consequently a numberless of algorithms were designed to answer the problematic of grouping data with notably different performances. [33] organised and vulgarised the major algorithms used in map application: K-mean, DBscan and Hierarchical Clustering.

Conceived in 1967, K-mean is the most common algorithm in clustering analysis due to its relative simplicity and performance. DBscan is relatively new (1996) in comparison and some research found that it is less efficient [10]. However, it has a lot of advantages: it does not require either a parameter indicating the number of clusters, or that points are within the same shape. DBscan is more flexible and allow arbitrarily shaped clusters. Finally, hierarchical clustering make use of the prominent tree structure largely used in geospatial. In practice inside the clustering web map 'community', it was popularised by Dave Leaver on the plugin Markercluster for the Leaflet library and seems to be the most efficient [3]. Experiments have been made with other algorithms like sweep and prune which determine clusters by simulating collisions between markers. Grid-based clustering methods were also mentioned in an earlier version of the Google Maps documentation [29]. That said, the performance benefits were not really demonstrated for the sweep and prune method, and grid-based definitely clustering lack of meaning.

Spatial Indexes. The launch of the 'supercluster' library [3] illustrated that pre-calculating spatial indexes in addition to a good algorithm has a considerable repercussion. Spatial indexes are at the core of spatial database, but tend to be useful to optimise as well the client-side. Without, a database would need to sequentially compare every record to respond to a search query. Spatial indexes instead build a tree to retrieve the data at the fastest speed. Building an index certainly impact in some way the loading time which is precious in our case, but this initial cost is valuable later when used in conjunction with a clustering algorithm [4]. Supercluster, which manages to handle millions of points, use R-tree, but at least fifteen potential algorithms are known and use in the field.

5.3   Client-Server Load Distribution

The typical implementation of clustering does not involve the server except for serving the data files. Optimisation of the data transmission was for a long period restrained from handling the lowest number of files. Each new file involves a round of costing Hypertext Transfer Protocol (HTTP) requests. Developers had to balance between the cost-benefit of the requests compared to the sizes of file. Icons' sprites is assuredly the culminating example method of this period. Sprites targeted especially icons due to their small sizes. Icons were combined together to constitute a single file and a single transfer over the network. The icons were then separated by a masking mechanism. Since the end of 2015, major web browsers support version 2 of HTTP which completely change this paradigm by empowering concurrent transfers without degradation. The practice of chunks slicing emerged in multiple places. Today, the good practice in web development is to deliver the minimum piece of code only related to the current displayed page to minimise transmission and parsing time [51]. This innovation will also certainly benefit long-established technology like Web Map Service (WMS).

Streaming. In reality before version 2 of HTTP, it was already possible to avoid the cost of multiple requests by using Chunked Transfer Encoding function of HTTP version 1.1. Plug-in combined with libraries which support the streaming of GeoJSON exists. However in our case, this technique will only improve the First Meaningful Paint (the time it takes for an essential content to appear on the page). Markers will appear one after another and the user will still have to wait to have the big picture. The user could also be more confused without a clear feedback indicating the completion of loading. Streaming should be reserved for data which change over time with a short lifespan.

Preloading and Prefetching. As mentioned previously, zoom and panning can induce markers flashing due to computation or loading time. Recently, web browsers implemented the possibility to suggest that resources be preloaded and prefetched in priority via a simple Hypertext Markup Language (HTML) attribute. HTTP2 also added the possibility to the server to push resources directly to the client without the need to request them.

In the field of web mapping, these methods are hard to apply alone without wasting bandwidth. Indeed the map navigation in three dimensions would mean multiple level of preloading or prefetching. In this area, Google published a library using Machine Learning to try to predict user behaviour in terms of navigation [16]. Currently the library try to anticipate which page the user will choose to display after the current one and prefetch it, but we can envision such approaches applied to web mapping in the future and avoid issues like in Fig. 6.

Leverage the Server. Web mapping fields use since a long time ago tilling techniques which subdivide an image into a grid of multiples small square called tile and produce a pyramid of grids to serve these tiles according to the third dimension – the zoom. Since 1999, we use Web Map Service (WMS) servers to provide use with these grid of bitmaps. The method, still actively used, bring a relative simplicity to the web browser with the only job to rearrange the tiles in a grid without heavy calculations.

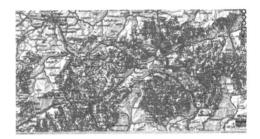

Fig. 8. Video example of Markers Flashing with WMS https://doi.org/10.6084/m9. figshare.9332309 https://map.geo.admin.ch (Terrestrial images swisstopo black and white), © Données:swisstopo

Nowadays, it is essentially used to display base layers like terrestrial images or a background map. However some organisations present markers or clusters of markers on a map with it. The technology calculate the position of the markers and renders the markers into a transparent grid of bitmaps which can be added on top of base layers. Basic interaction with markers is achieved with a request on the server and the coordinates of the click on the map as parameters. Loading time and transmission issues are avoided, but this technique also has disadvantages. The client has a reduced flexibility. When there is a need to filter or customise markers, the only way is to request the server for new bitmaps. In the example of Fig. 8, we can observe that each zoom requires to load new images which create an experience of Markers Flashing.

Through the years, experiments have been envisioned to leverage the server while still using the potential of the client [1,12,40,44], though none was ever democratised. The usual gap between academic research and real application may explain the situation. Moreover some of this research were too specific or missed a good practical documentation. These days, the popularity of the Node.js framework might change behaviour in the future since it employs JavaScript –

the client-side programming language. For example, supercluster was designed to be client-side, but [5] mentioned that it could be implemented on a server.

In the Drupal community, the Geocluster plugin introduced by [12] has been presented into a case study at a technical conference [42]. On the one hand, the demonstration shows a good performance in response time, but, on the other hand, as the interactivity still suffer with sluggish rendering (Fig. 9). The only responsible left to blame is the Document Object Model (DOM) on the client-side which takes care of the HTML markers. In another experiment, [36] tried to generate this markup on the server rather than on the client-side, but he terminated in no time seeing that the performance was even poorer.

Fig. 9. Video Case Study of Geocluster Drupal Plugin https://doi.org/10.6084/m9. figshare.9331547 https://www.vistacampus. gov/map, Leaflet—Tiles © Esri

5.4 Rendering

In the previous sections, we noticed that the majority of listed user experience issues in chapter "Perceived performance issues" can be solved excepting Markers Flashing (Fig. 3) and Rendering Latency (Fig. 4) issues. In this section, we will cover the last level of optimisation which happens exclusively on the client-side.

Enhancing the DOM. In the last decade, one major attempt was made to improve the DOM. The concept of virtual DOM appeared several years ago, but was mainly popularised by React, the JavaScript framework which uses it as a primary argument to promote their technology. The principle is to create an abstraction of the DOM in memory and synchronise only needed changes. The whole concept was misunderstood and advertised by third parties to something which would be faster than the DOM itself. As a matter of fact, virtual DOM allows developers to build applications with a good default performance, but it does not improve in any way the performance of the DOM [18]. This outcome is presumably also relevant to all alternatives of virtual DOM like Memoized DOM, hyperHTML, etc.

The DOM has a serious reputation to be slow among developers, but benchmark demonstrations like [48] explains that competences and knowledge of its functioning are key for good performance while also confirming the benefit of virtual DOM to reduce the risk of extremely poor performance. However, the notion of DOM is relatively old and was not built for applications like appending thousands of points on a page. Recommendations issued by Google for Web developers argue for a maximum 1,500 nodes per page [14]. Naturally, clustering methods help to mitigate the problem by limiting the numbers of nodes, but circumstances where the number of nodes rapidly inflates are not extraordinary and perceived performance issues appear (e.g. Fig. 9 has 2,071 nodes at the time of writing, visually way more than at the time of [42] publishing). Therefore alternatives should be taken into consideration.

Drawing Markers. The revolution and alternatives to the DOM came with three technologies: Canvas API (around 2004), WebGL API (around 2011), the hardware acceleration of the HTML Canvas element (2012) [20]. Sometimes, there is a certain confusion when talking about canvas as both Canvas API and WebGL API render graphics inside the HTML Canvas element.

In theory, many would have bet on the abandon of Canvas API as WebGL API is able match and enhance greatly this API. However, the Canvas API is still used widely. Assuredly, canvas API is often used as a fallback for compatibility when WebGL is not supported and also due to its less austere API. The adoption of WebGL inside the web community was mainly driven by the conception of intermediary JavaScript libraries like three.js, babylon.js or Pixi.js which try to translate the complex language behind WebGL. Talking to the GPU require to use a special language – the OpenGL Shading Language (GLSL) – and to tessellate data into triangles.

For cases like rendering markers, the following question arises: which of the two should we use. WebGL is a low-level API giving you a total freedom whereas with the Canvas API you are not fully aware of how the browser choose to opti-mise the rendering. Therefore, optimising performance of the Canvas API is possible (and a number of tips are known) but quite limited. In this perspective, many comparisons have emphasised the superiority of WebGL with a consider-able number of objects [7, 22, 28].

In practice, the adoption of WebGL in web cartography is still in its infancy, but the Mapbox company is well determined to change this. The use of WebGL in web cartography is highly linked to the research for a vector tiles specification. One of the main reasons given to this innovation, saw as a replacement of WMS, is the possibility of styling elements directly in the browser. Aside from this main characteristic and in terms of user experience, the use of WebGL allow dynamic rendering mentioned by [15]. Regular mechanisms used to render HTML markers try to keep a seamless experience between level of zooming by using some transitions on current zoom data until the next zoom data have been charged in memory. Vector data eliminate this kind of workaround with their ability to be rendered multiple time according to the zoom without any additional network requests. Markers Flashing (or flickering) and Rendering Latency are avoided with this only ability (Fig. 10). Moreover, WebGL bring an evident advantage to our research of an optimised experience. All points rendered with WebGL are displayed in a unique HTML element which renders like a simple bitmap, allows theoretically unlimited of points (by using instancing property of WebGL2 - [39]) and therefore remove the risk of too many markers performance issues.

Meanwhile version 2 of WebGL is only supported by a limited number of web browsers, multiple proposals have been initiated for the future replacement of WebGL. The efficiency and reliability of WebGL is contested from all parts and there is multiple need like accessing low-based GPU capacity, multithreading or access to the GPU memory [53]. Apple, Google and Mozilla are developing and experimenting their own proposal for an API, all encompass with the project working name of WebGPU. At the end of 2019, early implementation of Safari and Chrome browser already show that WebGPU outperforms WebGL and allows much more complex scene rendering [31,52].

Fig. 10. Video example of OpenLayers Icon Sprites with WebGL https://doi. org/10.6084/m9.figshare.9332366 https:// openlayers.org/en/master/examples/ icon-sprite-webgl.html, Certain data © OpenStreetMap contributors, CC-BY-SA National UFO Reporting Center

6   Discussion

In this last section, we will explore two questions: why technologies discussed in this paper are not widely adopted and why we should rethink the usage of aggregation in projects involving web mapping.

6.1   A Call for Documented Workflows Combining Technologies

Multiple causes may explain the slow adoption of new technologies in web cartography.

Leaflet—the biggest and the most popular web cartography library (according to the stars ranking on Github.com)—is supporting the Canvas API only since a few years and tend to not explicitly promote it [24]. In addition, the author of Leaflet wants to keep the relative simplicity of the implementation and does not want to integrate WebGL at the heart of the library [2]. Developers have to rely on imperfect third-party plugins to add a layer of WebGL on Leaflet no without user experience issue (e.g. Fig. 11. Beyond the addition of a generic WebGL overlay, no straightforward solution for Leaflet has been published to bring a solution which would render clusters and not only markers. Concurrently, Mapbox has successfully implemented a workflow in their Mapbox GL library using their supercluster library client-side and a process to convert the resulting clusters and points into their own Mapbox vector tiles specification [30].

The creator of Leaflet has developed and published for Mapbox—the company he works for—multiple open source tools (like GeoJSON-vt, vt-pbf, tippecanoe, etc.) for their stack solutions which provide a complete end-to-end for serving clusters of markers efficiently by taking advantage of both client and server. However, it is becoming increasingly difficult for developers to avoid being overwhelmed by such an extent of tools at different levels and to resist to only embrace the default pattern to display markers on a map for this reason.

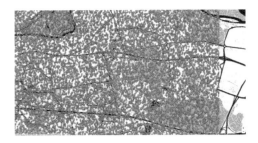

Fig. 11. Video of Leaflet.PixiOverlay – One million markers Demo https://doi.org/10.6084/m9.figshare.9332153 https://manubb.github.io/Leaflet.PixiOverlay/many-markers.html, Leaflet—Map tiles by Stamen Design, under CC BY 3.0. Data by OpenStreetMap, under ODbL.

In the domain of data visualisation, some practical research highlighted the fact that we should not choose a perfect technology but rather try to combine them and exploit their best aspect [35,55]. More and more we see new way to fill the gap between technologies like the implementation of 'offscreenCanvas' which allow drawing without affecting the main thread with a clear benefit for Canvas API and WebGL users especially if it is combined with web workers [46].

In the end, we cannot lean on another tool or library which will encompass fine-tuned technologies and all the gain of each tool. The real true absent is a better documentation of workflows or even a way to interactively assess a technology stack and pinpoint performance issues early.

6.2   Questioning the Systematic of Clustering

The overview of technologies and potential optimisations calls into questions the choice of choosing aggregation for better performance, outlined in the second chapter of this paper. Clustering aggregation tends to be systematically applied in a situation where POIs need to be displayed on a map without really judging the necessity. Figure 12 illustrates this tendency well—clusters are everywhere at low levels of zoom, albeit when we zoom in, icons of clusters and individual markers are mixed and visually obstruct the field of view. The user cannot anymore quickly compare the areas and find the most active region in the capture of mosquitoes, for instance.

As stated by [37], the meaning of clustering all too often lack of sense for many reasons, but mainly because grouping points together with variable distance misrepresent density as long as the cluster position is only the result of mathematical depiction. Additionally clustering can become a source of inconvenience. In some situation, it introduces other problems like the obfuscation of the distance between points illustrated by Fig. 5. In practice, developers or designers tend to make minimal customisation of the cluster icon resulting in a lack of proper comparison attributes like variable sizes or colours other than just numbers on a text label (Fig. 5). Some system like Google MarkerClusterer encourage the use of different colours and restrict the possibility to change the size of the cluster icon in the percentage of the number of points that it contains (Fig. 12). A majority of maps represent POIs with the Google Maps Pin or an imitation despite the research of other ways to transmit the meaning like the concept of Generative Marker [34] which exhort to use representative markers of the data and to display different icons to reflect the number of elements behind a cluster.

Nevertheless, clustering in some exceptional case can be meaningful. When this aggregation method is used to depict a sum of attributes inside a common depicted area, for example. Region-aware clustering method exist as an alternative to mathematical one. In this case, aggregations are constructed with a database of territory like countries, states or smaller (administrative) area.

Fig. 12. The Mosquito Atlas of Germany 2018   https://mueckenatlas.com/karte-der-sammler-2018, Kartendaten © 2019 GeoBasis-DE/BKG (©2009), Google, Inst. Geogr. Nacional

After all in terms of clutter reduction methods, aggregation is only one of the height methods according to the classification of [25]. Some libraries are exploring other clutter reduction methods like animation of the overlapping markers [21]. However recently in the usage and with the power of WebGL, alternatives have been chosen over clustering (Fig. 13). One day, the trend of 'symbolisation simplified' method will certainly become the norm. A lot of websites would benefit from it, but the change of development habits and the sharing of knowledge will take some time to propagate.

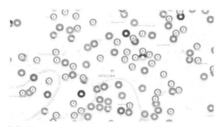

(a) Current map with clustering method
https://doi.org/10.6084/m9.figshare.9331985
https://recyclemap.ru, Map data © 2019 Google

(b) Beta map with symbolisation simplified method https://doi.org/10.6084/m9.figshare.9332051 https://beta.recyclemap.ru, © Mapbox © OpenStreetMap

Fig. 13. The transition of clutter reduction method on the Greenpeace Russian recycling map project

6.3   A Note on Accessibility

Eventually, we cannot finish this technical overview without making a general reminder of accessibility.

The choice of technology may have an impact on accessibility. Although WebGL has interactive functionalities like click recognition and mapping, it would be an illusion to think that it has the same accessibility level as the DOM. Basically, the construction of the DOM allows the user to access each node with the keyboard whereas WebGL, as mentioned before, build a static bitmap. Hit region functionalities which would give the ability to navigate with the keyboard is only supported on two major browsers currently [38]. The proposed and promising Accessibility Object Model (AOM) will certainly make a great difference in this situation. This JavaScript API will allow developers to create virtual nodes exclusively for the accessibility purpose and leave the DOM as it is. However if keyboard navigation is an essential mechanism for accessibility in a standard web page, an abundance of markers or clusters are not easy to review without hierarchies. Mapbox is currently experimenting with the development of a plugin which converts important markers to HTML nodes [19], but defining the importance of markers is largely dependent on a use case and it is difficult to generalise.

Google has implemented another form of accessibility combination their Google Maps Platform. The map view is sliced in the region or area like a city and the user is invited to select an area. Blind users also benefit of this mechanism, because each area is named and have a common sense. Though, this kind of technique is difficult to replicate and, like the experimentation of Mapbox, might not suit every usage. In the end, it should be noted that keyboard navigation on a map is experimental or very tailored to a use.

Eventually, we went through a lot of web map during the writing of this paper, but only one (Fig. 1 and Fig. 2) differentiate cluster icons with colours as well as with their shape. People with low-vision or colour blindness will gain a lot if it were broadly adopted.

7   Conclusion

A large spectrum of approaches to enhance perceived performance of clustering in web mapping was proposed and discussed in this paper. Most of them are available for several years, but there is a certain reluctant to use it. Furthermore, the best performance is a matter of combining technologies. We think that straightforward documented workflows are needed to change this general behaviour.

Above all, whether the performance was one of the main reasons to adopt clustering in web mapping, we exposed through examples that the introduction of new techniques and technology make this statement obsolete. No clutter reduction method is perfect, though web practitioners need to rethink their usage of clustering and enlarge their vision of the possibilities to reduce cluttering.

Acknowledgments. The present thesis was written as a part of the Certificate of Advanced Studies in Interaction Science and Technology (CAS) organised by the Human-Centered Interaction Science and Technology Institute (Human-IST) of the University of Fribourg.

References

1. Adam, P.: Pre-clustering Google Maps Markers using KMeans in Django, September 2017. https://medium.com/@padam0/pre-clustering-google-maps-markers-using-kmeans-in-django-aeabc6eb2c0b
2. Agafonkin, V.: Leaflet, WebGL and the Future of Web Mapping, March 2015. https://www.youtube.com/watch?v=lj4SS1NTqyY
3. Agafonkin, V.: Clustering millions of points on a map with Supercluster, March 2016. https://blog.mapbox.com/clustering-millions-of-points-on-a-map-with-supercluster-272046ec5c97
4. Agafonkin, V.: A dive into spatial search algorithms, April 2017. https://blog.mapbox.com/a-dive-into-spatial-search-algorithms-ebd0c5e39d2a
5. Agafonkin, V.: Client-side clustering or server-side clustering · Issue 91 · mapbox/supercluster, July 2018. https://github.com/mapbox/supercluster/issues/91
6. Alstad, K.: New Findings: State of the Union for Ecommerce Page Speed and Web Performance [Spring 2015], April 2015. https://blog.radware.com/applicationdelivery/wpo/2015/04/new-findings-state-union-ecommerce-page-speed-web-performance-spring-2015/
7. Andrews, K., Wright, B.: FluidDiagrams: web-based information visualisation using JavaScript and WebGL. In: EuroVis - Short Papers. The Eurographics Association (2014). https://doi.org/10.2312/eurovisshort.20141155
8. Bernstein, M.: 5 Reasons to Use Protocol Buffers Instead of JSON For Your Next Service, June 2014. https://codeclimate.com/blog/choose-protocol-buffers/
9. Burigat, S., Chittaro, L.: Decluttering of icons based on aggregation in mobile maps. In: Meng, L., Zipf, A., Winter, S. (eds.) Map-Based Mobile Services. LNGC, pp. 13–32. Springer, Heidelberg (2008). https://doi.org/10.1007/978-3-540-37110-6_2
10. Chakraborty, S., Nagwani, N.K., Dey, L.: Performance Comparison of Incremental K-means and Incremental DBSCAN Algorithms, June 2014. arXiv:1406.4751 [cs]
11. Corbacho, D.: Debouncing and Throttling Explained Through Examples, April 2016. https://css-tricks.com/debouncing-throttling-explained-examples/
12. Dabernig, J.: Geocluster: Server-sideclustering for mapping in Drupal based on Geohash. Master's thesis, Fakultät für Informatik der Technischen Universität Wien, Vienna, June 2013. http://dasjo.at/files/geocluster-thesis-dabernig.pdf
13. Delort, J.: Vizualizing large spatial datasets in interactive maps. In: 2010 Second International Conference on Advanced Geographic Information Systems, Applications, and Services, pp. 33–38, February 2010. https://doi.org/10.1109/GEOProcessing.2010.13
14. Developers, G.: Uses an Excessive DOM Size, May 2019. https://developers.google.com/web/tools/lighthouse/audits/dom-size
15. Eriksson, O., Rydkvist, E.: An in-depth analysis of dynamically rendered vector-based maps with WebGL using Mapbox GL JS. Master's thesis, Linköping University, August 2015. http://urn.kb.se/resolve?urn=urn:nbn:se:liu:diva-121073
16. Gechev, M., Osmani, A., Hempenius, K., Mathews, K.: Guess.js. https://guess-js.github.io/docs

17. Gibbs, S.: Google Maps: a decade of transforming the mapping landscape. The Guardian, February 2015. https://www.theguardian.com/technology/2015/feb/08/google-maps-10-anniversary-iphone-android-street-view
18. Harris, R.: Virtual DOM is pure overhead, December 2018. https://svelte.dev/blog/virtual-dom-is-pure-overhead
19. Harvey, A., Brown, T., Vakil, A.S., Wood-Santoro, M.: mapbox-gl-accessibility - an accessibility control for Mapbox GL JS, May 2019. https://github.com/mapbox/mapbox-gl-accessibility, original-date: 2017–11-16T14:34:49Z
20. Heikkinen, I.: Taking advantage of GPU acceleration in the 2D canvas—Web, July 2012. https://developers.google.com/web/updates/2012/07/Taking-advantage-of-GPU-acceleration-in-the-2D-canvas?hl=fr
21. Here: Ordering Overlapping Markers - Maps API for JavaScript. https://developer.here.com/api-explorer/maps-js/markers/ordering-overlapping-markers
22. Horak, T., Kister, U., Dachselt, R.: Comparing rendering performance of common web technologies for large graphs. In: Poster Program of the 2018 IEEE VIS Conference, VIS, vol. 18 (2018). https://imld.de/cnt/uploads/Horak-2018-Graph-Performance.pdf
23. Huang, H., Gartner, G.: A technical survey on decluttering of icons in online map-based mashups. In: Peterson, M. (ed.) Online Maps with APIs and WebServices. LNGC, pp. 157–175. Springer, Heidelberg (2012). https://doi.org/10.1007/978-3-642-27485-5_11
24. Karambelkar, B.V.: Canvas renderer? · Issue #463 · rstudio/leaflet, September 2017. https://github.com/rstudio/leaflet/issues/463#issuecomment-329014257
25. Korpi, J., Ahonen-Rainio, P.: Clutter reduction methods for point symbols in map mashups. Cartogr. J. **50**(3), 257–265 (2013). https://doi.org/10.1179/1743277413Y.0000000065
26. Krebs, B.: Beating JSON performance with Protobuf, January 2017. https://auth0.com/blog/beating-json-performance-with-protobuf/
27. Larsgård, N.: Comparing sizes of protobuf vs json, April 2017. https://nilsmagnus.github.io/post/proto-json-sizes/
28. Lee, A.: Drawing 2D charts with WebGL, May 2019. https://blog.scottlogic.com/2019/05/28/drawing-2d-charts-with-webgl.html
29. Mahe, L., Broadfoot, C.: Too Many Markers! - Google Maps API - Google Developers, December 2010. https://web.archive.org/web/20121113185947/. https://developers.google.com/maps/articles/toomanymarkers/
30. Mapbox: Create and style clusters (2020). https://www.mapbox.com/mapbox-gl-js/example/cluster/
31. Maxfield, M.: WebGPU and WSL in Safari, September 2019. https://webkit.org/blog/9528/webgpu-and-wsl-in-safari/
32. McConnell, J.: WebAssembly support now shipping in all major browsers, November 2017. https://blog.mozilla.org/blog/2017/11/13/webassembly-in-browsers/
33. Meert, W., Tronçon, R., Janssens, G.: Clustering Maps. Master's thesis, Katholieke Universiteit Leuven, Leuven (2006). http://citeseerx.ist.psu.edu/viewdoc/download?doi=10.1.1.132.6977&rep=rep1&type=pdf
34. Meier, S.: The marker cluster: a critical analysis and a new approach to a common web-based cartographic interface pattern. Int. J. Agric. Environ. Inf. Syst. (IJAEIS) **7**(1), 28–43 (2016). https://doi.org/10.4018/IJAEIS.2016010102
35. Mikkolainen, T.: Canvas filled three ways: JS, WebAssembly and WebGL, December 2018. https://compile.fi/canvas-filled-three-ways-js-webassembly-and-webgl/
36. Nebel, P.: Dynamic Server-Side Clustering for Large Datasets, January 2018. https://geovation.github.io/dynamic-server-side-geo-clustering

37. Nemeth, A.: "How do I do clustering on a map correctly" is a common question in mapping applications, March 2015. https://ux.stackexchange.com/a/75190/116603
38. Network, M.D.: Hit regions and accessibility. https://developer.mozilla.org/en-US/docs/Web/API/Canvas_API/Tutorial/Hit_regions_and_accessibility
39. Ninomiya, K.: Webinar Recap: WebGL 2.0, What You Need to Know, May 2017. https://www.khronos.org/blog/webinar-recap-webgl-2.0-what-you-need-to-know
40. Ortelli, G.: Server-side clustering of geo-points on a map using Elasticsearch, August 2013. https://blog.trifork.com/2013/08/01/server-side-clustering-of-geo-points-on-a-map-using-elasticsearch/
41. Osmani, A.: Speed is now a landing page factor for Google Search and Ads!, July 2018. https://twitter.com/addyosmani/status/1022005088058073088
42. Paul, E.: Case Study: Large-Scale, Server Side Mapping with the Leaflet-Geocluster Stack, June 2015. http://2015.tcdrupal.org/session/case-study-large-scale-server-side-mapping-leaflet-geocluster-stack
43. Poskanzer, J.: Clusterer.js - marker clustering routines for Google Maps apps (2005). http://www.acme.com/javascript/Clusterer2.js
44. Rezaei, M., Fränti, P.: Real-time clustering of large geo-referenced data for visualizing on map. Adv. Electr. Comput. Eng. **18**, 63–74 (2018). https://doi.org/10.4316/AECE.2018.04008
45. Sandvik, B.: How to minify GeoJSON files?, November 2012. http://blog.mastermaps.com/2012/11/how-to-minify-geojson-files.html
46. Sitnik, A.: Faster WebGL/Three.js 3D graphics with OffscreenCanvas and Web Workers, April 2019. https://evilmartians.com/chronicles/faster-webgl-three-js-3d-graphics-with-offscreencanvas-and-web-workers
47. Svennerberg, G.: Handling Large Amounts of Markers in Google Maps - In usability we trust, May 2009. http://www.svennerberg.com/2009/01/handling-large-amounts-of-markers-in-google-maps/
48. Teller, S.: Building an interactive DOM benchmark, preliminary results, February 2018. https://swizec.com/blog/building-interactive-dom-benchmark-preliminary-results/swizec/8219
49. Tihonov, I.: Speed up web maps - minify geojson, November 2014. http://igortihonov.com/2014/11/12/speedup-web-maps-minify-geojson/
50. Urbica: Visualising large spatiotemporal data in web applications, July 2018. https://medium.com/@Urbica.co/visualising-large-spatiotemporal-data-in-web-applications-8583cf21907
51. Wagner, J., Osmani, A.: Reduce JavaScript Payloads with Code Splitting—Web Fundamentals, May 2019. https://developers.google.com/web/fundamentals/performance/optimizing-javascript/code-splitting/
52. Wallez, C., Cabello, R.: Next-Generation 3D Graphics on the Web (Google I/O 2019), May 2019. https://www.youtube.com/watch?v=K2JzIUIHIhc
53. Weissflog, A.: Thoughts about a WebGL-Next, August 2016. https://floooh.github.io/2016/08/13/webgl-next.html
54. Wen, T.: Is Protobuf 5x Faster Than JSON?, April 2017. https://dzone.com/articles/is-protobuf-5x-faster-than-json-part-ii
55. yWorks: SVG, Canvas, WebGL? Visualization options for the web, March 2018. https://www.yworks.com/blog/svg-canvas-webgl

Environmental Control Units for Inpatient Care at Veterans Affairs Spinal Cord Injury Centers: Heuristic Evaluation and Design Recommendations

Gabriella M. Hancock[1]([⊠]), Sam Anvari[2], Matthew T. Nare[1], Nicole B. Mok[1], Aram Ayvazyan[1], Kelsey M. McCoy[1], Xiaolu Bai[1], Gregory P. Mather[1], Amanda S. McBride[3], and Natalia Morales[4]

[1] Department of Psychology, California State University, Long Beach, 1250 Bellflower Boulevard, Long Beach, CA 90840, USA
Gabriella.Hancock@csulb.edu
[2] School of Art, California State University, Long Beach, 1250 Bellflower Boulevard, Long Beach, CA 90840, USA
[3] College of Health and Human Services, California State University, Long Beach, 1250 Bellflower Boulevard, Long Beach, CA 90840, USA
[4] Department of Biological Sciences, California State University, Long Beach, 1250 Bellflower Boulevard, Long Beach, CA 90840, USA

Abstract. Heuristic evaluation is a valid and widely accepted method for evaluating system usability. Findings from such evaluations provide valuable insight concerning which system elements should be targeted in future design iterations for improved functionality and user experience. This paper details a heuristic evaluation, utilizing Nielsen's Heuristics and Shneiderman's Golden Rules of Interface Design, of an inpatient environmental control unit used at the VA Spinal Cord Injuries and Disorders (SCI/D) Centers nationwide. Results identified a number of usability issues inherent to the currently deployed interface at varying levels of severity. Design recommendations for addressing these significant issues in future iterations of this system are provided in an effort to foster independence and enhance quality of life in veterans with spinal cord injuries and disorders.

Keywords: Usability evaluation · Heuristic evaluation · User interface · Environmental control units

1 Introduction

The U.S. Department of Veterans Affairs is the federal agency charged with providing any and all healthcare services to eligible military veterans. As a result, it comprises the largest integrated healthcare system in the country. In its mission to provide the highest quality healthcare to over 9 million veterans, the VA has established 14 Cross-agency

© Springer Nature Switzerland AG 2020
S. Yamamoto and H. Mori (Eds.): HCII 2020, LNCS 12184, pp. 23–38, 2020.
https://doi.org/10.1007/978-3-030-50020-7_2

Priority Goals for the future [1]. Four of these goals explicitly address information technology and usability issues with technologies that directly impact veterans: modernizing information technology to increase productivity and security; improving customer experience with federal services; sharing quality services; and improving transfer of federally-funded technologies from lab-to-market [1]. In an effort to support these goals, this project analyzed a multiple-purpose user interface currently deployed throughout the VA's 25 Spinal Cord Injuries and Disorders Centers in order to assess its usability and provide design recommendations for its improvement.

The user interface in question is an autonoME Hospital Environmental Control Unit (ECU; Accessibility Services, Inc., Homosassa, FL). ECUs are "devices that allow individuals who have functional limitations and/or disabilities (such as persons with SCI/D) to increase their independence to control aspects of their environment" [2; pg. 58]. Due to the varying range of functional limitations that result from spinal cord injuries or disorders (SCI/D), the individual needs of each patient are varied and wide-ranging; patients may have paralysis in all four limbs (tetraplegia), or only in their lower limbs resulting in continued use of their hands and arms (paraplegia) [2]. Consequently, the ECU in question includes four modes of interaction to maximize its utility for users with various abilities: a touch interface, sip-and-puff (pneumatic tube), eye-tracking, and voice-control modes. The data herein relate to the touch mode functionality exclusively.

Increased levels of perceived control of environment (via lights/bed functionality), and increased social support (via email/phone/internet functionality) have been forwarded as mechanisms to foster independence and improve subjective well-being [3, 4]. As veterans diagnosed with SCI/D undergo rigorous physical, mental, and emotional rehabilitative care, the effective usability and user experience associated with these technologies is imperative for improving quality of life and alleviating workload of hospital staff. Based on self-reports, patients most often use the systems for watching television and other media, communicating with medical staff, and adjusting their immediate physical environment such as lighting conditions and bed position [5]. Consequently, these were the tasks selected for the current usability assessment. While veterans have reported being largely satisfied with these systems (71%), only 42% of those surveyed felt that this technology met their need for independence [5]. Such a low success rate is most likely due to the prevalence of usability problems inherent to the system. Seventy-five percent (75%) of surveyed users encountered significant problems, identifying the major issues as relating to both the technology (i.e., a non-working system) and the user (i.e., a lack of sufficient training) [5].

Previous usability assessments of Environmental Control Unit (ECU) technologies deployed by the VA note that among the eight identified reasons in which an ECU was out-of-use (ECU was not being used though use was desired), 89% of downtime was due to the patient's need for assistance and maintenance [2]. Problems with startup protocol for ECU use (patient admission, education, and ECU configuration) accounted for 28.8% of this unproductive time, and the remaining 71.2% was due to maintenance (troubleshooting, repair), with troubleshooting alone contributing to 13%-37% of wasted time [2]. Moreover, the majority of staff interactions (51%) with the ECU was due to their necessitated intervention for troubleshooting [2]. Of the issues affecting patients' usability of the system, 53% were considered minor and easily correctable, while 47% of problems were considered major due to their eliciting long delays, the need for additional resources, or both [2]. Given these serious considerations, this work performed a heuristic analysis on the autonoME ECU interface to identify catastrophic, major, and minor usability issues in order to better inform recommendations for the iterative design of ECU systems that seek to aid veterans in accomplishing necessary tasks, and thereby foster independence as well as better usability and user experience.

2 Methods

Seven evaluators from California State University, Long Beach (CSULB) completed a heuristic analysis of the autonoME Hospital Environmental Control Unit designed to assist SCI/D patients (Fig. 1). Though the system has multiple functionalities, this analysis exclusively addresses those issues raised by interacting via the touch-based mode. The analysis was conducted on operational inpatient systems at the VA Long Beach Spinal Cord Injury and Disorders Center in Long Beach, CA.

2.1 Task Description

Four tasks were selected to simulate typical actions that a patient would expect to make while interacting with the touch control interface of the device, thus assessing the system's range of functionality. These specific tasks have moreover been previously identified as some of the most common tasks for which the system is used [5]. Again, these activities broadly encompass communication with medical personnel, entertainment,

Fig. 1. ECU Home Screen Interface. The display shows the buttons and icons for completing the tasks including the room control, TV, telephone, and interest.

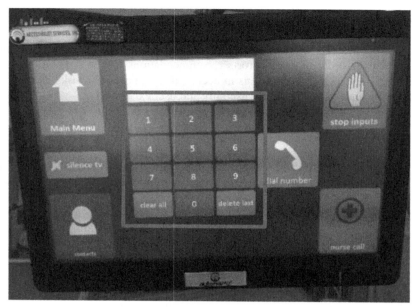

Fig. 2. Display used to enter phone numbers in the ECU call function. Keypad interface is highlighted within the red box. (Color figure online)

and manipulating their immediate physical environment. Therefore, the evaluators used the touchscreen to navigate through the interface in order to: 1) enter a phone number (Fig. 2), 2) send an email (Fig. 3), 3) change the television channel (Fig. 4), and 4) re-position the bed (Fig. 5).

Task 1. The first task was to simulate the steps required for the patient to make a phone call using the ECU's touchscreen interface. Each evaluator used the keypad as illustrated in Fig. 2 to enter their personal phone number to replicate the familiarity the patient would have with entering their physician's phone number.

Task 2. The second task was to compose an email to a medical professional, friend, or family member. Again, without access to veridical email addresses of VA personnel, evaluators performed the task by inputting their own personal email addresses to reflect users' familiarity with their own personal contacts.

Task 3. The third task was to turn on the television screen and then navigate to a particular channel. Despite the presence of shortcut buttons on the television function screen as seen in Fig. 4, evaluators were required to navigate to and change the channel by physically entering channel 20 (i.e., TNT) using the number pad to determine how well manual input completed the task.

Task 4. The fourth and final task was to adjust the head and foot positions of the bed. While the patients do not have the option to change the overall height of the bed, they do have the choice of adjusting various settings in order to sit upright, at an angle, or lay supine.

Fig. 3. The display illustrating multiple internet options. The red box indicates the button used to access the email function. (Color figure online)

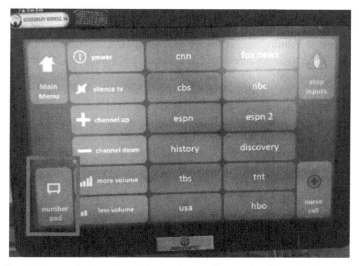

Fig. 4. Red box indicates the location of the number pad button for changing the television. (Color figure online)

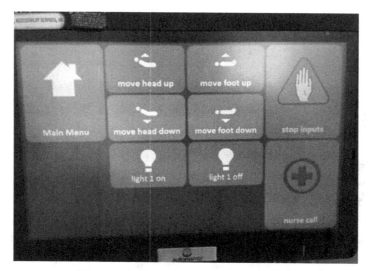

Fig. 5. Display options for bed adjustments

2.2 Heuristics

The seven researchers completed their evaluations independently. Each evaluator completed each task twice; the first assessment concentrating on overall work flow, and the second assessment for individual elements of the interface. The interface was evaluated for its adherence to Shneiderman's Eight Golden Rules for Interface Design [6] as detailed in Table 1, and Nielsen's 10 Heuristics for Interface Design [7] as presented in Table 2. The fact that Nielsen's heuristics and Shneiderman's rules share many common principles emphasizes their importance in effective design. After the violations of these heuristics were identified, each violation was rated for severity on Nielsen's Severity Rating Scale [8]. This instrument utilizes a five-point scale (0 to 4) to reflect the importance of the usability issue in terms of frequency, impact, and persistence, and provides a method for quantifying how to prioritize them in the re-design process (and see Table 3). Severity ratings were averaged across evaluators to determine the end rankings displayed in the following tables.

Table 1. Shneiderman's Eight Golden Rules for Interface Design [6].

Number	Rule	Description
S1	Strive for consistency	Information (i.e., icons, colors, symbols, etc.) presentation should be standardized throughout the entire system in order to reduce user confusion
S2	Enable frequent users to use shortcuts	There should be an option for experienced users to be able to expedite task completion

(continued)

Table 1. (*continued*)

Number	Rule	Description
S3	Offer informative feedback	The user should always know the status of the system's response by providing feedback to the user based on their completed action (e.g., page loading message or bar)
S4	Design dialogue to yield closure	The users should be presented with the required message that allows them to know when their task has been completed
S5	Offer simple error handling	Error message should be presented with language that explains what error occurred, why it occurred, and what can be done with normal language and not an error code of numbers and letters
S6	Permit easy reversal of actions	The system should allow the user to easily undo any action that was accidental or inappropriate
S7	Support internal locus of control	Users should not be surprised by how the system reacts to their actions. The system should respond in a way that is consistent with a user's expectations for an action
S8	Reduce short-term memory load	The user should easily be able to recognize the information that is being displayed (i.e., icons, symbols, etc.)

Table 2. Nielsen's 10 Heuristics for Interface Design [7].

Number	Heuristic	Description
N1	Visibility of System Status	The system should always keep users informed about what is going on, through appropriate feedback within reasonable time
N2	Match Between System and the Real World	The system should always keep users informed about what is going on, through appropriate feedback within reasonable time
N3	User Control and Freedom	Users often choose system functions by mistake and will need a clearly marked "emergency exit" to leave the unwanted state without having to go through an extended dialogue. Support undo and redo
N4	Consistency and Standards	Users should not have to wonder whether different words, situations, or actions mean the same thing. Follow platform conventions

(*continued*)

Table 2. (*continued*)

Number	Heuristic	Description
N5	Error Prevention	Even better than good error messages is a careful design which prevents a problem from occurring in the first place. Either eliminate error-prone conditions or check for them and present users with a confirmation option before they commit to the action
N6	Recognition Rather that Recall	Minimize the user's memory load by making objects, actions, and options visible. The user should not have to remember information from one part of the dialogue to another. Instructions for use of the system should be visible or easily retrievable whenever appropriate
N7	Flexibility and Efficiency of Use	Accelerators—unseen by the novice user—may often speed up the interaction for the expert user such that the system can cater to both inexperienced and experienced users. Allow users to tailor frequent actions
N8	Aesthetic and Minimalist Design	Dialogues should not contain information which is irrelevant or rarely needed. Every extra unit of information in a dialogue competes with the relevant units of information and diminishes their relative visibility
N9	Help Users Recognize, Diagnose, and Recover from Errors	Error messages should be expressed in plain language (no codes), precisely indicate the problem, and constructively suggest a solution
N10	Help and Documentation	Even though it is better if the system can be used without documentation, it may be necessary to provide help and documentation. Any such information should be easy to search, focused on the user's task, list concrete steps to be carried out, and not be too large

Table 3. Nielsen Severity Rating Scale [8].

Rating	Description
0	Not a usability problem
1	Cosmetic – only fix if time allows
2	Minor – low priority fix
3	Major – high priority fix
4	Catastrophe – imperative to fix

3   Results

After reviewing the environmental control unit, the identified usability issues were categorized as either catastrophic, major, or minor by taking the average of the evaluators' severity ratings. Four catastrophic, eight major, and fifteen minor usability issues were identified (Fig. 6). For the sake of clarity and brevity, only the three most severe usability issues from each category will be herein discussed.

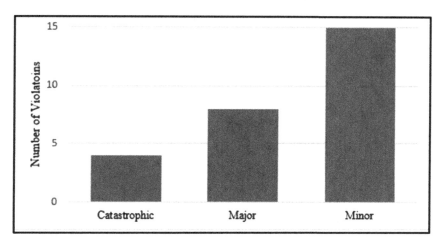

Fig. 6. Frequency counts of catastrophic, major, and minor usability violations.

3.1   Catastrophic Usability Issues

As illustrated in Figs. 7 and 8, the screens for dialing phone numbers or selecting TV channels have no option to "go back" to the previous screen or undo selections. As a result, users are forced to return to the home screen and again navigate through any and all screens to reach their previous decision point and select another option. With no capability to move backward in the workflow, users waste time and energy going through the process a second time and can become frustrated (Table 4).

While writing an email, no assistance is provided for completing tasks such as logging in or inputting contacts, nor is there support when the system experiences server connection issues. Figures 9 and 10 show the lack of "Help" options in any email-related menus. Such a lack of feedback as to how to troubleshoot issues leaves users confused about how to effectively progress in the workflow, and increases the likelihood that they will have to ask medical staff for assistance as help tools are not available through the system. While attempting to send an email, the system experienced server login issues which prevented the fabrication of email or even drafts. Again, no feedback or help was offered to address how the user could mitigate the server login issues. As a result, users could not even begin the task.

Fig. 7. Images of interface for dialing phone number (left)

Fig. 8. Selecting TV channel (right).

Table 4. List of top three Catastrophic Usability Issues with heuristic violations and final average severity ratings.

Issue	Heuristics violated	Rating
Phone Dial/TV dial menus lack dedicated "Go Back" button. Phone screen lacks button entirely; TV menus do not label them consistently (e.g., "favorite channels" instead of "go back")	N3, N5, N7; S5, S6	4
No help documentation in case user has a problem or needs to troubleshoot (e.g., when having server/login/email contact issues)	N9, N10; S3	4
No system feedback given to user for troubleshooting issues (e.g., unable to login to server)	N1, N3, N5, N9; S3, S4, S5, S6	4

Fig. 9. Images of interface for selecting email function (left)

Fig. 10. Starting email composition (right).

3.2 Major Usability Issues

Contacts must be added to the system prior to composing emails; however, the system does not provide the user with any instruction regarding this requirement. Without being told of this stipulation, users can waste time attempting to begin a draft of the body of the email and become confused when this is not possible due to a missing contact (Table 5).

Table 5. List of top three Major Usability Issues, with heuristic violations and final average severity ratings.

Issue	Heuristics violated	Rating
User must input and save contact before they are allowed to compose an email. System does not give feedback/inform user of this requirement	N1, N2, N7, N9, N10; S3, S7	3
Interface uses Red and Green as key colors for function coding; can be detrimental to Red/Green colorblind individuals	N2, N4, N7; S3	3
In email menus: "Jump Back" button does not work properly; can sometimes send user back several screens in email writing process	N3, N5, N7, N8; S2, S5, S6	3

Furthermore, multiple menus rely on red and green color-coding for key functions. Figures 11 and 12 demonstrate this color scheme for multiple screens of the phone call task. Confusion can arise as green buttons that users depress briefly flash red, which can confuse users as to which button has actually been pushed. Red-green is the most common congenital color vision deficiency and it disproportionately affects males [9]. As US male veterans outnumber female veterans (16.3 million versus 1.6 million) [10] and self-reports identify 95% of users as male [5], this design choice places the typical user at as significant disadvantage for navigation and interpretation of system feedback.

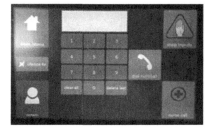

Fig. 11. Interfaces for choosing phone dialing function (left) (Color figure online)

Fig. 12. Inputting phone number (right). (Color figure online)

While in the process of composing an email, the "Jump Back" button can work improperly. If the user is composing an email after a contact is input, they are sent back to the menu seen in Fig. 10. After selecting to compose an email, should the user press "Jump Back", they will not be sent back to the immediately previous menu found in Fig. 10. The user is instead sent back several screens to where they first initiate the process of inputting contacts (Fig. 10).

3.3 Minor Usability Issues

Figures 9, 13 and 14 illustrate how the ECU has no feature to give users feedback for a chosen channel. The only way to determine if the desired channel is actually selected is to have the TV next to the ECU on and visible. Figure 15 shows the home screen and how, in order to access email functions found in Fig. 16, users must first press the "Internet" button on the screen to send an email. This design makes it more difficult to find email function. Moreover, while dialing the phone or selecting a channel, pressing green buttons provides feedback by turning red. Figure 17 shows how this scheme can be confusing as buttons such as "Clear All" and "Delete" are present and coded in red. Seeing only a collection of red buttons may therefore confuse the user as to which button has in actuality been depressed (Table 6).

Fig. 13. Interfaces for selecting TV channel by inputting channel number directly (left)

Fig. 14. Using channel shortcuts (right).

Fig. 15. Interface of ECU home screen (left)

Fig. 16. Location of email function in "Internet" sub-menu (right).

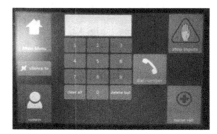

Fig. 17. Image of the keypad used for entering the phone number. (Color figure online)

Table 6. List of top three Minor Usability Issues detected, with heuristic violations and final ratings.

Issue	Heuristics violated	Rating
When selecting TV channel; ECU gives no feedback that task was successful. User must check TV to ensure success; needs element displaying 'TV now on channel "X"'	N1; S3, S4	2
User must press "Internet" button first before finding "email" button; user may not be aware, and might be hard to find the email button	N1, N2, N3; S3, S9	2
For dialing numbers (e.g., phone/TV channel); Numbers are green, while "Clear All"/"Delete" buttons are red. Pressing green buttons give visual feedback by turning red. Can be confusing, given that buttons turn the same color as the delete functions	N1, N3; S3	2

4 Discussion

4.1 Major Findings

The frequencies of usability violations identified in the heuristic evaluation of the ECU interface are illustrated in Fig. 6. In terms of severity, 15% of the usability problems were categorized as catastrophic, 30% were major usability problems, and 55% were minor usability problems. For catastrophic violations, the three most violated heuristics were "user control and freedom," "error prevention," and "offer informative feedback."

The most important catastrophic usability issue was the lack of a dedicated "go back" button across screens. As shown in Figs. 7 and 8, the screens for dialing a phone number and selecting a TV channel completely lack the "go back" button. Without this control, the user is unable to recover from navigation errors without backtracking to the home page. For veterans with spinal cord injuries and other special populations with severe motor skill impairments, using the ECU provides users with communication and entertainment benefits, however, using the ECU necessitates significant cognitive effort. Using an inflexible system that restricts user control and freedom increases cognitive load and causes user frustration [11]. As a result, this can negatively impact the user's ability to effectively engage with the system and accomplish task goals. To address issues of user interface inconsistency, the authors propose the inclusion of a permanently visible, clearly defined backward navigation button (e.g., "go back") at the top of every screen that returns the user to the previous screen. The "go back" button should always be available, in the same location, and work in the same fashion, allowing the user to retrace one step at a time rather than restarting the task every time [12]. Additionally, the button should be a fairly large target, especially when designing for users with motoric impairments, who benefit greatly from having a large target [12].

The second catastrophic issue identified was the absence of help documentation when the user runs into an error, as shown in Figs. 9 and 10. The lack of help documentation can impede the user's ability to use the system correctly [13], especially when the user is not in the presence of a healthcare provider. Help documentation is also critical for nurses and healthcare providers who are required to learn how to use the system prior to teaching their patients [5]. As a result, not being able to troubleshoot errors while learning how to navigate the ECU can lead to faulty training when teaching patients how to use the device. A clearly defined "Help" button should be made visible throughout the application. It should be designed to allow the user to search for context specific information relevant to their issue by clicking on a drop-down menu. Instructions for troubleshooting issues should consist of clear, consistent, sequential, and actionable items that instruct the user on how to perform the task.

The final catastrophic problems were the lack of informative system feedback given to the user when troubleshooting errors and the inability to login and draft an email due to no internet connection/no offline mode. When attempting to login and draft an email without internet connection, the user receives an error ("Unable to login to server"). However, this error message does little to assist the user in diagnosing and solving the system issue. Such confusion can hinder the user's ability to understand, detect, and manage the appropriate errors when they occur [14].

Effective feedback should keep the user informed of system state at all times [7]. An error message should be designed to give the user troubleshooting options on how to connect to the server and list specific instructions on how to manage the connectivity error. If the issue persists, an additional option should provide the user with instructions on how to contact a product representative for the autonoME Hospital Environmental Control Unit or a service provider to troubleshoot the connectivity issue.

A major usability issue was the lack of system feedback to inform the user that he/she is required to add a new contact to the system before composing an email. Lack of informative feedback to enter information in a mandatory data entry field can lead to user frustration and dissatisfaction. To bypass this issue, the system should be designed to either restrict the user from inputting text in the email body section prior to entering a new contact or instruct the user to enter a new contact first, prior to composing an email. A design element of emphasis that highlights the first step of completing the task, such as a red box around the specific section to be completed should be implemented, while also making other sections inaccessible by greying them out.

The second major usability issue is the interface's color coding. Using color for function coding is unfavorable for users with color vision deficiencies. The interface relies on color to convey a message. For example, Fig. 11 demonstrates the use of red for "hang up" and green for "answer phone". Certain users with red-green color vision deficiencies might have difficulties distinguishing the colors on the buttons and have to read the text instead. Thus, the color-coding in the interface is inefficient and lacks accessibility for different user populations. A suggestion is to use both color and symbols to indicate the purpose of a button. In addition, in order to prevent the users from choosing the unwanted function by mistake, all the buttons should clearly describe the location where users will be redirected. For example, the "Jump Back" button in the email menu would send the users several screens back, instead of only to the previous one. For users who intend to go back to the previous screen, this design causes confusion and frustration. To improve efficiency, the button name can be changed to the location that will be redirected to, such as "Main Menu".

Minor usability issues are the violations that receive the lowest priority for fixing, though failure to identify and address these issues can still cause negative user experiences. For instance, the system should always keep users informed about the system's status after a selection. However, the interfaces failed to provide feedback when selecting TV channels. If users are uninformed about the current channel, they might waste effort on clarifying whether they have successfully made the desired selection. Thus, the interface should contain a message about current channel selection. In addition, the design of the menu should match users' past experiences. The evaluators found difficulties related to the location of the "Email" button as it is listed on a secondary menu that is accessed after the "Internet" button has been selected, while the "Telephone" button is listed as an option on the primary menu. This layout is inconsistent with our mental models of the email function as a primary option on the home screen, prioritized in other touch-centric interfaces (i.e., smartphones and tablets). Therefore, we recommend moving the "Email" button to the primary menu and place it next to the "Telephone" button. Furthermore, the interface should be consistent and eliminate any ambiguous or confusing feedback. However, evaluators found the current design to be misleading for users due to the green buttons flashing red when pressed, changing to the same color as the "Clear All" and "Delete" buttons. A recommendation is to simply darken the same color when pressing button (i.e., green flashes a darker green).

4.2   Continuing Line of Research: Next Steps

The goal of this project is to research various user interface design approaches and standards for the purpose of enhancing the usability of the ECU device, with VA Hospital patients in the SCI/D Centers as the target user-base. The authors plan to accomplish this goal in multiple phases, beginning with this heuristic evaluation of the design of the currently deployed ECU system. In the upcoming second phase, the authors will administer validated questionnaires and conduct structured and semi-structured interviews with end-users to examine usability issues. In the third phase of the project, the authors will re-design the ECU digital interface in keeping with Nielsen's heuristics, Shneiderman's golden rules, and end-users' input from the second phase. Interactive prototypes will be generated to conduct A/B user testing to measure the effectiveness of the design and user experience. Systems will be evaluated for task completion rates and times across myriad tasks that necessitate interacting with elements both within and outside of the VA hospital. The final phase of this research project is to test the effectiveness of the CSULB re-designed user interface with end-users (i.e., Veterans), VA Staff, at-home caregivers, and CSULB students for comparisons of usability in a general population. Findings will facilitate the empirically-driven re-design of such systems to improve the independence and quality of life of our veterans and other stakeholders of the ECU system (i.e., both inpatient and outpatient caregivers).

5   Conclusion

Veterans with spinal cord injuries and diseases typically find environmental control units to be useful technological tools [5]. However, the current design and functionality of these systems suffer from numerous usability issues that compromise performance and undermine a strong sense of independence in its intended end users, our veterans [5]. The heuristic analyses herein evaluated this system's usability across a range of different tasks to identify specific design elements that led to these undesirable outcomes. Results indicated that the interface currently has issues ranging in severity from relatively minor to catastrophic. Design recommendations for rectifying these violated heuristics and enhancing usability were provided to ensure that veterans' technological support tools are designed in such a way that promotes successful task completion, fosters independence, and decreases workload and frustration for veterans and hospital staff.

References

1. U.S. Department of Veterans Affairs: FY2020/FY2018 annual performance plan and report [PDF file] (2019). https://www.va.gov/oei/docs/VA2020appr.pdf
2. Bidassie, B., et al.: Evaluating the roll-out of environmental control units in Veterans Affairs spinal cord injury centers: workflow observations. Int. J. Healthcare 3(2), 57–67 (2017)
3. Schulz, R., Hanusa, B.H.: Experimental social gerontology: a social psychological perspective. J. Soc. Issues 36(2), 30–46 (1980)
4. Cohen, S., Syme, S.L.: Issues in the study and application of social support. In: Cohen, S., Syme, S.L. (eds.) Social Support and Health, pp. 3–22. Academic Press (1985)
5. Etingen, B., et al.: Patient perceptions of environmental control units. Experiences of Veterans with spinal cord injuries and disorders receiving inpatient VA healthcare. Disabil. Rehabil.: Assistive Technol. 13(4), 325–332 (2017)
6. Shneiderman, B.: Eight golden rules for interface design. In: Designing the User Interface, 3rd edn. Addison Wesley, Boston (1998)
7. Nielsen, J.: Ten usability heuristics for user interface design (1995). http://www.useit.com/papers/heuristic/heuristic_list.html. Accessed 26 Jan 2020
8. Nielsen, J.: Severity ratings for usability problems. Pap. Essays 54, 1–2 (1995)
9. Birch, J.: Worldwide prevalence of red-green color deficiency. J. Opt. Soc. Am. A 29(3), 313–320 (2012)
10. US Census Bureau: B21001: Sex by age by veteran status for the civilian population 18 years and over (2018). https://data.census.gov/cedsci/table?hidePreview=true&table=B21001&tid=ACSDT1Y2018.B21001&lastDisplayedRow=38&q=B21001%3A%20SEX%20BY%20AGE%20BY%20VETERAN%20STATUS%20FOR%20THE%20CIVILIAN%20POPULATION%2018%20YEARS%20AND%20OVER. Accessed 29 Jan 2020
11. Shneiderman, B., Hochheiser, H.: Universal usability as a stimulus to advanced interface design. Behav. Inf. Technol. 20(5), 367–376 (2001)
12. Nielsen, J., Loranger, H.: Prioritizing Web Usability. New Riders Press, Berkeley (2006)
13. Nielsen, J.: Iterative user-interface design. Computer 26(11), 32–41 (1993)
14. Tang, Z., Johnson, T.R., Tindall, R.D., Zhang, J.: Applying heuristic evaluation to improve the usability of a telemedicine system. Telemed. J. E-Health 12(1), 24–34 (2006)

A Generalized User Interface Concept to Enable Retrospective System Analysis in Monitoring Systems

Viviane Herdel[1], Bertram Wortelen[2(✉)], Mathias Lanezki[2],
and Andreas Lüdtke[2]

[1] Carl v. Ossietzky University, 26129 Oldenburg, Germany
viviane.herdel@uni-oldenburg.de
[2] OFFIS - Institute for Information Technology, 26121 Oldenburg, Germany
{wortelen,lanezki,luedtke}@offis.de

Abstract. Many technical work environments nowadays face the situation that large technical systems are controlled by semi-autonomous software systems that process a huge amount of information. Human operators are still required to monitor the system, but only at sporadic time points to assure that the system is healthy or to analyze any fault conditions that have occurred since the last observation. However, a problem with such a monitoring situation is that the operator is often out-of-the loop when observing the system (after a long time of not observing it). The objective is to develop a graphical user interface concept that supports operators in developing valid situation awareness of the system and furthermore provides an easy to use functionality for efficient retrospective system analysis. We discuss requirements for retrospective system analysis and present a concept for a user interface (UI) that efficiently supports the operator in getting back in the loop and developing a valid situation awareness of the current system state. It furthermore supports the operator in recognizing the global system health state, identifying and localizing current and past fault conditions and easily tracing how the system and especially error states have evolved over time. The UI concept is applied to a software application for controlling and monitoring hybrid energy systems. However, we argue, that the UI concept is applicable for a wide range of applications.

Keywords: Human-machine interaction design · Retrospective system analysis · Monitoring systems · Visualization concepts · Hybrid energy systems

1 Introduction

The last years have seen an increase in complexity of technical systems due to their ever-advancing development. One dominant factor that increases the complexity of technical systems is the huge amount of data that can be processed fast, precisely and often in parallel by machines – a task that requires great effort for humans to the point where cognitive limitations regarding workload and attention hinder error-free processes. Thus automated systems that

© Springer Nature Switzerland AG 2020
S. Yamamoto and H. Mori (Eds.): HCII 2020, LNCS 12184, pp. 39–57, 2020.
https://doi.org/10.1007/978-3-030-50020-7_3

analyze huge amounts of data provide a reasonable solution and became indispensable. However in many systems humans are still involved in the overall process for instance by making decisions based on complex information provided by a system. Accordingly operators have to monitor systems to control and interpret outcomes provided by a system interface. Examples, where humans have to deal with complex data of automated systems are numerous, come from diverse domains (e.g. aviation, health care, energy management) and often involve safety-critical systems (SCS) [16]. Hence many operators (e.g. pilots, aircraft controllers, nurses, power plant operators) have in common that they must know which pieces of information - displayed on an interface - are important and how these should be integrated and interpreted with respect to specific job tasks. The overall process of assessing a situation leads to a state called situation awareness - a critical and thus highly important factor for decision making and task performance [8]. In the following section we will define situation awareness in general and describe it in more detail regarding its relevance, levels and accompanied errors [5].

Situation awareness (SA) can be shortly defined as:

> the perception of the elements in the environment within a volume of time and space, the comprehension of their meaning and the projection of their status in the near future [4, p. 97].

The importance of the multi-dimensional construct SA for designing systems originates from the fact that valid SA increases the probability of good decision making and good performance, whereas poor SA increases the probability for poor decisions and poor performance that may end fatal [5,8]. Consequently the interface of a system must provide a design that assists operators to achieve valid SA.

As described by Endsley [5], SA consists of three different levels. The first level comprises the perception of relevant information in terms of job tasks and is the foundation of SA. It is followed by level two that deals with the comprehension and integration of information according to current goals of operators. The third level comprises the ability to project meaning of information and their integration onto future events and consequences. These levels build on one another - meaning that level two can only be achieved correctly based on accurate information from level one, and level three only if all relevant information at level two was combined and interpreted correctly. Accordingly Endsley [5] argues that errors related to SA are due to incomplete (e.g. missing or unattended information) or inaccurate SA (e.g. misunderstanding or wrong integration of information). Since level three SA is primarily achieved by operators who have acquired expert knowledge or at least advanced knowledge for their work tasks, it can be implied that SA is not only formed through bottom-up (information-driven), but also through top-down (concept-driven or hypothesis-driven) processes. The latter is based on knowledge, prior experiences, training and automaticity as well as goals and expectations that all have an influence on how the situation is assessed [12,21]. For example, a high level of automaticity (e.g. knowing which information belongs together and how information needs to be integrated without the need of conscious effort) allows operators to perform tasks without being occupied with low-level details so that the workload of operators can be reduced. Therefore automaticity can generally facilitate SA, but may also lead to biased and possibly wrong decisions. This might be the case when relevant information is neglected, because it does not belong to the schema (e.g. problem pattern) expected by an operator or when information is misinterpreted, due to a wrong mental model that is usually used within a specific context. Hence top-down processes have a major impact on the selection of information that is taken into account and how it is interpreted or integrated within different contexts [8,28].

Now that we specified the different levels of SA, we will shortly describe particular errors that go along with different levels of SA and prevent the accomplishment of reaching them. For the specification of errors we will use the taxonomy of SA errors provided by Endsley [5]. If for instance relevant information is hard to notice or not even provided by an interface, the achievement of level one SA will be highly limited. This might also be the case when operators are distracted, too focused on a task or have a high workload with the consequence of missing available information (see: attentional narrowing [19]). Failures in reaching level two SA are related to misinterpretations or incomprehension of perceived information. Furthermore operators may fail to connect pieces of information with each other or may be biased towards inappropriate schemata in recognition-primed decision making [17]. And even in the case that the knowledge about how to connect specific information is available in general, operators may fail to memorize it. Aside from level one and two, reaching level three SA can be hindered, when the understanding of a complex system along with its underlying processes and principles is too superficial on the part of the operator, as that the integration and meaning of information could be projected to future events.

2   Motivation

In the following section we discuss the relevance of situation awareness (SA) within the context of monitoring tasks. As discussed above operators often have to handle rich in content user interfaces that reflect system complexity and thus are not easy to overlook. In order to approach resulting problems (e.g. safety-critical issues due to human errors) owing to complexity, automated functions are a favored possibility to help operators managing the system. Increased automation, however, changes tasks and the workflow of operators and does not automatically mean that operators have to deal with less, but with processed data. Hence the function of many operators strongly shifted towards monitoring systems. Monitoring tasks in general may include to ensure system health, act on unusual events as well as to analyze and resolve failures that the system cannot cope with.

Although monitoring tasks are often meant to decrease the mental workload of operators, they comprise another set of problems that should not be disregarded. One of the issues in monitoring tasks is the out-of-the-loop problem [9] that comprises, amongst others, the inability of operators to trace back processes that caused errors due to their passive role in automated systems [6]. Conceived in general terms monitoring tasks can cause a lack of SA:

> The traditional form of automation which places humans in the role of monitor has been shown to negatively impact situation awareness and thus their ability to effectively perform that function. Losses in situation awareness can be attributed to the unsuitability of humans to perform a monitoring role, assumption of a passive role in decision making, and inadequate feedback associated with automation. As a result many automated systems have been suboptimized, with infrequent, but major errors attributed to a failure of the human component [6, p. 9].

An additional point is that some systems require to be monitored over the entire process, whereas some systems must only be monitored irregularly. In case of infrequent monitoring, operators face the challenge of gaining SA for error states in the past that possibly evolved over the time span in which the system was unobserved. Consequently user interfaces of complex technical systems require solutions that enable a retrospective analysis of errors to tackle problems that occur in infrequent monitoring tasks. We argue that this can be achieved by providing information in a way that supports operators to gain valid SA regarding the following questions:

1. Is the system currently healthy?
2. Did any problem occur since the last observation?
3. If there was a problem: where did it appear and how did it evolve over time?

To approach further development in this direction, our work aims towards building design guidelines for a particular class of monitoring systems with a specific workflow. In the main part of the paper we present requirements for the visualization of user interfaces that support a retrospective analysis of errors. Furthermore we illustrate the concept by means of an application used to monitor hybrid energy systems. The development of such system is expected to increase in the near future [10, 27].

3   State of the Art

Monitoring software for technical systems are a broad class of applications. A key objective in monitoring software is that operators maintain or regain valid SA of a technical system. Several methods for designing Human-Machine Interfaces (HMIs) that improve monitoring tasks already exist. This includes design guidelines (e.g. [18]), design methods (e.g. [11]) and real-time intervention systems (e.g. [24]). Endsley [7] gives a good overview and practical recommendations to achieve the objective of maintaining good SA.

For our use case demonstrated further down, we used the Konect method [11] for designing many of the HMI elements. It is a structured step-by-step approach which is particularly useful for creating elements that enable a quick perception of the system health status. In addition to that we used some of the Konect concepts to create an HMI for infrequent and irregular monitoring intervals.

4   Retrospective System Analysis in Monitoring Systems

In this section we first describe how different levels of automation affect the monitoring behaviour of operators. We then define the class of systems, for which retrospective system analysis during system monitoring is an essential aspect of the operator's tasks. Finally, we introduce a use case that we use throughout the paper to illustrate the UI design concept developed in this work.

4.1   System Monitoring and Automation

Nowadays more and more technical systems can operate autonomously in most of their everyday situations. Think for example about autonomous lawn mower or vaccum cleaner. However in some situations human interaction is needed, for example if the robot got stuck or when the dirt disposal bag needs to be emptied. Most of the time, the robot is able to detect the problem, but is unable to solve it on its own. Formulated in more general terms, this means that monitoring by a human operator is especially important, if the system is not able to automatically interpret every situation and detect or solve every relevant event. This is certainly the case for most of today's complex system. Consequently a human operator has to monitor the system, although, the operator is typically assisted by some sort of semi-automatic machine-agent that detects critical or abnormal states and emits a warning thereupon.

An important characteristic of a monitoring system is the monitoring frequency, respectively the rate with which operators observe a technical system or individual subsystems. As mentioned earlier the monitoring frequency influences how well the operator can maintain or regain valid SA. For experienced operators, the monitoring frequency depends primarily on the Expected Value of an observation [23, 29]. Wickens [29] defines the Expected Value of an information source (i) as the product of the expectancy (E) of the operator that new information (e.g. new events) are accessible in the information source (e.g. a UI view) and the value (V) of that information for the operator.

$$\text{Expected Value}(i) = E_i \cdot V_i = E_i \cdot \sum_{t \in T} R_{i,t} \cdot I_t$$

The value depends on how relevant (R) the information is for each of the tasks (T) of the operator and how important (I) each task is for the operator. If events are highly relevant for operator tasks, then they are of great value to the operator and the expected value of an observation is high. The Expected Value is also high, if the operator highly expects new events and information. This means that the expectancy typically rises over time.

In many surveillance environments, the value of an observation can be described very well by the costs that are incurred if an event is not responded to in time [3]. So the value of an observation is that these potential costs are avoided. This can be illustrated by the example of driving a car. Manual driving is an extreme example where the cost of not observing the traffic can be very high (injury or even death from an accident). This means that the value of an observation (of the surrounding traffic) is high, because it avoids paying the costs. In addition, due to the high speed and the dynamics of the surrounding traffic, the time to react in time is extremely short. For this reason, driving requires a high –nearly continuous– monitoring rate. Estimating the effects of new in-vehicle systems on the driver's monitoring rate is therefore very important and has become a standardized procedure [13,14].

Introducing automated functions can reduce the required monitoring rate or the time-criticality or even both. Today's advanced lane keeping and distance keeping systems (Level 2 in Society of Automotive Engineers (SAE) definition of driving automation [20]) enable the driver to slightly decrease the monitoring rate in some restricted situations. But still, controlling and supporting a suitable and safe monitoring rate of the human driver is one of the most critical aspects of this level of automation [2]. In SAE Level 3 the time-criticality of events is reduced, because the vehicle can bring itself into a temporarily safe state when a critical event occurs. All events that the vehicle cannot handle on its own are not time-critical, e.g. traffic alerts (traffic jam, bypass rerouting) or technical alarms (low fuel, A/C malfunction). No immediate response of the driver is required in order to ensure safety, while in Level 4 no response at all for ensuring safety is required. However, the vehicle cannot act autonomously in all situations, but may give back control to the driver in a safe state.

4.2   Addressed Class of Systems

The above mentioned levels of autonomy are found similarly in many other domains. The work of this paper addresses systems that

1. can operate autonomously for extended periods of time, i.e. for a few hours or even days, without the need for human intervention,
2. typically require no time-critical, immediate response to alarms,
3. are complex (i.e contain very large amount of parameters),
4. may have transient alarm states.

Due to the first and second condition the expected value of an observation is relatively low. The first condition means that the system controls itself and the user does not have to control it manually when the system status changes. Therefore, the expectation for events to which the operator must react is low. The second condition means that even when events occur, they are usually associated with relatively little information values, because it does not incur high costs if the operator does not respond to the events immediately. These two conditions therefore result in a low monitoring frequency. This is in contrast to the third condition, in which observations take a lot of effort and time. Due to the complexity of the system, the achievement of valid SA (up to level three SA) regarding system health can be time-consuming. The fourth condition is about the nature of alarms in the system. An alarm is often viewed as a signal that indicates critical system state changes, which require timely response by

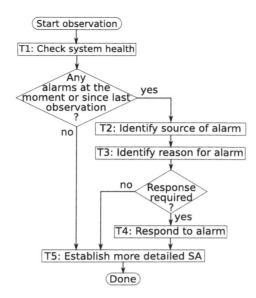

Fig. 1. Workflow of the operator during a system observation.

a human operator. But this is not always the case. Stanton [25] discusses the nature of alarms extensively and provides different definitions of alarms. In many systems an alarm is an unexpected and undesired change in system state. That is the definition of alarm used in this work. Errors are state changes that result in non-functional subcomponents. For simplicity we often use the terms error and alarm synonymously. In this respect, a transient alarm is an alarm that is only active for a certain period of time. The system enters an alarm state, but leaves the state after some time, without intervention of the operator, e.g. a navigation system that shortly looses contact to GPS satellites. Transient alarms can be problematic when the monitoring rate is low, since they can appear and disappear without the operator noticing it.

The objective of our work is to develop HMI design concepts for complex monitoring system, that enable a fast and efficient assessment of the current system state and also an efficient retrospective analysis of (transient) alarms. During an observation of the system, we assume that the operator has a workflow similar to the one shown in Fig. 1. The operator checks the system's health state, looking out for alarms and errors (T1). If there are any alarms or errors, the source and root causes are identified (T2, T3). If required, the operator takes countermeasure (T4) and finally, the operator establishes are more detailed SA that goes beyond alarm states (T5). All the above mentioned operator tasks not only consider the current state of the system, but importantly also past system states. Due to the low monitoring frequency, a lot of time may have passed since the last observation. The operator therefore also has to retrospectively analyze past issues that occurred since the last observation.

4.3   Use Case: Hybrid Energy Systems

The energy sector is currently undergoing major changes and has become a research field of high interest and a matter of importance. Hence we have chosen a use case within the energy sector and demonstrate a visualization concept by means of an user interface for the management of hybrid energy systems. These systems have the characteristic that electrical and thermal energy generation and storage facilities are coupled. Furthermore they have several advantages: they can increase the share of renewable energy by storing or converting excess energy, reduce carbon emission and increase their overall system efficiency. Beyond that the advancements in renewable energy technologies, operations of local heating grids and rise in prices of petroleum products are expected to make operations of hybrid energy systems more profitable in the future. Therefore the development of hybrid energy systems is likely to be expedited in near future [10,27]. The study "cellular energy system" from the German Association for Electrical, Electronic & Information Technologies proposes how supply security and stability of electrical grids can be improved by combining different forms of energy in hybrid systems, described as "energy cells" [1]. A core element is the energy management of the cell itself and the ability of cells to coordinate their functionality with neighbouring cells. The application of the proposed visualization concept is demonstrated based on such a local energy management system in a new district in Oldenburg in northwestern Germany. The hybrid energy system is still in the planning phase and will contain a set of energy consumers and suppliers (combined heat and power (CHP) and photovoltaic (PV) plants), district heating as well as heat and power storage facilities [22].

In hybrid energy systems, several plants and components are used, which all have to be considered to support the achievement of valid SA of current, past, as well as future processes. However the integration of all energy components brings up new challenges regarding the operation, control and monitoring of the entire system. The complexity of system operation is significantly increased, because in the future it will not only be necessary to adapt energy production to current consumption, but also to control the consumers according to the current energy offer. Most of these systems are designed to run autonomously, but are monitored continuously or every once a while by an operator. In general operators have the task to maintain the technical availability of machines and systems. This includes the planning of maintenance and repair work as well as monitoring the systems and reacting in case of an alarm. To do this, operators need a comprehensive overview of all systems, notifications of alarms and a display of current and historical measured values of certain sensors (e.g. temperature of the heating network, filling level of the thermal energy storage, operating status of the CHP).

5   Support for Efficient Error Detection During Infrequent and Irregular Monitoring Intervals

As mentioned above we developed guidelines for designing systems that support the gain of valid SA in infrequent monitoring tasks. As valid SA is the result of perceiving and categorizing errors correctly, it is a precondition to act on them properly and is thus indispensable for good decision making in case of error states. The design guidelines were created based on the requirements that we discuss in the following section. For each of the generalizable requirements for retrospective system analysis in monitoring systems we present a design solution for the use case described in the previous section (hybrid energy system). We would also like to briefly highlight what our specific design solutions can and cannot be used for.

The concept visualizations provide a structured overview of monitoring systems in the course of time in order to gain valid SA for past and current error states. A typical situation could be for instance that an operator returns to his or her workplace in the morning and then wants to check whether there are or were erroneous components within the system. If this is the case our design solution enables the operator to explore the system over time and space. Knowledge that operators can gain from the usage of the interface might be the classification of errors into a known error pattern, or to identify root causes, or connections between errors over time or space. However our design solutions do not incorporate a data analysis tool to scrutinize and analyse data related to error states, but focuses on efficiently communicating the system state to the operator.

5.1   Global System Health State

The first task during an observation is to check the system health state (see Fig. 1, T1). Design elements should enable operators to inspect past and current system health at a glance. Hence the first aim is to provide an overview of the system and an idea about when and where errors occurred in order to give an idea how to further explore the system in greater detail. In addition the overview should support the development of valid level two SA functions, such that operators can classify and interpret errors with a high automaticity based on previously observed and similar error patterns. In order to realize the first requirement, we used the Konect method [11] and developed a glyph that visualizes the system health in a way that allows fast perception relying on pre-attentive processes. The effect that facilitates fast perception of objects is the so called pop-out effect which is a key element of feature-integration theory (FIT) [26]. The pop-out effect refers to the ability to easily detect an object that differs from other objects by a unique feature (e.g color). Consequently we chose the color red for errors and only for errors, and a light gray for error-free states. Since the design guidelines aim to support retrospective system analysis, the glyph concept needs to be extended by a third color that indicates errors that occurred in the past, but are no longer present in the system. These components are indicated by a yellow coloring. Figure 2 illustrates the pop-out effect. For an effective pop-out-effect this color concept should be used throughout the entire HMI system.

Correspondingly the glyph (Fig. 3) shows whether errors or alarms are currently present (red components) or had been present in the past without confirmation (yellow components). Thus the operator can differentiate between current and past errors. We assume that the recognition of each error or alarm needs

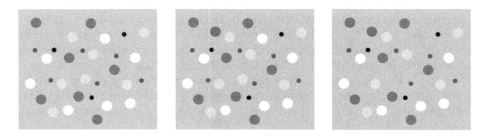

Fig. 2. Color concept and visualization of the pop-out effect. (Color figure online)

to be actively confirmed by the operator. Otherwise past errors are not cleared, which means that the component remains colored yellow. Red components are active until the error state of the element has been solved by an operator or by the system itself. Moreover the glyph displays where problems are localized approximately to support task T2. In our chosen use case this means that the glyph is arranged in a matrix-like 2 × n structure where each element corresponds to a component of the energy system (e.g. combined heat and power plant (CHP), buffer storage...). The first column contains n categories that are related to electricity, whereas the second column contains n-1 categories that are related to heat. In case that an element belongs to both the electricity and heat category (e.g. CHPs) it is located between the intersections. Categories might be amongst others: production (e.g. CHP, PV systems), storage (e.g. buffer storage, battery storage), transducer (e.g. Power-to-Heat), transportation (water pipes, power supply lines) and consumer (buildings, charging stations) (see Fig. 3).

This approach additionally supports the operator regarding the recognition of recurring error patterns or meaningful combinations of errors in the system, simply by recognizing a recurring graphical pattern. For instance, an operator could check the glyph of the system after a few hours and receives the information that the CHP is currently in an error state, as well as two categories related to heat - namely transportation (e.g. there might be a leak in one of the water pipes) and consumer (e.g. some of the buildings might not be supplied with hot water) (see Fig. 3b).

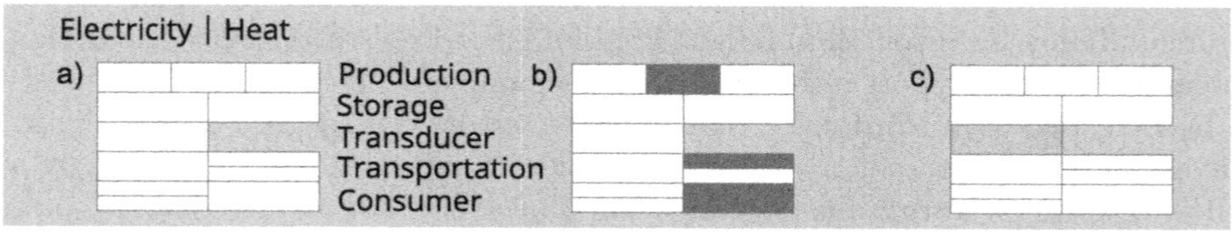

Fig. 3. a) Glyph structure. b) Current error status. c) Unconfirmed past error status. (Color figure online)

5.2   Traceability of Alarms and Errors

Besides the enhanced human performance in error detection, the design of the interface should provide elements that facilitate the traceability of causal error-relationships. Thus operators can detect past and current errors as well as error patterns, but are additionally able to inspect error progressions in the course of time. In order to be able to analyze possible causes and the time course of errors fast and easy, we introduce an application-wide mechanism based on time bars. The designed time bars are again small glyphs based on the Konect method [11]. They show the time course of errors within the time bars using red areas that begin and end together with the start and end times of errors or alarms. Moreover the slider of the time bars can be used to navigate the entire system visualization through the past, in order to make a detailed analysis of the root causes of error states. When the slider is placed at a time point where components are or were erroneous, the slider turns red to prevent that small red areas - thus error states - disappear unnoticed behind the slider.

Fig. 4. First type of time bar. Summary time bar indicates the time course of all errors that occurred within the components of a system. Triangles indicate the starting point of errors. (Color figure online)

We realized two types of time bars. The first type of time bar is a summary of all errors that occurred within the components of a system (see Fig. 4). The triangles indicate the starting point of errors within the same or multiple components. As this summary gives a rough idea about the time course of errors without great detail, the operator can expand the summary time bar using the arrow at the right side. This will open the second type of time bars that are specific for each of the components within the system (see Fig. 5a). Components that are displayed in the interface can be added and removed as system components might also be added or removed within a hybrid energy system. For example in our use case a second CHP could be supplemented to the district's hybrid energy system.

We argue that the causal arrangement of time bars of erroneous components support operators in analyzing errors throughout the entire system and time. The operators might identify causal relationships between errors and easily recognize recurring error patterns, based on the graphical pattern that the red sections of the time bars create.

It is also possible to select one of the system components via the toggle buttons or double-click to inspect the chosen component in detail. The detail view of each component contains aspects that are critical for the component's health state (see Fig. 5b) and supports the operator in identifying the reason for an

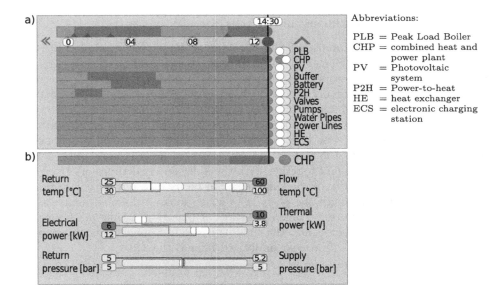

Fig. 5. a) First and second type of time bars. Component time bars indicate the time course of all errors that occurred within a particular component of a system. b) Time bars and detail view for the selected component CHP. (Color figure online)

alarm (task T3) and choosing appropriate responses (task T4). In our use case an operator may select the CHP to open the corresponding detail view. The operator is then provided with information regarding return and flow temperature [°C], electrical and thermal power [kW], as well as return and supply pressure [bar]. The lower boxes show the ideal value for each element (e.g. 3.8 kW thermal power) that comes along with a range of tolerance indicated by the surrounding white area. The upper boxes are the actual values (e.g. 10 kW thermal power), which turn red when the actual value is outside the range of tolerance.

The design of the detail view strongly depend on the use case. We recommend to use appropriate design methods for designing the HMI elements. For the hybrid energy system use case in this work we again used the Konect method [11].

In many monitoring applications, the representation of system behavior over time already plays a role. However, this is mostly limited to the display of individual important system parameters, which are shown in diagram components as curves over time. These representations make it possible to quickly observe the behavior of the selected parameters separately from the rest of the system behavior. The proposed time bar concept can be easily integrated into such displays of system parameters over time. The same sliders as for the time bars are now inserted into these diagrams. Here, too, they always indicate which time is currently displayed. These sliders can also be moved to change the system time. In the case of hybrid energy systems, for example, schedules for individual system components play an important role. These schedules provide target values

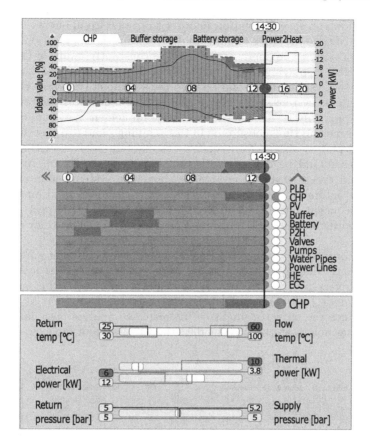

Fig. 6. Overall view - present day and current time. (Color figure online)

over time for the respective components (e.g. the electrical power generated by the CHP). The operator compares the target values with the actually measured values. A corresponding visualization of the schedules including the time slider can be seen in Fig. 6 (top). Within this view, the operator can select schedules for particular system components that display target values that a component should approach (dashed line), actual values that a component approached (gray bars) and also mark discrepancies between ideal and actual values, when these exceed a threshold (marked in red).

5.3   Exploration of Past System States

Due to the fact that operators have to explore past and current states in systems that are non-constantly monitored, operators should be provided with a functionality that allows them to explore the complete system over time. As shown in Fig. 6 all described views are interconnected by an orientation line of a slider.

The slider allows an easy navigation in order to inspect components thoroughly in the course of time. In order to gain valid SA within the exploration of current and past error states, the operators have to be constantly aware of the selected HMI mode (HMI displaying the current state of the system vs. HMI displaying a past state of the system). One solution is to use a complete different HMI design for displaying past system states than for current system states. However, such a solution may not only be expensive to develop, implement and maintain, but is also not intuitive and time-consuming in the handling - and can therefore lead to poor SA and poor usability. Consequently the system analysis within different system modes should be realized with the same systems design. At the same time it should create a strong awareness about the system mode with which operators are interacting. To realize these requirements we used on color used in the color-concept introduced in Sect. 5.1. We colored structural parts (e.g. component borders) of some HMI components using the yellow color to indicate past time.

Based on our design concept the HMI can be in three different modes regarding the currently displayed system time. In our use case the first system mode (see Fig. 6) refers to the present day at the current time, whereas the second system mode (see Fig. 7a) displays also the present day, but at a selected past time. Since the operator might be interested to analyse past days and not only past time points at the present day, the third system mode was realized.

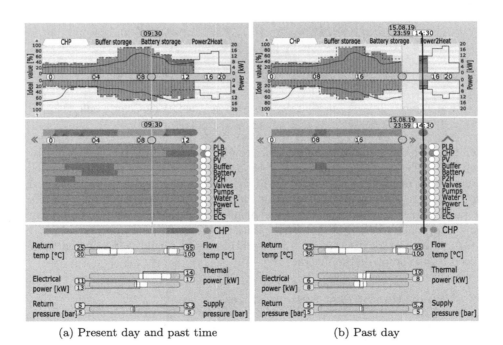

(a) Present day and past time   (b) Past day

Fig. 7. Overall view (Color figure online)

For this purpose we used the color concept and additionally some structure changes of the time bars (see Fig. 7b). Instead of ending in a semicircle the time bars are unaltered rectangles. Nonetheless the system should still call the operators attention while exploring past events in case of incoming new errors. This is why the third system mode is equipped with a circle for each component, which appears red in case of an incoming current error. As a result the operator can end the exploration of past days and return to the first system mode to analyse the current error state. In our example (see Fig. 7b) the operator is performing an retrospective analysis (15.08.2019) of the system, when an incoming error of the CHP is calling the attention of the operator.

When comparing Fig. 6 and Fig. 7 it is easy to see, that the operator can instantly recognize, whether the current system state or a past system state is displayed, based on the yellow colors.

5.4 Error Localization

Another requirement is that errors must be spatialized - meaning that operators must not only know which and when errors occurred, but also where erroneous components are located in the system.

Many HMIs for monitoring – especially in process control applications – contain a main view that uses mimic displays [15] showing all main components of the system and their interconnections and associated measurements in a topologically correct view. Figure 8 shows the topology view for the hybrid energy system. Errors should not only be displayed within the time bars, but importantly also within the topology. By default, we color the border of currently faulty components red (see Fig. 9a).

As described in Sect. 5.2, the system can be navigated through time using time bars and sliders. A miniature version of the time bars is also available below each faulty components (see Fig. 9). When the mouse courser is placed on a mini time bar within the topology, the slider enlarges and can be used for a retrospective analysis of the system. Hence moving the slider in the topology will – like all other sliders (see Fig. 6) – navigate the entire system through the course of time.

The mini time bars use the design concept presented in Sect. 5.3 for displaying different system modes. As in the further up discussed views of the system (Fig. 6, 7a, 7b) the slider turns red when placed at a time point where errors within the system occurred (indicated by red areas within the time bars).

5.5 Visualisation of Measured Physical Parameters

Finally, the HMI design should of course also support the last subtask of an observation well (T5 – establish more detailed SA). Even if there are currently no alarms or errors, the operator should get a good overview of the current system status. This applies generally to monitoring systems and is not specific to retrospective system analysis. We therefore recommend using established design methods at this point. We consistently used the Konect method [11] for the

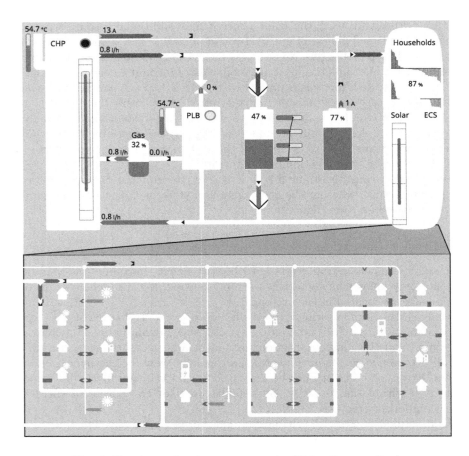

Fig. 8. Topology of system components. (Color figure online)

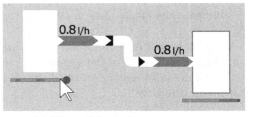

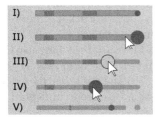

(a) Time slider below components   (b) Time slider states

Fig. 9. Error visualisation within topology. a) Erroneous components are encircled red and shown with a time bar. b) States of time bars: I) Present day and current time. II) Mouse-over enlarges the slider. III) Slider is placed onto a past time point of the present day. IV) Slider is placed onto a time point where the corresponding component was erroneous. V) Time bar of a past day; slider is reduced in size since no mouse courser is placed on the corresponding time bar. (Color figure online)

presented use case. With the Konect method, the system parameters are not presented purely numerically or textually, but translated into visual forms that optimally use the capabilities of human perception so that the operator can perceive the system parameters as quickly and correctly as possible. For example, Fig. 10 shows the design for different lines (pipes and cables). The flow in these lines is represented by a bar length proportional to the measured physical quantity. Thresholds are shown as a position on this bar and the type of line by the color of the bar. The Konect methods provides similar arguments for the visualization of all components in the topology (see Fig. 8).

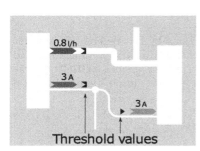

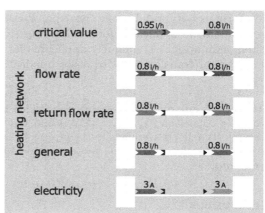

(a) Bars and threshold points visualizing physical values

(b) Color scheme of our use case applied in the topology of system components.

Fig. 10. Physical parameter values are indicated by bars whose length corresponds to the size of the parameters values. Threshold values are identifiable by threshold symbols positioned on the bars. Color indicates the measured physical quantity. (Color figure online)

6 Discussion

In this paper we outlined a graphical user interface concept that supports sporadic monitoring of large technical systems. The main objective is to support the operator to 1) identify the current and past health state of the system efficiently, 2) identify alarms and error states and localize the source and root causes for the error, 3) trace the development of errors over time and space as well as 4) understand how the system in general evolves over time. The named points were discussed and implemented under the condition that there are typically longer periods between the observations, such that the operator usually has to analyze error conditions retrospectively. Furthermore, the operator typically does not want to spend too much time observing the system and therefore needs an efficient interface concept. To enable an efficient identification of the system's health state and localization of sources of errors, we heavily relied on pre-attentional visual processing and adequate visualizations tailored to the task of the operator. The resulting concept was developed using the Konect method and is used within the entire application. In order to support the operator in understanding how the system and especially error states evolve over time, we developed a time bar concept that enables operators to easily visualize the entire system state in the course of time. Timebars are automatically placed near erroneous components and allow the operator to select a point in time. The UI then displays the state of the system at that point in time.

We integrated the time bar concept and the visualization of error states in a coherent visualisation concept. The concept was applied to a single use case: Monitoring of Hybrid Energy Systems. However, we believe that the concept itself should be applicable for a wide range of applications, since none of the system assumptions is uniquely applicable for hybrid energy systems. But still, the practical transferability to other applications needs to be shown in future work.

Acknowledgement. This research was funded in parts by the Federal Ministry for Economic Affairs and Energy (BMWi) and the Federal Ministry of Education and Research (BMBF) of Germany in the project ENaQ (project number 03SBE111). The authors thank the other ENaQ project partners for support, inspiration and fruitful discussions.

References

1. Bayer, J., et al.: Zellulares Energiesystem - Ein Beitrag zur Konkretisierung des zellularen Ansatzes mit Handlungsempfehlungen. Technical report, Verband der Elektrotechnik Elektronik und Informationstechnik e.V., May 2019
2. Blanco, M., et al.: Automated vehicles: take-over request and system prompt evaluation. In: Meyer, G., Beiker, S. (eds.) Road Vehicle Automation 3. LNM, pp. 111–119. Springer, Cham (2016). https://doi.org/10.1007/978-3-319-40503-2_9
3. Carbonell, J.R.: A queuing model of many-instrument visual sampling. IEEE Trans. Hum. Fact. Electron. **7**(4), 157–164 (1966)
4. Endsley, M.R.: Design and evaluation for situation awareness enhancement. In: Proceedings of the Human Factors Society Annual Meeting, vol. 32, pp. 97–101. SAGE Publications, Los Angeles (1988)
5. Endsley, M.R.: A taxonomy of situation awareness errors. Hum. Fact. Aviat. Oper. **3**(2), 287–292 (1995)
6. Endsley, M.R.: Automation and situation awareness. Autom. Hum. Perform.: Theory Appl. **20**, 163–181 (1996)
7. Endsley, M.R.: Designing for Situation Awareness: An Approach to User-Centered Design. CRC Press, Boca Raton (2016)
8. Endsley, M.R., Garland, D.J., et al.: Theoretical underpinnings of situation awareness: a critical review. Situat. Aware. Anal. Meas. **1**, 24 (2000)
9. Gouraud, J., Delorme, A., Berberian, B.: Autopilot, mind wandering, and the out of the loop performance problem. Front. Neurosci. **11**, 541 (2017)

10. Gui, E.M., MacGill, I.: Typology of future clean energy communities: an exploratory structure, opportunities, and challenges. Energy Res. Soc. Sci. **35**, 94–107 (2018)
11. Harre, M.C.: Supporting supervisory control of safety-critical systems with rationally justified information visualizations. Ph.D. thesis, C.v.O. University Oldenburg (2019)
12. Irtel, H., Goldstein, E.: Wahrnehmungspsychologie: Der Grundkurs (2007)
13. ISO: ISO 15007-1:2014. Part 1: Road Vehicles: Measurement of Driver Visual Behaviour with Respect to Transport Information and Control Systems - Definitions and Parameters. ISO, Genf, Schweiz (2014). Stage 90.92
14. ISO: ISO 15007-2:2014. Part 2: Road Vehicles: Measurement of Driver Visual Behaviour with Respect to Transport Information and Control Systems - Equipment and Procedures. ISO, Genf, Schweiz (2014). Stage 90.92
15. Javaux, D., Colard, M.I., Vanderdonckt, J.: Visual display design: a comparison of two methodologies. In: Proceedings of the 1st International Conference on Applied Ergonomics ICAE, vol. 96, pp. 662–667 (1996)
16. Knight, J.C.: Safety critical systems: challenges and directions. In: Proceedings of the 24th International Conference on Software Engineering, pp. 547–550. ACM (2002)
17. Lipshitz, R., Shaul, O.B.: Schemata and mental models in recognition-primed decision making. In: Zsambok, C.E., Klein, G. (eds.) Naturalistic Decision Making. Lawrence Erlbaum Associates, Inc. (1997)
18. Pikaar, R.N.: HMI conventions for process control graphics. Work **41**(Suppl. 1), 2845–2852 (2012)
19. Prinet, J.C., Mize, A.C., Sarter, N.: Triggering and detecting attentional narrowing in controlled environments. In: Proceedings of the Human Factors and Ergonomics Society Annual Meeting, vol. 60, pp. 298–302. SAGE Publications, Los Angeles (2016)
20. SAE On-Road Automated Driving Committee and others: SAE j3016. Taxonomy and definitions for terms related to driving automation systems for on-road motor vehicles. Technical report, SAE International, 2016. Cited on (2018)
21. Salerno, J., Hinman, M., Boulware, D.: Building a framework for situation awareness. Technical report, Air Force Research Lab Rome NY Information Directorate (2004)
22. Schmeling, L., Schönfeldt, P., Klement, P., Wehkamp, S., Hanke, B., Agert, C.: Development of a decision-making framework for distributed energy systems in a German district. Energies **13**(3), 552 (2020)
23. Senders, J.W.: Visual scanning processes. Ph.D. thesis, University of Tilburg, Netherlands (1983). Lawrence Erlbaum Assoc., Hillsdale (1984)
24. Singh, H.V., Mahmoud, Q.H.: EYE-on-HMI: a framework for monitoring human machine interfaces in control rooms. In: 2017 IEEE 30th Canadian Conference on Electrical and Computer Engineering (CCECE), pp. 1–5. IEEE (2017)
25. Stanton, N.A.: Human Factors in Alarm Design. CRC Press, Boca Raton (1994)
26. Treisman, A.: The perception of features and objects. Vis. Atten. **8**, 26–54 (1998)
27. Werner, S.: International review of district heating and cooling. Energy **137**, 617–631 (2017)
28. Wickens, C.: Engineering psychology and human performance theory (1992)
29. Wickens, C.D., McCarley, J.S.: Applied Attention Theory. CRC Press, Boca Raton (2008)

Utilizing Geographical Maps for Social Visualization to Foster Awareness in Online Communities of Practice

Markus Jelonek$^{(\boxtimes)}$ (iD)

Ruhr University Bochum, 44780 Bochum, Germany
markus.jelonek@rub.de

Abstract. Finding information in online communities is crucial, as the content gives users of a community value to use and participate in it. However, information retrieval can be hindering, as the amount of information can be overwhelming for users or stay undiscovered. To support the exploration of communities and foster the awareness about the activity inside a community, social visualization is applied by creating five different mashups utilizing geographical maps paired with additional data of an online Community of Practice (CoP) for Public Employment Services (PES). The visualizations focus on different aspects of the community and associate it with the locations of members to raise awareness inside the community. The views display data that focuses on the own participation of members, the most prominent tags for topics per location, an egocentric visualization of the own social network, the overall activity inside the community, and the participation in groups and topics. To evaluate the visualizations, an expert evaluation was conducted with five participants in a Thinking Aloud test. Results show that the tool motivates to explore the online community and raises awareness about the activity inside the community as well as the topics that are being discussed.

Keywords: Awareness · Communities of Practice · Information visualization · Social visualization

1 Introduction

Information retrieval in online communities can be hindering, as the amount of information can be overwhelming and one has to know the specific terms or topics for the information he or she is looking for. A common way to explore an online community is using the search function in hope to find the topic of interest in more or less recent threads. As online communities do not follow fixed schedules and users can contribute whenever they want, these systems work in a "chaotic manner" [1] and therefore the topics of interest might not be visible to a user directly. However, information retrieval is a crucial activity in online communities. Information is what gives users a value inside the community and supporting the process of finding relevant information helps to gain valuable knowledge from the data inside the community they are a part of. In online Communities of Practice (CoP) practitioners within the same field of profession use the

© Springer Nature Switzerland AG 2020
S. Yamamoto and H. Mori (Eds.): HCII 2020, LNCS 12184, pp. 58–71, 2020.
https://doi.org/10.1007/978-3-030-50020-7_4

CoP to gain knowledge about their domain of practice through learning and supporting each other in a group of professionals [2].

In this exploratory study, practitioners of Public Employment Services (PES) in Slovenia had the possibility to participate in an online CoP for their field of practice. As multiple PES locations (regional offices) around Slovenia were involved in the CoP, the research question was to visualize regional emphasis on topics, to gain awareness about topics inside the CoP and to make the activity in the community more transparent. To support various information retrieval mechanisms, five different map visualizations for presenting information to users were implemented in the CoP in form of mashups by combining geographical maps with data of the online community. The map-views were evaluated in five semi-structured interviews with experts on the field of PES. The views focused on displaying certain information in the CoP: Visualizing own activity in the community, highlighting often discussed topics, visualizing the own social network, visualizing the total activity in the community, and adding a contextual geographical view to a forum. The goal of this tool was to foster the motivation to use the online community, to raise awareness about the activity and to enable exploration of the community.

2 Social Visualization in Online Communities of Practice

2.1 Online Communities of Practice

Online communities can be widely defined as groups of people that interact with each other on a website [3]. In 2000, Preece proposed a working definition, that online communities consist of people with a shared purpose, specific policies and that interact via computer systems [4]. However, as the term is so widely used, there are different ways to define online communities, for example on a social perspective, focusing on the activities of the community, or on a technical perspective [5]. Categorization of online communities can be done by their area of focus [6]. Online Communities of Practice (CoP) are groups of practitioners from the same field or profession [2]. These groups focus on learning from each other by sharing and exchanging knowledge that is part of their domain or field [7, 8]. Therefore, CoP are built around practitioners' commitment and passion for a specific discipline and serve the purpose of learning, developing members' capabilities and skills. They are social learning systems in which informal learning takes place [2, 9]. Additionally, CoP support reflection among community members by giving and receiving support from each other [10].

In the case of a PES, the objectives and interests of the an online CoP include individual and organizational learning, as well as to support PES practitioners to develop competences that address their need to help and support people that are searching for jobs. To achieve these objectives, PES practitioners should be engaged in an ongoing transformation process. This process includes activities as reflection, networking, learning and facilitating the learning of others via peer-model interventions. However, due to the vertical organization of PES, communicative exchange between PES offices is mostly limited to the level of the upper management, whereas PES practitioners are bound to the practitioners inside their own office. Exchange on the practitioner level beyond those boundaries is hardly possible. Here, an online CoP that is accessible for

PES practitioners from their workplace might help to address the problem and enable exchange between them (see Fig. 1).

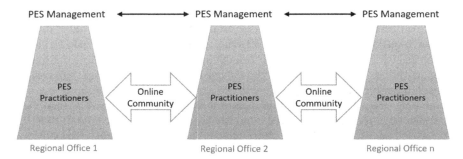

Fig. 1. The online community of practice should allow practitioners to communicate with colleagues of other offices and encourage them to exchange best practices.

However, starting an online community is faced with challenges: Is the number of active contributing users too small, a community will most likely struggle and not take off, a challenge usually described as getting to critical mass [11]. Additionally, in CoP direct contribution after joining a community as a new member is not always possible: Before one can actively participate in a CoP, new members have to evolve by lurking until enough knowledge is accumulated for an active participation, a process also described as 'legitimate peripheral participation' [9, 12]. This peripheral lurking-phase contributes to the difficulty of starting an online community, as contribution of all members to a community is what gives value.

To promote active participation and to highlight the value of the online CoP, this work uses examples to visualize social interaction to encourage members in actively participate and explore the online CoP. Besides these motivational aspects, the social visualization raises awareness about activity and content in the CoP itself.

2.2 From Data to Social Visualization

To visualize information, data has to be put into a specific context in order to gain knowledge. Whereas data can be described as raw symbols and facts, which are non-interpreted, information uses data that got a meaning by interpreting data. Knowledge describes information that was cognitively processed and integrated into existing knowledge structures of a human being [13]. Visualization of information is a process of transforming data, information and knowledge into graphical presentations to support the explanation of information, the exploration of information or other tasks [14]. From an epistemological view, information visualization serves to develop insights from collected data [15]. Using this process, social visualization focuses on people and their social surroundings by visualizing social information for social purposes [16].

Social visualization can be used to create awareness of other users and content of online communities [17] by integrating principles of visibility, awareness and accountability [18]. In addition, visualization can be used as a way to encourage reflection and support organizational learning in peer-based communities [1].

In order to use social visualization in an online CoP, the structure of PES was focused. As PES consist of multiple regional entities that might have differences in the work to be found around their regional areas, different demographic structures of the population and therefore differing emphases on consultations, the social visualization should take these aspects into account and use them to foster awareness on the variety of content that occurs in the CoP.

3   Mashups for Geographical Visualization of Data

Based on the structure of PES and the design ideas for social visualization, mashups for geographical visualization of information were used in the CoP. Mashups are software modules that mix and combine multiple information sources. Mapping-mashups are used to show any kind of data on geographical maps. Examples for this kind of visualization can be found in modern map services (e.g. E-Commerce platforms) or in community based collaborative Geo-Tagging applications [19]. In the case of e-commerce applications, geographical maps are used to display online search results and give the users the possibility to explore the map for further information. This way, users receive the search results with the added geographical context. Such tools can also be used to enable communities to visualize their distribution of members geographically [20].

A visualization on a map allows including the geographic context and adding it to the mental image one creates as the surroundings can be integrated into that image. For example, without the geographic knowledge one would not expect the city of Koper to be located on the Mediterranean Sea. However, this is directly clear when looking on the map (see Fig. 2). Therefore, with the presentation on the map, one could easily indicate that in Koper many jobs might have a reference to the sea (e.g. touristic) and therefore require different skills than in other areas of the country.

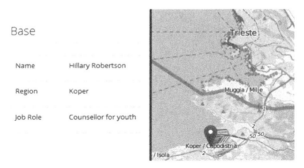

Fig. 2. Tables (left) give no further context to a location, whereas maps allow contextualizing the geographic surroundings.

The online platform for the CoP allowed typical functions of online communities: users could join different (thematic) groups inside the forum, could start new topics, add new comments to a topic (threads), could add 'like' to a post and add tags to categorize topics, which were then shown in a tag cloud. The community also used a social network function that allowed users to add 'friends' to their own network.

Using Scenario-Based Design (SBD) [21] multiple scenarios were defined for a requirements acquisition of mashups for the online community. As high-level vision, the tool should contribute the online community by fostering the motivation of community members to use and explore the community as well as contribute to it. As stakeholders, community members and managers were identified. Members should be supported by finding relevant topics and helpful answers, whereas managers should gain overall knowledge about the community.

To support information visualization, three solution ideas in particular were selected after an analysis of possible usage scenarios. The requirements for the tool were: (1) it should allow exploration of the community, (2) increase overall awareness of what is happening within the community and (3) allow content to be found in a different way than using a search. The implemented views allow members to understand the community distribution over the country. All views exposed more or less details in pop-up windows on the map, when zoomed in or out. Every view allowed several filtering options, e.g. to filter by specific job role of the members. If pop-up windows were closed, the highlighted location markers (red) indicated that information is available at that location, otherwise the marker was gray (see Fig. 3).

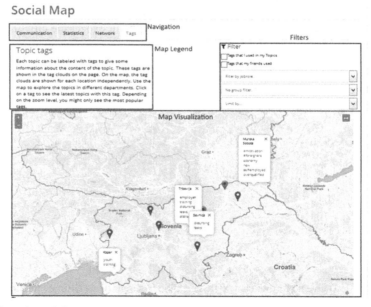

Fig. 3. Overview of the general mashup showing a navigation bar, a map legend, filters and the map. (Color figure online)

3.1 Communication View

The Communication View represents the past communication of a user in an egocentric way (see Fig. 4). The map shows which users one have had contact with and in which threads this contact has happened. In principle, this view should also enable reflection, as users are able look at their past communication and call it up again if necessary. Additionally, this view is intended to increase awareness of one's own communication and also allows exploration of the online community, as it is possible to click on the shown users to find out in which other topics they might have been active. By visualizing the number of times other members have answered to the own topics, this view tries to motivate to repaying behavior (reciprocity). As users might recognize they have received more input from specific members than they have given, their motivation to help them could increase.

Fig. 4. The Communication View shows the own communication inside the community.

3.2 Tag View

The Tag View depicts regional focal points of the CoP. By using tags when creating new topics, the community platform creates a tag cloud for each user on the users' landing page. This view uses the same data as the tag cloud, but adds the location of the user who used the tag. This makes it possible to filter the tags according to the regions and thus create and display them location-based.

The more often a tag is used in topics from a specific region, the bigger its font size is inside the tag cloud (see Fig. 5). This view allows users to gain a fast overview of which topics are discussed in which region and can work as a tool to explore the community to visit topics that are associated to their own interests.

3.3 Social Network View

The Social Network View is intended to show how the own network presents itself in the community via the respective regions. In addition, the thickness of the individual connections shows an aggregation of data, whether one communicates with someone more or less frequently (see Fig. 6). It is an egocentric view of the own network and is designed to help members understand who is part of their network and what their contacts are writing about. Social network visualization can lead to new insights about

Fig. 5. The Tag View shows most prominent tags location-based.

network structures and subnetworks [22]. Additionally, it can facilitate and promote increased awareness of the community and support discovery of people, connections and communities [23]. An ego-centered network view is used, that provides a view from the perspective on oneself [24].

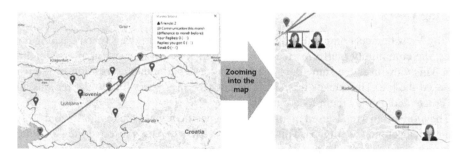

Fig. 6. The Social Network View showing all contacts in the own network.

As the view does also show users in which regions they do not have any contact, this could motivate to expand the network and accelerate their participation.

3.4 Statistics View

The Statistics View allows a basic overview of quantitative data of the community, for example: How many topics, replies or users are active in which location (see Fig. 7). This view should help, above all, to assess at which locations users are particularly active.

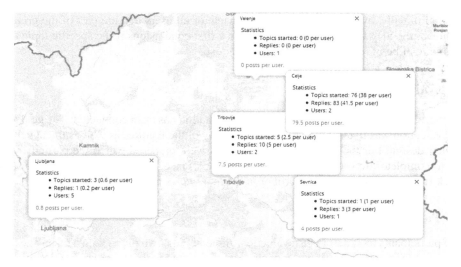

Fig. 7. The Statistics View showing topics, replies and active users per location.

By visualizing the activity, this view allows community members as well as managers to gain insights about the activity in total. This knowledge, in turn, could be used to introduce the online community differently in other locations and to derive best practices. In addition, managers might gain insights about which locations need further advertising for the community.

3.5 Map Widget

The Map Widget is displayed peripherally as a widget next to the actual content (e.g. group, topic etc.) of the online community. By clicking on the widget, the map displays which users are active in the group or this topic accompanied with the job role of each user. This allows to further explore the other users that are active in this group, for example to see what they have posted lately (see Fig. 8). Compared to the other views, the context remains given by the actual content of the website and allows a direct contextualized exploration of the online community.

Fig. 8. The Map Widget that is displayed in groups and topics.

Additionally, by proposing a direct overview of all users that are part of the group or thread, the map widget allows users to draw first conclusions if the specific topic or group might be of regional or nationwide interest.

4 Evaluation

For the evaluation of the mashups, an expert evaluation has been conducted. The goal of the evaluation was to test both usability and utility of the features as well as the novelty of their design. For the evaluation, several tasks were prepared which the participants had to complete. Before the actual evaluation took place, a pre-test was carried out to check if any changes in the platform or in the map-views needed to be done.

4.1 Participants

Five participants took part in the evaluation (three female, two male) with a mean age of $M = 43.4$ ($SD = 10.37$). All participants were associated to the overall research project and were at least partly familiar with the online platform, but did not know the map-views prior to the evaluation. The interviews were conducted via video conferences. In order to be able to understand the use of the map-views and to follow their actions, the participants shared their screens during the tests.

4.2 Procedure

To prepare the evaluation, the online platform was enriched with demo data (topics, threads, tags, users etc.). A demo user was used for the evaluation that had seven connections in his social network and participated in several discussions. About one hour before the start of an evaluation session, the participants received an e-mail with the login-data for the platform and were told to login five minutes before the start.

All semi-structured interviews followed the same procedure. After a short introduction, the permission to record interviews was obtained, followed by questions depending personal information. The participants were also informed that the interviews could be stopped at any time.

The evaluation was structured in two parts. First, the participants were asked to perform certain tasks with the map-views of the online platform. During these tasks, they were asked to 'think aloud'. If they did not know what to do at a certain point, or other problems arose, the action or problem was documented and the experimenter gave them hints to get on. The participants were also asked to give honest feedback as the map-views and the CoP would benefit from it.

5 Results

The results are considered on two levels: First, general statements of the participants are presented and discussed. Then, the statements for each view are considered in a differentiated manner. In the following, "tool" is used when referring to all views at once. When only one specific view is meant, it is referred to by its name.

5.1 Overall Results

Generally, all participants acknowledged the explorative characteristic of the map-views. All participants believed that, except for the social network view, all views bring useful functions. For example, two participants pointed out that the social visualization tool would raise awareness for the community itself and support social networking.

Visual Presentation. The design used was described as minimalistic and was positively highlighted. However, the popup windows on the map were described as overwhelming, since all popups were open when the tool was opened (see also 'Usability'). The tool could be used intuitively, since the participants were familiar with such maps from their everyday life.

Transferability. The transferability to other settings was addressed by several participants. Three participants mentioned that the social visualization tool might be also of use in other online CoP. Additionally, one participant mentioned it would be worth to try it in educational learning communities. Another stated it could be also of use in bigger and more international organizations or corporations that have multiple locations and could therefore benefit from the geographic context of the tool by visualizing location-based structures of teams or the whole organization.

Usability. Several comments were made about the usability of the tool. One reoccurring aspect was that the pop-up windows inside the map were directly displayed whenever a map was opened. Participants mentioned that this could overwhelm users and make the map itself unusable when too many popups are shown directly, so that the presentation becomes confusing. A functionality to reorganize the popups was missing, but one participant mentioned a wish for such function explicitly. In addition, one participant wanted a preview of topic content inside the tool in order to explore it inside the tool itself and not always have to click to the actual forum posts, as this was accompanied with switching the view to the topic and having to go back to the map-tool.

Utilization. For each view, the participants were asked what they would use it for or what context of use they could imagine. The results are shown in Table 1. In general, only the social network view did not give any benefit to the participants in the presented form. In their opinion, the other views would add a value to the CoP, as participants could imagine specific use cases.

One participant highlighted the quality of the location information in the context of PES: If you know that colleagues at another location often deal with a certain topic and you are confronted with the same topic, you know which colleagues you can ask for information. The map allows you to set yourself mental anchors, as the map visualizes which colleagues work in which location and what kind of topics might be regional focused.

Motivational Aspects for Exploration. Participants addressed the motivational character of the plugins several times. In general, the visual presentation of the data via the interactive map was interpreted as motivating to use. One participant mentioned that every visual presentation of data is more appealing than plain textual information. The

Table 1. View specific results considering their utility and an example use case.

View	Utility	Example Use Case
Communication	Useful	Exploration; Find prior discussions
Social Network	Not very useful	To see the own network in the community
Tags	Very useful	Find geographic emphases; Explore topics
Statistics	Not very useful for members; very useful for managers	See number of active users and their activity
Widget	Useful	Direct overview of participating members in a thread

interactivity would provide the opportunity for exploration. For example, exploratory searches can be made for topics of interest. One participant also pointed out that the map might also help to find practitioners who work in the same facility, which could then lead to face-to-face meetings rather than only digital contact via the platform.

5.2 View-Specific Findings

In addition to the general results, the participants' comments were also categorized by view. During the evaluation, the participants commented on the advantages of the views as well as problems or the meaningfulness of the views. The general utilization of views is shown in Table 1.

Communication View. This view visualizes with which other members of the community one had contact (in groups or topics) accompanied with the possibility to see in which other topics the members were active.

Overall, this view was considered helpful, although it could be enriched by more content. For example, it would be helpful to see a preview of the content of posts where members have written something. One participant also noted that it would be helpful to see the job role of other members in this view. This information was already stored as a tool tip in the view, but was not found intuitively by every participant. This view emphasizes the exploratory nature of the tool. Several participants said they would use this view to see what other members of the community were writing or to find their prior discussions.

Social Network View. This view visualizes the own social network inside the community location-based from an egocentric view.

Here, participants struggled with the usefulness of the view. Although two participants mentioned that it is nice to see how the own network is distributed regionally, all participants mentioned that such view might not be important for a single user. However, two participants added that the distribution of the network on the level of regional offices could be more interesting. Such networks, on the collective rather than the individual level, could show how the connections between locations evolved, as this knowledge would allow seeing where networks developed and where exchanging practices evolved.

Tag View. In this view, tag clouds are shown at every regional office with the most important tags used in topics coming from these locations.

All participants interpreted the view as very helpful. It allows an intuitive exploratory search for topics, as well as to find geographically focused topics. One participant added that this view should integrate temporal tag clouds, as the importance of topics might change over time. In total, the view highlights geographical focuses of PES and makes them easily accessible for practitioners.

Statistics View. This view gives an overview of the general activity of each office within the online community. Among other things, it shows how many members are registered at this location and how many contributions they have written.

Overall, this view was evaluated with mixed impressions. There was a consensus among the usefulness of the view for the individual community member which one participant summarized as using the community to 'look for answers'. Although the statistics provide a general overview of the activity at the individual locations, they do not help the practitioners with their needs, as no content-based information is shown in this view. The statistics could even put pressure on individual members to post something so that they can keep up with other offices.

From the perspective of managers, however, this view was considered as very helpful, which the participants underlined with many examples. For example, this view allows monitoring the community and compare the activity of different regional offices. The activity figures give managers the opportunity to see at which locations they might still want to advertise the community. One participant pointed out that to gain knowledge about how many potential users are at the location and what percentage is actually active the used normalization (number of topics divided by all users) should be changed (number of topics divided by active users).

Finally, the view allows to do further investigations to find out reasons for the total number of activity. If the community is not used in a specific location, one could investigate the reasons (e.g., do members have no time to use the community or does the community give them value etc.).

Social Map Widget. The widget is shown directly aside of a group or a forum thread and shows users that are active in the given context. For example, the map widget in a thread shows all users that are active in that thread.

Participants found the widget very helpful. Due to the context of the subject area, the widget allows to identify geographical characteristic of a subject, even if the widget is closed, as the markers on the map give a first information (see Fig. 8). By opening it, it allows to look at more details and maybe explore the activity of other users. As the widget is placed peripheral to the content, it does not distract or disrupt users from the content and can be quickly opened. One participant also highlighted that the map is a quick visual way to show the data rather than to scroll down a long list.

6 Discussion and Conclusion

In this study, an information retrieval mechanism to explore an online CoP was evaluated that uses using social visualization to display community data on geographical maps. As form of presentation, mashups with maps were chosen, as such tools might be already known from other online platforms. In this work, the regional information of data was linked with social data of the online community.

One major limitation of this work is that the evaluation could only be carried out with experts and thus feedback from potential users is unfortunately lacking. However, the experts were able to give very insightful feedback and comments on the presented map-views and repeatedly pointed out that such approach of information retrieval is different compared to standard tools like, e.g. a text-based search or lists and tables. The evaluation showed that all experts were able to use the tools without further introduction, although some minor usability problems occurred. The implementation also showed that especially the data aggregation and presentation on the map was difficult, as too many pop-up windows on the map made the visualization confusing.

Some map-views were highlighted to gain awareness about the activity in the community and the topics that are discussed (e.g. Communication View, Statistics View, and Map Widget). For all views, participants in the evaluation acknowledged that the design could lead to an exploration of the community (especially Tag View, Communication View). Further, the Statistics View has shown that geographical visualization also offers additional value to community managers, by drawing conclusions about the total activity of to the community on a regional level.

In conclusion, the results indicate that social visualization has the potential to shape an exploratory search for information in online Communities of Practice. Comments made by the participants confirm that such map-views have the potential to increase the users' motivation for exploration of online communities. It can give users the ability to gain awareness about their activity and role in the community.

Acknowledgements. I would like to thank Michael Prilla for his guidance and his feedback during the study and for the opportunity to support the EU funded project *EmployID* with this work. Furthermore, I would like to thank Oliver Blunk for his technical support and especially the participants of the study for their insightful feedback and their valuable time.

References

1. McAuley, J., O'Connor, A., Lewis, D.: Exploring reflection in online communities. In: Proceedings of the 2nd International Conference on Learning Analytics and Knowledge, pp. 102–110. ACM, New York (2012). https://doi.org/10.1145/2330601.2330630
2. Wenger, E.C., Snyder, W.M.: Communities of practice: the organizational frontier. Harv. Bus. Rev. **78**, 139–145 (2000)
3. Buss, A., Strauss, N.: Online Community Handbook: Building Your Business and Brand on the Web. New Riders, Indianapolis (2009)
4. Preece, J.: Online Communities - Designing Usability, Supporting Sociability. Wiley, Chichester (2000)

5. Preece, J., Maloney-Krichmar, D.: Online communities: design, theory, and practice. J. Comput.-Mediat. Commun. **10** (2005). https://doi.org/10.1111/j.1083-6101.2005.tb00264.x

6. Seufert, S., Moisseeva, M., Steinbeck, R.: Virtuelle communities gestalten. In: Hohenstein, A., Wilbers, K. (eds.) Handbuch e-learning. Dt. Wirtschaftsdienst, Kölkn (2001)

7. Lehner, F.: Wissensmanagement: Grundlagen, Methoden und technische Unterstützung. Hanser, Carl (2014)

8. Wenger, E.: Communities of practice: a brief introduction (2011). http://hdl.handle.net/1794/11736

9. Gray, B.: Informal learning in an online community of practice. Int. J. E-Learn. Distance Educ. Rev. Int. E-Learn. Form. À Distance **19**, 20–35 (2004)

10. Nyhan, B.: Collective reflection for excellence in work organizations: an ethical "community of practice" perspective on reflection. In: Boud, D., Cressey, P., Docherty, P. (eds.) Productive Reflection at Work: Learning for Changing Organizations, pp. 134–145. Routledge, London (2006)

11. Kraut, R.E., Resnick, P.: Building Successful Online Communities: Evidence-Based Social Design. MIT Press, Cambridge (2012)

12. Lave, J., Wenger, E.: Situated Learning: Legitimate Peripheral Participation. Cambridge University Press, Cambridge (1991)

13. Tergan, S.O., Keller, T.: Knowledge and Information Visualization: Searching for Synergies. Springer, Heidelberg (2005). https://doi.org/10.1007/b138081

14. Zhang, J.: Visualization for Information Retrieval. Springer, Heidelberg (2008). https://doi.org/10.1007/978-3-540-75148-9

15. Fekete, J.-D., van Wijk, J.J., Stasko, J.T., North, C.: The value of information visualization. In: Kerren, A., Stasko, J.T., Fekete, J.-D., North, C. (eds.) Information Visualization. LNCS, vol. 4950, pp. 1–18. Springer, Heidelberg (2008). https://doi.org/10.1007/978-3-540-70956-5_1

16. Donath, J., Karahalios, K., Viégas, F.: Visualizing conversation. J. Comput.-Mediat. Commun. **4** (1999). https://doi.org/10.1111/j.1083-6101.1999.tb00107.x

17. Sun, L., Vassileva, J.: Social visualization encouraging participation in online communities. In: Dimitriadis, Y.A., Zigurs, I., Gómez-Sánchez, E. (eds.) CRIWG 2006. LNCS, vol. 4154, pp. 349–363. Springer, Heidelberg (2006). https://doi.org/10.1007/11853862_28

18. Gilbert, E., Karahalios, K.: Using social visualization to motivate social production. IEEE Trans. Multimed. **11**, 413–421 (2009). https://doi.org/10.1109/TMM.2009.2012916

19. Ebersbach, A., Glaser, M., Heigl, R.: Social Web. UTB (2016)

20. Wenger, E., White, N., Smith, J.D.: Digital Habitats: Stewarding Technology for Communities. CPsquare (2009)

21. Carroll, J.M.: Making Use: Scenario-Based Design of Human-Computer Interactions. MIT Press, Cambridge (2000)

22. Viégas, F.B., Donath, J.: Social network visualization: can we go beyond the graph? In: Workshop Social Networks, CSCW, vol. 4, pp. 6–10 (2004)

23. Heer, J., Boyd, D.: Vizster: visualizing online social networks. In: IEEE Symposium on Information Visualization, INFOVIS 2005, pp. 32–39 (2005)

24. Garton, L., Haythornthwaite, C., Wellman, B.: Studying online social networks. J. Comput.-Mediat. Commun. **3** (1997). https://doi.org/10.1111/j.1083-6101.1997.tb00062.x

SeeMe2BPMN: Extending the Socio-Technical Walkthrough with BPMN

Ufuk Kacmaz$^{(\boxtimes)}$ ⓘ, Thomas Herrmann ⓘ, and Markus Jelonek ⓘ

Ruhr University Bochum, 44801 Bochum, Germany
{ufuk.kacmaz,thomas.herrmann,markus.jelonek}@rub.de

Abstract. This work introduces a tool that converts socio-technical SeeMe diagrams to BPMN diagrams within the scope of the Socio-Technical Walkthrough (STWT) method. SeeMe is the established modeling notation for performing the method. STWT analyzes the requirements of a process and captures the different views of stakeholders in a workshop setting with considering the socio-technical aspects. The tool extends the STWT to have more capabilities and improve the accessibility of the generated results as BPMN is a highly well-known notation across different domains.

For providing this tool we first introduce the involved modeling aspects for socio-technical systems. Following, we point out similarities and differences of both involved modeling notations. Based on the elaborations we established conversion rules to match the expectation for BPMN diagrams while preserving as much information as possible from the SeeMe diagrams. Additionally, the visualization of the generated BPMN diagram is described. We demonstrate the tool's generated results by comparing them with the elaborated rules. Furthermore, we compare the converted diagram with the expectation that a modeler of BPMN would possibly have.

Keywords: Requirements analysis · Socio-technical systems · Socio-technical design · Process modeling

1 Introduction

Process modeling is an essential tool for supporting requirements engineering or accompanying design projects. Even though there are diverse types of modeling, the target is mainly the same as of supporting the development and maintaining of processes [1].

A method to support the socio-technical view in process modeling - the socio-technical Walkthrough (STWT) - allows for capturing the views of different stakeholders in workshop settings. Importantly, the STWT is simply designed to be used even with stakeholders that have no prior knowledge in process modeling. Using analytical questioning, combining the views of multiple stakeholders for each process step as well as visualizing the process model, the method allows to gain a deep understanding of a projected process and uncovers previously hidden problems, challenges, redundancies etc. in the process [1].

© Springer Nature Switzerland AG 2020
S. Yamamoto and H. Mori (Eds.): HCII 2020, LNCS 12184, pp. 72–84, 2020.
https://doi.org/10.1007/978-3-030-50020-7_5

The applied modeling notation for supporting the STWT needs to cover formal descriptiveness as well as providing a certain degree of vagueness and incompleteness [2]. For this purpose, the modeling notation SeeMe is well approved. SeeMe allows for initially sketchy modeling with incompleteness or omissions on purpose. If required, it is possible to incrementally improve the depth and extend of details of a SeeMe-diagram [1].

Business Process Model and Notation (BPMN) in contrary is strongly focused on formal descriptions. The constraints allow an exchange of formally represented concepts of processes with solely mastering the notation. Therefore, BPMN became popular and is in common use in a variety of domains [3]. The degree of formality serves as a basis for automatically deriving the configuration of workflow engines [4].

In our work we focused on the benefits of both introduced modeling notations and tried to extend the STWT method with a tool for an automatic conversion of a SeeMe process into BPMN diagrams. This allows applying the advantages of the STWT to generate process models in the SeeMe notation. Once reaching the final stages of the STWT the SeeMe process gets matured and well-engineered. At this point it turns beneficial to be able to utilize the advantages of BPMN diagrams.

2 Modeling Socio-Technical Systems

Initially it is elementary to understand the concepts of both modeling notations and the involved techniques before being able to identify translation rules and targets. Therefore, it is crucial to point out their similarities and differences.

2.1 Socio-Technical Walkthrough (STWT)

The Socio-Technical Walkthrough (STWT) is a methodological approach to create and review socio-technical process diagrams by capturing the views of different stake-holders in workshop settings. The STWT is based on two parts: the socio-technical, semi-structured modeling method SeeMe (see Sect. 2.2) to create and document socio-technical diagrams, and special workshops where walkthroughs are applied to inspect and improve SeeMe-diagrams step-by-step by guiding through the workshop and asking certain questions [1].

The workshop settings are characterized by a participatory design process that use specific activities to support cooperation and coordination during the workshops. Usually the workshop starts with a 'Getting started' where the workshop facilitator prepares a diagram or the results of a previous workshop. In this part, the modeling method SeeMe is explained, so that every participant is able to follow and participate during the workshop. Then, the facilitator has to ask prepared questions to gain detailed information for the diagram of the workshop participants (e.g. "Which information/tool support is needed for this activity?"). These contributions have to be collected and to be inserted into the diagram which integrates the varying perspectives of all participants into a larger picture. Therefore, the diagram has to be modified constantly during the workshops and the facilitator has to deal with conflicts, for example, if the opinions of participants differ with regard to specific activities in a process. To deal with conflicts, the modeling language SeeMe supports vagueness, to visualize that certain tasks may be completed in different ways.

The outcome of such workshops can be a concept or an outline of a socio-technical system or process which is represented by diagrammatic models. Such models can be developed from scratch or be derived from previous or existing work processes. They are inspected step-by-step and will be incrementally modified with every workshop before a model is considered as the final solution [1].

Importantly, the STWT is designed to be used even with stakeholders that have no prior knowledge in process modeling. Using analytical questioning, combining the views of multiple stakeholders for each process step as well as visualizing the process model, the method allows to gain a deep understanding of created process models and uncovers previously hidden problems, challenges, redundancies etc. in the process.

The extension of SeeMe will therefore allow to make the results of the STWT workshops available to a wider audience, as there are two main advantages. Firstly, it is possible to present the results in an industry-wide standard so that many people can read and understand the results, even if they have no knowledge in SeeMe. Second, the extension allows to create BPMN models with a socio-technical focus.

2.2   SeeMe as Modeling Method

SeeMe (semi structured, sociotechnical modeling method) – as being emphasized by its name - aims to describe the interaction between technical and social aspects [5]. Since social aspects cannot be completely formally described, SeeMe-diagrams are just partly structured. The main idea behind SeeMe is the possibility to understand and generate diagrams with a short introduction into the notation. Even though there is the possibility to detail the model with additional elements, it is not mandatory.

The generic process being illustrated in Fig. 1 gives a good capture of the important elements of the notation while describing the process of deciding about an application. The process consists of an *application form*, which is evaluated by the *quality control* department and a decision is taken based on the *requirements* fulfillment. The *decision* is being documented and handed back to the *applicant*. The whole process is supervised by a *responsible official*.

As being described SeeMe uses three basic elements. The (yellow) activities are used for describing the actions that were taken. The (red) roles represent persons or groups executing the activity or being affected by them. The (blue) entities show the utilities being used for the activity or being changed by the activity. The arrows illustrate relations between elements as the order of execution for the case of activities or the type of involvement for the case of other elements. Even though SeeMe is not restricted to the described notational characteristics they form the basic frame for most diagrams [5].

A characteristic for this notation is the representation of possible incompleteness up to a certain amount. The modeler can additionally express some vagueness. One example is shown in Fig. 1 as the name of the parent activity of the grouped activities *accept/decline application* is intentionally omitted. The specific naming is not necessarily important to understand the meaning of the process and thus is being left out. Another example is given by the semi-circle at the bottom line of the activity *process application*.

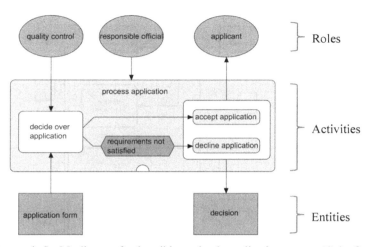

Fig. 1. A generic SeeMe diagram for describing a simple application process (Color figure online)

It indicates that there might be more sub-activities to be taken into consideration that are not explicitly displayed in the diagram.

Another remarkable feature of this notation is the possibility to embed elements into each other to represent their relational togetherness. Generally, this feature is not restricted to any of the basic element types. However, for the case of activities the embedding enables additional ways of representing vagueness. For presenting them without explicitly specifying, whether they are completely or only partially sequenced, or even can be executed in parallel is possible by embedding the activities into a super-activity or parent element.

2.3 BPMN

The Business Process Model Notation (BPMN) aims to describe and manage business processes. Its intention is to standardize the modeling for complex processes with notations. BPMN tries to cover the main aspects of these complex processes with including organizational entities and the flow of data. It specifies which symbols should be used for different elements related to the process. This uniform notation allows the exchange of the modeled ideas with anyone being confident with the notation [6].

As illustrated in Fig. 2 the basic structure of BPMN consists of a regulated flow between tasks. While not being mandatory, the notation allows the usage of pools or swimlanes to express the responsibility for the executed task. The representation of involved documents or general entities is also supported. Another important part of BPMN is covered by events. They might appear in different styles for different purposes. The three general event types are start, intermediate and end events, which are generally visualized as empty circles. They differ in their stroke width being thin for start events, being thick for end events and being double thin circles for intermediate events [7].

BPMN focuses on the flow of activities for additionally allowing the executability of the modeled process. Therefore, the regulation flow between the tasks need to be

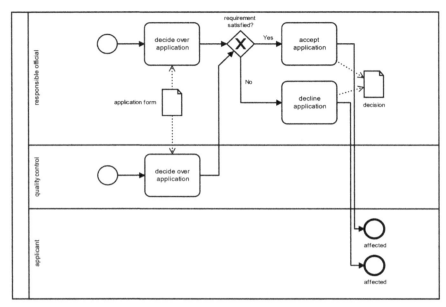

Fig. 2. This BPMN diagram describes a mostly similar application process being introduced in Fig. 1 as a SeeMe diagram.

well regulated. One example is being illustrated in Fig. 2. The gateway '*requirements satisfied?*' is the preferred choice to keep the diagram valid while splitting it explicitly into two possible flows.

2.4   SeeMe vs. BPMN: Similarities and Differences

Even though both modeling notations try to describe processes with including affected roles and utilized technical tools, they do not coherently overlap. This is mainly due to the fact of being semi structured for the case of SeeMe in comparison to being strongly regulated for the case of BPMN. Furthermore, SeeMe has a much stronger focus on the tools and documents being used than BPMN.

One of the main aims of both notations is to express a relation between tasks. This leads to many visually equal structures. The activities (or tasks) are mainly represented the same way in both notations. They are executed by the involved roles (or persons). Also, the way of attaching the entities (or documents) are mostly similar. But BPMN allows different symbols for specifying their type of involvement while SeeMe treats them without distinction.

Both notations differ noticeable with how they represent the roles. In SeeMe they are directly attached to the activities. It is possible to attach multiple roles to a single task. It is also common to repeat the same role at different parts of the diagram to prevent intersections and support local readability. BPMN in contrast provides for every role an individual swimlane. This difference is caused by the pursued aim to express the collaboration between roles in the case of SeeMe and clearly identify the responsible person for any task in the case of BPMN.

The major difference is the usage of events in BPMN. The tasks are triggered or affected by them and exist in different types and shapes for different occasions while events are not present in SeeMe at all. The start and end points are also visualized as events. Their usage is optional, but they are common and recommended for complex diagrams. SeeMe has also the optional possibility to point out the start and end points with specific labels but their usage is rather uncommon.

Some minor objects are similarly represented in both notations. As mentionable examples there are the possibility to comment every element in SeeMe while BPMN allows annotations. Furthermore, BPMN consists of gateways to enable the control of data flow while SeeMe features the same target with connectors. Small variations are present since BPMN provides event-based gateways as addition.

Another special feature for SeeMe is the usage of vagueness or omissions on purpose with the usage of semi-circles (see Fig. 1) as an example which is not covered by BPMN. The embeddings provided by SeeMe are also remarkable differences as some type of vagueness.

3   Transforming SeeMe to BPMN

The key challenge being part of this work is the identification of applicable rules for translating the SeeMe notation into the BPMN notation. Another additional task is to keep the generated results for the BPMN diagram organized and readable by enabling dynamical growing.

3.1   New Translation Rules

Picking out the described similarities it is easy to define translation rules for them. Many of them can remain mostly unmodified. With referring to Fig. 3, which describes the trivial process of programming being carried out by a programmer using a computer as his tool, the activity can be translated without any changes. The roles carrying out the activity differ much in their way of representation. However, they are translatable with less effort. Every role in SeeMe can be transferred into a swimlane in BPMN. Even the entities can be translated in terms of representation without any change. It should be noted, that in BPMN there is no overall term for entities. There are different symbols for representing the information in respect to the type of data or even being a data storage. Due to the fact there is no explicit difference between entities in SeeMe we decided to keep all entities to stay documents after conversion.

For each role being involved into the process, an individual swimlane should be added to the BPMN diagram. Going further, the direction of the used relation is important to express the type of involvement within the process. The direction of the relation towards the role in SeeMe expresses that the role is affected by the activity. To express this idea the modeler can use events in BPMN. In Fig. 4 an example is illustrated to represent the way of involvement of the user into the activity of programming which is executed by the programmer: The diagram is extended with another role and entity. The process

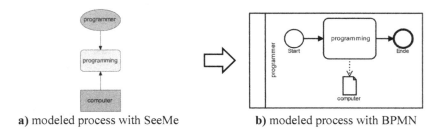

a) modeled process with SeeMe   **b)** modeled process with BPMN

Fig. 3. An exemplarily simple process consisting of three basic elements. The examples used in this chapter are derived and modified from [5].

describes the creation of a software designed for the end-user. The programming changes the user interface and therefore affects the users. For the entities, direction of data access can remain the same as before.

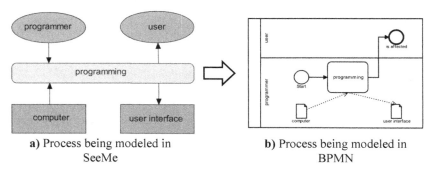

a) Process being modeled in   **b)** Process being modeled in
SeeMe   BPMN

Fig. 4. Extended diagram with an affected role

So far, the translation is obviously trivial. However, the more complex the constellation gets the more conditions need to be considered. In SeeMe, embedding elements into each other as illustrated in Fig. 5 is a common case. This process consists of a main activity named running a project and a few sub-activities. The sub activities meeting, delegating tasks and exception handling are parallel executed sub activities. The sub activity of carrying out tasks is explicitly denoted as following the task of delegating tasks. The semi-circle indicates some sub elements may be missing. For the process of exception handling the following task is not specifiable for now.

From two options of either preserving those embeddings as subprocesses in BPMN or resolving the embedding we decided for the latter option. A main reason is the fact that embeddings can reach complicated structures. Another reason is that embedding is also applicable for roles and entities. Therefore, a generalized solution is a reasonable decision. The resolving process is easily achieved by dissolving the surrounding parent elements and representing them with a concatenated name-structure of the child elements. This is performed recursively until the last child elements remain. For highlighting the usage of this process of dissolving, we used the notation of content of parent

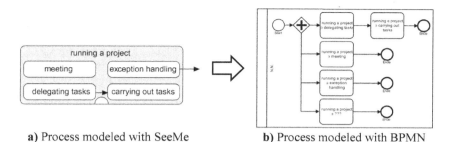

a) Process modeled with SeeMe   **b)** Process modeled with BPMN

Fig. 5. Translation of embedded activities

element ∋ content of child element. The used symbol ∋ is derived from the mathematical operator with preserving its meaning of 'contains as member'. With resolving those kinds of embedding, some incidental parts of them need also to be reconsidered for deriving the BPMN diagram. With respect to the relations that connect those remaining child activities with other elements, the connections between outside elements and the initial parent element must be reconsidered. Firstly, all sub-activities that are not put into a sequence by relations need to be aggregated and presented as tasks to be executed in parallel. For the illustrated diagram in Fig. 5b, the start event is the preceding element of the parent task. The child elements are connected to it with a parallel gateway for forking parallel paths. The task carrying out tasks is not connected to the preceding event since it is explicitly following on another subtask delegating tasks. The possibility of sub-processes that are not presented in the diagram and therefore indicated with a semi-circle, is easily translatable with adding a new sub task with the name '???'. Thus, it is as represented as an existing sub task for which the name is not known. At this point, we define to not join the forked path. This decision leads to the problem of possibly not well synchronized paths. However, the benefits of saving further trouble with overcomplicated diagrams gives preference to this decision. We assume that every forked path will reach an ending event and the process will finally terminate.

Another reduction of an embedding with respect to roles is illustrated in Fig. 6 by extending the previous diagram with including the involved roles. The process itself is simplified to focus on multiple embedded roles belonging to a team. The leader of the team precedingly executes another activity of initiating a project. SeeMe is constructed to easily involve several roles (Fig. 6a) while it needs including additional swimlanes in BPMN (b). With this representation of each role with a separated swimlane in BPMN, the assigned tasks need to be duplicated over all the considered lanes. As it is not necessarily determined which of the roles really executes which task, the duplicated tasks are forked with an inclusive gateway allowing that only one path is activated or several of them. Additionally, another swimlane with the name '???' is created as specified in the SeeMe diagram with the semi-circle.

Finally, the structure for start and end events need to be considered. By definition of SeeMe, it is not mandatory to label the entry and end points. But the absence of the entry point turns out difficult to identify the correct entry for generating the BPMN diagram as most of the activities could be potentially a start point. Therefore, it is required to

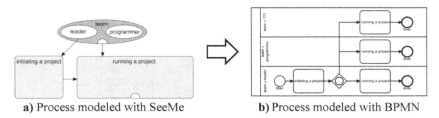

a) Process modeled with SeeMe   **b)** Process modeled with BPMN

Fig. 6. Extended diagram with embedded roles

define the entry points with extra labels. However, the end points are not necessarily to be mentioned as every final activity without outgoing relations would lead automatically to end points.

3.2 Dynamical Layout Creation

For the aim of generating the visual components, we focus firstly on the structure of the activities to reduce the amount of represented overlaps and of relations that indicated repetitions by pointing back to activities. For this purpose, we benefit from the structure of the process flow. As illustrated in Fig. 7 we consider our input diagram (Fig. 7a) as a tree (Fig. 7b). The result of this procedure determines the final placement for the tasks in the BPMN diagram. On this tree, we apply a slightly modified breadths first search algorithm for determining the depth of each node. Regularly, in each iteration the depth of each node is noted down (Fig. 7c–Fig. 7f). If the algorithm reaches an already marked node, we try to shift it down as if it is a descendant of the currently evaluated node. As seen in Fig. 7g and 7h for the case of the path <9, 5, 8> this performed as desired and the node 5 can be shifted down with its children with increasing the depth to the fourth depth. Therefore, the back leading relation (9, 5) could be dissolved. For the case of the path <9, 4, 7, 9> in Fig. 7g we encounter a cycle and therefore cannot shift the path any lower. In that case we need to accept the pointing back of a relation (between 9 and 4). Finally, we rotate the tree in the direction of reading and consider the depths of the tree column-wise. As visible in the automatically generated diagram in (Fig. 7i), the algorithm generated a well spanned BPMN diagram with some minimal downsides.

Another aspect of placement is illustrated in Fig. 8. Each swimlane has for each depth a stack-like area which can grow downwards as much as needed with respect to the number of tasks. The width of the whole diagram depends on the greatest depth of the diagram. The height of each swimlane is individually dependent on the biggest stack size of the lane. Additionally, the presence of any document in this lane adds a constant size to the height.

The last part of this diagram generation tool treats the optional presence of events and gateways. They always correspond to a task. Thus, every task has four spots, two on each side, reserved for optionally displaying them. An example is shown in the first depth of Fig. 8.

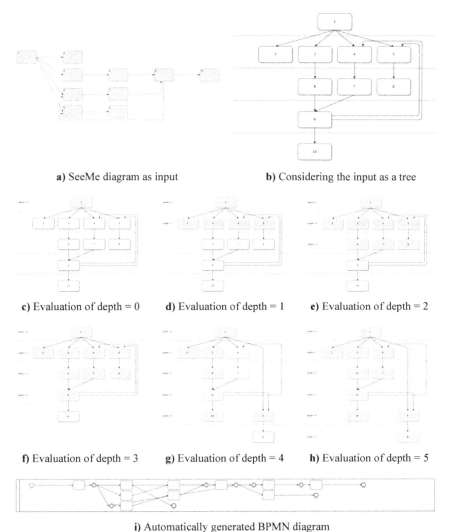

a) SeeMe diagram as input

b) Considering the input as a tree

c) Evaluation of depth = 0

d) Evaluation of depth = 1

e) Evaluation of depth = 2

f) Evaluation of depth = 3

g) Evaluation of depth = 4

h) Evaluation of depth = 5

i) Automatically generated BPMN diagram

Fig. 7. Each step of calculating the depth for each activity and final placement

4   Results

The tool is in general fulfilling the pursued goal of transforming a semi-structured process diagram into a formal process presentation where the vagueness and incompleteness is still indicated. For initial testing, the process described in Fig. 1 is used as input for the conversion tool and is displayed in Fig. 9. The ideal reference for the result is Fig. 2. The main content is correctly transferred. All desired tasks, lanes, documents and the start and end events are generated. As the exclusive gateway from Fig. 2 is not explicitly modeled in Fig. 1 it is not shown in the generated diagram. However, there are multiple

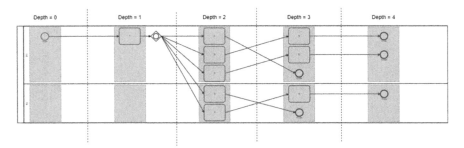

Fig. 8. Stack-Visualization of the tool for layout generation

inclusive gateways present which can be considered redundant at most points. They are generated due to the fact, that the tool is not aware of the context-related intentions and tries to preserve most of the possible process flows. Additionally, the single condition from Fig. 1 is preserved as an event as it is not explicitly belonging to any connector. Generally, the generated diagram matches mostly the expectations with respect to Fig. 2.

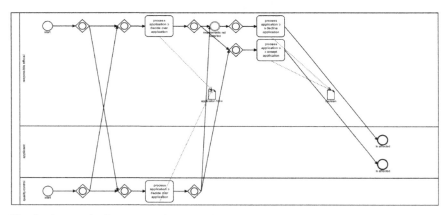

Fig. 9. Automatically generated BPMN diagram based on the process in Fig. 1 and Fig. 2

Another exemplarily generation is visualized in Fig. 10 which represents a simple process of purchasing a smartphone. The process describes the desire of a potential buyer who wants to purchase smartphone and therefore searches the internet or asks some advisers and finally uses his purchased smartphone. The diagram itself is moderately detailed but it still covers a well described process flow. The SeeMe diagram and the final version after being automatically generated as a BPMN diagram are visualized. Most of the introduced rules are being covered and thus suits well for testing the functionality of the tool. Additionally, it is a challenging conversion as it consists of multiple roles attached to activities, embeddings and a cycle in the activity flow.

As being visualized in Fig. 10 the process flow is mostly linearly preserved. For the activities with multiple roles (a) the tool generates the desired swimlanes with many

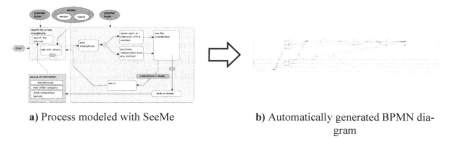

a) Process modeled with SeeMe   **b)** Automatically generated BPMN diagram

Fig. 10. An exemplarily diagram consisting of embedded elements, semi-circles and a cycle

duplicated tasks which are distributed over those lanes (b). However, the circle is disturbing the readability as it causes relations that point back and cross each other. Even though initial SeeMe-diagram is moderately matured and lacks clarity with regards to the content, the tool anyways performs the conversion and it works well in terms of syntactical correctness. The diagram reaches its end event, when the task of writing a review is performed. At this point, the conversion tool has proven that it is in general able to satisfy the overall goal.

5   Discussion and Conclusion

With the current state, the conversion tool is still not yet fully perfected, but the main idea is well covered. As elaborated previously, the described translation rules are well implementable. Anyways the translation rules are not entirely complete, since both notations allow special but rare representations and were not considered as part of the current stage.

Furthermore, the tool has its limiting aspects. The possibility of complex embedding, concatenations or complex structures are some potential sources of trouble. Even if those are possibly resolvable in terms of translation, the results probably might not be reasonable. Thus, the modeler might need to adjust or modify the generated results to match his or her expectations. Extensive usage of vagueness or intentional omissions in SeeMe might also turn out to be breaking points for the tool.

However, the main aim to extend the STWT process is achieved. This conversions tool aims to support the final phases of the STWT process which provides well-engineered SeeMe diagrams. Therefore, the problem of possible omissions is in general avoided. For the case of incompletely developed diagrams, it is up to the modeler to clarify if his or her needs are coverable for the situation.

Whether the reasons for establishing this conversion tool are fulfilled or not, is not yet clarified. For the future, it remains to observe how the tool is assisting the modelers of the STWT process. Additionally, it is up to observe if the goal of employing the widespread accessibility of the finalized results in BPMN notation is matched. The conversion from one modeling notation usually allows for reflecting the quality of the model. With respect to using BPMN, the modeler is urged to decide how far incompleteness should be maintained or reduced. The visual complexity of the resulting BPMN-diagrams might also be an indicator to decide at which points a reduction of elements or relationships might be reasonable.

As outlook for future work, it needs to be validated by modelers if the tool is useful for the targeted case and on this basis the tool might be improved relating the inferred shortcomings with performing refinement works and reevaluations.

References

1. Herrmann, T.: Systems design with the socio-technical walkthrough. In: Handbook of Research on Socio-Technical Design and Social Networking Systems, pp. 336–351. IGI Global, Hershey (2009). https://doi.org/10.4018/9781605662640.ch023
2. Herrmann, T., Loser, K.-U.: Vagueness in models of socio-technical systems. Behav. Inf. Technol. **18**, 313–323 (1999). https://doi.org/10.1080/014492999118904
3. Chinosi, M., Trombetta, A.: BPMN: an introduction to the standard. Comput. Stand. Interfaces **34**, 124–134 (2012). https://doi.org/10.1016/j.csi.2011.06.002
4. Ouyang, C., Dumas, M., Aalst, W.M.P.V.D., Hofstede, A.H.M.T., Mendling, J.: From business process models to process-oriented software systems. ACM Trans. Softw. Eng. Methodol. **19**, 1–37 (2009). https://doi.org/10.1145/1555392.1555395
5. Herrmann, T.: SeeMe in a nutshell – the semi-structured, socio-technical modeling method. **18** (2006). https://www.imtm-iaw.ruhr-uni-bochum.de/wp-content/uploads/sites/5/2011/09/Seeme-in-a-nutshell.pdf
6. Allweyer, T.: BPMN 2.0 - Business Process Model and Notation: Einführung in den Standard für die Geschäftsprozessmodellierung. Books on Demand, Norderstedt (2009)
7. OMG: Business Process Model and Notation (BPMN), Version 2.0. (2011)

Designing a Dashboard Visualization Tool for Urban Planners to Assess the Completeness of Streets

Greice C. Mariano[1]([✉]), Veda Adnani[1], Iman Kewalramani[1], Bo Wang[2], Matthew J. Roorda[2], Jeremy Bowes[1], and Sara Diamond[1]

[1] Visual Analytics Lab (VAL), OCAD University, Toronto, ON, Canada
{gmariano,vadnani,jbowes,sdiamond}@ocadu.ca
https://www2.ocadu.ca/research/val
[2] University of Toronto, Toronto, ON, Canada
brz.wang@mail.utoronto.ca, matt.roorda@utoronto.ca

Abstract. This paper presents a design study for a novel interactive web-based visualization tool that utilizes a "Complete Streets" model to support urban planners and engineers to design streets in urban areas more effectively. The proposed tool integrates a map and a dashboard view, where streets are analyzed and scored based on their overall completeness through six parameters of service; automobile, public transit, goods vehicles, environment, pedestrians and cyclists. In the map view, planners can assess streets based on their location, type and form and perform comparisons between multiple streets. In the dashboard view, planners can tweak a comprehensive set of instructions within each of the six parameters and view the effects of their changes in real time for both overall completeness and across parameters. Planners can also save versions to revisit and tweak them whenever necessary and may also download their dashboard data in different formats. We proposed that planners will be able to assess the completeness of existing streets in their current state and create multiple street prototypes exploring different scenarios and combinations virtually, instantaneously, minimizing costly pilots and prototypes. Future iterations will also promote collaboration and sharing across dashboards.

Keywords: Dashboard design · Urban systems · Transportation

1 Introduction

Urban sustainability is one of the most pertinent issues of the twenty-first century, given that more than half of the world's population now lives in cities [12]. Cities are becoming complex systems of systems, with spatial needs in urban areas increasing rapidly, while the available urban area that is available remains unchanged. Automobiles, public transport vehicles, pedestrians and cyclists are all competing within the same amount of space, and it is becoming imperative

© Springer Nature Switzerland AG 2020
S. Yamamoto and H. Mori (Eds.): HCII 2020, LNCS 12184, pp. 85–103, 2020.
https://doi.org/10.1007/978-3-030-50020-7_6

for urban planners and engineers to redesign streets in a way that is optimized and services the needs of all its stakeholders.

In the early 2000's, in the United States, a group of cyclists started a movement to require that bicycle facilities become part of all road construction plans [15]. In 2003, that movement was renamed to "Complete Streets". Since then, a new notion about how streets should be planned and built has changed over the years. Today, Complete Streets is a term used to identify streets that were built to safely accommodate automobiles, bicyclists, pedestrians and public transit users [17]. This concept changed the way the transportation industry plans transportation infrastructure, thinking more about how to create a safe environment for everyone, including people of all ages and abilities; those who walk, those who travel by bicycle, take transit, or drive.

Though the Complete Streets idea is compelling, not every type of street can accommodate all types of use, as it is necessary to plan a network of streets according to social, economic and environmental priorities. There is more than one way to make a street "complete"; the application depends on the context of its use. Planners need guidelines and policies that assess the completeness of streets and create priorities for types of usage.

"A Complete Streets policy ensures that transportation planners and engineers consistently design and operate the entire street network for all road users, not only motorists. Complete Streets offer wide ranging benefits. They are cost effective, sustainable, and safe." [4]. In fact, the number of policies to create Complete Streets has consistently increased over the years. In Canada, according to the website Complete Streets for Canada, the number of policies that have been adopted grew in the last twelve years, from only one in 2008 to 122 in 2018. Each city has its own guidelines and policies for designing Complete Streets. However, there remains a lack of tools that visually support urban planners to design and evaluate Complete Streets before any plan is implemented.

One way of evaluating Complete Streets or to measure the quality of service of one street is using a Level of Services (LOS) rating. According to the National Cooperative Highway Research Program (NCHRP) user guide [7], "Level of service (LOS) is used to translate complex numerical performance results into a simple letter grade system representative of the traveler's perception of the resulting quality of service provided by the facility". Thus, "Level of service is a quantitative stratification of quality of service into six letter grades with letter grade A representing the best quality of service, and letter grade F representing the worst quality of service" [7]. This method of rating is "widely used in transport Planning to evaluate problems and potential solutions. Because they are easy to understand (they are like school grades), Level of Service rating often influence transport planning decisions. Such ratings systems can be used identify problems, establish Performance Indicators and targets, evaluate potential solutions, compare locations, and track trends." [26].

This paper presents a design study for an interactive web-based visualization dashboard tool that uses a "Complete Streets" model to support urban planners and engineers to design streets in urban areas more effectively. The tool is composed of a map view and a dashboard view, where streets can be analyzed based on a score computed using Level of Services (LOS) for six different categories: automobile, public transit, goods vehicle, environment, pedestrians and cyclists. Users of the tool can evaluate the streets, and compare different scenarios based on the category's overall completeness. For example, a city planner may want to evaluate the trade-offs between additional landscape buffer zones versus an increase in private vehicle transport lanes or dedicated public transit lanes. Our research, and resultant dashboard work provides a model to test prototypical Complete Streets combinations. This supports urban design and transportation planning decision making.

2   Related Work

2.1   Complete Streets

The "Complete Streets" model has been introduced to ensure that streets are designed for all ages, abilities and modes of travel [14,15]. Complete Streets are a means to encourage active transport and are associated with health benefits [13]. The model ensures that planners and engineers employ an inclusive approach while designing and building streets in urban areas [3,17]. There are approximately a hundred Complete Street policies that exist across all ten provinces across Canada as of today and many others around the world, suggesting the relevance of this research [3].

2.2   HCI and Visualization Design Principles

According to Sedlmair et al. (2012) "design studies have become an increasingly popular approach for conducting problem-driven visualization research" [24]. In their paper, the authors define design studies for visualization in four steps: analyze a specific real world problem faced by domain experts; design many possibilities to address the problem; validate the proposed design with the domain experts (users); reflect the lessons learned during the design development. They also propose a nine-stage framework where the collaboration between visualization researchers and domain experts is mandatory.

These Nascimento et al. (2016) highlights that "User experience (UX) covers the relationship between usability, context of use, and user emotions regarding an application" [16], and usability is a critical point that can influence the prototypes acceptance by the users. Nielsen (1995) introduces ten usability heuristics for user interface design [18]. In his recent work, Nielsen (2012), defines usability by five quality components: learnability, efficiency, memorability, errors and satisfaction, and you can fix problems(implement solutions to problems) if the evaluation is performed in small tests [19], using the iterative design process and evaluation using heuristics, as suggested by Zuk et al. (2006) [27]. During our study design to develop the Complete Streets Dashboard visualization tool, we conducted a similar approach to that proposed by Sedlmair et al. (2012). We developed a user-centered interface using Nielsen's (2012) quality components for usability to enhance the user experience. Reynold's (2014) Basic Qualities of Good Design [21] provide a series of design principles that integrate well into user interface design. These are simple, clear, consistent, meaningful, extendable/longevity and collaborative.

Bowes et al. (2018) introduces a well-developed taxonomy of user-centered visualizations to "help designers understand which visualization techniques (or combination of them) best serve the goals and needs of user and stakeholder groups" [1]. Their paper outlines how to adapt abstract and spatial data categories, integrating the three major components of data, visual and navigation into the visualization approaches, along with levels of user engagement, to build a relationship between user engagement goals and visualization components. Based on Bowes et al. (2018) paper, Gordon et al., (2018) proposed a comparative visualization tool to visualize the attributes of software listed by the taxonomy work [8]. The tool is called Compara and allows users "to quickly understand the broad-scale application landscape of transit and transportation digital tools" [8]. A related tool Vizland matched typical visualization types to types of usages and users. From these sources we can correlate what kind of visualization task, visualization tool, and data type are the most important and have been used by users who need to undertake Complete Streets analysis to visualize their data. These principles are applied in developing the dashboard.

In 1987, Rowe introduced the concept of Design Thinking as a design process for architecture and urban planning [22]. Thirty years later, during a lecture in Harvard University Graduate School of Design, he described new ways in which design thinking can be applied in the digital age [23]. According to Tim Brown of IDEO [11], "Design thinking is a human-centered approach to innovation that draws from the designer's toolkit to integrate the needs of people, the possibilities of technology, and the requirements for business success". We used design thinking methods [2] that integrate human-computer interaction (HCI) factors proposed by Shneiderman et al. (2016) [25] to create user engagement.

In Nusrat's article on Task Taxonomy for Cartograms, she states "A cartogram should enable the viewer to quickly and correctly interpret the data encoded in the visualization" [20], and it is important to define the "visualization goals and a set of tasks that are suitable for cartogram visualization". In this case, we considered the kinds of tasks that users accessing Complete Streets Dashboard tool need to perform. The author also outlines the following tasks related to the use of a cartographic map: detect change (compared to a base map), Locate, Recognize, Identify, Compare, Find Top, Filter, Find Adjacency, Cluster and Summarize. These tasks can classify "along four dimensions: goals, means, characteristics, and cardinality". Based on the follow questions: "Goals: why is a task performed? Means: how is a task carried out? Characteristics: what are the features of a task? (level of complexity of the visualization task), and Cardinality: where in the data a task operates?" [20]. This was an important reflection to include in the map visualization in our Complete Streets Dashboard. Based on the map view, users can easily identify the streets that they are working with. In addition, users have a summarized visualization of complete-ness for one or multiple streets and can navigate, compare and visualize data for different types of streets or events though segments of streets.

3 Methodology

In this section, we discuss the process used to propose an interactive dashboard to support the evaluation of Complete Streets. Using heuristics, map-based visual-ization and dashboard guidelines, the tool was created to facilitate the analysis and evaluation of different Complete Streets scenarios by urban planners and engineers.

3.1 Process Overview

The first phase of the design study involved a collaborative research exercise between researchers from University of Toronto (UofT) and OCAD University (OCAD U). The UofT team introduced the OCAD U team to their spreadsheet tool developed for measuring the "completeness" of a Complete Street according to the concept presented by Hui et al. (2017) [10]. They developed a rich Excel display with: (i) a data sample in array; (ii) formulas based on authoritative Level of Service (LOS) model equations and criteria, such as NCHRP Report 616 [6] and Florida Department of Transportation - Quality/Level of Service (FDOT QLOS) main handout [9] to compute the different categories of LOS scores for streets with given roadway specifications and information; and (iii) visualizations in order to help individuals design Complete Streets. The dashboard's visual layout computes and presents information for a set of six categories: Walking, Cycling, Transit, Goods, Auto, Place, and Environment. Figure 1 provides an overview of the spreadsheet created by the UofT team (see Fig. 1).

For each category, the bar graphs and gauges charts show a comparison between the desired LOS scores and the target score obtained by the user's interactions with main five boxes control. In the first box, called "Roadway Specifications", the users can set the width of different parts of a symmetric roadway using sliders below each value. Users can select, for example, the width of the sidewalk, bike lane, buffer, among others. Below the sliders, the users can use drop-down lists to assign materials types, choosing if they are to be permeable or impermeable.

In the second box, "Roadway Information", the user can provide more detailed information selecting true or false from drop down lists for a set of three questions: *"Is there a raised buffer between sidewalk and other users (e.g. planters, trees)?", Is there unstriped parking in the curb lane?, Is the median actually a 2-way left turn lane?.*

The third, fourth and fifth boxes are considered as "Parameters" boxes, and the user can inform "Miscellaneous Design", "Auto Traffic Flow", and "Transit Flow Parameters". The miscellaneous design is used to get at some features related to the street and includes options in drop down lists or sliders. For

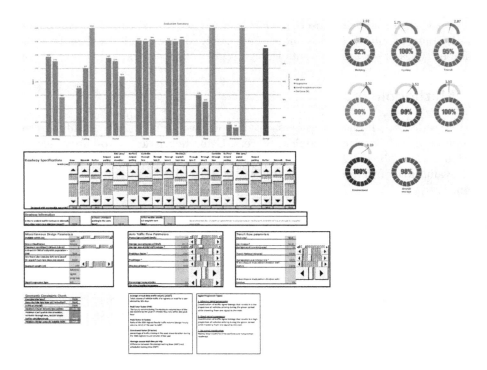

Fig. 1. Spreadsheet with data, logic, formulas, controls and projected output. This spreadsheet formed the basis for the dashboard visualization.

instance, in the streets' classification field, it is possible to select the type of the street (collector, local arterial, industrial street, residential street, etc.) using a drop-down list. At the same time, the user might inform the segment length using slider bars. Similarly, information related with automobile traffic flow can be selected, such as, average operation speed (km/h) and peak factor. Finally, information related to specific public transportation, such as, buses, streetcars and average transit operating speed can be informed.

The spreadsheet also has a "Geometric Constraints Check" table, where the user can identify if the street contains a bike lane, if the bike lane has a buffer larger than 0.7 m, if the street is an arterial street, and where streets fail to conform to guidelines that are designated within Complete Streets policies and guidelines.

When the user changes any parameter from the five boxes or from the table, the performance of a given roadway is evaluated. For each category, target scores are computed and compared with desired LOS scores based on roadway types according to Calgary's Complete Streets scoring tool [5]. The results are summarized and presented in the charts. Both bar graphs and gauge charts show the LOS score, and the target score. The bar chart also includes an additional bar to indicate the performance in percentage. In the gauge chart, green and red areas are determined by the target scores, and when a needle falls within the green area it means that LOS score meets the targets. The overall performance (in percentage) is also displayed for each category and the overall rating below each gauge. Since this dashboard is using a small data sample, some categories do not have data, as in the case of Goods and Auto. Their gauge chart has the green and red color inverted when compared with the others.

While the functionality of the dashboard was clear, there were many usability and visualization challenges posed with the use of the spreadsheet format. Users needed a scalable, simple application that could be used to design Complete Streets in accordance with regulations. The research team applied HCI and visualization principles from our prior research. We worked towards an intuitive map-based visualization dashboard that integrates graphs, is highly interactive and follows visualization design and dashboard principles. We applied lessons learned from Compara and Vizland [8] and our earlier taxonomy work [1] to select visualization strategies that were appropriate to the expert's needs. Sedlmair et al. (2012)'s [24] approach to developing visualizations through user engagement allowed the Complete Streets experts at UofT to provide requirements that the OCAD U team responded to. We used a design thinking process [2] to take the team through the process of understanding the spreadsheet, the requirements for the visualization and to create a solution, then to separate our design process into five phases, as follows:

Empathize: The cross-institutional team collaborated to understand the documents together by breaking out various parameters and finding consistent systems of representation for the various criteria within the Complete Streets document (outlined above). This process took 2–3 weeks to complete and required a series of collaborative workshops to break down and simplify the data at hand. In this phase, the team also discussed the visualization tasks and resulting interface elements that would support personas representing possible users.

Define: Once all the data had been broken down, the next step was to synthesize parameters and measures for Completeness in a way that was standard, easy to understand and accessible. Another workshop linked the background data science to the desired design outcomes, ensuring that the outcomes would be accurate.

Ideate: With agreement on data structure, the design team proceeded to ideate by drafting screen flows and content for the application. Sketching culminated with the creation of an application map.

Prototype: Once the application map was clear, wireframes for multiple screens were designed using the Adobe XD software. The wireframes were created to be interactive, and another workshop was held to generate feedback and address concerns. This development process was iterative, and experimental in nature.

Implementation: During the prototype development, programming the data structure for applications based on the information architecture commenced. After three rounds of updating the prototyping, the most final iteration was accepted.

Testing: Since the development process was iterative, the application was being tested internally as it was being developed. There were weekly team meetings to ensure that the vision was seen through to fruition. Our team validated the application with sample and hypothetical data. We are planning to apply Nielsen's heuristics in usability tests with stakeholders to evaluate the interface's usability [18,19].

3.2   Interface Design Approach

Reynolds' (2014) Basic Qualities of Good Design [21] were studied, and from them we derived the following design principles have been taken into consideration while designing and developing the User Experience and Interface for this application. They form the basis for the strategic thinking and design execution process. These principles have been adopted keeping in mind that the user lies at the center of the design process (user-centered design).

Simple: The focus of creating this application was to convert complex formulas for urban planning into a simplified and engaging user experience. The structure and design for the application has been built on a foundation of a five second rule, where the user should be able to easily to use the interface at any point. The goal for the application was not to restrict usage to urban planners, but also enable students, researchers and other audiences interested in exploring the design for Complete Streets models. Elements of content, function and visual design have been created keeping this principle in mind. Decorative elements have been minimized to avoid confusion; however, the application was created with a compelling design aesthetic.

Clear: Information is displayed clearly within the application, with one touch links with key explanations for theoretical concepts that seem new or unique to a user. Using the application is clear both in terms of content and design elements for input throughout the application. The strategic approach to design the application has been function first.

Consistent: Because of the many permutations and combinations used to configure Complete Streets, the interface has been simplified with easily recognizable, intuitive, analog and binary inputs that have been standardized to two formats for each type of input. For the binary inputs there are buttons and checkboxes and for analog inputs there are sliders and dropdowns. This structure has been followed to ensure consistency and ease of use to manipulate data throughout the application. The layout, structure, language, and aesthetic have been designed consistently so that the user may focus on the task at hand.

Meaningful: In order to ensure that the user is able to understand the purpose and use of the application, the flow of the application has been designed to proceed from overarching, holistic views of streets within an area, to manipulating of details within each street in a gradual progression. The approach has been centered around giving the user the right information at the right time. This ensures that the user has the flexibility to browse through streets and draw comparisons between them across areas, before moving into a detailed street redesign or designing a new street.

Extendable/Longevity: This application has been designed with the flexibility to add and remove parameters in the future, to adapt to changing laws and amendments, and with the ability to be applied across different cities to ensure its future usability.

Collaborative: The team understands that often designing or redesigning streets is a collaborative effort and plans to include collaborative street design in the next iteration of this application.

In addition to the above design principles, Five Quality Principles of Usability proposed by Nielsen (2012) [19], Learnability, Efficiency, Memorability, Errors and Satisfaction, were also considered when designing this application. They have been central to the structure and design of this application. The application has been designed keeping in mind that not all users will be urban planners, and not all will be adept with urban planning terminology, software, or process. Content has been simplified and additional information on concepts, terminology, and literature have been provided across the application to help users understand core concepts and processes within Complete Streets with ease. A first-time user, will be able to easily browse streets, filter them, study parameters and even simply customize a street through the application. Once users have navigated through the application for the first time, they will find it easy, quick and intuitive to use the application to customize streets repeatedly. Repeated use after long breaks is also easy. Internal testing thus far has resulted in a low error rate, and future iterations will comprise external user testing as well.

3.3   Implementation Details

Once the design prototype was completed, the search for frameworks and libraries capable of handling the complexities of the user interactions and user interface began. Ultimately, the development team settled on using Deck.gl, a powerful layered-based data exploratory, analysis and visualization framework; and Mapbox, an open source custom mapping platform; both in conjunction with HTML and JavaScript.

The next step was to obtain the data set of streets in the Toronto area along with their necessary parameters to calculate completeness, such as street widths, speed limits, number of lanes, and location coordinates. Once obtained, the development team used data manipulation and wrangling techniques to render the data format compatible with the technologies used. With the linkage of the data file to the preliminary web application, we successfully implemented a major part of the project, the map view.

The development team then worked on implementing features one at a time, beginning with the tooltip pop-up, then the sidebar, followed by the navigation bar and finally, the dashboard. During this process, multiple issues were raised by the development team about the flow of the application, especially in the dashboard view. The biggest technical hurdle during the implementation phase was the creation of complex User Interface (UI) elements such as the dual handle slider with labels, which had to be designed from scratch.

Once all the features were implemented, and rigorous testing of individual features was completed, it was time to implement the styling of each UI element in the application which was an extremely time-consuming process. The backend of the web application is written in Python. The primary web framework used is Flask. The backend database contains user login information, a log of sessions, files of saved preferences that are stored in individual folders. The backend also contains converted code of the calculation of completeness used in the prototype spreadsheet mentioned above.

The limitations of the application lie in the lack of accurate street information in the dataset obtained. As a result, much of the completeness parameters had to be estimated based on averages across Toronto, which is not ideal. Another limitation is the fact that streets in the dataset spanned the whole length of the street with equal parameter values throughout, which is not realistic since streets can differ widely from one end to another.

4   Complete Streets Application Prototype

The proposed layout for the tool is comprised of a map and dashboard view, where streets are analyzed and scored based on their overall completeness through six parameters: automobile, public transit, goods vehicles, environment, pedestrians and cyclists [10]. In the map view, planners can assess streets based on their location, type and form, and can perform comparisons between multiple streets. In the dashboard view, planners can tweak a comprehensive set of instructions within each of the six parameters and view the effects of their changes in real time for both overall completeness across parameters, saving various versions. They may also download their dashboard data in various formats. For image-based versions, users can download a PDF format or a high-resolution JPEG format. These file types are valuable when presenting and sharing the street combinations. For text-based versions users can download a CSV or TXT formats. There are useful for further altering, categorizing, integrating or visualizing the data outside of this application.

Consistency has been maintained across User Interface (UI) elements. These include elements for navigation, call to action, input controls and information. The elements offer simple yet familiar usability affordances and clear feedback mechanisms to ensure that urban planners can focus their attention on the task at hand as opposed to the interaction with the interface itself. In addition, the interface has been designed keeping principles of usability in mind [19]. It is easy for first time users to learn how to navigate the interface, and thereafter be able to use it with further ease and reduced cognitive load. The prototype has also been designed keeping prolonged use and to be light, loading easily and working on all browsers. The following visualization components were considered for this application:

Colour Usage: The interface has been designed in black to minimize the load on the eyes. Colour use is minimal, function first. Key action colours such as green and red that are easily recognizable have been used to denote positive and negative actions.

Typography: Clean sans-serif fonts have been used to allow the user to focus on the task at hand. They provide visual relief and make it easy to read at all sizes.

User Interface Elements: Typical usability patterns for buttons, sliders, checkboxes and dropdowns have been used so that the user does not have to expend cognitive load on figuring out what the elements can do. These elements can be found on most web and mobile interfaces.

A detailed application flow for the tool is shown below. New users can register, and existing users can login to the application. New users are verified through a moderator, and the application is accessible through any web browser on desktop or laptop screens for this iteration.

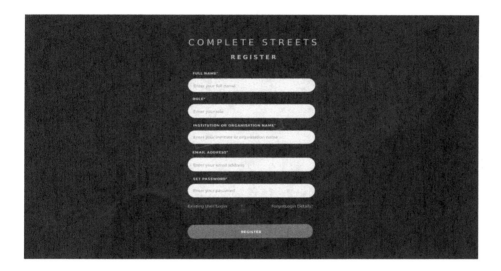

Fig. 2. Registration screen for first time users.

Upon logging in or registering (see Fig. 2), the user arrives at a map view screen where they can search for a street through the search bar in the header, or hover over streets on the map to get an overarching view of how complete each street is. The map view has been provided to give users a spatial understanding, and a sense of the shape of streets prior to customization. It is necessary for planners to first see the location, neighbourhood, size, shape and environment around the street before they can begin assessing it, and therefore this view is the first point of interaction within the application. When a user hovers over a street in this view, a tooltip with completeness details of the selected street pops up (see Fig. 3). The user can browse through multiple streets consecutively to be able to draw comparisons, gain insight into streets in that neighbourhood, or see how similar shaped streets are designed for completeness. Once the designer understands the spatial details of the selected street, the next step is to study the street in further detail before they begin transforming it. This pop-up gives them instant overviews into the overall completion of the selected street along with summarized category-wise completion rates. Colours for Level of Service scores indicate if categories are complete or not to make it easy for the user to comprehend. The user can also gain a deeper understanding of how the scores are derived, by clicking on detail information pop-ups for Level of Service. This feature has been added for those users who are new to urban planning and would like to familiarize with the relevant literature and formulas.

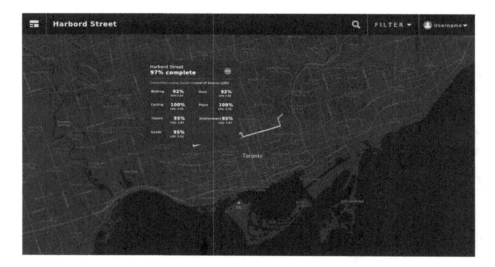

Fig. 3. Map view with tooltip to provide a completeness overview on the selected street.

Because browsing experiences and preferences can differ for different users, the application also provides the user the option to choose to filter streets within a city, based on parameters for completeness, street types, or length of streets (see Fig. 4). This type of browsing is also helpful when users need to compare similar street types, lengths or find other similar Complete Streets or categories to set benchmarks for their own design.

Users can click into a street to obtain more detail around how completeness scores are derived for each parameter (see Fig. 5). They can also find relevant literature here and choose to navigate to the dashboard to begin customizing the selected street at hand. Because the tooltips only provide an overview of completeness this view is critical for users to investigate each parameter in detail,

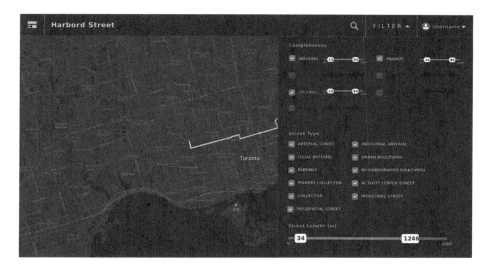

Fig. 4. Filter window for map view that allows users to locate streets by Completeness across categories, street type and length.

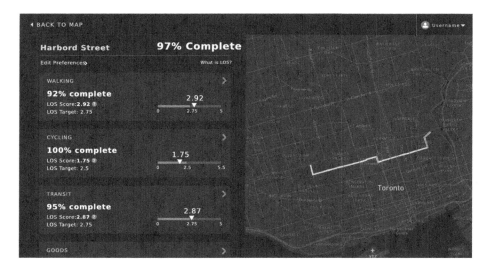

Fig. 5. Detail window for map view. This view provides in depth insight into the completeness of an individual street, along with details about each category of completeness

in correlation to the street's spatial presence on the map. Users can also dig deeper into the various criteria for assessment at this stage to better understand the science behind the scoring system (see Fig. 6).

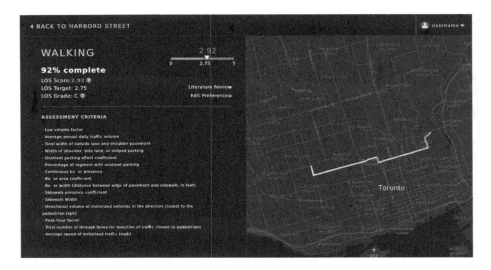

Fig. 6. Category wise details within the Detail Window (Fig. 5). This provides the user insight into criteria of completeness assessment for that category within the selected street.

The dashboard view was the most challenging to design during this process. Some of the key challenges faced were; ensuring the controls fit within one-fold of the screen so users do not miss adjusting any parameters while designing their street. Another challenge was ensuring that the dashboard looks clear and uncluttered. The third was to create visual relief between sections of the dashboard view as subtle demarcations for the user. The fourth was to standardize input elements – both analog and binary to ensure that the interface is easy and intuitive to use.

The screen has been designed in a modular format. It begins with real time data visualizations for overall completeness and completeness across different parameters. Thereafter there are sliders to allow designers to adjust the width of the street for each parameter mentioned. And lastly, they can make further customizations to roadway information, design parameters, and traffic and transit flow parameters (see Fig. 7).

Users can choose to augment an existing street, or to create a new street from scratch within the dashboard. It is also easy for them to start over if they would like to, in which case they are given the option to save their work prior to moving away. On the second fold, users can view streets they have adjusted in the past as rectangular cards. These consider both new streets which have blank map names and existing streets, of which the names are near the map markers within the cards.

Users can search for existing streets within the search cards, or through the search box in the top menu bar (see Fig. 8). This is a critical component given the volume of streets within urban areas.

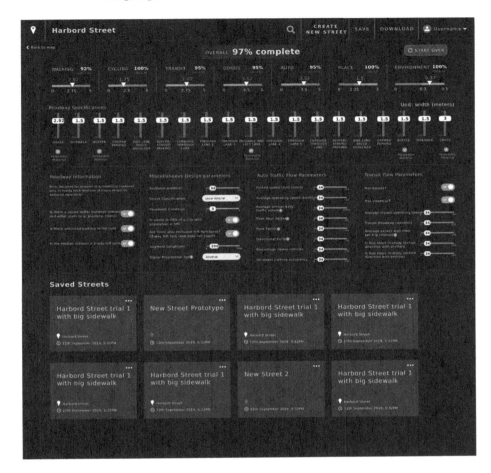

Fig. 7. Complete Dashboard View. This view comprises two folds of a screen, the first fold lasts up to the Saved Streets section, and that is where the user can manipulate data to build a Complete Street. The second fold is where the user's saved work is archived and easily accessible for future use.

Users can create a new street from scratch (see Fig. 9). This feature has been created to accommodate the expansion of urban areas through development.

Users can choose to save their work at any point, using the top menu bar controls (see Fig. 10). This will help users to archive their work, create multiple versions of completeness for the same street, and revisit their data with ease.

Users can choose to download their work in an array of image and text-based formats to ensure compatibility with multiple applications (see Fig. 11). Text based formats aid with data integration, analysis and application, and image-based formats aid with presentation of data.

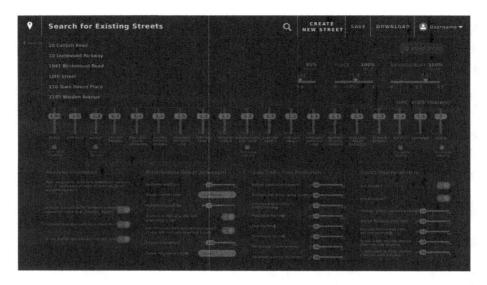

Fig. 8. Dropdown for street search bar. Users can choose to search for a street within the database by its name. Upon picking a street the dashboard will auto-populate with current data from that street.

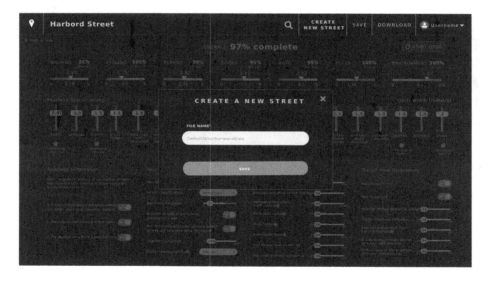

Fig. 9. Create new street window for users who want to build a new street from scratch.

Future versions of the prototype will be responsive to tablet and mobile platforms to afford usability on the move and future iterations will also promote collaboration and sharing across dashboards.

Fig. 10. Save work window for user's who have manipulated an existing street. It also shows the original street name for future reference.

Fig. 11. Download window. Users can choose to download data in text or image-based formats depending on their needs at the time.

5   Conclusions and Future Work

The Complete Streets application presented in this research is currently in its first iteration, with a working coded prototype ready for detailed user-testing that will commence later this year. We feel that the proposed tool enables planners to assess the completeness of streets in their current state, and to create a variety of virtual scenarios to model changes immediately with minimal cost. Prior to developing future iterations, we plan to user test the prototype with domain experts and implement feedback. We will test this interface and improve its accessibility and usability to ensure inclusive design. Furthermore, we plan to develop increased functionality to allow multiple users to collaborate on the dashboard and maps simultaneously and make the application more responsive and accessible. This will be useful for users on-site, or at remote locations.

As next steps, we will work together with Esri Canada, an industry partner of OCAD U and UofT in the iCity Urban Informatics for Sustainable Metropolitan Growth research consortium, to incorporate the Complete Streets Dashboard inside of the ArcGIS platform, combining the 2D and 3D map visualizations. We envision that this will improve the user experience and the quality of evaluation of Complete Streets, because users will be able to explore their changes in real time in a simulated environment. We would also like to see this application scale across cities.

Acknowledgments. The authors gratefully acknowledge the support of OCAD University and the Visual Analytics Lab, University of Toronto, Canada Foundation for Innovation, the Ontario Ministry of Research & Innovation through the ORF-RE program for the iCity Urban Informatics for Sustainable Metropolitan Growth research consortium; NSERC Canada CreateDAV, and MITACS for support of graduate internships.

References

1. Bowes, J., et al.: User-centered taxonomy for urban transportation applications. In: Nah, F.F.-H., Xiao, B.S. (eds.) HCIBGO 2018. LNCS, vol. 10923, pp. 577–593. Springer, Cham (2018). https://doi.org/10.1007/978-3-319-91716-0_46
2. Brown, T.: Change by Design. Harper Business Books, New York (2009)
3. City of Toronto. Complete Streets Guidelines by Chapter. https://www.toronto.ca/services-payments/streets-parking-transportation/enhancing-our-streets-and-public-realm/complete-streets/complete-streets-guidelines/. Accessed 30 Jan 2020
4. Complete Streets for Canada. https://www.completestreetsforcanada.ca/locations/. Accessed 29 Jan 2020
5. Complete Streets for Canada, Complete Streets Guide (2014). https://www.completestreetsforcanada.ca/wp-content/uploads/2014/09/www.calgary.ca_Transportation_TP_Documents_CTP2010_complete-streets-guide-2014-web.pdf. Accessed 30 Jan 2020
6. Dowling, R.-G., et al.: NCHRP Report 616: Multimodal Level of Service Analysis for Urban Streets. Transportation Research Board of the National Academies, Washington, DC (2008)
7. Dowling, R.-G., Reinke, D.-B.: NCHRP Web-Only Document 128: Multimodal Level of Service Analysis for Urban Streets: Users Guide. Transportation Research Board (2008)
8. Gordon, M., Diamond, S., Zheng, M., Carnevale, M.: Compara. Encount. Theory Hist. Educ. **19**, 163–185 (2018). https://doi.org/10.24908/eoe-ese-rse.v19i0.11867

9. Florida Department of Transportation, Quality Level of Service Handbook (2013). https://fdotwww.blob.core.windows.net/sitefinity/docs/default-source/content/planning/systems/programs/sm/los/pdfs/2013_qlos_handbook.pdf?sfvrsn=22690bd2_0. Accessed 30 Jan 2020
10. Hui, N., Saxe, S., Roorda, M., Hess, P., Miller, E.: Measuring the completeness of complete streets. Transp. Rev. **38**, 1–23 (2017). https://doi.org/10.1080/01441647.2017.1299815
11. IDEO Design Thinking. Design Thinking Today. https://designthinking.ideo.com/#design-thinking-today. Accessed 29 Jan 2020
12. Keivani, R.: A review of the main challenges to urban sustainability. Int. J. Urban Sustain. Dev. **1**, 5–16 (2009). https://doi.org/10.1080/19463131003704213
13. Laplante, J., And, P., Mccann, B.: Complete streets: we can get there from here. Inst. Transp. Eng. (ITE) J. **78**(5), 24–28 (2008)
14. Lynott, J., et al.: Planning complete streets for an aging America (2009). https://www.aarp.org/home-garden/livable-communities/info-08-2009/Planning_Complete_Streets_for_an_Aging_America.html. Accessed 29 Jan 2020
15. McCann, B.: Completing Our Streets: The Transition to Safe and Inclusive Transportation Networks. Island Press, Washington, DC (2013)
16. Nascimento, I., Silva, W., Gadelha, B., Conte, T.: Userbility: a technique for the evaluation of user experience and usability on mobile applications. In: Kurosu, M. (ed.) HCI 2016. LNCS, vol. 9731, pp. 372–383. Springer, Cham (2016). https://doi.org/10.1007/978-3-319-39510-4_35
17. National Complete Streets Coalition: The best complete streets policies of 2015 (2016). https://www.smartgrowthamerica.org/app/legacy/documents/best-cs-policies-of-2015.pdf. Accessed 30 Jan 2020
18. Nielsen, J.: 10 usability heuristics for user interface design. Nielsen Norman Group (1995). https://www.nngroup.com/articles/ten-usability-heuristics/. Accessed 26 Jan 2020
19. Nielsen, J.: Usability 101: Introduction to Usability. Nielsen Norman Group (2012). https://www.nngroup.com/articles/usability-101-introduction-to-usability/. Accessed 26 Jan 2020
20. Nusrat, S., Kobourov, S.: Task taxonomy for cartograms. In: Bertini, E., Kennedy, J., Puppo, E. (eds.) Eurographics Conference on Visualization (EuroVis) - Short Papers. Theu Eurographics Association (2015). https://doi.org/10.2312/eurovisshort.20151126
21. Reynolds, G.: Presentation Zen Design: A Simple Visual Approach to Presenting in Today's World, 2nd edn. Pearson Education, London (2014)
22. Rowe, P.: Design Thinking. The MIT Press, Cambridge (1987)
23. Rowe, P.: Design Thinking in the Digital Age. Harvard University Graduate School of Design, Cambridge (2017)
24. Sedlmair, M., Meyer, M., Munzner, T.: Design study methodology: reflections from the trenches and the stacks. IEEE Trans. Visual Comput. Graphics **18**(12), 2431–2440 (2012). https://doi.org/10.1109/TVCG.2012.213
25. Shneiderman, B., Plaisant, C., Cohen, M., Jacobs, S.: Designing the User Interface: Strategies for Effective Human-Computer Interaction, 6th edn. Pearson, London (2016)
26. Victoria Transport Policy Institute. Introduction to multi-modal transportation planning (2019). https://www.vtpi.org/tdm/tdm129.htm. Accessed 30 Jan 2020
27. Zuk, T., Schlesier, L., Neumann, P., Hancock, M. S., Carpendale, S.: Heuristics for information visualization evaluation. In: Proceedings of the 2006 AVI Workshop on Beyond Time and Errors: Novel Evaluation Methods for Information Visualization, pp. 1–6. ACM, May 2006. https://doi.org/10.1145/1168149.1168162

Exploring Ontology-Based Information Through the Progressive Disclosure of Visual Answers to Related Queries

Dalai S. Ribeiro$^{(\boxtimes)}$, Alysson Gomes de Sousa$^{(\boxtimes)}$,
Rodrigo B. de Almeida$^{(\boxtimes)}$, Pedro Henrique Thompson Furtado$^{(\boxtimes)}$,
Hélio Côrtes Vieira Lopes$^{(\boxtimes)}$, and Simone Diniz Junqueira Barbosa$^{(\boxtimes)}$

Pontifícia Universidade Católica do Rio de Janeiro,
Rio de Janeiro, RJ 22451-900, Brazil
dalai.ribeiro@gmail.com, {asousa,rbarbosa,lopes,simone}@inf.puc-rio.br,
pedrothompson@petrobras.com.br

Abstract. Web search has become the predominant method for people to fulfill their information needs. Although widespread, the traditional model for search result pages is only satisfactory if the user knows quite precisely how to phrase their query to match their intended information. We propose a new model for search page results, which goes beyond providing a navigable list of visualization search results, by implicitly generating related queries to expand the search space and progressively disclosing the corresponding results.

Keywords: Design · Information design · Information retrieval · UX and usability · User interface of search result pages

1 Introduction

"In a little more than a decade, the Web has become the default global repository for information" [15]. Search has remarkably contributed to this result and it has become ubiquitously associated with the Web itself, to the point of becoming a default tool in any modern browser and one of the most popular activities online, already in 2008 [5].

As stated by Wilson et al. (2010) [15], "Web search, as provided by Google, Microsoft, Yahoo, etc., allows users to find the information they need via the simplest of interaction paradigms": the user types in keywords or a natural language query and obtains a related ranked result list. If the results do not fulfill the user's information needs, he/she may create a new query to obtain new results, making the information seeking process naturally iterative [3].

Our work focuses on searches whose results can be represented as data visualizations. At first glance, this may seem similar to "image search" mechanisms.

Supported by the Coordenação de Aperfeiçoamento de Pessoal de Nível Superior - Brasil (CAPES).

S. Yamamoto and H. Mori (Eds.): HCII 2020, LNCS 12184, pp. 104–124, 2020.
https://doi.org/10.1007/978-3-030-50020-7_7

However, as data visualizations usually represent underlying structured data, the known relations between the data points and data sets can be used as input to search expansion mechanisms. In our work, we assume that the data are described by an ontology [7], such as those we can find in linked-open data (LOD)[1], *e.g.*, DBPedia[2].

Traditionally, a user submits a search query through a search dialog box and, in response to the query, a search engine delivers one or more search result pages (SRPs) to the user. SRPs often consist of multiple pages of items that are related to the search query submitted by the user. Most of the initial search results are closely related to the query but, as the user navigates to later results, they are increasingly less related to it.

As the users may need to navigate through many SRPs [2], from their point of view, the traditional model is only satisfactory if they know quite precisely how to phrase their query to match their intended search for information.

Let us consider as an example a user named Jack who wants to know the movie *genre* that generated the highest box office in 2018, but who formulates the following query: "Which *movies* had the highest gross revenue in 2018?" In this case, the search results would likely contain a list of the top individual grossing movies, with links to details about each movie. Jack might then think he would need to inspect the movies one by one to try to figure out to which genre most of them belong, a very tedious task. When inspecting a movie, Jack may see that there is genre information associated to each movie and, realizing this is the term he should include in the query, he might reformulate the query to "Which *movie genre* had the highest gross revenue in 2018?", which then brings the intended information in the search results. This scenario has a successful ending, but in many other situations the user cannot figure out the specific query formulation needed to find the intended information.

In this paper we propose a new model for search user interfaces, focusing on the search results page. Our proposal goes beyond providing a navigable list of visualization search results. It includes an API for implicitly generating related queries to expand the search space, and progressively discloses the corresponding results. Our hypothesis is that such mechanism can improve the user interaction with search results, especially in situations where users cannot figure out how to formulate the precise query to yield the intended results.

2   Related Work

Wilson (1999) [16] defines information-seeking behavior as a set of activities that people engage in when identifying their information need, searching for it through an information resource, and using the results to satisfy that need.

Understanding human information-seeking processes is the foundation for the design of effective and usable search systems [16]. In the next sections, we describe existing models of information-seeking behavior.

---

[1] https://lod-cloud.net/.
[2] https://wiki.dbpedia.org/.

2.1   Iterative Model of Information-Seeking Behavior

Marchionini (1997) [11] laid the foundation for the traditional information-seeking process, defining it as a set of "systematic and opportunistic" subprocesses.

In this work, we will use a simplified version of this process defined by Hearst (1999) [9]. This model also assumes the process is iterative and that the user information need does not change. The model comprises the following sequence of steps [9]:

1. "Recognize the information need.
2. Select the information repository to search.
3. Form a search query.
4. Send the query to the system.
5. Receive the results.
6. Evaluate and interpret the results.
7. Stop, if the information need is fulfilled, or
8. Reformulate the query and return to Step 4."

Although widespread, the iterative model of information seeking does not capture the richness of genuine information-seeking processes [10], especially because the users' information demands may change during the search process as a result of their interaction with the search system. The user can at the same time present a behavior that is both systematic and unsystematic, starting their search processes following the hierarchical approach presented by Hearst (2009) [10], and then switching to a more dynamic behaviour that uses the initial result set as a starting point that informs further queries, as pointed out by Marchionini (1997) [11]. Marchionini also advocates that, because individual factors affect information-seeking interaction, there is a need for new models that better account for the dynamic nature of information seeking, i.e., models that can address the challenges of describing how users employ different search tactics and how they can make sense of the results.

2.2   Exploratory Search

The traditional information-seeking method is well supported by search engines, especially when the user has well-defined information needs. However, when the user lacks the knowledge or contextual awareness to formulate queries or navigate complex information spaces or the information, the search system should provide more support for a complex information seeking process, where the user is able to browse and explore the results in order to fulfill their needs [15].

Exploratory Search research tackles this issue by studying information-seeking models that blend querying and browsing with a focus on learning and investigating, instead of information lookup [12]. White et al. (2005) [14] distinguish three typical situations in which exploratory search happens:

- The user has partial or no knowledge of the search target

- The search moves from certainty to uncertainty as the user is exposed to new information
- The user is actively seeking useful information and determining its structure

O'Day and Jeffries (1993) [13] describe this incremental search behavior as a process of exploration through a series of related but distinct searches on a specific topic. They identify three distinct search modes:

- "Monitoring a well-known topic over time;
- Following a plan of information gathering;
- Exploring a topic in an undirected fashion."

This shows that even exploratory information seeking has structure and continuity, which could be supported by the search system.

3   Progressive Disclosure of Related Search Results

Many systems allow the user to navigate through search results by refining the search query. Although effective when the user has a clear vision of their interests, those interfaces may not be very suitable when the user is performing an exploratory search or cannot properly formulate their information need.

Some systems, such as Datatone [6], allows the user to navigate through related questions by direct manipulation of the query or through manual interactions with its user interface (in Datatone, through "ambiguity widgest"). In other words, Datatone requires users to plan and take action in order to obtain related search results.

We hypothesized that, instead of requiring users to manually adjust the queries to amplify their search results, user interfaces for searching data visualizations might continuously offer answers to related queries by navigating through an underlying ontology. Our proposed search user interface, named *JARVIS - Journey towards Augmenting the Results of VIsualization Search*, is based on the progressive disclosure model used by Google Images,[3] where the interface continuously appends content to the search results page. Rather than requiring users to refine their queries, JARVIS automatically amplifies the set of results with answers to related queries.

3.1   Research Context

Our work focuses on understanding how to better support the user by designing a result page that is both effective and efficient. More specifically, we propose and evaluate a progressive disclosure mechanism for related questions. For that to happen, many other parts need to be in place.

Figure 1 presents the JARVIS architecture. The topmost part represents the interface of the system, where the user can input their questions and visualize

---

[3] https://images.google.com/.

the answers. Take the question "Which actresses won the most Golden Globe awards last year?" as an illustration. The interpreter, fed with a movie ontology, identifies the known entities, such as *actresses (Actress → is → Person), Golden Globe Awards (Award → has_name → Golden Globe Awards)*, relationships, in this case, *won (Person → awarded → Award)* and the temporal attributes like *last year*. With this information, the system transforms the question into an RDF query that accesses the domain database and gathers the answers.

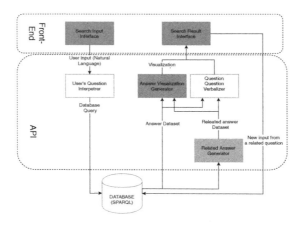

Fig. 1. JARVIS architecture

Also crucial is the generation of the relevant related questions whose answers that will be represented as data visualizations to the user. Figure 3 shows an example of how the system generates its related questions. In the question "What were the 5 highest rated movies from Viola Davis this decade?", after identifying the known entities from the ontology in the question, it looks for the structure of their relationships. In this case: actress → is_actress_in → movie → has_rating → imdb_rating.

In order to improve the effectiveness of the system, a domain expert can enrich the ontology with relationships that they find interesting to the users of the search engine. Figure 2 shows the simplified ontology proposed by Calvanese et al. (2017) [1], with annotations. This process is especially important when dealing with large and complex ontologies. In our case, the ontology used is fairly small and simple. This aspect enables us to have good results even when we have skipped this stage when building our system. We applied the same methodology for a different domain for a large company of Oil & Gas in Brazil. This latter ontology was significantly larger and presented more complex relationships. Because we did not have access to domain experts in this case, the related question could present variations that would make no sense to the final user of the search system. In a case like this, developers of such system should prioritize direct relationships in the ontology to build the related questions mechanism.

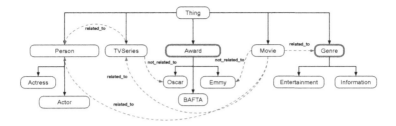

Fig. 2. Simplified ontology of Calvanese et al. (2017) [1] with annotations

With that structure defined, it starts to scan for possible traversals in the ontology which are relevant for generating a related question. Those traversals can occur in various ways, for example from an entity to its parent (movie → production) or, like in Fig. 3, to a sibling entity, that is, an entity that belongs to the same structure to the one identified in the user query. In this case, the system can change 'Movies' to 'TV Series' and select "What were the 5 highest rated *TV series* from Viola Davis this decade?" as the new query.

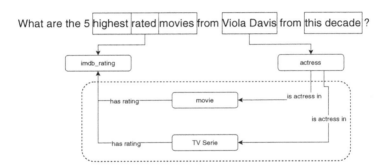

Fig. 3. Relation between a question in natural language and the corresponding elements in an ontology.

3.2 The Related Question Mechanism

In order to enhance the answers generated by the interpreter and to reduce the user's cognitive effort to formulate other related questions which may interest them, our group developed a mechanism that recommends answers to questions related to the initial question the user searched. This mechanism applies operations to the ontology, taking into consideration the entities that were detected in the initial question (see Fig. 3).

Figure 4 depicts the JARVIS interface. Let us take the example described in Sect. 1: the information needed by the user is the movie *genre* that generated the highest box office in 2018, but when formulating their query they typed: "Which *movies* had the highest gross revenue in 2018?". JARVIS sends, through an API, the natural language query written by the user. The API looks for the literal answer or answers to the question and ranks the results. It then exhibits the n highest ranked direct, literal results for the query on the topmost area of the interface, in a slightly shaded area (Fig. 4). Below that area, it progressively displays results from related questions, which are gradually received from the API. Those results are the outcomes of a search mechanism that, given a domain ontology (*e.g.*, related to the IMDB), navigates through the ontology looking for useful relationships between the elements presented in the search query to expand the given question into related ones. JARVIS may offer, for example, results for questions such as "Which *studios* had the highest gross revenue in 2018?" (through a movie–produced by–studio relationship), "Which *movies* had the highest gross revenue in 2018 per country?" (through a movie–produced in–country relationship), and "Which *movie genre* had the highest gross revenue in 2018?" (through a movie–classified as–genre relationship). These related questions may offer the information needed by the user, as well as different perspectives on the data related to the query, without any manual interaction by the user.

In this work, we focus on the delivery mechanism for the results and on how the users interact with it. The challenges of translating a natural language question to a database query, and of navigating in a ontology to find the useful relationships for related questions are relevant research topics, which are currently being developed by other members of our research group, and therefore lie outside the scope of this work.

4   Evaluation

Our proposed solution progressively discloses results for related queries. To evaluate the effectiveness and efficiency of our solution, we have devised two other search user interface (SUI) models for the same search task. The first uses the traditional search interaction method described by Wilson (1999) [16] (henceforth called *Traditional* SUI (J1)), and the second is built showing the related questions as links to explore the results (henceforth called *Related-links* SUI (J2)). We then conducted a comparison test of three SUIs. We invited graduate students from different areas to serve as volunteer participants in the study.

The *Traditional* SUI (J1) (Fig. 5) is an almost direct representation of the work described by Wilson (1999) [16]. The user types a search query and receives the highest ranked result for their question. The only way they can obtain further search results is by manually editing or typing a new query for the system, which again will only return the highest ranked result. This model represents a baseline for our work, whereas the interface, although pedestrian, is straightforward and familiar to the participants.

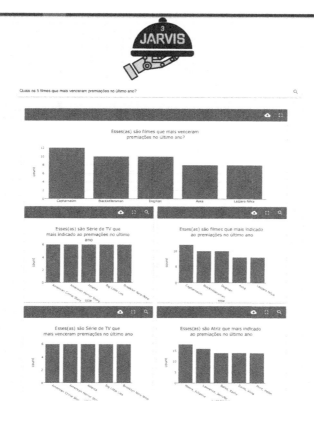

Fig. 4. JARVIS search user interface

The *Related-links* SUI (J2) (Fig. 6) introduces a suggested list of related questions. The user is now presented not only with the highest ranked result, but also with a set of related questions on a lateral pane. This allows the user to navigate through related questions more quickly, but still requires manual interaction with the user interface. Model J2 is presented to the participants so we can attempt to understand whether the mere introduction of related questions is enough to reduce the users' cognitive overload and to build a more effective search interface.

To evaluate the interface models, we conducted an empirical comparative test of the three SUIs. We invited graduate students from different areas to serve as volunteer participants in the study. To reduce the learning effects, we varied the order in which each SUI is presented to the users, using the configuration shown in Table 1. With this, we attempted to see if the order on which the user experienced each model affected their evaluation. Since model J1 required more effort to complete the suggested task, we hypothesized that users that had contact with the model J1 prior to the other models would find the introduction

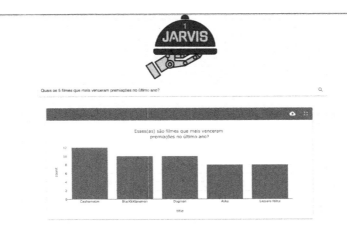

Fig. 5. User interface of the Traditional SUI (J1)

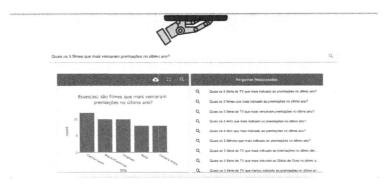

Fig. 6. User interface of the Related-links SUI (J2)

of mechanisms for searching the related queries more useful. That would be especially true with users in group A, where the mechanism scaled in complexity gradually. The user started the experiment with only a straightforward search mechanism in J1, to later test an interface that presents he/she with related queries in J2, to finally evaluate our proposal. This order would help to gradually raise the awareness of the related questions and its answers. By contrast, we also hypothesized that participants in group C might get confused with non-traditional features of model J3 and evaluate it poorly.

Fifteen people participated in the experiment to evaluate the delivery mechanism of the related queries: three females (P01, P04, P14) and 12 males (P02, P03, P05, P06, P07, P08, P09, P10, P11, P12, P13, P14). They were all graduate students at PUC-Rio (11 Master's students, and 4 PhD students). Apart from P14, who is a psychology student, all the participants were Computer Science students. Eleven participants (P01, P02, P03, P04, P05, P06, P07, P08, P10, P11, P15) fell within the 18–24 age group. Only four participants (P09,

Table 1. Experiment groups

Group	Order of SUIs
A	J1 J2 J3
B	J2 J1 J3
C	J3 J2 J1

P12, P13, P14) were 25 to 44 years old. Regarding their previous knowledge of the models, all participants were familiarized with traditional search tools. Four of the participants had already seen a search user interface similar to J3 in another context, but had not used it (P02, P03, P05, P06). We henceforth call these "participants with little previous knowledge". One participant – henceforth "Developer" – helped develop J3 for an R&D project (P11). The other ten participants had no knowledge of models J2 and J3 – henceforth "participants with no previous knowledge.

For each SUI, the user received six search tasks, each one representing a search query. We devised the queries in two groups, one which had two related queries and other with four related queries, but we did not inform users of such grouping. Such grouping was designed so that in the Related-links SUI (J2) and our proposal (J3), participants would need to type only two queries, and then they would have quick access to the remaining related queries through the links at the right-hand panel. In the Traditional SUI (J1), however, the user would need to type in each of the six queries manually. For each group, when the participant asked the first question, the results pages also presented either the questions of the following tasks (on J2) or their answers (on J3). The groups were also designed in such a way that the related question ranked high in each related queries mechanism of J2 and J3, except for the last question of the first group (Quais as 5 Séries de TV de menores durações? – What are the 5 TV Series of shortest duration?), which was intentionally more distant and thus required the user to scroll the related queries component (on J2) or the screen (on J3).

The content of the tasks varied: to discover the five movies that had won the most awards last year (through a *Movie–won award–Awards* relationship) and related information such as the 5 TV Series that won most awards last year (through a *TV Series –won award–Awards* relationship) and in the last decade (through a time variation).

After interacting with each SUI, we asked the participant to fill out a questionnaire regarding the perceived ease of use and utility of the SUI – based on the Technology Acceptance Model (TAM) [4] –, and their subjective workload assessment – based on the NASA Task Load Index[4] [8]. At the end of the session, we briefly interviewed the users, asking them to choose their preferred SUI and explain the factors that led them to their choice. We also collected performance data in terms of effectiveness (correctness of the result) and efficiency (time on task). In particular, we used the number of searches as a proxy for efficiency.

---

[4] https://humansystems.arc.nasa.gov/groups/TLX/.

We expected that model J3 followed by J2 would present better results in the TAM questionnaire due to the introduction of mechanisms that offer more ways to explore the search results. However, participants might find that the new interfaces require from them a more significant effort, resulting in poor results on the NASA TLX.

Unfortunately, a few days before the experiments, the API we used as a service to our work became faulty and behaved erratically. During the pilot test, we identified that too often the user interactions with the system would cause the server to restart or not to load data correctly. To build a workaround solution significant changes in the performance of the interface were needed, slowing down the chart load in several seconds in order to ensure that the data presented to all the participants would be consistent. This prevented us from analyzing the time on task.

5   Results

5.1   NASA Task Load Index Results

Figure 7 shows the results of the entire NASA Task Load Index questionnaire, discussed in detail in the next subsections.

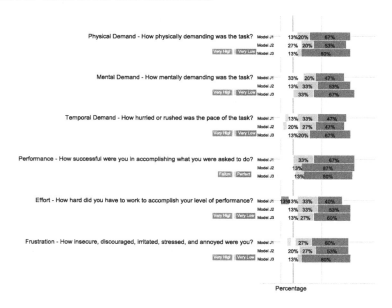

Fig. 7. NASA Task Load Index results

Mental Demand: The task in the experiment was relatively simple. However, as the complexity of the models grew (J2 is more complicated than J1, and J3 is more complex than J2), we expected that the questionnaire scores for J1 would be better than for J2 and J3. During the interviews, this hypothesis seems to gather even more support mainly because of what participants (P01, P02, P03, P04, P010, P13, P14) called "lack of resources" of model J1 and their assessment of J2 and J3. Regarding the other models, we expected results from the questionnaire to follow the comments of the participants that the models J2 (P11, P14) and J3 (P3, P4, P5, P8, P9, P11, P13, P14) would be better suited to multiple search tasks, thus ranking worse than J1. Figure 7 seems to be in accordance with our hypothesis and shows an advantage of J1 for the *Mental demand* measurement over the other models.

Physical Demand: The measurement may be a reflection of the number of clicks or the number times the user has to manually inform the query in the main search bar to complete the tasks. In J1, the user had no other choice but to insert the search queries six times, so we might hypothesize that, although the task itself was not physically troublesome, models J2 and J3 would be rated slightly better because they offered options that did not involve typing or copy-and-pasting new queries in to the system. Figure 7 seems to show a slight advantage of J3 for the *Physical demand* measurement over the other models.

Temporal Demand: Since model J1 required more interaction and clicks at the user interface than models J2 and J3, we hypothesized that J1 would perform worse on this measurement than the other models. However, during the interviews, we noticed that the model J2 had drawn polarized opinions from participants. This may have been an effect from the limitations of J2. However, we believe that faulty design implementation presented in J2 played a prominent role on those participants' commentaries. Considering the component was not intuitive, and the text font was quite small, the interaction with the component was deeply affected, and its problems may have overshadowed its virtues. Figure 7 seems to be in accordance with our hypothesis and shows an advantage of J3 for the *Temporal demand* measurement over J1. Unsurprisingly, model J2 seems to have a slight worse temporal demand evaluation than J1 and J3.

Performance Demand: The results may have been profoundly affected by a severe problem with the experiment: the server performance. Because the server was very fragile, the system was slower than usual. This problem affected primarily the user interface of the J3 model, which is, by far, the model that needs to receive a larger volume of data to build the visualizations at the user interface. These issues may have influenced the performance scores in the questionnaire, leaving J2 slightly better ranked than J3. Figure 7 seems to be in accordance with our hypothesis, showing an advantage of J2 for the *Performance demand* measurement over the other models.

Effort: Similar to the Physical demand measurement, the effort measurement may be a reflection of the number of times the user had to manually inform a query in the main search bar to complete the tasks. Surprisingly, users ranked even J3 poorly, acknowledging that the user interface could further reduce the user effort on searching. Moreover, J1 is the only model that offers no other option to complete the task, *i.e.*, it requires that all queries be informed, one by one, in the search bar. For that matter, we hypothesized that J3 would perform better than J2 and that J2 would perform better than J1. Figure 7 seems to be in accordance with our hypothesis and shows an advantage of J3 for the *Effort* measurement over the other models.

Frustration: Because J3 is the model that it was more complicated than the others, it also had the effects of the problems with the server being more prominent in the J3. When the participants were exploring the interface of J3, the server would often crash and require a reboot in other to become functional again. Because of that, we expected to J3 to be lowest-ranked model in this measurement. Surprisingly, Fig. 7 seems to debunk our hypothesis and shows a slight advantage of J3 for the *Frustration* measurement over the other models, even with the problems on the interface design and the server malfunctions. However, the Kruskal-Wallis hypothesis tests for each measurement of the questionnaire showed no significant difference among the models, at $\alpha = 0.05$ (either considering all users, only users with little knowledge, and only users with no knowledge).

6 Technology Acceptance Model (TAM) Results

Figures 8 and 9 show the results of the Technology Acceptance Model questionnaire, discussed in detail in the next paragraphs.

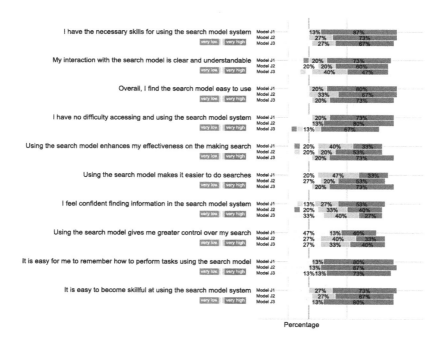

Fig. 8. TAM results (part 1)

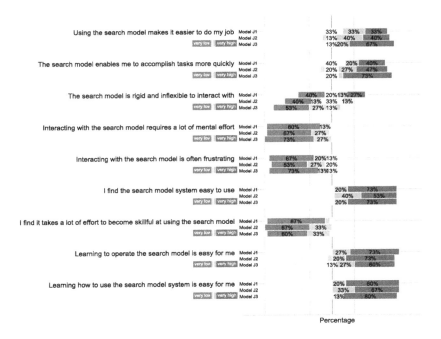

Fig. 9. TAM results (part 2)

Because the questionnaire is fairly long, we decided to not discuss each result in full detail. Instead, since the Technology Acceptance Model evaluates the *perceived usefulness* and the *perceived ease of use*, we will discuss the overall results of these dimensions with a selected example.

Regarding the *perceived ease of use*, because of the nature of the task, all models performed reasonably well. For example, in the question *"I find the search model system X easy to use"*. The figure shows model J2 as worse than models J1 and J3. This seems to contradict our hypothesis that the model J1 is easier to use than models J2 and J3. Instead, it shows identical results to J1 and J3. This means that users do not think JARVIS (J3) is harder to use than the other models, even though it has more complex features than the other models. The unfortunate result of the model J2 may be a consequence of the faulty user interface design choices, that some participants reported as "confusing".

The *perceived usefulness* was evaluated with questions such as *"The search model X enables me to accomplish tasks more quickly"*. With this item, our goal was to evaluate whether the perceived evaluation from the participants matched their actual time on task. Unfortunately, due to the problems experienced in the server, we were unable to execute this analysis. We expected that model J2 and J3 would perform better than J1 in this item because it offers the answer or question for the other task more efficiently, not requiring the participant to type each search query to finish the experiment tasks. The results shown in Fig. 9

confirms our prediction for the model J3, which had the best evaluation among the participants. Despite presenting to the user an alternative way to search, the model J2 was the worst-ranked among all three models. These results may indicate that the mere recommendation of related questions is not enough to support the user while navigating on search result pages more quickly, or be an outcome of an unrefined user interface design.

7   Interviews

Table 2 shows a compilation of the common critiques reported by the participants of the study. We categorized each comment into four categories: Model, Design, Configuration, and Implementation. In *Model*, we selected the comments more closely related to intrinsic aspects of each model and which would likely remain true even if significant changes to the design or implementation of the system were made. In *Design*, we summarized comments related to the user interface design. The comments reported under the *Configuration* category are those that may be related to the parameterization and flexibility of how the related questions are calculated and prioritized. In *Implementation*, we compile the observations strongly associated with the system performance.

7.1   Model

Regarding the Model, most of the comments from the participants are related to the occasions in which they seem to be adequate and what the model's intrinsic, positive or negative characteristics are and which had the biggest influence on the participants' experience. Participants mostly commented on the differences between model J1 and models J2 and J3. Most of them (12 participants) found that the model J1 is simple or straightforward, a characteristic that they consider a positive aspect of the model. In contrast, they found that executing the task using the model J1 was very time consuming for multiple searches (5 participants) and better suited for when the user knows what they want (4) or only needs to do a quick search (4 participants). Although in the participants' view the model J1 lacks resources (7 participants), some of the participants perceive this as a positive aspect, because the user interface does not distract the user from the task they are executing (2 participants).

These perspectives of model J1 contrast with what participants said about the models J2 and J3. Furthermore, whereas they found it difficult to use model J1 in long or exploratory tasks, they highlighted the benefits of using the other models for those scenarios. For example, two participants reported that, because both models presented them with related questions, they were able to have insights of new questions that they may not have had if they were only exploring the data following the traditional interface of model J1. They also found that both models support scenarios where the user needs to make multiple searches or search tasks that are broader or exploratory (2 participants for J2 and 4 for

Table 2. Compilation of interview results

		Total	P01	P02	P03	P04	P05	P06	P07	P08	P09	P10	P11	P12	P13	P14	P15
The model fits the screen better	Implementation	5				X	X	X				X			X		
Simple/Straightforward	Model	12	X	X	X		X	X	X	X	X			X	X	X	X
Lacks resources		7	X	X	X	X					X				X	X	
Time-consuming for multiple searches		5	X			X					X	X			X		
Better for a quick search		4	X									X			X	X	
Better for when the user knows what it wants		4	X									X			X	X	
Don't distract the user		2					X									X	
Can be confusing for the user	Configuration	4	X			X						X	X				
The recommendation can be better ranked		2		X					X								
Reading questions is worse than reading charts	Design	8	X		X		X	X	X			X			X	X	
Exhaustive		3							X			X			X		
The model fits the screen better	Implementation	2			X			X									
Recommendations make the task easier	Model	7			X	X	X	X			X				X	X	
Makes the search task broader/explorative		5			X				X					X	X	X	
Better for multiple search tasks		2										X			X		
The model gives me insights of new questions		2		X											X		
The recommendation can be better ranked	Configuration	5		X		X				X		X					X
The need to scroll is bad	Design	3						X			X			X			
Can be confusing/distracting for the user		3					X	X					X				
Too slow	Implementation	2				X				X							
Has an information overload problem		1										X					
Recommendations make the task easier	Model	10	X		X	X	X	X		X	X	X			X	X	
Better for multiple search tasks		8			X	X	X			X	X	X			X	X	
Makes the search task broader/explorative		4		X			X		X							X	
The model gives me insights of new questions		2		X												X	
Better for when the user doesn't know what it wants		2	X													X	

J3). Those comments are in line with the conceptual design of those models, as described in Sect. 4.

Besides that, a crucial point for this research is how the recommendations affected the user interaction. We did not directly ask of participants questions about the perceived effectiveness of the recommendation to avoid inducing certain answers. However, participants spontaneously evaluated aspects of the recommendation. The majority (7 for model J2 and 10 for model J3) agreed that the recommendation makes it easier to achieve the search task. Those comments are an indication that the models J2 and J3 are potentially efficient and useful for the search task, especially when the user is on an exploratory task.

7.2   Design

In the Design category, we outline here the most common complaints from the participants that we believe could be solved by redesign the user interfaces. These include the related questions component from model J2. Although it does what is supposed to do, the component could have been better designed to highlight the differences between questions to reduce the amount of text the user needs to read. Eight participants evaluated that the model J2 was harder to interact with because it had too much text to read, and they evaluated it as worse to read than charts. Three of those participants even added that the model J2 was exhausting for them to use.

However, regarding the differences from J1 to models J2 and J3, there is a trade-off between using the chart or the text component. Although participants noted that the use of text could be exhausting, they also elucidated on problems with model J3, such as the need to scroll the interface (3 participants) and some (3 participants) even stated that they found the interface distracted them from the task they needed to perform.

7.3   Configuration

The Configuration category represents issues that may be related to either the parameterization or the flexibility in how the related questions are calculated and prioritized.

In models J2 and J3, users complained about the selection of the related questions/answers that were exhibited. Although this mechanism is out of the scope of this work, we must develop a better algorithm for related questions/answers in order to better evaluate the models we have proposed. Participants even commented about the lack of coherence between the related questions and the main query they searched. In other words, in order for models such as J2 and J3 to thrive, as a better alternative to the design of search result pages, it is vital that the ranking engine of those questions/answers be effective.

7.4   Implementation

Concerning the implementation category, we were interested in how the system performance affected the participants' experience with each model. Since our implementation suffered from many issues, as mentioned before, we looked in the interviews for what how those problems influenced their evaluation.

In that regard, two participants reported that the model J3 was too slow. This is a direct effect of the fact that the model J3 was the one most affected by those problems.

7.5   Efficiency

As mentioned before, we were unable to directly measure the time on task. However, we counted the number of explicit searches the participants did during the experiment. This can be considered as an indirect indication of efficiency of each model. It is flawed, however, as it does not take into account the actual time it took for participants to locate the related questions when using models J2 and J3.

Figure 10 shows the number of searches made in each model, by each group, according to the participants' previous knowledge. It shows the median number of searches and corresponding interquartile range using each model, in the group of all users. We note that model J1 always requires six searches to complete the task.

We conducted statistical analyses of the differences in the number of searches across models in three different groups: all users, users with little previous knowledge of the models, and users with no previous knowledge of the models, as described in the next subsections. We ran a Kruskal-Wallis rank sum test, which showed a **significant difference** at $\alpha = 0.05$ level ($\chi^2 = 14.600$, df = 3, p-value = 0.0022). We therefore ran a Conover-Iman post-hoc test, with Bonferroni correction. There was a significant difference in the number of searches between J1–J2 and J1–J3, in the group of all users.

We also investigated whether there was a significant difference between the number of searches across models considering only users with little knowledge of the models. We ran a Kruskal-Wallis rank sum test, which showed a **significant difference** at $\alpha = 0.05$ level ($\chi^2 = 9.900$, df = 2, p-value = 0.0071). We therefore ran a Conover-Iman post-hoc test, with Bonferroni correction and found that

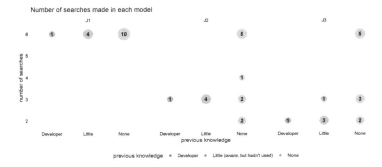

Fig. 10. Bubble plot of number of searches using each model

was a significant difference in the number of searches between J1–J2, J1–J3, and J2–J3, in the group of users with little previous knowledge of the models.

Considering users with NO knowledge of the models, we ran a Kruskal-Wallis rank sum test, which showed no significant difference at $\alpha = 0.05$ level ($\chi^2 = 5.872$, df $= 3$, p-value $= 0.1180$).

8 Discussion

Although many of the results presented in this work are not statistically significant, it is essential to note that the evaluation of JARVIS (model J3) did not perform worse than the other models and, in most cases, it received a better evaluation from the user than models J1 and J2. These results indicate that, even though JARVIS is more complex and less familiar than the other models, from the user perspective it is a potential solution for the design of search result pages that enhance the user experience when doing an exploratory search.

The results in Sect. 5 imply that, between the traditional search behaviour of model J1 and the exploratory based of models J2 and J3, there is a significant difference. These differences imply that since the results from the TAM and NASA TLX were mostly in pair with the other models, the alternative models are possible useful solutions and should be explored more in-depth in future works.

Based on our results, we believe a possible alternative solution for the design of search results pages such as the one we proposed in this study may be a hybrid of from the models evaluated in this research. This hybrid model can be displayed in at least two forms of interface design:

1. A new model that shows the related question as a preview and only unfolds the visualization when the user explicitly ask.
2. An adaptive interface model that increases the personalization of search results pages by showing or hiding the related answers to the user.

We leave these hybrid models for future work.

9 Conclusion

The main contribution of this paper is a model to amplify cognition for search tasks. The model involves generating and presenting related queries to expand the search space and progressively disclosing the corresponding results.

We conducted an evaluation of the proposed model (J3) in comparison with two distinct search user interface models for data visualization: a *Traditional* SUI Model (J1), inspired by the work of Wilson (1999) [16], and a *Suggested-links* SUI (J2), which combines J1 with a suggested list of related questions.

The outcomes of the analysis suggest that the model proposed with JARVIS may be a promising path for the design of new SUIs. The results from the Task Load Index and Technology Acceptance Model Questionnaires showed that, although J3 presents a more complex user interface and more features, it did not perform worse than the other models evaluated by the questionnaires. Moreover, even in the simple experiment we conducted, the number of searches made with J3 was significantly lower than the number of searches made with the Traditional SUI (J1), as shown in Sect. 5.

References

1. Calvanese, D., et al.: Ontop: Answering SPARQL queries over relational databases. Semant. Web **8**(3), 471–487 (2017)
2. Chen, H., Dumais, S.: Bringing order to the web: automatically categorizing search results. In: Proceedings of the SIGCHI Conference on Human Factors in Computing Systems, pp. 145–152. ACM (2000)
3. Chowdhury, G., Chowdhury, S.: Introduction to Digital Libraries. Facet Publishing, UK (2002). https://strathprints.strath.ac.uk/2603/
4. Davis, F.D.: Perceived usefulness, perceived ease of use, and user acceptance of information technology. MIS Q. **13**(3), 319–340 (1989). https://doi.org/10.2307/249008
5. Fallows, D.: Search Engine Use—Pew Research Center, August 2008. https://www.pewinternet.org/2008/08/06/search-engine-use/
6. Gao, T., Dontcheva, M., Adar, E., Liu, Z., Karahalios, K.G.: DataTone: managing ambiguity in natural language interfaces for data visualization. In: Proceedings of the 28th Annual ACM Symposium on User Interface Software & Technology. UIST 2015, pp. 489–500. ACM Press, New York (2015). https://doi.org/10.1145/2807442.2807478
7. Gruber, T.R.: A translation approach to portable ontology specifications. Knowl. Acquis. **5**(2), 199–220 (1993). https://doi.org/10.1006/knac.1993.1008
8. Hart, S.G.: NASA-task load index (NASA-TLX); 20 years later. Proc. Hum. Factors Ergon. Soc. Annu. Meet. **50**(9), 904–908 (2006). https://doi.org/10.1177/154193120605000909
9. Hearst, M.A.: User Interfaces and Visualization, vol. 2. Addison-Wesley, Boston (1999). https://ci.nii.ac.jp/naid/10022005353/en/
10. Hearst, M.A.: Search User Interfaces, 1st edn. Cambridge University Press, New York (2009)
11. Marchionini, G.: Information Seeking in Electronic Environments. Cambridge Series on Human-Computer Interaction. Cambridge University Press, Cambridge (1997)
12. Marchionini, G.: Exploratory search: from finding to understanding. Commun. ACM **49**(4), 41–46 (2006). https://doi.org/10.1145/1121949.1121979
13. O'Day, V.L., Jeffries, R.: Orienteering in an information landscape: how information seekers get from here to there. In: Proceedings of the INTERACT 1993 and CHI 1993 Conference on Human Factors in Computing Systems. CHI 1993, pp. 438–445. ACM, New York (1993). https://doi.org/10.1145/169059.169365
14. White, R.W., Kules, B., Bederson, B.: Exploratory search interfaces: categorization, clustering and beyond: report on the XSI 2005 workshop at the human-computer interaction laboratory, University of Maryland. SIGIR Forum **39**(2), 52–56 (2005). https://doi.org/10.1145/1113343.1113356

15. Wilson, M.L., Kules, B., Shneiderman, B., et al.: From keyword search to exploration: designing future search interfaces for the web. Found. Trends® Web Sci. **2**(1), 1–97 (2010)
16. Wilson, T.: Models in information behaviour research. J. Doc. **55**(3), 249–270 (1999). https://doi.org/10.1108/EUM0000000007145

A Template for Data-Driven Personas: Analyzing 31 Quantitatively Oriented Persona Profiles

Joni Salminen[1,2(✉)], Kathleen Guan[3], Lene Nielsen[4], Soon-gyo Jung[1], and Bernard J. Jansen[1]

[1] Qatar Computing Research Institute, Hamad Bin Khalifa University, Doha, Qatar
`jsalminen@hbku.edu.qa`
[2] University of Turku, Turku, Finland
[3] Georgetown University, Washington, DC, USA
[4] IT University of Copenhagen, Copenhagen, Denmark

Abstract. Following the proliferation of personified big data and data science algorithms, data-driven user personas (DDPs) are becoming more common in persona design. However, the DDP templates are seemingly diverse and fragmented, prompting a need for a synthesis of the information included in these personas. Analyzing 31 templates for DDPs, we find that DDPs vary greatly by their information richness, as the most informative layout has more than 300% more information categories than the least informative layout. We also find that graphical complexity and information richness do not necessarily correlate. Furthermore, the chosen persona development method may carry over to the information presentation, with quantitative data typically presented as scores, metrics, or tables and qualitative data as text-rich narratives. We did not find one "general template" for DDPs and defining this is difficult due to the variety of the outputs of different methods as well as different information needs of the persona users.

Keywords: Personas · Data-driven personas · Information design · Algorithms

1 Introduction

Quantitative data-driven user personas (DDPs) provide an alternative to qualitatively created personas (QCPs). DDPs can represent user populations in ways that are statistically valid, replicable via algorithms and verifiable by statistical metrics [1, 2]. The proliferation of DDPs is driven by the rise of "personified big data" [3] from social media and online analytics platforms that provides new opportunities to generate personas describing digital user populations.

Moreover, data science algorithms and machine learning libraries have made it possible to automate persona creation processes [4, 5] and to automatically update the personas when the underlying user data changes [6]. Based on these advantages, Human-Computer Interaction (HCI) scholars have proposed many types of profiles and layouts

© Springer Nature Switzerland AG 2020
S. Yamamoto and H. Mori (Eds.): HCII 2020, LNCS 12184, pp. 125–144, 2020.
https://doi.org/10.1007/978-3-030-50020-7_8

for DDPs [7–10], with varying complexity and informational content. The general goal is to increase quantitatively reliable information in personas.

Nonetheless, the multitude of layouts and templates for DDPs has resulted in two challenges: (1) *there is a lack of a general template for DDPs*, meaning that researchers and practitioners are uncertain of what information to include when using quantitative methods and online user data for the creation of DDPs. Moreover, (2) *it is not well-known what the boundaries are of DDPs relative to QCPs.* QCPs are based on social constructivism and human meaning-making [11] and the understanding that human persona creators infer from other humans (the users) when creating the persona. It has been postulated that persona creation is an immersive practice that in itself enhances understanding about the users. In turn, DDPs, might be limited in their ability to capture human nuances and understand meanings of social importance, as the persona creation takes place via probabilistic calculations that humans have little or no interaction with.

Thus, there is a need for research that critically examines the boundaries of the practice of DDPs and the information included in such personas. Figure 1 illustrates this concern with an example of a statistically valid but potentially non-useful persona. Previous research on DDPs fails to deliver a critical analysis such as this, focusing primarily on evaluating DDPs using technical accuracy metrics [1]. While Nielsen et al. [12] have analyzed the templates of user personas developed by Danish companies, such a review has not been conducted for DDPs personas specifically that, as we argue, require a dedicated analysis of their own.

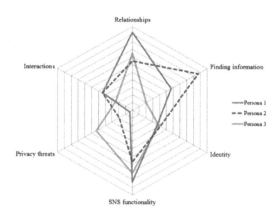

Fig. 1. DDP based on a quantitatively identified patterns of user behavior [13]

Understanding DDPs is important because in-depth information about user motivations and pain points may not be readily available when relying solely on quantitative methods. This is because machine learning methods rely on probabilistic learning rather than a true understanding of human nature, and thus have limited ability to detect human pain points, needs, and wants, as well as goals of individuals [14]. Algorithms are unable to capture tacit information or to understand why a person acts the way he or she does. This limitation might form a fundamental obstacle for the value and usefulness of DDPs, as personas traditionally rely on their ability to convey human-centric information. For

HCI, it is a principle of primary importance that personas appear as realistic profiles of otherwise cold and unempathetic "target groups" (as descriptions that cannot evoke empathy), thus enhancing stakeholders' focus on end user needs [15]. Personas typically contain demographic information, as well as user goals and motivations [12]. The principle of rounded personas [16] calls for the persona to contain all the necessary information for stakeholders using the personas.

Thus, it is important to identify and discuss the boundaries of the information design of DDPs for research and practice. For this, a review of layouts and information of DDPs is needed. To this end, this analysis specifically focuses on DDPs, specifically on their layouts and information designs. Using systematic review methods, we locate and retrieve 31 DDP templates from prior research. We analyze the information in these templates using an extended version of the categories by Nielsen et al. [12].

Relevant studies containing persona profiles were identified, and the content of the persona profiles was extracted to answer the following research questions (RQs):

- **RQ1:** What information do quantitative personas typically contain?
- **RQ2:** What patterns can be found in quantitative persona layouts?
- **RQ3:** How are purely quantitative personas different from qualitative or mixed quantitative-qualitative ones?

Our results indicate gaps in information design for DDPs, demonstrating the limitations of purely quantitative methods to generate rounded personas that serve stakeholders' information needs in a holistic way. To remedy these gaps, we outline potential avenues for the use of algorithms, both independently and in collaboration with humans, to generate more holistic, more rounded DDPs than the current state of the art provides. As such, we provide an important contribution of combining algorithms and machine learning techniques with online user data and human judgment in order to create user personas that involve the benefits of quantitative data but also contain the type of information needed to understand the humans being behind the profile.

2 Related Literature

Persona templates are characterized by influencing each other and very few have looked at research for inspiration. Anvari et al. [17] have looked at cognitive psychology and learning for inspiration on what to include in the persona description. Nielsen [18] takes inspiration from filmscript writing.

Looking at the literature concerning what to include in the descriptions, there are some variations. Bornet and Brangier [19] describe in their study of the literature how three categories define the persona: (a) identity of the persona, (b) attitude towards the product or service, and (c) context of usage. Their study is built upon nine texts written between 2001 and 2009. Floyd et al. [20] report from 13 papers written between 1999 and 2006 and differentiates between seven kinds of personas that have different characteristics. Some types refer to authors of persona literature and advocacy, others to variations in use context. The types vary in how detailed they have, according to how much and what data they are built upon and the purpose of creation.

Nielsen et al. [12] analyzed 12 templates from 2006–2013. The study shows that the attitude towards the product and the context of use is often intertwined; thus the information can be divided into two main areas: (a) personality that includes various information about demographics and personality traits (b) information related to the specific area to design for such as technology use, a-day-in-the-life, products goals and behavioral information. Apart from this, some researchers suggest adding business information such as market size and brand relationships [21–23]. Finally, a few researchers suggest indicating differences that can affect the persona, such as differences between international markets [21, 22, 24] and different behavior according to disabilities [25].

Looking at recommendations from personas based on design team's assumption, the literature recommends a limited amount of information such as name and demographics, behaviors and beliefs, needs and goals [26].

Common is that for both the qualitative data-based personas and the assumption-based personas is that the suggestions are not based on research across disciplines and large amounts of cases but are based on individual experiences and single case studies.

When it comes to the application areas, there is almost no area where personas has not been applied; digital services [27], learning [28], health care [29] are among the most common areas and target groups are both children [30], adults and users with special needs [31] using both mobile devices [32], and web services.

Previous research has shown that DDPs can take many forms and shapes. For example, Aoyama [7] used conjoint analysis to create DDPs for software embedded in digital consumer products. Holden et al. [9] developed "biopsychosocial" DDPs of elderly patients with heart failure using quantitative survey data. DDPs have also been applied in fashion [8], ecommerce [33], news [34], and many other domains. The diversity in persona information design, thus, appears to originate on one hand from *the specificity of the methods applied* – with the intuition that the outputs of different methods enable different information to be used for persona development – and, on the other hand, from *the varying information needs of persona users*, which inarguably affect the goals of the persona development endeavor. Thus, the consequence is that the field is embedded in the diversity of proposed design templates for DDPs. This diversity reflects the increasing relevance of DDPs for researchers and practitioners in user-centric industries.

Moreover, the design of DDPs has been explored both empirically, using experimental designs, and conceptually, by crafting research agendas that entail open questions for what is considered as "optimal" persona template. For example, Hill et al. [35] experimented with two persona designs: one that includes multiple pictures (consisting both of males and females) for a given persona and another one that has only one picture. Using a controlled laboratory study with eye-tracking measurement, they found that the use of multiple pictures may represent an appropriate technique to expand the persona users' understanding of the persona as a gender-free (or, "multi-gender") user segment rather than evoking gender stereotypes [35].

Similarly, Salminen et al. [34] experimented with persona profiles: one with lifestyle photos and the other with a single portrait picture. Contrary to Hill et al. [35], their findings indicated the use of multiple photos can distract and confuse the persona users, possibly because these are more used to the conventional template of the persona including only one photo [34]. Nonetheless, neither Hill et al. [35] or Salminen et al. [34] found that multiple photos would decrease the user engagement with the persona.

In another experimental study, Salminen et al. [36] presented 38 professionals with two alternate layouts: one that used numbers-oriented information presentation style and another one that used text-oriented style. They found that the numbers-oriented template was perceived significantly more usefulness by analysts but significantly less complete by both marketers and analysts [36]. The visual engagement with the persona profiles was found not to vary significantly between the templates [36].

Conceptually, persona information design in the context of DDPs has been raised as one of the prominent research areas [14, 37]. For example, Anvari et al. [38] discuss the use of personality traits in personas: it is unclear how well such traits that require subject-matter expertise and human analysis could be automatically added to DDPs.

3 Methodology

The persona layouts analyzed in this research were retrieved using systematic review methods. Two academic databases (Google Scholar and ACM Digital Library) were consulted for initial identification of articles. Identical literature searches were carried out for both databases in June 2019. The search phrases were devised with references to DDPs ("quantitative personas", "data-driven personas", "procedural personas") in addition to specific methodologies ("automatic persona generation", personas + cluster analysis | clustering | conjoint analysis | factor analysis | latent semantic analysis | matrix factorization | principal component analysis).

Snowball sampling was also applied [39] to identify additional DDP articles. In total, the searches yielded 138 unique articles, which were first assessed by reading the titles and abstracts and, subsequently, reviewing the full texts. The criteria for including an article in the final sample were:

- full research article (no short articles, books or theses)
- published in peer-reviewed journal or conference
- written in the English language
- empirical paper that develops personas using quantitative data

After a full text review, 49 (35.5%) articles remained. For the purposes of this researchers, we further excluded articles, which did not attach graphical representations of their final personas (i.e., persona layouts). At this stage, 30 final articles remained, and their persona layouts were extracted for further analysis. Data from each paper's persona layout(s) was recorded using a standardized data extraction form [40] with sub-categories built on the previous work of Nielsen et al. [12] (see Table 1). In addition, the methodology conducted by each study (i.e., whether the paper used statistical and/or numerical techniques such as k-means cluster analysis, solely or in combination with qualitative methods such as ethnography) was also recorded.

Furthermore, the categories were analyzed within the contexts of the authors' methods and goals in their respective papers. This included three papers that contained illegible layouts (i.e., too small or blurry), but nonetheless offered sufficient details in their text regarding the individual components of the persona layouts.

Table 1. Information extracted from each persona layout, with examples

Subcategory	Description of information content	Examples (verbatim whenever possible)
Name	Full name, first name, or epithet	Eric Transon [41] (p. 632), "Lazy Experts" [42]
Age	Age (or age range) ascribed to the persona	Age 23, "senior student" [7] (p. 6)
Gender	Gender ascribed to the persona	Male/female
Personality and psychographics	Character traits and disposition of the persona	"Very satisfied with life, usually gets the social support she needs" [43] (p. 66)
Lifestyle	Living situation, leisure, work-life balance	"Lives in central California, frequently walks and gardens" [43] (p. 66)
Experience	The person's experience with the product	"Never interacted with a robot before (…)" [44] (p. 8)
Daily work context	The persona's role and duties in the workplace	"Daily use of e-mail, browsing the web" [7] (p. 6)
Product related behaviors	How the persona interacts with technology and/or tools in the workplace	"During the interaction she kept saying that AIBO was cute and she was enjoying it" [44] (p. 8)
Product goals	What the persona hopes to achieve	"Wants reliable access to all journal articles he needs" [41] (p. 632)
Scenarios	Specific events involving the persona in relation to the product	"I mainly use the library website to find citations or to check whether I can get articles I've found in Google Scholar for free" [41] (p. 632)
A day in the life	Daily context for persona in relation to the product	"She goes out at least once in every two weeks with fellow hikers … frequently jogs in the field of Shenzhen University" [45] (p. 599)
Market size	Sample size of analyzed population that matches a particular persona	Percentage of time spent in a knowledge worker action section [46]
Color-coding to indicate segment	Color tagging for details of the persona	Yellow highlight
Use of facial picture	Photograph of real person included	N/A

(*continued*)

Table 1. (*continued*)

Subcategory	Description of information content	Examples (verbatim whenever possible)
Use of cartoon picture	Cartoon image to represent persona	Cartoon image depicting girl
Reference to sources	Source of data or explanation of metrics	Link to research references [47]
Disabilities	Handicaps of the persona (particularly for papers written in healthcare contexts)	Heart health metrics [9]
International considerations	Cultural heritage, ethnicity and/or citizenship	Non-aboriginal [48]
Explanations	Tooltip definitions	Link to research references [47]

The following section presents the findings. Appendix 1 shows the recorded data.

4   Findings

4.1   Levels of Information Richness

The persona layouts varied in "richness," which we define as *containing multifaceted, well-rounded information regarding the persona*. We quantitatively calculated the richness of personas by tallying the total pieces of information (i.e., subcategories present) within each persona layout. The most complex persona layout contained information for 14 subcategories [47], while the least complex contained only 4 [8, 13]. The mean number of subcategories was 8.83, while the standard deviation was 2.57.

Based on the descriptive statistics, the persona layouts were divided into three levels of richness styles: "simple" (4 to 7 subcategories), "moderate" (8 to 10 subcategories), and "high" (11 to 14 subcategories) (see Table 2 for examples). We selected the number of subcategories for the levels after examining the entire dataset and identifying the natural 'breakpoints' in the number of subcategories. Half of the persona layouts (50%) fell under the "moderate" category, with the remainder falling relatively evenly between either "simple" (26.6%) or "high" (23.3%) richness.

The graphical complexity and information richness of the personas do not necessarily correlate. For example, one persona layout [13], while an interesting graphical way of presenting personas, was questionable in its informativeness for end users; such extreme cases of abstraction were thus categorized under "simple" style despite their graphical complexity (see Table 2).

Persona layouts falling under the most "simple" information style, as exemplified by the layout from Dupree et al. [42] in Fig. 2, contained sparse information limited to bullet points detailing common behaviors. The persona is not identified with characteristics to make it human, like a name, or demographic and psychographic information; instead, it

Table 2. Examples of each category of persona layouts with varying richness

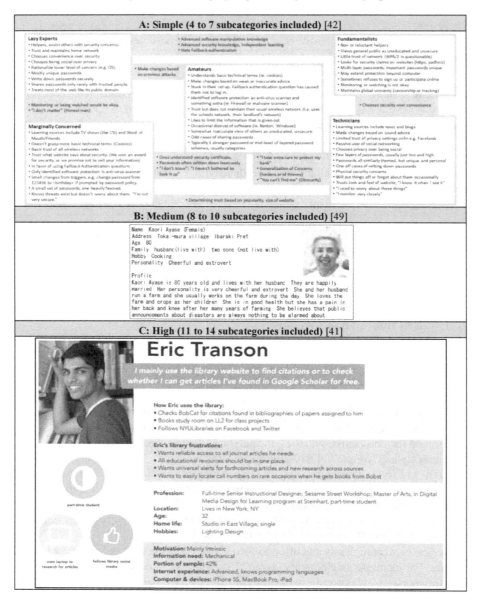

may only be labeled with a general epithet, such as "Lazy Experts" (close to what Floyd et al. [20] term as user archetypes).

Most "simple" persona layouts could be regarded as "skeleton personas" [43] that can be further enriched with details once time, costs, or limited data are removed as barriers.

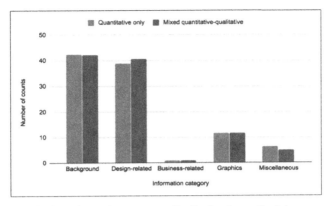

Fig. 2. Information category distribution by methodology

Persona layouts falling under the "moderate" information style – the most common category – reflect what such an upgrade in resources can result in. As exemplified by Kanno et al. [49], personas in this category are enriched with human-like elements, such as a full name, age, gender, and details on leisurely activities and temperament. In many cases, a photo of a real person is enclosed. The persona layout also contains a short narrative (or in some cases, detailed bullet points) about the persona's daily life scenarios and design-related goals.

Finally, persona layouts falling under the "high" information category are enriched with the most details (see "C" in Table 2). They extend beyond "moderate" information layouts through the inclusion of quotes, graphical representations, and categorization of the persona's information. In short, persona layouts in this category contain not only more comprehensive information on demographic and psychographic details, but also categorize details in direct relation to the authors' objectives. For example, Tempelman-Kluit and Pearce [41] categorize specific details under library usage and frustrations, which are in direct line with the authors' topics of inquiry. Graphical symbols illustrate what relevant devices or subscriptions the persona has (the authors' point of interest). This contrasts with the personas in the "moderate" category ("B" in Table 2), which usually contain only a short narrative with details that are not necessarily arranged into meaningful categories. As such, persona layouts in the "high" category go beyond mere personification and become mediums of analysis, as users can view these layouts to quickly discern between relevant information from various categories.

4.2 Mixed Methods Vs. Purely Quantitative Methods

Most articles (56.7%, N = 17) adopted solely quantitative methods, while 43% (N = 13) of the papers adopted mixed methods (i.e., used both qualitative and quantitative methods). Among the articles that adopted quantitative methods only, 29.4% (N = 5) fell under the "simple," 47.1% (N = 8) under the "medium," and 23.5% (N = 4) under the "high" information styles. Among the articles that adopted mixed methods, 23.1% (N = 3) fell under the "simple," 53.8% (N = 7) fell under the "moderate," and 23.1% (N = 3) fell under the "high" information styles.

As such, quantitative articles fell relatively more often under the "simple" category (29.4% versus 23.1% for mixed method studies). Beyond this, no other major differences in richness could be observed between papers, either adopting quantitative methods solely or in combination with qualitative methods. These findings are similar to Nielsen et al.'s, who found in their analysis that companies with the lack of a formal quantitative data collection protocol nonetheless still resulted in final personas as lengthy and with descriptions just as thorough as those with data [12].

When analyzing the number of information pieces from personas from papers adopting mixed methods, 42.1% fell under the background, 40.5% under the design-related, 0.8% under business and marketing related, 11.6% under the graphics, and 5.0% under miscellaneous categories. A similar distribution was observed for personal layouts from papers adopting only quantitative methods, 42.3% of details fell under the background, 38.7% under the design-related, 0.9% under business and marketing related, 11.7% fell under the graphics, and 6.3% under miscellaneous categories (see Fig. 2).

Table 3 displays examples of how solely quantitative versus mixed method approaches differ in presentation of persona layouts. Each of the example layouts (quantitative from Goodman-Deane et al. [50] and qualitative from Tu et al. [45]) detail mostly background and design-related information. Nonetheless, the solely quantitative approach [50] results in a chart-like presentation of the details, with "scores" directly representing the quantitative data from the survey. On the other hand, the mixed method approach [45] results in more narrative-like, contextual descriptions.

Table 3. Purely quantitative versus mixed method persona

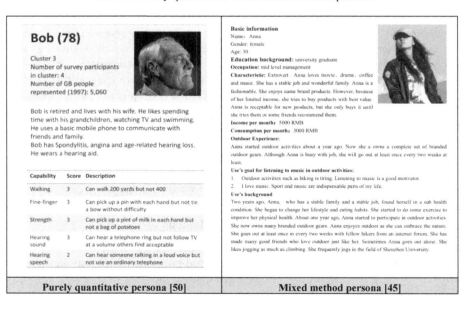

| Purely quantitative persona [50] | Mixed method persona [45] |

Furthermore, the former only captures "work related issues," "daily life context," and "product related issues" in subcategories with the design-related category, while the latter captures these in addition to the "product goals," "scenarios," and "a day in the life" subcategories. The former also does not capture any personality and psychographic information within the background category, while the latter infuses many of these details into narrative form. Thus, we surmise that the type of information collected for persona development (i.e., quantitative vs. qualitative) may carry over to the actually design of the persona, with numerical details such as graphs, scores, metrics, and tables being more common with purely quantitative personas and text-focused, narrative-like descriptions more prevalent in mixed method personas.

However, most layouts (especially in the "high" information richness category) combine both information styles, with some numerical cues and some textual information. The degree of text vs. numbers in data-driven personas is an open research question, with some previous research showing that the persona developers' choices can affect the persona perceptions of users [36].

5   Discussion

While Nielsen et al. [12] found that most persona layouts from Danish organizations had a "strict distinction" between personas and scenarios, our analysis found that personas were generally intertwined with descriptions of present scenarios. Many of the richest personas (i.e. falling under the "high" information category) had narratives infused into the persona layouts' descriptions to give them a more human-like quality. Interestingly, Nielsen et al. [12] reported that companies found this style "difficult to use (…) for the design of future solutions and as a result cancelled using the method [of intertwining]" (p. 6). This suggests the importance of considering the layout and categorization of information in a persona in conjunction with the researchers' and/or practitioners' needs. From our analysis, the persona layout from dos Santos et al. [44] is an example of how pertinent scenarios can be embedded into personas in a manner that remains relevant to stakeholders (see Fig. 3).

Lyanna is 23 years old and she loves dogs. She is an outgoing person that likes the fellowship of other people. Has a lot of energy and is proactive. Besides, she worries about social harmony, is honest, decent and trustful. Prefers to make plans rather them to act spontaneously, also being too self-disciplined. Rarely gets upset and is too calm. She is always looking for new experiences and thinks of a different way than other people. Her expectation for AIBO is that it will behave like a real dog, been capable to respond to her commands and seek for attention to play. She has never interacted with a robot before AIBO, but she had no difficult to perform the tasks with AIBO. During the interaction she kept saying that AIBO was cute and she was enjoying it. Her preferred tasks were the dancing one and the one that she gave voice commands to AIBO. After the test she said that AIBO attended to her expectations and would like to play with it again.

Fig. 3. Example of scenarios embedded into personas [44]

Furthermore, while Nielsen et al. [12] found a "noteworthy difference" in the "lack of information on income, urbanicity, and lifestyle" (p. 5) in their analysis, we did not find this to be the case. Moreover, Nielsen et al. also found that market segments were rarely captured in persona templates from Danish companies, which we also did not find to be the case. This may be attributed to a greater diversity in contexts observed in our set of persona layouts. As we only included studies that were data-driven and did not exclude by geographical region, such demographic details were intentionally included in many of the persona layouts. For example, studies developing personas for e-health devices found it pertinent to capture lifestyle and subpopulation distribution percentages [9], while studies conducted in market research and business contexts captured relevant income, lifestyle, and urbanicity data of potential customers [2, 45].

Nielsen et al.'s [12] finding that Danish persona descriptions lacked business and marketing related information was also reflected in our analysis of international, data-driven persona layouts. We also found it to be the case that "even though it is stated in several interviews that personas are used as a strategic tool and in marketing, the descriptions do not reflect this" (p. 6). Specifically, information pertaining to competitors, business objectives, and brand relationship were not captured in any of the persona layouts we analyzed. Rather, relevant information to businesses was mostly indirectly captured in the design-related categories, in relation to the personas' product goals, work-related issues, and daily life or work context. This may suggest that the persona layouts were designed to envision common product usage scenarios among customers rather than to explicitly to illustrate and correspond to business objectives.

Moreover, the persona layouts in our analysis also reflected Nielsen et al.'s [12] observation that researchers developed "different ways of fostering identification (…) the use of keywords, headlines, and quotes give a quick understanding of the kernel of the persona description" (p. 6). Our own analysis found that a variety of visual cues across persona layouts, from color coding, use of icons, visual scales, and even data charts [47] (see Fig. 4 for an example).

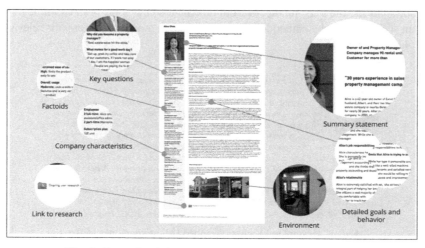

Fig. 4. Example of visual identification aids in personas [47]

The field is in dire need of empirical user studies. Nascent work shows promise in applying methodologically diverse methods such as eye-tracking, think-aloud, observer notes [34, 35], and examining multiple aspects of persona design, such as photos, text vs. numbers, and so on [36, 51, 52]. Yet, there is a lack of systematic research that would incrementally advance the design practice of personas into a more *optimal* state. Currently, some of the empirical findings are conflicting (such as those by Hill et al. [35] and Salminen et al. [34] regarding the use of multiple photos). We surmise that this is due to variations in the implementation of persona templates – both small and large variations can affect user experiences in crucial ways. In other words, the persona templates tested by different research "look and feel" different and thus are perceived as and engaged with in different ways. The only way, it thus appears, to produce consistent research insights that are generalizable across the nuanced implementations of DDPs, is to include more design variations in these user studies. This would, consequently, require the use of large-scale data collection, potentially prompting for more scalable data collection such as persona crowd experiments. There are already existing examples of using crowdsourcing for data collection in persona studies [51, 52]; however, more efforts are needed.

6   Conclusion

An empirical analysis shows that DDP layouts draws heavily from both quantitative and qualitative data. Some persona information (e.g., lifestyle, personality) is difficult to obtain using purely quantitative methods, thus requiring qualitative insights to realistically portray this information. We also find that graphical complexity and information richness do not necessarily correlate. The range of information categories is high, as the most information-rich persona template has more than 300% more information categories than the least information-rich template. Furthermore, the choice of the persona development methodology may carry over to the information design of DDPs, with quantitative data typically presented as scores, metrics, or tables and qualitative data as text-rich narratives. We did not find one "general template" for DDPs; this cannot be defined easily if at all, due to the variety of the outputs of different methods as well as differences in the information needs of the persona users.

Appendix 1: Full Coding Results

Year	Title	Only quantitative	Mixed quant-qual	Name	Age	Gender	Personality and psychographics	Urbanity	Work related issues	Daily life or work context	Product related issues	Product goals	Scenarios	A day in the life	Market size, segment	Color-coding	Use of facial picture	Use of cartoon picture	Reference to sources	Disabilities	International considerations	Explanations
							Background				Design-related				Business	Graphics			Miscellaneous			
2005	Persona-and-scenario based requirements engineering for software embedded in digital consumer products	X		X	X	X	X	X	X	X	X	X							X				
2007	Persona-scenario-goal methodology for user-centered requirements engineering	X		X	X	X	X	X	X	X	X	X							X				
2008	A Latent Semantic Analysis Methodology for the Identification and Creation of Personas	X		X	X	X	X	X	X	X	X	X	X					X					
2008	Data-driven persona development	X		X			X	X	X			X		X	X		X						
2009	Developing and validating personas in e-commerce: A heuristic approach	X		X	X	X	X	X			X	X					X						
2010	Combine Qualitative and Quantitative Methods to Create Persona		X	X	X	X	X	X	X	X		X	X	X			X						
2010	Using cluster analysis in persona development		X		X		X	X	X	X	X	X	X				X						
2011	Integrating Human Modeling and Simulation with the Persona Method		X	X	X	X	X	X	X		X	X	X	X			X						

Year	Title	Background							Design-related						Business	Graphics			Miscellaneous			
		Only quantitative	Mixed quant-qual	Name	Age	Gender	Personality and psychographics	Urbanicity	Work related issues	Daily life or work context	Product related issues	Product goals	Scenarios	A day in the life	Market size, segment	Color-coding	Use of facial picture	Use of cartoon picture	Reference to sources	Disabilities	International considerations	Explanations
2011	Behavioral Persona for Human-Robot Interaction: A Study Based on Pet Robot		X	X	X	X	X	X	X	X	X	X	X						X				
2012	Basic senior personas: a representative design tool covering the spectrum of European older adults	X		X		X	X	X	X	X	X	X	X				X	X			X		
2013	Learning Latent Personas of Film Characters	X		X	X	X	X	X												X		X	
2014	Personas in the Middle: Automated Support for Creating Personas As Focal Points in Feature Gathering Forums	X		X		X	X	X															X
2014	Explaining predictive models to learning specialists using personas	X		X		X	X			X		X	X				X						
2014	Invoking the User from Data to Design		X	X	X	X	X	X	X	X	X	X	X		X		X					X	
2015	Demystifying online personas of Vietnamese young adults on Facebook: A Q-methodology approach		X				X		X		X					X							
2016	A Factor Analysis Approach to Persona Development using Survey Data	X						X	X	X	X	X										
2016	Privacy Personas: Clustering Users via Attitudes and Behaviors Toward Security Practices	X		X	X	X	X	X	X	X	X	X										
2017	Animal personas: representing dog stakeholders in interaction design		X	X	X	X	X	X	X	X							X				X	

Year	Title	Only quantitative	Mixed quant-qual	Background					Design-related						Business	Graphics			Miscellaneous			
				Name	Age	Gender	Personality and psychographics	Urbanicity	Work related issues	Daily life or work context	Product related issues	Product goals	Scenarios	A day in the life	Market size, segment	Color-coding	Use of facial picture	Use of cartoon picture	Reference to sources	Disabilities	International considerations	Explanations
2017	ID3P: Iterative Data-driven Development of Persona Based on Quantitative Evaluation and Revision	X		X	X	X			X		X	X					X					X
2017	Know thy eHealth user: Development of biopsychosocial personas from a study of older adults with heart failure	X		X	X	X	X	X	X	X	X	X	X				X			X	X	
2017	SOPER: Discovering the Influence of Fashion and the Many Faces of User from Session Logs using Stick Breaking Process	X						X				X	X			X						
2017	The Use of Data-Driven Personas to Facilitate Organizational Adoption–A Case Study		X	X		X	X	X	X	X	X	X	X	X		X	X		X			X
2017	Characterizing Software Engineering Work with Personas Based on Knowledge Worker Actions						X		X	X	X	X			X							
2018	Analysis of Regional Group Health Persona Based on Image Recognition		X	X	X	X	X	X	X	X		X						X				
2018	Customer segmentation using online platforms: isolating behavioral and demographic segments for persona creation via aggregated user data	X						X	X	X	X					X	X					
2018	Evaluating Inclusivity using Quantitative Personas	X		X	X	X			X	X	X				X		X					
2018	From 2,772 segments to five personas: Summarizing a diverse online audience by generating culturally adapted personas		X	X	X	X		X	X	X	X	X				X	X					X

Year	Title	Only quantitative	Mixed quant-qual	Name	Age	Gender	Personality and psychographics	Urbanicity	Work related issues	Daily life or work context	Product related issues	Product goals	Scenarios	A day in the life	Market size, segment	Color-coding	Use of facial picture	Use of cartoon picture	Reference to sources	Disabilities	International considerations	Explanations
							Background				**Design-related**				**Business**	**Graphics**				**Miscellaneous**		
2018	Imaginary People Representing Real Numbers: Generating Personas from Online Social Media Data		X	X	X	X		X	X	X	X	X				X	X					
2018	Research on the Annual Reading Report of Academic Libraries Based on Personas		X			X		X	X	X	X	X										
2019	Creating Persona Skeletons from Imbalanced Datasets - A Case Study using U.S. Older Adults' Health Data		X	X	X	X	X	X	X	X	X		X				X			X		X

References

1. Brickey, J., Walczak, S., Burgess, T.: Comparing semi-automated clustering methods for persona development. IEEE Trans. Softw. Eng. **38**, 537–546 (2012). https://doi.org/10.1109/TSE.2011.60
2. Tu, N., Dong, X., Rau, P.P., Zhang, T.: Using cluster analysis in persona development. In: 2010 8th International Conference on Supply Chain Management and Information, pp. 1–5 (2010)
3. Stevenson, P.D., Mattson, C.A.: The personification of big data. In: Proceedings of the Design Society: International Conference on Engineering Design, vol. 1, pp. 4019–4028 (2019). https://doi.org/10.1017/dsi.2019.409
4. Jung, S., Salminen, J., An, J., Kwak, H., Jansen, B.J.: Automatically conceptualizing social media analytics data via personas. In: Proceedings of the International AAAI Conference on Web and Social Media (ICWSM 2018), San Francisco, California, USA (2018)
5. Jung, S., Salminen, J., Kwak, H., An, J., Jansen, B.J.: Automatic Persona Generation (APG): a rationale and demonstration. In: Proceedings of the 2018 Conference on Human Information Interaction & Retrieval, pp. 321–324. ACM (2018)
6. Jung, S., Salminen, J., Jansen, B.J.: Personas changing over time: analyzing variations of data-driven personas during a two-year period. In: Extended Abstracts of the 2019 CHI Conference on Human Factors in Computing Systems, pp. LBW2714:1–LBW2714:6. ACM, Glasgow (2019). https://doi.org/10.1145/3290607.3312955
7. Aoyama, M.: Persona-and-scenario based requirements engineering for software embedded in digital consumer products. In: Proceedings of the 13th IEEE International Conference on Requirements Engineering (RE 2005), Washington, DC, USA, pp. 85–94 (2005). https://doi.org/10.1109/RE.2005.50
8. Dhakad, L., Das, M., Bhattacharyya, C., Datta, S., Kale, M., Mehta, V.: SOPER: discovering the influence of fashion and the many faces of user from session logs using stick breaking process. In: Proceedings of the 2017 ACM on Conference on Information and Knowledge Management - CIKM 2017, pp. 1609–1618. ACM Press, Singapore (2017). https://doi.org/10.1145/3132847.3133007
9. Holden, R.J., Kulanthaivel, A., Purkayastha, S., Goggins, K.M., Kripalani, S.: Know thy eHealth user: development of biopsychosocial personas from a study of older adults with heart failure. Int. J. Med. Inform. **108**, 158–167 (2017). https://doi.org/10.1016/j.ijmedinf.2017.10.006
10. An, J., Kwak, H., Jung, S.-g., Salminen, J., Jansen, Bernard J.: Customer segmentation using online platforms: isolating behavioral and demographic segments for persona creation via aggregated user data. Soc. Netw. Anal. Min. **8**(1), 1–19 (2018). https://doi.org/10.1007/s13278-018-0531-0
11. Denzin, N.K., Lincoln, Y.S.: Introduction: entering the field of qualitative research. In: Strategies of Qualitative Inquiry, pp. 1–34. Sage, Thousand Oaks (1998)
12. Nielsen, L., Hansen, K.S., Stage, J., Billestrup, J.: A template for design personas: analysis of 47 persona descriptions from danish industries and organizations. Int. J. Sociotechnol. Knowl. Dev. **7**, 45–61 (2015). https://doi.org/10.4018/ijskd.2015010104
13. Dang-Pham, D., Pittayachawan, S., Nkhoma, M.: Demystifying online personas of Vietnamese young adults on Facebook: a Q-methodology approach. Australas. J. Inf. Syst. **19**, (2015). https://doi.org/10.3127/ajis.v19i0.1204
14. Salminen, J., Jansen, B.J., An, J., Kwak, H., Jung, S.-G.: Automatic persona generation for online content creators: conceptual rationale and a research agenda. Personas - User Focused Design. HIS, pp. 135–160. Springer, London (2019). https://doi.org/10.1007/978-1-4471-7427-1_8

15. Cooper, A.: The Inmates Are Running the Asylum: Why High Tech Products Drive Us Crazy and How to Restore the Sanity. Sams - Pearson Education, Indianapolis (1999)
16. Nielsen, L.: Personas - User Focused Design. Springer, New York (2019)
17. Anvari, F., Tran, H.M.T.: Persona ontology for user centred design professionals. In: The ICIME 4th International Conference on Information Management and Evaluation, Ho Chi Minh City, Vietnam, pp. 35–44 (2013)
18. Nielsen, L.: Engaging personas and narrative scenarios (2004). http://personas.dk/wp-con tent/samlet-udgave-til-load.pdf
19. Bornet, C., Brangier, E.: La méthode des personas: principes, intérêts et limites. Bulletin de psychologie 2, 115–134 (2013)
20. Floyd, I.R., Jones, M.C., Twidale, M.B.: Resolving incommensurable debates: a preliminary identification of persona kinds, attributes, and characteristics. Artifact. 2, 12–26 (2008). https://doi.org/10.1080/17493460802276836
21. Jones, M., Marsden, G.: Mobile Interaction Design. Wiley, Hoboken (2006)
22. Mulder, S., Yaar, Z.: The User is Always Right: A Practical Guide to Creating and Using Personas for the Web. New Riders, Berkeley (2006)
23. Pruitt, J., Adlin, T.: The Persona Lifecycle: Keeping People in Mind Throughout Product Design. Morgan Kaufmann, Boston (2006)
24. Goodman, E., Kuniavsky, M., Moed, A.: Observing the User Experience: A Practitioner's Guide to User Research. Morgan Kaufmann, Boston (2013)
25. Pichler, R.: A template for writing great personas (2012)
26. Seiden, J., Gothelf, J.: Lean UX: Applying Lean Principles to Improve User Experience. O'Reilly, Sebastopol (2003)
27. Miaskiewicz, T., Kozar, K.A.: Personas and user-centered design: How can personas benefit product design processes? Des. Stud. 32, 417–430 (2011)
28. Dantin, U.: Application of personas in user interface design for educational software. In: Proceedings of the 7th Australasian conference on Computing education-Volume 42, pp. 239–247. Australian Computer Society, Inc., Newcastle (2005)
29. LeRouge, C., Ma, J., Sneha, S., Tolle, K.: User profiles and personas in the design and development of consumer health technologies. Int. J. Med. Inform. 82, e251–e268 (2013). https://doi.org/10.1016/j.ijmedinf.2011.03.006
30. Antle, A.N.: Child-personas: fact or fiction? In: Proceedings of the 6th Conference on Designing Interactive Systems, pp. 22–30. ACM (2006)
31. Loitsch, C., Weber, G., Voegler, J.: Teaching accessibility with personas. In: Miesenberger, K., Bühler, C., Penaz, P. (eds.) ICCHP 2016. LNCS, vol. 9758, pp. 453–460. Springer, Cham (2016). https://doi.org/10.1007/978-3-319-41264-1_62
32. Sedlmayr, B., Schöffler, J., Prokosch, H.-U., Sedlmayr, M.: User-centered design of a mobile medication management. Inform. Health Soc. Care 44, 152–163 (2019)
33. Al-Qirim, N.: Personas of e-commerce adoption in small businesses in New Zealand. J. Electron. Commer. Organ. (JECO) 4, 18–45 (2006)
34. Salminen, J., Nielsen, L., Jung, S.-G., An, J., Kwak, H., Jansen, B.J.: "Is More Better?": impact of multiple photos on perception of persona profiles. In: Proceedings of ACM CHI Conference on Human Factors in Computing Systems (CHI2018). ACM, Montréal (2018). https://doi.org/10.1145/3173574.3173891
35. Hill, C.G., et al.: Gender-inclusiveness personas vs. stereotyping: can we have it both ways? In: Proceedings of the 2017 CHI Conference, pp. 6658–6671. ACM Press, Denver (2017). https://doi.org/10.1145/3025453.3025609
36. Salminen, J., Liu, Y.-H., Sengun, S., Santos, J.M., Jung, S.-G., Jansen, B.J.: The effect of numerical and textual information on visual engagement and perceptions of AI-driven persona interfaces. In: Proceedings of the ACM Intelligent User Interfaces (IUI 2020). ACM, Cagliary (2020)

37. Salminen, J., Jung, S., Jansen, B.J.: The future of data-driven personas: a marriage of online analytics numbers and human attributes. In: ICEIS 2019 - Proceedings of the 21st International Conference on Enterprise Information Systems, pp. 596–603. SciTePress, Heraklion (2019)
38. Anvari, F., Richards, D., Hitchens, M., Babar, M.A.: Effectiveness of persona with personality traits on conceptual design. In: Proceedings of the 37th International Conference on Software Engineering - Volume 2, pp. 263–272. IEEE Press, Piscataway (2015)
39. Radjenović, D., Heričko, M., Torkar, R., Živkovič, A.: Software fault prediction metrics: a systematic literature review. Inf. Softw. Technol. **55**, 1397–1418 (2013)
40. Zhu, E., Hadadgar, A., Masiello, I., Zary, N.: Augmented reality in healthcare education: an integrative review. PeerJ **2**, e469 (2014)
41. Tempelman-Kluit, N., Pearce, A.: Invoking the User from Data to Design. CRL **75**, 616–640 (2014). https://doi.org/10.5860/crl.75.5.616
42. Dupree, J.L., Devries, R., Berry, D.M., Lank, E.: Privacy personas: clustering users via attitudes and behaviors toward security practices. In: Proceedings of the 2016 CHI Conference on Human Factors in Computing Systems, pp. 5228–5239. ACM, New York (2016). https://doi.org/10.1145/2858036.2858214
43. Zhu, H., Wang, H., Carroll, J.M.: creating persona skeletons from imbalanced datasets - a case study using U.S. older adults' health data. In: Proceedings of the 2019 on Designing Interactive Systems Conference - DIS 2019, pp. 61–70. ACM Press, San Diego (2019). https://doi.org/10.1145/3322276.3322285
44. dos Santos, T.F., de Castro, D.G., Masiero, A.A., Aquino Junior, P.T.: Behavioral persona for human-robot interaction: a study based on pet robot. In: Kurosu, M. (ed.) HCI 2014. LNCS, vol. 8511, pp. 687–696. Springer, Cham (2014). https://doi.org/10.1007/978-3-319-07230-2_65
45. Tu, N., He, Q., Zhang, T., Zhang, H., Li, Y., Xu, H., Xiang, Y.: Combine qualitative and quantitative methods to create persona. In: 2010 3rd International Conference on Information Management, Innovation Management and Industrial Engineering, pp. 597–603 (2010). https://doi.org/10.1109/ICIII.2010.463
46. Ford, D., Zimmermann, T., Bird, C., Nagappan, N.: Characterizing software engineering work with personas based on knowledge worker actions. In: Proceedings of the 11th ACM/IEEE International Symposium on Empirical Software Engineering and Measurement, pp. 394–403. IEEE Press, Piscataway (2017). https://doi.org/10.1109/ESEM.2017.54
47. Miaskiewicz, T., Luxmoore, C.: The use of data-driven personas to facilitate organizational adoption–a case study. Des. J. **20**, 357–374 (2017)
48. Brooks, C., Greer, J.: Explaining predictive models to learning specialists using personas. In: Proceedings of the Fourth International Conference on Learning Analytics and Knowledge, pp. 26–30. ACM, Indianapolis (2014). https://doi.org/10.1145/2567574.2567612
49. Kanno, T., Ooyabu, T., Furuta, K.: Integrating human modeling and simulation with the persona method. In: Stephanidis, C. (ed.) UAHCI 2011. LNCS, vol. 6766, pp. 51–60. Springer, Heidelberg (2011). https://doi.org/10.1007/978-3-642-21663-3_6
50. Goodman-Deane, J., Waller, S., Demin, D., González-de-Heredia, A., Bradley, M., Clarkson, J.P.: Evaluating inclusivity using quantitative personas. Presented at the Design Research Society Conference, 28 June 2018 (2018). https://doi.org/10.21606/drs.2018.400
51. Salminen, J., Santos, J.M., Jung, S.-G., Eslami, M., Jansen, B.J.: Persona transparency: analyzing the impact of explanations on perceptions of data-driven personas. Int. J. Hum.–Comput. Interact., 1–13 (2019). https://doi.org/10.1080/10447318.2019.1688946
52. Salminen, J., Jung, S.-G., Santos, J.M., Jansen, B.J.: Does a smile matter if the person is not real?: The effect of a smile and stock photos on persona perceptions. Int. J. Hum.–Comput. Interact., 1–23 (2019). https://doi.org/10.1080/10447318.2019.1664068

Does Visualization of Health Data Using an Accelerometer Be Associated with Promoting Exercise Among Elderly People?

Yurika Shiozu[1]([✉]), Shoki Muramatsu[2], Ryo Shioya[3], Katsuhiko Yonezaki[4], Mizuki Tanaka[3], and Katsunori Shimohara[3]

[1] Kyoto Sangyo University, Kyoto, Kyoto 603-8555, Japan
yshiozu@cc.kyoto-su.ac.jp
[2] Aichi University, Nagoya, Aichi 453-8777, Japan
[3] Doshisha University, Kyotabe, Kyoto 610-0394, Japan
[4] Taisho University, Toshima, Tokyo 170-0001, Japan

Abstract. Most people in developed countries know that exercise is good for health and recommended by the government. However, even if the numerical goal of steps is suggested by the government, we often fail to achieve the goal. Behavioral analytics shows that it needs to give information about evidence-based health to promote changes in individual's activities.

This study aims to determine whether self-monitoring using an accelerometer is associated with behavioral changes and to demonstrate the relationship between the visualization of the data brought by an accelerometer and willingness to exercise continuously. The data were collected using a social experiment and investigation, and the analysis adopted statistical methods, t-test and chi-test.

Our results clarify the following points. First, even considering the difference between individuals, statistically, the subjects increased neither their number of steps nor exercise by using the accelerometer continuously. According to Tong and Laranjo (2018), self-monitoring is an effective behavior change technique for most people, however, this study shows that self-monitoring does not associated. Second, statistically, at 10% level, a change in awareness of exercise was associated with the willingness to use the accelerometer continuously. Third, some people want to use their accelerometer and understand their own data even without a financial reward.

Keywords: Visualization · Exercise · Accelerometer

1 Introduction

Today, developed countries face aged society. Elderly people hope to maintain their health and are aware of their daily activities like eating, exercising, and sleeping. As some previous studies (e.g. Takahashi et al. (2007)) show that exercise prevents the development of lifestyle-related diseases, governments usually recommend exercise for its citizens. Additionally, communication with others is also important to maintain mental and physical health.

© Springer Nature Switzerland AG 2020
S. Yamamoto and H. Mori (Eds.): HCII 2020, LNCS 12184, pp. 145–155, 2020.
https://doi.org/10.1007/978-3-030-50020-7_9

The activities considered desirable for individuals are also good for public health insurers as they contribute in financial improvement. Behavioral economics shows that nudges are effective when the government voluntarily guides citizens to perform desired activities. For instance, to encourage savings on electricity, if the government displays the amount to use of nearby electricity on a collection table, people save on electricity.

However, more efforts are needed to continue such activities than merely understanding that one needs to continue exercising, eating balanced nutritious meals, and sleeping at regular times. It is known that nudge does not keep the effect and it is important problem how to improve the sustainability of nudge.

Regarding this problem, fun theory suggests the application of gamification. Moreover, behavioral analytics report the need to provide information about evidence-based health to promote changes in individuals' activities.

In this study, we verified the hypothesis that introduction of the accelerometer encourages subjects to walk or become active. Additionally, we clarified the relationship between the visualization of the data such as the number of steps, amount of activities and willingness to exercise continuously.

The contents of this study are as follow. In Sect. 2. we focus on previous studies and describe our data in Sect. 3. Section 4 shows the results of statistical analysis and our conclusion and future work are described in Sect. 5.

2   Previous Studies

In behavioral economics, Thaler and Sunstein (2009) denote that the government decides the desired behavioral policy to promote the desired behavior in residents. For instance, to encourage savings on electricity, if the government displays the amount to use of nearby electricity on a collection table, people save on electricity. The means to promote the desired behavior is called "Nudge". However, it has a problem in terms of sustainability of its effect. In addition, randomized controlled trial (RCTs) are required to verify their efficacy, but it sometimes has ethical difficulties involving some subjects. As RCTs require significant research costs, accumulation of research does not in progress in social science.

In some cases, people can expect to benefit from changing their behavior, both at the individual and government level. For example, because Plassman et al. (2010) showed that exercise habits reduce the risk of dementia, U.S. government recommends to its citizens, the performance of exercise twice per week across 6 months. However, even if the suggestion is an evidence-based policy, as it is not enforced, some citizens do not change their behavior.

Applied behavior analysis has accumulated a great deal of research to solve such social problems with changing one's behavior. Abraham and Kools (2012) list the mechanisms for behavior change based on incentives, which can promote the desired behavior. According to the list, changing the normative belief of people's behavior and gaining approval for one's behavior is one mechanism for behavior change. Moreover, to strengthen one's self efficacy is another mechanism. The techniques for the mechanisms include providing information about others, suggesting comparison with others, encouraging one to acquire others' approval for one's behavior, encouraging self-monitoring, and providing feedback performance.

Many researches describe the effect of providing feedback on one's performance. For example, Blok et al. (2006) described that feedback is provided using a pedometer, some people try to walk more steps. Enjoying activity is important to continue it. To make someone continue the desired behavior, applying the elements of game is valid. Whitton (2009) calls it gamification and shows that comparison with others is an important element for gamification. In other words, by comparing oneself with others, people enjoy the desired action and continue to perfume it.

However, the mechanism has not yet been systematized, and it is not clear what combination of techniques will lead to solving each social issue such as promoting exercise.

3   Overview of the Data

3.1   Overview of Our Experiment and Investigation

In this study, we conducted an experiment and an investigation with the cooperation of Makishima Kizuna no Kai, a non-profit organization of Makishima, in Uji City, Kyoto Prefecture, Japan. The number of subjects was 20, and their average age was 70 years. We conducted the experiment from September 1 to October 31, 2019 and the survey was held on December 17 and 18, 2019. In the experiment, we obtained subjects' steps using the accelerometer, and at the investigation, we conducted a cognitive function test and a questionnaire survey on awareness about exercise and communication.

Before the experiment, we received ethical approval from Doshisha University.

We lent the subjects smartphone and accelerometer, the *Calori Scan* HJA-405T made by OMRON. This accelerometer can measure the number of steps, distance, total calorie consumption and the amount of active exercise and so on. In our research, we used the data on number of steps and amount of active Ex. Ex is a unit of exercise using Metabolic Equivalents (METs). METs defined as the amount of oxygen consumed while sitting at rest and are equal to 3.5 ml O_2 per kg body weight $\times$ min. For example, cooking counts as 2.0 METs and walking(67 m/min) counts as 3.0 METs.

Equation 1 shows the relationship between Ex and METs.

$$Ex = METs \times min/60 \tag{1}$$

To clarify the effect of visualization using the accelerometer, we asked the subjects about their willingness to use the accelerometer continuously, changes in awareness about exercise, and recognition of change in minutes of exercise.

3.2   Data

This section is divided into description of data obtained through the experiment and the investigation.

Outline of the Data Obtained Through the Experiment. The system of collecting data was as explained below. The accelerometer can store data for two weeks and the users transfer their data to their smartphone by the press of a button. The data obtained using the accelerometer were collected from subjects' smartphone with Bluetooth and input to OMRON's web server through the application as Fig. 1 shows.

These data stored in the web server can be accessed with the application. The application shows the data through graphs and values. It can include one's annual, monthly, or daily data; however, it cannot contrast one's data with that of other individuals. If someone tries to compare it with others' data, it needs to other individuals' permission to show their data with or without the application.

We obtained the data from the OMRON's web server once a day.

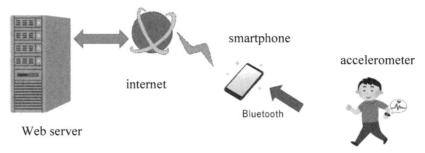

Fig. 1. Data collection

The valid number of responses from subjects was 11. Table 1 describes the descriptive statics for the number of steps and amount of active Ex. The total number of observed steps or active Ex data was 684 and the average steps per a day was 5483.52. According to the survey of Ministry of Health, Labour and Wealth of Japan in 2018, the average steps per day of elderly men was 5417 and that of elderly women was 4759. Based on this result, it can be said that the subjects walked more than the national average.

Table 1. Descriptive Statistics for the number of steps and amount of active Ex

	Total	
	Steps	Amount of active Ex
Min	0	0
Max	21254	11.300
Average	5483.52	2.981
Standard deviation	3683.233	2.101
Variance	13566204.997	4.415
N	684	

To verify the hypothesis that visualization of data of the number of steps using the accelerometer increases steps or the amount of active Ex, we divided the data into two groups by month. If the steps or the amount of active Ex in October increase compared to the data of September, it suggests that the accelerometer contributed in encouraging individuals to become active.

From Table 2, it can be said that the September data were not very different from October data. However, the data of each variable in October increased compared to that of September.

Table 2. Descriptive Statistics for each month's number of steps and amount of active Ex

	September		October	
	Steps	Amount of active Ex	Steps	Amount of active Ex
Min	0	0	0	0
Max	15851	9.3	21254	11.30
Average	5234.09	2.83	5759.05	3.14
Standard deviation	3562.48	2.07	3798.65	2.13
Variance	12691268.56	4.28	14429739.49	4.52
N	359		325	

Table 2 describes the tendency of all the subjects. However, the standard deviation indicates that the error between individual was large. Figure 2 shows the situation of each individual.

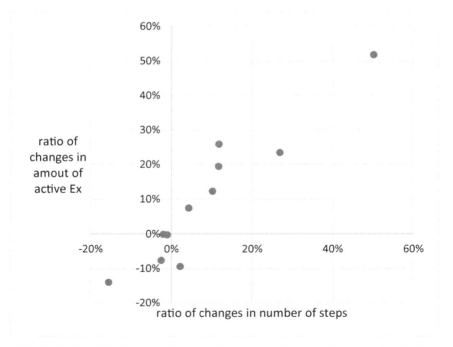

Fig. 2. Scatter plot of ratio of changes in the number of steps and amount of active Ex

Figure 2 shows that most subjects became more active, considering the ratio of changes in the number of steps and amount of active Ex. It also suggests a positive correlation between in the number of steps and the amount of active Ex. Evidently, the number of steps is one factor of the increase in the amount of active Ex, however, other activities such as cleaning can also become factors.

Outline of the Data Obtained Through Investigation. In our investigation, we administered a questionnaire to 20 participants who participated the experiment explained above. We adopted placement method. To clarify the relationship between the willingness to exercise continuously and visualization of the data, the questionnaire consisted of items on the changes in recognition of exercise time, changes in awareness about exercise and the willingness to use accelerometer continuously. The valid number of responses was 16. The cross tabulations are shown in Tables 3 and 4.

Table 3. Cross tabulation between change in recognition of exercise time and willingness to use accelerometer continuously

		Willingness to use accelerometer continuously		Total
		Yes	Don't know	
Change in recognition of exercise time	Increase	7	1	8
	No change	3	5	8
Total		10	6	16

Table 4. Cross tabulation between change in awareness of exercise and willingness to use accelerometer continuously

		Willingness to use accelerometer continuously		Total
		Yes	Don't know	
Changes in awareness of exercise	Need more exercise	6	3	9
	As usual	4	2	6
	Feel nothing	0	1	1
Total		10	6	16

Table 3 and Fig. 3 suggest that the individuals who changed their recognition of exercise time apparently wanted to use the accelerometer continuously. Table 4 also suggests that those who changed their awareness of exercise wanted to use the accelerometer continuously.

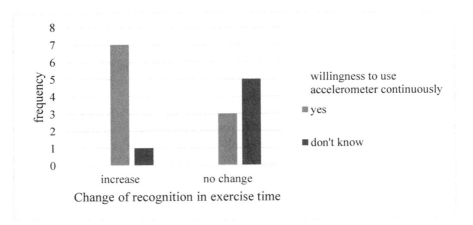

Fig. 3. The relationship between the change of recognition in exercise time and willingness to use accelerometer continuously

4   Results of Analysis

First, we statistically confirmed that introduction of the accelerometer encourages subjects to walk or become active. We verified the hypothesis that the number of steps and the amount of active Ex were changed beginning and continuing to use the accelerometer. Hence, the t-test was applied to the data shown in Table 2. Then, to verify the hypothesis that change in awareness of exercise is associated with the willingness to use accelerometer continuously, chi-squared test was applied to the data in Table 3.

4.1   Relationship Between the Ratio of Changes in the Number of Steps and Amount of Active Ex

Table 2 and Fig. 2 suggest that visualization of the data obtained using the accelerometer seems to have positive correlation. However, in the previous section, this was not statistically established. First, we confirmed that visualization of the data obtained using the accelerometer encouraged subjects become more active cannot be established.

Table 5. Result of t-test for all subjects

	Levene's test		The difference between the population mean test		
	F-value	P-value	t - value	df	P-value
Steps	1.228	0.268	−1.865	682	0.063
Amount of active Ex	0.102	0.749	−1.936	682	0.053

In Table 5, as the P-value of Levene's test was over 0.05, it can define homogeneity of variance. Thus, t-test could be applied to this data. As p-values of the difference between the population mean test were over 0.05, there was no difference between steps in September and October. The same can be said about the amount of active Ex.

This means that the subjects did not become more active statistically using the accelerometer continuously.

However, as Fig. 2 suggests that most of subject walked more in October, this result may have been influenced by the differences between individuals. To exclude this effect, subjects without any missing values during the experimental period were selected and the same test was applied to their data. The number of subjects was 8, and the results were the same as that mentioned above (see Table 6). In other words, even after considering the difference between individuals statistically, the subjects neither took more steps nor exercised more after using the accelerometer.

Table 6. Results of t-test for each individual

		Levene's test		The difference between the population mean test		
		F-value	P-value	t -value	df	P-value
1	Steps	0.001	0.977	−0.217	59	0.829
	Amount of active Ex	0.107	0.745	0.678	59	0.5
2	Steps	0.762	0.386	1.125	59	0.265
	Amount of active Ex	0.009	0.927	1.157	59	0.252
3	Steps	1.234	0.271	−1.208	59	0.232
	Amount of active Ex	3.84	0.055	−1.94	59	0.057
4	Steps	0.002	0.965	0.362	58	0.719
	Amount of active Ex	0.004	0.948	0.656	58	0.514
5	Steps	1.285	0.261	−1.444	59	0.154
	Amount of active Ex	0.067	0.797	−2.844	59	0.006

(*continued*)

Table 6. (*continued*)

		Levene's test		The difference between the population mean test		
		F-value	P-value	t -value	df	P-value
6	Steps	0.376	0.542	0.06	59	0.953
	Amount of active Ex	0.063	0.803	0.003	59	0.997
7	Steps	1.389	0.243	−0.464	59	0.645
	Amount of active Ex	0.317	0.576	−0.558	59	0.579
8	Steps	2.408	0.126	0.102	59	0.919
	Amount of active Ex	3.215	0.078	0.019	59	0.985

4.2 Relationship Between Change in Awareness of Exercise and Willingness to Use Accelerometer Continuously

In this part, we verified the hypothesis that change in awareness of exercise is associated with the willingness to use accelerometer continuously. As Table 3 involves a 2 × 2 matrix and Fig. 3 shows that the frequency of 2 bars are less than 5, Fisher's exact test was adopted. As the test showed a statistically significant difference, the group who recognized increase in exercise time by using the accelerometer showed the willingness to use the accelerometer continuously. The result is as below (Table 7).

Table 7. Result of Fisher's exact test

	Value	Exact p-value
Fisher's exact test		0.059
n	16	

The exact p-value was over 0.05 but under 0.1. This means that the null hypothesis could be rejected at 5% level but not at 10% level. In other words, at 10% level, a change in awareness of exercise was associated with the willingness to use the accelerometer continuously.

5 Conclusion and Remarks

Our results clarify the following points. First, even after considering the difference between individuals, statistically the subjects increased neither the number of steps nor exercise by using the accelerometer continuously. Second, statistically, at 10% level, a change in awareness of exercise was associated with the willingness to use the accelerometer continuously. Third, some people want to use their accelerometer and understand their own data even without a financial reward.

Based on the research using behavioral analysis, our results can be considered to suggest that the visualization of data was associated with the behavioral changes. In other words, this study suggested that though visualization of the number of steps and the amount of active Ex becomes support of self-monitoring, self-monitoring does not change the behavior immediately. This result is different from previous studies.

Our results showed that self-monitoring was statistically related to change in awareness of exercise, at the 10% level. This result suggests that visualization of data is related to changes in awareness, however, not to changes in behavior immediately.

However, strategies to help participants enjoy using the accelerometer continuously does not always increase the number of steps or the amount of active Ex actually.

From the perspective of developing policy, if the government tries to make financial improvement in public healthcare insurance or long-term care insurance, the government needs to not only indicate the target steps and the amount of active Ex, but also develop programs that induce enjoyment is recommended. Moreover, to ensure sustainable programs, non-monetary factors such as camp game, to induce enjoyment is recommended.

In generally, many previous studies (e.g. Matthews et al. (2001)) showed that the number of steps and the amount of activity decrease in winter than in summer in the Northern Hemisphere. However, after controlling such seasonal changes, this study could not address whether visualization of the number of steps and amount of active Ex using the accelerometer is related to behavioral changes. In other words, in our study, though the statistical analysis were not significant, the number of steps and activity may have increased due to the appropriate season for exercising. To solve this problem, the long-term panel analysis is required to apply.

As the number of subjects was too small, the results cannot be generalized. In addition, it should be noted that the experiment does not use an RCT. In other word, this study cannot show causality of using the accelerometer.

We are currently developing the program including elements of fun for users comprising of non-monetary factors. We plan to start small-scale experiments in the future. The challenge in the future is to conduct large-scale experiments to confirm the robustness of the results of this analysis and verify the effects of the program under development.

Acknowledgement. The authors acknowledge and thank the members of the Makishima Kizuna Association non-profit organization for their cooperation in preparation of this paper. This study was funded by JSPS Kakenhi (Grants-in-Aid for Scientific Research by Japan Society for the Promotion of Science) Nos. JP16K03718 and JP17KT0086. This study was supported by the foundation of Kyoto Sangyo University (No. E1910).

References

Abraham, C., Kools, M.: Writing Health Communication, 1st edn. Sage Publications, London (2012)

Blok, B., Greef, M.H.G., Hacken, N.H.T., Sprenger, S.R., Postema, K., Wempe, J.B.: The effects of a lifestyle physical activity counseling program with feedback of a pedometer during pulmonary rehabilitation in patients with COPD: a pilot study. Patient Educ. Couns. **61**(1), 48–55 (2006)

Matthews, C.E., et al.: Seasonal variation in household, occupational, and leisure time physical activity: longitudinal analyses from the seasonal variation of blood cholesterol study. Am. J. Epidemiol. **153**, 172–183 (2001)

Plassman, B.L., Williams Jr., J.W., Burke, J.R., Holsinger, T., Benjamin, S.: Systematic review: factors associated with risk for and possible prevention of cognitive decline in later life. Ann. Int. Med. **153**, 182–193 (2010)

Takahashi, H., Kuriyama, S., Tsubono, Y., Nakaya, N., Fujita, K., Nishino, Y., et al.: Time spent walking and risk of colorectal cancer in Japan: the Miyagi Cohort study. Eur. J. Cancer Prev. **16**, 403–408 (2007)

Thaler, R., Sunstein, C.: Nudge, 1st edn. Penguin Books, London (2009)

Tong, H.L., Laranjo, L.: The use of social features in mobile health interventions to promote physical activity: a systematic review. npj Digit. Med. **1** (2018). https://doi.org/10.1038/s41746-018-0051-3. Article no. 43

Whitton, N.: Learning with Digital Games: A Practical Guide to Engaging Students in Higher Education. Routledge, New York (2009)

Ministry of Health, Labour and Welfare: National Health and Nutrition Survey in 2018. https://www.mhlw.go.jp/stf/newpage_08789.html. Accessed 27 Jan 2020

A Visualization Tool for the CIRMMT Distinguished Lecture Series

Marcelo M. Wanderley[(✉)], Mathias Bredholt, and Christian Frisson

Input Devices and Musical Interaction Laboratory - IDMIL,
Centre for Interdisciplinary Research in Music Media and Technology - CIRMMT,
McGill University, Montreal, Canada
{marcelo.wanderley,christian.frisson}@mcgill.ca,
mathias.bredholt@mail.mcgill.ca

Abstract. The CIRMMT Distinguished Lecture (DL) series consists of over seventy 1-h videos of leading scholars and artists discussing their interdisciplinary work, a unique video encyclopedia of Music, Science and Technology. Though this collection in itself is already an invaluable research and pedagogical tool, searching videos in the collection is not a trivial task given the diversity of fields and topics. To facilitate the navigation in the collection, we developed a visualization tool representing textual metadata of videos in a hierarchical bubble chart. In this paper we describe the distinguished lecture series and discuss the iterative prototyping of the visualization tool, as well as avenues for future developments.

Keywords: Data visualization · Video lectures · Music · Science and technology · CIRMMT

1 Introduction

The Centre for Interdisciplinary Research on Music Media and Technology (CIRMMT)[1], based in Montreal, Quebec, Canada, is a leading research institution aimed at fostering interdisciplinary research across sound/music, science and technology. Founded in 2001, it has quickly established itself at the forefront of research institutions at the intersection of these areas. Thanks to strong support from McGill University and its partners (Université de Montréal, Université de Sherbrooke and recently École de technologie supérieure), to a large number of individual and group grants from provincial and federal agencies, as well as to a variety of industrial partnership projects, CIRMMT has built unique facilities for the scientific study of sound and music. Among such facilities, a novel 400+ square meter ultra-quiet, large-scale multimedia room which is one of the most advanced research and performance spaces using the latest virtual acoustics techniques and cutting-edge performance measurement equipment. Altogether, CIRMMT serves around 130 members and collaborators, more than 200 graduate and undergraduate students, and many industrial partners.

---

[1] http://www.cirmmt.org.

© Springer Nature Switzerland AG 2020
S. Yamamoto and H. Mori (Eds.): HCII 2020, LNCS 12184, pp. 156–169, 2020.
https://doi.org/10.1007/978-3-030-50020-7_10

1.1   CIRMMT Research Structure

CIRMMT's research is currently organized in four research axes (RA). These axes are guiding the selection of speakers for distinguished lectures. A short summary of each research direction is presented here, a full description is available on the Centre's website[2].

- *Instruments, Devices and Systems* (RA1) encompasses engineering and mathematics research applied to sound and music. Topics include instrument and room acoustics, digital signal processing and new interfaces for musical expression.
- *Music Information Research* (RA2) focuses on computer applications for music information research. Research topics include digital music libraries, optical music recognition and computer-aided analysis of large amounts of music.
- *Cognition, Perception and Movement* (RA3) focuses on the scientific study of music, from the performer to the listener. Research topics include embodiment and movement synchronization and music cognition & perception.
- *Expanded Musical Practice* (RA4) focuses on artistic research. Research topics include the creation of works involving science and technology, the documentation of creative processes and the evaluation of the impact of technology in the arts.

1.2   CIRMMT Distinguished Lecture Series

The *Distinguished Lecture* (DL) series is one of the main public events organized by the Centre. Together with the *live@CIRMMT* concert series, it aims to foster interdisciplinary research by inviting world-class researchers to present an overview of their research to a broad audience, with typically 6 or 7 lectures yearly. To date, 94 lectures were held, of which 71 videos are available online constituting a unique, freely accessible resource for the community.

Starting in October 2005, distinguished researchers and artists from around the world have been invited to Montreal to present a 1-h overview of their research, which most of the time spans over several decades. Video recordings of the talks were made early on, though initially only as a means of archiving the events for internal records.

Over the years, with the increase of the number of talks, the CIRMMT direction realized the strong potential of the DL as pedagogical tool for anyone interested in the intersection of science, technology and sound/music. A dedicated YouTube channel[3] was then established and the lectures were posted online, cf. Fig. 1.

---

[2] http://www.cirmmt.org/research/axes.
[3] https://www.youtube.com/c/CIRMMT.

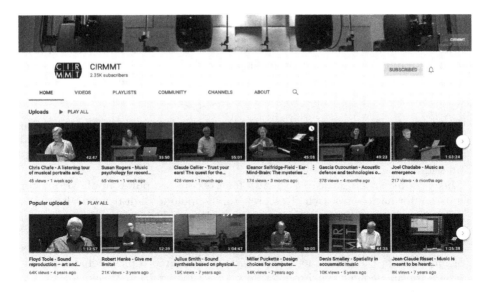

Fig. 1. Front page of CIRMMT's YouTube channel. Note the large spectrum of topics, but also the wide variation in the number of views for each lecture. Screenshot taken on January 27, 2020.

The Distinguished lecture series showcase researchers who made crucial contributions to their fields, with topics varying from computer music/sound and music computing, to psychology, cognition and neuroscience of music, from audio processing and music information retrieval to music composition and education. It not only provides accurate and recent information spanning many research careers, it has also an invaluable historical importance. This is the case for the videos of seminal researchers and artists such as David Wessel and Jean-Claude Risset, who sadly already passed away. Their videos illustrate their research and artistic achievements in what constitutes a first-hand, sometimes unique reference to their outstanding work.

It is important to note that the CIRMMT video channel actually encompasses more than the DL videos, as it also hosts videos of other high-profile CIRMMT events such as CIRMMT Student Symposium Keynotes and CIRMMT Seminars[4]. Though we refer to the DL series in this paper, we actually included these other videos in the DL series video collection and in the visualization tool, raising the current total number of available videos to 84.

---

[4] *live@CIRMMT* concert videos, although regularly recorded, are unfortunately not available to the public due to more complex copyright management.

2   Archiving Lectures and Establishing a DL Dataset

Apart from the YouTube channel, CIRMMT created a webpage dedicated to the DL videos around 2012[5]. Though meaningful when a handful of videos were available, it rapidly became less useful due to the constant increase in the number of videos. This can be seen in Fig. 2, that although only displaying a few of the most recent DLs, already shows the limitations of this solution.

2019-2020

- Nov 21, 2019 – Susan Rogers: Music psychology for record makers [NEW!]
- Oct 24, 2019 – Claude Cellier: Trust your ears! The quest for the optimum (digital) audio representation
- Sep 19, 2019 – Eleanor Selfridge-Field: Ear-Mind-Brain: The mysteries of musical similarity

2018-2019

DISTINGUISHED LECTURES

- May 02, 2019 – Joel Chadabe: Music as emergence
- Apr 11, 2019 – Udo Zölzer: DAFX digital audio effects and applications
- Mar 21, 2019 – Daniel Russell: Animations as educational tools for understanding the acoustics of musical instruments
- Feb 21, 2019 – Steven Takasugi: A machine for deception: Electro-acoustic composition as sleight of hand
- Nov 29, 2018 – Sally Jo Cunningham: Engagement with personal music collections
- Oct 18, 2018 – William Hartmann: Sound source localization: How the auditory system copes with confusing data
- Sep 20, 2018 – Richard Lyon: Extracting meaning from sound: Experiences in machine hearing

CIRMMT-OICRM-BRAMS STUDENT SYMPOSIUM (COBS) KEYNOTE

- May 09, 2019 – Gascia Ouzounian: Acoustic defence and technologies of listening during the First World War

2017-2018

DISTINGUISHED LECTURES

- Mar 15, 2018 – Sylvie Gibet: Gesture: a language to sense, express, control
- Feb 01, 2018 – Trevor Wishart: Composing the real
- Dec 13, 2017 – Bill Seaman: Recombinant music: Generative approaches
- Nov 09, 2017 – Toshifumi Kunimoto: YAMAHA's musical instruments and audio products as DSP applications
- Oct 09, 2017 – Joseph Myers: Recital halls, rehearsal rooms, and research spaces

CIRMMT STUDENT SYMPOSIUM KEYNOTE

- May 17, 2018 – Eric Heller: Journey into psychoacoustics

2016-2017

DISTINGUISHED LECTURES

- Apr 20, 2017 – Dan Gauger: Giving people control of our most important human sense – hearing
- Feb 23, 2017 – Benoit Fabre: Musical instruments and players – an acoustical approach to the relations between

Fig. 2. Top part of the CIRMMT Video page showing in list form the most recent DL dates, speaker and title with links to the videos. Screenshot taken on January 27, 2020.

---

[5] http://www.cirmmt.org/video.

2.1   Distinguished Lecture Dataset

In early 2018, a collaborative effort, headed by CIRMMT administrator Jacqueline Bednar, was carried out to create a DL dataset of all available lecture videos, as well as of videos of student symposium keynotes and selected seminars. This dataset includes basic information such as lecturer's name, affiliation, date, talk title and newly prepared 100-word summaries and keywords for each talk.

Nine CIRMMT graduate students were hired to watch from 4 to 6 videos each and prepare the required information for each video. After receiving the data from each student, the administrator verified the consistency across the various contributions, aiming to achieve a coherent description of the videos.

2.2   Homogenizing Keywords

A complex issue when describing information, notably in interdisciplinary research, is to select an optimal number of keywords to describe each item uniquely and, at the same time, restrict the number of choices to a minimum. For our prototype, a list of keywords was created taking into account a balanced distribution of topics for each research axis, with 5 or 6 keywords per axis.

In the current implementation of the visualization, each DL is associated with only one keyword, a choice needed to facilitate the implementation of the visualization, though a simplification considering the interdisciplinary nature of the talks. On the other hand, research axes do share keywords (Table 1).

Table 1. Choice of keywords per research axis.

Research axis	Keywords
RA1	Audio processing, Computer music systems, Musical acoustics & instruments, New interfaces for musical expression, Room acoustics
RA2	Audio processing, Computer music systems, Music information retrieval, Music theory, Musicology
RA3	Composition, Movement, Music performance & education, Music theory, Neurosciences, Perception & cognition
RA4	Composition, Computer music systems, Music performance & education, Music production, Musicology, Perception & cognition

3   Improving Video Production, Edition and Visibility

As previously mentioned, though filming of the DL series has been implemented early on, videos were mainly aimed for archiving. To make the talks openly available and take into account the constant increase of the video collection, apart from inherent copyright issues, a few other actions were needed:

– Improve on the quality of the videos.
– Streamline the editing of video recordings.
– Increase visibility of the collection.

3.1   Video Production and Editing

Improving the limited quality of the videos was mostly solved with a simple administrative decision: move the DL series to an auditorium already equipped with theatrical lights[6]. To streamline the editing of the recordings, it was decided to hire CIRMMT students to both film the talks and later edit the videos right after they were recorded, speeding up the whole process[7] (Fig. 3).

(a) Early recording example, lecture by Butch Rovan, January 2008.

(b) Example of setup after 2012, lecture by Ed Campion, February 2016.

Fig. 3. Screen shots of two distinguished lectures eight years apart.

Since 2013, the talks take place at McGill University's Tanna Schulich Hall, a 170-seat auditorium equipped with theatrical lights that are easily adjusted to fit the needs of the DL series. While keeping the original two-camera setup, a dedicated video feed for the slides was added to the recordings so that slides can be easily read. Finally, CIRMMT also provides courses to students on how

---

[6] Issues such as the availability of theatrical lighting for videos were not initially considered. The result was that sometimes the speaker was barely seen in the videos due to the high intensity of the slide projector. Similarly, given that the talks typically took place in the late afternoon in a room with several windows, daylight changes between the beginning and the end of the talks did cause drastic light variations.
[7] Until then, students filming the lectures did it in a volunteer basis. Editing of the early recordings was mostly done by the CIRMMT administrator or by a professional editor.

to operate the cameras and edit the videos, with the added benefit of offering them training that can be useful for their careers.

The result is that the quality of the videos has skyrocketed and now the Centre has a proven, streamlined procedure to film and make edits to the talks which become available in a short lapse of time. Furthermore, dozens of students have received training and have done a professional-level job editing the various videos.

3.2   Visibility of the Collection

Though in itself a useful tool, the CIRMMT webpage displaying the list of videos is certainly of limited use, cf. Fig. 2, calling for a better solution to help navigate the video collection in the form a visualization of its main characteristics.

A more complex issue is the wide variability in the number of views for the different videos, as seen in Fig. 1. While some of the lectures have excellent visibility (i.e. sometimes way more than ten thousand views), others are not well-known, with only a few hundred views each.

Clearly, this discrepancy does not correlate to variations in the quality of, or interest in, the different lectures. Rather, it seemed clear that access to the talks is overwhelmingly based on YouTube recommendation, not from the CIRMMT homepage. This situation brings both advantages, e.g. academic talks might get visibility that greatly overdoes typical academic video views, and drawbacks, in this case the fact that viewers who arrive at a given lecture do not necessarily learn about the others.

One of the main goals of the visualization tool is to provide a more user-friendly way of discovering the DL videos, helping viewers get a better sense of the richness of the information available in the DL series as a whole.

4   Visualization Iterations

Information visualization is a well established research field. Decades ago, Card, MacKinlay and Schneiderman edited an overview of seminal works in information visualization [2]. Though more recently works provided guidelines to carefully design information visualizations, e.g. [8], making sense of available data visualization techniques and tools can still be a complex endeavour [4].

Our dataset is composed of video recording of lectures, associated with textual metadata, partially obtained through manual annotation. Creating techniques and tools to browse and analyse these diverse types of data requires combining knowledge from research communities such as multimedia information retrieval, text mining, and natural language processing; human-computer interaction, information visualization, and search user interfaces [3]. Previous works addressing similar topics include those by Schoeffmann et al. [6], who recently surveyed tools for video interaction including browsers with visual displays and by Kucher and Kerren [5], who proposed a taxonomy of visualization techniques specific to textual datasets.

4.1 Initial Prototypes

Initial explorations with visualizations for CIRMMT DL videos were made during McGill's Music Technology graduate seminar MUMT 620 in the winter of 2019. A class assignment was proposed in which groups of students should devise and implement visualizations for the distinguished lecture dataset. Initial visualization strategies included a Sunburst [7], shown in Fig. 4, and a Dendrogram, shown in Fig. 5.

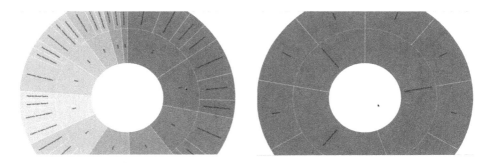

Fig. 4. Sunburst visualization of distinguished lectures.

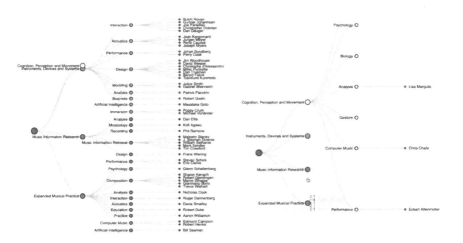

Fig. 5. Dendrogram visualization of distinguished lectures.

4.2   Current Prototype

After discussing the pros and cons of the initial prototypes, a third visualization technique was chosen, featuring a hierarchical bubble chart[8], as seen in Fig. 6. In this visualization, at the first viewing level, dark circles represent the four CIRMMT research axes and are not interactive.

Chosen keywords appear in brighter circles that can be clicked upon. The relationship between the keywords and their associated axes is indicated by traces uniting keywords to axes when the cursor passes over the corresponding area in the visualization.

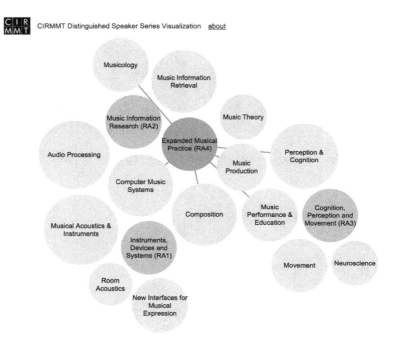

Fig. 6. The hierarchical bubble chart visualization of the DL series. Darker circles indicate CIRMMT research axes, while brighter ones are associated with keywords. In this case, as the cursor was placed on top of the dark circle representing RA4, related keywords are shown connected to it.

When clicking on a given keyword circle, another view appears (2nd level) showing the chosen keyword in the centre of the screen with its associated talks around it. Information displayed for each talk include speaker name, talk title and date, as well as the current number of views in YouTube. Examples of two keywords with their associated talks are shown in Fig. 7.

---

[8] The visualization tool is available from http://www.cirmmt.org/video.

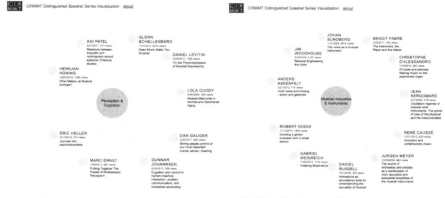

(a) Perception & cognition.   (b) Musical acoustics & instruments.

Fig. 7. Examples of keywords-based lists of lectures.

When in the second level, by clicking on a bubble representing a talk, the YouTube video of the talk appears on the right of the screen and includes the information already displayed around the bubble (talk), plus the speaker affiliation and the 100-word summary of the talk. Once here, the talk is visible as an embedded YouTube video (Fig. 8).

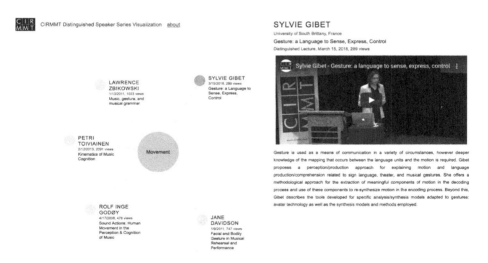

Fig. 8. The final level of the visualization showing the talks associated with a chosen keyword on the left and on the right the video and information of a specific talk chosen (darker bubble).

By clicking on the keyword at the second level, the user is taken back to the first level where they can start again exploring the set of keywords.

5   Prototype Implementation

The visualization is implemented in JavaScript using the data visualization library d3.js [1], which is a Document Object Model (DOM) manipulation library that allows for generating data-driven documents and visualizations.

The visualization is based on a force directed graph layout provided by the module *d3-force*. The module implements a force simulation and provides parameters for charge, link, center, and collision forces. These parameters were hand-tuned to match the visualization.

The video dataset is stored in a file with comma-separated values, which is loaded into an array containing all the nodes in the graph. The links between the nodes are created by iterating through the nodes, adding a link for each connection. This results in two arrays describing the nodes and links of the graph. The arrays are passed to the *forceSimulation* of the d3-force function which generates the coordinates for each node and link. The node array is also passed to the *select* function of d3, which generates a Simple Vector Graphics (SVG) group for each node. A circle is drawn in each group along with a text label. As SVG doesn't support text wrapping, the label is attached as a HTML tag using the *foreignObject* tag of SVG, which allows for embedding HTML in a SVG drawing. For animating the shapes, the object returned from the *forceSimulation* function provides the *tick* event that updates the coordinates of the nodes and links at each frame.

The search functionality is implemented using fuse.js, a JavaScript fuzzy-search library. The data from the .csv file is passed to a *Fuse* object along with the search options such as which keys to search in. The searchable keys are

- Lecture title
- Lecturer
- Topic
- Keywords
- Summary
- Affiliation
- Country

The search is executed when the user releases a key on the keyboard using the *search* function of the Fuse object. The video player is embedded using the YouTube Player API, and the video view count is obtained by sending a request to the YouTube Data API. The source code for the visualization is released under the MIT License at https://github.com/IDMIL/CIRMMT_visualizations (Fig. 9).

Search for lecturers, topics, affiliation, country, etc.

Latest videos (5 of 83)

SUSAN ROGERS
November 21, 2019
Music psychology for record makers

CLAUDE CELLIER
October 24, 2019
Trust your ears! The quest for the optimum (digital)
audio representation

ELEANOR SELFRIDGE-FIELD
September 19, 2019
Ear - Mind - Brain: The mysteries of musical similarity

GASCIA OUZOUNIAN
May 9, 2019
Acoustic defence and technologies of listening during
the First World War

JOEL CHADABE
May 2, 2019
Music as emergence

Fig. 9. The right side of the initial visualization screen, when the page is loaded. It shows a space for entering text to be searched as well as the latest videos uploaded in reverse chronological order. Screenshot taken on January 27, 2020.

6   Conclusions and Future Work

This paper presented a visualization tool created to help explore the talks in CIRMMT's Distinguished Lecture Series, a collection of more than 70 videos of leading scholars and artists discussing their work.

After reviewing the DL series characteristics and evolution over time, different visualizations were proposed to help present the talks in a coherent way, allowing viewers to navigate in the video collection. Finally, a detailed description of a fully functional visualization prototype featuring an hierarchical bubble chart is discussed in detail.

Since its completion in the summer of 2019, the visualization tool has been used by the CIRMMT community showing the potential as an entry door to the richness of the content in the DL video series.

6.1   Future Work

Several improvements are currently planned:

- More advanced choice of keywords. While the present choice of keywords solved our initial needs, for a more advanced solution a novel set of keywords should be selected in collaboration with the staff at the McGill Music Library to ensure coherence and homogeneity.
- Other visualization techniques. The exploration of other visualization possibilities should be carried out to eventually find more adapted techniques to display the contents of the DL series.
- Automatic extraction of features from videos and their transcriptions. Automatic extraction of features can provide a more adapted way to obtain meaningful information to populate the dataset, reduce the manual workload to create metadata associated to the videos, and inform their browsing.

Acknowledgments. The CIRMMT Distinguished Lecture Series and the visualizations presented in this paper are a joint effort of dozens of people that started some 15 years ago.

Essential players in establishing and maintaining the DL series include former and current CIRMMT directors & associate directors (Stephen McAdams, Sean Ferguson, Gary Scavone, Isabelle Cossette, Fabrice Marandola, Catherine Guastavino, Jean Piché and Jérémie Voix) and staff (Sara Gomez, Jacqueline Bednar, Julien Boissinot, Yves Méthot, Harold Kilianski and Sylvain Pohu, among others), as well as axis leaders, student representatives and the dozens of students involved in the organization, recording and editing of the lectures, and the creation of the dataset.

Thanks also to the other graduate students who took the seminar MUMT620 in the winter of 2019: Mark Bennett, Mathias Kirkegaard, Josh Rohs and Evan Savage.

Thanks to Michael McGuffin and Guillaume Boutard for many suggestions for future work and to Isabelle Cossette and Jacqueline Bednar for commenting on this manuscript.

Funding allowing for the development of the final visualization prototype was provided through a Natural Sciences and Engineering Research Council of Canada (NSERC) Discovery Grant to the first author.

References

1. Bostock, M., Ogievetsky, V., Heer, J.: D^3 data-driven documents. IEEE Trans. Visual Comput. Graphics **17**(12), 2301–2309 (2011). https://doi.org/10.1109/TVCG.2011.185
2. Card, S.K., MacKinlay, J.D., Schneiderman, B. (eds.): Readings in Information Visualization: Using Vision to Think. Morgan Kaufmann, Burlington (1999)
3. Hearst, M.: Search User Interfaces. Cambridge University Press, Cambridge (2009). https://www.searchuserinterfaces.com
4. Heer, J., Bostock, M., Ogievetsky, V.: A tour through the visualization zoo. Commun. ACM **53**(6), 59–67 (2010). https://doi.org/10.1145/1743546.1743567

5. Kucher, K., Kerren, A.: Text visualization techniques: taxonomy, visual survey, and community insights. In: 2015 IEEE Pacific Visualization Symposium (PacificVis), pp. 117–121 (2015). https://doi.org/10.1109/PACIFICVIS.2015.7156366
6. Schoeffmann, K., Hudelist, M.A., Huber, J.: Video interaction tools: a survey of recent work. ACM Comput. Surv. **48**(1) (2015). https://doi.org/10.1145/2808796
7. Stasko, J., Catrambone, R., Guzdial, M., McDonald, K.: An evaluation of space-filling information visualizations for depicting hierarchical structures. Int. J. Hum.-Comput. Stud. **53**(5), 663–694 (2000). https://doi.org/10.1006/ijhc.2000.0420
8. Ware, C.: Information Visualization: Perception for Design. Interactive Technologies, 3rd edn. Morgan Kaufmann, Burlington (2012)

Gender Difference in Preference for Apple Watch Dial Interface

Jian Wang[1,2(✉)] and Yen Hsu[1]

[1] The Graduate Institute of Design Science, Tatung University, Taipei 10491, Taiwan
wangjian_168@nuaa.edu.cn
[2] Jincheng College of Nanjing University of Aeronautics and Astronautics, Nanjing 210000, China

Abstract. This study uses the dial interface of Apple Watch Series 5 as a research sample to explore the preferences of different genders for the visual style of the Apple Watch dial interface, and analyze the gender differences in consumer visual perception of the Apple Watch interface. In order to summarize the aesthetic emotions of the visual style of the Apple Watch dial interface by different genders. A total of 114 observers participated in this experiment, and analyzed the experimental data collected from 58 males and 56 females. The single-sample t-test and independent sample t-test results show that the visual style of the Apple Watch dial interface is favored by consumers. In terms of visual aesthetics, compared with females, males have a higher preference for the visual interface of Apple Watch. In addition, it is also speculated that males are more receptive to visually complex interfaces than females. According to the results of regression analysis, male groups tend to be more rational and regular, and prefer technological visual interface; while female groups tend to be more active and sensitive. The simple interface, simple style and diversified functions make female consumers have great fun and practicability, and they pay more attention to intelligent life. This study can help to understand the aesthetic preferences of different gender consumers for the visual interface style of products, and provide design strategies for the interface design of consumer electronic products.

Keywords: Gender difference · Aesthetics · Interface · Apple Watch

1 Introduction

Consumer electronic products are increasingly being used by people. In order to meet the market demand for differentiated or segmented consumer electronic products, the company is paying more and more attention to the market positioning of products. Apple's consumer electronic products are good at grasping fashion trends and leading fashion. For example, the Apple Watch is equipped with a choice case and a matching band. The style is available to consumers to meet the needs of the segmented market. Furthermore, because different consumer groups have different consumer psychologies and behaviors, they show various preferences for consumer electronic products. Previous studies have suggested that male group tends to be more rational and regular in consumer

S. Yamamoto and H. Mori (Eds.): HCII 2020, LNCS 12184, pp. 170–182, 2020.
https://doi.org/10.1007/978-3-030-50020-7_11

behaviors, while female group is more sensitive with active thinking and strong initiative in consumer behaviors [1]. Moreover, female group prefers to pursue fashion and novelty, purchase some new products and try new life. Therefore, gender is one of the important influencing factors in the individual's visual cognition. In addition, gender differences are one of the most common forms of segmentation used by marketers. Gender differences in consumer behavior, though recognized as an important topic, have attracted only limited research attention. This study helps to fill this gap and combines consumers' preference for aesthetic emotion, which is emerging as a valuable theoretical perspective in the field of marketing.

Consumer electronic products, especially smartwatches, are considered a new fashion in the minds of consumers. Watches are commonly worn as an adornment, so a smartwatch with a pleasingly aesthetic design will attract more consumer attention [2]. Recent evidence indicates that smartwatches have been marketed as devices that allow for the presentation of information in a manner that is simple and easier to access than smartphones [3]. Based on the consumer's perspective, such experience plays a fundamental role in determining their preferences, which then influence their purchase decisions [4]. The Apple Watch Series 5, unveiled at Apple's 2019 autumn press event, is not significantly different from its predecessor in terms of the interface design, with all the dials adjusted for the new display. The press event also launched different styles such as Nike and Hermès, targeting consumer groups that like sports or consumers who prefer fashion life. On the latest Apple Watch Series 5, its dial is filled with a lot of information, all graphically and in colorful colors, making full use of the dial space and corner, though complicated without being too crowded. In addition, the color and materials of the case and band are significantly more abundant than before to meet the aesthetic needs of different consumer groups.

So far, although there have been many researches on smartwatches, few researchers have experimentally explored the visual preferences of smartwatch dial interfaces from the perspective of gender based on the factors of visual aesthetics, and there is little information about the gender-specific preference of user interface design. Therefore, this study responds to this gap, and taking the dial interface of Apple Watch Series 5 as a research sample to explore the preferences of different genders for the visual style of the Apple Watch dial interface, and analyze the gender differences in consumer visual perception of the Apple Watch interface. In order to summarize the aesthetic emotions of the visual style of the Apple Watch dial interface by different genders. As discussed by Bezruczko and Schroeder (1996), preference for visual stimuli is important theoretically because preference has been linked to personality positioning, consumer behavior, and adaptive capacity, which then affect their purchasing decisions [5]. In addition, due to Apple still does not allow the use of third-party dial interfaces. Therefore, it is necessary to study the gender differences in the visual aesthetic perception of the Apple Watch interface, and provide a reasonable and effective basis for the interface designer to develop graphical user interface of smartwatch in the future.

2 Literature Review

2.1 Smart Watch Definition and Related Research

Smartwatches are considered as a new technology in the mind of consumers. Despite the wide use of technology adoption's theories to investigate new technologies, limited research has been devoted so far to analysis consumers' adoption of smart wearable devices [6]. The academic literature does not provide a well-accepted definition of smartwatch. According to Dehghani (2018), we can define the smartwatch as a multi-functional wrist-worn device that provides a convenient, fast access to data and applications via short-range wireless Bluetooth connection with a paired smartphone [6]. Jung, Kim, and Choi (2016) found that aesthetic appeal has a significant positive impact on consumers' intention to adopt smartwatches [7]. Smartwatches have come to the forefront as not only the next killer product following smartphones but also the first popularized wearable device. In the mature diffusion stage, diversified designs are required to meet the aesthetic needs of consumers, and the details of design factors may affect consumers' decision to purchase smartwatches as well as other wearables [7]. The aesthetics of the product's appearance is an important factor influencing the acceptance of new technologies [8, 9]. When consumers judge their aesthetic value, they even decide whether to buy or not. Since watches can be used to signify status and are worn on body, smartwatch designers should pay more attention to design aesthetics than smartphone device designers do [6]. Design aesthetics has the strongest direct impact on the attitude towards using smartwatches, and also has a positive impact on social values [10]. Hsiao et al. (2013, 2018) defined the convenience of graphical user interface as the extent to which a user believes that the vendor's smartwatches can provide an efficient and easy user–system interaction. They believe that interface convenience plays an important role in attracting users to adopt smartwatch technology and enhancing users' positive feelings. If users feel that the smartwatch interface is convenient, they will have a better impression of the device [10, 11].

2.2 Gender Difference

Gender is one of the important factors in the individual cognitive process. Psychologists have long been concerned about gender differences in visual cognition. Research results of Collins and Kimura (1997) show that compared with females, males are more dominant in visual spatial tasks [12]. However, Researchers such as Herlitz (1997) found that females had an advantage in episodic memory tasks [13]. Feng et al. (2007) studied gender differences in spatial attention allocation, and females were superior to males in spatial attention and psychological activity tasks [14]. However, some researchers have suggested that gender differences do not necessarily exist in the process of visual cognition. For example, in a recent study, Notarnicola et al. (2014) studied the gender difference in visual spatial ability between volleyball and tennis players and non-athletes, and the results showed that males in non-athletes' groups performed better than females, while there was no significant gender difference in trained tennis and volleyball players [15]. Gender differences have always been an important research topic in various academic fields. But studies on gender differences in visual preferences are rare. Many researchers believe that the characteristics of things (such as color, brightness, and brightness) lead to visual search, which in turn leads to preferences for visual stimuli [16]. As subjects of the test, the visual differences of population variables and gender factors will inevitably affect their preferences. However, there is no clear conclusion as to whether gender factors are significantly different in user interface design.

3 Methods

3.1 Semantic Scales of Aesthetic Emotion

The semantic scale of aesthetic emotion in this study refers to scholars' literature research on smartwatch. From the hedonic perspective, users may see smartwatches with large screens as more attractive than those with small screens [17]. Individuals are drawn to objects that appear aesthetically pleasing [18]. This is especially true for smartwatches, while people buy watches to tell time, the number one criterion in choosing a smartwatch for most people is how it will look [17]. Smartwatch screens may serve as an aesthetic or novelty cue that triggers the coolness heuristic, i.e., "a conscious acknowledgment of the hipness of the digital device suggested by its newer modalities" [19]. Pleasing aesthetics have a positive impact on consumer acceptance, especially in today's market, where fashion and product design are important aspects of personal feeling formation. In the case of smartwatches, fashionability can be defined as an individual's perception towards the fashion aspects (design, uniqueness, size, etc.) of smartwatches for using in every occasion and activity [6]. Choi and Kim (2016) believes that smartwatches are fashion products and are more likely to be seen as luxury goods. And, according to their model, fashion factors play an important role in understanding how consumers respond to smartwatches [20]. The uniqueness of a smartwatch will influence users' positive attitude toward the product. Moreover, the uniqueness can satisfy the need of self-expression and enhance social values [10]. Hong, Lin, and Hsieh (2017) believe that the simplicity of smartwatches should be paid attention to according to the specific situation of using smartwatches or different research objectives [21]. Researchers such as Jung et al. (2016) believe that it is necessary to study the influence of more detailed design factors on consumers' recognition of smartwatches and wearables [7]. Lu and Chang (2013) focused on the design framework of watch appearance and applied it to the analysis between watch appearance design and aesthetic emotion on the basis of Kansei Engineering, to explore the difference of aesthetic emotion between groups of high and low age and groups of males and females [22]. Table 1 shows 10 semantic scales of aesthetic emotions collected from references.

3.2 Sample Selection

The sample for this study is the dial interface in Apple Watch Series 5, and the sample is from the user manual on the official website of Apple Watch (https://support.apple.com/zh-tw/guide/watch/apd6ce85daf4/watchos). There are a total of 26 surface categories of Apple Watch. For each category, select the dial graph shown in the Apple Watch user manual. The size and proportion of 26 dial interface samples are the same (see Fig. 1).

Table 1. 10 semantic scales of aesthetic emotions collected from references

Semantic scales of aesthetic emotions	Author(s)	Year
Complex-simple	Lu and Zhang	2013
Traditional-modern	Lu and Zhang	2013
Popular-unique	Hsiao and Chen; Dehghani	2017, 2018
Crowded-spacious	Lu and Zhang	2013
Serious-entertaining	Kim	2017
Retro-fashionable	Sundar; Bajarin; Choi and Kim	2008, 2014, 2016
Luxurious-minimalist	Lu and Zhang; Hong et al.	2013, 2017
Multifunctional-single	Lu and Zhang	2013
Archaic-technological	Lu and Zhang	2013
Unrecognizable-recognizable	Jung, Kim, and Choi	2016

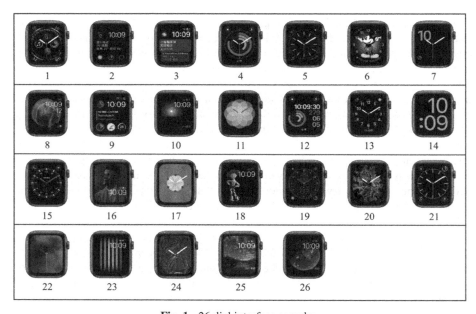

Fig. 1. 26 dial interface samples.

3.3 Test Procedure

Test Terms and Scales. In this study, 10 semantic scales of aesthetic emotions were selected from the references and semantic words of "dislike-like" were included to measure the preference of the observers. On the 7-step scale used in the test, a score of 1 indicates the high intensity of aesthetic emotion on the left side, and a score of 7 indicates the high intensity of aesthetic emotion on the right side. The ten semantic scales of aesthetic emotions are presented in Chinese during the experiment. An English translation of the ten scales is shown in Table 2.

Table 2. Ten semantic scales of aesthetic emotions.

Chinese	English	Chinese	English
1. 复杂的-简单的	Complex-simple	2. 传统的-现代的	Traditional-modern
3. 大众的-独特的	Popular-unique	4. 拥挤的-宽敞的	Crowded-spacious
5. 严肃的-娱乐的	Serious-entertaining	6. 复古的-时尚的	Retro-fashionable
7. 奢华的-简约的	Luxurious-minimalist	8. 多功能的-单一性的	Multifunctional-single
9. 古老感的-科技感的	Archaic-technological	10. 难识别的-易识别的	Unrecognizable-recognizable

Display. This study used two Apple 27-inch iMacs (model: MD095CH/A) as the display. The two monitors were under the same indoor environment and light source. During the experiment, other interference factors were avoided, and the same brightness and display calibration was set for the two monitors. During the test, an image was displayed for 10 s to avoid interference with the next image.

Observers. A total of 114 observers tested in this study were trained in graphic design, 58 males and 56 females, aged 22–41 years old, all with professional backgrounds related to visual communication design.

During the test, each observer was asked to sit in front of a monitor that was placed approximately 55 cm away from him/her. Each observer then rated his/her preference of the 26 Apple Watch dial interface.

4   Results and Discussion

4.1   Overall Preferences of the Sample

From the average of the overall preference of male and female samples, as shown in Table 3, the highest preference for males and females is sample 10. Surprisingly, the lowest preference for males and females is sample 17. According to the previous research on the interface of the Apple Watch dial, the dial interface of sample 10 has a simple visual style and related functions, while the dial interface of sample 17 has high visual complexity and single function. Compare respectively the gender differences in preferences between sample 10 and sample 17 by The Semantic Differential Scale (SD), as shown in Fig. 2. The overall trend of the blue and red lines of sample 10 is close, and the difference is not significant, indicating that males and females have similar aesthetic emotion towards the dial interface, and both prefer a dial interface that is simple in visual style and has related functions. Moreover, sample 10 has a concise visual style with moderate visual complexity, and can convey effective information more reasonably within the limited interface space. However, the function of the dial interface of sample 17 is too singular. It can be seen from the SD that males and females have similar aesthetic emotion towards the dial interface, and only significant differences are shown on the "traditional-modern" semantic scales. The sample takes the "Kaleidoscope" as the dial background. The "Kaleidoscope" has a neat and orderly beauty, concealing the rational logic to the structure of the spatial order, achieving a constant and quiet regularity and beauty. Wang and Shan (2017) believe that male group tends to be more rational and regular in consumer behaviors, while female group is more sensitive with active thinking and strong initiative in consumer behaviors [1]. Therefore, the male group believes that sample 17 is more modern and rational, while the female group believes that it reflects the traditional rhythm aesthetic.

Table 3. Independent Sample t-Test.

SAM	GEN	M	SD	t	df	p	SAM	GEN	M	SD	t	df	p
1	MA	4.38	1.72	3.633	102.198	0.000*	14	MA	4.91	1.72	2.580	112.000	0.011*
	FMA	3.38	1.20					FMA	4.11	1.61			
2	MA	4.81	1.30	0.873	112.000	0.384	15	MA	4.88	1.33	2.981	112.000	0.004*
	FMA	4.59	1.40					FMA	4.13	1.38			
3	MA	4.93	1.47	0.886	112.000	0.377	16	MA	4.52	1.68	1.439	112.000	0.153
	FMA	4.70	1.35					FMA	4.07	1.63			
4	MA	5.12	1.48	3.197	112.000	0.002*	17	MA	4.26	1.81	3.168	112.000	0.002*
	FMA	4.25	1.43					FMA	3.23	1.64			
5	MA	5.41	1.32	1.037	112.000	0.302	18	MA	4.41	1.62	0.665	112.000	0.507
	FMA	5.18	1.08					FMA	4.23	1.26			
6	MA	4.16	2.03	0.542	112.000	0.589	19	MA	5.22	1.23	2.021	112.000	0.046*
	FMA	3.96	1.71					FMA	4.73	1.37			
7	MA	5.26	1.60	1.712	112.000	0.090	20	MA	4.36	1.67	3.606	112.000	0.000*
	FMA	4.75	1.58					FMA	3.23	1.67			
8	MA	5.16	1.45	1.860	112.000	0.065	21	MA	4.95	1.25	0.887	112.000	0.377
	FMA	4.61	1.69					FMA	4.75	1.13			
9	MA	4.38	1.74	2.408	112.000	0.018*	22	MA	4.90	1.57	0.612	112.000	0.542
	FMA	3.66	1.43					FMA	4.71	1.60			
10	MA	5.62	1.12	0.840	112.000	0.403	23	MA	4.76	1.44	3.658	112.000	0.000*
	FMA	5.45	1.09					FMA	3.80	1.34			
11	MA	4.79	1.58	1.807	112.000	0.073	24	MA	4.66	1.49	2.191	112.000	0.031*
	FMA	4.23	1.74					FMA	4.04	1.53			
12	MA	4.53	1.67	2.230	103.813	0.028*	25	MA	4.81	1.48	3.250	112.000	0.002*
	FMA	3.93	1.20					FMA	3.89	1.53			
13	MA	5.07	1.36	1.228	112.000	0.222	26	MA	4.91	1.38	2.917	112.000	0.004*
	FMA	4.77	1.25					FMA	4.18	1.31			

Note: SAM- sample; GEN- gender; MA- males; FMA- Females
*$p < 0.05$.

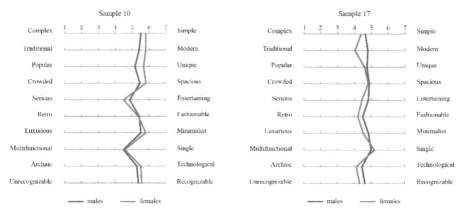

Fig. 2. The Semantic Differential Scale of sample 10 and 17.

With the increase of elements such as icons or symbols, it is easy to improve the visual complexity of the graphical user interface, and increase the negative effects such as long search time, operation errors, and user burden. Visual complexity has a certain impact on visual stimuli perception, which increases the user's muscle tension and cognitive load, reduces the pleasure of interaction, the visual aesthetics and usability of the user interface. Therefore, a graphical user interface with appropriate visual complexity tends to have higher aesthetics, usability, and accessibility, resulting in higher user satisfaction [23]. This is consistent with Berlyne's aesthetic theory that complexity plays a crucial role in the perception of visual stimuli, showing an inverted U-shaped curve [24]. Berlyne proposed that aesthetic appraisal is determined by the arousal potential of an object. The psychobiological theory posits that objects with a moderate arousal potential result in the most favorable response in a perceiver, whereas stimuli with either a very low or a very high arousal potential are perceived as being unpleasant [25]. Therefore, the appropriate combination of visual information in the dial interface not only reduces consumers' fear of information overload, but also increases the possibility of their positive emotional response.

4.2   Gender Differences in Visual Style Preferences

One-Sample t-Test. This study used a 7-point scale in the experimental test, so 4 points represent the neutrality of preference. A one-sample t-test was used to analyze the observer's preference for the dial interface, as shown in Table 4. The averages of 7 samples (Sample 1/6/9/12/16/17/20) are close to 4 ($p > 0.05$), with no significant difference. However, the averages of sample 1 (t (113) = -0.78; $p = 0.437$), 17 (t (113) = -1.46; $p = 0.147$) and 20 (t (113) = -1.17; $p = 0.244$) are all less than 4, indicating that observers have a lower preference for this dial interfaces. The averages of the other 4 samples are greater than 4, indicating that observers have a higher preference. In addition, the averages of the preferences of the other 19 samples (Sample 2/3/4/5/7/8/10/11/13/14/15/18/19/21/22/23/24/25/26) have significant differences. On the whole, the averages of the 19 samples with significant differences are significantly higher than 4, showing that both males and females prefer these dial interfaces. In general, the visual style of the Apple Watch dial interface is still very satisfactory. The quality and performance of Apple's products are usually superior to those of other brands' products, so that the relative advantage can be favored by more consumers.

Table 4. One-Sample t-Test.

Sample	M	SD	t	df	p	Sample	M	SD	t	df	p
1	3.89	1.56	−0.78	113	0.437	14	4.52	1.71	3.23	113	0.002*
2	4.70	1.35	5.55	113	0.000*	15	4.51	1.40	3.89	113	0.000*
3	4.82	1.41	6.17	113	0.000*	16	4.30	1.66	1.92	113	0.058
4	4.69	1.51	4.89	113	0.000*	17	3.75	1.80	−1.46	113	0.147
5	5.30	1.21	11.44	113	0.000*	18	4.32	1.45	2.38	113	0.019*
6	4.06	1.87	0.35	113	0.727	19	4.98	1.32	7.97	113	0.000*
7	5.01	1.60	6.74	113	0.000*	20	3.81	1.76	−1.17	113	0.244
8	4.89	1.59	5.95	113	0.000*	21	4.85	1.19	7.62	113	0.000*
9	4.03	1.63	0.17	113	0.863	22	4.81	1.58	5.44	113	0.000*
10	5.54	1.11	14.81	113	0.000*	23	4.29	1.47	2.11	113	0.037*
11	4.52	1.67	3.30	113	0.001*	24	4.35	1.53	2.44	113	0.016*
12	4.24	1.48	1.71	113	0.091	25	4.36	1.57	2.45	113	0.016*
13	4.92	1.31	7.50	113	0.000*	26	4.55	1.39	4.25	113	0.000*

*$p < 0.05$.

Independent Sample t-Test. In this study, the scale of "dislike-like" was used in the experimental test to judge the preferences of observers for different dial interfaces. An independent sample t-test was used to analyze the gender differences of preferences for 26 samples, as shown in Table 3. The preference of different genders for the 13 samples (Sample 2/3/5/6/7/8/10/11/13/16/18/21/22) showed no significant difference ($p > 0.05$), indicating that different genders had the same preferences for them. However, the preference of different genders for the other 13 samples were significant ($p < 0.05$), which means that different genders have significant differences in the preference of the 13 dial interfaces. Judging from the 13 different dial interfaces, these dial interfaces usually consist of multiple icons, text, or control elements. The proper combination of the visual information of these dial interfaces as a whole is more complicated and has more functions. Therefore, the male group prefers more functional dial interfaces than the female group. It can also be speculated that in visual aesthetics, males are more likely to accept interfaces with higher visual complexity than females. But there is no empirical research to prove this. And importantly, what we found from the data is that the average level of preference of the male group is higher than the female group. Even when there was no significant difference, the average level of preference of the male group is slightly higher than that of the female group. Males are generally more technology and females more fashion-focused [26]. Therefore, compared with females, males have a higher preference for the visual interface of Apple Watch.

Regression Analysis. Multivariate linear regression analysis was performed on the data collected by male and female observers, respectively with "dislike-like" as the dependent variable and 10 semantic scales of aesthetic emotions as the independent variable. Table 5 shows the analysis results of male observers, and the adjusted coefficient of determination ($R^2 = 0.605$) indicates that the regression equation can explain the high variation of "dislike-like". In ANOVA's analysis ($F = 13.751$, $p < 0.001$), there was a significant linear regression relationship between "unrecognizable-recognizable" (x_1), "archaic-technological" (x_2), "serious-entertaining" (x_3) and "dislike-like" (y), and the regression equation was significantly valid. Moreover, the three independent variables of "unrecognizable-recognizable" ($p = 0.001$), "archaic-technological" ($p = 0.002$) and "serious-entertaining" ($p = 0.019$) are significant by t-Test. The regression equation can be established as follows: $y = 1.214 + 0.544x_1 + 0.551x_2 - 0.386x_3$. It indicates that the male preference for the visual style of Apple Watch dial interface has a positive linear correlation with "unrecognizable-recognizable" (x_1) and "archaic-technological" (x_2), while it has a negative linear correlation with "serious-entertaining" (x_3).

Table 5. Analysis results of male observers.

Coefficients[a]

Model		Unstandardized coefficients		Standardized coefficients	t	p
		B	Std. Error	Beta		
1	(Constant)	1.520	0.873		1.741	0.094
	Unrecognizable-recognizable	0.663	0.175	0.611	3.784	0.001*
2	(Constant)	−0.560	1.022		−0.548	0.589
	Unrecognizable-recognizable	0.567	0.155	0.523	3.663	0.001*
	Archaic-technological	0.525	0.174	0.431	3.016	0.006*
3	(Constant)	1.214	1.157		1.049	0.306
	Unrecognizable-recognizable	0.544	0.140	0.501	3.891	0.001*
	Archaic-technological	0.551	0.157	0.452	3.511	0.002*
	Serious-entertaining	−0.386	0.153	−0.319	−2.528	0.019*

a. Dependent Variable: dislike-like
*$p < 0.05$.

Table 6 shows the analysis results of female observers, from which it can be seen that two sets of regression models can be established. For one thing, the adjusted coefficient of determination ($R^2 = 0.541$) indicates that the regression equation can explain the high variation of "dislike-like". In ANOVA's analysis ($F = 15.732$, $p < 0.001$), there was a significant linear regression relationship between "luxurious-minimalist" (x_1), "multifunctional-single" (x_2) and "dislike-like" (y), and the regression equation was significantly valid. Moreover, the two independent variables of "luxurious-minimalist" ($p < 0.001$) and "multifunctional-single" ($p = 0.006$) are significant by t-Test. The regression equation can be established as follows: y = 0.645 + 0.999x_1 − 0.317x_2. It indicates that female preference for the visual style of Apple Watch dial interface has a positive linear correlation with "luxurious-minimalist" (x_1), while it has a negative linear correlation with "multifunctional-single" (x_2).

Table 6. Analysis results of female observers.

Coefficients[a]

Model		Unstandardized coefficients		Standardized coefficients	t	p
		B	Std. Error	Beta		
1	(Constant)	0.727	0.866		0.840	0.409
	Luxurious-minimalist	0.703	0.172	0.641	4.089	0.000*
2	(Constant)	0.645	0.750		0.860	0.399
	Luxurious-minimalist	0.999	0.178	0.911	5.608	0.000*
	Multifunctional-single	−0.317	0.105	−0.490	−3.016	0.006*
3	(Constant)	2.113	0.707		2.987	0.007*
	Luxurious-minimalist	0.072	0.281	0.066	0.256	0.800
	Multifunctional-single	−0.518	0.098	−0.802	−5.261	0.000*
	Complex-simple	0.845	0.221	1.128	3.823	0.001*
4	(Constant)	2.263	0.388		5.826	0.000*
	Multifunctional-single	−0.524	0.094	−0.811	−5.577	0.000*
	Complex-simple	0.894	0.109	1.193	8.208	0.000*

a. Dependent Variable: dislike-like
*$p < 0.05$.

Second, the adjusted coefficient of determination ($R^2 = 0.723$) indicates that the regression equation can explain the high variation of "dislike-like". In ANOVA's analysis ($F = 33.689$, $p < 0.001$), there was a significant linear regression relationship between "complex-simple" (x_1), "multifunctional-single" (x_2) and "dislike-like" (y), and the regression equation was significantly valid. Moreover, the two independent variables of "complex-simple" ($p < 0.001$) and "multifunctional-single" ($p < 0.001$) are significant by t-Test. The regression equation can be established as follows: y = 2.263 + 0.894x_3 − 0.524x_2. It indicates that female preference for the visual style of the Apple Watch dial interface has a positive linear correlation with "complex-simple" (x_1), while it has a negative linear correlation with "multifunctional-single" (x_2).

Multiple regression analysis was conducted to analyze the preferences of different genders for the visual style of the Apple Watch dial interface. The results showed that in the regression model for male observers, "unrecognizable-recognizable", "archaic-technological" and "serious-entertaining" had significant effects on preferences. The more recognizable, technological and serious visual style of the Apple Watch dial interface, the more males like it. In the regression model for female observers, "luxurious-minimalist", "complex-simple" and "multifunctional-single" had significant effects on preferences. The more minimalist, simple and multifunctional visual style of the Apple Watch dial interface, the more females like it. Therefore, this is consistent with the results of Wang and Shan (2017) [1], the male group tends to be more rational and regular and prefer technological visual interface; however, the female group tends to be active and sensitive, and pay more attention to intelligent life. Simple interface, minimalist style and diversified functions make female consumers get great fun and practicality.

5   Conclusions

This study takes the dial interface of Apple Watch Series 5 as a research sample to explore the preferences of different genders for the visual style of the Apple Watch dial interface, and analyze the gender differences in consumers' visual perception of the Apple Watch interface. In order to summarize the aesthetic emotions of the visual style of the Apple Watch dial interface by different consumer groups. This study can help to understand the aesthetic preferences of different gender consumers for the visual interface style of products, and provide design strategies for the interface design of consumer electronic products. In addition, this study only takes Apple Watch Series 5 as an example, and the research results are consistent with the purposes of this study, but not necessarily for other brands of smartwatches. Future research can explore the visual style of different brands of smartwatches to understand consumers' preferences. And, attention is paid to the preferences of different age groups for the visual style of the dial interface of smartwatches.

References

1. Wang, T., Shan, F.: Research on discussion of gender difference in preference for smart watches based on fuzzy analytic hierarchy process. In: Kurosu, M. (ed.) HCI 2017. LNCS, vol. 10272, pp. 263–275. Springer, Cham (2017). https://doi.org/10.1007/978-3-319-58077-7_21
2. Yang, H., Yu, J., Zo, H., Choi, M.: User acceptance of wearable devices: an extended perspective of perceived value. Telematics Inform. **33**(2), 256–269 (2016)
3. Giang, W.C., Shanti, I., Chen, H.-Y.W., Zhou, A., Donmez, B.: Smartwatches vs. smartphones: a preliminary report of driver behavior and perceived risk while responding to notifications. In: Proceedings of the 7th International Conference on Automotive User Interfaces and Interactive Vehicular Applications, pp 154–161. ACM (2015)
4. Gentile, C., Spiller, N., Noci, G.: How to sustain the customer experience: an overview of experience components that co-create value with the customer. Eur. Manag. J. **25**(5), 395–410 (2007)
5. Bezruczko, N., Schroeder, D.H.: The development of visual preferences in art-trained and non-art-trained schoolchildren. Genet. Soc. Gen. Psychol. Monogr. **122**(2), 179–196 (1996)

6. Dehghani, M.: Exploring the motivational factors on continuous usage intention of smartwatches among actual users. Behav. Inf. Technol. **37**(2), 145–158 (2018)
7. Jung, Y., Kim, S., Choi, B.: Consumer valuation of the wearables: the case of smartwatches. Comput. Hum. Behav. **63**, 899–905 (2016)
8. Cyr, D., Head, M., Ivanov, A.: Design aesthetics leading to m-loyalty in mobile commerce. Inf. Manag. **43**(8), 950–963 (2006)
9. Nanda, P., Bos, J., Kramer, K.-L., Hay, C., Ignacz, J.: Effect of smartphone aesthetic design on users' emotional reaction: an empirical study. TQM J. **20**(4), 348–355 (2008)
10. Hsiao, K.-L., Chen, C.-C.: What drives smartwatch purchase intention? Perspectives from hardware, software, design, and value. Telematics Inform. **35**(1), 103–113 (2018)
11. Hsiao, K.-L.: Android smartphone adoption and intention to pay for mobile Internet: perspectives from software, hardware, design, and value. Libr. Hi Tech **31**(2), 216–235 (2013)
12. Collins, D.W., Kimura, D.: A large sex difference on a two-dimensional mental rotation task. Behav. Neurosci. **111**(4), 845 (1997)
13. Herlitz, A., Nilsson, L.-G., Bäckman, L.: Gender differences in episodic memory. Mem. Cogn. **25**(6), 801–811 (1997)
14. Feng, J., Spence, I., Pratt, J.: Playing an action video game reduces gender differences in spatial cognition. Psychol. Sci. **18**(10), 850–855 (2007)
15. Notarnicola, A., Maccagnano, G., Pesce, V., Tafuri, S., Novielli, G., Moretti, B.: Visual-spatial capacity: gender and sport differences in young Volleyball and Tennis athletes and non-athletes. BMC Res. Notes **7**(1), 57 (2014)
16. Kanan, C., Tong, M.H., Zhang, L., Cottrell, G.W.: SUN: top-down saliency using natural statistics. Vis. Cogn. **17**(6–7), 979–1003 (2009)
17. Kim, K.J.: Shape and size matter for smartwatches: effects of screen shape, screen size, and presentation mode in wearable communication. J. Comput.-Mediated Commun. **22**(3), 124–140 (2017)
18. Dion, K., Berscheid, E., Walster, E.: What is beautiful is good. J. Pers. Soc. Psychol. **24**(3), 285 (1972)
19. Sundar, S.S.: The MAIN model: a heuristic approach to understanding technology effects on credibility. In: Metzger, M.J., Flanagin, A.J. (eds.) Digital media, Youth, and Credibility, pp. 72–100. The MIT Press, Cambridge (2008)
20. Choi, J., Kim, S.: Is the smartwatch an IT product or a fashion product? A study on factors affecting the intention to use smartwatches. Comput. Hum. Behav. **63**, 777–786 (2016)
21. Hong, J.-C., Lin, P.-H., Hsieh, P.-C.: The effect of consumer innovativeness on perceived value and continuance intention to use smartwatch. Comput. Hum. Behav. **67**, 264–272 (2017)
22. Lu, J.-C., Chang, S.-C.: The study of design watch-shape by using Kansei engineering. J. Comm. Modern. **7**(1), 49–69 (2017)
23. Miniukovich, A., Sulpizio, S., De Angeli, A.: Visual complexity of graphical user interfaces. In: Proceedings of the 2018 International Conference on Advanced Visual Interfaces, p. 20. ACM (2018)
24. Berlyne, D.E.: Studies in the New Experimental Aesthetics: Steps Toward an Objective Psychology of Aesthetic Appreciation. Hemisphere (1974)
25. Moshagen, M., Thielsch, M.T.: Facets of visual aesthetics. Int. J. Hum.-Comput. Stud. **68**(10), 689–709 (2010)
26. Chuah, S.H.-W., Rauschnabel, P.A., Krey, N., Nguyen, B., Ramayah, T., Lade, S.: Wearable technologies: the role of usefulness and visibility in smartwatch adoption. Comput. Hum. Behav. **65**, 276–284 (2016)

A Detailed Examination of User Interactions with Two Different Data Interfaces

Rui Wang and Tamara Babaian[✉]

Bentley University, Waltham, MA 02452, USA
{wang_rui,tbabaian}@bentley.edu

Abstract. We present results of a detailed analysis of ten screen capture videos documenting how participants in a laboratory user study used two different interfaces to complete data exploration tasks. Findings presented in this paper include methodological observations as well as those concerning the design of both interfaces. On the methodology side, we demonstrate that observation and analysis of videos that capture how people used a system can uncover aspects of interface learnability, different approaches to problem solving and efficiencies associated with good design. In the context of the two compared interfaces, we document the details of how participants used each interface: the affordances they used and patterns of interface exploration they followed. Combined with the data on task completion time and accuracy, these analyses provide empirical evidence to our assumptions regarding what makes a particular interface efficient. These analyses can greatly inform re-design efforts after pilot evaluations, complementing time and accuracy data. They can also help guide user training and automated user support.

Keywords: Usability · Visualization · Visual interface · Evaluation

1 Intro and Motivation

User interfaces are commonly evaluated in a laboratory setting with the efficacy of an interface assessed based on user performance metrics, such as task completion time and accuracy. In addition to the objective measures, a variety of survey instruments can be used to elicit subjective assessments related to user satisfaction, perceived interface difficulty, cognitive load and other factors. Eye movement and biometric measurements offer a promising approach to investigating the cognitive aspects of interface use, such as attention, situational awareness and others. However, eye movement tracking and biometric tools remain invasive, costly and offer mostly an indirect assessment of the strategies people employ in problem solving. An alternative approach, which is described in this paper, is to perform a close inspection and analysis of system-user interactions, based on the actions taken by users in pursuit of their goals.

In this paper we describe what we have learned via a detailed analysis of videos capturing users' interactions with two different data interfaces: a visual and a tabular one. This analysis revealed patterns of interaction and learning that can be used to

© Springer Nature Switzerland AG 2020
S. Yamamoto and H. Mori (Eds.): HCII 2020, LNCS 12184, pp. 183–197, 2020.
https://doi.org/10.1007/978-3-030-50020-7_12

improve interfaces and guide user training. When combined with objective performance measures, such as task completion time and accuracy, this analysis may offer an empirical basis for explaining performance gains, supporting reasoning about the advantages of one interface over another and helping identify efficiency traps.

1.1 Background

The work presented here originated from an experimental side-by-side comparison of two alternative interfaces AM2.0 [1] and Oracle SQL Developer [2] Reports (henceforth, OR) for working on data exploration and analysis tasks. Both interfaces present views of ternary relationships (i.e. associations of three different entities) and are intended to support reasoning about such associations to solve enterprise tasks. The AM2.0 (see Fig. 1) is a visualization-based interface, while the OR (see Fig. 2) uses the table-based representation of data traditionally employed in the major enterprise systems, such as Oracle, SAP, PeopleSoft and others. In the laboratory user study described in [1], users worked with each of the two interfaces to solve tasks of varying difficulty. The analysis of user performance data along with user responses to the post-usage questionnaire regarding their experiences, has shown statistically significant comparisons in favor of AM2.0 for measurements of time, correctness, and user satisfaction [1]. As a part of this study, we recorded screen capture videos for ten out of forty one participants working with both interfaces.

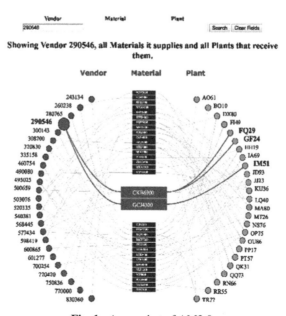

Fig. 1. A snapshot of AM2.0.

We performed a detailed analysis of the ten videos with the purpose of getting some insight into how the users go about solving the tasks using each interface. The analysis

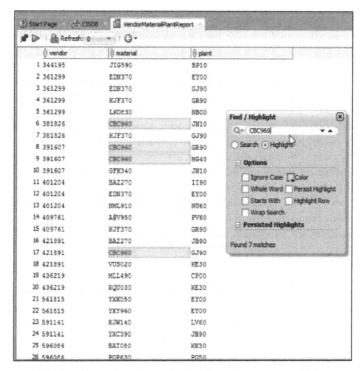

Fig. 2. A snapshot of Oracle SQL Developer Reports (OR).

unveiled certain patterns of interactions that would not be captured using other means of analysis. We present some of the results of this analysis here and argue that this kind of close analysis of interaction data captured in a video is useful for understanding the realities of use of interfaces. Results from close observation of usage videos can suggest explanations for performance gains, inform fine-tuning of the design, and direct user guidance. In the context of this study, our observations of usage videos offered empirical justification to our assumptions regarding what makes the visual interface more effective.

2   Related Work

Former studies undertook systematic reviews of visualization evaluation methods using different approaches. Lam et al. [3] categorize evaluation methods into seven scenarios based on evaluation goals and questions. Furthermore, they present most common evaluation goals and outputs, evaluation questions, and common evaluation methods for each scenario. Work presented in our paper falls under the Evaluating Visual Data Analysis and Reasoning (VDAR) category, as our analysis presented here examines how the visualization tool as a whole supports the analytics and reasoning process. Lam et al. suggest three types of techniques that can be used under the VDAR category, which are

Case Studies, Laboratory Observation and Interviews, and Controlled Experiment, and provide some sample evaluation approaches under each technique. The detailed analysis of coded videos that we report on here adds to the example approaches presented in [3].

Yen and Bakken [4] reviewed and categorized health IT usability study methods into five stages of an integrated usability specification and evaluation framework that was based on a usability model and the system development life cycle (SDLC) – associated stages of evaluation. The paper categorized usability evaluation stages based on the number of involved components, which are user, tool, task, and environment. Our study fits Stage 3 category, which evaluates interaction performance in the laboratory. According to Yen and Bakken, objective measures that researchers use at Stage 3 include system validity (accuracy and completeness), efficiency (speed and learnability) and user satisfaction. In addition to time, accuracy and user satisfaction measures described in our earlier paper [1], this paper includes analysis of learnability (as adoption), but uses different methods than those listed in [4].

A systematic review of visualization evaluation strategies, data collection methods and other characteristics is presented by Merino et al. [5], who argue that an effective software visualization should boost not only time and correctness but also recollection, usability, engagement and other emotions.

In this paper, we demonstrate that observation and analysis of videos that capture *how* people used the interfaces can uncover aspects of interface learnability, different approaches to problem solving, and efficiencies associated with good design. The analyses presented here are not described in any literature we found so far, although Kang et al. [6] describe how they used analysis of videos and system logs to derive activity patterns and problem solving strategies employed by users of visual analytics system called Jigsaw in a laboratory study.

The analyses presented here can be put to use in directing design efforts after pilot evaluations of interfaces in order to improve the designs. Such improvements may consist of eliminating unused redundant interface affordances, directing user attention to useful features they do not employ, reducing the number of affordances and redesigning the interaction model.

3   Video Data Collection

The analyses presented here are based on the data collected in a laboratory side-by-side comparison of two alternative interfaces for working on data exploration and analysis tasks, AM2.0 [1] and Oracle SQL Developer [2] Reports (OR). The snapshots of these interfaces are shown in Fig. 1 and Fig. 2.

3.1   AM2.0 and OR Interfaces

AM2.0 is an interactive visualization (Fig. 1), in which the instances of three entities Vendor, Material and Plant, are shown as labeled geometric primitives on the left and the right sides of a circle (Vendor and Plant) and inside along the vertical diameter line (Material). AM2.0 is a version of a node-link diagram, in which related items are connected via links; selection of an item causes the associated links and related items to be highlighted to create a pop-out effect. For example, Fig. 1 depicts selection of a vendor node 290546 (left), which highlights two materials supplied by this vendor (CKB6900, GCJ4300, center) and the plants (FQ29, GF24, LM51, right), to which each of the two materials are supplied by vendor 290546.

The node-link diagram in AM2.0 is supplemented with a search interface displayed above it, which allows to select items of one or more types on the diagram by entering the values in the search fields.

OR (Fig. 2) is a typical table-based interface for displaying data. Each column represents a single entity, and each row presents an instance of an association. For example, the associations which are highlighted in Fig. 1 by AM2.0 and described above, would be represented by the following three rows of data:

290546	CKB6900	FQ29
290546	CKB6900	GF24
290546	GCJ4300	LM51

The table can be searched, using a dialog box shown in Fig. 2. The search is performed across all rows and fields of the table, with the found items simultaneously highlighted in the selected color. The table can also be sorted by a column value and filtered to select only the rows with matching items.

Note that data which is presented on one screen of AM2.0 may occupy multiple pages in the tabular representation of OR. The node-link representation along with the zooming capability of AM2.0 allow for a compact representation of multiple rows, in which no item of an entity is ever repeated. In contrast, the tabular representation includes an item as many times as there are relationships in which it participates.

3.2 Data Collection

Ten participants recruited from a graduate student population of a small business school in the Northeastern US were asked to perform nineteen tasks using AM2.0 and OR. Prior to performing these tasks, the participants were shown brief tutorials on using each interface and given two problems with solutions and explanations in a practice session. The two interfaces were supplied with data that was isomorphic in structure, but used different labels; likewise, the task questions were similar, with the only difference being the item labels involved. Tasks ranged from very simple, like finding all plants that supply a specific material, to more difficult ones, which required more reasoning and multiple actions with the interface to determine the answer. An example of a more difficult task is finding a replacement for a vendor; this task requires identifying materials supplied by the vendor, and then finding a set of other vendors who supply these materials. The seven most difficult tasks appeared in the end of the sequence of nineteen tasks.

4   Video Data Analysis

Analysis of performance and accuracy measures from the side-by-side comparison of AM2.0 and OR are presented in [1]. The same paper also presents responses to a questionnaire that included learnability and engagement parameters assessed on a Likert scale as well as open-ended questions regarding user preferences and suggestions from using the two interfaces. Here we report on the analysis of ten screen capture videos of ten anonymous participants who self-selected to perform the study in a laboratory setting with screen capture.

Our first step involved coding each video. The coding schema consisted of interface actions performed by users as they were solving each of the nineteen tasks using each of the two interfaces. We used the following coding procedure: for each task performed using each interface we first identified the steps required to answer the task question. This yielded 57 AM2.0 steps and 82 steps in OR. Then, for each step, we recorded all actions that the user took to finish it. Each action used for a task step was recorded once per task step, even if it was invoked multiple times. The list of action *codes* and action descriptions classified into *categories* is presented in Table 1. Action codes were created as different user actions were observed; upon finishing the coding, we derived the action categorization, which we describe next.

Table 1 starts with actions in **SF** (Search and Filter) category. This category encompasses actions that enact search and filter capabilities implemented via controls that are separated from the representation of the data, visual or tabular. In the AM2.0 such controls consist of the search interface that is displayed above the visualization (see top of Table 2). The AM2.0 search interface includes three input boxes for entering each of the three entity values, along the Search and Clear buttons. In OR, the search and filter tools accessible outside of the table itself include a search dialog box (shown in Fig. 2) that is revealed via a key combination or a press of a mouse button.

The second category, called **SFV** (Search and Filter, Visual), lists those search and filter actions that are executed *while the cursor is positioned on the visual representation of the data itself*. Notably, only the OR interface allows to invoke search and filter from within the table cells. A dialog box appears when the cell is selected with a click of a mouse. AM2.0 interface does not implement similar capabilities.

The **V** category contains those actions that implement direct interaction with the visual representation of the data but do not invoke a search. Examples include clicking on a data item, selecting items, clicking on them, moving between them, and others. This category actions occur while the user's attention is focused on the data directly.

In the meta or mental actions listed in category **M** we included clearly observed actions to verify the correctness of the result, including any checks users performed after the answer was already entered.

O category includes a single action of typing in an answer into an answer box. It is separate from category V, because it does not involve interaction with the data, though it is based on the viewing of the data.

The created categorization is based on the *intent* behind the action (search and filter, selection, mental actions) as well as the *locus* of interaction: whether the user is interacting through the data items directly or with the user interface controls separated from the data.

Table 1. Action codes and descriptions.

Category	Code	Interface	Description of the corresponding action
SF	C	AM2.0	Clear search fields by writing over or cutting out content
	Cb	AM2.0	Clear search fields by using the Clear Fields button
	FH	OR	Find/highlight; find (involves typing the material name, analog of Se)
	FHa	OR	Click up and down arrow in find/highlight search box to iterate over matched results
	Sb	AM2.0	Type value in search box, press Search button
	Se	AM2.0	Type value in search box, press Enter
	Sp	AM2.0	Copy/paste value into search box
	Spb	AM2.0	Copy/paste value into search box, press Search button
	Spe	AM2.0	Copy/paste value into search box, press Enter
	Stb	AM2.0	Partial search, type value in search box, press Search button. Highlights all items for which the search value is just the starting substring
SFV	FI	OR	Type value into the filter box, then select target item by double clicking on the item
	FIE	OR	Type value into the filter box, then press enter
	FIP	OR	Copy/paste target item into the filter box and select target item by double clicking on the item
	FIPE	OR	Copy/paste target item into the filter box and press enter
	FIS	OR	Select target item from the filter box without typing or copy/pasting target item by double clicking on the item
	FITE	OR	Invoke partial filter by typing in partial words and press enter
	RF	OR	Remove filter by clicking on the filter icon, then double click 'Remove filter'
	RFb	OR	Remove filter by clicking on the filter icon, then press enter
	T	OR	Sort
V	A	Both	Seemingly aimless clicking/mouse movement.
	B	Both	Browse over items
	K	Both	Select item by clicking
	L	OR	Scroll
	P	Both	Copy/paste (usually from visualization into answer box, sometimes to record item for future use)

(*continued*)

Table 1. (*continued*)

Category	Code	Interface	Description of the corresponding action
	SH	Both	Select/highlight several items within visualization, i.e. select manually, without invoking Find/Highlight. Selecting a single item is coded by K
	W	Both	Move mouse over observed fields
	Y	OR	Use keyboard to move between columns/rows
O	M	Both	Manually type in answers
M	R	Both	Take some time to review the result after it is entered
	V	Both	Perform a step (additional action) to verify the result

Table 2. Action categories.

Category	Description
SF	Search and filter using controls separated from the data itself
SFV	Search and filter using controls that are embedded within the data visualization/table
V	Direct interaction with data visualization/table
M	Mental work and additional actions involved in reviewing and checking results
O	Other

5 Analytics

5.1 Range and Frequency of Actions

Figure 3 summarizes the use of specific actions for solving tasks. In it, each action is depicted with a percentage number (also visualized with a horizontal bar). The total number from which the percentage is computed is the count of all actions taken by all users while working on all tasks, where within each separate task step and user, the action is counted only once even if it was used multiple times (see Sect. 4 for the coding procedure description). The bar thus depicts the percentage of the count of a *specific* action over the total count of *all* actions performed by all users on all tasks.

From Fig. 3 we see that users executed fewer different actions with AM2.0 than with OR. Among all action categories, when using AM2.0 participants used SF (Search and Filter) actions the most. The frequency of SF category actions is about three times that of the frequency of direct interaction with the visualization (V) category.

Usage of OR shows a much broader spread of actions: users interacted directly with the data, including for search and filter (V and SFV categories, respectively). Scrolling (L), highlighting multiple items using a mouse (SH), moving the mouse over the data of interest (W), moving between the data items using the keyboard arrow buttons (Y), and seemingly aimless clicking on data items (A) are actions that users engaged in with OR,

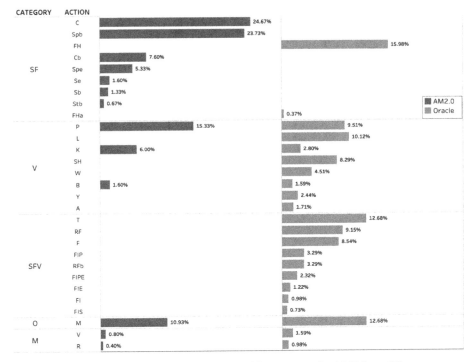

Fig. 3. Frequency of actions grouped by category for AM2.0 vs. OR

but did not within AM2.0. Of these five actions only two (scrolling and moving between items with keyboard, L and Y) are available exclusively in OR.

Although AM2.0 has fewer affordances tied to the data items than OR, participants used less time and achieved greater accuracy with AM2.0 (see [1]) in all categories of question difficulty. Hence, the availability and use of multiple UI controls that are enacted via interacting directly with data items is not necessary for the efficient operation of an interface.

Data in the M category indicates users reviewed and verified answers more when using OR than AM2.0. The verification is twice as prevalent with OR, which may indicate a lower confidence in the correctness of the final answer, when working with OR than with AM2.0. The explanation may be that the visualization in AM2.0 displays data in one screen, whereas the OR interface takes multiple screens, which users need to scroll on occasion. The ability to view all information pertinent to the answer in one screen reduces the user's need to perform additional verification of the correctness of the answer.

5.2 Adoption of Different Actions

The next series of figures visualizes how users adopt actions while working with the interfaces. Recall, that each of the participants worked on nineteen tasks (also referred to as *questions*) using AM2.0 and then OR interface. We categorized the questions by difficulty: questions 1–7 were simple, the next five (8–12) were of moderate difficulty and the last seven were higher difficulty questions (13–19).

Each of the figures in this subsection is drawn based on data from AM2.0 or OR usage. Each figure depicts curves associated with specific actions. The points on the curve indicate how many participants have used that action at the time of or before answering the given question. For example, from Fig. 4 we see that action P (the top curve) was used by five people while working on the first question, and all ten participants have used it by question number 15.

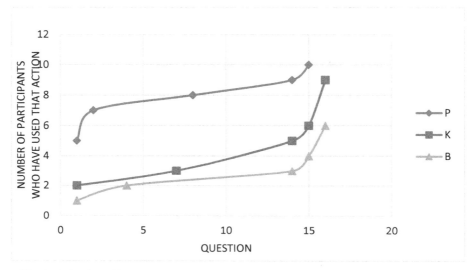

Fig. 4. Adoption of V category actions (direct interaction with the visualization) in AM2.0.

Note that all actions used, except for filtering in OR, were demonstrated in the tutorial shown to participants before they started working on tasks independently.

Figure 4 and Fig. 5. Adoption of V category actions (direct interaction with the visualization) in OR. Figure 5 present adoption curves for actions in category V (direct interaction with the visualization, see Table 1). Figure 4 shows that out of six category V actions available in AM2.0 only three were used:

- P – Copy/paste a value from the visualization into some other area.
- K – Select item by clicking, and
- B – Browse over items.

We can observe a notable increase in the use of K and B starting at question 14. As question 14 is one of the higher difficulty questions, we may assume that higher difficulty questions caused more users to select items by clicking on them and to browse over the data.

We do not observe a similar pattern in the use of OR (Fig. 5). The graph shows that scrolling (L) is one of the fastest adopted actions in OR. Clicking on a single data item

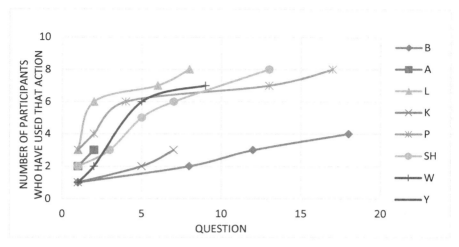

Fig. 5. Adoption of V category actions (direct interaction with the visualization) in OR.

(K) is not used by as many users as within AM2.0, because it yields no useful effect in OR. Instead, manual selection of multiple items (SH) is gradually adopted. Interestingly, none of the V category actions in OR are adopted by more than 80% of the users, and only one category V action (P-copy/paste) of AM2.0 is adopted by 100% of users.

Figure 6 illustrates how users of AM2.0 gradually learn to use more ways of interacting with the search interface. All actions in the SF category pertain to clearing and entering values into the search box (either by typing or pasting) and executing the search command (by button click or via keyboard). We see that with time users learn to use the Search and Clear Fields buttons. Though 80% of users start of by clearing the content of a search field via writing it over or erasing (C), the users of the Clear Fields button increase from 20% to 60% in the end (Cb), presumably as the more difficult questions require multiple search boxes to be used, hence cleared at once with a button. As in the case of V category actions with AM2.0 (Fig. 4), there also seems to be a pattern of an increase in use of different SF mechanisms after question 14, when working on higher difficulty questions. Two-three people used the partial search (STB, highlights all items which start with the searched string), on the last two questions of higher difficulty (Fig. 7).

When it comes to the Search and Filter actions in OR, the action adopted by all users is Find/Highlight (FH), which is executed via the ubiquitous Ctrl-F key combination. It is used from the very beginning by six out of ten participants and is gradually adopted by all. Most users also adopt sorting (T) very early on. One user discovered and used the partial filtering action (FITE) after answering a dozen questions.

To summarize: as participants become more familiar with the visualization and as the questions become more difficult, users gradually adopt different actions and use different strategies to find answers to task questions. As time progresses, more users engage with the visual part of the interface. However, the fact that most action curves

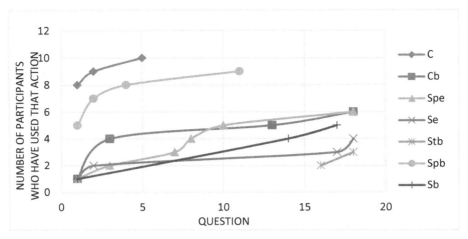

Fig. 6. Adoption of SF (Search and Filter) Functions in AM2.0.

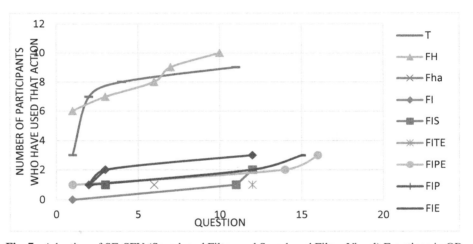

Fig. 7. Adoption of SF, SFV (Search and Filter, and Search and Filter, Visual) Functions in OR.

stop growing before reaching the maximum number of participants suggests that as the time progresses, users settle in on their chosen set of action.

5.3   Comparison of Prevalence of Actions Between Interchangeable Actions in AM2.0

The next set of analyses examines individual users' choices of actions among actions with the same effect, in other words, among interchangeable actions.

Figure 8 visualizes the prevalence of different selection mechanisms in the use of AM2.0. Each bar represents one user. Each bar is subdivided into rectangular components, depicting the number of actions found in the user's transcript: the blue (bottom) rectangle represents selection via the search interface actions ending with a click on the Search button (Spb, Sb, Stb), the green (middle) rectangle represents similar actions ending with a press on the Enter keyboard key (Spe, Se), and the purple (top) rectangle represents actions (K, B) of selecting items by a click on its visual representation (circle or rectangle) and browsing.

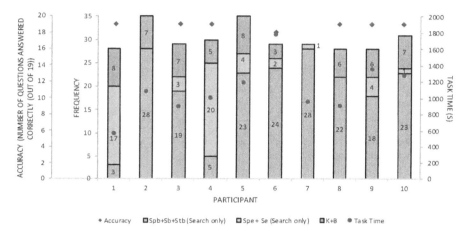

Fig. 8. Comparison between item selection enacted via the Search button (Spb, Sb, Stb), via Enter key press (Spe, Se), and via browse and click actions (K, B) in AM2.0.

The same figure also displays the accuracy measure (a higher value is better) as a rhombus and the completion time measure (lower is better) as a circle.

We observe that all but two users (User 1 and User 4) relied mostly on the selection via the search interface ending with a Search button click. Eight participants have a count of (K, B) actions ranging from 5 to 8. There is no visible influence of the reliance on Search button versus keyboard Entry key on total completion time.

The next figure (Fig. 9), constructed to examine preferences between clearing search fields with a click on Clear Fields button (bottom rectangle) versus manual erasure in the field (top rectangle), shows that users tend to prefer to erase or overwrite the field content to using the button. Four out of ten users have never used the button and two users used it very little compared to the manual erasure. Looking back at Fig. 6, we observe a slight increase of use of the button associated with more complex questions.

Finally, the graph in Fig. 10 shows that users overwhelmingly preferred using copy/paste (P, shown in blue, bottom rectangle) to manual entry (M, green, top rectangle). Notably, using mostly manual entry did not slow down user 3 compared to many others, who relied mostly on copy/paste.

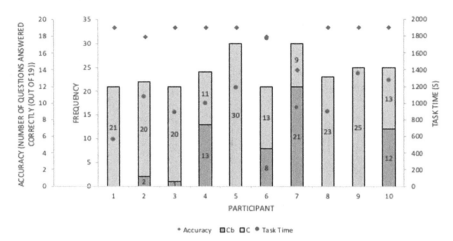

Fig. 9. Comparison between clear content actions using the Clear Fields button (Cb) or erasing/overwriting the content of the search field (C).

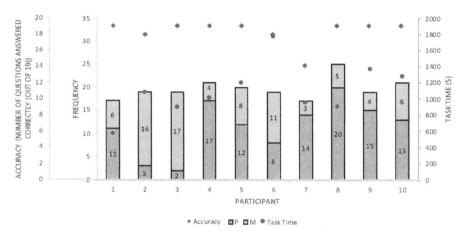

Fig. 10. Comparison between using copy/paste (P) and manual keyboard entry (M) to enter the search parameter. (Color figure online)

6 Conclusions and Limitations

The screen capture data was collected from 10 randomly chosen participants of a laboratory study ([1]) comparing user performance using the Association Map (AM2.0) with the performance using Oracle SQL Developer reports (OR). We have demonstrated that the data collected in this way can be analyzed to assess a number of factors, for example:

- What was the relative usefulness of each action for an individual user and overall?
- What are the different action categories? Did users employ the action categories in the same or in different ways when using two different interfaces to solve problems?

- For a set of interchangeable actions, what were the patterns of use and patterns of discovery of the alternatives?
- Are there clear efficiency gains associated with different patterns of action use?

Specifically for the two interfaces that were examined and compared, we have several useful findings that could not have been observed without the close examination of screen capture videos. For example, that the multiple search and filter features of the OR interface enacted directly via the data items did not help users in completing the tasks faster or more accurately than when using AM2.0, which lacks such features. Furthermore, using AM2.0 incurred fewer user actions aimed at verifying answer correctness as the use of OR. This finding confirmed our intuition that the one-page node-link diagram provides a representation of ternary relationships that is more intuitively clear and easier to work with than the tabular representation. Lastly, users tend to gradually expand their repertoire of actions in both interfaces. In case of AM2.0 there were no easily observable efficiency gains associated with a specific way to execute a search interface.

The observations made in this analyses, although useful in confirming hypothesized user behaviors or revealing insights, cannot be used for a definitive assessment of interface features. They offer insights that can be further investigated with more thorough multi-method investigation. The summary results presented here are also influenced by some degree of subjectivity involved in the coding and categorization methods performed by the authors of the paper. Nevertheless, we believe that the types of analyses presented here can be used during the formative stage of interface evaluation to understand patterns of learning and use (or non-use) of the different affordances. The learning patterns discovered in this way can be used in guiding user training or to offer suggestions to users, pointing their attention to overlooked features that were found to be useful by others.

References

1. Babaian, T., Lucas, W., Chircu, A.: Mapping data associations in enterprise systems. In: Tulu, B., Djamasbi, S., Leroy, G. (eds.) DESRIST 2019. LNCS, vol. 11491, pp. 254–268. Springer, Cham (2019). https://doi.org/10.1007/978-3-030-19504-5_17
2. SQL Developer. https://www.oracle.com/database/technologies/appdev/sql-developer.html. Accessed 31 Jan 2020
3. Lam, H., Bertini, E., Isenberg, P., Plaisant, C., Carpendale, S.: Empirical studies in information visualization: seven scenarios. IEEE Trans. Vis. Comput. Graph. 18, 1520–1536 (2012)
4. Yen, P.-Y., Bakken, S.: Review of health information technology usability study methodologies. J. Am. Med. Inform. Assoc. 19, 413–422 (2012). https://doi.org/10.1136/amiajnl-2010-000020
5. Merino, L., Ghafari, M., Anslow, C., Nierstrasz, O.: A systematic literature review of software visualization evaluation. J. Syst. Softw. 144, 165–180 (2018). https://doi.org/10.1016/j.jss.2018.06.027
6. Kang, Y., Gorg, C., Stasko, J.: Evaluating visual analytics systems for investigative analysis: deriving design principles from a case study. In: 2009 IEEE Symposium on Visual Analytics Science and Technology, pp. 139–146. IEEE, Atlantic City (2009). https://doi.org/10.1109/VAST.2009.5333878

Service Design and Management

Feature Analysis of Customers Purchasing Cars in Japan

Kenta Hara[✉] and Yumi Asahi[✉]

School of Information and Telecommunication Engineering, Department of Management Systems Engineering, Tokai University, Tokyo, Japan
kh@fuji.tokai-u.jp, asahi@tsc.u-tokai.ac.jp

Abstract. Car sales in Japan are decreasing year by year. In addition, it will be affected by consumption tax increase and oil prices increase. Therefore, it is assumed that Car sales will be affected by external factor in Japan. Japan has problems with the declining birth rate and aging population. Car sales in Japan will be decrease caused by it, so it is necessary for Car industry in japan to know needs of customers. In this study, we analyze customer data from a car sales company "I" based in prefecture "A" in Japan to know customer needs. It is assumed that Cars in Japan have customers who purchase new or used cars, so their needs differ. Today, there are more customers buying new cars than customers buying used cars, however the opposite could happen for car industry affected by external factors in the future. So, it is important for car industry to know the needs of both customers. We use logistic regression analysis and decision tree analysis to know the difference between the two. After that, we evaluate the accuracy of AUC and confusion matrix as evaluation of both analyses. The analysis shows that customers who buy new cars are affected by the salesperson, and customers who buy used cars are less likely to be affected by the salesperson.

Keywords: Car · Logistic regression analysis · Decision tree analysis

1 Introduction

1.1 Background

The current state of the automobile industry in Japan has high international competitiveness and Supporting the local economy with vast supporting industries and employment [1]. It shows that the car industry in Japan plays an important role economically. In addition, it shows that there are five issues that the Japanese car industry will face in the next 10 to 20 years. The first, it is growing environmental and energy constraints. It shows the future task which will be reduce carbon dioxide emissions when driving a car. The second, it is population growth and personal income growth. It shows the future task which will be increase population and economic growth and increase the middle class in several emerging countries, including China. The third, it is aging population. It shows the future task which will be fear that aging will lead to a decrease in the number of cars

© Springer Nature Switzerland AG 2020
S. Yamamoto and H. Mori (Eds.): HCII 2020, LNCS 12184, pp. 201–211, 2020.
https://doi.org/10.1007/978-3-030-50020-7_13

owned and an increase in traffic accidents. Figure 1 shows the population in Japan is decreasing year by year and declining birth rate and aging population.

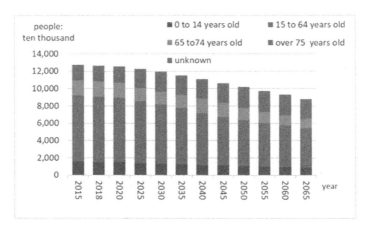

Fig. 1. Change of aged and future population projections in Japan [2]

The fourth, it is the progress of urban congestion and rural depopulation. It shows the future task which will be important to effectively cooperate with the problem of car congestion, infrastructure such as roads, and public transportation systems such as railways in order to ensure smooth movement of people in overcrowded cities, also rural areas where depopulation is advancing, it is difficult to maintain public institutions in rural, so there is a possibility that demand for car will increase. However, it is feared that maintaining infrastructure such as gas stations that supports automobiles will also be difficult. Figure 2 shows that there is a demand for cars in metropolitan areas than in provincial areas. Therefore, it is assumed that the car ownership rate changes depending on the location.

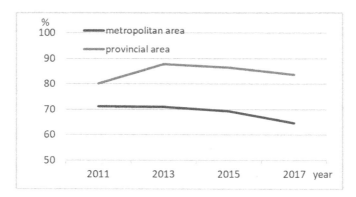

Fig. 2. Car ownership rate in metropolitan area and provincial area

The fifth, it is change in one's sense of values. It shows the future task which will be people born after 1990 are digital generations with a strong affinity for IT, and attractive cars including active use of IT are required. In addition, that this generation does not always share the previous generation's values about owning and driving a car because of its diverse values. It is an issue to determine what strategy to carry out as car departure progresses in Japan under 30 years old. We need to consider given the increasing tendency to not drive in the under 30 years old of generations in Japan, what kind of strategy should be addressed.

Figure 3 shows Car sales in Japan have been declining since 2004. In addition, significant decrease in car sales between 2004 and 2011. It is assumed that caused by soaring oil prices started around 2004. Most recently, 2013 had the highest vehicle sales. It is due to the consumption tax increase. Therefore, it is assumed that Car sales will be affected by external factor in Japan.

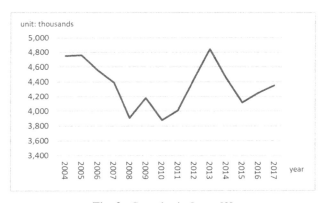

Fig. 3. Car sales in Japan [3]

1.2 Propose

There is much research on automotive technology in Japan. On the other hand, few studies focused on customers purchasing cars in Japan. Owaki et al. [4] conducted an analysis by attribute of consumers and considered sales promotion of passenger cars from the viewpoint of age and gender. It shows that the domestic car market showed a mature market and replacement demand was more important than new demand. However, did not focus on the used car market. They consider age, gender and job separately. It is assumed that we can't get the right approach it and it's not right to consider separately. Otsuka et al. [5] used logistic regression analysis and decision tree analysis to predict the presence or absence of a criminal which is record from case data on a single murder case created from 2004 to 2009. To create both models, logistic regression analysis used a stepwise backward regression method with a likelihood ratio test, and decision tree analysis used CHAID. As an evaluation, the AUC calculated from the ROC was calculated, and no significant difference was found. It was proved that both models were useful as a method for predicting the criminal history of the criminal.

We have shown from the research background that car sales will be affected by external factors. In addition, car sales are on a declining trend, and it is feared that auto sales will continue to decline due to the aging of the population and the declining birthrate. Therefore, the car industry must know its needs and make strategies. It is assumed that Cars in Japan have customers who purchase new or used cars, so their needs differ. Today, there are more customers buying new cars than customers buying used cars, however the opposite could happen for car industry affected by external factors in the future. So, it is important for car industry to know the needs of both customers. We use logistic regression analysis and decision tree analysis to know the difference between the two. After that, we evaluate the accuracy of AUC and confusion matrix as evaluation of both analyses.

2 Data Summary

2.1 Data Overview

Provide: provided in car sales corporation "I" based in prefecture "A" in Japan.
    Period: Dec 4, 2000 to Oct 4, 2019 (For 19 years)

2.2 Data Cleaning

No abnormal values were found in the data used, however missing data and duplicate data were found when coupled data was performed. The processing method is shown below.

At first, we dealt with missing data. Since the data used is qualitative data, if there are missing data in the variables used for analysis, the method of deleting all data rows was used. Many studies have shown how to deal with missing data. However, there is no clear solution for polynomial qualitative variables, and compatibility problems have been pointed out [6].

The second, we dealt with duplicate data. Duplicated data was deleted based on the customer code, age, and car name because the data was duplicated when the data was combined. After that, in order to confirm that there are no duplicate codes, totaling was conducted based on the number of vehicles owned, and it was confirmed whether there was data exceeding the number of vehicles owned for each customer code.

2.3 Basic Aggregate

Table 1 show customers living in prefecture "A" account for 96.42% of the total data. This is because the sales corporation "I" who received the data is located in prefecture A. The feature of prefecture A is that the area of the continent is larger than other prefectures. The ranking of the number of cars owned by prefecture A is intermediate when compared to 47 prefectures in Japan. Prefectures B and C are neighbors of prefecture A, so it is assumed car ownership rate is no change depending on the location.

Table 1. Residential district ratio by prefecture

Prefecture	A	B, C	Unknown	Other
Rate (%)	96.42	0.54	0.07	2.98

Table 2 shows among the customers who purchased cars, men account for about 60% of the entire data, and women account for about 30% of the entire data. Males have a higher ratio than females, and male customers are the main customers, but women also account for 30%, indicating that the market is not male-only.

Table 2. Sex ratio

Sex	Male	Female	Corporation	Unknown
Rate (%)	59.23	30.97	9.5	0.29

Figure 4 show that new cars account for 62% of purchased cars, used cars account for 23%. Therefore, the demand for new cars is higher than the demand for used cars, however it is also clear that there is demand for used cars, so it is necessary to think about used cars.

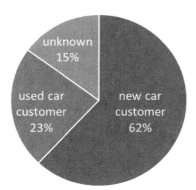

Fig. 4. Customer ratio

2.4 Data Processing

We used three variables as a method of selection criteria. The first, Car ownership rate changes depending on the location, so we use prefectures A, B, C that are not affected. The second, we use men and women for gender classification. The corporation and unknown do not use the car, judging that there is no favorite car purchase by the customer. The third, we do not use unknown to find the difference between customers buying new cars and used cars. As a result, we create a new dataset containing 36,097 records.

3 Analysis

3.1 Analysis Method

At first, we use a resampling method that splits new dataset into training and test data to increase model accuracy. In the resampling method, a holdout method is used in which the learning data was divided into 80% (28,877 records) and the test data into 20% (7,220 records) from the new dataset (36,097 records). We use logistic regression analysis and decision tree analysis using test and training data, then evaluate accuracy. As the evaluation method of both models, the accuracy of the models is evaluated using the confusion matrix that shows the results of the classification and the AUC that is under the ROC area.

3.2 Logistic Regression Analysis

The purpose of this analysis is to understand what affects the objective variable. We use binary objective variables new car customers and older car customers in logistic regression analysis. We check whether there is a correlation between the explanatory variables used in the logistic regression analysis, that is, whether multicollinearity might occur during the analysis. Because, if the analysis is performed when there is multicollinearity, the solution becomes unstable even if the solution is obtained, and the reliability decreases, so the possibility that the necessary explanatory variables are not selected increases. In other words, no matter how good the value is, we can't assert that a suitable model is complete.

Table 3 shows that the four explanatory variables have no correlation. Therefore, we use it as explanatory variables. We use the stepwise backward regression method of variable selection reduction method to reduce the variables until the optimal model based on AIC and continue until the optimal model with variable selection.

Table 3. Result of Cramér's V for each classification

Correlation coefficient	Age	Regular customer	Light car	Contact
Age	1	0.05	0.08	0.02
Regular customer	0.05	1	0.06	0.02
Light car	0.08	0.06	1	0.01
Contact	0.02	0.02	0.01	1

Table 4 shows in the stepwise backward regression method based on AIC, where contact is not required for the model and contact is not included in the model variables. New car customer has a positive effect when Exp (B) is greater than 1 and negatively when it is less than 1. Therefore, ages 30 to 70 and regular customer 1 to 3 have a positive effect, and light car have been selected as a negative effect. In addition, regular customer

1 to 3 have a higher effect than other variables, and that in age, Exp (B) increases with age. On the other hand, the light car is the negative effect of customers who buy new cars, so it can be interpreted that customers who buy used cars purchase light cars.

Table 4. Analysis result of logistic regression analysis

Variables	Estimate	Exp(B)	P value
Light car	−3.25	0.04	0.00E+00
30 s	0.24	1.27	1.22E−05
40 s	0.33	1.40	5.21E−10
50 s	0.34	1.41	1.57E−10
60 s	0.50	1.65	1.67E−19
70 s	0.51	1.67	4.81E−13
Regular customer 1	0.93	2.54	1.11E−23
Regular customer 2	0.85	2.34	1.67E−27
Regular customer 3	1.31	3.71	2.92E−73

3.3 Decision Tree Analysis

The purpose of this analysis is to understand the relationships between variables that could not be revealed by logistic regression analysis. We use partitioning method uses CART and uses Gini coefficients as the partitioning criterion. In addition, the tree pruning method uses the Min + 1 × SE criterion, which is the minimum mean cross-validated misclassification rate + 1 × standard deviation. Figure 5 show the dotted line indicates the Min + 1 × SE standard. It is necessary to prune at $0.0011 < cp < 0.022$, which is lower than the dotted line, to use it, and prune at $2 < size of tree < 5$. Therefore, We use No3 from Table 5 as pruning a decision tree.

Figure 6 shows customers who buy used cars have a high probability of purchasing a light car, and that customers who buy a new car have a high probability of purchasing a regular car. In addition, the percentage of customers who purchase new cars with maintenance packs is about the same as the percentage of customers who purchase new cars without contracts. On the other hand, customers who buy used cars are more likely not to contract a maintenance pack. In particular, the characteristics of customers who do not contract for maintenance packs, there is a high probability that the fixed regular customer into 1 to 3.

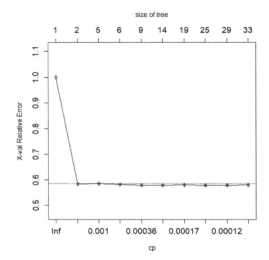

Fig. 5. Complexity per tree size

Table 5. List of pruning decision trees

No	CP	N split	Rel error	X error	X std
1	0.417527	0	1	1	0.008671
2	0.001135	1	0.582473	0.582473	0.007226
3	0.000988	4	0.579069	0.584999	0.007238
4	0.000403	5	0.578080	0.580716	0.007218
5	0.000384	10	0.575994	0.580387	0.007216
6	0.000293	14	0.574456	0.580167	0.007215
7	0.000220	17	0.573578	0.582144	0.007225
8	0.000176	29	0.570942	0.582363	0.007226
9	0.000146	39	0.569185	0.584230	0.007235
10	0.000141	42	0.568746	0.584011	0.007234
11	0.000137	50	0.567538	0.584011	0.007234
12	0.000110	59	0.566000	0.584011	0.007234
13	0.000100	68	0.565012	0.585219	0.007239

3.4 Accuracy Evaluation

AUC and confusion matrix are used for accuracy evaluation. The reason for using AUC is that the proportion of customers who buy new cars and those who buy used cars is uneven. Figure 7 shows the red curve shows the logistic regression analysis and the

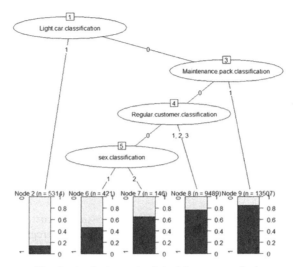

Fig. 6. Analysis result of decision tree analysis

blue curve shows the decision tree analysis, showing that there is no difference between the two models. In other words, there is no difference in the accuracy of both models (Table 6).

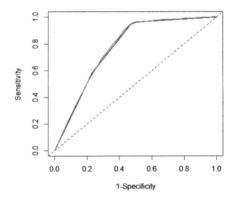

Fig. 7. ROC for both models (Color figure online)

Table 6. Evaluation list of both models

Evaluation	Logistic regression analysis	Decision tree analysis
AUC	0.7758	0.77
Accuracy	81.37	81.61
Precision	95.72	95.36
Recall	80.63	81.06

4   Consideration

The purpose of this study was to know the characteristics of customers who buy new cars and those who buy used cars. From the results of logistic regression analysis and decision tree analysis, it was possible to find the characteristics of customers who buy new cars and those who buy used cars and showed that the accuracy evaluation was of the same level.

The results of logistic regression analysis showed that customers purchasing new cars were more positively affected by the regular customer 1 to 3, and that the older the age, the greater the positive impact. Therefore, it is assumed that as we age, we like new cars. Owaki et al. research shows that the tendency to go to the store to purchase a car increases as the age increases. I can guess that as a result, customers purchasing a new car may be affected by the salespersons. The results of decision tree analysis showed that probability of a customer purchasing a new car contracting a maintenance pack is close to the probability of a customer not contracting. On the other hand, customers who buy used cars are more likely not to contract a maintenance pack. It is assumed that customers buying new cars may be interested in maintenance packs, but customers buying used cars are less likely. Therefore, customers buying new cars may be affected by the seller, but customers buying used cars may be less affected by the seller.

5   The Future Tasks

In this study, we used two analyzes to examine the characteristics of customers who buy new cars and those who buy used cars. Both models will be adaptable to data where the background does not change well. However, the data in this study are susceptible to external factors. Therefore, it is assumed that we need to use a flexible model. Bayesian network should be used as flexible models in this study in the future. It expresses dependencies between random variables by network structure and expresses the relation between random variables by conditional probability. Since the data used in this study is binary data, we would like to create a model as shown in Fig. 8 in the future.

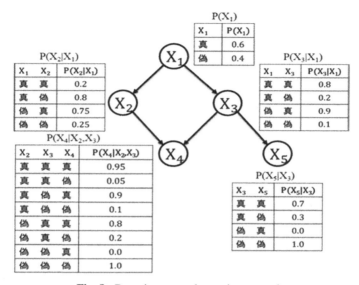

Fig. 8. Bayesian network creation example

References

1. Car industry strategy (2014). https://www.meti.go.jp/shingikai/sankoshin/seizo_sangyo/pdf/003_s02_02.pdf. Accessed 03 Dec 2019
2. Chapter 1 Aging Situation. https://www8.cao.go.jp/kourei/whitepaper/w-2019/html/zenbun/s1_1_1.html. Accessed 25 Nov 2019
3. Changes in vehicle demand in 2018. http://www.jama.or.jp/stats/outlook/20180315/change2018fy.html. Accessed 10 Nov 2019
4. Owaki, T., Matsumoto, Y., Hirohisa, W.: A study on information seeking and sending for consumer's buying behavior (2) case of passenger Car. Res. Inst. Mark. Distrib. **20**, 23–54 (2014)
5. Otsuka, Y., Hirama, K., Yokota, K.: Methods for predicting offender's criminal history in single homicide cases. Comparison of logistic regression analysis and decision tree. Jpn. J. Forensic Sci. Technol. **22**(1), 25–34 (2017)
6. Watanabe, M., Takahashi, M.: Missing data processing: single substitution method and multiple substitution method by R. Kyoritsu (2017)

Waiting Time Analysis at University Hospitals Based on Visitor Psychology

Shigeyoshi Iizuka[1,2(✉)], Shozo Nishii[2], Eriko Tanimoto[2], Hiro Nakazawa[2], Asuka Kodaka[2], and Takanori Takebe[2]

[1] Kanagawa University, 2946, Tsuchiya, Hiratsuka, Kanagawa 259-1293, Japan
`iizuka@kanagawa-u.ac.jp`
[2] Communication Design Center, Yokohama City University, 3-9 Fukuura, Kanazawa-ku, Yokohama, Kanagawa 236-0004, Japan
{`snishii,nakazawa,ttakebe`}`@yokohama-cu.ac.jp`,
`erispc05572@gmail.com`, `asuka.k19@gmail.com`
`http://y-cdc.org/`

Abstract. Hospital waiting time is an important issue for improving patient satisfaction. The problem is described as the necessity of shortening not only "direct waiting time" a physical quantity, but also "sensory waiting time," so that patients spend the same amount of time without frustration and do not feel waiting times to be overlong. It is thus necessary to devise ways to reduce the subjective feeling of waiting. This study is an exploratory/preliminary study focusing on how patients wait based on the mother's attending experience of a medical graduate who is aware of the issue of waiting time. A patient journey map and a mental model of attitudes toward waiting time in hospitals and feelings when waiting are created. It is suggested that the user experience (UX) will be improved by providing more sufficient services using the "time" and "space (place)" in the hospital.

Keywords: Waiting time · Patient satisfaction · University hospital · Journey map · Mental model

1 Introduction

Visitor dissatisfaction with the length of time spent waiting at a healthcare facility is a significant matter needing improvement in healthcare management. It is a daily occurrence as hospitals become larger and the waiting times become longer than 30 min in medical institutions with multiple departments. This tendency is said to be particularly strong in large hospitals such as university hospitals. Considering financial transactions after consultation and additional waiting times at dispensing pharmacies, the stress on the visitor is physically and psychologically burdensome. In recent years, competition has been intensifying in medical management, and it is also necessary to implement waiting time improvements as a means of differentiating the hospital from other medical institutions. Although

© Springer Nature Switzerland AG 2020
S. Yamamoto and H. Mori (Eds.): HCII 2020, LNCS 12184, pp. 212–221, 2020.
https://doi.org/10.1007/978-3-030-50020-7_14

there have already been numerous academic and practical research on hospital waiting time [1–3], it remains an important issue. This study explores the possibilities of hospital communication design focusing on how visitors perceive waiting time in hospitals. Visitors' emotional response to their waiting time may vary depending on how they wait. We sought to clarify this relationship to help reduce the negative emotions caused by long waiting times and provide a means of improving how visitors perceive waiting times. This is a preliminary exploratory study conducted from the above point of view with an university medical graduate.

In some cases, there are waiting times from the reception of a patient receiving chemotherapy for cancer to the start of therapy, the time until the drug is handed to the patient after the in-hospital prescription is issued, and the time from the reception of the prescription at the out-of-hospital pharmacy to the handing of the drug. However the term "waiting time" in this paper refers to the time spent visiting a medical institution and staying in the hospital from receiving medical treatment to accounting.

2   Measures for Waiting Time

2.1   What Is Waiting Time

In our lives, we encounter the need to "wait" in various situations, for example, when waiting in a hurry, waiting for a signal, waiting in line with a theme park attraction, waiting at a bank counter, meeting on a date. On the other hand, the perception of that time is different between one minute waiting for a signal when you are in a hurry and 30 min waiting for the first data. In other words, how waiting time is felt naturally depends on physical duration, but that is not the only factor [4,5]. From this point of view, "waiting time" can be analyzed under two concepts, "direct waiting time" and "sensory waiting time". Reducing "sensory waiting time" means that patients spend the same amount of time without frustration and do not feel long waiting. Hospitals point out that it is necessary to reduce "sensory waiting time" in addition to "direct waiting time," and it is necessary to institute measures to reduce waiting time, as patients dissatisfied with waiting time consider waiting time "wasted", and especially to reduce subjective "waiting feeling," that is, "sensory waiting time." Psychological research on waiting time also faces the problem of subjectively felt "psychological time," which is thought to affect not only the length of the physical time but also the awareness of the passage of time and the segmentation of time. It has also been pointed out that the evaluation of the quality of the waiting time is affected by how the patient perceives the waiting time, and it has been reported that those who have negative feelings or thoughts while waiting report longer waiting time.

2.2   Concept of Measures for Waiting Time

In order to reduce the waiting time, it is necessary to consider the above-mentioned "direct waiting time" and "sensory waiting time" separately to ensure improvements in patient satisfaction (Fig. 1). There are some approaches that can be taken from the hardware side, such as buildings and reservation machines, and others from the software side, such as changes in hospitality, traffic flow, and treatment order. However, depending on the method, even if the direct waiting time increases, the perceived waiting time may decrease. In other words, when considering measures to reduce waiting time, it is necessary to consider the balance between the two when judging the effects of the measures.

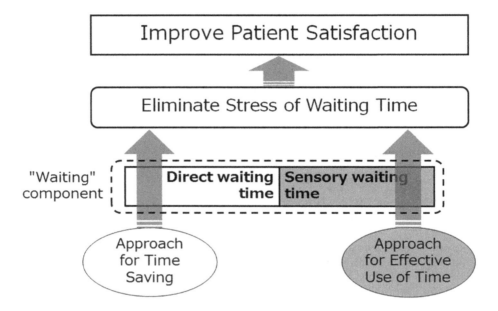

Fig. 1. Waiting time and improving patient satisfaction.

What kind of approach has being taken to the problem of waiting time, which can be said to be an eternal theme of hospitals and clinics? Table 1 shows the countermeasures respectively, the measures to reduce "direct waiting time" and "sensory waiting time" that have been implemented so far to comfortably reduce waiting time. For example, there are many cases where a reservation system (for returning patients) has been introduced. While these are effective in shortening the waiting time for medical treatment, there often lead to numerous inquiries and complaints by patients without reservations, consultations at concurrent departments, an a lack of understanding of the system, which can all present difficulties.

Patients and their families who use hospitals often have various mental burdens such as anxiety about illness, injury, and sometimes financial anxiety, as well as physical distress itself, such as illness, injury, and fatigue. In addition, hospitals are an unfamiliar environment for many patients, families and visitors, which entails a variety of anxieties, including feelings of alienation among

Table 1. Measures to reduce waiting time.

1. Measures to reduce direct waiting time
1) Job improvement
Review staffing/role assignment
Review of work flow/quality
Review patient flow
Review medical hours
2) Improve information flow and management
Improvement of paper chart management system
Introduction of electronic medical records
Order entry system
3) Patient Flow Management: Reservation System
2. Measures to reduce sensory waiting time
1) Information on waiting status
2) Ingenuity of waiting rooms
3) Liberalizing where to wait
4) Effective use of waiting time
Interview
Nurse
Patient education
Other ideas

strangers in large numbers in an unfamiliar place, and the stresses they bring [6–8]. Therefore, it is desirable that the hospital environment functions to reduce users' anxiety and improve their mood. In other words, it is necessary to design an environment that goes beyond the framework of functions and efficiency to take the patient's mind into account.

In order to improve the environment so that waiting time for consultation can be spent more comfortably, the following waiting time environment improvements have been made.

- Outpatient information guide
- Additional psychiatric outpatient toilets
- TV extension
- Install paintings that create a friendly atmosphere
- Renovation of the psychiatric outpatient entrance
- Install more comfortable waiting room chairs

Other studies have focused on the waiting room environment where the user spends the longest time by examining the waiting room chair arrangement and patient consciousness in, traditional and modern hospital waiting rooms [9]. Investigations of the effects of impressions on the physical characteristics of the waiting room and exterior of the hospital on the use of hospitals and factor analyses of the results of evaluations of the impressions of hospital waiting rooms among university students examples of this [10].

3   Derivation of Issues from Attendant Experience

In this chapter, a collaborator (a woman in her twenties, a graduate of the Faculty of Medicine) went to two university hospitals in Tokyo with her mother, with the aim of understanding in detail how the visitor spends time in the hospital. This report summarizes the behavior of patients in hospitals, especially during waiting times, based on their experience in the series of observations. Since she graduated from medical school, she understands the problem of waiting time and is aware of related problems at the hospital. Therefore, we expected to obtain sufficient information.

First, we created a journey map (Fig. 2) and summarized in-hospital behaviors and changes in emotions over time (Fig. 3). As is clear from this journey map, most of the time during the hospital stay is "waiting time", and the line representing the emotion at that time indicates a negative mode. In addition, characters and touchpoints in certain situations and scenes were identified, and their contact models were created (Fig. 4).

These efforts led to the identification of the following two issues concerning waiting time common to the two hospitals.

- The two areas involving the patient (medical/clerical) are clearly divided and the lack of coordination breeds patient dissatisfaction with waiting times and prevents further reductions in waiting times.
- The fact that facilities that should be available for patients (canteens, shops, gardens, etc.) are not used or not available to patients during waiting time causes feelings of silence and irritation while waiting.

The first task is related to "direct waiting time" and the second task is related to "sensory waiting time". In particular, the second problem as follows: When waiting in the waiting room of a hospital, there is the concern that "I do not know when I will be called (if I am not there when I am called, my turn will be skipped)"; therefore, it is not possible to reduce the "sensory waiting time" by utilizing facilities such as cafeterias, shops, and gardens.

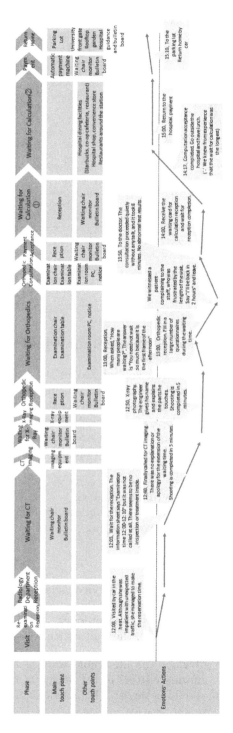

Fig. 2. Outpatient situation in a hospital (patient journey map).

- 58 year old female. A housewife who lives with her eldest daughter (26 years old) during job hunting, eldest son (23 years old), and disabled husband (61 years old).
- In June 2018, she underwent surgery at the Tokyo National University Hospital and Orthopedic Surgery for lumbar spondylolisthesis caused by her husband's care.
- Since then, he has been discharged from the hospital with a good postoperative course and is following an outpatient department.
- Follow-up once every six months from 2019, and the second outpatient regular check-up today.
- Lately, stoic pampering with gardening and dog walking can recur during work.
- Although pain control is good only with rest, I am worried about the results of diagnostic imaging.
- Other concerns are my menopause and where my children work.

Fig. 3. Persona.

4   "Wait" in the Service Management Field

The psychology of the waiting person is analyzed in the field of service management, and devices and measures to make the waiting time less burdensome are studied and implemented. David Meister, an American management consultant, has discussed the psychology of waiting times and the eight measures that customers take to reduce waiting times in response [11], to which business scholar Christopher Lovelock has added two yielding the following ten principles of latency psychology:

- Waiting times without doing anything feels long
- The waiting time before and after the original service feels long
- If you are worried, you will feel longer waiting
- Indeterminate waiting times feel long
- Waiting for an unknown reason feels long
- Unequal waiting times feel long
- There is a willingness to wait long if the service value is high
- When you wait alone, you feel long waits
- Uncomfortable or painful waiting times seem long
- When waiting in an unfamiliar place, the waiting time seems long

These indicate that to alleviate the inevitable waiting times in providing services, a mechanism that informs visitors of the length of the wait and holds their attention while waiting should be devised. For example, if only the reception number is displayed, this does not provide information on how many minutes a

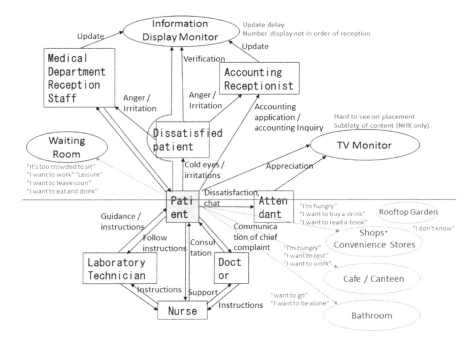

Fig. 4. Interaction during waiting time.

visitor is likely to wait. Most patients will this wait in the waiting room until consultation time, even though there are places to spend waiting times, such as restaurants, shops, and book spaces.

Even if it is not possible to physically reduce the waiting time, a service that displays expected waiting time or sends a message indicating that the visitor's number has been called can change a highly frustrating time into a more acceptable time. That is, the patient's waiting time can mode to feel freer. In using medical services, the hospital UX includes not only the medical treatment itself but also such waiting time. It is estimated that the burden of waiting time has been reduced in some ways by the spread of smartphones. However, it is expected that the UX can be further improved by providing more services that ensure sufficient "time" and "space (place)" within the hospital.

5   Conclusion

We have focused on "waiting time," which remains an important issue in large-scale hospitals such as university hospitals, focusing on reducing "sensory waiting time," which is distinct from physical waiting time. In this paper, we conducted an exploratory, preliminary study focusing on how patients spend their waiting time, based on the experience of attending with her own mother, with graduates of the medical school as a collaborator. Based on her findings, she presented a journey map and a contact model of her attitudes toward waiting at hospitals and her feelings about how she was spending waiting time. In order to reduce waiting time, it is necessary to adopt costly measures or measures that would cause greater dissatisfaction than waiting time improvements, such as lowering the quality of medical examination, even if the waiting time can be reduced. Thus, in order to improve the waiting time (feeling of waiting) for the patient, it is important to understand how to reduce the waiting time without lowering the quality of the examination, reduce the psychological burden of waiting time on the patient, and how to provide a more comfortable waiting time.

D. A. Norman proposed the following six queuing design principles to enhance the queuing experience, adding insights based on David Meister's classic 1985 paper, "The psychology of queuing."

- Provide a conceptual model
- Make sure that it is appropriate to wait
- Meet or exceed expectations
- Keep people in mind
- Be fair
- Emphasize the end and start

A structural model of patient satisfaction from the viewpoint of "patient satisfaction" has been shown. It has been reported that "satisfaction with medical treatment and treatment attitudes from doctors" has a greater effect on the overall satisfaction of outpatients with consultations. On the other hand, it has also been reported that "the effect of satisfaction on building comfort and convenience such as waiting time is weaker." In other words, "waiting time" is also a significant influencing factor on overall satisfaction, but "communication with doctors" should be given priority in improving overall satisfaction. In light of the "Kano model" [12] of the relationship between product/service quality and satisfaction, a "short waiting time" is considered "naturalness" as a part of service quality. On the other hand, it has been pointed out that "If you think the value of the service is high, you are willing to wait longer." Hospitals have a "place" and a "time" to spend waiting time. By making effective use of these and providing further services to make the waiting time meaningful, it is possible to make the "waiting time at the hospital" an "attractive quality." Based on these ideas, we will not only contribute to solving the problem of waiting time, but also conduct research to improve the in-hospital experience value of patients.

Acknowledgments. This research was supported by the Hideo Yoshida Memorial Foundation, 2019 (53rd) Research Grant.

References

1. Ouchi, K., Kawarada, A., Ono, J., Otsuki, M., Inake, E.: Relationship between patient waiting time and patient's feelings at an outpatient department of ophthalmology. Bull. Fukushima Med. Univ. Sch. Nurs. **15**, 1–7 (2013). (in Japanese)

2. Mitsui, S., Yanagihara, K., Maruyama, H., Yanagihashi, T.: Survey on outclinic patient waiting time at Shinshu University Hospital. Ann. Nurs. Res. Shinshu Univ. Hosp. **29**(1), 57–64 (2000). (in Japanese)

3. Tokunaga, M., Watanabe, S., Nakane, N.: Survey on outpatient's waiting time and satisfaction level. J. Jpn. Soc. Health Care Manag. **7**(2), 324–328 (2006). https://doi.org/10.11191/jhm2006.7.324. (in Japanese)

4. Aoi, T., Azuma, M.: A study of patient waiting time for plain radiographic examination and continuous quality improvement. Memoirs Osaka Kyoiku Univ. Hum. Soc. Sci. Nat. Sci. **49**(1), 161–173 (2000). (in Japanese)

5. Kato, T., Uetsuka, Y.: Considerations over the effectiveness of introducing electronic medical record system in shortening the waiting hours at out-patient department: comparison between the initial phase of the implementation and 20 months later. J. Tokyo Women's Med. Univ. **80**(1, 2), 9–13 (2010). (in Japanese)

6. Carver, A.M.: Hospital design and working conditions. In: Moran, R., Anderson, R., Paoli, P. (eds.) Building for People in Hospitals, Dublin, Ireland, pp. 85–92, European Foundation for the Improvement of Living and Working Conditions (1990)

7. Veitch, R., Arkkelin, D.: Environmental Psychology: An Interdisciplinary Perspective. Prentice Hall, Englewood Cliffs (1995)

8. Zimring, C., Carpman, J.R., Michelson, W.: Design for special populations: mentally retarded persons, children, hospital visitors. In: Stokols, D., Altman, I. (eds.) Handbook of Environmental Psychology, pp. 919-949. Wiley, New York (1987)

9. Leather, P., Beale, D., Santos, A.: Outcomes of environmental appraisal of different hospital waiting areas. Environ. Behav. **35**, 842–869 (2003)

10. Arneill, A.B., Devlin, A.S.: Perceived quality of care: the influence of the waiting room environment. J. Environ. Psychol. **22**(4), 345–360 (2002)

11. Maister, D.H.: The Psychology of Waiting Lines. http://www.columbia.edu/~ww2040/4615S13/Psychology_of_Waiting_Lines.pdf. Accessed 2 Mar 2020

12. Kano, N., Seraku, N., Takahashi, F., Tsuji, S.: Attractive quality and must-be quality. Hinshitu (Quality) **4**(2), 147–156 (1984). https://doi.org/10.20684/quality.14.2_147. (in Japanese)

Creating New Strategies for the Changing Sports Business ~The Case of Nippon Professional Baseball~

Masaru Kondo[1][✉] and Yumi Asahi[2]

[1] School of Information and Telecommunication Engineering, Course of Information Telecommunication Engineering, Tokai University, Tokyo, Japan
6bjm1219@star.tokai-u.jp
[2] School of Information and Telecommunication Engineering, Department of Management System Engineering, Tokai University, Tokyo, Japan
asahi@tsc.u-tokai.ac.jp

Abstract. Baseball is a popular sport mainly in Japan, Asia, and the United States, and over the past five years, Japanese baseball teams have made significant changes to the way business strategies are created. They brought content from major league baseball fields and created new content in home stadiums such as Ferris wheels and merry-go-rounds in case of Tohoku Rakuten Golden Eagles. The content to the home stadium they are working hard to create content that will entertain us every day. However, the size of the Japanese and Western sports markets is very different now. The reason is that Europe and America have better ideas than Japan and have a wide range of uses other than sports. In particular, there is income and investment from the private sector and various facilities and equipment, but Japan is limited. We were wondering what impact this changing sports business would have on viewers. Reach different elements such as date, time, event, present, game situation. Using the open data on the official website of the Japanese baseball team and the historical weather data on the weather site, we investigated the effect of the number of spectators on the event factors.

This study used random forest analysis and correspondence analysis. Traditionally, multiple regression analysis has been used to determine the effect of audience size, but there is an error between the predicted and actual measurements. Therefore, we adopted a classification method performed in the random forest. This is an ensemble learning algorithm that integrates weak learners to improve generalization ability. since the main influence is on the number of spectators, which is a sports business, there is a problem that an error appears between the predicted value and the actually measured value. Since the number of people that can actually be accommodated at baseball stadiums in Japan varies between large and small stadiums, the spectator mobilization is based on an analysis using a random forest by calculating the seat occupancy rate based on the average number of spectators/capacity. Since the factor that increases the number can be calculated, it can also be used in sports other than baseball in the future. Furthermore, because it is possible to see the impact on popularity due to event details in the correspondence analysis, it is possible to derive a new sports business idea.

Keywords: Sports marketing · Random forest analysis · Baseball event contents

© Springer Nature Switzerland AG 2020
S. Yamamoto and H. Mori (Eds.): HCII 2020, LNCS 12184, pp. 222–235, 2020.
https://doi.org/10.1007/978-3-030-50020-7_15

1   Introduction

This study is an analysis of the marketing business in Nippon Professional Baseball (NPB). Japanese baseball consists of two leagues, Central League and Pacific League, and 12 teams.

In 2019, the Pacific League recorded the most audiences and the Central League recorded the mobilization of the crowd that came in 1992 (Fig. 1).

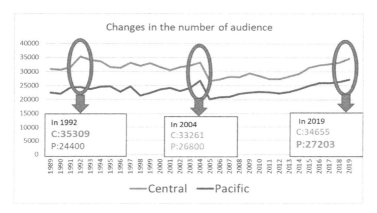

Fig. 1. Changes in the number of audience in Nippon Professional Baseball

Among them, Rakuten Eagles introduced cashless payment at the stadium in 2019. Park facilities such as a ferris wheel are also located in the stadium (Fig. 2) (Fig. 3).

Fig. 2. Charge electronic money place   **Fig. 3.** Rakuten Golden Eagles Home stadium

Other teams also perform live distribution using VR and live broadcasts using movie theaters at Softbank Hawks, and beer gardens at Yokohama Baystars.

In recent years, the Japanese sports community has brought new business strategies, including the birth of new leagues such as basketball. However, the average annual income of the world's major leagues is very different in Japanese sports from other countries. Specifically, there is a difference in the concept of a stadium. In the case of Japan, only the sports business strategy is given, and the company only has naming rights and income (Fig. 4).

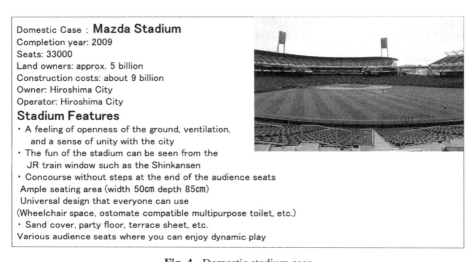

Fig. 4. Domestic stadium case

Ricoh Arena in the UK, on the other hand, has non-sport hotels, conferences and casinos. This gives a total of 60–70% (Fig. 5).

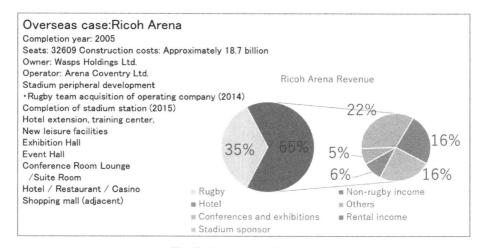

Fig. 5. Overseas stadium case

The table above shows the average annual income of the major leagues in the world. Among them, Japanese sports organizations are NPB and J-League (Fig. 6).

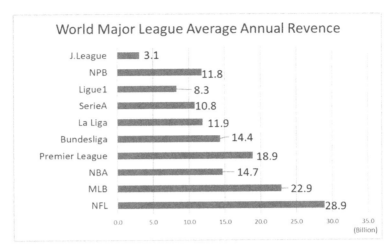

Fig. 6. World major league average annual revence

As you can see, Japan is 10 billion distant from the NFL and Premier League. Looking at this graph, it seems that there is a difference in how to get income between Japan and other countries. Also, in the American Major League, with the aim of providing an experience that cannot be enjoyed unless it is a stadium, which is an important basis for watching sports, the emphasis is on responding to the needs of the audience, and a mechanism to stimulate the potential needs of the audience is provided. As a result, they have been creating spectator spaces that are more closely related to extraordinary events such as games, such as the Seattle Mariners' hometown of T-Mobile Park, where different events and handouts are held every game. The first attraction is that you can enjoy a variety of craft beers and local restaurants in Seattle, and the Yankees has a sports bar and a hard rock cafe in the stadium, free live baseball In the major league baseball stadiums, there is a combination of content that can be seen and experiences that can only be enjoyed at the stadium. The other hand, which is to have a different content, in Japan there is also a part that is common, a major challenge is to not fully taking advantage of all the features of the baseball team. We were wondering what impact this changing sports business would have on viewers. The purpose of this study is to examine how Nippon Professional Baseball's business strategy drives demand for audiences. In particular, the Pacific League seat occupancy is significantly lower than the Central League seat occupancy. Therefore, the analysis focused on the Pacific League.

2 Data Summary

This survey uses the official websites of six baseball teams participating in the Nippon Professional Baseball Pacific League and viewer data released by the Japan Baseball Organization. In addition, we analyzed the game data of companies that handle sports data in Japan and the past weather published online by the Japan Meteorological Society. The outline is as follows.

Table 1. Part of usage data

Team	Date	Day	Weekdays	Holiday	Opponent team	Start time	Night game	Day game	Audience	Maximum capacity
1.Tohoku Rakuten	April.3	Tuesday	1	0	Fighters	16:00	1	0	26622	30580
1.Tohoku Rakuten	April.4	Wednesday	1	0	Fighters	13:00	0	1	24179	30580
1.Tohoku Rakuten	April.5	Thursday	1	0	Fighters	13:00	0	1	24071	30580
1.Tohoku Rakuten	April.6	Friday	1	0	Hawks	18:00	1	0	20721	30580
1.Tohoku Rakuten	April.7	Saturday	0	1	Hawks	14:00	0	1	22857	30580

Table 2. Part of usage data

Place	Percentage	Weather	Main weather	Sunny	Cloudy	Rain	Event details
Rakuten Seimei Park	87%	Cloudy then sunny	2. Cloudy	1	1	0	Opening match for the home ※Opening ceremony Kazumasa Oda Fleece hoodie gift (all visitors) ※Memorial to Senichi Hoshino Wearing 77 Uni Noodle Festival Smile Glico Park Opening Event
Rakuten Seimei Park	79%	Cloudy then sunny	2. Cloudy	1	1	0	Noodle Festival @ Smile Glico Park Opening Event
Rakuten Seimei Park	79%	Sunny	1. Sunny	1	0	0	Noodle Festival @ Smile Glico Park Opening Event
Rakuten Seimei Park	68%	Rain	3. Rain	0	0	1	Fan Club Limited Wheeler Players Players Figures First 7,000 Gifts 500 Yen Collectible Garapon Lottery Noodle Festival Smile Glico Park Opening Event
Rakuten Seimei Park	75%	Cloudy with occasional rain	2. Cloudy	0	1	1	Baseball Music Festival Noodle Festival Smile Glico Park Opening Event 47 Cap Festa (Original Product Presented by Purchase) The first 1000 people to purchase uniforms Parker and Blanket Garapon Lottery

Table 3. Explanation of variables used

Variable	Example data	Description	Format
Match ID	2017033101	Match unique ID (date and game number)	10 digit integer
Date	2017/3/31	Match date	Date
Home team ID	1	Home Team Unique ID	1 to 3 digit integer
Home team name	巨人	Home team name	String
Away team ID	2	Unique ID of the other team	1 to 3 digit integer
Away team name	阪神	Opponent team name	String
Stadium ID	1	Stadium unique ID	1 to 5 digit integer
Stadium name	Tokyo Dome	Stadium name	String
Match type	Official match	Match type	String
Match type details	Sereg Official Game	Details by type of match	String
Home team scoring	3	Home team score	1 to 2 digit integer
Away Team Score	0	Opponent team score	1 to 2 digit integer
Match inning	9	Inning after the match	1 to 2 digit integer
Number of visitors	45000	Number of visitors	4 to 5 digit integer
Commentary	The giant won	Details of the match	String

Variable used: Number of audiences, maximum capacity, game date, weekdays, holidays, day games, Night game, weather, event contents (2018 Pacific League official game 6 teams 429 games) (Tables 1 and 2).

The study also uses the following data. The outline is as follows.

Data name: 01. Baseball game

Period: 2017, 2018 season

Range of use: 143 games of 12 teams in 2017, 143 games of 12 teams in 2018, totaling 286 games (Table 3).

3 Analysis Result

3.1 Analytical Method

This study used random forest analysis and correspondence analysis. Traditionally, multiple regression analysis was used to examine the effect of audience size. However, multiple regression analysis introduces an error between the predicted value and the actual measured value. We adopted a classification method that is performed in a random forest. This is an ensemble learning algorithm that integrates weak learners to improve generalization ability. In the random forest, the decision tree analysis was performed first, and then the significance of the explanatory variables was determined in the random forest in order to check for misinterpretation. In addition, many studies have analyzed many factors, so we assigned 0 or 1 data to each event and performed aggregate correspondence analysis to analyze the event details.

3.2   Analysis Result: Basic Aggregation

Before beginning the analysis of this study, we calculated the seat occupancy for 2018 in the Central League and the Pacific League. Because the actual number of people that can be accommodated in a Japanese baseball stadium differs between a large stadium and a small stadium, audience recruitment calculates the seat occupancy based on the average number of people/capacity and solves the problem that occurs with multiple regression analysis. Here is the result (Table 4).

Table 4. Nippon professional Baseball seat occupancy rate

CentralLeague	2018	2018Night	2018Daygame	2018Weekday	2018Hoilday
Giants	93%	92%	97%	91%	97%
Swallows	86%	86%	92%	81%	95%
Baystars	92%	91%	93%	91%	93%
Dragons	83%	75%	97%	75%	96%
Tigers	89%	85%	97%	84%	96%
Carp	95%	95%	96%	95%	96%
PacificLeague	2018	2018Night	2018Daygame	2018Weekday	2018Hoilday
Hawks	95%	93%	97%	93%	97%
Eagles	79%	78%	82%	76%	83%
Marines	76%	68%	92%	65%	91%
Lions	75%	68%	90%	64%	90%
Fighters	69%	62%	81%	61%	80%
Baffloes	64%	63%	66%	57%	73%

The table above shows the percentage of seats occupied by the Japan Professional Baseball 2018 season.

While the Central League has a relatively high figure, the Pacific League has four teams with significant challenges in weekday and night games.

3.3   Analysis Result: To Get the Audience

Frist of all, we performed a decision tree analysis and random forest to determine the factors that get the audience.

The objective variables are "popularity" and "remaining seats", calculated from seat occupancy. These variables are based on 80%. The reason is that the maximum capacity is determined based on the Japanese Fire Service Law. The variables used and Branching method for it are as follows.

Variables used: Date and time of the event (weekday holiday @ night game 4 items, weather 3 items (sunny and cloudy rain), event details 17 items in total (contents: number of distributions, distribution target audience, number of events, event content, limited Sales (goods sales, etc.))

Branching method: entropy (information amount)

Post decision tree analysis first.

In the decision tree above, you can see that the branch is split around the item "holiday". In addition, if it does not fall on a holiday, you will find that "Distribution to all visitors" and "Distribution of uniforms and products" are required.

Next, to determine whether this interpretation was correct, we calculated the importance of explanation using a random forest.

The result is shown on the next page. In Fig. 6, "Holiday" has the highest value. The next highest are "Number of Items Distributed", "Weekdays", and "Distribute Team Products". From the above, We think that there is no problem in the way of interpretation.

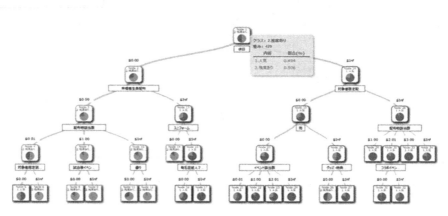

Fig. 7. Decision tree analysis results

Table 5. Evaluation of random forest model

Popularity.objective variable.key	Popularity.judgment result popularity	Judgment result.number
1. Popular	True	161
1. Popular	False	51
2. Remaining seats	True	168
2. Remaining seats	False	49

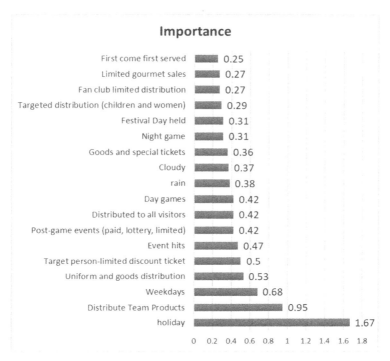

Fig. 8. Explanatory variable importance

Also, when the model evaluation of the random forest was examined, the correct answer rate was 75% from the above table, and it is considered that there is no problem with the evaluation (Table 5).

3.4 Analysis Result: Characteristics of Each Team

Next, we investigated the content of the event content using correspondence analysis. When performing the survey, if $p < 0.05$ was significant, it was determined by performing a chi-square test. This is to determine if the variables used can make a difference in the characteristics of the event factor.

The analysis was performed using the following variables based on the results of the performed chi-square test.

Variables used: 2 items for popularity (popularity, remaining seats available) 15 event details (Distribution on a first-come-first-served basis, limited distribution to fan clubs, limited distribution to target audience (children and women), ticket discounts, discount tickets for limited audiences, tickets with goods, festival events, collaboration events, post-game events (free/all), Post-game events (pay, lottery, limited), limited goods sale, food and beverage discounts, campaigns, limited gourmet sales, fireworks, free lottery) (Fig. 9).

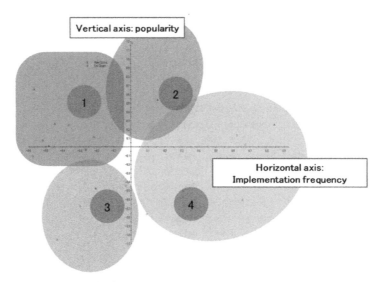

Fig. 9. Results of correspondence analysis

The results of the correspondence analysis are shown in Fig. 7, where the vertical axis is the degree of popularity and the horizontal axis is the frequency of implementation, and the relationships between the categories were interpreted.

The summary of the results is as follows and is described together with the target team.

1. Holding events with different contents for each season
   Target teams: Hawks, Eagles
2. Many tickets with special benefits. Target team: Fighters
3. Conducting events and services targeting fans and targets
   Target team: Lions
4. There are many first-come, first-served and lottery events.

   Target teams: Marines, Buffaloes
   Classification is based on the four interpretations above. Popular teams like Eagles and Hawks provide content that doesn't get tired of changing content every season.
   Other teams had low seat occupancy due to poor location and event content.
   In particular, teams that are far away may need more attractive content.

4   Interpretation and Ideas Based on Analysis Result

4.1   For Other Sports and the Olympics

In this study, we investigated the event factors of baseball games. It is thought that it can predict the demand of spectators such as soccer and basketball. Especially in Japan, there is a difference in the maximum capacity of a soccer field. Basketball has also recently been running and has also been operating the B-League for four years. We think it can be used to expect more customers in the future. Especially in recent years, the operation of facilities has not been successful in the operation of facilities after the Olympics, and the Olympic Games held in Beijing and the Rio de Janeiro Olympics have become ruined.

4.2 To Attract a Large Audience

Sports events need compelling content that appeals to as many people as possible. For example, in the Japanese sports world, rugby representatives are performing well in the World Cup Top 8. In the basketball world, Louis Hachimura was ranked number one by the NBA Draft Washington Wizard. It was noted that this was the first Japanese achievement, and many people visited the place where the international friendly match was held.

There may be some causal relationship in attracting attention to sporting events in this way, but We think that the event factor surveyed this time will need to be done in the future. Especially after the Olympics, as a sacred place, we think that content specialized for it is preferable. Even at Nippon Professional Baseball surveyed this time, we sometimes challenge the game with a different uniform than the one usually worn by players. At that time, a commemorative replica uniform may be distributed to all visitors free of charge to commemorate the event. In this way, as a way to use it after the Olympics, it would be good to distribute the scenes that left an impression at the time of the event at the time of the event as T-shirts every time the event is held.

In addition, children who are candidates for future competition need to purchase equipment at low prices and set up facilities as a place to practice. In particular, there are baseball games at the Tokyo Olympics, but there are currently few places where you can play the catch ball. To overcome the current situation, it is desirable to create an environment that provides a place for many children to exercise. The figure below shows the current sports population of junior high school students in Japan (Figure 8).

Japanese junior high school students have recently been affected by a decline in motor skills. Japanese junior high school students have recently been affected by a decline in motor skills. This is thought to be mainly due to the regulation of ball games in the park and the spread of smartphones. Simply put, you lose the feeling of playing outside. After the Tokyo Olympics, Japan felt that it would be desirable to provide content that appeals to parents and children, including children, for Japan facing the problems of aging, declining birthrate, and the Internet (Fig. 10).

A specific example is the introduction of facility management where you can play on the spot whenever your schedule is free. Professional baseball players and athletes will eventually find what they do not use. Rather than throwing it away, donating equipment so that adults and children can play, and operating facilities so that they can always play, will create healthy and strong children and future athletes.

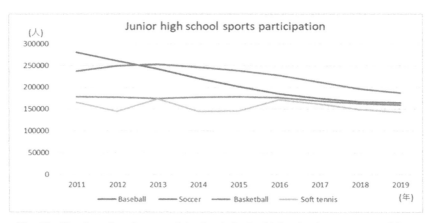

Fig. 10. Number of students participating in junior high school sports competitions

5   Conclusion

The study conducted an attribution analysis based on open data described in three updated sites and found that it was desirable to provide engaging content to audiences. However, there are some areas where accurate data cannot be obtained, and there is also individual subjectivity, so it is necessary to improve accuracy and processing. In addition, we have seen papers on the prediction of visitors in terms of price and the degree of impact when famous players enter, and we hope that the relevant section can be calculated using the method used this time.

References

1. Nippon Professional Baseball Organization (Statistical Data). http://npb.jp/statistics/. Accessed 24 Jan 2020
2. Tohoku Rakuten Golden Eagles Official site. https://www.rakuteneagles.jp/. Accessed 24 Jan 2020
3. Sports Agency Ministry of Economy, Trade and Industry: Sports Future Development Conference Interim Report (2016)
4. MLB Mariner.com. https://www.mlb.com/mariners. Accessed 20 Feb 2020
5. MLB Yankees.com. https://www.mlb.com/yankees. Accessed 20 Feb 2020
6. Hokkaido Nippon-Ham Fighters Official Site. https://sp.fighters.co.jp. Accessed 24 Jan 2020
7. Saitama Seibu Lions Official Site. https://www.seibulions.jp. Accessed 24 Jan 2020
8. Chiba Lotte Marines Official Site. https://www.marines.co.jp. Accessed 24 Jan 2020
9. ORIX Buffaloes Official Website. https://www.buffaloes.co.jp. Accessed 24 Jan 2020
10. Japan Meteorological Association@Tenka.jp. https://tenki.jp. Accessed 7 Dec 2019
11. Shigemura, T., Kuroki, S., Kitakami, H., Mori, Y.: Estimating the number of spectators in professional baseball games using LVQ. In: 2nd Forum on Data Engineering and Information Management DEIM 2010 Online Proceedings, Hiroshima City University (2010)
12. Ozaki, T.: Data mining for business. Technol. Rev. 119–162 (2014)
13. Kraussen, S.E., Fujimoto, K.: Introduction to Correspondence Analysis: From Principles to Applications, Ohmsha (2015)

14. Business Insider: Pyeongchang, Tokyo OK? Competition facilities around the world where the Olympics are held. https://www.businessinsider.jp/post-161687. Accessed 19 Feb 2020
15. Japan Junior High School Physical Education Federation Member schools. http://njpa.sakura.ne.jp/kamei.html. Accessed 13 Jan 2020

Consumer Analysis of High Sensitivity Layer

Yoshio Matsuyama[✉] and Yumi Asahi

School of Information and Telecommunication Engineering, Department of Management
System Engineering, Tokai University, Shibuya, Japan
ym@fuji.tokai-u.jp, asahi@tsc.u-tokai.ac.jp

Abstract. Today, test marketing is often performed in order to perform marketing
efficiently. The purpose of this study is to conduct test marketing of food more
efficiently. We focus on the Innovation Theory and report on "food" from the
study purpose. Matsuyama and Asahi are conducting similar study. Matsuyama
and Asahi created a generalized model with a deep learning model to achieve a
similar goal. In this study, logistic regression analysis is performed using the same
objective variables and explanatory variables, and the results are compared with
the Matsuyama and Asahi study results. In addition, in the analysis of Matsuyama
and Asahi, they did not see the text information when posting the report. This time
we analyzed this text information in addition to the logistic regression analysis.
We searched the word which is likely to come to make reports easy to emphasize
and hard to emphasize about the report. In this study, we used data from an SNS
site called Minrepo, which may be applicable to other platforms.

Keywords: Innovation Theory · Natural language processing · Logistic
regression analysis

1 Introduction

Today, test marketing is often performed in order to perform marketing efficiently. Test
marketing is a method of selling products on a trial basis before actually selling or
deploying the products, performing a preliminary simulation, and identifying issues
based on the results before conducting full-scale sales. The advantages of test marketing
are that it can reduce the risk of failure, make efficient sales plans, and accurately
understand the target users. Test marketing is generally done in representative cities, e.g.
Tokyo, Kyoto, Osaka and Shizuoka in Japan. Among them, Shizuoka is the area most
often selected for test marketing (see Fig. 1). Reasons include "they tend to be close to
the national market" and "excellent in logistics". In this way, before the development
of the Internet and its associated services, test marketing was common in some regions.
However, in recent years when the Internet and the like have developed, test marketing
using SNS and crowdfunding has been performed. Despite the Internet's development,
using such techniques, except for products sell only on EC sites, can lead to erroneous
decisions unless you are aware of the bias. Attention must be paid to that point.

We propose ways to make test marketing more efficient. The research target is "food",
the place of sale is a store, and the selling party is assumed to be a general consumer.

© Springer Nature Switzerland AG 2020
S. Yamamoto and H. Mori (Eds.): HCII 2020, LNCS 12184, pp. 236–249, 2020.
https://doi.org/10.1007/978-3-030-50020-7_16

Fig. 1. Location of Shizuoka in Japan

There are three reasons for this. For one thing, the food contains dairy products that need to be refrigerated and can be easily purchased at convenience stores. Another reason is that if you do not care much, in Japan where there is a convenience store nearby, you will not stock up the same food on EC sites in large quantities. Finally, new food products are easier to develop than new varieties such as cars and vegetables.

In this study, we focus on Innovation Theory. Innovation Theory [1] was proposed in 1962 by Professor E. M. Rogers. This theory has been successful in a wide variety of fields, including communication, agriculture, public health, criminal justice, and marketing. In Japan, research using Innovation Theory has been researching the introduction of new vegetable varieties with a long sales period. Another study similar to this study is "High Sensitivity Layer Feature Analysis in Food Market" by Matsuyama and Asahi [2]. This study is discussed in depth in Sect. 2.

From Innovation Theory, if it can be disseminated to Innovators and Early Adopters, it is known that leading to Early Majority and Late Majority (see Fig. 2), the market share will rise significantly (see Fig. 3). The characteristics of the Innovator and Early Adopter are that they are interested in product innovation and are sensitive to trends and constantly collect new information themselves and have a great influence on other consumers.

In this study, these two layers are called "High Sensitivity Layer". We think that "High Sensitivity Layer" with keeping them eyes open, and products that them sympathize will

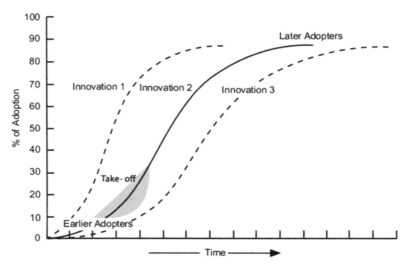

Fig. 2. Diffusion process

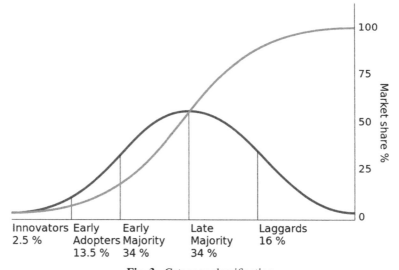

Fig. 3. Category classification

diffusion from the innovation theory to the Early and Late Majority and the market share is expanded to expand. We think that those that collect a lot of empathy in the "High Sensitivity Layer" are diffusive in the innovators and the early adopters, and grab the characteristics of highly sensitive consumers who gather many empathies. We think that it may be able to fulfill the purpose of test marketing by seeing the response of new products of food to this consumer. In this study, logistic regression analysis is used to analyze the factors that make reports easy to empathize. In addition, in the analysis of

Matsuyama and Asahi, they did not see the text information when posting the report. This time we analyze this text information in addition to the logistic regression analysis. We search the word which is likely to come to make reports easy to emphasize and hard to emphasize about the report.

2 Previous Study

As a previous study, I will mention Matsuyama and Asahi. Matsuyama and Asahi reported the characteristics of consumers belonging to the "High Sensitivity Layer" defined in this study. They prepared a generalized model with a deep learning model and report features of highly sensitive consumers, visually and numerically clearly, using decision tree analysis from that model. Table 1 lists the variables they used primarily.

Table 1. Mainly used variables of previous study

Variables name	Data type1	Data type2	Details
Genre	Text	SA	Kinds of report (objects report, places report, foods report, note report)
Sub-Genre	Text	SA	Detail of genre
Foods report type	Text	SA	Detail of foods report. Set only foods report. (eaten out, cooked, bought or received)
Feelings	Text	SA	Report feelings (excitement, pleasure, favorite, puzzle, reglet, angry)
Gender	Text	SA	User set up
Age	Integer	SA	User set up
Number of favorites	Integer	-	Represent empathy to the report
Number of wish	Integer	-	Number entered in other user's wish list
Number of activity	Integer	-	Number tapped by people who did similar actions

Then, the analysis was performed using the two values defined by them as the "sympathy report" and the "non-sympathetic report". From the data we handle, they used a network structure called multilayer perceptron (see Fig. 4) to construct a deep learning model.

Table 2 shows the hyperparameters set for the creation of the deep learning model. As a result, the correct answer rate in the deep learning model was 73.263%.

In addition, a decision tree analysis is performed, and Table 3 shows the settings used. Figure 5 shows the result of performing a decision tree analysis using the settings.

From Matsuyama and Asahi, high sensitivity consumers write an empathic report as "the number of images is the most important", "the age is important next", and "the emotions and gender when writing the report are less relevant".

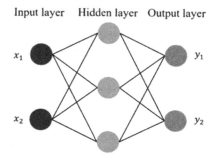

Fig. 4. Architecture of multi-layer perceptron

Table 2. Parameter adjustment method and the hyperparameters set for the creation of the deep learning model

Parameter adjustment method or parameter name	Value
Parameter adjustment method	Bayesian optimization using random forest
Parameter adjustment index	Accuracy
Optimization function	AdaDelta
Learning rate	0.0001
Mini-batch size	64
Number of epochs	100

Table 3. Setting of decision tree analysis

Explanatory variable	Max branch	Parameter	Contents
Number of images	5	Objective variable	Empathy or non-empathetic
Feelings	Unlimited	Branching method	Gini coefficient
Gender	Unlimited	Min number of data	0.80%
Age	5	Max branch	5
		Node impurity	0.01
		Height limit	Unlimited
		Weighting	Nothing

3   Data Summary

We analyzed the report posted on the living post & enterprise co-creation SNS application "Minrepo". In this study, 6,367 reports with genre "Foods report" and type "Bought or Received" were targeted. The used data period is from January 1, 2016 to June 30, 2016. "Minrepo" is a Japanese SNS service, but it is "Twitter" when compared to famous

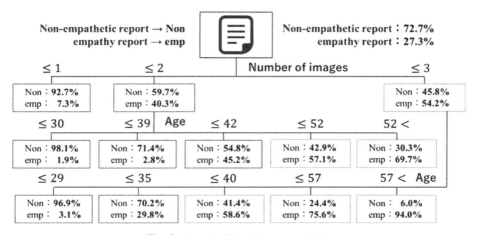

Fig. 5. Result of decision tree analysis

SNS. The user is different from Twitter. According to the official Minrepo site [3], high sensitivity consumers are users. The high sensitivity consumer's post "Reports" of "Minrepo users" will receive responses from the same highly sensitive consumers. Minrepo's popular tabs sort and display "favorite" in descending order on reports posted within a few days. In this study as in previous study, we define "empathy report" for favorite number of 10 or more, and "non-empathetic report" for less than 10 favorites. The 2 values are taken as objective variables and analyzed.

Here, basic tallying is performed on the data to be analyzed. Figure 6 shows the distribution of "Number of Favorites" for each report. Figure 7 shows the report type ratio and gender ratio, and Fig. 8 shows the report type ratio for each gender. From Fig. 6, it can be seen that reports having "favorites" of less than 10 occupy most of the entire report, and that it is slightly difficult for "favorites" to be 10 or more. From here you can see the difficulty of writing a report that fits into the popular tab. Figure 7 shows the report type ratio and gender ratio of the people who wrote the food report. It can be seen that the ratio of empathy reports is lower than the ratio of non-empathetic reports, and that many women write food reports.

From Fig. 8, it can be seen that men write about half the number of people who write empathy reports compared to those who write non-empathetic reports, and that women write about the same number of people who write empathy reports and non-empathetic reports.

Figure 9 shows the ratio of emotions specified in the food report. About a quarter were "nothing" and 3.29% were negative. In the food report, about 70% were posted with positive emotions.

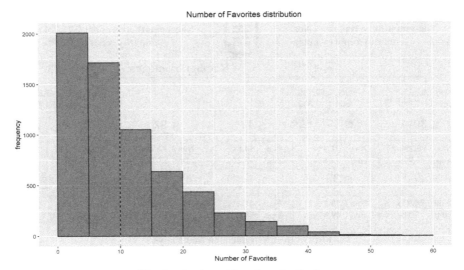

Fig. 6. Number of favorites distribution

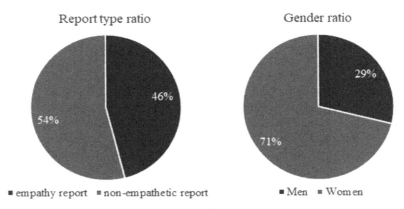

Fig. 7. Report type ratio and gender ratio

4 Logistic Regression Analysis

Logistic regression analysis is a regression analysis that predicts the probability of becoming a target variable. The equation is as shown in Eq. (1).

$$Y = \begin{cases} 1, & f(x) \geq 0.5 \\ 0, & f(x) < 0.5 \end{cases}$$

$$f(x) = \text{logit}^{-1}\left(\beta_0 + \sum\nolimits_{t=1}^{m} \beta_{it}x_{it} + r_i\right) \tag{1}$$

The difference between ordinary regression analysis and logistic regression analysis is that the scale of the objective variable to be predicted is different [4]. Logistic regression

Report type ratio per gender

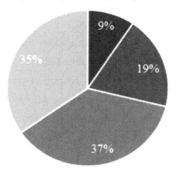

■ Men-emp ■ Men-non ■ Women-emp ▪ Women-non

Fig. 8. Report type ratio per gender

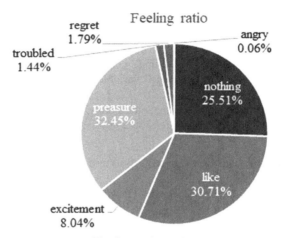

Fig. 9. Feeling ratio

analysis is a regression equation that predicts qualitative probabilities, and is also a regression analysis that can predict data on a scale below the ordinal scale. The method is a non-linear regression analysis using a link function called a logit function. By using this link function, the range can be restricted from 0 to 1. Logistic regression analysis does not predict the value of the objective variable according to the explanatory variable, but predicts the probability of becoming a specific objective variable. In other words, it is an analysis method that predicts the odds, which is the ratio of the probability that a target event occurs and the probability that it does not occur.

Perform logistic regression analysis using the data in Sect. 3. Table 4 shows the variables used in the analysis.

An explanatory variable scale that can be used in logistic regression analysis is a proportional scale. The explanatory variables used included an ordinal scale. If this variable is used as an explanatory variable as it is, it deviates from the assumption of

Table 4. List of variables used for logistic regression analysis

Kind of variables	Variable names
Objective variable	empathy report or non-empathic report (Binary)
Explanatory variables	Number of attached images
Explanatory variables	Feelings when posting a report
Explanatory variables	Gender of the person who posted the report
Explanatory variables	Age of the person who posted the report

logistic regression analysis, and an incorrect result is obtained. Therefore, variables of "Number of attached images", "Feelings when posting a report", and "Gender of the person who posted the report" were processed. Since "Number of attached images" takes only four values from 0 to 3, it was changed to a dummy variable. "Gender of the person who posted the report" was also made a dummy variable. Furthermore, since "Feelings when posting a report" was a discrete value of 7 values, it was too large to be used as a dummy variable. Therefore, we changed the three variables "like", "excitement", and "pleasure" to "Positive" and changed the three variables "troubled", "regret", and "angry" to "Negative". These and "Nothing" were combined into three values, which were used as dummy variables. The "Age" variable was used as is as an explanatory variable.

Table 5 shows the log odds ratio, the standard error, the z value, and the significance probability of the results of logistic regression analysis.

Table 5. Logistic regression analysis results (log odds ratio)

	Estimate	Std. error	z value	Pr (> |z|)
(Intercept)	−7.6396	0.7422	−10.2935	0.0000
Women	1.4309	0.0707	20.2431	0.0000
Ages	0.0606	0.0034	17.9693	0.0000
feelings.category2Posi	0.6582	0.0690	9.5423	0.0000
feelings.category2Nega	0.3024	0.1677	1.8034	0.0713
image.number1	2.8220	0.7211	3.9133	0.0001
image.number2	3.5864	0.7223	4.9656	0.0000
image.number3	4.3157	0.7228	5.9708	0.0000

Table 6 shows the odds ratio, standard error, and 95% confidence interval.

AIC is called Akaike's information criterion and is a relative evaluation value for comparing statistical models based on data. Defined by Eq. (2), where the dimension of parameter a is k [5].

$$AIC(k) = -2L(a_{k0}|x) + 2k \qquad (2)$$

Table 6. Logistic regression analysis results (odds ratio)

	Estimate	Std. error	2.5%	97.5%
(Intercept)	0.0005	2.1005	0.0001	0.0016
Women	4.1827	1.0732	3.6443	4.8080
Ages	1.0625	1.0034	1.0556	1.0696
feelings.category2Posi	1.9313	1.0714	1.6878	2.2119
feelings.category2Nega	1.3531	1.1826	0.9727	1.8780
image.number1	16.8110	2.0568	5.2286	102.8327
image.number2	36.1050	2.0591	11.1943	221.1525
image.number3	74.8626	2.0602	23.1768	458.8511

5   Text Mining

The data used in this study included comments as text data. We search the word which is likely to come to make reports easy to emphasize and hard to emphasize about the report.

In this study, spaCy and GiNZA were used for morphological analysis. spaCy is an open source natural language processing library implemented in Python/Cython developed by Explosion AI. It supports many languages and comes with trained statistical models and word vectors. However, the "many languages" did not include Japanese. Japanese has three writing styles, "Hiragana", "Katakana", and "Kanji", and the subject is often omitted in sentences. Furthermore, unlike English, it is very difficult to extract words because words are not separated by spaces. For these reasons, Japanese may not have been included in spaCy's corresponding "many languages". Here, GiNZA, a research result of Recruit Co., Ltd. and the National Institute for Japanese Language and Linguistics, will appear in April 2019. According to Recruit Co., Ltd. [6], GiNZA has three main features. The first is "Complete introduction of advanced natural language processing in one step". The second is "corresponding to high-speed, high-precision analysis processing and internationalization of dependent structure analysis level". The third is "Providing a learning model for the results of joint research with the National Institute for Japanese Language and Linguistics". With the development of GiNZA, it is now possible to analyze in Japanese using spaCy. Using spaCy and GiNZA, morphologically analyze the comments in the empathic report and the non-empathic report. After morphological analysis, only nouns and verbs were extracted and their frequencies were counted. Some emoticons that were incorrectly identified as nouns/verbs when counting the frequency were excluded.

Figure 10 shows a histogram of words of the "empathy report", and Fig. 11 shows a word cloud. Note that the words in Fig. 10 were translated into English, but the exact nuances may be different. Figure 12 shows a histogram of words of the "non-empathy report", and Fig. 13 shows a word cloud. Note that the words in Fig. 12 may also have different exact nuances.

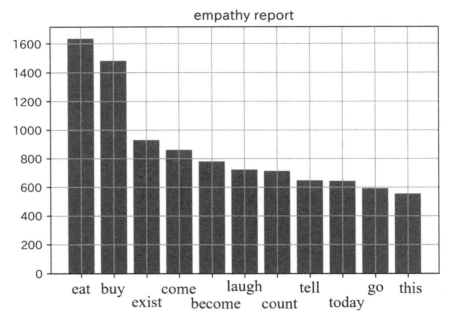

Fig. 10. Histogram of words in empathy report (top 10 words)

Fig. 11. Word cloud (empathy report)

6 Conclusion

6.1 Discussion

This Section discusses and concludes the analysis performed in Sects. 4 and 5.

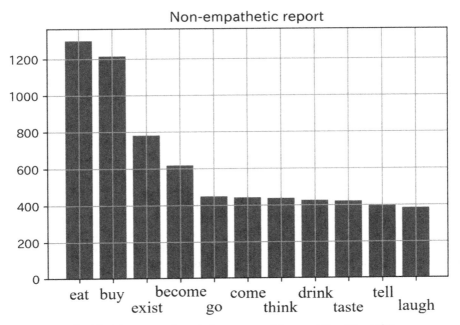

Fig. 12. Histogram of words in non-empathic report (top 10 words)

Fig. 13. Word cloud (non-empathic report)

The results of the logistic regression analysis showed that the number of images attached to the report had the greatest effect. It can be seen from the odds ratio that the effect of the number of attached images is very large compared to other variables.

Furthermore, among the number of attached images, it was found that the greater the number of attached images, the higher the probability of becoming an empathic report. Gender women are the second most influential. It turns out that women are more likely to write empathy reports than men. On the other hand, "emotion" and "age" were also used as explanatory variables in logistic regression analysis. These two variables were shown to be less important.

When developing a new product of food, it is necessary to care about the sensitive layer from Innovation Theory. In conclusion, from the results of logistic regression analysis, it was found that it was important to look at the response of the person who attaches many images even in the high-sensitivity layer, and then to look at the response by gender. Taken together with the results of previous studies in Sect. 2, it is shown that the number of attached images is the most important factor. What has been identified as the most important factor in the two alternative approaches is that it is so important.

Next, we will look at the results of text mining. In the empathy report and the non-empathic report, the first to third words were exactly the same. The words were "eat", "buy", and "exist". It can be seen from the food report that was analyzed in this study that many people actually posted sweets that could be easily purchased at convenience stores. So what was the difference between the empathy report and the non-empathic report? The major difference was the word "photo". The empathy report ranked 14th in frequency, while the non-empathetic report ranked 38th. This result was consistent with the results of the logistic regression analysis of this study and the results of previous studies, and provided evidence that the attached images were important. From the results of this research, it is thought that test marketing can be performed more efficiently by observing the reaction of the person who attaches many images.

6.2 Future Work

This time, using logistic regression analysis, we analyzed the variables that affect the "empathy report". Together with previous studies, it was well demonstrated that the number of images to attach was important. In this study, text mining was performed on comments. However, other text mining techniques include "word co-occurrence network" and "negative/positive determination". We would like to use these techniques to deepen my knowledge of words that can be more widely used by high-sensitivity consumers. Furthermore, it was shown that the number of images to be attached is important in three methods of decision tree analysis, logistic regression analysis, and text mining using a multilayer perceptron. We want to analyze this image in the future. Specifically, images are first tagged using Google's Vision API. Then, text mining is performed on the tags as in this study. I want to analyze images by this method.

References

1. Rogers, E.M.: Diffusion of Innovations, 3rd edn. Macmillan Publishers, London (1962)
2. Matsuyama, Y., Asahi, Y.: High sensitivity layer feature analysis in food market. In: Yamamoto, S., Mori, H. (eds.) HCII 2019. LNCS, vol. 11570, pp. 232–243. Springer, Cham (2019). https://doi.org/10.1007/978-3-030-22649-7_19

3. INTAGE Inc.: Minrepo SNS analysis. https://www.intage.co.jp/solution/process/market/min reposns. Accessed 20 Oct 2018
4. Wang, J.: Ippanka sennkei moderu (Generalized Linear Model). Asakura shoten, Tokyo (2016)
5. Akaike, H., et al.: Moderinngu -Hiroi shiya wo motomete- (Modeling -Seeking a wide field of view-). Kindai kagakusya, Tokyo (2015)
6. Recruit Co., Ltd. https://www.recruit.co.jp/newsroom/2019/0402_18331.html. Accessed 24 Feb 2020

Comprehensive Evaluation of an Educational Information Management Solution for Parents: MyStudentScope

Theresa Matthews[1](), Jinjuan Heidi Feng[2](), Ying Zheng[1], and Zhijiang Chen[1]

[1] Towson University, Towson, MD 21252, USA
tscott2@students.towson.edu
[2] Frostburg State University, Frostburg, MD 21532, USA
jfeng@towson.edu

Abstract. Existing electronic student information systems used by schools were designed from the perspective of the educators or students, not the parents. Parents and caregivers have challenges optimizing their use of information regarding their children's education (Matthews and Feng 2017). To address this challenge, we developed MyStudentScope (MSS), a web portal that aims at assisting parents in managing information regarding their children's education. MSS has four primary functions to aid its users in accessing and analyzing collected data: monitoring, retrieving, communication and decision making (Matthews et al. 2018a).

A preliminary study was conducted to compare the effectiveness of task completion between the MyStudentScope (MSS) web portal and the traditional paper-based methods by simulating situations parents/caregivers may encounter related to their children's education and extracurricular activities (Matthews et al. 2018b). Although the small group of participants from this study provided an indication of the effectiveness of MSS versus paper, a study with a larger group of users was needed to further validate the results. For this reason, we decided to conduct another study based on the lessons learned from our prior user study with a larger sample size using a refined version of MSS with improved design in several key functions. Detailed results from this study, the implication of the findings and future research are reported in this paper.

Keywords: Parents · Education · Personal information management · PIM · Information organization · Web portal

1 Introduction

Researchers have explored the use of paper in work practices where complexity made the transition to or the use of technology difficult (Bishop 2002; Marcu et al. 2013, Piper et al. 2013; Turner 2010). Extensive research also exists in the area of information management (Bruce et al. 2004; Buttfield-Addison et al. 2012; Oh and Belkin 2011; Trullemans and Signer 2014). No previous research, aside from our prior user study, has been conducted to empirically investigate the use of technology versus paper when

© Springer Nature Switzerland AG 2020
S. Yamamoto and H. Mori (Eds.): HCII 2020, LNCS 12184, pp. 250–264, 2020.
https://doi.org/10.1007/978-3-030-50020-7_17

managing children's educational information. Although the small group of participants from the first user study provided an indication of the effectiveness of MyStudentScope versus paper, a study with a larger group of users was needed to further validate the results. For this reason, we decided to conduct another study based on the lessons learned from our prior user study with a larger sample size. The study aimed at answering the following research questions.

- Are parents able to complete information retrieval tasks more quickly using paper-based methods or MyStudentScope?
- Are parents more frustrated completing information retrieval task using paper-based methods or MyStudentScope?
- Are parents able to make decisions more effectively using paper-based methods or MyStudentScope?
- What are the challenges for parents when using MyStudentScope to complete tasks?
- How can we improve the design of MyStudentScope to better meet the needs of parents?

The design of the study was modified to address challenges that may have negatively impacted prior results. For example, the scrolling function was improved to make it easier to view all available data. The course selection function was also revised to improve selection efficiency.

The pre and post-test questionnaires that had been completed on paper during the preliminary studies were converted into four online surveys. Some of the tasks were also modified to reduce the amount of writing required by the participant to express his/her answers. The motivation for these changes was to decrease participant's fatigue due to writing while completing the test, so that he/she would be willing to provide more complete and informative feedback to the survey questions.

Twenty-three (23) participants took part in this study. Situations parents encounter related to receiving or interacting with information regarding their children's education and extracurricular activities were simulated during the study. A within-group design was adopted and each participant completed functionally equivalent tasks using paper-based methods and MSS. The task completion time, success rate, and perceived level of frustration were documented. Participants also provided feedback regarding their preferences and challenges related to the tasks when using MSS and the paper-based method. The results suggest that, compared to the paper-based solution, MyStudentScope significantly improved the efficiency and reduced the level of frustration for parents when managing educational information.

2   Method

2.1   Participants

Participants include 1) parents of students in grades Kindergarten through 12 that currently use a school-provided electronic student information system, 2) parents having children in grades Pre-Kindergarten through 12 and older children who have used a school-provided electronic student information system in the past and 3) parents of young children who may use a school-provided electronic student information system in the future. Overall, 23 parents having at least one child between the ages of 0–18 participated in the study (7 males and 16 females). Some of the participants also had children over the age of 18. Thirteen (13) of the participants were between the ages of 31 and 40 (average: 41, stdev: 8.01). The majority of participants have more than one child (95.45%). Figure 1 reflects the grade level distribution of the children of the participants. Four parents who participated in study 1 also participated in this usability study.

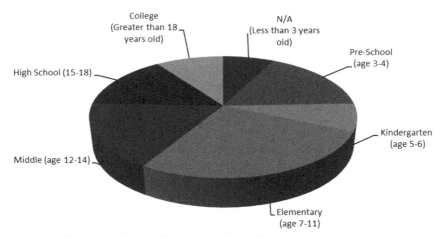

Fig. 1. Grade level distribution of the children of study participants

All participants have been using a computer, smart phone or tablet daily for more than ten years. Sixteen (16) of the participants have a school system-provided education management system available to them. The majority (13) of those with access to an education management system access the system at least once per quarter. Three of the respondents with access to a system do not access it. Table 1 shows the general demographic information for each participant. It includes answers to questions of whether or not an education management system is available to the parents through their child's school and, if available, whether it is used by the parent.

2.2   Experimental Design and Procedure

A within-group design was adopted for this study. Each participant completed similar tasks related to the management and use of educational information for two students under two conditions: paper-based condition and MyStudentScope condition. The order of conditions was balanced to control the learning effect. 11 of the participants completed the tasks under the paper condition first and 12 completed the study under the MyStudentScope condition.

At the beginning of the study, the participants completed a pre-test questionnaire to provide information regarding their demographics, computer and information management experience and preferences. During the formal task session, participants completed

Table 1. General demographic information for participants

ID	Gender	Age	Number of children	Availability of education management system	Education management system in use
P1	F	31–40	3	Yes	No
P2	M	31–40	3	Yes	No
P3	F	31–40	3	Yes	No
P4	F	31–40	3	Yes	Yes
P5	M	51–60	4	Yes	Yes
P6	F	41–50	4	Yes	Yes
P7	F	31–40	3	No	N/A
P8	F	41–50	5	Yes	Yes
P9	M	41–50	3	No	N/A
P10	F	41–50	3	Yes	Yes
P11	F	31–40	3	Yes	Yes
P12	F	51–60	5	Yes	Yes
P13	M	31–40	3	No	N/A
P14	F	41–50	3	Yes	Yes
P16	F	31–40	3	N/A	N/A
P17	F	41–50	3	Yes	Yes
P18	F	31–40	4	N/A	N/A
P19	F	31–40	2	Yes	Yes
P20	F	31–40	3	Yes	Yes
P21	M	51–60	3	Yes	Yes
P22	F	31–40	4	Yes	Yes
P23	M	31–40	3	No	No

a total of 24 tasks; 14 using MyStudentScope and 10 using paper. At the beginning of the MyStudentScope condition, each user was given a brief demo of the MyStudentScope web portal. A MyStudentScope user guide was also available to participants as a reference during the test. Upon completion of tasks for each condition, the participant was asked to complete a questionnaire regarding their satisfaction and frustration. Upon completion of all tasks participants were asked to complete a questionnaire comparing their experience using paper to MyStudentScope. All participants completed the tasks; however pre and post-test survey responses were only recorded for 22 participants. In general, each session lasted approximately 1 ½ to 2 h.

To avoid privacy concerns, four fictional student data sets were created for the study: Amelia, Jack, Emily and Oliver. Two of the test data sets represented high performing elementary school students; one female and one male (Amelia and Jack). The other two test data sets represented average performing elementary school students; one female and one male (Emily and Oliver). Each test data set included assignment grades; course/report card grades; samples of the student's work; and communications, schedules and notices from the school and extracurricular programs. The data was organized in a paper folder and in MyStudentScope for each data set. Depending on the test data set, the paper folder contained between 105 and 140 pages. The documents included report cards, interim reports, sample assignments, extracurricular schedules and sign-ups for the current school year and school newsletters for the current school year. The documents were organized chronologically with the most recent documents on top. The electronic equivalents of the documents and/or information reflected in the paper documents were uploaded into MyStudentScope for each test data set.

Experiment Environment. The study was conducted in participants' homes. The website was hosted on a DigitalOcean cloud server. Participants used laptop computers owned by the test facilitators and the Google chrome browser to perform pre and post-test questionnaires and MyStudentScope tasks.

Tasks. The paper condition consisted of 10 tasks. The MyStudentScope condition had 14 tasks. The mapping of MyStudentScope and paper tasks to monitoring, communication, recovery and decision making functions is presented in Table 2. A single unpaired paper task asked participants what information they would use to remember their student's accomplishment. The additional MyStudentScope tasks are specific to portal functionality and they all map to the monitoring function (see Table 3).

The tasks were presented as scenarios parents may face while their children are in school or participate in extracurricular activities. For MyStudentScope task 4, and corresponding paper tasks 1 and 2, a participant using the Emily test data set would be presented with the following task:

Emily's teacher, Mrs. Keller, sent you the following message:

Dear Emily's Parent,

The quality of Emily's handwriting is poor. At times is it is difficult for me to read the answers on her assignments. Please work with Emily to improve her penmanship.

Sincerely,

Mrs. Keller

You believe Emily's teacher is mistaken. Show the test facilitator evidence in MyStudentScope/the folder that you could use to support your belief that Emily's teacher is mistaken.

3   Results

Twenty-three participants completed the study. All participants conducted 14 tasks under the MyStudentScope condition and 10 tasks under the paper condition. Task performance

Table 2. Function to task mapping for study conditions

Function	Paired Task	MSS Task Number	Paper Task Number	Task Descriptions
	1	4	1 and 2	Identify facts to support belief regarding child's performance
	2	5	3	Determine average grade for specified subject area for school career (all years)
	3	6	4	Determine grade for specified grade level and marking period
	4	7	5	Determine if there are schedule conflicts for specific date
	5	9	6	Determine if recent grade is normal for student
	6	10	7	Identify data in MSS/folder used to determine if the student's recent grades are normal, above average or below average based on his/her usual performance
	7	11	8	Document trends about the student's grades from K through the current year
	8	13	9	Determine if a similar incident has occurred in the past

Monitoring   **Communication**   **Recovery**   **Decision Making**

was measured through 3 variables: the time spent completing a task, the success rate, and the total number of pages visited to complete a specific task. Comparing the total number of pages visited with the minimum number of pages needed to complete a task can provide insight about the efficacy of the navigation design of the MSS web portal.

Table 3. Function to task mapping for additional MyStudentScope tasks

Function	MSS Task Number	Task Descriptions
N/A	1	Login to MyStudentScope
	2	Enter an assignment grade in MyStudentScope
	3	Save/upload a file to MyStudentScope
	8	Add a new event to the MyStudentScope calendar
	12	Record an entry about a student accomplishment in MyStudentScope
	14	Add a grade alert in MyStudentScope

Monitoring   Communication   Recovery   Decision Making

3.1 Task Completion Time

Among parents who participated in the final study (N = 23), a paired samples t test suggests that there is a significant difference between the MyStudentScope condition and the paper condition in paired tasks 3, 4, 7 and 8; the time it took to determine grade for specified grade level and marking period ($t(8) = 5.36$, $p < 0.05$) (Task 3), determine if there are schedule conflicts for specific date ($t(8) = -4.73$, $p < 0.05$) (Task 4), determine trends in student grades ($t(8) = -2.10$, $p < 0.05$) (Task 7) and determining if a similar incident occurred in the past ($t(8) = -6.28$, $p < 0.05$) (Task 8).

The comparison between the times to complete paired tasks 3, 4, 7, and 8 using MyStudentScope and paper is presented in the graphs below (see Fig. 2, Fig. 3, Fig. 4 and Fig. 5). With the exception one participant's completion time for paired task 4, all participants completed paired tasks 3, 4 and 8 in less time using MyStudentScope than paper. Paired samples t tests find no significant difference between the MyStudentScope condition and the paper condition in the time it took to complete the other tasks (Task 1: $t(8) = -.79$, n. s.; Task 2: $t(8) = -.50$, n. s.; Task 5: $t(8) = .20$, n. s.; Task 6: $t(8) = 1.47$, n. s.).

3.2 Failed Tasks

An indicator of the efficacy of using MyStudentScope to complete tasks versus paper is the number of failed tasks under each condition. A successful entry indicates that

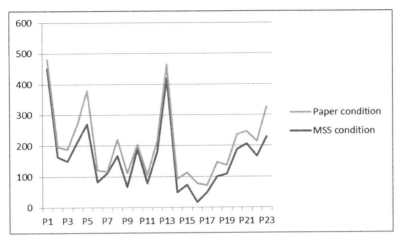

Fig. 2. Completion times (seconds) for paired task 3 - determine grade for specified grade level and marking period

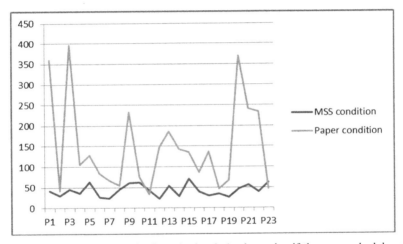

Fig. 3. Completion times (seconds) for paired task 4 - determine if there are schedule conflicts for specific date

the participant was able to find the desired information and/or complete the required action. Failure means the participant found incorrect information, failed to complete the required action or indicated by task response that he/she was unable to determine the answer to the task.

The majority of the failures were observed when users attempted to determine if there are schedule conflicts for specific date and determine if a similar incident had occurred in the past using paper. Only one participant failed to complete one of those tasks using MyStudentScope. For all but that single instance, participants were able to successfully complete each task using MyStudentScope.

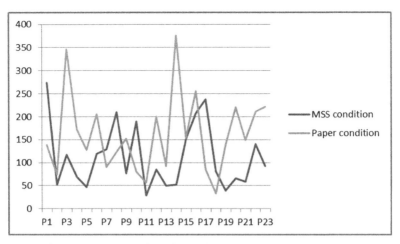

Fig. 4. Completion times (seconds) for paired task 7 - document trends about the student's grades from K through the current year

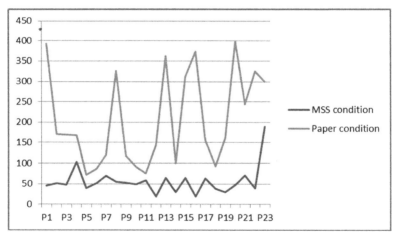

Fig. 5. Completion times (seconds) for paired task 8 - determine if a similar incident occurred in the past

3.3 Pages Visited

An indicator of the efficiency of using MyStudentScope to complete tasks is the number of pages visited to perform each activity. In general, more pages visited indicate that the user did not know how to use the tool and was searching for the means to complete the task. In most cases this resulted in more time spent and therefore lower efficiency. An optimal path was defined for each MyStudentScope task. The optimal path consists of the minimum number of pages necessary to complete each task accurately.

The ratio between the number of actual pages visited and the optimal pages needed is an indicator of how effective the task is completed. Higher ratio indicates that users are substantially deviated from the optimal path. The lowest ratios were observed on three tasks: (a) determining if there were schedule conflicts for specific date (1.05), (b) recording an accomplishment (1.05), and (c) adding a new event to MyStudentScope (1.07). Most users navigated to the Events page and completed the task easily without any error. The highest ratio was observed on identifying and documenting trends in the student's academic performance (3.05). Users should have been able to complete the task by visiting the Dashboard only, but some participants visited as many as 11 pages before completing the task (Fig. 6).

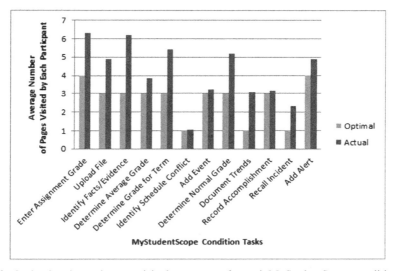

Fig. 6. Optimal and actual pages visited on average for each MyStudentScope condition task

3.4   Observed User Frustration

Observed user frustration was measured by comments made by the participant while completing each task as well as the participant's body language. Non-verbal signs that signaled to facilitators that participants were frustrated included changes in breathing like sighing or long exhales, rubbing the back of the neck or shaking the head. Time taken to complete a task was not automatically assumed to factor in to a participant's level of frustration because overall, they were very patient with completing task under both conditions.

The observed levels of user frustration for the MyStudentScope tasks with equivalent paper tasks were recorded. Based on observed behavior, the two most frustrating tasks were determining if there are schedule conflicts for specific date (Task 4) and determining if a similar incident has occurred in the past (Task 8) using paper. For these two tasks, 13 out of 23 participants had a high or very high observed level of frustration. This drastically contrasts with the fact that no participants experienced frustration at any level while completing paired task 4 using MyStudentScope. When completing the tasks, users made comments like, "I cannot figure out how to answer this!", "[There are] a lot of paper to look through. This is a pain!" and "This is why we are stressed, right?"

Figure 7 is a depiction of the observed user frustration during the study. The width of the red lines indicates the number times the level of frustration was observed. Red lines in the lower left quadrant (unshaded area) indicate that participants showed low or no frustration completing tasks using MyStudentScope and paper. Red lines in the upper left quadrant (blue shaded area) indicate that participants showed more frustration using paper than MyStudentScope. Red lines in the upper right quadrant (unshaded area) indicate that participants showed high or very high levels of frustration under both conditions. Red lines in the lower right quadrant (gray shaded area) indicate that participants showed more frustration using MyStudentScope than paper. The very wide red line in the lower left-most box indicates that there were nearly 100 tasks for which no frustration was observed in the paper and MyStudentScope condition. The thin red line in the gray shaded area indicates that there were a few incidents where completing tasks using MyStudentScope was observed to be more frustrating than paper. The thickness and number of lines in the blue shaded area compared with those in the gray shaded area show that overall, using paper was more frustrating to user than using MyStudentScope.

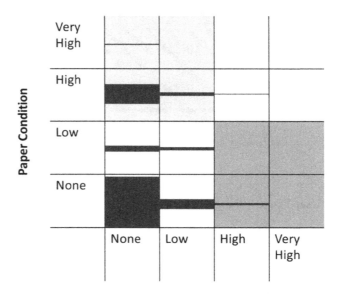

MyStudentScope Condition

Fig. 7. Observed levels of user frustration (Color figure online)

3.5 Preferences Based on Survey Responses

To understand the participants' preference for managing information and technology experience, each participant completed a questionnaire before the test. Most parents indicated that they use both paper and technology to manage information. All participants agreed that managing information regarding their children's education is important (Question 4). All also began the study with a positive opinion of the ease with which technology can be used to manage their children's educational information (Question 5).

All participants answered a questionnaire after each test condition to evaluate their experience. Although users experienced some frustration with MyStudentScope due to their lack of familiarity with it, the majority of the participant feedback was positive in favor of the portal. By the responses to Question 1 the majority of participants, 19, agreed or strongly agreed that it was easier to use MyStudentScope than paper. The majority of participants, 20, also agreed or strongly agreed that they could be more productive using MyStudentScope than paper per response to Question 3.

4 Implications

The knowledge of the needs and preferences of parents when managing and using information regarding their children's education can help designers create more functional information management tools to support them. This knowledge could also be applied to the design of electronic student information systems available in most school systems, thereby extending their functionality to support both the needs of parents and educators. When designing these tools, developers should keep the recommendations of experts in education in mind. Per the experts, parents need to document teacher phone calls, keep records of requests for appointments by the parent or teacher, keep copies of school work/assignments especially those with which that parent or teacher has expressed concern, keep copies of any official reports that have been signed and dated, keep children's pre-school portfolio and retain baseline assessment results. Therefore any system built for parents should have a means for accepting and saving this information. Designers should keep in mind the reasons parents use the information they keep. This will drive the metadata parents are able to record with information saved in the system. Dates are particularly important because parents may be able to use a timeframe to recall or recovery information when needed. Designers should remember that parents may need to look across many years' worth of educational data at one time to get a good understanding of the child's progress. For this reason, graphical representations of the data should be designed and made available as much as possible.

Keeping in mind that the system is only as useful as the data in it, it is important for parents to remain diligent in recording information in MyStudentScope. The more information they add regarding grades, behaviors, and observations, the more clear the picture of their child's academic progress will be. This is especially important when entering metadata about uploaded documents, grades or comments. The data is important, but the details associated with it like the date, subject area, comments about whether the data point reflects a positive or negative situation are invaluable to being able to search for and recover the data efficiently in the future. Parents' awareness of the types of data they should retain regarding their children's education and having a means to manage that information as a whole may motivate more parents to more regularly review their children's academic progress. Having the ability to quickly detect trends and anomalies will also empower parents to be proactive in addressing concerns with respect to their child's educational development instead of relying on educators to point out potential areas of concern. Taking action early may improve their child's chances of educational success.

Educating children is team effort between the parent, student and educator. Informed, activated parents communicating effectively with educators will lead to improved outcomes in the child's academic development. Parents' use of MyStudentScope to remain aware of their children's progress and identify areas of concern with tangible evidence will allow them to have more meaningful and effective conversations about issues with the child's progress. Educators will benefit from parents' ability to provide actual evidence to support their views regarding their children's academic progress or concerns instead of having to weed through anecdotal thoughts that may be difficult or impossible to verify. This clarity in communication and identification of issues will enable educators to more quickly develop a strategy to address concerns raised by the parent. Parents and teachers will be able to track whether changes are leading to the expected results with respect to the child's development.

5   Limitations and Future Research

The research only involved testing of novice users of MyStudentScope. The participants completed their interaction with MyStudentScope in only one session. In reality, parents must manage information regarding their children's education over many years. As stated by many participants in their post-test survey responses, with more experience using MyStudentScope their productivity may improve. A longitudinal study of several weeks or even months is needed to understand the true efficacy of the MyStudentScope web portal versus the traditional paper-based approach. A six month time period might be ideal because it will cover approximately three marking periods or terms for most schools. It is possible that significant difference might be observed with some of the tasks as users gain more experience in MyStudentScope. In addition, the longitudinal study will also allow the researchers to observe the learning curve with the MyStudentScope web portal and examine how the interaction patterns and strategies evolve as users gain more experience in MyStudentScope.

The study was conducted using manually generated test data based on fictional students. Parents have greater familiarity with their own child's academic performance, extracurricular activities and other factors that impact their educational development. Future studies are needed to investigate how parents use the MyStudentScope web portal in a realistic setting with actual data of their children. Those studies will allow the researchers to better gauge the effectiveness of the portal in managing the educational information.

Finally, the MyStudentScope web portal was designed and implemented as a traditional website. With the rapid development in mobile computing, more and more educators and parents have started to use mobile devices and applications to communicate, access, and manage students' educational information. Compared to the traditional website, a mobile application delivered through a smart phone or other mobile devices could be easier to access in a variety of environments (e.g., work, public space) in addition to home. Another advantage of mobile applications is the alert and notification functions that are usually easier to check than emails. We plan to design and implement a mobile application that delivers similar functions of the MyStudentScope web portal.

6 Conclusion

The results of the comprehensive study are consistent with the results of the preliminary studies in demonstrating that MyStudentScope is a viable solution for improving the efficiency and efficacy of parental management and use of their children's educational information. A significant difference in task completion time was achieved for half of the paired tasks completed using MyStudentScope and paper. User responses in post-test questionnaires, observed levels of user frustration and the success rates all show that using MyStudentScope is generally less frustrating and more effective. We plan to further examine the efficacy of the design and users' interaction pattern through a long term field study.

References

Bishop, P.: Information and communication technology and school leaders. In: Seventh World Conference on Computers in Education. Australian Computer Society, Inc, Copenhagen (2002)

Bruce, H., Jones, W., Dumais, S.: Information behaviour that keeps found things found. Inf. Res. Int. Electron. J. **10**(1), n1 (2004)

Buttfield-Addison, P., Lueg, C., Ellis, L., Manning, J.: "Everything goes into or out of the iPad": the iPad, information scraps and personal information management. In: Proceedings of the 24th Australian Computer-Human Interaction Conference, pp. 61–67. ACM, Adelaide (2012)

Jones, W., Dumais, S., Bruce, H.: Once found, what next? A study of 'keeping' behaviors in the personal use of web information. In: Proceedings of ASIST 2002, pp. 391–402. Information Today, Inc., Philadelphia (2002)

Ma, Y., Fox, E.A., Goncalves, M.A.: Personal digital library: PIM through a 5S perspective. Proceedings of the ACM first Ph.D. workshop in CIKM, pp. 117–124. ACM (2007)

Marcu, G., Tassini, K., Carlson, Q., Goodwyn, J., Rivkin, G., Schaefer, K. J., et al.: Why Do They Still Use Paper? Understanding Data Collection and Use in Autism Education. In: Proceedings of the SIGCHI conference on human factors in computing systems, pp. 3177–3186. ACM (2013)

Matthews, T., Feng, J.H.: Understanding parental management of information regarding their children. In: Yamamoto, S. (ed.) HIMI 2017. LNCS, vol. 10273, pp. 347–365. Springer, Cham (2017). https://doi.org/10.1007/978-3-319-58521-5_28

Matthews, T., Feng, J.H., Zheng, Y., Chen, Z.: MyStudentScope: a web portal for parental management of their children's educational information. In: Yamamoto, S., MoriHuman, H. (eds.) Interface and the Management of Information. Information in Applications and Services. LNCS, vol. 10905, pp. 108–121, Springer Cham (2018a). https://doi.org/10.1007/978-3-319-92046-7_10

Matthews, T., Feng, J.H., Zheng, Y., Chen, Z.: User evaluation of MyStudentScope a web portal for parental management of their children's educational information. In: Proceedings AHFE 9th International Conference on Applied Human Factors and Ergonomics 2018, Orlando, Florida, 22–26 July (2018b)

Oh, K.E., Belkin, N.J.: Cross analysis of keeping personal information in different forms. In: Proceedings of the 2011 iConference, pp. 732–733. ACM, Fort Worth (2011)

Piper, A.M., D'Angelo, S.D., Hollan, J.D.: Going digital: understanding paper and photo documentation practices in early childhood education. In: Proceedings of the 2013 conference on Computer supported cooperative work, pp. 1319–1328. ACM (2013)

Trullemans, S., Signer, B.: From user needs to opportunities in personal information management: a case study on organisational strategies in cross-media information spaces. In: IEEE/ACM Joint Conference on Digital Libraries, IEEE (2014)

Turner, E.: Technology use in reporting to parents of primary school children. SIGCAS Comput. Soc. **40**, 25–37 (2010)

Ontology Construction for Annotating Skill and Situation of Airline Services to Multi-modal Data

Satoshi Nishimura$^{(\boxtimes)}$ ⓘ, Yuichi Oota, and Ken Fukuda ⓘ

National Institute of Advanced Industrial Science and Technology (AIST), Tokyo 1350064,
Japan
`satoshi.nishimura@aist.go.jp`

Abstract. The integration of the physical space and the cyberspace by the cyber-physical system such as Indrie 4.0 and Society 5.0 attracts the attention. Annotations to the data, which is measured in the physical world, is one of the ways to manage human activities in physical space for information retrieval and inferences in cyberspace. If annotations are performed with no controlled vocabulary, it is difficult to share and reuse the annotated data. This study provides an ontology for annotating service skills occurred in customer-contact service scene. The ontology was constructed according to a top-level ontology as guide for constructing domain concepts and based on the analysis of service scene movies. The evaluation of the ontology was carried out by annotating 4 to 6 min movies of the service scene by 4 different staffs. As a result, 24 of the 77 prepared terms in the proposed ontology were used for annotations and we found the ontology covers the test movie scenes. We also provide the use case scenarios for the annotated movies as a summary of this study.

Keywords: Ontology engineering · Controlled taxonomy for customer contact · Airline services

1 Introduction

The Japanese government advocates a notion, so called Society 5.0 [4]. In the society, new services are produced by technologies integrating physical space and cyberspace. For instance, Amazon Go [1] is the service that recognizes physical space and handles data in cyberspace. It is interpreted as new service that replaces existing service, such as supermarket. Services which improve existing services are also expected to realize in Society 5.0. A staff training service is one of its candidates.

Airlines and restaurants provide services through interaction among persons. It is important that staffs perform this interaction in high quality. Such high-quality interaction is performed based on the staff skills. Therefore, the importance of staff training is well known [19]. Virtual Reality system (Hereafter referred to as VR) can be interpreted as a training system using cyberspace technology and is carried out in various industries including the service industry [6].

© Springer Nature Switzerland AG 2020
S. Yamamoto and H. Mori (Eds.): HCII 2020, LNCS 12184, pp. 265–278, 2020.
https://doi.org/10.1007/978-3-030-50020-7_18

There are some research efforts [14] that human body and motion models for using in VR. However, the model of the internal condition of the customer and the cognitive interaction has not been considered yet.

In this paper, we focus on modeling the service skills which are performed in customer-contact service situation. The situation contains services which staffs provide based on their skills and is one of the components of cognitive interaction. Modeling such situations is an important element for staff training and support systems. The objective of this research is to provide the model of situation and to organize concepts which represents the situation and service skills as an ontology. The proposed ontology is intended to use as controlled vocabulary for annotating multi-modal data.

2 Related Work

2.1 Ontology for Annotating Scene Information

Framester. Gangemi et al. constructed Linked data hub called Framester [11] which connects language resources such as FrameNet [2], WordNet [25], VerbNet [16], BableNet [31], DBpedia [3], Yago [34], DOLCE-Zero [33]. FrameNet is a useful resource describing Frame semantics. Gangemi et al. pointed out that its coverage lacks for processing general sentences in the web. Framester makes possible to identify a semantic frame from a natural language sentence by association with various other language resources. Amnestic Foregery [12] is an example system of its application, and an ontology of metaphors is constructed for the system that generates new metaphors using Framester.

Such system and ontology are not intended to describe scenes in movie. They are used for expression of frame semantics in natural language sentences based on the ontologies. It means the studies can be treated as a framework to express the scene which described by sentences with the relation among an actor and an object, the effect of the action of the actor on the object, etc.

Drammar. Damiano et al. built Drammar [5, 23] as an ontology for annotating data on dramas. In this ontology, a drama is regarded as a series of actions by characters. It is applied to annotate some movie works in [22].

This ontology can be useful to describe service scenes because the service scene also consists with actors and actions. However, it is a schema made from the viewpoint of bibliographic record, and it has not been examined whether it is sufficient to express the service skills. We also need to construct taxonomies to express service skills.

Semantic Question Answering with Movie Data. Suchan and Bhatt have developed a framework that combines computer vision and knowledge representation to enable semantic question answering in movie [37]. They analyzed how the audience perceives the scenes when they watch a movie from the viewpoint of Cognitive Film Studies. Feature extraction in a movie is processed and detection of the location of the entity and the gazing point by spectators. Such information is handled as qualitative representation so that the system can answer the semantic question, such as "How is the spectator attention shifting, when the camera is moving/after a cut/during a long shot?"

We aim to analyze movies from the qualitative perspective as same as the study, however the viewpoint is different. Suchan and Bhatt pay attention to analyze the gazing point of spectators. Our standing point is service engineering rather than cognitive film studies or bibliographic archiving.

Autonomous Vehicle. Recognition of real-world entities and making them interpretable from qualitative perspective are gathering attention not only in movie analysis and also the field of autonomous driving [15, 39].

Zhao et al. [39] constructed map information as instance data based on ontology and qualitative description of traffic rules in advance. In addition to the information and rules, they acquired information of external world by the sensor. The combination among the map information, sensed information and traffic rules helps the autonomous driving system solve the problem of "Which car should be given priority when driving on each road at a three-forked road consisting of a wide road and a narrow road?"

Kaleeswaran et al. [15] proposed a concept to combine formal analysis method and qualitative representation for evaluation of the design of autonomous driving system. The study seems different with annotating movie but the qualitative representation of the external world when the autonomous vehicle recognize can be considered as a scene information like customer-contact service. In autonomous driving research, it is also important to recognize human behavior, but it does not deal with internal conditions such as human skills or emotion. This point is crucial difference from this study.

3   Analysis of Customer-Contact Services Based on Movie Data

3.1   Data Collection and Identification of Key Concepts in Customer-Contact Services

Interview-Based Data Collection. An interview-based survey of airport ground staff skills was conducted under a research project [36] on training support for cognitive interaction using VR. This interview was conducted with five ground staff members. Three of them are experts and two are intermediates. The interviews were conducted with 1 person each and took 105 min while showing a movie of a skill contest being held by the airline company. We referred to the result for constructing an ontology of skills in this study.

Movie Recording of Pseudo Customer-Contact Service Settings. The customer-contact service was simulated in the pseudo airport environment which contains the ticket counter and gate to the airplane in the project [36]. They recorded the scene including skills which occurs in the scene as movie data. The simulated service was provided by three experts and two intermediates and was based on four different scenarios in about 5 min each. We analyzed one scenario of four staffs, two experts and two intermediates. We omitted a data of one staff because the staff is expert for international line.

The movie was analyzed by manual. We identified who performs a service in the scene, who is received the service and who and what exists in the scene. There are not many kinds of actions, and it is necessary to pay attention to the conversation content since it is the customer-contact service.

First, we wrote down the utterances and labeled them with abstract category. For instance, the utterance "いらっしゃいませ。こんにちは。" (English translation: Hello, How are you?) is acquired and it is categorized as "greeting". Second, we identified what actions are performed. The actions are categorized into two types, actions with physical behavior and verbal actions. The customer-contact service is mainly telling the information which is necessary for customers. These categories were used for ontology construction described in the Sect. 4. At the result, 8 action types and 15 utterance categories were obtained. A rough hierarchical structure was constructed with labeling process.

3.2 Alignment of Elements with Concepts in Existing Top-Level Ontology

YAMATO as Top-Level Ontology. We employed a top-level ontology, so called Yet Another More Advanced Top-level Ontology (YAMATO) [26] as a guide to construct domain concepts. One of the role of top-level ontology is enhancing ontology construction by giving developers a general guideline about how to view the target domain, and some domain ontologies, including sustainability science [20], abnormal state in clinical domain [38], color emotions in psychology [28, 29] and an ontology of gene [24] are constructed with reference to YAMATO. We introduce following key concepts in this study: process (action), event, representation and its related concepts, and property, in the next section.

Key concepts in YAMATO

Process and Event: Processes and events are distinguished in YAMATO [10]. The major differences are as follows. A process has a feature "ongoing" on the other hand an event has a feature "completed." Therefore, a process is mutable, but an event cannot be changed, and it exists exactly an entire time duration from the start to the end. A process is dissective but an event is not. For instance, an athletic event can be decomposed into its opening ceremony, a footrace and the closing. Such distinction criteria can be useful for this study to identify the actual service scene and its components as a process or an event.

Action: YAMATO defines action as a process which needs an intention of the doer. The process can be represented by using the notion of function decomposition [17] and its key feature is state change of its doer/operand. Based on the notion, the modeler of processes can describe a structure of goal accomplishment by examining the correspondence among goal process and sub processes. The notion introduce granularity of processes and it helps the modeler consider whole process and fine-grained processes in consistent manner.

Representation, Representation Form, Content and Representing Thing: YAMATO provides a concept "representation," "representation form," "content," and "representing thing" for description of information. Representation consists with representation form and content. Well-known subclasses of representation form are character strings, image and movie which are used to represent contents. The distinction among representation form and content is useful to describe different representing thing which contains same content. For instance, "Hamlet" can be represented as drama or movie. The form is different, but the content is almost same. We employed this notion to describe customer-contact service scene.

Property: "A property is as a complex attribute that can be represented as a pair of quality and some value." [26] YAMATO provides fine-grained concepts about attribute, quality and property to describe measurement and its qualitative and quantitative result. For instance, we can consider about to describe "impatient" of the staff. The impatient can be treated as dependent entity belonging to the staff. It is described as "impatient" is a property which the staff has, and its value is "true". On the other hand, heartrate is a measurable attribute and can be treated quantitatively. We assume that a staff is impatient if his/her heartrate is over 100 bpm. Then, we measure a heartrate of one staff is 110 bpm. We can describe it as a pair of an attribute "heartrate" and its value "110 bpm" corresponds to a property "impatient" and its value "true." Such description contributes to handle both quantitative data which are measured by sensors and internal state of staffs such as emotion which are usually handled as qualitative data.

Alignment of Elements in Service Scene with Concepts in YAMATO. We interpreted customer-contact service scene as a subclass of event in this study. Customer-contact service scene is composed of ground staffs who provide service, customers who receive the service, service actions, customer actions, states of each participant, and location where the service actions are performed. The components can be aligned with each component of event in YAMATO. The service scene is completeness, so that its wholeness is not same as its parts. For instance, the wholeness describes customer-contact service and it is decomposed into greeting, providing information about the flight and seeing the customer off to the gate. These subevents are not same as the whole event but its components. We employed event notion because of its features.

We defined a skill event as an event which a staff perform a skill. An employee can be considered to have a certain skill if s/he can perform the actions corresponding to the skill in the event. It is possible to describe the customer-contact service scene by preparing such skill events as the component of the scene according to the notion. The description of customer-contact service scene makes trainers to search specific scene by querying with a term of specific skill event. Moreover, we can detect the commonality and differences among experts or intermediates by analyzing from the qualitative perspective.

As a result, we conceptualize the event, action, content, representation, property, human, human body in order to describe the customer service scene through the analysis of skill events.

4 Skill Event Ontology

4.1 Hozo as Ontology Editor

We used Hozo [18] as an ontology editor. Hozo has a function to manage context-dependent concept, so called role concept. YAMATO is originally constructed by using Hozo, so it is useful for us to use Hozo to construct a skill event ontology by specializing YAMATO. Hozo also has a function to export Web Ontology Language (OWL) [1] from its original language, therefore the proposed ontology can be used through web standard technology like SPARQL [2].

Figure 1 shows an overview of ontology representation in Hozo. Orange nodes represent concepts which can be interpreted as whole thing (Bike in Fig. 1). Each concept has attributes which are represented as slots in Hozo. There are two types of slots (p/o and a/o). A p/o slot represents a part-of relation (Handlebar in Fig. 1) and an a/o slot represents an attribute-of relation (weight(kg)) in Fig. 1). All slots are managed as a role concept which has class restriction as a player of the role. In this example, Wheel is a basic concept and it is called as Front wheel when it plays Front wheel role, on the other hand, it is called as Rear wheel when it plays Rear wheel role. The properties are inherited to the specified concepts which is linked by is-a link as same as other ontology representation tools.

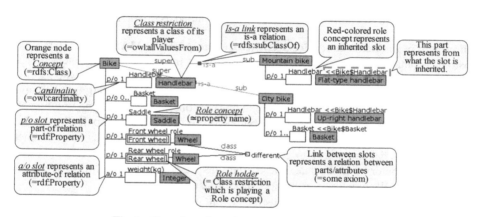

Fig. 1. Overview of ontology representation in Hozo

4.2 Key Concepts in Hozo Representation

We specialized concepts including the event, action, content, representation, property, human, human body in YAMATO to describe skill events. First, we analyzed the movie as mentioned in Sect. 3.1. We picked up some skills which the ground staffs performed in

[1] https://www.w3.org/TR/owl2-overview/.
[2] https://www.w3.org/TR/sparql11-overview/.

the movie based on the analysis. Second, the characteristics of each skill was considered. The consideration was performed based on the analysis what the differences among experts and intermediate staffs. For instance, one expert staff calls out a customer as his name rather than general word like "sir." We considered what actions are performed in each skill event and who participates in the event. At the result of this consideration, we got a schema to describe skill event as shown in Fig. 2. The skill event is described as a subclass of event in YAMATO. Every skill event has a ground staff and more than one customer as participants of the event. The skill event is also constituted by three actions, two of them by the staff and one of them by the customer. The number of actions is determined by the former analysis in Sect. 3. The last component is the location where the event occurred.

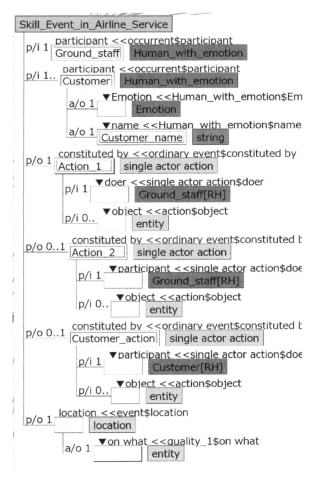

Fig. 2. Definition of skill event

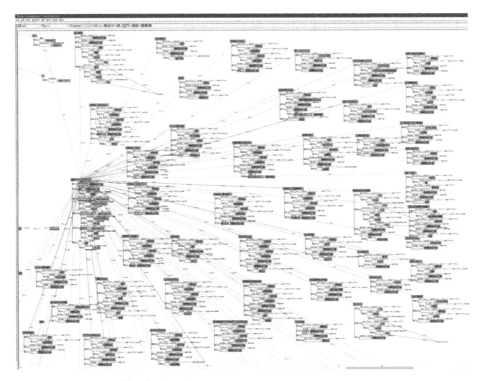

Fig. 3. Overhead view of the classes of skill event

We constructed 77 subclasses of the skill event in airline service according to the schema. Figure 3 shows an overhead view of the part of the proposed ontology. Table 1 shows statistic information of the proposed ontology. The left side shows statistics from Hozo and the right side shows statistics of OWL version from Protégé [30].

Table 1. Statistic information of proposed ontology

Hozo statistics	#	OWL statistics	#
Basic concept	736	Axiom	13605
Role concept	1135	Class	1707
Role holder	110	Object property	1334
Class constrain	1135		

Figure 4 shows a specific example of skill event, so called calling out customer by name. The red characters denote specialized slots from their super classes. For instance, "constituted by" slot is derived from "Skill_Event_in_Airline_Service" and its class restriction (it is equivalent to owl:allValuesFrom) is specialized into "talk" from "single actor action." The operand of "talk" is "Customer_name," which is defined as a "name" of "Customer." Based on the definition, when the ground staff talks and his/her utterance includes customer's name, then the ground staff is identified that s/he has a skill "Calling out customer by name." Such detailed definition will be helpful for human annotators to identify whether the skill event is occurred or not.

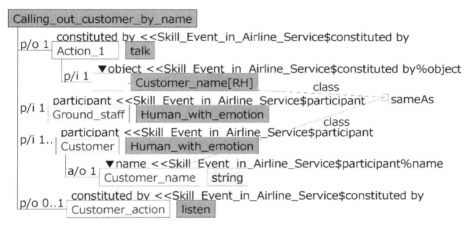

Fig. 4. An example: Calling out customer by name (Color figure online)

5 Evaluation of the Ontology Competence

5.1 Annotation-Based Evaluation

We evaluated the proposed ontology by annotating the movies which represent customer-contact service scenes as mentioned in Sect. 3.1. Four movies, which are same scenario performed by different staffs, were annotated based on the ontology. Each service situation is constituted by the interaction among one ground-staff and one customer at the airport. The customer missed his scheduled flight due to his fault, but he complained to the ground-staff. The pseudo service situation was finished after the customer was satisfied and it took 4 to 6 min. We annotated actions of both the ground staff and the customer with their utterance. At the result, we found ground staffs performed 33.25 actions and customers performed 18.75 actions on average. Based on the actions, we analyzed which skills were occurred in each service scene. Then, we found 24 types of service skills can be annotated by using the proposed ontology.

5.2 Use-Case Scenario

The proposed ontology and annotated data based on the ontology can be used for information retrieval and computer-supported analysis after generating Resource Description

Framework (RDF) [3] graphs. Fukuda et al. proposed a proof-of-concept (POC) framework which generates knowledge graphs of high-end service provision movies massively annotated with human interaction semantics [9]. The feature of the system is combination of Deep Neural Network (DNN) detectors [27, 35] with ontology based rich annotated movie data and RDF converter. The input movie is spitted into image frames for DNN detector and bounding boxes in the frame are annotated based on the ontology. The combined information is converted into RDF to store in a triple store for computation. The proposed ontology in this paper will contribute in the system to provide controlled vocabulary and schema for describing service scene.

The flow of RDF data generation is described as follows (Fig. 5). First, movie of customer service scene and the proposed ontology of skill event exist as a premise. Second, the annotation is carried out manually for the move. The annotator uses the schema and vocabulary specified in the proposed ontology. The manual annotation content is an action such as "The staff calls the customer's name.", and each vocabulary is provided by ontology in a structured form such that the subject is a "staff", the action is "call," the object has a "customer name", and the customer has a "customer name". Third, the DNN detector detects which object is person, where s/he is, his/her pose, and which direction s/he is facing to. Fourth, the results of manual annotation and DNN detector are integrated and a knowledge graph, which represents the service scene is generated. It will be possible to calculate following facts: how many times the expert calls a customer by his/her name, how many times the interaction among the staff and the customer occurred before making final decision, thanks to the knowledge graph. In addition, by generalization of the proposed ontology, we will apply this same framework to other industries.

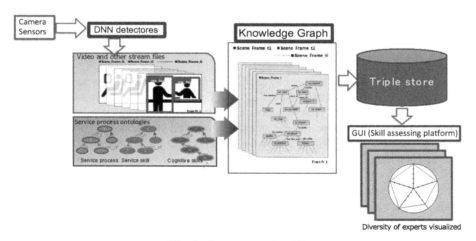

Fig. 5. System overview [9]

---

[3] https://www.w3.org/TR/rdf11-primer/.

6 Discussion

6.1 Considerable Concepts

Empathy. Showing empathy by a staff is thought as an important skill in high-class customer-contact services, such as high-class hotel and full-service carriers [32]. The proposed ontology also contains empathy for representation of such skill of the staff and annotation of movies. While the term is contained in the ontology, its definition is not well considered yet. Empathy is interpreted as emotion and subclass of quality. The notion represents the empathy depends on someone who feel empathy to another person. However, the definition does not mention for the "another person." Showing empathy is considered if and only if another person who is a target of empathized exists, but the definition does not mention it. It means the concept empathy also depends on the empathized person. In this case, we should consider about the entity on which is depended, so called context, for the empathy. Although Elliot et al. [8] classified empathy to subclasses, the definition of the empathy is not clear yet in psychology. Therefore, it is future work to make clearer definition of empathy.

Emotion. In this study, we treated emotion as a subclass of a quality, and we do not define it yet. Some emotion ontologies were proposed [13, 21] and classification of facial expression is well known in psychology domain [7]. The ontology [13] is developed based on the mental functioning notion with deep consideration. On the other hand, some emotion recognition system is based on the psychological findings. Our proposed ontology is intended to use for annotation of multi-modal data and for analysis from service engineering perspective. Therefore, the ontology should combine internal states of actors, such as emotion, and psychological features, such as heartrate, which is observed from external world. We also remain this issue as future work.

6.2 Event Based Representation of Skills or Quality Based Representation of Skills

We employed a notion of event as a frame to describe service scene including skills of a staff in this study. The notion is based on the intuition which the skill is observed as an occurrence in an event. The intuition is partially correct as I mentioned in Sect. 5 from the viewpoint of observation or recognition by computer. On the other hand, a skill has another feature which depends on a holder of the skill. For instance, the ground-staff is required to get a skill to learn broadly for acquisition of customer-contact service methods. Such skill is not occurred in the airport but more internal motivation and ability. Therefore, we should consider the both side of service skills as a future work.

7 Conclusion

7.1 Contribution to the Human Computer Interaction Community

This study provides intuitive ontology construction method for annotation service skills and situation to multi-modal data and constructed ontology. In this study, the ontology is intended to use as controlled vocabulary. The controlled vocabulary enables researchers, who have own multi-modal data of service scenes, to share and integrate the data from the qualitative perspective. It means once measured data can be re-used for multi-purpose in cyber-physical system. Especially, human-computer interaction community needs not only computer-interpretable description but also human-understandable description for accomplishment of explainability. The proposed ontology and its use case scenario show one example.

7.2 Summary

We reported ontology construction for annotating skill and situation of airline services to multi-modal data with its use case scenario in this paper. The ontology was constructed with reference to a top-level ontology. The focus concept is an event which includes specific service scene and service skills occurred in it. We called the event as skill event and characterized with its participants and processes. We also defined 77 specific skills which usually occurred in customer-contact service. The ontology was evaluated by using as annotation vocabulary for four service scenes provided by an airline company. The result indicates 24 skills are occurred in the pseudo-situation of customer contact. The annotation result can be used to detect expert features or distinct experts and novices in the framework which we mentioned as use-case scenario.

Acknowledgements. The part of this was supported by Council for Science, Technology and Innovation, "Cross-ministerial Strategic Innovation Promotion Program (SIP), Big-data and AI-enabled Cyberspace Technologies". (funding agency: NEDO).

References

1. Amazon.com, Inc.: Amazon go. https://www.amazon.com/b?node=16008589011
2. Baker, C.F., Fillmore, C.J., Lowe, J.B.: The berkeley framenet project. In: Proceedings of the 17th International Conference on Computational linguistics-Volume 1, pp. 86–90. Association for Computational Linguistics (1998)
3. Bizer, C., et al.: DBpedia - a crystallization point for the web of data. J. Web Semant. **7**(3), 154–165 (2009)
4. Cabinet Office: Society 5.0. https://www8.cao.go.jp/cstp/english/society5_0/index.html
5. Damiano, R., Lombardo, V., Pizzo, A.: The ontology of drama. Appl. Ontol. **14**(1), 79–118 (2019)
6. Dávideková, M., Mjartan, M., Greguš, M.: Utilization of virtual reality in education of employees in Slovakia. Procedia Comput. Sci. **113**, 253–260 (2017)
7. Ekman, P.: Facial expression and emotion. Am. Psychol. **48**(4), 384–392 (1993)
8. Elliott, R., Bohart, A.C., Watson, J.C., Greenberg, L.S.: Empathy. In: Norcross, J. (ed.) Psychotherapy Relationships that Work, 2nd edn, pp. 132–152. Oxford University Press, New York (2011)
9. Fukuda, K., Vizcarra, J., Nishimura, S.: Massive semantic video annotation in high-end customer service - example in airline service value assessment. In: Proceedings of International Conference on Human-Computer Interaction 2020, pp. 1–16 (2020)
10. Galton, A., Mizoguchi, R.: The water falls but the waterfall does not fall: new perspectives on objects, processes and events. Appl. Ontol. **4**, 71–107 (2009)

11. Gangemi, A., Alam, M., Asprino, L., Presutti, V., Recupero, D.R.: Framester: a wide coverage linguistic linked data hub. In: Blomqvist, E., Ciancarini, P., Poggi, F., Vitali, F. (eds.) EKAW 2016. LNCS (LNAI), vol. 10024, pp. 239–254. Springer, Cham (2016). https://doi.org/10.1007/978-3-319-49004-5_16

12. Gangemi, A., Alam, M., Presutti, V.: Amnestic forgery: an ontology of conceptual meta-phors. In: Borgo, S., Hitzler, P., Kutz, O. (eds.) Formal Ontology in Information Systems. Frontiers in Artificial Intelligence and Applications, vol. 306, pp. 159–172. IOS Press, Amsterdam (2018)

13. Hastings, J., Ceusters, W., Smith, B., Mulligan, K.: Dispositions and processes in the emotion ontology. In: Martone, O.B.M.E., Ruttenberg, A. (eds.) Proceedings of the 2nd International Conference on Biomedical Ontology, vol. 833, pp. 71–78. CEUR (2011)

14. Inamura, T., et al.: Simulator platform that enables social interaction simulation—SIGverse: sociointelligenesis simulator. In: 2010 IEEE/SICE International Symposium on System Integration, pp. 212–217. IEEE (2010)

15. Kaleeswaran, A.P., Nordmann, A., Mehdi, A.U.: Towards integrating ontologies into verification for autonomous driving. In: Suárez-Figueroa, M.C., Cheng, G., Gentile, A.L., Guéret, C., Keet, M., Bernstein, A. (eds.) Proceedings of the ISWC 2019 Satellite Tracks (Posters & Demonstrations, Industry, and Outrageous Ideas) co-located with 18th International Semantic Web Conference (ISWC 2019), pp. 319–320 (2019)

16. Kipper, K., Dang, H.T., Palmer, M.: Class-based construction of a verb lexicon. In: Proceedings of the Seventeenth National Conference on Artificial Intelligence and Twelfth Confer-ence on Innovative Applications of Artificial Intelligence, pp. 691–696. AAAI Press (2000)

17. Kitamura, Y., Koji, Y., Mizoguchi, R.: An ontological model of device function: industrial deployment and lessons learned. Appl. Ontol. 1(3–4), 237–262 (2006)

18. Kozaki, K., Kitamura, Y., Ikeda, M., Mizoguchi, R.: Hozo: an environment for building/using ontologies based on a fundamental consideration of "role" and "relationship". In: Gómez-Pérez, A., Benjamins, V.Richard (eds.) EKAW 2002. LNCS (LNAI), vol. 2473, pp. 213–218. Springer, Heidelberg (2002). https://doi.org/10.1007/3-540-45810-7_21

19. Kumar, V., Pansari, A.: Measuring the benefits of employee engagement. MIT Sloan Manag. Rev. 56(4), 67 (2015)

20. Kumazawa, T., et al.: Initial design process of the sustainability science ontology for knowledge-sharing to support co-deliberation. Sustain. Sci. 9(2), 173–192 (2014)

21. Lin, R., Amith, M.T., Liang, C., Duan, R., Chen, Y., Tao, C.: Visualized emotion ontology: a model for representing visual cues of emotions. BMC Med. Inf. Decis. Making 18(Suppl 2), 64 (2018)

22. Lombardo, V., Damiano, R., Pizzo, A., Terzulli, C.: The intangible nature of drama documents: an FRBR view. In: Proceedings of the 2017 ACM Symposium on Document Engineering (DocEng 2017), pp. 173–182. Association for Computing Machinery, New York (2017)

23. Lombardo, V., Damiano, R., Pizzo, A.: Drammar: a comprehensive ontological resource on drama. In: Vrandečić, D., Bontcheva, K., et al. (eds.) ISWC 2018. LNCS, vol. 11137, pp. 103–118. Springer, Cham (2018). https://doi.org/10.1007/978-3-030-00668-6_7

24. Masuya, H., Mizoguchi, R.: An ontology of gene. In: Cornet, R., Stevens, R. (eds.) Proceedings of the 3rd International Conference on Biomedical Ontology (ICBO 2012), vol. 897, pp. 1–5. CEUR (2012)

25. Miller, G.A.: WordNet: An Electronic Lexical Database. MIT press, Cambridge (1998)

26. Mizoguchi, R.: Yamato: yet another more advanced top-level ontology. In: Proceedings of the Sixth Australasian Ontology Workshop, pp. 1–16 (2010)

27. Moon, G., Chang, J.Y., Lee, K.M.: Camera distance-aware top-down approach for 3D multi-person pose estimation from a single RGB image. In: The IEEE International Conference on Computer Vision (ICCV), October 2019

28. Muramatsu, K., Togawa, T., Kojima, K., Matsui, T.: Proposal of a framework to share knowledge on consumer's impressions. In: Proceedings of the Third International Conference on Agents and Artificial Intelligence, vol. 1, pp. 388–393 (2011)
29. Muramatsu, K., Togawa, T., Kojima, K., Matsui, T.: Ontology of psychological attributes on color emotions. Trans. Jpn. Soc. Artif. Intell. **30**(1), 47–60 (2015). (in Japanese)
30. Musen, M.A.: The protégé project: a look back and a look forward. AI Matters **1**(4), 4–12 (2015)
31. Navigli, R., Ponzetto, S.P.: Babelnet: the automatic construction, evaluation and application of a wide-coverage multilingual semantic network. Artif. Intell. **193**, 217–250 (2012)
32. O'Connell, J.F., Williams, G.: Passengers' perceptions of low cost airlines and full service carriers: a case study involving ryanair, aer lingus, air asia and malaysia airlines. J. Air Transp. Manag. **11**(4), 259–272 (2005)
33. Paulheim, H., Gangemi, A.: Serving DBpedia with DOLCE – more than just adding a cherry on top. In: Arenas, M., et al. (eds.) ISWC 2015. LNCS, vol. 9366, pp. 180–196. Springer, Cham (2015). https://doi.org/10.1007/978-3-319-25007-6_11
34. Rebele, T., Suchanek, F., Hoffart, J., Biega, J., Kuzey, E., Weikum, G.: YAGO: a multilingual knowledge base from wikipedia, wordnet, and geonames. In: Groth, P., et al. (eds.) ISWC 2016. LNCS, vol. 9982, pp. 177–185. Springer, Cham (2016). https://doi.org/10.1007/978-3-319-46547-0_19
35. Redmon, J., Divvala, S., Girshick, R., Farhadi, A.: You only look once: unified, real-time object detection. In: Proceedings of the IEEE conference on computer vision and pattern recognition, pp. 779–788 (2016)
36. Sato, H., Ujike, H.: Developments of vr/ar cognitive training in air travel service based on behavioural and emotional measurements. In: Aviation XR Weekend 2019 (2019)
37. Suchan, J., Bhatt, M.: Semantic question-answering with video and eye-tracking data: Ai foundations for human visual perception driven cognitive film studies. In: Proceedings of the Twenty-Fifth International Joint Conference on Artificial Intelligence (IJCAI 2016), p. 2633–2639. AAAI Press (2016)
38. Yamagata, Y., Kozaki, K., Imai, T., Ohe, K., Mizoguchi, R.: An ontological modeling approach for abnormal states and its application in the medical domain. J. Biomed. Semant. **5**(1), 23–37 (2014)
39. Zhao, L., Ichise, R., Liu, Z., Mita, S., Sasaki, Y.: Ontology-based driving decision making: a feasibility study at uncontrolled intersections. IEICE Trans. Inf. Syst. **100**(7), 1425–1439 (2017)

Proposal for the Tablet-Based Disaster Response Evacuation Drill for Elementary School Children

Makoto Oka[1,2]([⊠]), Chiharu Terui[1,2], Sakae Yamamoto[1,2], and Hirohiko Mori[1,2]

[1] Tokyo City University, 1-28-1 Tamadutumi, Setagaya-ku, Tokyo, Japan
{moka,g1323050,hmori}@tcu.ac.jp, sakae.yamamoto@rs.tus.ac.jp
[2] Tokyo University of Science, 1-3 Fujimi, Chiyoda-ku, Tokyo, Japan

Abstract. In elementary schools, disaster prevention education is provided during the integrated learning period or in school events. Evacuation drill is a subject in this category. In recent years, the move by the Central Council for Education to revise the curriculum to include disaster prevention in the subjects is fully in progress. However, specific policies and lesson plans have not yet been finalized. This research aims to work out how to use tablets in evacuation drills, which is a subject in disaster prevention education, in consideration of the class method to use the acquired knowledge of children, and the method to use mental map and ICT equipment. In order to consider how to use ICT equipment, two tablet-based learning methods, MAP learning (displaying a planar map) and StreetView learning are prepared. Then the effectiveness of these tablet-based disaster response evacuation drills for children is investigated. In the tablet-based evacuation drill, children were able to take different approaches to the same task. As a result, each child was able to make different discoveries. MAP learning is considered to be suitable for the learning to work out evacuation routes and evacuation sites, such as drills on disaster maps. StreetView learning is considered to be suitable for learning that can provide similar experiences to those in actual disasters, such as evacuation simulations. Through the learning that combines these two learning methods, the ability to carefully consider the disaster situation and select the best route with a bird's-eye view could be developed.

Keywords: School children · Mental map · Tablet device

1 Research Background

1.1 Current Status of Disaster Prevention Education

In elementary schools, disaster prevention education is provided during the integrated learning period or in school events. Evacuation drill is a subject in this category. It is aiming to develop the practical attitude and ability of children for safe evacuations and the willingness to act for the safety of other people, groups, and communities at home and in the community, at the time of disaster [1].

© Springer Nature Switzerland AG 2020
S. Yamamoto and H. Mori (Eds.): HCII 2020, LNCS 12184, pp. 279–289, 2020.
https://doi.org/10.1007/978-3-030-50020-7_19

The evacuation drills currently conducted at elementary schools are, in many cases, venue-based drills in which children gather at an evacuation site in response to the siren and announcement. In this type of drills, children tend to participate passively and have difficulty acquiring practical skills. On the other hand, in the disaster response evacuation drills, disasters are caused suddenly during an evacuation action to make the participants decide and take necessary actions. Children would be able to acquire more practical skills useful in the event of a disaster through the disaster response evacuation drills carried out as part of the emergency drills at elementary schools. In recent years, the move by the Central Council for Education to revise the curriculum to include disaster prevention in the subjects is fully in progress. However, specific policies and lesson plans have not yet been finalized.

1.2 Current Status of ICT Education

The Ministry of Education, Culture, Sports, Science and Technology has developed the "Acceleration Plan for informatization of Education" [2] based on the discussion at the "Informal gathering to discuss informatization of education for the 2020s" [3]. Therein "the staged development to realize the educational computer environment where every student is provided with a computer" was presented as a vision of ICT utilization. Active utilization of ICT equipment is required in educational settings to enable teachers to use ICT freely to design their classes based on the lesson content and the children's attitudes. Also, the "survey on the informatization of education at schools in 2015" [4] led by the Ministry of Education, Culture, Sports, Science and Technology revealed that the number of children per computer was 6.2, which was far from the targeted "one for every student". However, the number of educational computers increased from 900,700 in 2015 to 918,799 in 2016. Also, the number of tablets used in FY2016 was 253,755, which is more than 1.5 times the number in the previous year (156,018 in 2015). The use of tablets in the classrooms at schools is attracting attention.

2 Related Research

Researches on the disaster response evacuation drill and ICT equipment have been conducted as part of disaster prevention efforts in communities. Hisada et al. [5] conducted the experiment on the disaster response evacuation drill on the streets and the experiment of collection & sharing of disaster information by using ICT equipment, simultaneously. As a result, the effectiveness of the drill was confirmed. Also, it was found that the disaster response evacuation drill generated more realistic feels than in the conventional venue-based drill. It increased the awareness of disaster prevention and regional cooperation. However, the studies and cases for the disaster response evacuation drill targeting children are few.

While disaster prevention education and utilization of ICT equipment are attracting attention, the researches on the usage of ICT equipment in disaster prevention classes have been conducted. In the previous research, Shirai et al. [6] proposed the class where children create a hazard map on a tablet, as a disaster prevention hands-on learning using ICT equipment for elementary school students. They developed an app to create hazard maps tailored to the characteristics of the school children's viewpoints, thoughts, and actions. Also, they created the curriculums for tablet-based classes. As an experiment for evaluation, children were asked to make a hazard map in a disaster prevention education class at an elementary school. They started to change the scale of the map themselves and naturally learned how to view and handle the map on the tablet. Through this experiment, their awareness of disaster prevention improved, and they were able to acquire disaster prevention knowledge. In the future, these children would be able to develop more practical skills through the classes in which they can use their acquired knowledge.

3   Research Purpose

This research aims to work out how to use tablets in evacuation drills, which is a subject in disaster prevention education, in consideration of the class method to use the acquired knowledge of children, and the method to use ICT equipment.

4   Suggestions

In this research, the classes that incorporate the disaster response evacuation drill are conducted, in which children are directed to use their disaster prevention knowledge. In order to consider how to use ICT equipment, two tablet-based learning methods, MAP learning (displaying a planar map) and Street View learning (displaying a google Street View, hereafter referred to as SV learning), are prepared. Then the effectiveness of these tablet-based disaster response evacuation drills for children is investigated.

5   Apps Developed

Two types of apps for Android devices (MAP learning app and SV learning app) as an educational material to be used by children in the disaster response evacuation drills in the classroom are developed. In the disaster response evacuation drill on a tablet, routes are inputted with the lines drawn on a map on the MAP learning app (Fig. 1 left), and by going forward on the SV learning app (Fig. 1 right). In the case where the inputted route is closed off due to a disaster, an alert to direct to bypass the route will be generated.

Fig. 1. Left: MAP learning app, Right: SV learning app

6 Comparison of Learning Methods

The disaster response evacuation drill in the classroom (with tablets) and the disaster response evacuation drill on the streets (without tablets) were conducted at an elementary school as part of the disaster prevention class as an experiment in order to observe the effectiveness of the two tablet-based disaster response evacuation drills (MAP learning and SV learning) and the differences in the way of thinking, action, and route selection among children when they were working on the tasks for these tablet-based drills.

6.1 Subjects

The subjects of this research were 43 fifth grade students at Shinjuku Municipal Aijitsu Elementary School. These children were divided into ten groups (A to J). Each group consists of 4–6 children living in the same neighborhood. In the experiment, these ten groups were divided into two groups: MAP learning group and SV learning group.

6.2 Experiment Contents

The experiment consisted of two types of disaster response evacuation drills. One is conducted in the classroom with tablets, and the other is conducted on the streets without tablets.

6.3 Experiment Schedule

The following Table 1, in the experiment, a total of three disaster response evacuation drills were carried out in three days. The drill in the classroom was conducted twice, and the drill on the streets (Field work) was conducted once. At the beginning of each session, children were given an explanation on the task and a lecture on the operation of the tablet and apps to be used as educational materials. At the end of each session, the activities on the day were reviewed and summarized. In order to maintain the fairness of the education, the MAP learning group and the SV learning group were switched. For this reason, the disaster response evacuation drill in the classroom was carried out twice.

Table 1. Table of lesson plan

Session	Date	Group A, D, F, I, J	Group B, C, E, G, H
1st	Sep. 23	SV learning	MAP learning
2nd	Oct. 14	Field work	
3rd	Oct. 21	MAP learning	SV learning
4th	Nov. 4	Field work	
5th	Nov. 11	Summary class	
6th	Dec. 3	Final presentation	

6.4 Experimental Tasks

Under the hypothetical situation immediately after an earthquake, children were given a task to safely evacuate from the designated starting point to the evacuation site (goal point). Then, they were directed to select a route to the goal point each time upon facing a forked road. When encountering a road closure due to a disaster during the evacuation, children were directed to select a new route.

Table 2 shows the starting point and goal point set in advance for the task. Task 1 and Task 3 were set for the first experiment, task 3 and Task 4 were set for the second experiment, and Task 2 and Task 3 were set for the third experiment. Each task had a time limit of 20 min. When a task was completed early, the participants were directed to work on the same task again in the disaster response evacuation drill in the classroom.

Table 2. Starting point and goal point in tasks

Task No.	Starting point	Goal point
Task 1	Aijitsu elementary school	Edogawa elementary school
Task 2	Tokyo university of science	Aijitsu elementary school
Task 3	My house	Aijitsu elementary school
Task 4	Friend's house	Aijitsu elementary school

6.5 Data Collection

The experiment observation record sheets were distributed to the experimenters. The experimenters were asked to fill out what they noticed on the behaviors of children and the questions from them. In the second experiment, a wearable camera was attached to two experimenters to record the drill scenes. In the first and third experiments, a camera was set in the classroom to record the entire class scenes.

7   Results and Discussion

From the collected data, 29 evacuation routes, 166 route selections, and 364 comments of the experimenters were extracted for analysis.

7.1 Route Selection Strategy

In order to understand the route selection tendency of children in each learning, route selection strategies were classified into the following three based on the analysis data.

1. Shortest route: The shortest route to the goal. The routes selected based on the "proximity" or "speed".
2. Safe route: The routes selected based on the "safety".
3. Known route: The routes selected because "they know it" or "it is a school road".

Note that these three strategies are not independent from each other. Therefore, they may be counted repeatedly upon the classification.

In both MAP learning and SV learning, the "safe route" strategy appeared most frequently. However, the second most common strategy was different between MAP learning (shortest route) and SV learning (known route). In MAP learning, the tendency to select the shortest route was increasing upon route selections in the latter half of the task.

7.2   Route Selection in MAP Learning

Figure 2 and Table 3 shows the route created by children and the experiment record of the experimenter. Place No. in Table 3 refers to the numbers in Fig. 2. In MAP learning, children were often observed to reduce the scale to check the current location and goal point. In No2 and No3, children checked the current location and the goal point when selecting a route and selected the "main street" as a relay point to the goal. At the time, children seemed to select the route to take in consideration of the route to the goal point by setting a relay point to the goal point. Based on these facts, it is conceivable that, children reduced the scale to check the current location and goal point upon route selection to work out the best route to the goal point. Children selected routes with the process shown in the Fig. 1 in MAP learning. Therefore, they tended to use the strategy to select the shortest route in the route selection in MAP learning. This tendency increased in the latter half of the task. It would be because the path options, which connect the current location to the goal point, decrease as the goal point approaches. It is obvious when seeing the intersections where a route selection occurs as nodes and the map as a

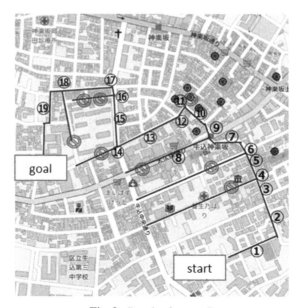

Fig. 2. Result of group G

Table 3. Comments on group G (RS: Route Selected, AO: Accident occurred)

No.	Place No	Comments	Strategy
1	1/RS	Children selected the route to the right residential area. Opinions were divided on which way to go first	2 and 3
2	2/RS	Children checked the goal and selected the shortest route. Headed to get to the main street first	1
3	3/RS	Children checked the goal and selected the shortest route. Headed to the main street first	1
4	4/RS	Halfway through, children thought to take another person's school road and headed to the left (Ushigome Chuo-dori)	3
5	AO	Children took the disaster marker appeared to be above the house as that the house was collapsed	
6	5/RS	Halfway through, children thought to take another person's school road and decided to turn the next corner	4
7	6/AO	Children took the disaster marker appeared to be above the house as the fence was misaligned	2
8	7/RS	Children headed to the main street (Okubo-dori). They assumed that the traffic on the main street was low in the norning and high in the day line	
9	8/RS	Halfway through, children thought to take another person's school road and decided to turn the next corner to the left	3
10	AO	Children took the fire marker on the main street as a traffic accident because of the large traffic volume on the street	1
11	9/RS	Children selected the shortest route	1
12	10/RS	Children selected the shortest route	1
13	11/AO	Children took the location of the disaster mirker far from the current location as the traffic closure due to fire and the smoke	1
14	12/RS	Children considered forcing their way through the closed road	
15	13/RS	Children selected the shortest route	
16	14/RS	Children selected the shortest route	
17	14/AO	Children rejected thinking!	1
18	15/RS	An advisor suggested going back, but children rejected it and selected a path they could go on	
19	16/RS	Children selected the shortest route	1

(*continued*)

Table 3. (*continued*)

No.	Place No	Comments	Strategy
20	AO	Children took the two disaster milkers generated due to an operation enor as a widespread road closure due to cracks on the ground	1
21	17/RS	Children selected the shortest route	1
22	18/RS	Children selected the shortest route	1
23	AO	Children were upset. They took it as a fire	1
24	19/RS	Children selected the shortest route	1
25	Consideration	Any route can be dangerous during a disaster	
		They should head for the goal quickly before another disaster occurs	
		Want to move quickly	

network diagram. Upon route selections, children reduced the scale of the map to search for dangerous places or places that could be a temporary evacuation site. Based on such information from the map, they seemed to decide the route to take. In this way, children could discover dangers that they would not usually notice in MAP learning, find safe places, and select the shortest path. During this process, they changed evacuation sites flexibly. In summary, children took the following process.

1. Reduce the scale of the map to check the current location and the goal point.
2. Create a route from the current location to the goal point.
3. Determine the relay point to the goal point.
4. Select the shortest route from the current point to the relay point.

7.3 Route Selections in SV Learning

Figure 3 and Table 4 shows the route created by children and the experiment record by the experimenter. Place No. in Table 4 refers to the numbers in Fig. 3. In No.1-6, children checked each route that appeared at intersections. In such times, the comments like "This road is XX, so I won't go" were observed many times. Children scrutinized each route at intersections to confirm "whether they know it" before selecting a route. In SV learning, children seemed to scrutinize all the routes to make a decision in the process shown in the Fig. 1 right side. Also, children used such information as steepness and car traffic on the path when selecting a route or upon disaster. From this, it is conceivable that children used information extracted from the photo to determine the route to take. In this way, they discovered many dangers and selected safe routes in SV learning. In summary, children took the following process.

1. Check the surrounding routes at intersections.
2. Scrutinize each route based on whether they know it, and whether there is any danger.
3. Select the route to take.

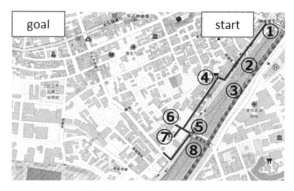

Fig. 3. Result of group H

Table 4. Comments on group H (RS: Route Selected)

No.	Place No	Comments	Strategy
1	1/RS	Concerned about the danger of encountering many slopes if going up on Kagurazaka, children proceeded to Sotobori-dori with a wide sidewalk	2 and 2
2	2/RS	There was a forked road (slope) on the way, but it was ignored because they didn't know the road very well	3 and 3
3	3/RS	A child who knew the road said it should lead to Ushigome-dori. There was an objection to it. As in No.2, they hit a slope on the way and turned risht	3 and 3
4	4/RS	They judged the slope was too steep but kept going on this path until another path appears. They followed the path parallel to Sotobori-dori	2 and 2
5	5/RS	The slope became gentle. The path leading to Ushigome-dori appeared, so they followed the path	2 and 2
6	6/RS	There were stairs leading to a dead end on the StreetView, so they turned back	
7	7/RS	Headed to Sotobori-dori but jumped to a distant place as it was not supported on StreetView	
8	8/RS	The path to Ushigome-dori appeared, so they selected it	
9		Children got quite bored because they just had to go straight along Sotobori-dori	
10		It seemed that children had only two criteria for the path to take: "shortest" and heading "to Ushigome-dori". It seemed that they do not take account of the danaer upon selection	

7.4 Effectiveness of the Disaster Response Evacuation Drill Using Tablets

In the disaster response evacuation drill on the streets, children scrutinized each route at intersections to select the route to take, which was a similar route selection method as in SV learning. Also, the comments similar to those in MAP learning were observed upon route selections, such as the comments referring to the distance to the goal point, and temporary evacuation sites. From this, it is conceivable that the disaster response evacuation drill in the classroom can give children similar learning as in the drill on the streets. That is, the tablet-based disaster response evacuation drill in the classroom is effective. Also, it is reported that children consider more as the experiment is repeated and selected the route to go based on their previous experiences. From this, it is conceivable that children were able to utilize their disaster prevention knowledge acquired through the disaster prevention classes that incorporate disaster response evacuation drills.

8 Conclusion

In the tablet-based evacuation drill, children were able to take different approaches to the same task. As a result, each child was able to make different discoveries.

Through the experiment, it was found that children thought proactively and scrutinized to select a route to the goal in MAP learning. Therefore, MAP learning is considered to be suitable for the learning to work out evacuation routes and evacuation sites, such as drills on disaster maps. On the other hand, children thought carefully and scrutinized all the routes upon route selection in SV learning. Therefore, SV learning is considered to be suitable for learning that can provide similar experiences to those in actual disasters, such as evacuation simulations. Through the learning that combines these two learning methods, the ability to carefully consider the disaster situation and select the best route with a bird's-eye view could be developed.

9 Future Outlook

In this research, focusing on the evacuation behavior of children in MAP learning and SV learning, the route selection strategy was divided into three categories: "the shortest route", "the safe route", and "the known route". However, we may be able to find new characteristics of MAP learning and SV learning by considering different viewpoints, such as other classification methods and other methods to grasp the current state. Also, this experiment used the town where children lived. However, we may be able to discover new features of each learning method by comparing the results of this experiment with the results of the experiment using unknown towns.

References

1. Ministry of Education, Culture, Sports, Science and Technology of Japan: Guide to creating a school disaster prevention manual (2012). (in Japanese) https://www.mext.go.jp/a_menu/kenko/azen/1323513.htm. Accessed 01 Mar 2020

2. Ministry of Education, Culture, Sports, Science and Technology of Japan: Acceleration Plan for informatization of Education (2016). (in Japanese). https://www.mext.go.jp/b_menu/hou dou/28/07/__icsFiles/afieldfile/2016/07/29/1375100_02_1.pdf. Accessed 01 Mar 2020
3. Ministry of Education, Culture, Sports, Science and Technology of Japan: Informal gathering to discuss informatization of education for the 2020s (2018) (in Japanese). https://www.mext.go.jp/b_menu/houdou/28/07/__icsFiles/afieldfile/2016/07/29/1375100_01_1_1.pdf. Accessed 01 Mar 2020
4. Ministry of Education, Culture, Sports, Science and Technology of Japan: survey on the informatization of education at schools in 2015 (2016). (in Japanese). http://www.e-stat.go.jp/SG1/estat/Pdfdl.do?sinfid=000031462110. Accessed 01 Mar 2020
5. Hisada, Y., et al.: Earthquake drill for effective emergency response and quick collection of damage information by collaboration between local government and residents. J. Jpn. Assoc. Earthq. Eng. **9**(2), 130–147 (2009). (in Japanese)
6. Shirai, D., Oka, M., Yamamoto, S., Mori, H.: Proposal of educational curriculum of creating hazard map with tablet-type device for schoolchildren. In: Yamamoto, S. (ed.) HIMI 2017. LNCS, vol. 10274, pp. 74–84. Springer, Cham (2017). https://doi.org/10.1007/978-3-319-58524-6_7

Hearing Method for User Requirement Extract in Participatory Design -Designing for Service Involving Local Residents-

Fuko Oura[1,2](✉), Takeo Ainoya[1], and Keiko Kasamatsu[1]

[1] Tokyo Metropolitan University, 6-6 Asahigaoka, Hino, Tokyo, Japan
fu.a7te@gmail.com
[2] National Institute of Advanced Industrial Science and Technology, Chiba, Japan

Abstract. In participatory design involving local residents, recently, interest in social issues has increased, and design approaches that focus on finding local issues and solving them or creating new value have emerged, such as social labs. In such approaches, it is important to organize needs extraction and requirements based on human-centered. However, there is no methodology that focuses on the hierarchical structure of human needs. Therefore, this paper focused on the application of a hierarchy of ergonomics and hedonomic needs. In the participatory design with residents living in Hachijo island, Tokyo, we conducted hearings and systematization from the perspective of Hedonomics. We report a case study in which the three types of hearings combined in a step-by-step was practiced in the participatory design with the local residents and a case study of systematizing them. Then we present its potential as a framework for grasping the living conditions surrounding the local residents and interacting with participants.

Keywords: Participatory design · User requirement · Hedonomics

1 Introduction

Participatory design involving local residents has been addressed in areas such as public construction, resource management, and urban planning. In these fields, the design target has already been determined, and it is common practice to set the requirements for the design through interaction with residents. On the other hand, recently, interest in social issues has increased, and design approaches that focus on finding local issues and solving them or creating new value have emerged, such as social labs [1]. One of the important thing in the latter approach is to recognize what the current situation is and what challenges there are. Here, the context of the residents is important, and it is important to derive information from the participant's perspective, such as actual experience and how they recognize the area, from the participants who live in the area. In the next step, it is important to systematize the current situation and issues that have been expressed in the dialogue, and create a foundation for discussion with participants. Here, systematization and visualization of the collected information leads to the sharing

© Springer Nature Switzerland AG 2020
S. Yamamoto and H. Mori (Eds.): HCII 2020, LNCS 12184, pp. 290–300, 2020.
https://doi.org/10.1007/978-3-030-50020-7_20

of a sense of problem and problem structure. Therefore, we report a case study in which the three types of hearings combined in a step-by-step was practiced in the participatory design with the local residents and a case study of systematizing them. Then we present its potential as a framework for grasping the living conditions surrounding the local residents and interacting with participants.

2 Application of Hedonomics to Participatory Design

In dealing with regional issues, it is necessary to consider at which layer various information about the current state of the region should be organized, depending on the purpose of participatory design at that time. One of the objectives of the approach starting from the discovery of regional issues is to search for the issues that the region has from the perspective of the parties involved, but there are a wide variety of regional needs. Therefore, we tried to practice participatory design based on the hypothesis that systematization of regional needs using "a hierarchy of ergonomics and hedonomic needs" would enable rearrangement of needs from a human-centered perspective. A hierarchy of ergonomics and hedonomic needs is derived from Maslow's five-stage theory, and is a hierarchical representation of ergonomics that satisfies safety and functionality, and hedonics with added experience and enjoyment [2]. Figure 1 shows a hierarchy of ergonomics and hedonomic needs.

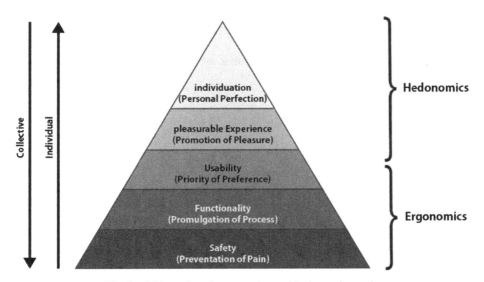

Fig. 1. A hierarchy of ergonomics and hedonomic needs.

3 Workshop to Grasp the Situation of Living

In order to understand the context of consumers, we do the workshop based on hearing. This chapter report about the project, summary of workshop and contents.

3.1 Summary of the Project

The project was in cooperation with Tokyo named "Island Activation Project" [3]. This workshop was conducted as a part of the project. Hachijo island is one of the islands which belong to Tokyo. It is 287 km far from the main island.

3.2 Summary of the Workshop

Through the workshop, we interviewed high school students living on the island about their lives. By analyzing the interview data from all direction, we attempt to find the possibility of new product or service for next generation.

The workshop is held in conference room of Hachijo Island High School on August 26th, 27th, 2019.

Participants included:

7 Hachijo island office clerk

7 high school students living on the island

5 university design students

4 university teachers

Here are 3 steps of the workshop.

1. Mapping of places related to life.
2. Make persona and experience model and do the presentation.
3. Depth interview with high school students about their present situation.

The workshop was including the seminar of university faculty members and conducted over two days.

3.3 Contents

Mapping
Behavior Mapping of Consumers

According to pre-interview, there are 5 areas (see Fig. 2) on the Hachijo island, and the situation of each area has a bit of difference. As result, we mapped the place and service which had become the key point of daily behavior in 5 areas at first, and wrote down at the map. It can be figured that the participant from the island, such as workers and high school students is scattered in the residential district, and their knowledge about the island has disparity. Hence, we are aiming to lead participants to be able to work and pass freely, rather than providing working group previously.

Mapping of Different Category

In order to understand area life situation, we assumed to summarize into 5 categories which are "Shopping", "Meal", "Public Service", "Hobby/Play", "Hospital" (referred to as Life Category). We asked participant to write down the place and service are used usually in each Life Category, and reflect on map as we did at chapter 3.3.1. Maps are finished according to each area separately, so there are 5 areas × 5 categories = 25 maps. (see Fig. 3).

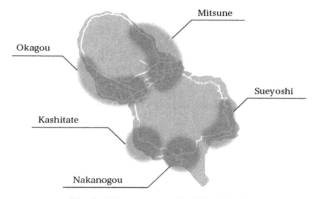

Fig. 2. Five areas on Hachijo island.

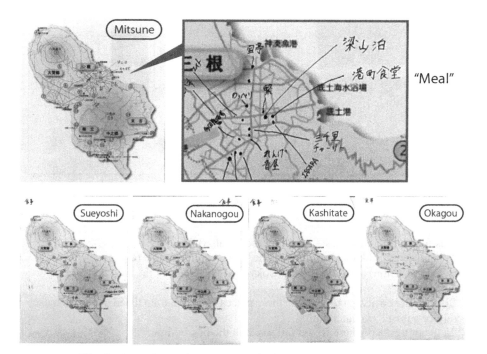

Fig. 3. Created maps in "*mapping of different category*" (ex. Meal)

Persona and Experience Model

Persona and Using Scene

First of all, based on 5 areas × 5 categories, we extracted the persona and using scene for 3 generations (youth, adults and seniors). We made 75 sheets (5 areas × 5 categories × 3 generations) on the provided format (see Fig. 4). The sheets were made according to the previous part of persona and using scenes. These scenes are including the following content.

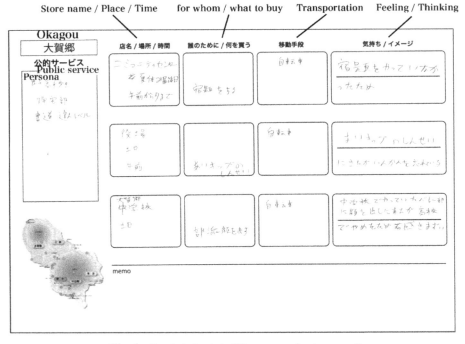

Fig. 4. Created sheets in "*Persona and using scene*"

"It is too far to go to the supermarket (south area)."

"When you get sick that hospitals on the island cannot handle (e.g. physical check-up and operation) and have to go to Tokyo, you have to pay the air ticket and spend a lot of time."

"Tourists are easily get together in these places like restaurant listed in the Japanese Yelp or subsoil seawater bath."

"You can't go anywhere if you fail to catch the bus in time."

"You can't get to the shop which is far from the bus stop."

Besides, the transportation options depicted in the scene shows that each generation has its own tendency.

Youth: bicycle, Scooter, Pick up by parents

Adult: Automobile, Taxi

Senior: Walking, Bus, Go out with fellow passenger

Persona and Experience Models

Then, we also made 9 persona and experience models for North area (youth, adult and senior), South area (youth, adult and senior) and Sueyoshi (youth, adult and senior) as representative participant model (see Fig. 5). In each area, typical individual was assumed and different attributes were added. In order to show the context of persona's life, one-day flow was described as experience model. According to the description, we discussed the problems that could be seen and gave presentations. Table 1 shows the problems extracted from each experience model.

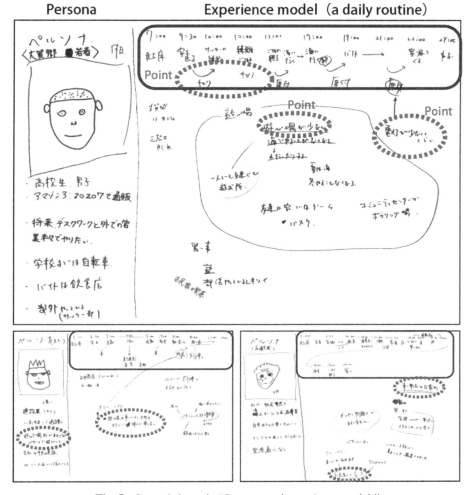

Fig. 5. Created sheets in *"Persona and experience models"*

Table 1. The problems extracted from each experience model

	Youth	Adult	Senior
North area Mitsune, Okagou	• Going to school by scooter are not allowed, so you have to go home once if you play after school • There are few playgrounds. Mostly sea or mountain.	• Hachijo iland is motorized society, so when you go to drink by car, return is a taxi or picked-up by someone • There are few playgrounds and they play pachinko	• They want more interaction with different generations. • Healthy people move by bus or walk. Otherwise, they are taked by family members or helpers, or ride with someone you know
South area Kashitate, Nakanogou	• Driving at night is a little scary because it is dark. Sometimes if it's rainly, we can't get through the road. • There are few women in their twenties on the island. There are no friends to meet soon	• we also work part-time on holidays as a side job, so we have no solid blocks of leisure time. • There are not many places to go out with my wife on holidays	• There are few opportunities for communication • If you have no one to drive In your family, you need help by one's friends and acquaintances
Sueyoshi	• We have to match our schedule with our parent to move, and this things make us inactive. • Word-our–mouth communications is so fast that everyone knows when something happens • They want to go to cram school	• Difficulty secure some transportation for after drinking alcohol • There are few new encounters even in hobbies	• You have to live according to the bus time

Depth Interview

We interviewed high school students about the impressions of each district, means of transportation and shopping. The interview was conducted in the presence of other participants. The interview took (about 1 h) in total. In regard to cognizing different area, participants had numbers of cognitions in common. On the contrary, sometimes the person living adjacent had different cognition.

4 Visualization of the Current Situation in the Region Based on Hierarchy Model of Life Category

4.1 In Order to Understand the Life Conditions, Create the Framework

It is an interpretation from the viewpoint of ergonomics corresponding to Maslow's five desires. By learning the 5 steps of a hierarchy of ergonomics and hednomic needs, we organized the elements of life category and made the framework (see Fig. 6). It included 6 parts, which are "Shopping", "Meal", "Public service", "Hobby/Entertainment", "Hospital" and "Job". At first, the part of job wasn't existence when we were doing the workshop. As the discussion of jobs occurred, we added the analysis of job into the framework.

4.2 Visualization of Current Situation of Service in Hachijo Island

Based on the data and research in the workshop, we analyzed the current situation of Hachijo island by the framework we made. According to the following information, we plotted the following 3 elements ("Elements existed on the island", "Elements which have parts of deficiency", "Elements which have deficiency").

- The information of services that have existed on the island: we gathered the information of the restaurant and facilities, such as the opening hours, service, described in "Mapping by category" on the Internet again.
- The scenario made by means of the workshop: contents of the created sheets by using "make persona and experience model".
- Contents of depth interview: the statement data in "depth interview".

Actually, everything plotted by each category is shown in the Fig. 7.

5 Discussion

To master the current life situation of residents in area, we listed 6 categories: "Shopping", "Meal", "Public Service", "Hobby/Entertainment", "Hospital", "Job". These 6 categories were extracted from the interview in Hachijo island. To apply them in other regions, we assumed that there would be new categories emerge if necessary. Furthermore, according to ergonomics and hedonic needs, visualization is feasible by using the framework that came up with the elements of current service situation. In this case, without being bound by class, residents' remark was based on their own context. So, undergraduates could do the analysis and make the data visualized according to the content of workshop. Therefore, although it was able to gather the real opinion based on resident's own experience, when analyzing though the framework, the information may be insufficient. When visualizing the current service situation, researchers need to plot the information on the basis of content of workshop. Then, using the data plotted, researchers exchanged views with residents and intensify the data so that it makes the visualization of more substantial current situation become possible.

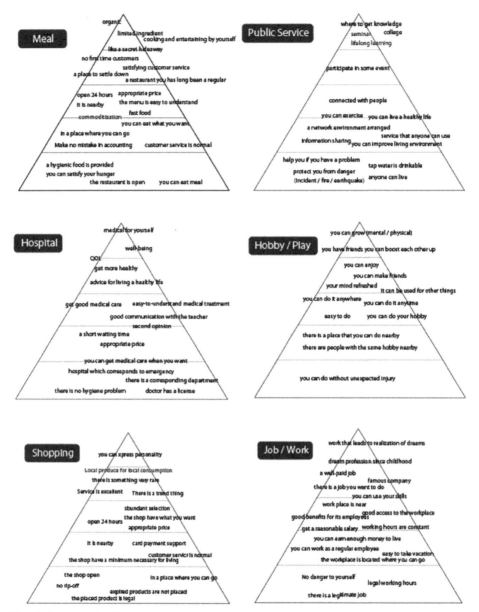

Fig. 6. Framework of the elements of life category based on a hierarchy of ergonomics and hedonomic needs

In the next phase of the project, the business creation phase, the staff of Hachijo island discussed based on the "Visualization of the current services situation of Hachijo island" (see Fig. 8) and another workshop about new service of the island in the future

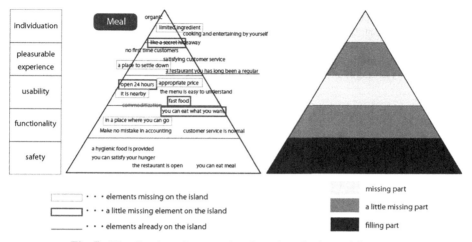

Fig. 7. Visualization of current situation of service in Hachijo island

was conducted, which helped them to participate in the subject about their area again and supported them to find the point of penetration.

Fig. 8. A look of the discussion based on the "Visualization of the current services situation of Hachijo island" in the business creation phase

6 Future Work

We are aiming to understand the current situation of local participant and based on the result we proceed into "Business Creation" phase, "Prototyping" phase although it is also analysis phase in this paper. Hearing phase seemed as first phase, but we are going to analyze that it will connect to what kind of dialogues and requirements. Eventually, linking to verification as a design process.

References

1. Hughes, H., Foth, M., Dezuanni, M., Mallan, K., Allan, C.: Fostering digital participation and communication through social living labs: a qualitative case study from regional Australia. Commun. Res. Pract. 4(2), 183–206 (2018)

2. Hancock, P.A., Pepe, A.A., Murphy, L.L.: Hedonomics: the power of positive and pleasurable ergonomics. Ergon. Des. **13**(1), 8–14 (2005)
3. Kasamatsu, K., Ainoya, T., Motegi, R., Kubota, N., Takesue, N., Ikei, Y.: Our approach for revitalization on Hachijojima using PXD. In: The 20th International Symposium on Advanced Intelligent Systems and 2019 International Conference on Biometrics and Kansei Engineering (2019)

Effective Disaster Prevention Map Creation Using Road Network Analysis

Kaname Takenouchi$^{(\boxtimes)}$ and Ikuro Choh

Department of Intermedia Art and Science, Waseda University, 3-4-1 Ookubo,
Shinjuku-ku, Tokyo 169-8555, Japan
takenouchi@ruri.waseda.jp

Abstract. As a disaster prevention measures based on self-help and mutual assistance, workshops have been conducted nationwide in Japan in which local disaster prevention maps are created by collecting information while walking around an area. The creation of disaster prevention maps in this way has attracted attention as an effective measure that can be done in advance for local disaster prevention and disaster mitigation. Although many support systems have been developed for creating disaster prevention maps, no system has been proposed that can handle all the steps of collecting information while walking around, elucidating disaster factors, and performing simulations of evacuation routes during a disaster. This research therefore proposes a disaster prevention map creation support system that focuses on the relationship between the road network and disaster factors with the potential to cause damage during a disaster and that can perform evacuation route simulations. To verify the usefulness of the proposed support system, a validation experiment was performed using a three-phase process up to the completion of the disaster prevention map, and the results confirmed that disaster prevention map creation using this system makes a useful contribution to disaster prevention measures.

Keywords: Disaster prevention map · Road network analysis · Space syntax · Disaster factors · Evacuation route simulation

1 Introduction

The lessons from the Great East Japan Earthquake of 11 March 2011 reaffirmed the importance of *self-help*, where people act to protect their own lives, and *mutual assistance*, where people help one another in their local community, as measures for disaster prevention. It is essential that self-help and mutual assistance initiatives be carried out not only when a disaster but also during normal times in order to be prepared for a large-scale disaster. It is therefore desirable to utilize the disaster prevention maps issued by various local government bodies as a disaster prevention measure that can be prepared in advance. In Tokyo, local earthquake hazard and risk assessment surveys are performed every 5 years under ordinances for earthquake countermeasures, and local risk levels are published. A risk level map of Tokyo has also been published that summarizes overall risk levels, evacuation sites, and other aspects.

© Springer Nature Switzerland AG 2020
S. Yamamoto and H. Mori (Eds.): HCII 2020, LNCS 12184, pp. 301–311, 2020.
https://doi.org/10.1007/978-3-030-50020-7_21

However, the utilization of these disaster maps is low and they do not play a role as a disaster prevention tool. One reason for this is that the information provided by the maps is not linked to the residents' evacuation behavior. The disaster prevention maps show disaster hazards over a wide area. For these reasons, disaster prevention maps can be considered insufficient in terms of providing disaster prevention information.

With the aim of reducing disaster damage, workshops are being conducted in various regions around Japan in which disaster prevention maps are created while walking around an area. The main purpose of these efforts is to illustrate on a paper map the information collected while walking around the area, but it is difficult to say that the completed maps can be utilized effectively as disaster prevention maps. Ushiyama et al. [1] analyzed the effect of disaster prevention workshops on non-resident participants noted that it was "important to deeply consider the natural factors and societal factors of the target region" in the disaster prevention workshop. In other words, to achieve the goal of reducing disaster damage through disaster prevention workshops, it is essential not only to raise awareness, but also to create a disaster prevention environment in which it is possible to perform disaster prevention simulations based on the discovered disaster factors and to hold discussions and perform verification so that cities can be created that have robust new disaster prevention measures. Furthermore, the role of disaster prevention maps is not just to spread disaster awareness and evacuation information. They are also essential for predicting and planning evacuation behavior for disasters that are likely to occur in the future. This research therefore performs analysis focusing on the relationships between the latent disaster factors in an area and the road network, and proposes a system that supports creation of disaster prevention maps that can be used for simulation of evacuation routes during a disaster.

2 Background and Related Work

2.1 Creating Disaster Prevention Maps

As a result of the Great East Japan Earthquake, activities and research into increasing disaster prevention awareness in communities as a whole have been conducted in which local residents create disaster prevention maps with the goal of raising disaster prevention awareness. For deeper understanding of local disaster risks, various disaster prevention education programs have been conducted. In these programs, disaster maps is usually done in a workshop format.

One activity of the Nigechizu Project [2] is a workshop that is held for creating maps of evacuation terrain and times. These maps enable visualization of the locations of hazards and the direction to a target evacuation site divided by time. Disaster prevention education programs held by the General Insurance Association of Japan involve activities such as walking around city streets and looking at the facilities related to disaster prevention, as well as "disaster prevention expeditions" in which disaster factors are summarized and illustrated on a map [3]. The main purpose of these disaster map creation workshops is to enable visualization of evacuation sites, locations of hazards, and so forth on paper maps. However, it is difficult to say that maps that show only evacuation sites and hazard locations can be utilized as a disaster prevention tool. Furthermore, disaster prevention maps on paper cannot provide information on local disaster risks that change on a daily basis. The role of disaster prevention maps is not just to spread disaster awareness and evacuation information. They also have a role to play in investigating disaster prevention measures for disasters where damage may occur in the future.

2.2 Road Network Analysis

When designing disaster prevention, it is extremely important to deepen residents' understanding of the area where they live. If a resident has an everyday understanding of the roads with high disaster risk in their area, they will be able to choose a safer evacuation route during a disaster. In other words, becoming familiar with the characteristics of the local road network on a daily basis can be an effective means for a person to protect themselves in the event of a disaster.

Space syntax proposed by Hillier et al. [4] is a method for analyzing road networks, and is able to analyze road characteristics by numerically representing the connection relationships between intersections (nodes) and roads (edges), which are the main elements in a road network.

Various studies have used space syntax theory to analyze spatial structures, and the following studies in particular sought to clarify relationships between road networks and phenomena that occur in an area. Takahashi et al. [5] analyzed the relationship between physical quantity of greenery according to people's perception and the road network, revealing trends in greenery in an area. Nagaie et al. [6] analyzed the relationship between the occurrence of street crime, the crime risk recognized by police, and the road network, revealing trends in the crime risk of an area. These studies are able to clarify road network properties by quantitatively analyzing factors that are inherent to a city.

In this study, we expected that methods for analyzing spatial structure by focusing on factors on the road network as in the preceding research could be applied to local disaster prevention. Accordingly, this research proposes a support system for creating disaster prevention maps for analyzing the relationships between road networks and disaster factors by using space syntax and performing simulations of effective evacuation routes during a disaster.

3 Support System for Disaster Prevention Map Creation

3.1 Approach

This research shares some common points with previous studies in terms of the method of learning about local disaster prevention and then completing a disaster prevention map by collecting disaster prevention information while walking around an area. However, the distinguishing features of the disaster prevention map creation support system proposed here are that it uses space syntax to analyze the relationships between the road network and latent disaster factors in an area and can perform simulations of effective routes for evacuation during a disaster. In this support system, disaster prevention maps are completed through a three-phase process (Fig. 1) involving collection, evaluation, and analysis of disaster factors as well as evacuation route simulations.

Phase	Task
Phase 1	Collection and evaluation of disaster factors using prototype device (Field work).
Phase 2	Visualization of disaster factors and analysis of road network using Online Map (Google Maps).
Phase 3	Simulation of effective evacuation routes at the time of disaster.

Fig. 1. Three-phase process for creating disaster prevention maps

3.2 Space Syntax

The proposed disaster prevention map creation support system uses space syntax theory which is a method for analyzing road networks. This section explains space syntax.

Space syntax was developed by Bill Hillier [4] of London University starting from the 1970s in order to analyze connections between spaces. Space syntax is mainly used for research analyzing spatial structures in indoor spaces and in city spaces. One analysis method in space syntax is axial analysis, which treats indoor spaces and outdoor spaces separately and provides a numerical value called the integration value (Int.V) for the connectivity of a space from each of the connection relationships between intersections (nodes) and roads (edges). In other words, space syntax can clarify the structures of seemingly complicated indoor and outdoor spatial patterns by following a set of logical rules. The calculation of Int.V in axial analysis is described below.

In axial analysis, the space being analyzed is divided into spatial units called convex spaces. Next, axial lines (A-lines) that divide up the convex spaces are arranged to maximize their length and minimize the number of lines by using isovists (the area visible from a point in space) as hints (Fig. 2). In this way, the connections between convex spaces and A-lines can be represented using a graph (Fig. 3).

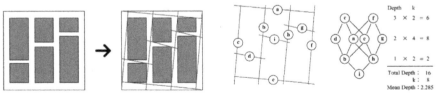

Fig. 2. Convex space and axial lines   **Fig. 3.** Conversion from axial lines to a graph

The mean depth (MD) can be found using Eq. (1).

$$MD_i = \frac{TD_i}{k-1} \quad TD_i = \sum_{j=i}^{k} Depth_{ij} \tag{1}$$

Next, the distance in the depth direction (RA_i) of all paths on a particular A-line is found by using Eq. (2).

$$RA_i = \frac{2(MD_i - 1)}{k - 2} \quad (k : \text{Total number of vertices}) \tag{2}$$

Because the value of RA_i depends on the vertex of the A-line being analyzed, RRA_i is found by normalizing RA_i as shown in Eq. (3).

$$RRA_i = \frac{(k - 1)(k - 2)}{2\left[k\left\{\log_2\left(\frac{k+2}{3}\right)\right\} + 1\right]} \tag{3}$$

Furthermore, Int.V is the reciprocal of RRA_i, as shown in Eq. (4).

$$IntV_i = \frac{1}{RRA_i} \tag{4}$$

Because Int.V is the reciprocal of depth, the space becomes shallower as Int.V increases, which indicates that the connection to other spaces is stronger. However, as Int.V decreases, the space becomes deeper, which indicates that the connection to other spaces is weaker. In other words, a particular A-line with a high value of Int.V can be said to be a vibrant space with many pedestrians in the target area.

When applied to all of the A-lines in the entire target region, Int.V is related to vehicle traffic and thus is called global (Int.V-G). On the other hand, when a limited area is studied, Int.V is related to pedestrian traffic and thus is called local (Int.V-L). Participants in this study were pedestrians, so Int.V-L (radius = 3) was used.

3.3 Disaster Factors

General disaster prevention maps provide information about an area such as zones where damage is expected, evacuation sites, and evacuation routes. The information is typically shown schematically to be used in disaster prevention measures and to reduce damage from natural disasters. However, more detailed disaster prevention information needs to be displayed on the map in order to implement disaster prevention measures. The main role of disaster prevention is to implement measures against disaster factors that have a possibility of occurring in the future. This research therefore defines disaster factors to be elements with a high probability of secondary damage to a road during a disaster, such as old wooden buildings, block walls, utility poles, and narrow roads (Fig. 4). Note that the proposed support system sets criteria for objectively evaluating these disaster factors in 3 levels while walking around using a device (Fig. 5).

3.4 Prototype Device

A prototype device was fabricated for collecting latent disaster factors in an area (Fig. 6). This device had an interactive design based on the importance of the experimental activity of collecting disaster factors.

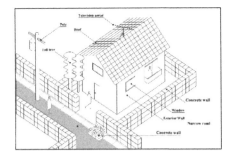

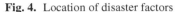

Evaluation 1	Disaster factors that need attention
Evaluation 2	Disaster factors that require caution
Evaluation 3	Disaster factors that require immediate improvement

Fig. 4. Location of disaster factors   **Fig. 5.** Evaluation of disaster factors

Fig. 6. Device for collecting and evaluating disaster factors

This device was designed based on the idea of a stone or cairn used as a landmark. The act of placing a stone indicates that there is a disaster factor. By placing the device on the ground, people can perform objective evaluation of disaster factors in 3 levels (Fig. 5) and collect position data. The operating environment was implemented using an Arduino micro. The device body was designed using Rhinoceros 5 (3D CAD software) and was output by a 3D printer.

A system was implemented using JavaScript to record the evaluation values and location data for the disaster factors collected by the device directly in a spread sheet (Google Sheets) via the Wi-Fi module built into the device (Fig. 7). Furthermore, a WEBGIS environment was implemented using JavaScript that updated an online map (Google Maps) with the data recorded in the spreadsheet (Fig. 8).

3.5 Simulation System

A system was constructed for simulating effective evacuation routes during a disaster (Fig. 9). The operating environment was implemented using the Grasshopper and Kangaroo plug-ins for Rhinoceros 5 (3D CAD software). When a road is closed, this system recalculates Int.V for each road in the road network and displays effective evacuation routes on the map using colors. Furthermore, we attempted to create disaster prevention maps that reflect changes in road condition by using aminations depicting people's movement in response to the road closures.

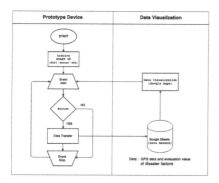

Fig. 7. Device configuration diagram

Fig. 8. Online map with data mapping

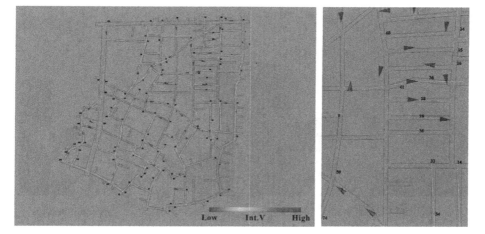

Fig. 9. Simulation system for disaster prevention map creation

In the proposed disaster prevention map creation support system, the disaster prevention maps are completed by using this simulation system via the three-phase process shown in Fig. 1.

4 Experiment

4.1 Purpose

To verify the usefulness of the proposed disaster prevention map creation support system, a validation experiment was conducted in which participants were asked to create a disaster prevention map for actual areas through the three-phase process shown in Fig. 1.

4.2 Study Areas

A validation experiment was conducted with reference to the Regional Risk Measurement Survey Report on Earthquakes (8th edition) published by the Tokyo Metropolitan

Government [7]. The targeted areas were the Machiya 4-chome area in Arakawa City, which is ranked number 1 in terms of overall risk level; the Senju-Yanagicho area in Adachi City, which is ranked number 2; and the Kyojima 2-chome area in Sumida City, which is ranked number 7.

4.3 Methods

In the validation experiment, participants were asked to walk around a set route for around 1 h and to perform the field work of collecting and evaluating disaster factors by using the device (Fig. 6). There were 9 participants in total, and they worked in groups of 3 in each area. After this, the participants reflected on the field work (Fig. 10) while viewing the online map (Fig. 8). Finally, we investigated road closures during an emergency by using the simulation system (Fig. 9), and simulated effective evacuation routes on the map (Fig. 11). The disaster prevention map was completed through this series of steps.

Fig. 10. Reflection on field work

Fig. 11. Simulation of evacuation route

5 Results and Discussion

5.1 Relationship Between Integration Values and Disaster Factors

The relationship between the disaster factors collected by participants and Int.V on the road network needs to be analyzed for each area, so the values of Int.V (which differs among the regions) were normalized to a minimum value of 0 and a maximum value of 1. Next, the total number of disaster factors for each road collected by the device was counted, and plotted on a graph showing the relationship between the road network and disaster factors. Note that in the validation experiment, all disaster factors were included in the total, regardless of the evaluation of the disaster factor (Fig. 5). We were able to clarify the characteristics of the disaster risk for each area by analyzing the relationship between the road network and disaster factors as a result of visually comparing the online map (Fig. 8) and the graph.

In the Machiya 4-chome area, the map and graph indicate a tendency for more disaster factors to be on roads near main roads that have many intersections (roads where Int.V is high) (Fig. 12).

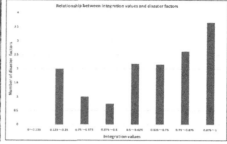

Fig. 12. Relationship between the road network and disaster factors (Machiya-4chome)

In the Senju-Yanagicho area, the map and graph indicate a tendency for the disaster factors to be more scattered throughout the entire area than expected, despite this being a city area arranged into zones (Fig. 13).

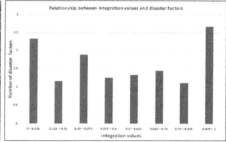

Fig. 13. Relationship between the road network and disaster factors (Senju-Yanagicho)

In the kyojima 2-chome area, the map and graph indicate a tendency for the disaster factors to be centralized on roads with low Int.V (Fig. 14).

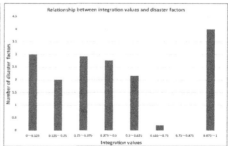

Fig. 14. Relationship between the road network and disaster factors (Kyojima 2-chome)

5.2 Support System for Disaster Prevention Map Creation

After creation of the disaster prevention maps was completed through the three-phase process shown in Fig. 1, the following positive opinions were received from the participants regarding the proposed disaster prevention map creation support system.

- The activity of collecting disaster factors using the device was considered enjoyable. Furthermore, it was an opportunity to gain deeper awareness of disaster prevention.
- The participants gained an understanding of the current state of the each area through the visualization of high disaster risk roads on the online map (Fig. 8).
- The disaster prevention map completed through the three-phase process shown in Fig. 1 was considered useful as a disaster prevention measure performed in advance by local residents.

However, the following negative opinions were also received.

- When moving around together in a group along the same route, the accuracy of evaluating disaster factors was limited by agreeability bias.
- Evaluating the disaster factors was difficult.
- While completing the disaster prevention maps, the participants felt it would be difficult to investigate effective routes for evacuation during a disaster by relying solely on the online map (Fig. 8). They felt material for reflection such as photos and videos would be needed during the collection of disaster factors.

6 Conclusion

In a validation experiment conducted to verify the usefulness of the disaster prevention map creation system proposed in this research, it was confirmed that the road network analysis (space syntax) used in the three-phase process shown in Fig. 1 was effective for creating disaster prevention maps.

In particular, by visualizing the relationship between the road network and collected disaster factors on an online map (Fig. 8), we were able to clarify the features of disaster risks in various area. This is an important result. Ultimately, by effectively utilizing this result, we were able to create disaster prevention maps that can be used for simulations of evacuations routes during a disaster.

In light of the above results as well as the opinions and evaluations by the participants, the proposed disaster prevention map creation support system was confirmed to make a useful contribution to disaster prevention measures that can be performed in advance.

In future research, we would like to improve the system by developing an application that combines the online map (Fig. 8) and simulation system (Fig. 9) into a single application. If it is possible to link the collection and evaluation of disaster factors by the device and to perform simulations of evacuation routes on a map in the app, prevention measures could be implemented more quickly by individuals and groups in preparation for disasters that could occur in the future. In other words, it would be possible to further reduce damage from disasters.

References

1. Ushiyama, M., Atumi, Y., Noriko, K., Seiichi, S., Yosuke, S.: Analysis of the effects of disaster workshop for non-residents on the participants. Nat. Disaster Sci. **27**(4), 375–385 (2009)
2. Nigechizu project team.: "Nigechizu" Making to Save Lives from Disasters. Gyosei Co., Ltd., Tokyo (2019)
3. Bousai-Tankentai.   https://www.sonpo.or.jp/about/efforts/reduction/bousai/index.html. Accessed 26 Jan 2020
4. Hiller, B., et al.: Space syntax. Environ. Plan. B **3**, 147–185 (1976)
5. Rie, T., Katsuya, H.: Street network characteristics and green space recognition. In: Lectures on Landscape and Design Studies, vol. 6, pp. 18–23. Japan Society of Civil Engineers, Tokyo (2010)
6. Tadashi, N., Kazunori, H., Takuro, I.: Analysis of the relationships between the accessibility of urban space based on the space syntax theory and the opportunity crime, the police's perceived risk of crime. J. City Plan. Inst. Jpn. **43**(3), 43–48 (2008)
7. Bureau of Urban Development, Tokyo Metropolitan Government: Regional Risk Measurement Survey Report on Earthquake (8th). Tokyo Metropolitan Government (2018)

Analysis of Mental Model of Users
with Network Malfunction

Haruka Yoshida[1]([envelope]), Kenta Tsukatsune[2], and Sumaru Niida[1]

[1] KDDI Research, Inc., Fujimino-shi, Saitama 3568502, Japan
ha-yoshida@kddi-research.jp
[2] Tokyo Metropolitan University, Hino-shi, Tokyo 1910065, Japan

Abstract. In order to improve the quality of communication networks, we adopted a research approach that realizes individual optimal control in consideration of the context and individual characteristics of the users, such as quality of experience (QoE) and co-created quality. In this paper, we report the results of a Web questionnaire survey of 722 participants to analyze the cognitive and behavioral characteristics under network malfunction. We analyzed the features of a mental model of users by the two-step cluster method. In the analysis, the data extracted by participants regarding the communication connection was regarded as a mental model. Characteristics of the mental model were examined by the element type (carrier, content providers, server, internet lines) included in the extracted data. The result showed the mental model of the users was classified into four classes with different characteristics. Analysis of the relationship with other attributes possessed by the users showed that there is a high possibility that the class of the mental model differs depending on the degree of ICT literacy. Moreover, it was found that the differences in mental models are likely to lead to differences in behaviors with network malfunction.

Keywords: Human-Network Interaction · Mental model · Prediction behavior · QoE · Co-created quality

1 Introduction

1.1 Background

With the spread of information and communication technologies (ICT), social networking has made use of artifacts, including information transactions through the communication network, now regarded as standard, and the communication network has become a lifeline for people. One of the long-standard issues that has not been solved is the dissatisfaction of users due to the malfunction of communication connection, despite high-performance ICT equipment that continues to improve its physical performance [1, 2]. Communication connection malfunctions are caused by various factors such as communication network problems including radio disturbance and congestion, and concentrated access to servers, in addition to failures and insufficient performance of communication devices and terminals. It seems that these problems will basically be solved

© Springer Nature Switzerland AG 2020
S. Yamamoto and H. Mori (Eds.): HCII 2020, LNCS 12184, pp. 312–328, 2020.
https://doi.org/10.1007/978-3-030-50020-7_22

by the progress of technology; however, in practice, the advanced ICT has not necessarily improved the malfunction of communication connections. For example, advanced ICT equipment increases the traffic volume due to the use of large screens and large-capacity contents. It is also a factor that increases network congestion. With the advanced ICT, people can use services anytime and anywhere, but this has led to the concentration of use in specific places and time zones, which has contributed to congestion [3, 4].

In communication service, many users use a system in which multiple devices are enjoyed. Therefore, many factors are complicatedly involved, and various problems probabilistically occur. In order to effectively solve such a problem that occurs with human behavior, a multidisciplinary approach to utilize users' adaptive behavior for changes in the state of communication services is required as well as an engineering approach to improve the system performance. Our research group proposes the Human-Network Interaction (HNI) framework as a part of the approach to analyze users' psychology and behavior when using the communication network [1]. Figure 1 shows a conceptual diagram of the HNI. In the framework, the communication network is regarded as cognitive artifacts. This model describes the cyclical interaction between people and networks in which users recognize the network state based on the information shown from the network and determine their behavior, and the communication systems change their state as a result of the users' behavior.

We work on issues of predicting users' behavior and controlling satisfaction in communication failure by using a cognitive approach as a study of communication networks considering users' behavior [4]. In the HNI framework, it is important to analyze cognitive aspects of how users understand the state of the network in order to predict the behavior of users using a communication network. If the behavior of users in communication failure can be predicted from the users' cognitive comprehension of the network state (mental model), the telecommunications carrier can take various measures to improve the user satisfaction.

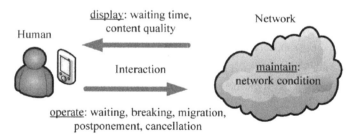

Fig. 1. Conceptual diagram of human-network interaction (HNI) [1].

1.2 Hypothesis Model

Our research team assumes that the User's behavior to deal with communication failure depends on two factors: a mental model and a causal attribution [5, 6, 11]. The mental model is an image that the user has regarding a communication connection in a normal

ICT usage environment. The causal attribution is a way of understanding the cause of the communication failure problem. For example, users who have a mental model in which their terminals are connected to some network according to the location and time and consider that the connection failure is on the network side are likely to move in search of a better network environment or change the connection time when the communication connection fails. On the other hand, users who have a mental model that their terminal communicate with something and think that connection failure is on their own terminal side, is likely to keep waiting or restart their terminals when the connection is failed.

Considering these features of users' mental models and behavior, we assume a hypothesis model of users' cognition and behavior based on the HNI framework in order to predict their behavior and satisfaction with communication networks. Figure 2 shows a diagram of the hypothesis model of users' cognition and behavior for communication networks. In this model, users have a mental model that is a cognitive comprehension for the network state based on their knowledge gained from their previous experience. Additionally, they predict a cause of the problems with network malfunction (causal attribution). Then, the mental model and the causal attribution result in users' behavior and satisfaction with waiting time as the output.

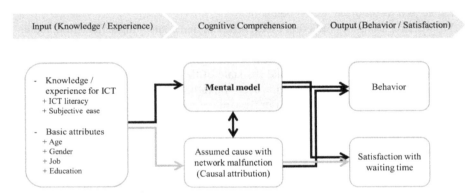

Fig. 2. The hypothesis model of users' cognition and behavior for communication networks

In order to verify the hypothesis model, our research group conducted a survey for each element shown in Fig. 2 with general users of communication services. The question items are about knowledge and experience of ICT (ICT literacy and subjective ease), cognitive comprehension of the network state, assumed cause and behavior with network malfunction, and satisfaction with waiting time. In this paper, we analyzed the characteristics of the mental model and relationships between the elements connected by black lines in Fig. 2. Analysis of the relationship between the elements connected by the grey lines was performed in existing studies. For example, Uemura et al. [5] analyzed the relationship among the causal attribution, ICT literacy, subjective ease and satisfaction with waiting time by using the survey data. The result showed that there was a positive correlation between the causal attribution and ICT literacy levels, namely users who use more advanced ICT technologies tend to attribute the cause to abstract equipment such as the communication foundation. Tsukatsune et al. [6] performed pattern classification of the causal attribution. As a result, different classes of the causal attribution were configured for computers (PC) and mobile phones (MP). Moreover, there was a difference in the satisfaction with waiting time between the classes of the causal attribution [7]. For example, users who attribute the cause to their own terminals were more tolerant of waiting time than users who attribute the cause to carriers, content providers, and servers. From the above, we concluded supporting the hypothesis model that causal attribution, which is one aspect of the cognitive comprehension of the network state that is formed based on ICT literacy, affects the satisfaction with waiting time. However, the analysis of the mental model, which is another aspect of the cognitive comprehension, has not been performed and the relationship with other factors has not been clarified yet. This paper reports the survey of the mental model of users for the communication networks and the results of the analysis. Then, we update the hypothesis model shown in Fig. 2 by clarifying the relationship among the mental model and other factors such as the ICT literacy, behavior with communication failure, and the satisfaction with waiting time.

2 Related Works

Research on communication quality has been developed from the approach that treats users as static entities that do not change temporally and spatially to the approach that treats users as dynamic entities that change their behavior based on the context or personal characteristics such as the Quality of Experience (QoE) [8]. With these developments, the subject of usability research has changed from efficiency and error reduction to learnability and social residuals. Similarly, the subject of communication quality research will change from the design of efficient communication networks to the study of dynamic control mechanisms of personalized networks that are easy to learn according to the social background and personality of users.

   In the HNI framework, users receive information indicating the state of the networks, recognize it, make a decision, and move on to the final action. In the QoE research, the quality of service (QoS) such as communication bandwidth, delay, and jitter is quantitatively given as a parameter. Then, factors that affect quality in the environment where the users are located are set and the subjective quality is measured. In addition to the research that deals with the users' cognitive aspects, research that deals with users' behavior is also performed. For example, Goto et al. [9] showed that the dissatisfaction of users is reduced in a dual task with two behavioral options. Yamori et al. [10] showed users selected the route with higher throughput when the system suggests a route that maximizes throughput. One goal of such an approach is co-creation quality, in which users and systems cooperate to control quality. There are two approaches to co-creation quality related to communication network systems. One is a system-controlled approach, in which the users provide various information to the system to adjust the network (e.g. [11]). The other is a behavior change approach, in which users' behavior is controlled by information provided from the system side (e.g. [12]).

   Attribution theory, the process of inferring the cause of consequences, has been studied in the framework of causal attribution in the field of psychology [13]. In a study on the causal attribution for communication use, Koyasu et al. [14] investigated the possible causes of PC malfunction estimated by students of information education classes. The result showed that there was no difference in how causes were attributed according to the experience and knowledge by the past information education.

There has been much research on mental models that people have for artifacts [15]. In the field of communications, there have been several studies on mental models for terminal operation [16, 17]. There is, however, no research that deals with mental models for communication connections that we focus on. In this paper, we survey and analyze the mental models for communication connections. We also analyze their relationships with satisfaction with waiting time and causal attribution. In the following, we define the users' image of connection structure for communication between PCs and mobile terminals as the mental model.

3 Survey

3.1 Participants

The survey was conducted from November 11th to 30th in 2009 [5]. Participants were recruited by voluntary application for a web search company recruitment. The number of participants in each segment by gender and age (10s, 20s, 30s, 40s, 50s) was adjusted to be 30 or more by the resource type attribute refinement method. The number of participants was 772 including 420 men and 352 women among the monitors registered by the research company. The participants were paid the prescribed reward.

3.2 Procedure

The survey asked the following questions in this order:

A) Questions about your profile such as gender, age, occupation, previous experience in information education, subjective ease/satisfaction with ICT use.
B) Question about the actual use of ICT such as PCs and mobile phones for ICT literacy measurement.
C) Subjective evaluation of waiting time in web link transition.
D) Drawing task for mental model measurement.
E) Question about behavior when the communication connection fails.
F) Question about assumed cause when the communication connection fails.

The participants visited the survey website and answered these questions in a browser.

3.3 Question Items

As for the profile in A), the subjective ease of ICT use was analyzed in addition to gender and age information. We asked about the four items of "making homepages on PCs," "making programs to run PCs," "setting up internet connections on PCs," and "constructing a LAN" on a five-point Likert scale, which is very easy to very difficult. As for the ICT literacy level in B), we asked about 20 specific actions using PCs and mobile phones, and whether or not they had performed them. The action items include making documents and address books using PCs, sending and receiving e-mails using PCs and mobile phones, searching for information, using internet shopping, and building LAN and web services. All question items are shown in [5]. The presentation order of the question items was fixed.

As for the subjective evaluation in the transition of the web link in C), based on the flow shown in Fig. 3, 14 types of waiting time (1 s, 2 s, 3 s, 4 s, 5 s, 6 s, 7 s, 8 s, 9 s, 10 s, 11 s, 12 s, 15 s, 20 s) between Screen 2 and Screen 4 were prepared, assuming the use of a browser on a PC. Then, the degree of satisfaction with each type of waiting time was inquired on a five-point Likert scale, which is very satisfied to very dissatisfied. As shown in Screen 3, the image of a rotating hourglass during the waiting time was displayed. The presentation order of the type of waiting time was random.

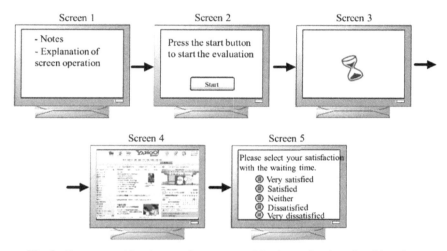

Fig. 3. Screen transition image of survey on subjective evaluation of waiting time.

As for the drawing task for measuring the mental model in D), in order to grasp the mental model for the internet connection using a PC and a mobile phone, participants drew what the communication connection would be like in the following two cases: when the target page is displayed and when the target page is not displayed due to communication failure by using the 48 icons such as PCs, mobile phones, servers, and towers. Figure 4 shows examples of icons used in the drawing task.

As for the behavior survey during communication failure in E), we asked two question items: frequency of experiencing situations where communication is difficult to connect and what action to take when communication is failed. The first question was asked on a six-point Likert scale, which is daily experience to never experience. For the second question, we asked to select the top three items from the 14 options shown in Table 1. The options were designed considering all possible components of the range of aggression and knowledge, and how behavior affects communication networks. The classification is shown for explanation in the table. In the survey, only options were shown to the participants.

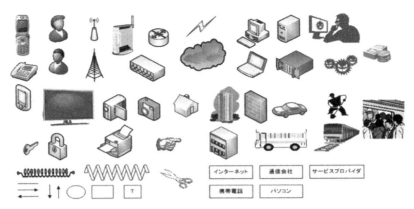

Fig. 4. Icons used for mental model drawing task

Table 1. The list of options for behavior when the communication connection of PC is failed.

Classification		Options
a. Active behavior	a1. Behavior affecting NW load	Access other websites and check if they are connected
		Reload the browser
	a2. Behavior not affecting NW load	Restart the PC
		Check if the LAN cables are connected correctly
		Close other applications and software
		Launch the task manager
		Launch another Web browser
		Send a ping
		Run the trace command
		Check the ipconfig
b. Passive behavior		Wait until connected
		Give up and see another web site
		Give up and do other things such as watching TV
Others		Others (free answer)

As for the survey of the causal attribution target when the communication connection fails, we asked two question items. The options for attribution are comprehensively prepared for elements that correspond to the depth and breadth of knowledge, from the terminals of the communication service users to communication infrastructures with higher abstraction. Details of the questions and the options are published in [6]. We asked the participants to select the top three items with a rank from eight options.

4 Result

4.1 Procedure of Data Analysis

Of the 772 participants, those who did not take the drawing task of D) seriously, and those who answered that they neither used "sending and receiving e-mail" nor "information retrieval" with PCs to the question about ICT use of B) were excluded as inappropriate answers. As a result, the responses of 715 participants including 393 men and 322 women were used as valid answers.

In the analysis of A), the score of subjective ease was calculated by inverting the sign of the scale value of subjective ease of answer to four items on the ICT use and summing them so that the higher the ease, the larger the value. In the analysis of B), multiple correspondence analysis (MCA) was performed from the results of answers to the 20 question items about experience in ICT in order to calculate the score of the ICT literacy level of each participant. MCA is a method to calculate the score considering the importance among multiple items. By using this method, it is possible to calculate the score of participants by statistically judging items that actually have important weights and items that are not. In the analysis of C), the Mean Opinion Score (MOS), which is the average of the evaluation value of each participant, was calculated.

In the analysis of D), two-step cluster analysis was performed as a method to classify the pattern of the drawing data. In this method, the first step is to use the data to find the centers of the clusters, and in the next step, the sub clusters are combined into larger clusters using a hierarchical cluster analysis technique. This method can handle large datasets efficiently since the optimal number of clusters for the data is automatically estimated.

In the analysis of E), the answers of each participant were classified into three classes: a1, a2, and b in Table 1. For the answer of "Others (free description)", we checked the contents and included any of the above classes.

In the analysis of F), the Latent Profile Analysis (LPA) [18] was performed as a method to classify the attribution patterns. This method is a type of Latent Mixture Model [19] and is widely applied in the fields of social science and behavioral science [20]. In this method, we assume that there is a group (class) of potential answers that have the same behavioral style and mindset, and explain the value of each question item (variable) by the difference between these classes. The analysis was performed with multiple variables in this method. It was possible to detect different patterns when the answer tendency for another variable is different even if the answer to a certain variable is similar.

4.2 Classification of Drawing Data

Classification was performed by two-step cluster analysis on the drawing data in the state of communication failure of the PC in D). The variable for classification was the type of icons used for drawing. That is, the data was classified according to the types of icons included in each drawing data. Icons that were not used by more than 90% of the participants were excluded from the input of the analysis since they had little effect on classification. The only variable for classification was the type of icons, and the number of used icons was not considered. This is because it was more important to consider which elements (icons) were composed than how many elements were used when discussing the mental model of communication connection.

The two-step cluster analysis classified 715 drawing data into four classes. Table 2 shows the classification results. We used IBM SPSS Statistics ver.26 for the statistical analysis tool. The frequencies in the table represent the number of data for each class, and the value in parentheses represents the percentage of the total data. In addition, the table shows the values of the top 10 variables that contributed to the classification for each class. For example, for the "Virus" variable (icon), the table shows that while 96.4% of the participants belonging to class 1 used this icon in their drawing data, 100% of the participants belonging to class 2 didn't use it. Interpreting each class in consideration of the used or not used variables in drawing data, the mental model corresponding to class 1 has the feature of the strong existence of third parties such as Virus and Hacker in addition to the existence of the carrier (Service P). The mental model corresponding to class 2 has a simple feature with a connection between the carrier (Service P) and the internet line (Internet). On the other hand, the mental model corresponding to class 3 has a feature including various elements such as icons indicating a radio wave (Wave) and cloud image (Cloud) in addition to a carrier (Service P) and an internet line (Internet). The mental model corresponding to class 4 has a feature that elements used in other classes, such as carrier (Service P) and the internet line (Internet), are hardly used. Instead, elements such as radio waves (Wave) and iron tower (Tower) are used in almost half the data. As described above, we interpreted and named the features for each class as shown in Table 2 in order to distinguish the features of each class.

Table 2. The classification result of drawing data

Class		1. Virus/Hacker	2. Provider/Internet	3. Multi-element mixture	4. Radiowave/Tower
Frequency		257 (35.9%)	242 (33.8%)	99 (13.8%)	117 (16.4%)
Variables contributed to the classification	Virus	1 (94.6%)	0 (100%)	0 (62.6%)	0 (100%)
	Cloud	0 (89.9%)	0 (100%)	1 (100%)	0 (80.3%)
	Service P	1 (68.1%)	1 (100%)	1 (76.8%)	0 (100%)
	Hacker	1 (57.6%)	0 (88.4%)	0 (79.8%)	0 (86.3%)
	Internet	0 (63.4%)	1 (59.9%)	1 (63.6%)	0 (89.7%)
	Worker	0 (70.8%)	0 (95.5%)	0 (90.9%)	0 (92.3%)
	Wave	0 (55.6%)	0 (69.8%)	1 (70.7%)	1 (52.1%)
	PC terminal	0 (70.4%)	0 (65.3%)	0 (74.7%)	0 (97.4%)
	Tower	0 (65.8%)	0 (83.9%)	0 (59.6%)	0 (56.4%)
	Text	0 (86.0%)	0 (66.1%)	0 (80.8%)	0 (82.9%)

4.3 Relationship Between the Mental Model and the ICT Literacy/the Subjective Ease

As described in the Sect. 4.1, the score of the ICT literacy level was calculated by performing MCA for answers among the 20 question items related to ICT experience. The score of subjective ease was calculated by inverting the sign of the scale value of subjective ease of answer to four items on the ICT use and by summing them. Here, in order to study the relationship between the mental model in PC connection failure and these values, we analyzed whether there is a difference in the ICT literacy level and subjective ease among the mental model classes.

Figure 5 shows the results of the average of ICT literacy level for each class of the mental model. Analysis of variance using the mental model class (4) as a factor in the ICT literacy level revealed that the main effect of the mental model class was $F(3, 711)$ = 4.44 (P = .004). Multiple comparison of the average value of the ICT literacy level among each mental model class revealed that there were significant differences between 1. virus/hacker class and 3. multi-element mixed class, between 3. multi-element mixed class and 4. radio/tower class, respectively. (Between class 1 and class 3: mean value difference = .344, P = .008, between class 3 and class 2: mean value difference = .415, P = .005).

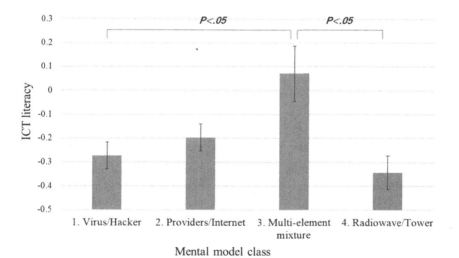

Fig. 5. Average of the ICT literacy level in each mental model class

Figure 6 shows the results of the average value of subjective ease for each mental model class. Analysis of variance using the mental model class (4) as a factor in subjective ease revealed that the main effect of the mental model class was $F(3, 711)$ = 3.20 (P = .023). Multiple comparisons of the average value of subjective ease among each class revealed that there was a significant difference between 1.virus/hacker class and 3.multi-element mixed class (mean value difference = 1.073, P = .047).

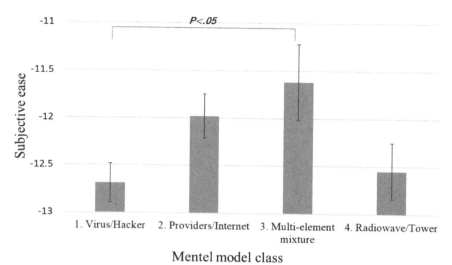

Fig. 6. Average of the subjective ease levels in each mental model class

The above results suggest that the mental model of users may be different depending on the ICT literacy levels and the subjective ease of the users. Especially, users with a low level of ICT literacy and subjective ease who think that ICT is difficult tend to have the mental model in network failure consisting of third party equipment that is not information and communication devices such as virus, hacker, radiowave, and tower. On the other hand, users with a high level of ICT literacy and subjective ease tend to have the mental model consisting of various elements such as carrier, provider, and internet connection.

4.4   Relationship Between the Mental Model and the Behavior

As described in Sect. 4.1, in this survey, participants selected the action to take when communication failures occurred on the PC from the options shown in Table 1. Here, in order to clarify the relationship between the mental model of users and the actions taken during communication failure, we analyzed the correlation between the mental model class and the behavior class, a1, a2, and b in Table 1.

Cross-tabulation of the mental model class (4) and the behavior class (3), and a chi-square test were performed. A significant difference was found ($P = .048$). Table 3 shows a cross-tabulation between the mental model class and the behavior class. As a lower level analysis, we performed residual analysis. The result showed that users in the mental model class 2 (Providers/Internet) were less likely to engage in behavior class b. (passive behavior) at the significant level of 5%. In addition, although there was no significance, users in the mental model class 2 (Providers/Internet) and 3 (Multi-element mixture) tend to engage in behavior class a2. (active behavior with small impact on the NW load) such as checking their peripheral equipment and environment, and are less likely to engage in behavior class b. (passive behavior) such as giving up and waiting. On the other hand, users in the mental model class 1 (Virus/Hacker) and 2 (Radiowave/Tower) are less likely to engage in active behavior such as checking peripheral equipment and environment, and reloading, and tend to engage in passive behavior such as giving up and waiting.

Table 3. Cross-tabulation table of the mental model class and the behavior class

			Mental model class			
			1. Virus/Hacker	2. Providers/Internet	3. Multi-elements mixture	4. Radiowave/Tower
Behaviour class	a1. Active(Large impact on NW load)	Frequency	202	197	80	90
		Percentage of total	28.3%	27.6%	11.2%	12.6%
		Adjusted residual	−.5	.9	.3	−.8
	a2. Active(Large impact on NW load)	Frequency	14	24	10	7
		Percentage of total	2.0%	3.4%	1.4%	1.0%
		Adjusted residual	−1.7	1.6	1.0	−.8
	b. Passive	Frequency	41	21	9	20
		Percentage of total	5.7%	2.9%	1.3%	2.8%
		Adjusted residual	1.9	−2.3	−1.2	1.5

4.5 Relationship Between the Mental Model and Satisfaction of Waiting Time

In order to confirm the relationship between the mental model of the participants in PC connection failure and subjective evaluation of the waiting time, we analyzed whether there was a difference in the waiting time evaluation among the mental model classes.

Figure 7 shows the results of the mean evaluation value (Mean Opinion Score: MOS) for the waiting time for each mental model class. As a result of a two-factor analysis of variance using the mental model class (4) and the waiting time (14) as the factors, the main effect of the mental model class was $F(3, 711) = 1.67$ ($P = .17$), and the main effect of the waiting time was $F(13, 9243) = 860.32$ ($P < .01$). The interaction between mental model class and waiting time was $F(39, 9243) = 2.29$ ($P < .01$).

We performed a simple main effect test since the interaction was significant. The results showed that there was a significant difference in the evaluation of the satisfaction only at the level of 1-s waiting time (between the 1. virus/hacker class and the 3. multi-element mixture class: mean value difference $= .48, P = .01$, between the 1. virus/hacker class and 4. radiowave/tower class: mean value difference $= .31, P = .01$). There was a significant difference in satisfaction between the levels of waiting time for all mental models. The above results indicate that there was almost no significant difference in the waiting time evaluation due to the difference of the mental model classes.

4.6 Relationship Between the Mental Model and the Causal Attribution

As described in Sect. 4.1, the causal attribution class is the result of classifying the answers about the causes with the malfunction of the communication connection by LPA. Here, we analyzed the relationship between the mental model class and the causal attribution class with PC connection malfunction. As for the causal attribution, we used

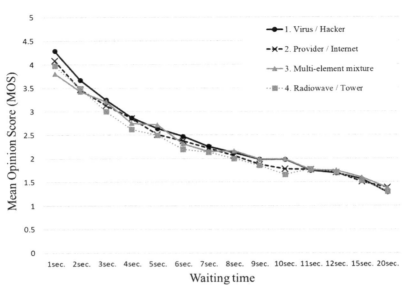

Fig. 7. Mean opinion score of waiting time in each mental model class

the four-class model based on the reference [6]. Each class name represents the feature of the cause with connection failure, namely, "Average/Foundation," "Terminal performance," "Provider," "Foundation."

Cross-tabulation of the mental model class and the causal attribution class, and a chi-square test were performed. The results showed that there was no significant difference ($P = .66$). Table 4 shows a cross-tabulation between the mental model class and the causal attribution class. The result suggests that there is little correlation between the mental model of users and the causal attribution in the communication network failure.

Table 4. Cross-tabulation table of mental model class and causal attribution class

			Mental model class			
			1. Virus/Hacker	2. Providers/Internet	3. Multi-elements mixture	4. Radiowave/Tower
Causal attribution class	Average/Foundation	Frequency	52	39	14	22
		Percentage of total	7.3%	5.5%	2.0%	3.1%
	Terminal Performance	Frequency	107	92	43	45
		Percentage of total	15.0%	12.9%	6.0%	6.3%
	Provider	Frequency	54	52	20	28
		Percentage of total	7.6%	7.3%	2.8%	3.9%
	Foundation	Frequency	44	59	22	22
		Percentage of total	6.2%	8.3%	3.1%	3.1%

4.7 Relationship Between the Causal Attribution and Behavior

Cross-tabulation of the causal attribution class and the behavior class, and a chi-square test were performed. The results showed that there was no significant difference. The result suggests that there is little correlation between the causal attribution and behavior of users.

5 Discussion

Updating the Hypothesis Model

From the results of Sect. 4.3 and 4.4, users in mental model class 1, virus/hacker, and class 4, radiowave/tower, have a relatively low level of ICT literacy and subjective ease for ICT, and tend to engage in passive behavior such as giving up and waiting with malfunction of the communication connection. On the other hand, users in mental model class 2, provider/Internet, and class 3, multi-element mixture, have a relatively high level of ICT literacy and subjective ease, and tend to engage in active behavior such as checking peripheral equipment and environment with malfunction of the communication connection. These results suggest that the mental model for the communication connection is formed from the knowledge and experience of the ICT accumulated so far, and that the mental model affects the behavior during the communication failure. Users with relatively advanced knowledge and experience of ICT use form a mental model that consists of multiple elements related to communication performance, such as carriers, service providers, and internet lines. Then, when communication network problems occur, it is inferred that they actively investigate where these problems are. On the other hand, users with little knowledge and experience of ICT use form a mental model that consists of elements frequently reported in news articles, such as viruses, hackers, and radiowaves. They themselves cannot investigate the elements, so it is inferred that they do not do anything and wait until connected when the communication connections fail. The model suggests that the behavior of users in the communication failure can be predicted by a survey of the users' knowledge and experience of ICT.

In this survey, it is suggested that the correlation between the mental model and the causal attribution/the waiting time satisfaction that are other factors affecting user behavior was low. In addition, a previous study [7] has shown that the difference in the causal attribution of users has a significant effect on the waiting time satisfaction when the communication fails.

Based on the above results, we updated the hypothesis model on the cognition and behavior of communication network users. Figure 8 shows the diagram of the updated model. In this figure, solid lines represent elements that suggest high correlation, and dotted lines represent elements that suggest low correlation in the previous and current studies. Especially, the black lines represent the relationship based on the results clarified in this paper. From the figure, the mental model and the causal attribution for the communication network are independently formed based on the users' knowledge and experience of ICT. And then, the mental model and the causal attribution affect behavior and satisfaction with waiting time, respectively.

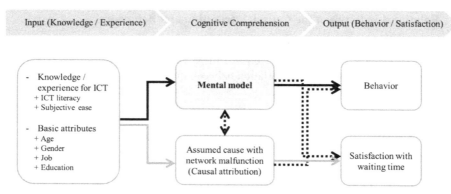

Fig. 8. The updated model of cognition and behavior of communication network users

Limitation

The analyzed data in this paper is the survey data obtained in 2009. At that time, terminals such as smart phones and tablet devices were not widespread. Therefore, there is a possibility that the user may have a different mental model and a different sense of causal attribution regarding the communication connection. The result of this paper suggests that in 2009, there was a correlation between the mental model and behavior when the communication connection failed. In the future, we will conduct a similar survey to clarify common and different points in the cognitive aspects and behavior of users from the viewpoints of the times. Such analysis is expected to develop the study of concrete methods for realizing co-creation quality that enhance QoE in this field.

In this analysis of the mental model, we performed two-step cluster analysis as a data classification method that can easily interpret the results. There are, however, many other methods for analysis and classification of the mental model. In order to clarify the relationship between the mental model and causal attribution and waiting time satisfaction, additional analysis is required to study the relationship between the mental model and other factors in depth, e.g. investigating the feature of mental models for each causal attribution class, and investigating the mental models of users whose satisfaction with waiting time is particularly high/low.

6   Conclusion

In order to improve the quality of communication networks, we adopted a research approach to realize individual optimal control in consideration of the context and individual characteristics of the users, such as quality of experience (QoE) and co-created quality. In this paper, as the first step, we conducted a survey on mental models of the users in 722 men and women when the communication connection failed and analyzed the feature by the clustering method. In the analysis, we regarded the drawing data for the communication state as the users' mental model and performed two-step clustering by using the types of elements (icons) contained in the drawing data as variables. As a result, the data were classified into four classes with different mental model features, 1. Virus/Hacker class, 2. Providers/Internet class, 3. Multi-element mixture class, 4. Radiowave/Tower class. This suggests that it is possible to analyze the features of the users' mental model by classifying the data drawn by the users according to the component types. Analysis of the relationship between the mental model and other attributes showed that the mental model is likely to be different depending on the level of ICT literacy and that users with different mental models are more likely to take different actions when the communication connections fail. On the other hand, the correlation between the mental model and the satisfaction with the waiting time/causal attribution, which are other factors related to users' behavior, was low. More detailed additional analysis is necessary to clarify how the differences in the mental models of the users affect the causal attribution and the satisfaction with the waiting time. Such research is expected to develop the study of concrete methods for realizing co-creation quality that enhances QoE in cooperation between the system and the user when the network connection fails.

References

1. Niida, S., Tsugawa, S., Suganuma, M., Wakamiya, N.: A survey on modeling of human states in communication behavior. IEICE Trans. Commun. **100**(9), 1538–1546 (2017)
2. Fiedler, M., Hossfeld, T., Tran-Gia, A.P.: Generic quantitative relationship between quality of experience and quality of service. IEEE Netw. **24**(2), 36–41 (2010)
3. Agboma, F., Liotta, A.: Quality of experience management in mobile content delivery systems. Telecommun. Syst. **49**(1), 85–98 (2012). https://doi.org/10.1007/s11235-010-9355-6
4. Niida, S.: Theory and applications of communication behavior engineering. IEICE Tech. Rep. **119**(125), 67–71 (2019). (in Japanese)
5. Uemura, S., Niida, S., Nakamura, H.: A study on the relation between one's mental model to communication service and the causal attribution. In: The Proceedings of the 28th Conference on the Japanese Cognitive Association, pp. 122–125 (2011). (in Japanese)
6. Tsukatsune, K., Niida, S.: Pattern classification of causal attribution in network malfunction situation with latent profile analysis. IEICE Tech. Rep. **119**(125), 89–94 (2019). (in Japanese)
7. Niida, S., Tsukatsune, K.: Influence of causal attribution in network malfunction on evaluation of satisfaction considering waiting time. IEICE Tech. Rep. **119**(367), 7–12 (2019). (in Japanese)
8. Abe, I., Ishibashi, Y., Yoshino, H.: State of the art and service quality. J. IEICE **91**(2), 82–86 (2008). (in Japanese)
9. Goto, Y., Niikuma, R., Honda, Y., Nojiri, H., Takahashi, R., Takahashi, T.: PoC of co-created quality with users in communication networks. IEICE Tech. Rep. **114**(209), 59–62 (2014). (in Japanese)
10. Yamori, K., Iwai, T., Nobukiyo, T., Oonishi, K., Satoda, K.: An economic approach for co-created quality in communication networks. IEICE Tech. Rep. **117**(386), 29–34 (2018). (in Japanese)
11. Niida, S., Uemura, S., Harada, E.T.: Design requirements for improving QoE of web service using time-fillers. IEICE Trans. Commun. **96**(8), 2069–2075 (2013)
12. Murase, T., Motoyoshi, G., Sonoda, K., Katto, J.: Quality of service of mobile users for longcut routes with congested access points. In: Proceedings of the 7th International Conference on Ubiquitous Information Management and Communication, ACM ICUIMC 2013 (2013). Article no. 40
13. Heider, F.: The Psychology of Interpersonal Relations. Wiley, New York (1958)
14. Koyasu, M., Goushiki, T., Nakamura, M.: Optimizing information literacy education for the first year course of the Faculty of Education. Kyoto Univ. Res. High. Educ. **6**, 65–76 (2000). (in Japanese)

15. Gentner, D., Stevens, A.L.: Mental Models. Erlbaum, Hillsdale (1983)
16. Matsui, H., Yokota, K., Tokunaga, Y.: Mental model of telephone operation. IEICE Trans. Commun. **J70-D**(11), 2058–2064 (1987). (in Japanese)
17. Doi, T., Tominaga, S., Yamaoka, T., Nishizaki, Y.: The elements for structuring the mental model in operation of user interfaces. Sci. Des. **58**(55), 53–62 (2012). (in Japanese)
18. Muthén, L.K., Muthén, B.: Mplus for applied researchers: User's guide (2016). http://www.statmodel.com/virg_nov_course.shtml
19. Takebayashi, Y.: Latent mixture distribution model. In: Kosugi, K., Shimizu, Y. (eds.) Introduction to Structural Equation Modeling with M-plus and R, pp. 224–228. Kitaooji Shobo Publishing, Kyoto (2014). (in Japanese)
20. Choi, W.S., Moon, O.K., Yeum, D.M.: Latent profile analysis of lifestyle characteristics and health risk behaviors among Koreans who have completed industrial accident care. Ind. Health **55**, 460–470 (2017)

Information in VR and AR

Virtual Reality Applications Using Pseudo-attraction Force by Asymmetric Oscillation

Tomohiro Amemiya$^{(\boxtimes)}$ (iD)

The University of Tokyo, 7-3-1 Hongo, Bunkyo, Tokyo 113-8656, Japan
amemiya@vr.u-tokyo.ac.jp

Abstract. Because virtual reality (VR) systems are accessible to anyone through inexpensive high-end consumer headsets and input devices, researchers are seeking a technique to enrich the VR experience using modalities other than audiovisual ones, such as touch. The author is developing a haptic display that utilizes the properties of human illusions, which makes humans experience an illusory force similar to the sensation of being pulled continuously in a particular direction through asymmetric vibrations. Using illusory force in the VR applications is not a popular concept. This paper discusses the possibility of whether such a pseudo-attraction force can be applied to VR applications and introduces several applications for the implementation of this pseudo-attraction force in real world scenarios.

Keywords: Haptics · Force sensation · Sensory illusion

1 Introduction

After several decades since the emergence of the virtual reality (VR) concept, the cost of the hardware for an immersive audiovisual VR experience, such as head-mounted displays (HMDs), has decreased drastically [17, 32]. Today, VR is accessible to everyone, owing to inexpensive high-end consumer-friendly HMDs and input devices. Humans experience the real world scenarios through various modalities; hence, to enrich their experience in VR, new modalities are being explored. Touch is often considered as promising candidate for modality because a lack of haptic feedback brings us back from VR quickly into the real world, enhancing the performance of VR applications [33, 34]. In spite of the importance of haptic feedback, a limited number of haptic interface displays, such as tactile or force feedback displays, have been adopted in VR systems, compared with the audiovisual ones. This is mainly due to the technical difficulty in reproducing a haptic or somatosensory experience with inexpensive haptic displays.

Innovative displays in VR systems that consider the characteristics of human perception and optimize information technologies can be designed. The perceptual limits of the human sensory system, or its characteristics, have often been considered to determine the guidelines for designing audiovisual displays, including proper video frame rates

© Springer Nature Switzerland AG 2020
S. Yamamoto and H. Mori (Eds.): HCII 2020, LNCS 12184, pp. 331–340, 2020.
https://doi.org/10.1007/978-3-030-50020-7_23

that produce perceptually smooth motion, and algorithms for lossy audio data compression to be perceptually lossless. In addition, human sensory illusions are often utilized to invent innovative audiovisual displays. Thus, some haptic interface displays can be built on the basis of the sensory-illusion-based approach without incurring much cost.

The author has focused on an approach that exploits the nonlinearity of human perception to develop mobile force displays. Because of the nonlinearity, a weak force stimulus is not clearly perceived, even if it is presented for a long period. A method that uses vibrations with asymmetric acceleration—brief, intense pulses of acceleration alternate with longer periods of low-amplitude recovery—to induce the sensation of being pulled or pushed in a particular direction [1], is proposed. This paper discusses the possibility of this pseudo-attraction force being applied to VR applications by demonstrating several cases of implementation.

2   Directed Force Perception by an Asymmetric Oscillation

2.1   Background

Over the past two decades, several force displays have been developed and studied. Most of them are grounded force displays, such as PHANToM [20] and SPIDAR [21], which use mechanical linkages to establish a fulcrum (grounding support), relative to the ground, or use huge air compressors [22, 23]. The fulcrum is required because of the action-reaction principle. However, because mobile devices lack a fulcrum, most conventional force display systems can produce neither a constant nor translational force, but only short-term rotational force (e.g., using the gyroscopic effect [18, 35] or momentum wheels [19, 29, 36]). Devices that use the gyroscopic effect are not suitable for miniaturization because the rotating wheels and gimbals needed to produce the gyroscopic effect require space. Devices that use the momentum wheels tend to produce an undesired and unintended torque generated by the gyroscopic effect when the flywheels are tilted, thereby adversely affecting the perception of force [35]. In general, a major problem of the non-grounded devices is their inability to generate a constant and translational force, which means that they can generate only a short-time rotational force. Thus, mobile devices, which are not grounded, use a simple vibrotactile cue as a haptic information display.

To resolve the issue, the author and his colleagues have proposed to utilize a characteristic of human perception and have succeeded in creating a force sensation of being pulled or pushed with various kinds of mobile apparatuses. The force display, called Buru-Navi [1, 2, 11], creates both a constant and translational force sensation, by utilizing the nonlinear characteristics of human perception. The key is to use different acceleration patterns for two directions to create a perceived force imbalance. A brief and strong force is generated in the desired direction, while a weaker one is generated over a longer period in the direction opposite to the desired direction. Although the temporal average of the net force is physically zero (e.g., the average of the forces in each direction is the same), the user holding a device that vibrates by acceleration patterns feels as if he/she is being pulled in one direction; this is because the amplitude of the weaker force is adjusted to be less than a sensory or perceptual threshold.

2.2 Prototypes and Underlying Mechanism

Over the past fifteen years, the author has worked on refining a method to create the sensory illusion of being pulled, such as a slider-crank mechanism [1, 2, 4, 5], a spring-cam mechanism [6], a knocking mechanism [16], or a linkage-cam mechanism [3]. Figure 1 shows various prototypes of ungrounded force displays that have been developed. Following the first prototypes, other researchers have implemented them using twin eccentric rotating masses [31], rotational motor's counterforce [25] and a magnetic levitation device [14]. The author has succeeded in reducing the size and weight of the force display remarkably by using a voice-coil vibrator [7, 11]. Because voice-coil vibrators are inexpensive and easily available, many researchers use them to create a force sensation [12, 15, 27, 28].

The prototype with a slider-crank mechanism (the third leftmost in Fig. 1) was designed to be held by the hand, while the prototype with a voice-coil vibrator (the second rightmost in Fig. 1) was designed to be pinched by the fingers. The former mainly stimulates muscle spindles in the forearm or the upper arm rather than mechanoreceptors on the palm. The authors found that 5–10 Hz of the asymmetric oscillation is effective for the former prototype to induce a clear sensation of being pulled or pushed.

In contrast, the latter stimulates mechanoreceptors on the finger pad, which is one of the most sensitive parts. The author has hypothesized that the Meissner corpuscles and the Ruffini endings contribute to the illusion because these mechanoreceptors are sensitive to force stimulus in a direction tangential to the skin. Moreover, the Pacinian corpuscles do not seem to contribute to the illusion because the Pacinian corpuscles cannot sense direction [26] or cannot discriminate the difference between symmetric and asymmetric acceleration change [7]. Furthermore, the authors found that around 40 Hz of the asymmetric oscillation is effective for the latter prototype, which falls below the frequency range of 100–300 Hz [8], where the Pacinian corpuscles are sensitive in the directions tangential to the skin [9]. In contrast, SA-I and RA-I fibers, whose signals are thought to be obtained from the Merkel disks and Meissner corpuscles, respectively, are sensitive to vibrations with lower frequencies (less than 100 Hz), and some of them can clearly code the sliding or tangential force direction [10]. The SA-II fiber innervating Ruffini endings are also sensitive to skin stretch, particularly to tangential forces generated in the skin. Therefore, to create an illusory force sensation of being pulled, an asymmetrical oscillation pattern should be designed that contains the frequency components stimulating these receptors (i.e., less than 100 Hz) and contains the asymmetric magnitude that exceeds the thresholds of shearing displacement in one direction, but not in the other.

In both the prototypes, psychophysical experiments on force direction discrimination of the asymmetric oscillation confirmed that almost all the participants felt an apparent illusory force of being pulled or pushed persistently and that they were able to distinguish the force direction correctly. However, the subjective impression of a force sensation tended to be different between the two prototypes.

2.3 Wayfinding Using an Illusory Force

Leading-by-hand is an intuitive manner for teaching body action or helping someone move in a certain direction. An illusory force of being pulled can be thought to be applied

Fig. 1. Prototypes of haptic displays generating an asymmetric oscillation to induce the sensation of being pulled or pushed. The second rightmost one is 18 × 18 × 37 mm (1 DoF), and the rightmost one is φ40 × 17 mm (2 DoF) [24].

for pedestrian navigation, without visual or auditory information, as if someone is being led by the hand physically.

The author has succeeded in providing directional cues for wayfinding using Buru-Navi for people with visual impairments (Fig. 2). The author, in collaboration with a fire department in Kyoto, performed an experiment for predefined route guidance using Buru-Navi to evaluate the time required to complete a walking task or error numbers. We built a human-size checkerboard-shaped maze in a gymnasium. The results showed that 91% of participants (N = 23) with visual impairment were able to walk safely along a predefined route without any prior training [3]. Smoke hinders the visual field of people at the scene in a fire emergency, which means that everyone, including sighted people, must rely on non-visual cues. Buru-Navi will be useful for everyone in such a situation.

During the experiment, a force display was developed to generate a force sensation in eight cardinal directions by the summation of linearly independent force vectors. Four vibration modules were stacked. By combining force vectors generated by each module, the force display can swiftly create a force sensation on a two-dimensional plane compared with "a module with a turntable" approach.

The author has developed another prototype that adopts the turntable approach that makes the force display thinner and the direction resolution of force vector finer. This prototype can express the direction in an open space, but not in a maze (Fig. 3). Furthermore, it has been shown that active manual movement in both the rotational and translational directions enhances the precise perception of the direction of an illusory force created by Buru-Navi [13], suggesting that the active exploration of force direction by moving the arm or hand is a good strategy for understanding the direction in a pedestrian navigation application. It is helpful to update the force direction and maintain the same direction in global coordinates depending on the orientation of the force display, similar to the operation of a compass.

Fig. 2. Haptic route guidance for pedestrian with visual impairments [3]. The visually impaired participants holding the force display walked in the predefined route in a maze, without prior notice.

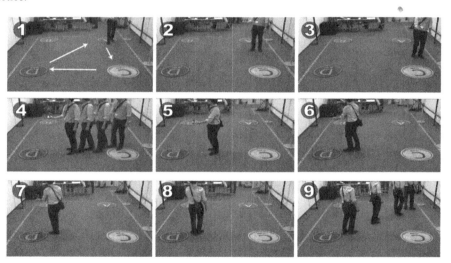

Fig. 3. A sequence of photos of a participant walking using haptic cues of asymmetric oscillation. The participant holding the force display walked in a predefined route in an open space, without prior notice of the route.

3   VR Application

3.1   Interaction with Virtual Objects

In VR environments, users frequently encounter difficulty in various scenarios, for example, in hitting a ball, touching a wall, or pushing a door. These occurrences are because of the absence of haptic sensation, when interacting with virtual objects. Though a simple vibration provides a binary feedback of contact or otherwise, it is very difficult to determine the property of a material, such as its shape or softness. Studies on grasping or manipulating virtual objects have been widely studied; in this study, however, the focus has been on a single point per hand.

A stiffness or elasticity of virtual objects is a prominent tactile feature and is relevant for many applications such as in medicine or teleoperation. Here, the author has tested whether an illusory force can be used to express a stiffness of virtual objects. The stiffnesses can be simulated using Hooke's law. A position of the hand was tracked by an infrared camera (leap motion controller). The amplitude of the illusory force was controlled proportionally to that of asymmetric oscillation. With this setup, a user can feel the stiffness of a virtual object using one or both hands (Fig. 4).

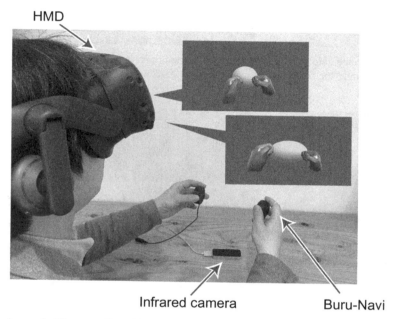

Fig. 4. A user holding two Buru-Navi devices in both hands; he can feel the elasticity of the virtual object.

3.2   Interaction with Virtual Creatures

In addition to virtual objects, virtual creatures are used in various forms of entertainments and in interactive arts. Virtual creatures move autonomously, and the interaction changes are time dependent on the state of both the user and the virtual creatures. An illusory force can be used to express the interaction in VR environments. For example, as a haptic experience in gaming, the illusory force has been implemented in an angling game; here, users can sense a virtual fish nibbling and pulling the hook of a fishing line. A fishing line with a small weight at its tip was attached to Buru-Navi as shown in Fig. 5. When the weight approaches the mouth of the virtual fish displayed on a touchscreen, the virtual fish bites it. When the virtual fish is caught, Buru-Navi generates the sensation of the virtual fish pulling the hook. The vibration of Buru-Navi enhances the sensation of catching a wiggling fish in the air.

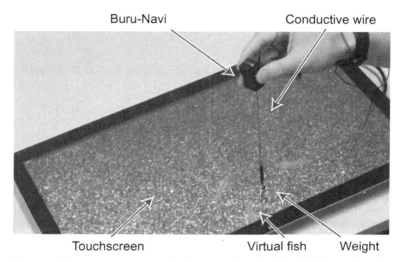

Fig. 5. Virtual angling game. A user can feel the sensation of a fish nibbling on a hook and being pulled by the fish without fishing lines [24].

The basic motion of a virtual fish is firstly modelled. The fish then repeatedly forms swirls with its fins, and its reaction force is used as a driving force. Therefore, the force pulling the string is intermittent and has a vibratory component. The larger the fish, the stronger the driving force and the lower the temporal frequency of the fin movement. The amplitude of the illusory force was changed by the amplitude of the asymmetric oscillation. The frequency of the illusory force corresponded to the fundamental frequency of the asymmetric oscillation. The result of a user study showed that the reality of a pulling sensation by a fish was improved by extending the time interval of the pulsive force (i.e., duration for brief and stronger force).

Previous haptic interaction systems for angling games used tension forces to express the fish pulling the string (for example [30]). In contrast, our system does not require mechanical linkages to establish a fulcrum relative to the ground, although the direction of pulling is limited.

4 Conclusion

This study introduced haptic displays based on perceptual illusions with the potential for VR applications. The sense of touch is very effective in presenting a feeling of object existence. To maximize the benefit of the haptic displays, utilizing human characteristics, such as sensory illusion, provides us with a new cues to develop innovative information displays. This study introduced a technique that creates the sensation of being pulled or pushed without using mechanical linkages to establish a fulcrum relative to the ground. It is worth noting that some VR systems may be accurate even if force displays are mechanically connected to the ground. There is a trade-off between higher fidelity force feedback and spatial workspace. It is important to select the types of force presenting methods suitable for the VR application. In future, adding other modalities such as vision and audition will create a richer haptic experience, enabling the VR systems to integrate them easily.

Acknowledgements. This work was supported in part by JSPS KAKENHI, Grants-in-Aid for Scientific Research (B) 18H03283.

References

1. Amemiya, T., Ando, H., Maeda, T.: Virtual force display: direction guidance using asymmetric acceleration via periodic translational motion. In: Proceedings of World Haptics Conference, pp. 619–622 (2005)
2. Amemiya, T: Haptic interface using sensory illusion. In: Tutorial in IEEE Virtual Reality 2008, Integration of Haptics in Virtual Environments: from Perception to Rendering, Reno, NV (2008)
3. Amemiya, T., Sugiyama, H.: Orienting kinesthetically: a haptic handheld wayfinder for people with visual impairments. ACM Trans. Access. Comput. 3(2), 1–23 (2010). Article 6
4. Amemiya, T., Maeda, T.: Asymmetric oscillation distorts the perceived heaviness of handheld objects. IEEE Trans. Haptics 1(1), 9–18 (2008)
5. Amemiya, T., Maeda, T.: NOBUNAGA: multicylinder-like pulse generator for kinesthetic illusion of being pulled smoothly. In: Ferre, M. (ed.) EuroHaptics 2008. LNCS, vol. 5024, pp. 580–585. Springer, Heidelberg (2008). https://doi.org/10.1007/978-3-540-69057-3_75
6. Amemiya, T., Ando, H., Maeda, T.: Hand-held force display with spring-cam mechanism for generating asymmetric acceleration. In: Proceedings of World Haptics Conference, Tsukuba, Japan, pp. 572–573 (2007)
7. Amemiya, T., Gomi, H.: Distinct pseudo-attraction force sensation by a thumb-sized vibrator that oscillates asymmetrically. In: Proceedings of Eurohaptics, Versailles, France, vol. II, pp. 88–95 (2014)
8. Bolanowski Jr., S.J., Gescheider, G.A., Verrillo, R.T., Checkosky, C.M.: Four channels mediate the mechanical aspects of touch. J. Acoust. Soc. Am. 84(5), 680–694 (1988)
9. Srinivasan, M.A., Whitehouse, J.M., Lamotte, R.H.: Tactile detection of slip: surface microgeometry and peripheral neural codes. J. Neurophysiol. 63(6), 323–332 (1990)
10. Maeno, T., Kobayashi, K., Yamazaki, N.: Relationship between the structure of human finger tissue and the location of tactile receptors. Bull. JSME Int. J. 41, 94–100 (1998)
11. Amemiya, T.: Perceptual illusions for multisensory displays. In: Proceedings of the 22nd International Display Workshops, IDW 2015, Otsu, Japan, vol. 22, pp. 1276–1279 (2015). Invited talk
12. Rekimoto, J.: Traxion: a tactile interaction device with virtual force sensation. In: Proceedings of ACM UIST, pp. 427–431 (2013)
13. Amemiya, T., Gomi, H.: Active manual movement improves directional perception of illusory force. IEEE Trans. Haptics 9(4), 465–473 (2016)

14. Tappeiner, H.W., Klatzky, R.L., Unger, B., Hollis, R.: Good vibrations: asymmetric vibrations for directional haptic cues. In: Proceedings of World Haptics Conference, pp. 285–289 (2009)
15. Choi, I., Culbertson, H., Miller, M.R., Olwal, A., Follmer, S.: Grabity: a wearable haptic interface for simulating weight and grasping in virtual reality. In: Proceedings of UIST, pp. 119–130 (2017)
16. Hamaguchi, H., Amemiya, T., Maeda, T., Ando, H.: Design of repetitive knocking force display for being-pulled illusion. In: Proceedings of 19th International Symposium in Robot and Human Interactive Communication, Viareggio, pp. 33–37 (2010)
17. Hirose, M.: The second generation virtual reality technology. In: Proceedings of 16th International Conference on Virtual Systems and Multimedia, Seoul, Korea (2010). Keynote/invited Speech
18. Yano, H., Yoshie, M., Iwata, H.: Development of a non-grounded haptic interface using the gyro effect. In: Proceedings of HAPTICS, pp. 32–39 (2003)
19. Tanaka, Y., Masataka, S., Yuka, K., Fukui, Y., Yamashita, J., Nakamura, N.: Mobile torque display and haptic characteristics of human palm. In: Proceedings of ICAT, pp. 115–120 (2001)
20. Massie, T.H., Salisbury, J.K.: The phantom haptic interface: a device for probing virtual objects. In: Proceedings of the ASME Winter Annual Meeting, Symposium on Haptic Interfaces for Virtual Environment and Teleoperator Systems, vol. 55, no. 1, pp. 295–300 (1994)
21. Sato, M., Hirata, Y., Kawarada, H.: Space interface device for artificial reality - SPIDAR. Syst. Comput. Japan 23(12), 44–54 (2007)
22. Gurocak, H., Jayaram, S., Parrish, B., Jayaram, U.: Weight sensation in virtual environments using a haptic device with air jets. J. Comput. Inf. Sci. Eng. 3, 130–135 (2003)
23. Suzuki, Y., Kobayashi, M., Ishibashi, S.: Design of force feedback utilizing air pressure toward untethered human interface. In: Proceedings of CHI 2002 Extended Abstracts on Human Factors in Computing Systems, pp. 808–809. ACM Press (2002)
24. Amemiya, T.: Haptic interface technologies using perceptual illusions. In: Yamamoto, S., Mori, H. (eds.) HIMI 2018. LNCS, vol. 10904, pp. 168–174. Springer, Cham (2018). https://doi.org/10.1007/978-3-319-92043-6_14
25. Yem, V., Okazaki, R., Kajimoto, H.: Vibrotactile and pseudo force presentation using motor rotational acceleration. In: Proceedings of IEEE Haptics Symposium, HAPTICS, Philadelphia, PA, pp. 47–51 (2016)
26. Culbertson, H., Walker, J. M., Okamura, A.M.: Modeling and design of asymmetric vibrations to induce ungrounded pulling sensation through asymmetric skin displacement. In: Proceedings of IEEE Haptics Symposium, HAPTICS, Philadelphia, PA, pp. 27–33 (2016)
27. Tanabe, T., Yano, H., Iwata, I.: Evaluation of the perceptual characteristics of a force induced by asymmetric vibrations. IEEE Trans. Haptics 11(2), 220–231 (2018)
28. Kim, H., Yi, H., Lee, H., Lee. W.: HapCube: a wearable tactile device to provide tangential and normal pseudo-force feedback on a fingertip. In: Proceedings of the 2018 CHI Conference on Human Factors in Computing Systems. Paper 501, pp. 1–13 (2018)
29. Choiniere, J.-P., Gosselin, C.: Development and experimental validation of a haptic compass based on asymmetric torque stimuli. IEEE Trans. Haptics 10(1), 29–39 (2017)
30. Noguchi, J., et al.: Powder screen: a virtual materializer. In: Proceedings of ACM SIGGRAPH 2006 Emerging Technologies. ACM (2006)
31. Nakamura, N., Fukui, Y.: Development of fingertip type nongrounding force feedback display. In: Proceedings of World Haptics Conference, pp. 582–583 (2007)
32. Jensen, L., Konradsen, F.: A review of the use of virtual reality head-mounted displays in education and training. Educ. Inf. Technol. 23(4), 1515–1529 (2018). https://doi.org/10.1007/s10639-017-9676-0

33. Georgiou, O., et al.: Touchless haptic feedback for VR rhythm games. In: Proceedings of IEEE Conference on Virtual Reality and 3D User Interfaces, VR, pp. 553–554 (2018)
34. Hebborn, A.K., Höhner, N., Müller, S.: Occlusion matting: realistic occlusion handling for augmented reality applications. In: Proceedings of IEEE International Symposium on Mixed and Augmented Reality, ISMAR, pp. 62–71 (2017)
35. Winfree, K., Gewirtz, J., Mather, T., Fiene, J., Kuchenbecker, K.: A high fidelity ungrounded torque feedback device: the iTorqU 2.0. In: Proceedings of IEEE World Haptics Conference, pp. 261–266 (2009)
36. Amemiya, T., Gomi, H.: Directional torque perception with brief, asymmetric net rotation of a flywheel. IEEE Trans. Haptics **6**(3), 370–375 (2013)

Galvanic Taste Stimulation Method for Virtual Reality and Augmented Reality

Kazuma Aoyama[1,2](✉)

[1] Graduate School of Information Science and Technology, The University of Tokyo,
Bunkyo-ku, Tokyo 1138656, Japan
[2] Virtual Reality Education and Research Center, The University of Tokyo,
Bunkyo-ku, Tokyo 1138656, Japan
aoyama@vr.u-tokyo.ac.jp

Abstract. The aim of this paper is to introduce our research into galvanic taste stimulation. Since galvanic taste stimulation can induce and modify taste sensations, it is expected to be applied in taste display technology for virtual and augmented reality. In addition, it is expected to be applied to support eating restriction systems. GTS has two stimulation types according to the polarity. The anodal stimulation where the anode is attached near the tongue can induce a metallic or electric taste. In contrast, a cathodal GTS in which the cathodes are near the tongue inhibits tastes induced by electrolyte water solution during stimulation and enhances tastes when GTS is stopped. Through our research, we investigated the mechanism of GTS and developed novel stimulation methods. Although some problems were resolved through our study, there are some problems using GTS for taste display in virtual and augmented reality systems. However, since GTS can modify and induce taste sensations without chemical materials, it can present attractive taste technology in the future.

Keywords: Galvanic taste stimulation · Electric taste · Taste display

1 Introduction

Recently, multisensory technologies such as visual, auditory, and haptic display technologies are being developed in virtual reality (VR) and augmented reality (AR), and human–computer interaction (HCI) study areas. These displays can induce and modulate sensations. For example, head-mounted display (HMD) and headphones are the most famous display technologies for visual and auditory displays.

In this wave of technological development, taste display technology has been progressing. Taste sensation strongly affects eating and drinking experience. These experiences are important in human life because delicious food makes humans happy. Therefore, the number of taste display studies has been increased in VR, AR, and HCI areas. For example, The Workshop on The Future of Computing & Food was held for the Association for Computing Machinery (ACM) Future of Computing Academy [1].

This paper explains what VR and AR technologies are being developed to modify the taste sensation and eating and drinking experiences.

S. Yamamoto and H. Mori (Eds.): HCII 2020, LNCS 12184, pp. 341–349, 2020.
https://doi.org/10.1007/978-3-030-50020-7_24

2 Previous Studies of Taste Display and Modulation Technology

Taste sensation is a chemical sensation that detects chemicals in the mouth. Generally, humans can perceive chemicals in the mouth with five basic tastes: sweetness, bitterness, saltiness, sourness, and umami. Here, hot and spicy sensations are not categorized as taste sensations. Then, all tastes that are induced by eating and drinking are virtually reproduced by inducing each of the five basic tastes with equal strength to the taste.

Therefore, a taste display system using chemical taste materials that induce all five basic tastes was developed by Iwata et al. [2]; this system was called a food simulator. The food simulator computer can spray taste chemical liquids into the mouth. Then, it can reproduce any taste sensation by controlling each taste's strength. Although it can reproduce the taste experience, it is difficult to use for VR and AR purposes because it requires taste liquids and opening the human mouth.

The taste sensation is also affected by smell and vision. For example, the ingredients of strawberry and lemon snowball syrups are the same except for the aroma chemical and color. Narumi et al. developed Meta Cookie to apply the interaction between taste, olfaction, and vision. In their system, users who put on a head-mounted display (HMD) and olfactory display eat plain cookies [3]. Then, cookies with different flavors such as strawberry, chocolate, and others are visually overlapped with plain cookies and the same odor is presented. Then users confuse the plain cookies with other tastes. Although this system confuses taste, it needs a large and heavy VR headset with an olfactory display.

3 Galvanic Tongue Stimulation Induces and Modifies Taste

3.1 Previous Studies of Galvanic Tongue Stimulation

Electrical Stimulation of the tongue has been known to induce electric or metallic taste sensations [4]. This perceptual phenomenon was first discovered by Sulzer in the 18th century and we call this stimulation method galvanic tongue stimulation (GTS). This technology is applied as a diagnosis method to detect taste disorders [5, 6].

In recent years, research about producing tastes by electric stimulation has boomed in human–computer interaction, VR, and AR areas because it can induce virtual taste sensations without the consumption of solids or liquids.

Nakamura et al. first proposed applying GTS for dietary restriction and taste augmentation display. They developed taste fork and taste cup that applies electric stimulation with natural eating and drinking behavior [7]. Aruga et al. developed a similar device to that of Nakamura et al. with which they tried to modify the taste of soup [8].

Ranasinghe et al. also developed a taste display using electrical stimulation. They developed a stimulation method that presents sourness, sweetness, bitterness, and saltiness by the square wave with a specific frequency and magnitude [9].

These studies used an anodal GTS. The effects of GTS are distinguished by whether anode was near the tongue. When an anode was attached near the tongue (anodal GTS), users felt electric or metallic taste, which is called the taste induction effect. Meanwhile, when only a cathode was attached near the tongue (cathodal GTS), the electric taste did not occur. When the cathodal GTS was applied with a salt-water solution, the salty taste was reduced during stimulation. Moreover, upon ending the stimulation, the salty taste briefly became stronger than the usual salty taste strength that would be induced by that concentration of salt-water solution. These effects are called the taste inhibition effect and taste enhancement effect.

These effects were discovered by Hettinger et al. [10] through human psychological experiments and animal physiological measurements.

Our research group has been researching the mechanisms of inhibition and enhancement effects to apply this phenomenon for taste modification display. The next chapter explains our research (Fig. 1).

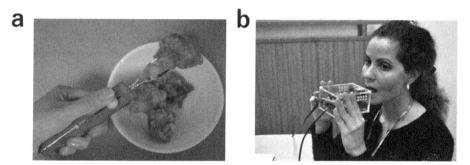

Fig. 1. (a) The electric fork developed by Nakamura et al. (b) The electric taste display developed by Ranashinghe et al. [9].

3.2   Mechanisms of Inhibition Effect of GTS

There are two rational theories of the taste inhibitory mechanism of cathodal GTS exist (i) ionic migration theory and (ii) nervous stimulation theory. The ionic migration theory explains the mechanism of the inhibition effect of the cathodal GTS in which the electrical field constructed by the GTS current migrates and removes taste ions from the tongue surface [10]. In contrast, nervous stimulation theory states that electrical stimulation disrupts nerve activation or habituates nerves. In anodal-GTS, Volta and Bujas considered that the stimulation current directly affects (may depolarize) taste cells or taste nerves [11]. Therefore, it is not wrong to consider that the cathodal GTS directly deactivates nerves.

The taste buds, which are human gustatory sensors, detect chemicals in the mouth. Each taste bud contains some taste cells that have receptors and/or ion channels at the surface [12] that detect chemicals in aqueous solutions [13]. Then, chemicals that generate tastes can be roughly divided into two categories: electrolytes and non-electrolytes. If the nervous stimulation hypothesis is adequate for the mechanism of the inhibition effect, the cathodal-GTS should inhibit tastes induced by both electrolytes and non-electrolytes. However, if the ionic migration hypothesis is valid for the mechanism, the cathodal-GTS should only inhibit tastes induced by electrolyte solutions.

Then, to demonstrate the validity of the ionic migration theory and nerve-stimulation theory, we conducted an experiment in which subjects were exposed to two types of aqueous solution: caffeine and $MgCl_2$. Caffeine and $MgCl_2$ exhibit bitter tastes and caffeine is a nonelectrolyte whereas $MgCl_2$ is an electrolyte [14].

In our experiment, subjects who joined our experiment were first exposed to modified concentrations of $MgCl_2$ with similar bitterness strength as 0.3% caffeine water solution. Then, subjects tasted two water solutions according to the experiment condition and chose which water solution was bitterer. There were four conditions for combining two water solutions: (a) $MgCl_2$ vs. caffeine, (b) $MgCl_2$ vs. $MgCl_2$ with GTS, (c) caffeine vs. caffeine with GTS, and (d) $MgCl_2$ with GTS vs. caffeine with GTS. For the GTS, 1.0 mA and two-second square current wave stimulation were used with anode attached to the back of the neck and cathode attached to the inner straw (Fig. 2).

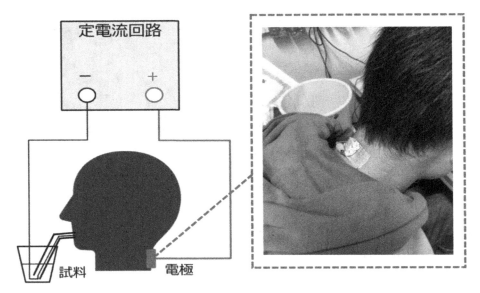

Fig. 2. The electrode positions in the experiment.

Figure 3 shows the results of this experiment. Figure 3d indicates that the bitterness of the caffeine and $MgCl_2$ solutions are at the same level even though the bitterness of caffeine with GTS is stronger than that with the $MgCl_2$ water solution. This means that GTS was effective for only electrolyte water solutions. Then, we concluded that the ionic migration theory is valid for the inhibitory effect of GTS.

3.3 Applying the Inhibitory Effect and Enhancement Effect for All Five Basic Tastes

We investigated the mechanism of inhibition effect for the cathodal GTS and cleared that ionic migration in the mouth is a critical phenomenon for evoking the inhibition effect. Then, we conducted the next experiment to investigate whether cathodal GTS inhibits all five basic tastes induced by electrolyte water solutions [14].

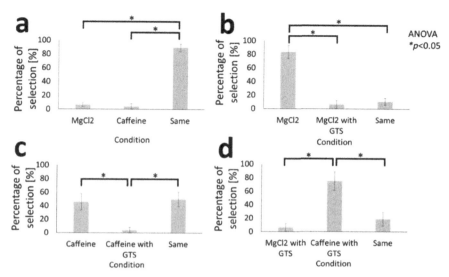

Fig. 3. Results of the experiment to investigate the mechanism of the taste inhibition effect. (a) The selection percentages in the $MgCl_2$ vs. caffeine condition. (b) The percentages of selection in $MgCl_2$ vs. $MgCl_2$ with GTS condition. (a) The percentages of selection in caffeine vs. caffeine with GTS condition. (a) The percentages of selection in $MgCl_2$ with GTS vs. caffeine with GTS condition.

Subjects were provided with five tastes aqueous electrolyte solutions: NaCl, $MgCl_2$, glycine, glutamic sodium, and citric acid, which tasted salty, bitter, sweet, umami, and sour, respectively. Each water solution was prepared at five concentrations (Table 1). The solution with the highest concentration for each taste water solution was called the "adjusting sample" and the others were termed "comparable samples." Subjects first tasted a comparable sample and then attempted to adjust the taste intensity of the adjusting sample to match it to that of the comparable sample by controlling the current strength of the cathodal GTS.

The results are as shown in Fig. 4. Each subfigure (a–e) shows the result of each taste materials. These figures show the normalized and averaged current strength needed to inhibit the taste of the adjusting sample so that its taste strength was similar to that of the comparable sample against each comparable sample concentration. The concentration of the comparable sample was negatively correlated with the strength of the current for all five types of electrolyte solution. Statistical analyses were performed using the Kruskal–Wallis ANOVA and Scheffe's method for each graph and demonstrated significant variations between conditions. These figures indicated that all five basic tastes induced by electrolyte water solutions were reduced by cathodal GTS. These results also indicated that the strength of the inhibition effects correlated to the stimulation strength.

Table 1. Concentration of adjusting material and comparable materials in the experiment of investigating the taste inhibition effect about all five basic tastes.

	Adjusting material [%]		Comparable materials [%]		
Glycine	5.0	4.0	3.0	2.0	1.0
$MgCl_2$	0.50	0.40	0.30	0.20	0.10
NaCl	1.0	0.80	0.60	0.40	0.20
Gritamic sodium	0.50	0.40	0.30	0.20	0.10
Critic acid	0.50	0.40	0.30	0.20	0.10

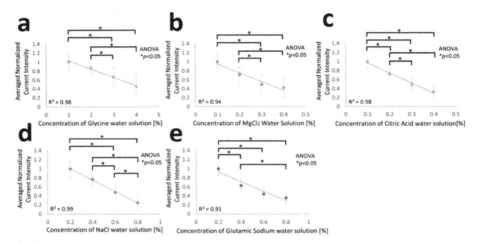

Fig. 4. Averaged and normalized current intensity required to attain the taste strength of the adjusting sample at same level for the concentration of each comparable sample. Each subfigure a–e shows the taste materials such as glycine, $MgCl_2$, citric acid, NaCl, and glutamic sodium.

It should be noted here that all subjects felt that the taste strength they experienced immediately after the stimulation offset was stronger than what they had experienced prior to stimulation for all the electrolyte solutions. Then, whether taste material is an electrolyte material would be an important condition when evoking the taste enhancement effect.

3.4 Continuous Square Current Stimulation

Since the GTS method can enhance the taste sensation, it would be attractive for VR and AR displays and applicable to support an eating restriction system. However, it has a critical problem. The timespan of the taste enhancement effect is extremely short (a few seconds). Using the GTS for taste display and eating restriction support system will require maintaining the enhancement effect during eating behaviors such as putting items in the mouth, biting, chewing, and swallowing.

To achieve long-duration enhancement effect, we developed continuous square current stimulation (CSCS) [15]. CSCS is the current form that repeats an on-and-off square current. We thought that the enhancement effects occurred by vibrating taste ions in the mouth. Then, the short-term taste enhancement effects would be repeatedly evoked by CSCS and users feel that it is "a taste enhancement effect."

We demonstrated whether CSCS evokes long-term taste enhancement effect through user study. In our experiment, users attached an anode to the back of their neck and drew a 1.0% NaCl–water solution into their mouth through a straw to which a cathode was attached.

Users were stimulated at 1 mA for 5.0 s CSCS at various frequencies (DC, 1, 5, 10, 20, 50, 100, 200, 500, and 1,000 Hz). Then, users controlled the volume slider. The center of this slider indicated the normal taste strength of 1.0% NaCl water solution and the right and left edges of this slider indicate the taste strengths of 3.0% and 0% NaCl–water solution, respectively. All users tasted 0, 1.0, and 3.0% NaCl water solutions.

Figure 5b shows the average taste enhancement duration against stimulation frequency. This figure indicates that CSCS evokes the longest enhancement effect at about 25 Hz, which is a similar duration to the stimulation duration. Through an additional experiment, we demonstrated that the duration of the enhancement effect for CSCS is no less than a minute.

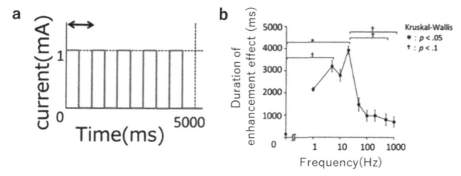

Fig. 5. The current pattern (a) and results of experiment. The duration of the salty taste enhancement effect of CSCS against the frequency.

3.5 Galvanic Chin Stimulation

In conventional cathodal GTS technology, a stimulation current was applied to the inner mouth with a utensil-type electrode such as a fork, spoon, or cup. The anode was attached to the forehead or back of the neck using a gel electrode. However, there is an important problem in using GTS for a taste display and eating restriction system; the electrode has to be attached to the inner mouth while eating.

In terms of electrophoresis in the mouth, it is assumed that the cathode does not need to be attached to the mouth. Taste ions in the liquid at the inner mouth would shift away from or come close to the current maw and current ingate. For example, when the back-of-neck anode and inner straw were used for stimulation electrodes, the stimulation current flowed from the skin at the inner mouth to taste the liquid and from the taste liquid to the straw. Then, we assumed that the key fact of GTS is the voltage difference between the tongue and taste liquid.

According to this hypothesis, we developed a cathode to attach to the chin and anode to attach to the back of neck; we call this stimulation method Galvanic Chin Stimulation (GCS) [16]. Our previous study showed that GCS can be used to induce, suppress, or enhance taste sensations.

In the experiment, electrodes were attached to the chin and back of participants' necks. A 3.0 mA square wave was applied with the chin as the anode or cathode. A taste sensation was not induced when the chin was used as the anode. However, the tasted sensation induced by a 1.0% NaCl water solution was reduced when the chin was used as the cathode. Participants were asked whether they tasted saltiness, sweetness, acidity, bitterness, umami, or an electrical taste when the chin was used as the anode. Participants adjusted the concentration of the NaCl solution so that the taste strength was similar to the taste during stimulation and stopped the stimulation, respectively (Fig. 6).

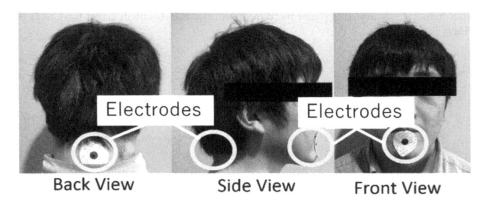

Fig. 6. The electrode positions in galvanic chin stimulation.

4   Conclusion

We investigated the mechanisms of the taste inhibition effect of GTS and developed novel stimulation methods such as CSCS and GJS. Although these stimulation methods can induce and modify all five basic tastes, the novel GTS method can affect tastes induced by either liquids or solids.

Moreover, how strong the effect is on eating restriction that supports GTS should be investigated. Since GTS is an attractive taste display, it is expected to be applied to support an eating restriction system. Then, we will demonstrate this effect in future works.

References

1. 2nd Workshop on The Future of Computing & Food. https://sites.google.com/view/fcfws2/
2. Iwata, H., Yano, H., Uemura, T., Moriya, T.: Food simulator: a haptic interface for biting, virtual reality, proceedings. In: Proceeding of IEEE Virtual Reality (2004)
3. Narumi, T., Tanikawa, T., Kajinami, T., Hirose, M.: Meta cookie: pseudo-gustatory display based on cross-modal integration. TVRSJ **15**(4), 579–588 (2010)
4. Stevens, D.A., Baker, D., Cutroni, E., Frey, A., Pugh, D., Lawless, H.T.: A direct comparison of the taste of electrical and chemical stimuli. Chem. Senses **33**(5), 405–413 (2008)
5. Krarup, B.: Electro-gustometry: a method for clinical taste examinations. Acta Otolaryngol. **49**(1), 294–305 (1985)
6. Cardello, A.V.: Comparison of taste qualities elicited by tactile, electrical, and chemical stimulation of single human taste papillae. Atten. Percept. Psychophys. **29**(2), 163–169 (1981)
7. Hiromi, N., Homei, M.: Controlling saltiness without salt: evaluation of taste change by applying and releasing cathodal current. In: Proceedings of the 5th International Workshop on Multimedia for Cooking & Eating Activities (CEA), pp. 9–14 (2013)
8. Yukika, A., Takafumi, K.: Taste change of soup by the recreating of sourness and saltiness using the electrical stimulation. In: The 6th Augmented Human International Conference, pp. 191–192 (2015)
9. Nimesha, R., Ryohei, N., Nii, H., Ponnampalam, G.: Tongue mounted interface for digitally actuating the sense of taste. In: Proceedings of the 16th IEEE International Symposium on Wearable Computers (ISWC), pp. 80–87 (2012)
10. Thomas, P.H., Marion, E.F.: Salt taste inhibition by cathodal current. Brain Res. Bull. **80**(3), 107–115 (2009)
11. Bujas, Z., Szabo, S., Kovai, M., Rohaek, A.: Adaptation effects on evoked electrical taste. Percept. Psychophys. **15**(2), 210–214 (1974)
12. Chandrashekar, J., Hoon, M.A., Ryba, N.J., Zuker, C.S.: The receptors and cells for mammalian taste. Nature **444**, 288–294 (2006)
13. Kandel, E., Schwartz, J., Jessell, T., Siegelbaum, S., Hudspeth, A.J.: Principles of Neural Science, 5th edn. Medical Sciences International (2014)
14. Kazuma, A., et al.: Galvanic tongue stimulation inhibits five basic tastes induced by aqueous electrolyte solution. Front. Psychol. **2**, 2112 (2017). https://doi.org/10.3389/fpsyg.2017.02112
15. Sakurai, K., Aoyama, K., Furukawa, M., Maeda, T., Ando, H.: Successive taste enhancement with saltiness and umami using continuance square wave cathodal current stimulation. TVRSJ **22**(2), 149–159 (2017)
16. Aoyama, K., Sakurai, K., Furukawa, M., Maeda, T., Ando, H.: New method for inducing, inhibiting, and enhancing tastes using galvanic jaw stimulation. TVRSJ **22**(2), 137–143 (2017)

Development of VR Learning Spaces Considering Lecture Format in Asynchronous E-learning

Takumi Baba[1,2(✉)], Toru Tokunaga[1,2], Toru Kano[1,2], and Takako Akakura[1,2]

[1] Faculty of Engineering, Department of Information Engineering, Tokyo University of Science, 6-3-1 Nijuku, Katsushika-ku, Tokyo 125-8585, Japan
{4616074,4616059}@ed.tus.ac.jp, {kano,akakura}@rs.tus.ac.jp
[2] Faculty of Engineering, Tokyo University of Science, 6-3-1 Nijuku, Katsushika-ku, Tokyo 125-8585, Japan

Abstract. E-learning has become more widespread with the progress of informatization. Active utilization of e-learning relaxes temporal and geographic restraints on learning, and furthermore allows visualization of learning status, because learning logs can be easily collected. Furthermore, learning effects are equivalent to or better than those of conventional learning methods, and further development is expected in the future. However, the lack of an in-person instructor and other students in e-learning can result in loneliness, causing learners to lose motivation and concentration and potentially leading to dropouts. We thus focus on asynchronous learning using lecture videos. By developing an e-learning system in which learners can feel the presence of instructors and other students like in conventional classes, learners can maintain motivation and avoid declines in concentration. This study aims to develop a lecture-style virtual reality-based learning system that displays instructors and other student avatars. We conduct an evaluation experiment to determine whether this system can maintain learner motivation. The results suggest that loneliness can be further reduced compared with conventional video lessons, that learning motivation is improved, and that the system can to some extent prevent decreases in concentration.

Keywords: E-learning · E-education · Interaction design · Virtual reality · Asynchronous learning

1 Introduction

1.1 Research Background

Spread of E-learning. With the rapid development of information and communications technology, companies and educational institutions have increasingly been introducing e-learning systems. According to a National Institute of Economic Research forecast [1], the e-learning market will expand by 9.3% to

S. Yamamoto and H. Mori (Eds.): HCII 2020, LNCS 12184, pp. 350–362, 2020.
https://doi.org/10.1007/978-3-030-50020-7_25

218.5 billion in FY2019. A survey on e-learning implementation at 360 Japanese companies [2] showed that 80% of those companies are utilizing e-learning. The reason for introducing e-learning is the potential and simplicity of simultaneous education. According to the Japan e-Learning Consortium's 2018 Investigative Committee [3], e-learning allows students to learn at any time and to study learning materials repeatedly. A growing number of users are taking courses not only on personal computers, but also on smartphones. According to Tominaga and Kogo [4], many studies comparing learning effects in e-learning versus paper-based or group-type lectures have found no significant difference, or found that e-learning performed better. The benefits and learning effects of e-learning have thus been evaluated, and we have entered an era in which both participants and learning media are diversified.

Issues in E-learning. The spread of e-learning has revealed some issues and problems. According to Tominaga and Kogo [4], questionnaires have shown that in e-learning, the lack of instructors and co-learners can make learners become bored. In the above-mentioned e-Learning Consortium survey [3], the number one complaint about e-learning was the difficulty of maintaining motivation to continue learning. According to a Goo Research survey [5] conducted in FY2003, the most frequently mentioned inconvenience of e-learning was the difficulty of maintaining a sense of tension in learning when using a personal computer alone. Tominaga and Kogo [6] compared e-learning and group-type lectures, and revealed that the former had significantly lower subjective evaluations, such as degree of interest and satisfaction. Such low evaluations are problematic, because these attitudes directly lead to dropping out.

1.2   Related Research

Many studies have addressed the problems described in the previous section. From among the potential solutions, we focused on research using a head-mounted display (HMD) and virtual reality (VR) to solve e-learning issues.

Nakamura et al. [7] focused on decreases in a sense of tension due to the absence of instructors in asynchronous e-learning, attempting to solve this problem by creating a VR lesson system in which an avatar (3D model) took the place of the instructor (Fig. 1). In that system, learners watched classes in VR using an HMD. Using gaze information obtained from the HMD, the instructor avatar could turn toward the user when the user looked at it. Test results suggested that the instructor's presence increased engagement and reduced loneliness.

Matsumoto et al. [8] focused on learner loneliness in problem-based e-learning and developed a practice-problem VR system implementing avatars that simulate other learners (Fig. 2). Their goal was to reduce or eliminate loneliness and to mitigate loss of concentration by placing other student avatars around users working on exercises in a VR space. However, this system had some issues to be addressed, such as making avatar movement more precise, incorporating interactivity, and applying the system in class delivery.

Fig. 1. VR lecture system with instructor avatar [7].

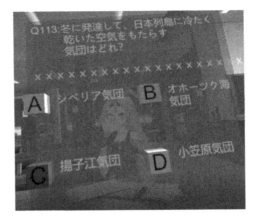

Fig. 2. Problem practice VR system [8].

1.3   Purpose of This Research

Based on the current state of e-learning and related research, this study aims to develop a VR lecture system that incorporates both instructor avatars and other-student avatars to maintain learners' motivation and prevent decreases in concentration. We then asked learners to use the developed VR lecture system and to evaluate its usefulness.

1.4   Structure of This Paper

In this paper, we describe the developed VR class system that incorporates avatars for the instructor and other learners, and describe its effectiveness.

The remainder of this paper is organized as follows. Section 2 gives an overview of the devices used in this experiment and describes functions of the system. Section 3 presents details of the experimental procedure, environment, and targets, along with learning contents and evaluation indices. Section 4 describes the test, questionnaire data, and log data of system use for each experimental group, and discusses the usefulness of the proposed system based on the results. Section 5 summarizes this study and discusses future issues and perspectives.

2   System Overview

2.1   Devices Used in This Study

HMD VR. We used an HTC Vive Pro Eye as the HMD device for the VR environment, which we constructed using Unity ver. 2018.1.1f. The VR system includes the HMD main unit, two controllers, and a base station for recognizing them three-dimensionally. Users can observe the VR space by wearing the HMD. The user's view is synchronized with the HMD, and users can move in the VR space by moving the position of the head. A virtual controller is displayed, so users can reproduce head and hand movements in the VR space.

The experiment used a Vive Tracker (described below) together with the HMD and controller to provide users with a high sense of presence and immersion.

Web Camera. A web camera (Logitech HD Pro Webcam C920) was used in the experiment to implement a memo creation function. Section 2.4 describes memo creation in the VR space.

Vive Tracker. We used a Vive Tracker in addition to the HMD and controller. The HMD can obtain head coordinates and the controller obtains coordinates of both hands, but waist and feet coordinates are additionally required to capture whole-body movements. Therefore, by attaching the Vive Tracker to the waist and both feet, we could record motions of the instructor and other learners and maintain an action log of the system user.

2.2   System Overview

Figure 3 shows an outline of the proposed system. Using a lecture recording system, we recorded voices, slide transitions, and whole-body instructor movements during a lecture. We then reproduced the lecture in the VR system, based on the recorded data. Learners can participate in the lesson in VR space via the HMD. The lesson recording system and VR lesson system were created using Unity, as described in Sect. 2.1. We used the HTC Vive and the Vive Tracker to record motions of instructors and other students.

The next section describes details of the created system.

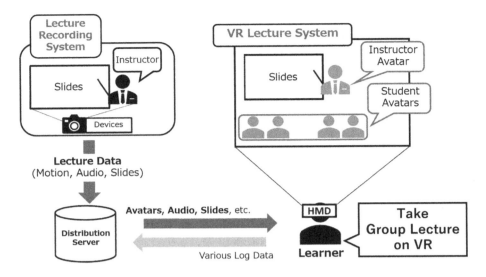

Fig. 3. System overview.

2.3   Lecture Recording System

Lectures in the VR space were presented using previously recorded motion, audio, and slide transition information. Motion recording for the instructor avatar was performed using an HMD, controller, and Vive Tracker to track the instructor's head, hands, waist, and feet (Fig. 4). Tracking data was saved in an

(i) Recording   (ii) Reflection on Avatar

Fig. 4. Instructor motion recording.

animation file format, allowing it to be easily applied to a VR lecture system. Audio was recorded using a pin microphone. Slide transitions were operated by a handheld controller, and operation logs including time information were saved in CSV file format. Instructors recorded these data as if actually teaching in a VR space, allowing the VR lecture system to reproduce natural lectures and avatar movements.

2.4   VR Lecture System

VR Learning Environment. We constructed a learning environment in the VR space using a model similar to an actual classroom (Fig. 5). The environment can reproduce slide presentations, instructor motions, and lecture audio stored in the lecture recording system. A desk is placed in real space at a position where a corresponding desk is displayed in VR. The VR desk is displayed in a different color than that of the actual desk, and calibration was performed via the controller at the start of the experiment.

Fig. 5. Learning environment in VR space.

Instructor and Other Student Avatars. The avatars in this experiment used materials that were distributed free of charge and models created using the 3D character modeling software VRoidStudio. The instructor avatar reproduced motions and voice data recorded by the lecture recording system, and other student avatars reproduced motion data that the authors prerecorded while receiving a lecture in VR space.

Avatar Interactivity. Instructor and other-student avatars reproduce recorded data as described above, and furthermore perform interactions based on the gaze information of the learner. Specifically, we created scripts causing other-student avatars to face the learner and smile when the learner's gaze was directed at them (Fig. 6). This provides the avatar with a social presence as if in a classroom with an instructor and other students.

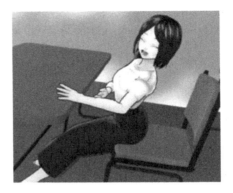

Fig. 6. Interaction based on learner gaze information.

Controller Operations. This section describes the details of functions activated by operating the left and right controllers. The right-hand controller implements pause, fast-forward, and rewind functions, as seen in many video-lecture-type e-learning systems. These functions allow users to take a longer look at writing on the board, repeat parts that were not understood from one explanation, or skip past parts that are already understood. Thus, learners can focus on what they want to learn from the course. The left-hand controller has functions for displaying lecture slide contents and changing the page.

MR Memo Function. Mixed reality (MR) is a technology that merges real and virtual spaces, allowing interaction between them. In both ordinary lectures and e-learning, students often take notes on important content or points that they did not understand well. However, it is difficult to take notes in VR space, due to controller tracking accuracy and the difficulty of drawing in 3D space. We therefore provided this system with a memo function that uses a web camera to partially project real space into the VR space. Figure 7 shows an image of this function, which allows students to take notes in VR space using notebooks and writing tools on their desk in real space, making note-taking feel more natural.

Acquisition of Learner Action Logs. Learners attend lectures in the above-described environment while performing controller and memo operations. To accurately capture learner behaviors and interests during the evaluation experiment, we implemented a system that uses 6-point tracking to log learner operations, gazes, and postures. Specifically, we created a program that records the learner's controller states and gaze direction in each frame to a CSV file, and another program that logs 6-point tracking posture as animation data.

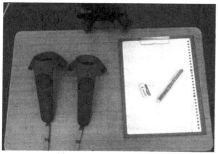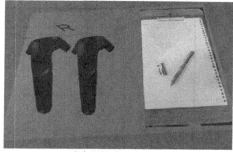

(i) Real Environment   (ii) VR Environment

Fig. 7. MR memo function.

3   Evaluation Experiments

3.1   Experimental Outline

Experimental Procedure. Twenty-one university students participated in the evaluation experiment. Participants were classified into three groups of seven, one group participated in VR lectures (experimental group), one watched video lectures (control group I), and one participated in real-space group lectures (control group II). Each group responded to a pre-questionnaire, took a pre-test, participated in the group's assigned class, and then responded to a post-questionnaire and took a post-test. This sequence took about 45 min.

Learning Environment for Experimental Group. Figure 8 shows the learning environment for the experimental group. These learners used the VR lecture system alone, in a learning environment with no other persons. To acquire posture logs, in addition to the HMD learners wore a Vive Tracker on their waists and both feet and held a Vive controller in each hand while participating in the lecture.

Learning Environment for Control Group I. A video-lecture-type e-learning system was used for control group I (the video lecture group). Learners watched lecture videos alone, in an environment with no other persons. We compared the experimental group with this control group to verify whether the presence of an instructor avatar mitigated loss of learning motivation and concentration. Learners watched video lectures, which allowed pausing, fast-forwarding, and rewinding by mouse operations. The system logged these operations along with corresponding elapsed times.

Learning Environment for Control Group II. Control group II (the group lecture group), participated in a group lecture. Learners listened to lectures in

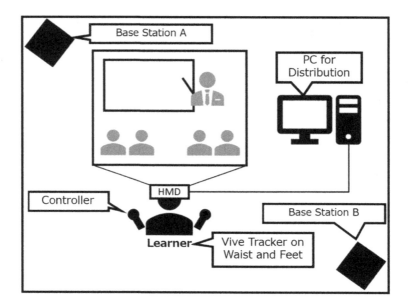

Fig. 8. Experimental group learning environment.

a classroom with six other students and one instructor, allowing them to feel the presence of others around them, unlike the e-learning system for video lectures. Comparing the experimental group with this group confirmed differences between real-space lectures and those reproduced in the VR space, and how any differences are related to mitigating loss of motivation or concentration in learning.

Lecture Content. The lectures in these experiments described problems in the field of artificial intelligence. This topic was selected because all participants were engineering students from science universities, so we hoped this would be a topic of interest about which learners had no prior knowledge. The pre- and post-tests verified learning effects in each group by measuring degree of understanding about this subject.

3.2 Evaluation Index

To test the hypothesis that reproduction of a natural class environment by introducing instructor and other-student avatars, etc., will mitigate loss of concentration and motivation to learn, we used the following data as the evaluation target.

Pre- and Post-tests. We calculated and compared degrees of knowledge acquisition for each lecture format. We also verified whether the developed system provides sufficient learning effects as an e-learning system. The tests asked the same five questions, scored with a total of 12 points.

Pre- and Post-questionnaires. We investigated differences in subjective evaluations of each lecture format and system. We also compared usefulness of the developed system with the conventional systems, and investigated points for improvement. We conducted pre- and post-questionnaires common to each group and a post-questionnaire unique to each group. Questionnaires used a five-point scale (with 1 as a highly negative evaluation and 5 as a highly positive one) and open-ended questions.

Action Log. We examined relations between maintaining concentration, motivation to learn, and learner behavior based on the operation, gaze, and posture logs and other data, and from the results of the tests and questionnaires.

4 Experimental Results

4.1 Results and Considerations of Pre- and Post-tests

Table 1 shows the average (Avg.) and standard deviation (SD) of on scores on the pre- and post-tests for each group. Table 2 shows the results of two-way analysis of variance (ANOVA) on score transitions between each group and between pre- and post-tests.

Table 1. Score averages and standard deviations for each group.

	Experimental			Control I			Control II		
	Pre	Post	Change	Pre	Post	Change	Pre	Post	Change
Avg.	5.86	10.43	4.57	6.57	10.00	3.43	6.00	10.14	4.14
SD	1.55	1.18	1.68	1.59	1.51	1.99	2.62	1.36	2.80

Table 2. Results of two-way ANOVA for pre- and post-test scores for each group.

Variable factors	Fluctuation	DOF	Variance	P value	Significance
Groups	0.33	2	0.17	0.95	n.s.
Pre & post	172	1	172	2.08×10^{-8}	**
Interaction	2.33	2	1.17	0.71	n.s

**: $p < .01$, n.s.: Insignificant

Analysis using two-way ANOVA found significant differences between pre- and post-tests ($p < .01$), but no significant difference among the three groups

($p > .10$). In addition, there was no significant difference in interactions, indicating a difference only between the pre- and post-test. However, despite there being no significant difference, the experimental group showed the highest score changes in Table 2, suggesting that lectures in this system had the same or better learning effects as seen in the other two groups.

4.2   Results and Consideration of Pre- and Post-questionnaires

Table 3 shows excerpts from the collected post-questionnaires.

Table 3. Summary of post-questionnaire results

5-point scale (positive rating: 5)

No.	Question
Q3 b-c-d	In this lecture format, I felt like I was taking a lecture alone.
Q6 b-c-d	I was strongly aware of the instructor's presence.
Q8a	I was able to concentrate on taking the lecture.
Q19b - Q13c	I want to use this system again.
Q21b	In the VR space, I felt like I was actually in the classroom.
Q24b	The pause, fast-forward, and rewind functions were easy to use.
Q25b	The slide display and operation functions were easy to use.
Q26b	The MR memo function was easy to use.

No.	Experimental		Control I		Control II	
	Avg.	SD	Avg.	SD	Avg.	SD
Q3 b-c-d	3.57	1.50	4.86	0.35	2.29	1.58
Q6 b-c-d	2.43	0.90	2.29	1.48	4.86	0.35
Q8a	3.43	0.90	4.43	0.73	4.00	1.07
Q19b - Q13c	4.00	0.76	3.00	1.20	-	-
Q21b	3.42	1.29	-	-	-	-
Q24b	4.29	0.70	-	-	-	-
Q25b	4.00	1.41	-	-	-	-
Q26b	2.29	1.03	-	-	-	-

Q3 b-c-d showed that control group I, the experimental group, and control group II were less likely to feel loneliness, in that order. Further, Q6 b-c-d suggests that the presence of instructors in VR lectures has nearly the same effect as in conventional video lectures, so it is unlikely that the presence of an avatar directly reduced loneliness. However, the relatively high evaluation in Q21 b suggests that the classroom performance of the entire system reduced loneliness.

Q19 b–Q13 c show that the VR system improved motivation for continuous learning in comparison with conventional video lectures. Also, from Q24 b,

Q25 b, and Q26 b for the experimental group and from free responses such as "I felt like taking a class," "I could feel the classroom," and "I felt immersed," we believe that reproducing lectures in the VR space increased learning motivation.

From Q8a, we found that the group using the VR lecture system tended to have reduced concentration than did the other groups. Regarding this result, free responses such as "the weight of the HMD is distracting" and "the overall image quality is low and characters are hard to read" from the experimental group suggest that the unfamiliarity and technical limitations of the HMD and VR inhibited concentration. Improving HMD resolution may mitigate this problem, but action logs collected for the experimental group showed that learners viewed lecture-related objects 80% of the time, suggesting that the system itself had a certain effect in preventing decreases in concentration.

These findings suggest that the VR system developed in this study produces a space similar to actual group lectures, reduces loneliness as compared to conventional video-lecture-type e-learning systems, improves learning motivation, and can prevent concentration loss to some extent.

5   Conclusion

5.1   Summary

We developed and evaluated a VR learning space that presents lectures in asynchronous e-learning. By constructing a realistic classroom in a VR space and presenting lectures viewed using an HMD, we aimed at improving motivation to learn and preventing decreased concentration. To allow recognition of instructor and other-student avatars as others, we reproduced prerecorded motions and replicated interactions according to the learner's gaze. In the VR classroom, we implemented an MR memo function simulating handwritten note-taking to produce a more realistic learning environment. We also implemented functions that allow independent learning, such as pause, fast-forward, and rewind functions typically seen in e-learning environments. Evaluation experiments conducted with university students verified whether classes in a VR space improved learning motivation and prevented decreased concentration. The results suggested that loneliness can be reduced in comparison with conventional video lectures, that learning motivation is improved, and that concentration loss is prevented to some extent. From these results, we consider the goals of this study to have been achieved.

5.2   Future Tasks

Future tasks will include improving lectures so that learners can concentrate more fully than with video lectures and feel more immersed. To that end, we will investigate development of experience-based lesson content utilizing the advantages of VR, creation of avatars that behave more naturally, and production of lectures that are more adaptive to learners.

Acknowledgements. This study was supported by PHOTRON LIMITED. Through Collaboration Research Project No. ~D19-195.

References

1. Yano Research Institute Co., Ltd.: Conducted e-learning market research (2019). https://www.yano.co.jp/press-release/show/press_id/2115. Accessed 23 Dec 2019
2. Nichino Study Group Management Center: Implementation status survey on e-learning for 360 domestic companies. https://www.jmam.co.jp/topics/1223801_1893.html. Accessed 23 Dec 2019
3. Japan e-Learning Consortium, 2018 Investigation Committee Report. http://www.elc.or.jp/files/user/doc/eLearningReport_2016.pdf. Accessed 23 Dec 2019
4. Tominaga, A.: Effects of Blending Lessons Combining E-learning and Peer Response on Writing Skills. Waseda University Press, Tokyo (2014)
5. Goo Research: Survey on the use of e-learning in business (2004). https://research.nttcoms.com/database/data/000134/. Accessed 23 Dec 2019
6. Tominaga, A., Kogo, C.: Progress and issues of practical research on e-learning. Ann. Rep. Educ. Psychol. Jpn. **53**, 156–165 (2014)
7. Nakamura, S., Unoki, T., Akakura, T.: Prototyping of a VR class distribution system that enables teacher avatars to interact with students. IEICE Tech. Rep. **119**(331), 43–46 (2019)
8. Nakamura, S., Matsumoto, T., Akakura, T.: Development and evaluation of a VR system that makes learners feel that they are working on exercises with others in e-learning. IEICE Tech. Rep. **118**(510), 111–116 (2019)
9. Asakawa, S., et al.: Deep Learning Textbook Deep Learning G Test (Generalist) Official Textbook. Shoeisha Inc., Tokyo (2018)

Augmented Reality Shopping System Through Image Search and Virtual Shop Generation

Zhinan Li[1]([envelope]) [iD], Ruichen Ma[1] [iD], Kohei Obuchi[1] [iD], Boyang Liu[1] [iD], Kelvin Cheng[2] [iD], Soh Masuko[2] [iD], and Jiro Tanaka[1] [iD]

[1] Waseda University, Kitakyushu, Japan
lizhinan@fuji.waseda.jp,
{mizutsu-ma,kohei76752109}@akane.waseda.jp,
waseda-liuboyang@moegi.waseda.jp, jiro@aoni.waseda.jp
[2] Rakuten Institute of Technology, Rakuten, Inc., Tokyo, Japan
{kelvin.cheng,so.masuko}@rakuten.com

Abstract. In this paper, we introduce an intelligent augmented reality shopping system that supports image search and 3D virtual shop generation. By capturing an image of the product that the user is looking at, and using image search, we can recommend similar products to the user. Based on the spatial understanding techniques, we developed a 3D virtual shop interface that would be automatically generated in the user's physical room, where products are arranged around the room at appropriate locations. With the virtual shop display, users would be able to interact with the products' life-size virtual models by full-hand manipulation. Our system provides more natural interactions such as grabbing and touching. We also carried out an evaluation study for using our system, the participants' feedback shows that our system provides a better shopping experience with its intuitive search process, immersive shop display, and natural interactions.

Keywords: Immersive shopping · Intelligent system · Image search · Spatial understanding · Full-hand manipulation

1 Introduction

After entering the 21st century, the advancement of Internet technology has promoted the vigorous development of e-commerce. Because of the flexibility and the ability to connect to a large information network, users are able to purchase products whenever and wherever they want [1, 17]. However, there exists limitations in current online shopping systems [2]. Users are usually limited to viewing product information in 2D, such as through photos on the PC or smartphone, instead of directly in the physical world [3]. Additionally, the method of searching products depends heavily on textural keywords. At the same time, many consumers still prefer offline shopping, which provide a more authentic shopping experience.

In our previous work, we have already developed an intelligent shopping assistant system in an augmented environment, which supports quick scene understanding of products' recommendation, using voice control and two-finger manipulations [4]. Based on

© Springer Nature Switzerland AG 2020
S. Yamamoto and H. Mori (Eds.): HCII 2020, LNCS 12184, pp. 363–376, 2020.
https://doi.org/10.1007/978-3-030-50020-7_26

this work, we observed that the 2D interface was inadequate in an immersive augmented shopping system, and two-finger manipulation [5, 6] is still very limited so that more natural interactions with the products' 3D models are needed in order to provide a better previewing experience.

Moreover, the search method was also limited to keywords extraction from voice input, and the use of the user's environment scene [3]. Users may sometime wish to purchase a similar product to the ones that they saw, as they go about their daily life, or that they have the desire to replace an old product. In these cases, simply using keywords to search for products is inadequate and imprecise. Understanding the shape and color of the product, and search by image search may be more effective.

Current online shopping systems are mostly limited to 2D information and usually cannot let users get an instant preview in the physical world [11]. Recently, emerging technologies that make use of Augmented-Reality (AR) and computer vision techniques brings new opportunities for intelligent shopping environments.

However, some consumers may still prefer offline shopping [12]. Offline shopping can provide a more authentic shopping experience. They can compare the size and shape of different products more clearly in offline shopping. Also, some offline furniture shop provides a sample room, where customers can have an immersive user experience. For example, in the real shop, the customer can see the true size of the products. To combine the benefit of online and offline shopping, we propose to bring the real shop to their home, virtually. Our system allows users to compare the color, shape, and size of each product as if they were in the real shop. Furthermore, customers do not need to leave their home. Users can place virtual items in their rooms directly to see if it fits their room style.

The system in our current work is aimed at building an augmented reality shopping system that supports image search, full-hand manipulation, and virtual shop generation. It can recommend similar products to users and bring the real shop to users' homes. Using our system, users will have an immersive shopping experience at their home and find it easier to interact with virtual product previews.

2 Goal and Approach

In this work, we envision an augmented reality shopping system that provides users with a better shopping experience at their own home. We consider the use of image search as well as 3D virtual shop display to enable a more effective way of searching a similar product and immersive previewing experience. At the same time, this system also involves hand-tracking based full-hand manipulation [7, 8], which provides a more natural interaction with the virtual shop interface and 3D product models.

Our image search component is aimed at recommending similar products to the product which the user is looking at. By capturing an image of the current product, the system can analyze the color and type of the item. We realized this by using the image search method. It first analyzes the image taken by the camera from the see-through type head-mounted display (HMD) [9, 14], recognize the objects in the image, then it would search the specific kind of products on the online shopping website.

Virtual shop generation is aimed at integrating an immersive shopping experience of the users. It allows users to decorate their own home into a virtual shop. The virtual object would then be automatically placed in the room according to the user's surroundings. For example, it would detect the largest flat surface in the room and show the first several products in the result in 3D form. We realized this with a spatial understanding method. We use the depth camera of the HMD to capture the surroundings and place the virtual products in the real room. Also, users can easily adjust the position of these 3D virtual objects and manipulate them manually.

Full-hand manipulation provides users with a more authentic experience of manipulating virtual products, users are able to interact with the interface and 3D objects through pushing, grabbing and touching, which is a more natural way comparing with two-finger manipulation in our previous work. This is realized by installing a full-hand motion detection device [10] on an ordinary HMD. These hand movements are also supported by the Mixed Reality Toolkit (MRTK) which we are using. Our system recognizes these hand movements by the hand tracking system and the operation result would be shown through the HMD.

This system connects all these features to make it easy for users to shop at their home as if in a real shop, or even better when they want to find a similar item and view the product in their rooms.

3 Intelligent Shopping Assistant

3.1 Image Search

In order to enable users to obtain information about the products around them at any time, we provide the image search feature. Compared with the previous manual text input method, this feature can help users get the information of the products around them faster. For example, if users want to buy a new television to replace their old one, one way is to type the letter "television", another way is to use image search. Obviously, taking a photo is faster than typing letters when using HMD.

When the user gives the voice command "Search this". The camera will take a photo of the current product. The image will be uploaded to the image search platform. Then

Fig. 1. A water bottle

the result will be returned to the user. As Fig. 1 shows, when the input product is a water bottle, the recommended products are also water bottles (Fig. 2).

Fig. 2. Recommended products

3.2 Virtual Shop Generating

In order to let users visually see whether the products that they are considering are suitable in their current environment, we designed an approach to generate a virtual shop in the real world.

Before getting the recommended products, we analyze the current scene and extract the dominant objects in the real environment. By recording the location of these key objects, we can place the recommended items in the physical location nearby. Different products have their own placement rules. For example, decorative paintings and racks are usually hung on the wall. Vases are usually placed on a table or other flat surfaces, and chandeliers are usually hung from the ceiling. In order for the virtual object to automatically follow the placement rules for placement, we needed a higher level of understanding about the user's environment.

We solved this problem by introducing the spatial mapping function. Using this, we analyzed the basic structure of the user's current environment and identify surfaces such as walls, ceilings, and floors. After scanning the whole room, the system will notify users to stop scanning, and the spatial understanding component in Microsoft Mixed Reality Toolkit will analyze the scanned data. Through this analysis, we can get the orientation (vertical or horizontal), position and size of the corresponding surface in 3D space.

Currently, not all the products have 3D models (Fig. 3). In these cases, 3D cubes with 2D images are being used instead (Fig. 4).

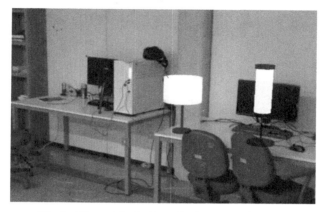

Fig. 3. 3D models displayed in the system interface

Fig. 4. 3D cube with 2D picture

3.3 Natural Interactions with Full-Hand Manipulation

In order to interact with an augmented reality system interface, hand gestures are often used for specific manipulation. In this work, it is necessary to use hands to move or rotate 3D objects for the preview experience. Some of the augmented reality (AR) systems use two-finger manipulation [5], like air-tap gesture. However, in daily life, we often use the entire hand for grabbing and placing objects. Two-finger manipulation does not conform to human natural behaviors. Therefore, monitoring and simulating full-hand manipulation is important to make it closer to human daily movements and let users act naturally when using our system.

In our previous work, we applied two-hand manipulation in the shopping system for dragging and rotating 3D virtual objects, but it was based on two-finger gestures: air-tap and hold [9]. This is very limited since it does not have much flexibility, we need to use both hands if we want to do a rotating operation.

To improve the manipulation method for interacting with our virtual shop interface and 3D virtual objects, we adopted an approach to enable hand motion detection by connecting an optical hand tracking module (Leap Motion) to an augmented reality HMD (Microsoft HoloLens). Apart from this, we applied Microsoft Mixed Reality Toolkit Version 2 (MRTK v2) [13] to enable user experience components (Table 1).

Table 1. Interactions of 3D objects

Interactable 3D objects	Related UI components	Input interactions
Buttons	Pressable button	Press
		Touch
Virtual products	/	Grab
	/	Air-tap
	Bounding box	Scale
		Rotate
	Tooltip	Gaze

As for the buttons in our system interface, we choose to use 3D pressable buttons (Fig. 5) to replace the previous 2D tap buttons. The pressable buttons provides feedback for touching and pressing. With pressing and touching enabled, the user can use one finger to interact with buttons, which is much easier than using an air-tap gesture.

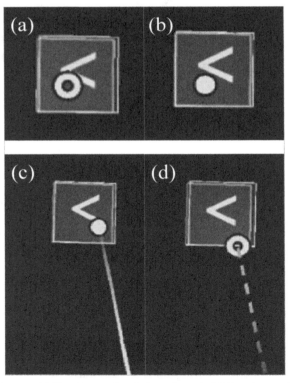

Fig. 5. Pressable button: (a) Near interaction, being released. (b) Near interaction, being pressed. (c) Far interaction, being released. (d) Far interaction, being pressed.

Since the virtual shop display is an important part of our system for previewing 3D virtual products in the user's room, we added plenty of interactions for manipulating these 3D objects (Table 1). In previous work, we need to use an air-tap gesture to move a virtual object, but now we can use the grabbing gesture as well. People usually grab things to move objects in daily life, so grabbing is a more natural way to interact with virtual objects. The grabbing gesture is not only be used for moving objects' position but also available for other direct manipulations like rotating the object by using hand movements. All these direct manipulations can be achieved by using the grabbing gesture (Fig. 6).

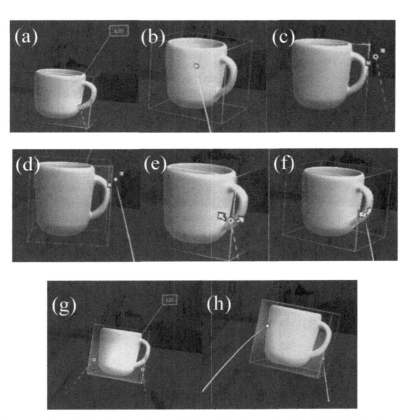

Fig. 6. Interactions of 3D virtual products: (a) Bounding box and tooltip. (b) Object being grabbed. (c), (d) Scaling the object by the bounding box. (e), (f) Rotating the object by the bounding box. (g), (h) Manipulating the virtual object with two hands. (Blue bounding box means object is being manipulated.) (Color figure online)

To make the operations understandable, we attached bounding boxes to virtual object models, which is invisible when the object is not being gazed at. The bounding box size is related to the size of the virtual objects. It enables handlers for scaling from eight apexes of the box and rotating from each edge's midpoint. We set the scaling range to be

1 to 5 times, according to the original scale of the object, so that users can see details by zooming in, and see the initial size by zooming out to the minimum size. With the new style of the bounding box, it is possible for users to do scaling and rotating operations with one or two hands, which is much more flexibility than our old system where the rotation operation must use completed with two hands. The accuracy of these operations is also improved by using the bounding box.

We also used tooltips for showing the price of the products. It is visible only when the object is being gazed at, so that users will not be overloaded with too much text or lines in the initial interface which may disturb the user's previewing experience.

Apart from close-up interactions such as touching and pressing, we also enabled distant interactions for both buttons and 3D objects, so that users can operate 3D objects from afar. Far interactions are supported by the hand tracking module, together with the feedback visualization from MRTK v2, which is shown as an imaginary line starting from the finger and ending with a circular pointer. Far interactions include grabbing, pointing and air-tap gestures. Each of them can be triggered by one or two hands. In our case, users can interact with buttons, bounding box or the object itself with the far interaction method, the user can feel more natural when interacting with our immersive shopping system.

3.4 Previous Work (Scene Understanding)

In previous work, we introduced a way to search for products based on the user's scene. By understanding the scene that the user is currently looking at, and extracting the detected scene information, the system can recommend related products that could potentially interest the user (Fig. 7).

Fig. 7. The system recommends relevant products to the user according to the current scene in the user's environment. Scene recognition results: a kitchen with a sink and a mirror.

A scene is a view of real-world environment where users are physically located, in which contains multiple surfaces and objects being organized in a meaningful way. By applying computer vision techniques, the scene can be understood quickly. After generating an overall description of the scene (e.g. kitchen, or restroom) in this way, the system would be able to recognize dominated objects (e.g. desktop computer, or desk) from the ambient environment. The keywords of the current scene (e.g. kitchen) can then be used to search products on an e-commerce platform which contains the related categories as the dominated objects in the scene (instead of the dominated objects themselves). In this way, this system recommends users with products that are strongly associated with the current scene.

In our system, the recommendation process is triggered by a speech command, "Show Something". After the detecting and searching process, the results would then be displayed in augmented reality in a virtual panel that floats in the real world by an HMD. Users can visually see the links between recommended products and the real world, and view the details of the recommended items, or directly filter the recommended items by voice command and quickly find the products they are interested in.

4   Implementation

Figure 8 shows the overview of our system. Our system includes the HMD client and the server.

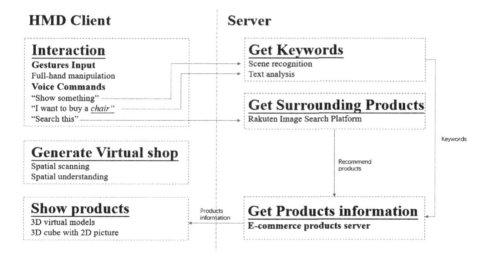

Fig. 8. System overview

4.1   Image Analysis

When the voice command "Search this" is issued, the camera of the HMD will capture the current product. The image will first be stored in the memory, and it will then be sent to the Rakuten Image Search Platform API. This API will analyze the image and return several similar products. We will visualize these products to the user.

4.2 Spatial Mapping

The system prompts users to walk around and start scanning the surrounding physical environment. Within the HMD, the camera group in front of the device are used to perceive the surface information in the surrounding environment. MRTK's spatial understanding component is used to analyze the metadata captured by the camera group to identify specific ceilings, floors, walls, and other flat information. Combined with the preset information for the virtual item placement feature, we calculate the location that is suitable for placing the virtual products and automatically place them.

4.3 MRTK v2

We built our system based on the Unity engine and Microsoft Mixed Reality Toolkit version 2 (MRTK v2). MRTK v2 for Unity is an open-source cross-platform development kit for accelerating the development of mixed reality applications. We used MRTK v2 for supporting camera system, input system, spatial mapping, UX and other functions. Compared with MRTK v1 we used in our previous system, MRTK v2 is modularized by different kinds of tools, which makes it possible for us to streamline our system. Since it configures many commonly used profiles in a foundation profile, our building procedure is simplified as well. Furthermore, our UX for full-hand manipulation and pressable buttons are supported by MRTK v2 which cannot be done in the previous version.

4.4 Hand Motion Detection

We used an optic hand tracking device, Leap Motion, to detect hand movements, and a see-through type HMD, Microsoft HoloLens 1, to detect user's head position information [15]. The Leap Motion controller is connected to a laptop PC through USB, and the PC and HoloLens are linked by Wi-Fi. We recreated a supporting frame [16] by 3D printing

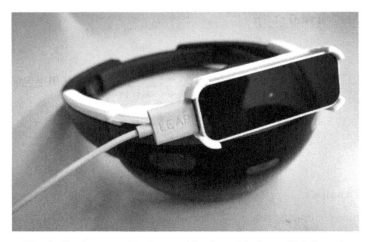

Fig. 9. Device assembly for attaching Leap Motion to HoloLens 1.

to fix the Leap Motion camera onto the HoloLens (Fig. 9) so that the Leap Motion camera would obtain a stable view as it can be moved with the HMD. Leap Motion camera captures the user's hand movements and sends it to the computer to analyze them, then exchanges the results with HoloLens to realize real-time feedbacks for hand interactions.

5 Preliminary Evaluation

In this section, we introduce our user study and result analysis. In our previous system, we asked participants to accomplish their shopping tasks. It shows the product in the form of a 2D panel. Users use two fingers to manipulate virtual products. The main purpose of this study was to test whether our new system can provide better display experience and better manipulate experience compared to the previous system. This study can help us figure out whether our system interests them. We will also discuss the received feedback from a questionnaire.

5.1 Participants

We asked 12 participants (5 females and 7 males), ranging from 20 to 26 years of age to participate in our experiment. All of them have basic computer skills. We divided them into two groups evenly.

5.2 Task and Procedure

Before the study, we introduced the basic operation of Microsoft HoloLens to each participant. We gave every participant 15 min to get familiar with the HoloLens. Then we asked them to search for three products (chair, water bottle, and monitor) in the room. Group 1 was asked to first use the old system for 15 min, and then use our new system for 15 min. Group 2 was asked the opposite, where they used the new system first. We asked all 12 participants to fill out a questionnaire with 5 questions to obtain qualitative feedback. Participants rated each question from 1 to 5 (1 = very negative, 5 = very positive).

5.3 Result and Discussion

After the experiment, we collected 36 sets of data from 12 participants using two systems. Then we analyzed the data we collected and performed preliminary evaluation.

As shown in Table 2, we divided the results into two parts, one is using our new system, and the other is using our old system. We calculated the average score of each question.

Question 1 judges whether the image search is faster. In our new system, the user tries to take a photo of the product and search. In the old system, users use voice command to search the product. From the result, we can see that when searching for a product that around us, the new system is faster than the old one. By using the image search, users can search the surrounding products quickly.

Table 2. Questionnaire

	Question	New system	Old system
1	I could search the products quickly	4.5	3.7
2	Search results are very accurate	4.5	4.5
3	I like the display interface very much	4.6	3.5
4	I felt the system operation was very easy	4.0	3.7
5	Gestures are very close to the real world	4.0	3.4

Question 2 is used to judge the accuracy of our new system. As we can see from the results, the participants gave the new system the same rating as the old one. It shows that although we use image search, the search results are not worse than the old system. Combining question 1 and question 2 we can know that we improved search speed while still maintaining high search accuracy.

Question 3 is used to compare the display interface of these two systems. The old system uses a 2D panel to show the products and the new system uses a 3D cube. As the result shows, most of the participants thought that the interface of our new system is better.

Question 4 and Question 5 is used to judge whether our new manipulate method MRTK v2 performs well. The new system's rating is higher than the old one. This is likely because when using the old system, the user has to use two fingers to manipulate, which is not similar to real life. Our new system uses full-hand manipulation, which is more realistic.

In general, all participants rated our new system higher than the old one. This signifies that our new system design is more reasonable and practical than the old one. It demonstrates that our new system can provide a faster, better and more realistic shopping experience than the previous version.

6 Related Work

6.1 Intelligent Shopping Assistant System

One of our related work is the intelligent shopping assistant system, which is also our previous work [3]. This work introduces an immersive shopping system supported by quick scene understanding and augmented reality 3D preview. This system can recommend related products that the user might interest in by understanding the scene the user is looking at. After returning the results of potential target products, the system provides users with an augmented reality preview experience. It automatically puts products to a suitable place in front of the user by using life-size 3D virtual products and spatial understanding. Users can use two-hand gestural manipulation to operate virtual products. It also allows searching and filtering for specific products by voice commands and keywords. We updated this system to a new environment to support MRTK v2 new UXs and more natural hand interactions to replace old type interface and two-hand manipulation methods. Our current work also extends the automatic placement method to generate our virtual shop interface at a proper position.

6.2 Spatial Recognition Based MR Shopping System Providing Responsive Store Layout

Another related work is a spatial recognition based mixed-reality (MR) shopping system providing responsive store layout [18]. This work is about building an MR shop system which could recognize the space and generate a virtual shop in the real environment. This system provides immersive virtual preview and interaction in the real environment. It also includes some in-store characteristics such as store layout, decoration, music, and a virtual store employee. It describes a new kind of online shop system by mixing virtual in-store characteristics and real environments, which may be the possible direction of the future online shop system. This research also introduced a new spatial understanding algorithm and layout mechanism to support a responsive spatial layout. This work inspired us to use spatial understanding techniques to generate our 3D virtual shop at a proper place in order to provide users with a better preview experience. In our work, we used spatial understanding to detect different kinds of surfaces in the user's room by the HMD and generate the augmented 3D virtual shop at a large platform in the user's environment, so that the user can have an immersive shopping experience.

7   Conclusion and Future Work

An augmented-reality online shopping system which allows users to experience in-store shopping at home is proposed. The system can recognize a specific object by camera and recommend similar products through an HMD. This system is also configured with a method for generating a virtual shop at the user's home. Users can use their full hand to manipulate the virtual object when using this system. This helps users to perform manipulation such as dragging and rotating more conveniently and naturally, and therefore the system enable the user to have an immersive preview for checking the details through the real model of the product that they want to buy.

Currently, the system is a single-user system, so it is not possible for others in the same room to view the virtual shop display during one is searching and manipulating the products. This would cause inconvenience when several users want to exchange opinions during shopping. For future work, we will try to make it into a multi-user system, in order to support two or more users sharing their preview information in the same room.

References

1. Luo, P., Yan, S., Liu, Z., Shen, Z., Yang, S., He, Q.: From online behaviors to offline retailing. In: Proceedings of the 22nd ACM SIGKDD International Conference on Knowledge Discovery and Data Mining, pp. 175–184. ACM, August 2016
2. Close, A.G., Kukar-Kinney, M.: Beyond buying: motivations behind consumers' online shopping cart use. J. Bus. Res. **63**(9–10), 986–992 (2010). Lu, Y., Smith, S. (2007)

3. Zhao, Y., Guo, L., Wang, X., Pan, Z.: A 3D virtual shopping mall that has the intelligent virtual purchasing guider and cooperative purchasing functionalities. In 8th International Conference on Computer Supported Cooperative Work in Design, vol. 2, pp. 381–385. IEEE, May 2004

4. Dou, H., Li, Z., Cai, M., Cheng, K., Masuko, S., Tanaka, J.: Show something: intelligent shopping assistant supporting quick scene understanding and immersive preview. In: Yamamoto, S., Mori, H. (eds.) HCII 2019. LNCS, vol. 11570, pp. 205–218. Springer, Cham (2019). https://doi.org/10.1007/978-3-030-22649-7_17

5. Tanikawa, T., Arai, T., Masuda, T.: Development of micro manipulation system with two-finger micro hand. In: Proceedings of IEEE/RSJ International Conference on Intelligent Robots and Systems, IROS 1996, vol. 2, pp. 850–855. IEEE, November 1996

6. Liu, J., Au, O.K.C., Fu, H., Tai, C.L.: Two-finger gestures for 6DOF manipulation of 3D objects. Comput. Graph. Forum **31**(7), 2047–2055 (2012)

7. Weichert, F., Bachmann, D., Rudak, B., Fisseler, D.: Analysis of the accuracy and robustness of the leap motion controller. Sensors **13**(5), 6380–6393 (2013)

8. Jailungka, P., Charoenseang, S.: Intuitive 3D model prototyping with leap motion and microsoft HoloLens. In: Kurosu, M. (ed.) HCI 2018. LNCS, vol. 10903, pp. 269–284. Springer, Cham (2018). https://doi.org/10.1007/978-3-319-91250-9_21

9. Microsoft HoloLens I Mixed Reality Technology for Business (2019). https://www.micros oft.com/en-us/hololens. Accessed 14 Dec 2019

10. Leap Motion (2019). https://www.leapmotion.com/. Accessed 14 Dec 2019

11. Lu, Y., Smith, S.: Augmented reality e-commerce assistant system: trying while shopping. In: Jacko, J.A. (ed.) HCI 2007. LNCS, vol. 4551, pp. 643–652. Springer, Heidelberg (2007). https://doi.org/10.1007/978-3-540-73107-8_72

12. Levin, A.M., Levin, I.P., Weller, J.A.: A multi-attribute analysis of preferences for online and offline shopping: differences across products, consumers, and shopping stages. J. Electron. Commer. Res. **6**(4), 281–290 (2005)

13. Getting started with MRTK version 2 - Mixed Reality (2020). https://github.com/Microsoft/MixedRealityToolkit-Unity/releases. Accessed 26 Jan 2020

14. Garon, M., Boulet, P.O., Doironz, J.P., Beaulieu, L., Lalonde, J.F.: Real-time high resolution 3D data on the HoloLens. In: 2016 IEEE International Symposium on Mixed and Augmented Reality (ISMAR-Adjunct), pp. 189–191. IEEE (2016)

15. Wozniak, P., Vauderwange, O., Mandal, A., Javahiraly, N., Curticapean, D.: Possible applications of the LEAP motion controller for more interactive simulated experiments in augmented or virtual reality. In: Optics Education and Outreach IV, vol. 9946, p. 99460P. International Society for Optics and Photonics, September 2016

16. Ababsa, F., He, J., Chardonnet, J.R.: Free hand-based 3D interaction in optical see-through augmented reality using leap motion, October 2018

17. Zhu, W., Owen, C.B., Li, H., Lee, J.H.: Personalized in-store e-commerce with the promopad: an augmented reality shopping assistant. Electron. J. e-Commer. Tools Appl. **1**(3), 1–19 (2004)

18. Dou, H.: Spatial recognition based mixed-reality shop system providing responsive layout. Unpublished master's thesis, Graduate School of Information, Production and System, Waseda University, Japan, September 2019

Multimodal Inspection of Product Surfaces Using Mobile Consumer Devices

Christopher Martin[✉] and Annerose Braune

Institute of Automation, Technische Universität Dresden, Dresden, Germany
{christopher.martin,annerose.braune}@tu-dresden.de

Abstract. Even though an increasing amount of products are bought online today, the remote evaluation of product surfaces remains a challenging task because of their multimodal nature. Despite the common use of modern mobile consumer devices for online shopping which would allow for multimodal user interfaces, current presentations of products mainly focus on the visual and (rarely) auditory presentation. However, tactile properties are also significant for a buying decision and should thus not be disregarded. Current multimodal approaches still use specific hardware, especially for the presentation of tactile properties. In this paper, we therefore present an approach for the multimodal inspection of product surfaces using only common mobile consumer hardware such as smartphones and tablets.

Approaches for the adaptation of the visual, auditory, and tactile output based on device features and user inputs are presented that enable an interactive multimodal evaluation of product surfaces. The tactile presentation is realized using only the vibration motor built into modern mobile devices. In order to deal with the restriction of mobile systems, a four-step tactile signal processing approach is introduced. The realization of the approaches is demonstrated by means of an Android application, which was used to conduct an initial user study that shows promising results but also the potential for future works.

Keywords: Virtual product surface representation · Multimodal user interface · Vibrotactile feedback · Mobile user interface

1 Introduction

Even with the e-commerce market size continuing to grow in recent years, the challenge of remote evaluation of product surfaces has not yet been solved. This mainly results from their multimodal nature, i.e. they are defined by multiple visual, auditory, and haptic properties. While the presentation of products currently focuses on the display of the visual and sometimes auditory properties, the haptic property remains a vital modality that should not be disregarded, e.g., when evaluating fashion [30]. Thus, a multimodal presentation of product surfaces – that incorporates all three modalities – is required and may also help

© Springer Nature Switzerland AG 2020
S. Yamamoto and H. Mori (Eds.): HCII 2020, LNCS 12184, pp. 377–392, 2020.
https://doi.org/10.1007/978-3-030-50020-7_27

to reduce the high number of product returns in online shopping that becomes an increasing challenge for the e-commerce sector [11].

A subjective inspection of the product surfaces is still essential for their comprehensive and genuine evaluation. For this task a representation of their visual, auditory, and haptic properties has to be displayed on a multimodal user interface. The visual and auditory properties are usually represented by photos and (on rare occasions) by prerecorded audio files using displays and speakers. Few approaches for the presentation of the haptic properties of product surfaces exist that mostly use vibration to represent the (tactile property) roughness. However, these approaches use specific hardware such as arrays of vibrating contactor pins [1, 22] or electrodynamic shakers [2] that are not mobile and not widely available to the public. This greatly hinders their use for e-commerce applications as most online shopping today is already done using common mobile devices such as smartphones and tablets [10] and does thus not require any additional hardware.

However, mobile devices today already allow for multimodal interactions without the need for additional hardware by offering distinct sensors and actuators: a touch sensitive screen for tactile input as well as visual output, speakers for auditory output, and a vibration motor for tactile feedback. In this paper, we therefore introduce an approach that allows the remote multimodal (auditory, visual, and tactile) inspection of product surfaces using only common mobile consumer hardware like smartphones or tablets. For this purpose, a multimodal user interface is presented that allows the adaptation of prerecorded auditory, visual, and tactile media data of product surfaces according to user interactions.

After a short introduction to the multimodal inspection of product surfaces (especially of textile fabrics) in Sect. 2, the processing of the multimodal signals is described in Sect. 3. The realization of these algorithms in an *Android* app is introduced in Sect. 4 and evaluated by means of a user study in Sect. 5. Finally, in Sect. 6 we will draw conclusions about the applicability of our approach for the multimodal inspection of product surfaces on common mobile devices and discuss future works.

2   Multimodal Properties of Product Surfaces

As stated earlier, product surfaces are defined by multiple properties of different modalities. In the following some of the most important properties are discussed subdivided by their modality. In order to achieve a realistic virtual representation of product surfaces, as many of these properties as possible should be presented in a multimodal user interface. In this section, textile fabrics are used as exemplary material of the product surfaces as their flexible nature results in the most diverse properties and hence poses the most challenging task for a virtual multimodal presentation.

2.1   Visual and Auditory Inspection

Color is a primary visual characteristic of product surfaces. In addition to the pure color tone, brightness and saturation play a separate role. These properties, also known as color depth, are, e.g., determined by dye concentration. For the objective evaluation of color depth, color tone metrics and standard type depths were defined and standardized [15]. However, as color must be evaluated by each person individually based on their personal taste, a photo may be used to show the color of the product surface. As colors may look different under certain light conditions, all photos should be taken using a constant light color. This way, the reflection behavior may also be represented by taking multiple photos with changing angles of the lighting system. Visual properties are today often already presented in online shops by presenting multiple photos of the product, e.g., by showing picture of the cloths worn by models or even close-ups of the textile fabrics. This way the design of the surface can also be presented.

An auditory description of a product surface may be obtained by mechanical interaction with the surface itself, e.g. by swiping over a textile surface with the finger or the aid of an object [2]. If audio is recorded during the swipe over motion, an audio profile of the fabric can be generated, which among others depends on the selected speed of the object [3]. This recording procedure can also be varied with regard to the coating head (different materials such as organic fabrics/finger) or the swiping direction in order to increase the significance of the audio recording. The resulting audio record may then give an impression of auditory properties such as the loudness of a fabric or the creaking sound of leather [20].

2.2   Kinesthetic and Tactile Inspection

The haptic properties of a product surface are usually the most diverse of the multimodal properties. In the textile industry, the totality of all sensory impressions associated with touching or manipulating a fabric by hand or finger is called *fabric hand* [13]. These impressions result from the mechanic properties of the product surface (e.g. its surface texture) and stimulate both the kinesthetic and tactile mechanoreceptors [19]: tactile due to the unavoidable skin contact with the surface and kinesthetic as a prerequisite for establishing contact and actively exploring the surface by moving the hand and fingers.

The first major haptic property to consider when evaluating product surfaces – especially of textile fabrics because of their flexible nature – is its stiffness, i.e. its resistance against deformation when applying force. It is therefore mostly recognized by the kinesthetic mechanoreceptors. A standardized test [8] for measuring a product's stiffness has already been established. It enables an objective comparison of the stiffness by means of a specific measurement value.

Physically a product surface is among others defined by its friction. While the coefficient of friction may be used to objectively describe this effect, the roughness of a surface may still be perceived different by every individual person [2]. The perceived roughness of a surface results from high-frequency vibration when swiping the finger over a surface due its structure as well as the softness of the textile fabric and is registered by the tactile mechanoreceptors (cf. [27]). A standardized measurement method [14] may be used to calculate the roughness depth of a surface by means of a 3D scan.

Other properties like the form, weight, compressibility, and temperature are also important when evaluating a product surface and may be measured.

3   Multimodal Signal Processing

As stated in the last section, the auditive and haptic presentation depends among others on the position, direction, and velocity of the finger movement. In order to provide an interactive multimodal user interface for the inspection of product surfaces, it is hence not only necessary to find an expressive representation of the properties described in Sect. 2 but also to continuously adapt the multimodal data to user inputs as displayed in Fig. 1. Therefore, representative multimodal media data that can be prerecorded are discussed in this section as well as algorithms for the adaption of this data to presentation devices and user inputs.

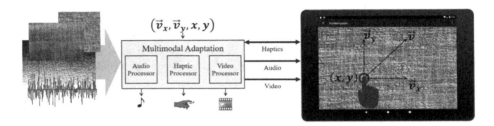

Fig. 1. Overview of the multimodal adaption process based on multimodal media data of the product surfaces and user interactions

3.1   Visual and Auditory Signal Processing

As discussed in Sect. 2.1, the visual properties of a product surface may be interpreted differently by each person and should thus best be presented by displaying a photo of it allowing the individual evaluation of the surface. An example of such photo is shown in Fig. 2a. Photos are shot as a top view to offer the best resemblance of a real fabric when shown on a touch screen. However, to allow an accurate evaluation of the surface, the photo must be displayed true to scale, because otherwise information about the design or surface structure may be distorted. For this, additional information about the presentation device's and photo's real dimension are required. While the former can be calculated from the pixel density that may be read from the system API (cf. [5]), the latter must be stored in a database as an additional image property. Based on these information, the photo can then be zoomed to be displayed on the device screen true to scale and thus enable an accurate evaluation of the surface.

Currently, there is no animated presentation of the deformation of the surface resulting from the physical interaction with the textile fabric as, e.g., proposed by Magnenat-Thalmann et al. [22]. As this could further enhance the visual evaluation, especially of flexible textile product surfaces, an animation of the surface deformation based on user interaction and information about the fabric stiffness should also be added in future work. Other visual information, such as the measured color depth, may be displayed in a tabular view and could, e.g., be used for finding further fabrics with similar colors.

Auditory properties may be represented by playback of prerecorded audio files. However, as the audio feedback – created by swiping over a product surface – changes based on the velocity of the motion, the output must be adapted continuously according to current user interactions. This can be accomplished by alteration of the playback speed by means of the *time stretching* mechanism, which allow change of playback speed without affecting the pitch. To allow for such processing, the audio file must be recorded using a swiping motion at a constant speed and this original velocity must be stored in a database. In addition, the velocity of the finger movement on the device screen must be tracked and may then be used for parameterization of the time stretching effect. On top of that, our studies have shown that the audio signal must also get louder with increasing finger velocity and vice versa for an higher acceptance of the virtual presentation. Hence, the amplitude of the audio signal should also be adapted based on the current finger velocity. To allow for a multimodal user interaction, the adaption is performed continuously while the user may interact with the photo of the product surface on the touch screen of the mobile device as shown in Fig. 1.

3.2   Tactile Signal Processing

While the auditory and visual modalities are already commonly supported by mobile user interfaces, tactile feedback is typically only used for alarming the user in case of new notifications or on button presses, e.g., on the on-screen keyboard. Different predefined vibration patterns may also be used for different kinds of notifications. However, during the inspection of product surfaces a continuous adaptive haptic feedback is required.

In this section, we therefore introduce a four-step algorithm that generates a tactile output using the vibration motor of mobile devices. Unfortunately, a kinesthetic output can not be provided using common mobile consumer devices as they lack actuators for the kinesthetic stimulation. Consequently, we will focus on the representation of the tactile property *roughness* (cf. Sect. 2.2) as it is currently the only tactile property that may be simulated on a touch display [2].

As stated earlier, the roughness of a surface is defined by its structure which may be recorded by 3D scanning the surface. The result of such 3D scan is a three-dimensional point cloud, an example of which is shown in Fig. 2b. However, as a very high resolution is required to record the fine structures of textile surfaces, the resulting point clouds usually become too large for processing on a mobile device. Hence, a data reduction is required in order to make the point clouds usable. Allerkamp et al. [1] propose a grayscale image as a representation of the surface profile which they calculated from a single photo of a surface. Adapting this approach, we propose transforming the point cloud into a grayscale image representing a physical map of the surface profile. Each pixel of this image represents an area on the x-y-plane of the point cloud with the brightness value $B(x, y)$ of a pixel representing the average height z of the area. An example of a resulting surface profile image can be seen in Fig. 2c.

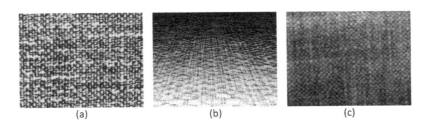

Fig. 2. Creation of the surface profile image (c) from a point cloud created by a 3D scan (b) of a textile fabric (a)

Based on the surface profile image, that can easily be processed by mobile devices due to its reduced amount of data, we propose a cyclic four step tactile signal processing algorithm that is shown in Fig. 3. The algorithm enables the continuous adaptation of a vibrotactile feedback to the user's swiping motion over the touch screen of a mobile device displaying the photo of a product surface (cf. Sect. 3.1).

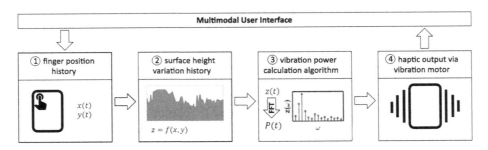

Fig. 3. Four step tactile signal processing procedure used for adaption of vibration output to the user's finger movement

Step ① of the process requires the continuous tracking of the finger position on the touch screen that corresponds to a specific position on the inspected product surface. As user inputs are usually only registered by discrete touch events, the continuous path of the user's swiping movements $\vec{x}(t)$ must be reconstructed. At first, the positions associated with the touch events $\vec{x}(t_i)$ must be converted from pixel values to real world dimensions to enable a later mapping of the finger position onto the surface profile image. As described in Sect. 3.1, the pixel density may be used for this step. In order to reconstruct a steady, continuous path, the ranges between consecutive sampling points of the touch events are interpolated using a linear function according to Eq. 1.

$$\begin{pmatrix} x \\ y \end{pmatrix} =: \vec{x}(t) = \frac{\vec{x}(t_{i+1}) - \vec{x}(t_i)}{t_{i+1} - t_i}(t - t_i) + \vec{x}(t_i) \text{ with } t_i \leq t < t_{i+1} \qquad (1)$$

Based on the finger position history from step ① and the surface profile image, the height variations $z(t)$, that a finger would have passed on the real surface during its trajectory, are calculated in step ②. Using Eq. 2, the height of the product surface z at a specific position $\vec{x}(t_i)$ can be reconstructed from the brightness values $(B(\vec{x}))$ of the surface profile image based on the resolution of the surface profile image $(R_p$ in $^{mm}/px)$ and scaling factor of the brightness value representing the height value $(R_h$ in $^{\mu m}/\text{grayvalue})$ that must be stored in a database in addition to the surface profile image.

$$z(t_i) = R_h \cdot B\left(R_p \cdot x(t_i), R_p \cdot y(t_i)\right) \qquad (2)$$

Figure 4 shows the resulting reconstructed surface height variation history $z(t) = z(\vec{x}(t))$ for an exemplary path and surface profile image.

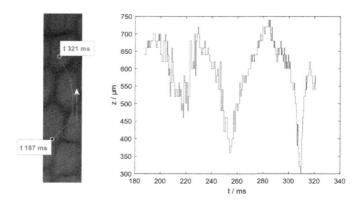

Fig. 4. Example for the reconstruction of the surface height variations (right) during a finger movement (left, green path) based on the product's surface profile image (Color figure online)

To allow an output to the vibration motor, an output signal $P(t) = P(z(t))$ is generated in step ③. This is done by analyzing the surface height variation history, as it resembles the surface structure that the tactile mechanoreceptors recognize as the roughness of the product surface. Common mobile systems usually only allow controlling the vibration motor by using predefined vibration patterns or setting a power level for a defined amount of time (see e.g. [6]). Hence, the output signal must be reduced to a set of discrete vibration power values allowing the representation of the roughness feeling of a surface.

Allerkampf et al. [1] proposed the decomposing of the vibration signal into two base frequencies of 40 Hz and 320 Hz based on the frequency spectrum created by a Fourier transformation. Comparable to this approach, we propose using a Fast Fourier Transformation [12] of the surface height variation history from step ② to enable the processing of the frequency spectrum: $F(\omega) = \mathcal{F}(z(t))$. To cope with the inertia of vibration motors in mobile system, 50 ms was defined as the window for the Fourier Transformation. The sample rate is set to 1600 Hz, which is twice as high as the upper sensory threshold of the pacinian corpuscles [18] – the tactile mechanoreceptors that mainly register vibration.

Based on the restrictions set by mobile systems, our algorithm requires the decomposition of the vibration signal into only a single vibration power value per execution cycle with an unknown frequency, as vibration frequencies may vary between mobile devices. In order to determine this single value, the weighted root mean square of the determined frequency spectrum is calculated as shown in Eq. 3. The root mean square is used to assign a stronger weighting to more dominant frequencies.

$$P(t) = \sqrt{\frac{1}{n} \sum_{i=1}^{n} [c_{rec}(\omega_i) \cdot F(\omega_i)]^2} \tag{3}$$

$$\text{with } c_{rec}(\omega) = \begin{cases} 1/6 & \omega < 10\,\text{Hz} \\ 1/2 & 10\,\text{Hz} \leq \omega < 40\,\text{Hz} \\ 1 & 40\,\text{Hz} \leq \omega \leq 800\,\text{Hz} \\ 0 & 800\,\text{Hz} \leq \omega \end{cases}$$

With lower frequencies usually representing static effects – e.g., when pressing the finger against a corner – and higher frequencies being primarily responsible for the perception of roughness (cf. [27]), frequencies lower than 10 Hz resp. 40 Hz are weighed lower by means of the factor $c_{rec}(\omega)$. Additionally, frequencies higher than 800 Hz are cut off, because they are above the human sensory threshold (cf. [18]), i.e. they cannot be recognized by the tactile mechanoreceptors.

With the vibration power $P(t)$ now determined, it may be output to the vibration motor in step ④ using the device's system API. For this, the value must be rescaled to match the expected value range of the mobile system (e.g., $0 \leq P_v(t) \leq 255$ in case of Android [6]): $P_v(t) = c_v \cdot P(t)$. The scaling factor c_v may however depend on the specific vibration motor or even user, i.e. it cannot be calculated and was therefore determined in a user study presented in Sect. 5.

4   Realization of a Mobile Application

In order to demonstrate our approach, an Android application was created that allows loading prerecorded multimodal media data from the internet and realizes a multimodal user interface by integrating the signal processing approaches described in Sect. 3. The application was tested on a *Sony Xperia XZ3* smartphone [25] that offers a high resolution screen, loudspeaker, and a linear resonant actuator as vibration motor as part of their *Dynamic Vibration System*, which offers better transient response [29] and thus allows a better tactile output.

At first, multimodal media data and measurements for 26 textile surfaces have been recorded and stored in a relational database as described in [20]. A RESTful web service interface[1] was then created that allows browsing the available products and provides the required multimodal media data as wells as the parameters for the multimodal signal processing in a JSON syntax. Furthermore, the media data are provided in an efficient way by support of multiple media codecs for file size reduction and a caching mechanism is implemented to avoid re-rendering of media data with previously used quality parameters (e.g. equivalent resolutions). To retrieve the data, a web service client was implemented in the Android application using the GSON[2] library. The products loaded from the web services are listed in the user interface shown in the left image of Fig. 5.

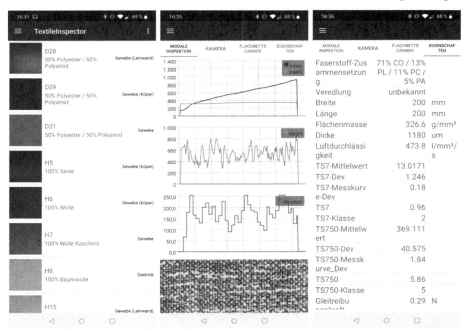

Fig. 5. Screenshots of the Android app showing the product selection screen (left), the multimodal interaction screen (center), and the tabular list of measured multimodal surface properties (right)

---

[1] The web service may be accessed at https://agtele.eats.et.tu-dresden.de/multimod.
[2] https://github.com/google/gson.

Upon selection of a product, the multimodal interaction screen is shown, the debug version of which is shown in the center image of Fig. 5. In the bottom of the screen, the top view photo of the product surface is shown true to scale as described in Sect. 3.1. In the non-debug version of this screen, the photo is also displayed instead of the three diagrams which show the finger position history (top, $x(t)$ resp. $y(t)$), the surface height variation history (middle, $z(t)$), and the resulting vibration signal (bottom, $P_v(t)$). When swiping over the photo of the product surface, a vibration signal is generated and output by continuous execution of the tactile signal processing algorithm described in Sect. 3.2. Furthermore, audio of the prerecorded swiping sound is played and adapted to the finger velocity as described in Sect. 3.1.

An alternate output mode was also implemented that allows audio and haptic output to external audio and haptic devices such as electrodynamic shakers via a stereo audio signal. For this, the left channel is used for audio output while the right channel may be used for pre-rendered haptic signals as, e.g., introduced in [2]. Haptic devices may then be connected to the mobile device using the headphone jack.

Additionally, the measured multimodal properties of the product surface (cf. Sect. 2) that are stored in the database are listed in a tabular view as shown in the right image of Fig. 5. These allow a comparison of products, e.g., based on the coefficient of friction or the fibre-composition.

The multimodal interaction design poses special challenges such as allowing only certain maximum latencies for haptic (36 ms [17]), auditory (30 ms [23]), or visual (25 ms [21]) feedback to a haptic input if a natural feeling of the user interface should be maintained. As the continuous tracking of the finger position in Android already raises certain delays and the calculation of the corresponding multimodal feedback signals adds further delay because of its 50 ms execution cycle time, an approximation of the future finger trajectory was also added to our application. The extrapolation is based on a regression of the finger position history $\vec{x}(t)$ from step ① of the tactile signal processing algorithm. The method of least squares with a quadratic model function was used for calculation of the extrapolated trajectory function. However, the error increases significantly on rapid finger movements, as shown in the exemplary extrapolated finger trajectory in Fig. 6, e.g., between 4 s and 4.6 s.

Therefore, the approximated time frame should be as short as possible. A bandwidth of up to 5 Hz for both arm and finger movement for a known or trained pattern has been determined as dynamic parameters for haptic user inputs according to [9,26]. Hence, the extrapolated range should not exceed 100 ms to avoid rapid changes of direction as a complete back and forth movement of the finger should take at least 200 ms.

5   User Study

As already discussed in Sect. 3.2, the scaling factor c_v required for the vibrotactile output is hardware- and user-specific. In order to determine a value for the

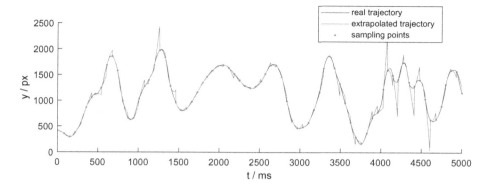

Fig. 6. Example for the extrapolation of the finger trajectory reducing output latencies

scaling factor and validate our application, we conducted a user study using a modified version of the Android application and the Sony Xperia XZ3 smartphone (cf. Sect. 4). The multimodal inspection screen – that was shown in the center of Fig. 5 – was modified for this user study by replacing the three debug diagrams with a slider that allows changing of the scaling factor c_v within the range $[0, 40]$. While a value of 0 would result in no vibrations, 40 generates a permanent maximum vibration for the roughest textile surface of the experiment. The three textiles shown in Fig. 7 were selected for the experiment as their surface structure ranges from very smooth (H71) to very rough (H31).

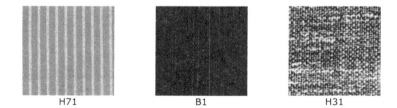

Fig. 7. Textile samples of the user study sorted from least rough (H71) to roughest (H31) surface texture

For the user study, the smartphone and textiles were fixated on a table, allowing the subjects to explore both the real and virtual textile surfaces by swiping their finger tips across the surfaces. The swiping motions were performed with a faster (10cm/s) and a slower velocity (2cm/s) which were visually monitored. Noise-canceling headphones were used for audio output to reduce possible outside influences as the sound of textile surfaces is very quiet and subtle.

13 subjects, 7 men and 6 women, aged between 21 and 34 resp. above 50 years, were asked to determine the point of subjective equality (PSE) as, e.g., introduced in [4]. That means, the subjects were ask to set the scaling factor c_v to a

value where they feel the vibration of the smartphone gives the most realisitic impression of the corresponding real textile surface. The experience level of the subjects in handling textiles ranged from beginners to experts, though most of them were beginners. All subjects had no previous experience with tactile simulation of surfaces. The order of the textiles and the swiping velocities were randomized. The subjects were given a training phase of approximately 5 min with the entire experiment taking approximately 20 min in average.

The resulting PSE values of c_v and their standard deviation are shown in Fig. 8. The mean PSE values increase with increasing surface roughness. For example, for the slow swiping motion, the PSE values range from 22.2 (H71) to 27.2 (H31). The relative standard deviation ranges from 23% (B1, fast) resp. 29% (B1, slow) to 34% (H71, fast) resp. 41% (H31, slow). PSE values of the fast swiping motion are in average 10% higher than for the slow velocity.

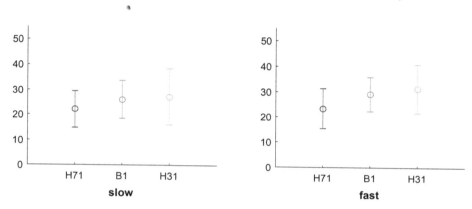

Fig. 8. Mean PSE values of c_v and their standard deviation, sorted in ascending order of surface roughness as shown in Fig. 7

The results show that an increase in roughness also requires an increased scaling factor c_v. An increase in vibration power is expected, as a bigger amplitude is usually perceived as a rougher surface texture. However, by using the surface height profile, the surface structure is already factored into our tactile signal processing algorithm. Hence, the scaling factor should be approximately even across all textiles for a defined hardware and user. Thus, an adaption of the algorithm should be considered for future works by integrating additional measured roughness values as, e.g., described in [20, 24].

The high relative standard deviations are caused by the user-specific perceptual characteristics. In order to set the user-specific scaling factor, an initialization phase should be provided in the application. The highest relative standard deviation was found for the roughest fabric (H31) at slow velocity which is an indication for an imperfect tactile user experience. This is due to the fact that the surface structure of this fabric is very sharp and is mainly perceived statically – i.e., at low frequencies as described in Sect. 3.2 – by the tactile mechanoreceptors, especially at lower velocities. This cannot be reproduced by the smooth glass surface of the smartphone or by the small amplitudes of the vibrations provided by vibration motors of mobile devices. On the other hand, the lowest relative standard deviation is found for the medium-rough jeans fabric (B1). This, in combination with comments by the subjects, shows that the vibrotactile output of a smartphone is best suited for rougher surfaces without distinct sharp structures.

Furthermore, subjects of the study were also asked to rate the haptic quality of the vibrotactile representation of the real textile surfaces from very unrealistic (1) to very realistic (7). The results depicted in Fig. 9 show no major difference in the assessed quality between the different surface textures or velocities.

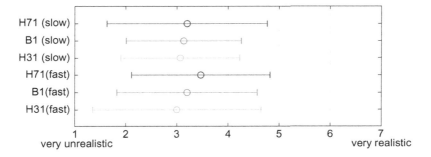

Fig. 9. Subjective assessment of the haptic quality of the experiment

As the mean evaluation shows an below average result (3.18), future work is still required regarding the tactile feedback. Criticism from the subjects included primarily the hard, cold, and smooth glass surface of the smartphone being too different from the soft and flexible nature of textile fabrics and the vibration intensity being too low for very rough surfaces (H31) even with the scaling factor set to maximum. However, when asked if such virtual tactile inspection options would support the decision to buy more clothes online in the future, most subjects thought it probable (40%) or were still undecided (27%). This underlines the great potential of virtual tactile inspection of product surfaces.

6   Conclusions and Future Work

In this Paper, we have presented an approach for the multimodal inspection of product surfaces by usage of common mobile devices such as smartphones. To create a virtual representation of the multimodal properties of product surfaces, we introduced algorithms for the adaptation of visual, auditory, and tactile pre-recorded media files to user interaction and device features. While visual and auditory presentation may already be found, e.g. within e-commerce applications, the vibrotactile presentation of surfaces using only the vibration motor of modern mobile device is very uncommon. We therefore introduced a four-step tactile signal processing algorithm that generates vibrotactile feedback based on the surface profile and user interactions with the virtual product surface.

We have demonstrated the applicability of this approach by realization of a web service – providing the multimodal media data – and an Android application. The application was tested using a modern smartphone with a linear resonant actuator for vibration output. Based on this application, a user study has been conducted in order to define the user-specific scaling factor c_v. Results of this user study show the potential of multimodal inspection of product surfaces but also the need for further developments, especially in the area of tactile output.

Initial tests with mobile devices with rotary vibration motors showed that the vibrotactile output produces very poor results due to the higher inertia. Some new technologies have already been introduced recently in the field of haptic feedback in mobile consumer devices such as Apple's *Taptic Engine* or Nintendo's *HD Rumble* that both also use a linear resonant actuator [16, 28]. The algorithm presented in this paper serves as a foundation for future developments and may well be adapted to new technologies.

Another result of the user study concerns the dependence of the vibration intensity on the installation location of the vibration motor. The vibration is perceived more strongly in direct proximity to the installation location than at a greater distance. For example, the vibration intensity decreased towards the top of the smartphone that was used in our user study as the actuator is situated at the bottom of the phone. The area of interaction should therefore be limited in the user interface in order to achieve a consistent, realistic tactile presentation. Since the position of the actuator cannot be detected automatically, a device database may be developed in the future, which could also be used to compensate the device dependency of the scaling factor.

Furthermore, the visual presentation may be enhance by adding a 3D animation of the fabric deformation when applying force to the surface (cf. Sect. 3.1). Measured information about the fabric stiffness may be used for this as well as live data about the pressure the user applies with his fingertip to touch screen, as provided by Apple's 3D Touch technology [7], for example.

Acknowledgments. The authors would like to thank Sebastian Artur Lehmann and Tung Le for their work on the Android application as well as Ugur Alican Alma, Kathrin Pietsch, and Cornelia Rataj for their contributions towards the virtual representation of textile fabrics.

The IGF proposal 19479 BG of the research association "Forschungskuratorium Textil e.V." is funded via the AiF within the scope of the "Industrial Collective Research" (IGF) by the German Federal Ministry for Economic Affairs and Energy (BMWi) on the basis of a decision by the German Bundestag.

References

1. Allerkamp, D., Böttcher, G., Wolter, F.E., Brady, A.C., Qu, J., Summers, I.R.: A vibrotactile approach to tactile rendering. Visual Comput. **23**(2), 97–108 (2007). https://doi.org/10.1007/s00371-006-0031-5

2. Alma, U.A., Altinsoy, E.: Perceived roughness of band-limited noise, single, and multiple sinusoids compared to recorded vibration. In: 2019 IEEE World Haptics Conference (WHC), Tokyo, Japan, pp. 337–342. IEEE (2019). https://doi.org/10.1109/WHC.2019.8816163

3. Altınsoy, M.E.: Auditory-tactile interaction in virtual environments. Ph.D. thesis, Ruhr-Universität Bochum, Aachen (2005)

4. Altinsoy, M.E., Merchel, S.: Electrotactile feedback for handheld devices with touch screen and simulation of roughness. IEEE Trans. Haptics **5**(1), 6–13 (2012). https://doi.org/10.1109/TOH.2011.56

5. Android Developers: DisplayMetrics (2019). https://developer.android.com/reference/android/util/DisplayMetrics

6. Android Developers: Vibrator (2019). https://developer.android.com/reference/android/os/Vibrator

7. Apple Inc.: 3D Touch - User Interaction - iOS - Human Interface Guidelines - Apple Developer (2019). https://developer.apple.com/design/human-interface-guidelines/ios/user-interaction/3d-touch/

8. ASTM D1388–18: Standard test method for stiffness of fabrics. Technical report, ASTM International, West Conshohocken, PA (2018). https://doi.org/10.1520/D1388-18

9. Brooks, T.L.: Telerobotic response requirements. In: 1990 IEEE International Conference on Systems, Man, and Cybernetics Conference Proceedings, pp. 113–120. IEEE (1990). https://doi.org/10.1109/ICSMC.1990.142071

10. Clement, J.: Global mobile retail commerce share 2021. https://www.statista.com/statistics/806336/mobile-retail-commerce-share-worldwide/

11. Dennis, S.: The Ticking Time Bomb of E-commerce Returns, February 2018. https://www.forbes.com/sites/stevendennis/2018/02/14/the-ticking-time-bomb-of-e-commerce-returns/

12. Douglas L.J.: Decimation-in-Time (DIT) Radix-2 FFT. OpenStax CNX (2006)

13. Hatch, K.L.: Textile Science. West Publishing Company, Minneapolis (1993)

14. ISO International Standard Organization: Geometrical Product Specifications (GPS) - Surface Texture: Profile Method - Terms, Definitions and Surface Texture Parameters. No. ISO 4287 (1997)

15. ISO International Standard Organization: Textiles - Tests for Colour Fastness - Part A01: General Principles of Testing. No. ISO 105-A01 (2010)

16. Porter, J.: Meet the minds behind Nintendo Switch's HD Rumble tech (2017). https://www.techradar.com/news/meet-the-minds-behind-nintendo-switchs-hd-rumble-tech

17. Kaaresoja, T., Hoggan, E., Anttila, E.: Playing with tactile feedback latency in touchscreen interaction: two approaches. In: Campos, P., Graham, N., Jorge, J., Nunes, N., Palanque, P., Winckler, M. (eds.) INTERACT 2011. LNCS, vol. 6947, pp. 554–571. Springer, Heidelberg (2011). https://doi.org/10.1007/978-3-642-23771-3_42

18. Kaczmarek, K., Webster, J., Bach-y-Rita, P., Tompkins, W.: Electrotactile and vibrotactile displays for sensory substitution systems. IEEE Trans. Biomed. Eng. **38**(1), 1–16 (1991). https://doi.org/10.1109/10.68204

19. Kern, T.A.: Entwicklung Haptischer Geräte: Ein Einstieg für Ingenieure. Springer, Heidelberg (2009). https://doi.org/10.1007/978-3-540-87644-1

20. Krzywinski, S., Pietsch, K., Boll, J., Alma, A., Martin, C., Rataj, C.: Advances in the field of digitalization by multimodal inspection of textiles - digital haptics. In: Proceedings of the 19th World Textile Conference-AUTEX 2019 (2019)

21. MacKenzie, I.S., Ware, C.: Lag as a determinant of human performance in interactive systems. In: Proceedings of the INTERACT 1993 and CHI 1993 Conference on Human Factors in Computing Systems, CHI 1993, pp. 488–493. ACM, Amsterdam (1993). https://doi.org/10.1145/169059.169431
22. Magnenat-Thalmann, N., et al.: From physics-based simulation to the touching of textiles: the HAPTEX project. Int. J. Virtual Reality **6**(3), 35–44 (2007)
23. Mäki-Patola, T., Hämäläinen, P.: Latency tolerance for gesture controlled continuous sound instrument without tactile feedback. In: Proceedings of International Computer Music Conference (ICMC), Miami, USA, p. 8 (2004)
24. Mooneghi, S., Saharkhiz, S., Varkiani, S.: Surface roughness evaluation of textile fabrics: a literature review. J. Eng. Fibers Fabr. **9**(2), 1–18 (2014). https://doi.org/10.1177/155892501400900201
25. Sony Mobile: Xperia XZ3 – official website (2019). https://www.sonymobile.com/global-en/products/phones/xperia-xz3/
26. Srinivasan, M.A., Cheng, J.S.: Human performance in controlling normal forces of contact with rigid objects. In: ASME Winter Annual Meeting: Advances in Robotics, Mechatronics and Haptic Interfaces, New Orleans, vol. 49, pp. 119–125 (1993)
27. Steinbach, E., et al.: Haptic codecs for the tactile internet. Proc. IEEE **107**(2), 447–470 (2019). https://doi.org/10.1109/JPROC.2018.2867835
28. Dixon, T.: Good Vibrations: How Apple Dominates The Touch Feedback Game (2019). https://de.ifixit.com/News/16768/apple-taptic-engine-haptic-feedback
29. Texas Instruments: Haptics: Solutions for ERM and LRA Actuators (2013). http://www.ti.com/lit/ml/sszb151/sszb151.pdf
30. Workman, J.E.: Fashion consumer groups, gender, and need for touch. Clothing Text. Res. J. **28**(2), 126–139 (2010). https://doi.org/10.1177/0887302X09356323

One-Handed Character Input Method for Smart Glasses

Toshimitsu Tanaka(✉), Yuri Shibata, and Yuji Sagawa

Department of Information Engineering, Faculty of Science and Technology, Meijo University, Shiogamaguchi 1-501, Tenpaku-ku, Nagoya 468-8502, Japan
toshitnk@meijo-u.ac.jp

Abstract. A character input method optimized for smart glasses is presented. The user grabs the input device with one hand and taps or strokes with the thumb. The entered text is displayed on the smart glass. A dynamic input guide is also provided to help users enter characters. The feature of this method is that the user can enter characters without looking at the fingertip. This allows the user to enter text while paying attention to the surroundings. Characters are selected by the movement of the thumb, so when a user enters text on a crowded street, people around him/her will not notice. Of course, the entered text will not be peeped.

Japanese hiragana and alphanumeric characters can be entered in each mode. One character is entered in two steps. In the first step, a group of 5 characters is selected by slide-in. This is a stroke from outside to inside the input area. In the second step, one character in the group is selected by a tap or a stroke.

In experiments, the average input speed for beginners was 21.4 [CPM] after using 15.5 min. The error rate was about 6%, but many misoperations occurred. These misoperations were mainly caused by determining the position of the fingertip by the feel of the touch. To reduce them, we shown an alternative to slide-in strokes. In addition, we have presented how to apply the proposed method to European languages.

Keywords: Character input · Smart glasses · One-hand operation · Non-visual · Mobile

1 Introduction

Recently, smart glasses, which are optical see-through type head mounted displays, are on the market. Smart glasses provide a large virtual screen in a mobile environment. Because the screen size is much larger than a smartphone, users can see more information at once. However, in order to enter characters in the posture shown in Fig. 1 (natural posture when walking on a street or riding urban traffic), a method that can be operated without looking at the finger is required.

We have developed a character input method named SliT [1] for smart watches. This method works on very small touch screens. When executed on a smartphone, it can be operated reliably within the reach of the thumb while grabbing the smartphone. Therefore, by optimizing SliT for blind operation, we will develop a character input method that does not require looking at a finger.

© Springer Nature Switzerland AG 2020
S. Yamamoto and H. Mori (Eds.): HCII 2020, LNCS 12184, pp. 393–406, 2020.
https://doi.org/10.1007/978-3-030-50020-7_28

Fig. 1. An example of posture when using the proposed method.

2   Related Researches

Many methods and devices have been developed for entering text in outdoor or moving.

Speech recognition technology commonly used in smart speakers [2–4] is a typical method of entering phrases without using hands. It is a standard input method in car navigation systems. But unfortunately, speaking in a crowd is probably heard by the people around, so privacy is not protected. Depending on the location and the situation, it is required to be quiet. Furthermore, it is difficult to correct sentences already entered using only voice commands.

Methods using gestures are available on mobile. However, in the method of drawing letters in the space by moving the arm, there is a risk that the arm hits the people around. Some methods require devices such as glove type [5] or ring type [6, 7] to detect movement. Cameras are required for methods based on image processing. Users need to carry these devices.

In virtual reality systems, several text input methods have been developed in which the user selects keys on the screen keyboard with finger or hand gestures [8–10]. These methods measure the finger position with a game controller or depth camera, so these devices must be carried on when using the methods outdoors. When using a camera, it is also necessary to take measures against outdoor backgrounds and lighting. Another problem is that the virtual keyboard takes up a lot of screen space.

There have been proposed methods of projecting a virtual keyboard to the back of the user's hand [11] or projecting it on the arm [12]. However, it is necessary to use both hands to enter characters in these ways. Devices to measure the position of fingers are also needed.

The methods of detecting the position of the thumb by attaching touch sensors to other fingers [13, 14] can be operated with one hand. The method of attaching the micro touch panel to the fingertip [15] is the same. However, the sensor-attached hand is not suitable for grabbing anything. The sensor can get in the way, but it is not practical to attach it every time before entering text.

A plate-type device named Tap Strap [16] selects a character based on the vibration of each finger. The device can be operated with one hand, but requires a flat plate to tap. It is also necessary to learn the finger combinations to tap that is defined to each character.

Several methods [17–19] specify the character from wrist orientation and rotation. These are also one-handed operations, but as the number of input characters increases, the user's wrist becomes quite tired. In addition, users need to learn the wrist movements assigned to each character.

We think the following functions are necessary for the character input system for smart glasses. The system must be able to operate in all situation of standing, sitting, and on the move. And it must be operable with one hand. This is because the user often must hold the bag or the handrail of the vehicle with the other hand. Small devices that are easy to carry are suitable for mobile use. Since small movements are not noticeable, it is desirable that the device can be operated with a finger. In addition, in order to concentrate on what is displayed on the smart glass, it is desirable that the position of the finger need not be visually confirmed. If these functions are fulfilled, you can enter text with your hand in your coat pocket without being noticed by the surrounding people. We have developed such a system by improving SliT to be operated without looking at the fingertips.

3   Character Input Method SliT for Smartwatches

Japanese text includes Kanji, Hiragana, Katakana, alphabets, numbers, and symbols. Kanji and Katakana characters are usually converted from Hiragana characters. The remaining characters must be entered directly, using a keyboard for example.

In SliT, users enter Hiragana or alphanumeric characters by switching input modes. As shown in Table 1, both characters are divided into groups of 5 characters each. Each group of Hiragana is a row of the Japanese syllabary table. Each member is specified by a column in the table. The alphabet is grouped in alphabetical order by 5 characters each. The numbers are divided into two groups: 0–4 and 5–9.

Each character is selected in two steps due to reduce the number of keys. Select one group in the first step and one character from the members of the group in the second step. Figure 2(a) shows the display before starting character input. The left, top, and right edges of the screen are each split into two segments, and two character-groups are assigned to each segment. In Hiragana mode, the names of two groups, such as "あ か", are written to the segment. Here, the first character of each group is used as the group name. In alphanumeric mode, the range of alphabets assigned to the segment is displayed. Because two groups are assigned to one segment, the range is 10 characters such as a–j. The bottom edge is divided into three parts to assign Backspace (BS), Space (SP), and Enter (ENT).

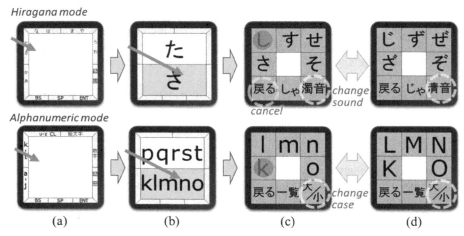

Fig. 2. Character selection. One character is entered by the following operations. (a) Slide-in your finger in from where the group name you want to select is written. (b) Select a group at the position where you release your finger. (c) Tap to select a character. (d) If necessary, tap the cell at the bottom right to change to voiced, semi-voiced, uppercase or lowercase. (Color figure online)

Table 1. Grouping of Hiragana and alphanumeric characters. 5 characters are grouped together. First the group is selected, then the members of the group. **CL** in this table means *Caps Lock*.

						Group (selected in the 1st step)											
					Hiragana mode								*Alphanumeric mode*				
		あ	か	さ	た	な	は	ま	や	ら	わ	a	f	k	p	u	z	0	5
Member (2nd)	い	き	し	ち	に	ひ	み	ー	り	。	b	g	l	q	v	CL	1	6
	う	く	す	つ	ぬ	ふ	む	ゆ	る	を	c	h	m	r	w	.	2	7
	え	け	せ	て	ね	へ	め		れ	、	d	i	n	s	x	,	3	8
	お	こ	そ	と	の	ほ	も	よ	ろ	ん	e	j	o	t	y	-	4	9

The user selects one segment in the slide-in. Slide-in is an operation of sliding the finger touching the outside of the screen inward. As the slide-in passes through one segment, the screen is split into two regions, each of which displays one of the two groups assigned to the segment as shown in Fig. 2(b). In Hiragana mode, the name of the group is written. This is because it is very easy for Japanese to understand the member characters from this group name. In alphanumeric mode, all characters are written. This is because people not unfamiliar with English sometimes take time to recall the characters between the first and last character. When the finger moves into one region, its background turns green. By leaving the finger from the screen, the group written in the region is selected.

Immediately, a keypad for member selection is displayed, as shown in Fig. 2(c). The five characters that are members of the selected group are displayed in the upper and middle cells, so the user taps to select one. If the user makes a mistake in selecting a group, tap the bottom left cell to cancel.

Some Hiragana characters have voiced, semi-voiced, or lowercase variations. Table 2 shows the variations. These can be selected after changing the display by tapping the bottom right cell in Fig. 2(c). Similarly, in alphanumeric mode, use the bottom right cell to change to uppercase, as shown in Fig. 2(d). This change is only valid for this input. To always use uppercase letters, select CL to toggle the default.

Table 2. Voiced, semi-voiced, and lowercase characters in Hiragana. These selections are available after tapping the bottom right cell of the member selection to change the display.

	Group							
type	L	V	V	V	L	V	SV	L
Member	ぁ	が	ざ	だ		ば	ぱ	ゃ
	ぃ	ぎ	じ	ぢ		び	ぴ	
	ぅ	ぐ	ず	づ	っ	ぶ	ぷ	ゅ
	ぇ	げ	ぜ	で		べ	ぺ	
	ぉ	ご	ぞ	ど		ぼ	ぽ	ょ

type	*meaning*
V	Voiced sound
SV	Semi-voiced sound
L	Lowercase

4 Proposed Method

A small smartphone that can be grasped by hand is used as an input device. Touch operation is performed with the thumb. The touch screen of the smartphone is covered with a partially cut plastic sheet as shown in Fig. 3, so that the position of the fingertip can be determined by tactile sensation. The thickness of the sheet is 1 [mm]. So that touch operation can be accepted only at the openings.

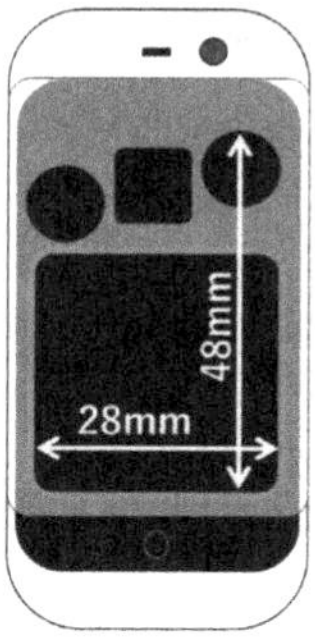

Fig. 3. Cover design

Fig. 4. A simulation image that displays an input guide on a smart glass.

Stroke gestures are performed within the large square opening. The functions assigned to the three small openings are selected with a tap. The shape of the central opening is square and the others are circular. This difference in shape is so that the three openings can be tactilely distinguished.

The cover shown in Fig. 3 is for right-handed. The vertical position of the small opening increases to the right. This is to reduce bending and stretching when turning the thumb to select the opening. For left-handed users, the cover reversed the frontside and backside is used.

An input guide showing the functions or character groups assigned to each area is displayed on the smart glasses to assist the user. Figure 4 is a simulation image of the input guide. This guide image is in the standby state before starting character input. The guide image changes according to the input stage.

The operation of the proposed method is an improvement of the operation of SliT so that the user can operate without looking at the finger. Therefore, like SliT, one character is entered in two steps. First select a group of characters, then select one character in the group.

Groups are selected by slide-in. The slide-in is performed from the surround of the large square opening in Fig. 3 to inside. It can be perceived by the tactile sensation of the fingertip which corner of the square is near of the fingertip. From this, the right or left side of the edge can be distinguished. The upper or lower side of the edge also is distinguished in the same.

The slide-in strokes are identified with only the start and end positions. So that, as shown in Fig. 5, the diagonal stroke of SliT can be replaced with a L-shaped stroke along two connected edges. The horizontal or vertical stroke can be replaced with a straight stroke along one edge. Therefore, by tracing edges, the slide-in strokes can be performed without looking at the fingertips.

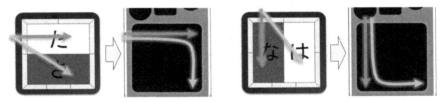

Fig. 5. Difference of slide-in strokes in the proposed method and SliT. Diagonal strokes are replaced by L-shaped strokes along the edges.

On the guide image in Fig. 4, each edge of the large square is split into two segments and name of two groups are written there. It is the same of SliT. However, Backspace (BS), Space (SP), and Enter (ENT) are each assigned to three small openings above a large square. They are selected by tapping. On the input guide, they are displayed side by side at the top. The assignment of these three functions are different from SliT. The reason is that it is difficult to correctly distinguish between the left, right, and center of the edge only by the tactile sensation of the finger.

Figure 6 shows the operation of entering one character. At the first, one group is selected by the slide-in stroke. The stroke displayed in the top of column (b) selects the "さ" group in Hiragana mode, group k–o in alphanumeric mode. This group selection is the same as SliT.

However the choice of members is different. The input guide displays the first member of the selected group in the center of the large square. Tap the large opening to

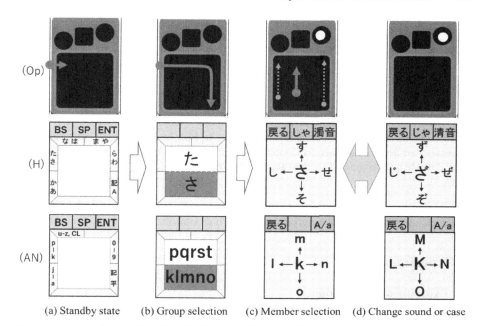

(a) Standby state   (b) Group selection   (c) Member selection   (d) Change sound or case

Fig. 6. A series of operations for selecting one character. The upper row shows the operations, and the middle and lower rows show the guide images in Hiragana mode and alphanumeric mode, respectively.

select this character. Other members appear on the left, top, right, and bottom of the square, according to the order in the group. Each is selected with a stroke in the direction indicated.

Taps are valid anywhere within the large square. Strokes are distinguished only by the direction in which the fingertip moves, regardless of the touch position. Therefore, the three strokes displayed in the image at the top of column (c) are equivalent. In Hiragana mode, select "す" by this stroke. In alphanumeric mode, select "m".

The ability to switch between voiced/unvoiced or upper/lower case is assigned to the upper right circular opening. In Hiragana mode, tap to change the sound of the selected group to voiced or semi-voiced, if existing, or change to lowercase. In alphanumeric mode, characters are switched to uppercase or lowercase. This change only applies to this character. When entering the next character, the sound returns to unvoiced. To enter consecutive capital letters in alphanumeric mode, toggle the state by selecting Caps Lock (CL) located after z.

The upper left circular opening is used to cancel the group selection. The center small square opening is only used in Hiragana mode. By tapping it, as shown in Fig. 7, the combinations of two characters are displayed on the guide. Each is the "い" column character of the selected group followed by a lowercase "や", "ゆ", or "よ". By a tap or a stroke, one is selected. These combinations often appear in Japanese sentences. This option is installed to enter them in one operation. Of course, they can also be entered as two characters.

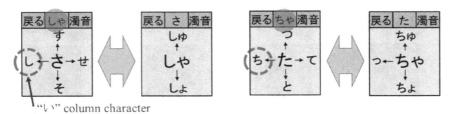

"い" column character

Fig. 7. Function assigned to the central small opening in Hiragana group selection. Change the selectable characters to the characters in the "い"column with the lowercase "や", "ゆ", or "よ" added. And change the guide display to show the assignment.

All operations of the proposed method do not need to visually identify the fingertip. Therefore, characters can be entered without visual confirmation.

5 Experiment

5.1 Experimental Conditions

The system was developed on Windows 7 using Android Studio and the Java language. It was then copied to the smartphone Unihertz Jelly Pro JPRO-03 running Android 7.0. Since the touch screen of JPRO-03 is used as an input device, the cover shown in Fig. 3 is attached to the screen. JPRO-03 is also used as a processing unit. The input system and the evaluation program run there.

The image displayed on the smartphone JPRO-03 is duplicated and displayed on Sony HMZ-T2 via USB-HDMI adapter 500-KC024HD. Sony HMZ-T2 is a non-see-through type HMD that completely covers the user's eyes and makes the surroundings invisible. The reason for using a non-see-through HMD is to eliminate the possibility that the subject will see the finger. The reason for connecting the smartphone and HMD with a cable is to reduce display delay. We tested the wireless connection on both Miracast and Chromecast, but the delay was too long for interaction.

We evaluated the input speed of beginners. Before the experiment, we gave a 5 min presentation on the operating procedure for inputting characters using the system, the meaning of display of the input guide, the experiment procedure, and some attentions. And we asked subjects enter characters as accurately as possible. Each subject sat on a chair in a comfortable position and wore the HMD. After confirming that the subject was unable to see the surroundings, the input device was handed over to the dominant hand. The subject checked the locations of the openings with the touch of his/her thumb. Then the experiment was started.

Subjects enter 5 Hiragana words in one trial. In the experiment, this trial is repeated 10 times every between with a 3 min break. Each trial starts when a subject touches the large opening on the input device. One test word is displayed in hiragana on the HMD screen. The characters entered by the test subject are underlined and appear immediately below the test word. After entering all the characters of the test word, tap the upper right opening to enter. The Enter key is accepted even if the input characters do not match the test word. This completes the input of one word. Then, the next word is displayed. When five words are entered, one trial is completed.

The test words were selected from the word list of the Balanced Corpus of Contemporary Written Japanese (BCCWJ) [20] of the National Institute for Japanese Language and Linguistics. From each of the 4, 5, and 6-letter nouns in Hiragana notation, 100 words were extracted in order of frequency, excluding numbers and quantifiers. Then words which are same in Hiragana notation but different in Kanji notation were merged. Frequency of the merged word is sum of frequency of the original words. Finally, the top 50 words in frequency from each of 4, 5, and 6-letter words were selected.

A total of 150 words were gathered in one list and sorted randomly for each test subject. After that, the list was divided to sets of 5 words from the first. Each set was used at only one trial. Therefore, one subject does not enter the same word twice. A different set of words is used for each test subject.

5.2 Experimental Results

The thin line in Fig. 8 shows the input speed for each subject. The thick blue line is their average. The average input speed of the first trial is about 11 [CPM: characters per min]. It increased with up and down fluctuations, as the trial progressed. In the tenth trial, the average speed reached 21.4 [CPM]. Total trial time averaged 15.5 min.

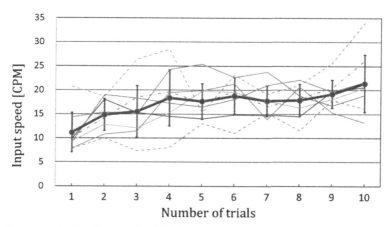

Fig. 8. Input speed of beginners. The thick blue line is the average speed. (Color figure online)

The reason why the average input speed does not increase from the fourth to eighth trials is probably because it took time to get used to this input method. The speed of a person familiar with the method was 41.1 [CPM] (standard deviation is 4.1) in the same experiment, so that, it is may possible to improve the input speed of the subjects by continuing the trials. The input speed of each subject varies greatly. The input speed is not always increasing through ten trials. This result also means that learning this method requires some practice.

Figure 9 shows the Total Error Rate (TER) of each test subject and their average. For each trial, TER is calculated by dividing the sum of the number of incorrect and corrected characters by the sum of the characters of the five words. The thick blue line in Fig. 9 is the average TER. After the fourth trial, it remained below 10%. And it dropped to 4.0% in the tenth trial. The average of TER in the last half is 6.3%. It is not so large, as SliT's TER was 4.7% in the fifth trial. The pattern of the average TER is similar to SliT, but decreases slowly. Compared to the SliT results, the differences between subjects are larger.

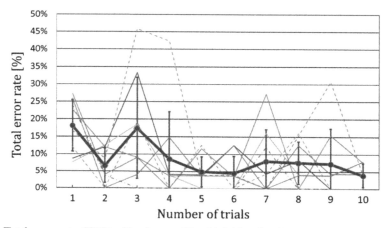

Fig. 9. Total error rate (TER) of beginners. The thick blue line is the average of TER. (Color figure online)

The input speed for beginners using SliT was 28.7 [CPM]. Therefore, the proposed method is 25% slower than SliT. Since the proposed method requires tactile positioning of the finger, a slowdown was expected. However, the experimental results are too slow than expected.

The reason for the slowdown is that there were many unnecessary operations that were canceled before the characters were entered. With the proposed method, if you select the wrong segment in the slide-in, you can cancel it by removing your finger from the touch screen before the background turns green or by returning your finger to the start segment. If you accidentally select the wrong group, you can still cancel by tapping the top left opening (which has been assigned a cancel function). Such operations are not counted as erroneous inputs because no characters have been entered. However, the time spent on these operations slows down the input speed.

The misoperation rate is defined as the total number of unnecessary operations during slide-in and member selection (but no characters entered) divided by the sum of the characters in the five test words. The red line in Fig. 10 is the average of misoperation rate for 8 test subjects. The blue line is the average of the TER displayed for comparison. Unnecessary operations occurred more than three times the number of erroneous characters. Therefore, the reason why the input speed decreased by 25% is presumed to be a high misoperation rate.

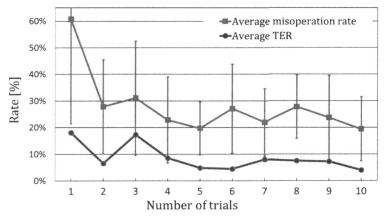

Fig. 10. Average misoperation rate. (Color figure online)

6 Discussion

6.1 Reduction of Misoperations

In order to improve the input speed, unnecessary operations must be reduced. Slide-ins that were canceled because the subjects noticed they started from the wrong segment accounts for 17% of the unnecessary operations for character input. Also, 40% of the unnecessary operations are taps to cancel the selected character group, but most incorrect group selections are caused by starting a slide-in from the wrong place. Thus, half of unnecessary operation is caused by mistakes in finding the start position of the slide-in stroke. This is because it was not easy to select the top/bottom or left/right side of the edge with a fingertip feel.

In a post-experiment interview, some subjects commented that "It was difficult to distinguish between the upper or lower sides of the edge, and the right or left sides". Another subject replied, "Because I am not confident, I checked the position by the display of the input guide immediately after touching and canceled it if it was wrong". Therefore, the solution is to make it easier to select the starting position of the slide-in stroke.

The proposed method uses 12 kinds of slide-in strokes. The strokes connect 6 segments (each 2 segments on 3 edges) to 2 regions. We will replace them by the strokes from each of 4 edges to 3 directions as show in Fig. 11(b). As a result, strokes starting from the wrong location are greatly reduced because each edge is not divided.

The remaining 43% of unnecessary operations are failures in slide-in. The reason is that the thickness of the cover moves the first touch point away from the edge. This can be solved by expanding the area used to judge the start segment of the stroke.

6.2 Extensions for Other Languages

The proposed method supports Hiragana and alphanumeric input. Therefore, users can enter English text using the alphanumeric mode. The system can be provided to those

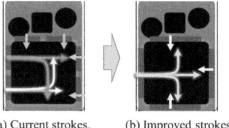

(a) Current strokes.   (b) Improved strokes.

Fig. 11. Improved slide-in strokes to reduce the misoperations.

whose native language is English, simply by changing the input guide language to English. Applying other European languages requires minor changes as described below.

The first way is to add groups of characters that are not included in the Latin alphabet (A–Z, 26 letters) but are needed for each language. As shown in Fig. 6, the right segment on the upper edge is empty. Therefore, two extra groups can be assigned. In addition, one more group can be assigned to the lower segment on the right edge. In Originally the function to switch to Hiragana mode is assigned here, but it is not necessary for European languages. The maximum number of characters that can be added is 15 in 3 groups.

The second way replaces the character set before member selection. The upper center opening is not used for member selection in alphanumeric mode as shown in Fig. 6. Here, we assign the function to add accent marks etc. to the character. For example, three types of accent marks (aigu, grave, and circonflexe), tréma, ç, and œ must been added for French language. These can be associated with the Latin alphabet, so convert from the associated alphabet. Figure 12 shows samples of guide images when this method is applied to a French language. Only group "a–e" has two additional states. Tap the upper center opening to cycle through the three states. Groups "f–j", "k–o", and "u–y" each have one additional state. Tap to switch between normal and additional states. The method for character input is same in all states.

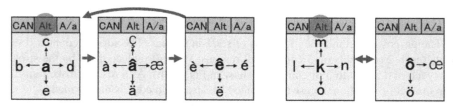

Fig. 12. The method adding characters by switching states. These guide images are examples applied to French. This is just an example. The layout and notation of letters and functions must be determined by a person who is familiar with French.

The first way is easy to implement, but learning where the additional characters are assigned may not be easy. So that, the method is more applicable to the languages with few additional characters, such as Spanish, Dutch, and German. The second way is appropriate when there are relatively many derivative characters, such as French and Portuguese. The input operation is a bit more complicated, but the user can easily select these derived characters by following the input guide.

7   Conclusion

We developed a character input method optimized for smart glasses. The user grabs the input device with one hand and operates by taps or strokes with the thumb. Feature of the method is that users can enter characters without looking their fingertips.

One character is entered in two steps. In the first step, a group of 5 characters is selected by slide-in, which is a stroke from outside to inside the input area. In the second step, one character in the group is selected by a tap or a stroke. Hiragana and alphanumeric characters are selected in each mode. In Hiragana mode, tap to change the characters of the selected group to voiced sound, semi-voiced sound, or lowercase. In alphanumeric mode, lowercase and uppercase are switched in the same way. Therefore, entering such characters is also easy.

In the experiments, the average input speed for beginners was 21.4 [CPM] after using 15.5 min. This speed was about 75% of SliT that is the original method of the proposed method. The cause of the slowdown is a high rate of unnecessary operations. This was caused by determining the position of the fingertip by the feel of the touch. In the discussion section, we shown an alternative to slide-in strokes to reduce unnecessary operations. In addition, we presented two small changes for applying the proposed method to European languages.

References

1. Akita, K., Tanaka, T., Sagawa, Y.: SliT: character input system using slide-in and tap for smartwatches. In: Kurosu, M. (ed.) HCI 2018. LNCS, vol. 10903, pp. 3–16. Springer, Cham (2018). https://doi.org/10.1007/978-3-319-91250-9_1
2. Alexa Voice Service Overview (v20160207). https://developer.amazon.com/docs/alexa-voice-service/api-overview.html. Accessed 16 Dec 2019
3. Use Siri on all your Apple devices. https://support.apple.com/en-us/HT204389. Accessed 16 Dec 2019
4. Google Assistant is better than Alexa or Siri. https://www.cnbc.com/2019/06/19/google-assistant-beats-alexa-and-siri-at-recognizing-medications.html. Accessed 16 Dec 2019
5. Fujitsu Develops Glove-Style Wearable Device. http://www.fujitsu.com/global/about/resources/news/press-releases/2014/0218–01.html. Accessed 16 Dec 2019
6. Ring-Type Wearable Device Enables Users to Write in the Air with Finger. https://journal.jp.fujitsu.com/en/2015/02/10/01/. Accessed 16 Dec 2019
7. Ring Zero. https://logbar.jp/en/index.html. Accessed 16 Dec 2019
8. Grubert, J., Witzani, L., Ofek, E., Pahud, M., Kranz, M., Kristensson, P.O.: Text entry in immersive head-mounted display-based virtual reality using standard keyboards. In: Proceedings of 2018 IEEE Conference on Virtual Reality and 3D User Interfaces, VR, pp. 159–166 (2018)
9. Boletsis, C., Kongsvik, S.: Text input in virtual reality: a preliminary evaluation of the drum-like vr keyboard. Technologies 7(2), 1–31 (2019)

10. Yu, C., Gu, Y., Yang, Z., Yi, X., Luo, H., Shi, Y.: Tap, dwell or gesture?: Exploring head-based text entry techniques for HMDs. In: Proceedings of the 2017 CHI Conference on Human Factors in Computing Systems, pp. 4479–4488 (2017)
11. Haier Asu Smartwatch. https://www.digitaltrends.com/smartwatch-reviews/haier-asu-rev iew/. Accessed 18 Dec 2019
12. NEC develops ARmKeypad Air, a contact-free virtual keyboard for a user's arm. https://www.nec.com/en/press/201607/global_20160713_01.html. Accessed 18 Dec 2019
13. Wong, P., Zhu, K., Fu, H.: FingerT9: leveraging thumb- to-finger interaction for same-side-hand text entry on smartwatches. In: Proceedings of the Conference on Human Factors in Computing Systems, 2018 CHI, p. 178 (2017)
14. Whitmier, E., et al.: DigiTouch: reconfigurable thumb-to-finger input and text entry on head-mounted displays. Proc. ACM Interact. Mob. Wearable Ubiquit. Technol. 1(3), 1–21 (2017)
15. Zheer, X., et al.: TipText: eyes-free text entry on a fingertip keyboard. In: Proceedings of the 32nd ACM Symposium on User Interface Software and Technology, pp. 883–899 (2019)
16. TAP STRAP 2. http://www.tapwithus.com. Accessed 18 Dec 2018
17. Sun, K., Wang, Y., Yu, C., Yan, Y., Wen, H., Shi, Y.: Float: one-handed and touch-free target selection on smartwatches. In: Proceedings of the 2017 CHI Conference on Human Factors in Computing Systems, pp. 692–704 (2017)
18. Gong, J., et al.: WristWhirl: one-handed continuous smartwatch input using wrist gesture. In: Proceedings of the 29th Annual Symposium on User Interface Software and Technology, pp. 861–872 (2016)
19. Gong, J. et al.: WrisText: one-handed text entry on smartwatch using wrist gestures. In: Proceedings of the 2018 CHI Conference on Human Factors in Computing Systems (2018). Paper No. 181
20. The word list of the Balanced Corpus of Contemporary Written Japanese of the National Institute for Japanese Language and Linguistics. http://pj.ninjal.ac.jp/corpus_center/bccwj/en/freq-list.html. Accessed 30 Dec 2019

Health Education VR

Sachiyo Ueda[1]([envelope]), Satoshi Fujisawa[1], Yasushi Ikei[2], and Michiteru Kitazaki[1]

[1] Department of Computer Science and Engineering, Toyohashi University of Technology, 1-1 Hibarigaoka, Tempakucho, Toyohashi-shi, Aichi 441-8580, Japan
ueda@cs.tut.ac.jp
[2] Graduate School of System Design, Tokyo Metropolitan University, 6-6 Asahigaoka, Hino-shi, Tokyo 191-0065, Japan

Abstract. We developed a full-body virtual-presence system in which users crawl to travel within the human body, and gain insight into the structures of digestive organs through visual, tactile, and auditory sensations. Digestive organs (esophagus, stomach, duodenum, small intestine, large intestine, rectum) are created in detail with 3-D images that users could look around using a head-mounted display, and an appropriate feeling of touch is presented to the abdomens and thighs of users by vibrotactile devices. Pressure sensors detect the crawling action of users so that they can travel in the digestive organs while hearing realistic 3-D sounds. Participants felt as if their body turned into digested food and was moving inside another person's body. Participants also felt as if their bodies became smaller. Thus, this system gives users the sensation of a reduced body size and provides a telepresence at improbable locations such as the stomach. Participants enjoyed the experience and were interested in the human body structure and function. This system can serve as an interactive, educational experience by simulating the contents of the human digestive system.

Keywords: Multi-modal sensations · Vibrotactile stimulus · Locomotion interface · Embodied learning

1 Introduction

Health education is important to gain necessary knowledge about one's health and make decisions about health problems. In particular, understanding one's own body structure is the basis for obtaining various kinds of health knowledge. However, the inner human body, such as the digestive organs, is usually a mysterious space for ordinary people. We can neither see nor touch digestive organs in daily life if we are not physicians. Learning about digestive organs through textbooks may not be interesting to most people because the organs cannot be easily visualized. Anatomical models of the human body have been used to visualize organs. Recently, virtual reality (VR) contents that provide experience and opportunities of looking around from inside the human body have been provided. With these VR contents, you can travel and look around inside the kidneys [1]. You can also get inside of Björk's mouth when she is singing [2]. In addition, an augmented reality (AR) system was developed to help visualize the anatomical organs and bones

© Springer Nature Switzerland AG 2020
S. Yamamoto and H. Mori (Eds.): HCII 2020, LNCS 12184, pp. 407–416, 2020.
https://doi.org/10.1007/978-3-030-50020-7_29

of an actual human body [3]. Using the system, people can view the outer surface of organs such as the lungs, heart, and stomach. These VR and AR systems involve an active and interactive experience, but they are limited to visual experience and serve as a realistic image-based anatomical model of the human body. People cannot touch organs. To understand a living and moving body, however, it will be effective to experience it not only through visual but also tactile sensation. In this study, we aimed to develop a full-body telepresence system in which users crawl to travel within the human body and study structures of digestive organs by visual, tactile, and auditory sensations.

Synesthesia Suit [4] and Teslasuit [5] used methods of presenting tactile stimuli to the whole body. In this study, a similar method of presenting multiple oscillators by manipulating the time difference and intensity difference was used, but the tactile stimuli were simply presented using only four oscillators. Users looked around the inside of the digestive tract, which was 3-D modeled on a head-mounted display (HMD), and traveled the human body by crawling. Vibration stimuli were presented to the abdomen and thighs, and a heartbeat sound was presented according to the user's current position inside the body. Crawling was used because we thought that active movement would increase user enjoyment. We expect that experiencing the process of being digested in the body as food would help us to understand the digestive function as our affairs. We also expected that the experience of combining visual, auditory, and tactile sensations would enhance reality and lead the good learning effect about the inner human body.

2   System Overview

The developed system consisted of a head-mounted display (HMD; Oculus DK2, 960 (width) × 1024 (height) pixel for each eye, 90 × 110 degrees of visual angle), four vibrotactile transducers (AcouveLab Vp408), a set of headphones (Bose quiet comfort 2), a computer (Dell XPS8900), a USB pre-amplifier (BEHRINGER FCA1616), a power amplifier (BEHRINGER EPQ304), four pressure sensors (Interlink electronics FSR408), and a microcontroller (Arduino Uno Rev3) (see Fig. 1). The computer (DELL XPS8900, Core i7-6700 2.4 GHz, 16 GB RAM, GPU AMD Radeon R9-370) controlled the entire system with software developed using Unity 5.

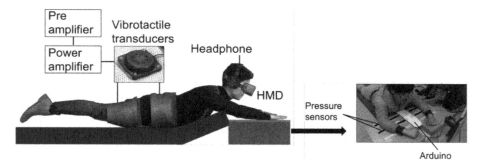

Fig. 1. Schematic of the apparatus

3   Contents

Users traveled through the digestive system of the human body as if they became food. At the beginning of the simulation, users were eaten by a person, and taken into his mouth (see Fig. 2). Then, the scene changed into the inside of the human body and users moved forward through digestive organs by crawling on a mat embedded with pressure sensors (see Fig. 3). They could look around inside of the digestive organs and move at their own pace. Some 3-D visual images showing each digestive organ (esophagus, stomach, duodenum, small intestine, large intestine, rectum) were presented to match the users' forward movement (see Fig. 4). The vibrator presented the tactile stimuli of rubbing the body, and sound accompanying movement was also presented from the headphones. The visual images and vibrations were different for different digestive organs, and they could learn their properties through vision and touch. 3-D sounds were arbitrarily created rather than relying on actual sounds because we could ascertain what the inside of organs sounded like. However, the sounds were made to enhance the different sensations of digestive organs. Moreover, simulated heartbeats were presented as auditory and tactile stimuli. The amplitude of the sound of heartbeats and touch increased as the user got closer to the heart. Users did not only move but also changed their appearance because they were food being digested, and they were able to see it from a subjective viewpoint (see Fig. 4).

Fig. 2. In the first scene, users were eaten.

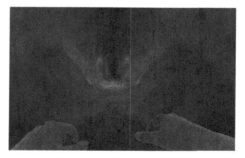

Fig. 3. Crawling inside of a digestive organ.

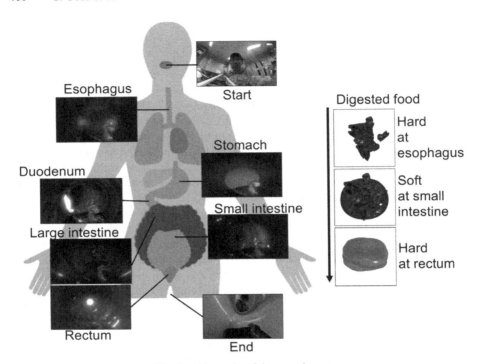

Fig. 4. Schematic of the experiences

3.1 Modeling of Organs

Digestive organs (esophagus, stomach, duodenum, small intestine, large intestine, rectum) were created in detail with 3-D models based on medical literature. However, the model did not reproduce details such as intestinal flora and villus and emphasized the surface shape and texture (see Fig. 5). The animation represented the peristalsis of the digestive organs and reproduced the specific movement of each digestive organ. We also reproduced the following movement to reproduce the characteristic phenomena occurring in each digestive organ.

Esophagus. Peristalsis is performed to transport the ingested food, causing the mouth to contract and the stomach to relax.

Stomach. First, large peristalsis is performed from the greater curvature to the pylorus. After that, the pyloric sphincter opens, and the pylorus performs fine peristalsis to send food to the duodenum. The inside of the organ is filled with gastric juice.

Duodenum. Bile is secreted from Vater's papilla. Moreover, digestive activity due to bile takes place, and feedback such as tactile stimulation starts to change.

Small Intestine. The segmentation contractions (movements that produce a constriction in the small intestine to create segmentation) and pendulum movements (movements in which the intestinal tract expands and contracts like a bellows) are performed to absorb nutrients from food. In addition, liquefaction of food due to digestion occurs.

Large Intestine. Performs the same movements as the small intestine, but performs only peristaltic movements as it approaches the anus. In addition, the solidification of digests starts and it becomes a stool.

Rectum. Stools are excreted by relaxation of the anal sphincter and contraction of the rectum wall.

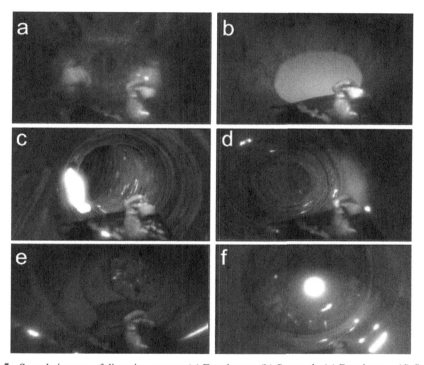

Fig. 5. Sample images of digestive organs. (a) Esophagus, (b) Stomach, (c) Duodenum, (d) Small intestine, (e) large intestine, (f) rectum.

3.2 Detection of Creeping Movement

To detect the creeping movement of the arms, two tape-type pressure sensors (Interlink Electronics FSR408) were placed in parallel on the left half and the right half of the mat, for each front and rear, for a total of four (see Fig. 6a). A similar locomotion device was proposed for navigating in a virtual world [6]. Two pressure sensors were bonded on two thick mats (50 × 41 × 6cm), which were independent on the left and right, and thin cushioning materials (1.5 cm thick) were pasted on them (see Fig. 6b, c). We put another thin cushioning material further forward as a mark to place the user's wrist. A thin, slippery material (Lycra® stretch mat) was placed on the surface to make the arm easier to move (see Fig. 6c). Users were told to move their arm from the upper protrusion to the lower protrusion.

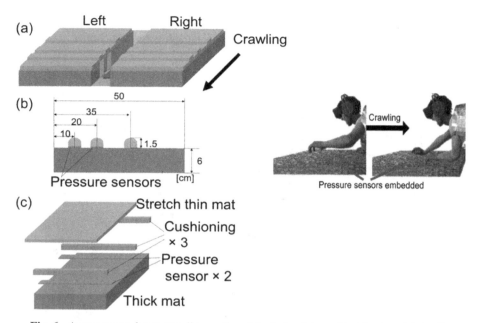

Fig. 6. Apparatus to detect crawling motion. (a) whole picture, (b) side view, (c) details.

The pressure sensor could measure the pressure applied anywhere on the tape between 0.1 and 10 kg. Users put the forearm on the two pressure sensors located in front and rear. The right and left arms were measured independently to determine the crawling movements. The outputs of the front and rear sensors were normalized to values from 0 to 1. If the front sensor position is 1 and the rear sensor position is 2, the center of gravity position M can be calculated by the following formula.

$$M = \frac{\text{Front sensor value} \times 1 + \text{Rear sensor value} \times 2}{\text{Front sensor value} + \text{Rear sensor value}} \tag{1}$$

The value of M ranges from 1 to 2. If the value of M is 1, the center of gravity is located directly above the front sensor, and if the value of M is 2, the center of gravity is located directly above the rear sensor. The value of M indicates where the center of gravity lies between the front and rear sensors. Crawling was detected by the sensors for the users' left and right hands independently, through a sequence in which the center of gravity is closer to the front sensor than the midpoint (M < 1.5), followed by the center of gravity moving to close to the rear sensor (M > 1.5). The judgment of the position of the center of gravity was made at 75 Hz frequency, but in to stabilize the operation, the average value of the immediately preceding 15 frames (200 ms) was used.

Each time it was judged as having performed a creeping movement, users experienced moving forward a preset distance in each digestive organ. During this, the movement accompanying the viewpoint change (i.e., optic flow and vibration) was presented. As an example, Fig. 7 shows the movement path in the duodenum. When the creeping movement was detected with either the left or right arm, users could move forward. There was no movement or swing to the left or right.

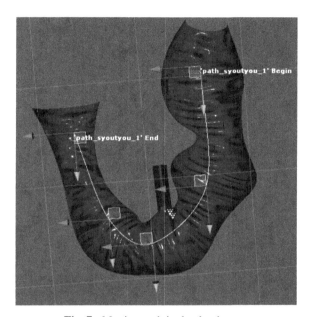

Fig. 7. Moving path in the duodenum.

3.3   Presentation of Visual, Haptic, and Auditory Stimuli

The 3-D models of the digestive organs described above were presented as visual stimuli on the HMD with binocular disparities as 3-D images, and users could look around scenes by moving their heads while both stationary and moving. Head motions were monitored by the HMD's gyro sensor sampling at 1 kHz, and reflected on visual images at 75 Hz.

Tactile stimuli were presented on users' abdomens and thighs by the vibrotactile transducers through the multi-channel audio pre-amplifier and the power amplifier for two s per movement (see Fig. 8). The vibration of the abdominal vibrator gradually increased for 1 s and reached the maximum value, and then decreased linearly in the next 1 s. The thigh vibrator started to vibrate at the maximum value after 1 s, and attenuated over 2 s. This vibration gave a feeling of movement to users. The vibration frequency changed according to the digestive organs experienced (see Fig. 9). The digested food, which is the user is initially solid and somewhat hard. Then, it becomes soft as a result of digestion in the stomach and small intestine. It hardens as a stool while it moves from the latter half of the large intestine o the anus (see Fig. 3). High-frequency vibration was presented when digested food is hard, and low-frequency vibration was presented when digested food is soft, considering digestive organ characteristics. For example, in the small intestine, a tactile stimulus as if crawls on mud was presented because the food was digested and becomes like porridge.

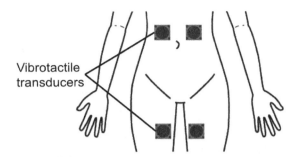

Fig. 8. Vibration locations.

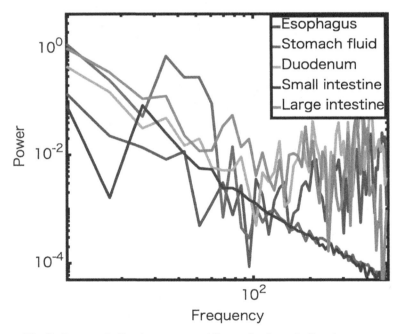

Fig. 9. Presented vibration patterns while moving in each digestive organ.

At the same time, the same frequency 3-D sound was presented through the headphones. In addition, the heartbeat sound was always presented. Distance from the heart to the current user position was calculated, and the beating sound was presented louder when closer and lower when far away.

4   Experience and Impression

We performed a preliminary demonstration at IVRC 2016 (The 24th International collegiate Virtual Reality Contest) [7]. About 100 people participated. Participants could move through the esophagus, stomach, duodenum, small intestine, large intestine, and rectum, and learn about them in a fun visual and tactile experience. Almost every participant was able to experience it to the end in about 5–10 min. They felt as if their own body became small and were moving inside of a person's bodily organs. Thus, this system would give us sensations of a change in one's own body size and a telepresence at improbable spaces.

Many participants reported the impressions that the experience was fun and they felt like actually moving inside the internal organs. There were also impressions or opinions such as "I was interested in the body structure through this system," "I want to experience the internal organs other than the digestive organs," and "It would be interesting to have feedback when eating and excreting." These responses suggest that our VR system might contribute to the improvement of learning motivation. Also, some opinions evaluate elaborateness such as "reproducing the movement of peristalsis accurately and it can be used as learning content". Also, some people opined that asking for further elaboration such as "reproducing small parts such as intestinal flora will make it more suitable for learning". On the other hand, there was an opinion that "I felt less resistance because it was more deformed than the actual internal organs." It will be necessary to balance the elaboration of models and sensory stimuli according to individual interests and knowledge levels. This system may serve as an interactive educational program of the inner human body.

5   Conclusion

The users enjoyed the experience and gave us the opinion that our VR system would be useful for learning. This suggests the possibility that our system is effective as educational content. In the education field, it is pointed out that linking knowledge with students' experiences facilitate their deeper understanding of learning contents. By applying multisensory stimuli, our system can provide a subjective experience of becoming the food that is digested and traveling inside the human body. This may help people to link their experience to knowledge of the structure and function of the internal organs of the human body, and encourage intellectual curiosity to human body and health. However, verification of the learning effect is a future topic.

Acknowledgement. This work was partly supported by Grant-in-Aid for Scientific Research (A) (#18H04118), Grant-in-Aid for Challenging Exploratory Research (#16K12477), and Inami JIZAI BODY Project, JST ERATO (# JPMJER1701).

References

1. NHK Special "Human Body" VR Pee Adventure. https://www.nhk.or.jp/vr/jintai/kidney/. Accessed 12 Jan 2020

2. Kanda, J.: Mouth Mantra VR (2016). http://www.bjork.fr/Mouth-Mantra-VR. Accessed 12 Jan 2020
3. Curiscope Virtuali-Tee, The Ultimate Way to Learn About the Body! https://www.kickstarter.com/projects/curiscope/virtualitee. Accessed 23 Nov 2016
4. Konishi, Y., Hanamitsu, N., Outram, B., Minamizawa, K., Mizuguchi, T., Sato, A.: Synesthesia suit: the full body immersive experience. In: Proceedings of 2016 ACM SIGGRAPH, VR Village, no. 20 (2016)
5. Teslasuit. https://teslasuit.io/. Accessed 12 Jun 2019
6. Couvillion, W., Lopez, R., Ling, J.: Navigation by walking around: using the pressure mat to move in virtual worlds. Stud. Health Technol. Inform. **85**, 103–109 (2002)
7. Fujisawa, S., Kondo, R., Okamoto, R., Team Bento Box: Food journey. In: Proceedings of the 24th International Collegiate Virtual Reality Contest, Tokyo, Japan (2017)

Feedback Control of Middle Finger MP Joint Using Functional Electrical Stimulation Based on the Electrical Stimulus Intensity-Joint Torque Relation Model

Kyosuke Watanabe[✉], Makoto Oka, and Hirohiko Mori

Tokyo City University, 1-28-1 Tamazutsumi, Setagaya-ku, Tokyo, Japan
{g1881852,moka,hmori}@tcu.ac.jp

Abstract. In this paper, we propose methods to control detailed finger movements by FES (functional electrical stimulation). It is difficult to control the detailed finger movement because the relationship between the electrical stimulus intensity applied to each muscle and the finger joint angle is discrete. However, since the relationship between the electrical stimulus intensity and the joint torque is close to a linear relationship, the relationship between the electrical stimulus intensity and the joint torque can be modeled by the two-piece linear regression model. Then, we propose a method to control the finger joint angle by adjusting the ratio of flexion torque to extension torque by PID control. Though, using the proposed method, it was possible to control to static target joint angle with high accuracy, it was necessary to correct the model by trial and error for some failed controls in some subjects. Therefore, we also propose a new method that can be modeled uniquely based on the relationship between the electrical stimulus intensity to both muscles and the joint angle. This model does not require trial and error model correction and can be modeled routinely. The new proposed model enable to control the finger to static target joint angle with high accuracy, to reduce individual differences, and to reduce the failure probability.

Keywords: Motor learning · Functional electrical stimulation · PID control

1 Introduction

In our dairy life, we often have opportunities to give some tips of finger motion or movement to others, such as how to use a pencil, sports, and so on. In such situations, we usually teach finger movements to others using explicit knowledge such as words and documents. On the other hand, human learn the movements through feeding back various information related to body movements, and there are various types of feedback. Among them, it is said that the most important one is to be sensitive to internal feedback, which is the feedback from autoreceptor, such as muscle receptors, skin receptors, and joint receptors [1]. Since it is difficult, however, to make human notice the internal feedback using only explicit knowledge, it is effective to teach the finger movements by directly performing the learning target movements using external stimuli.

S. Yamamoto and H. Mori (Eds.): HCII 2020, LNCS 12184, pp. 417–434, 2020.
https://doi.org/10.1007/978-3-030-50020-7_30

As a method of performing finger movement by external stimuli, FES (functional electrical stimulation) that causes body movements by applying electrical stimulus to muscles and nerves is often used [2]. The mechanism of body movements induced by FES is similar to voluntary body movements, and it is a method that makes it easy to notice internal feedback. Some studies have shown that electrical stimulation to muscles is effective in learning body movements [3, 4]. In addition, FES by the surface electrode method does not require surgery, so it can be used easily, and the device can be reduced the size and weight. Therefore, it is thought that if the detailed movements of the finger joint can be controlled by FES, learning various finger movements can be performed effectively.

Handa et al. [5] succeeded the finger movements such as grasping a cup by FES using the embedded electrode method, but have not been considered how to control the joint angle to arbitrary angle. Furthermore, since it is difficult to selectively stimulate muscles and nerves by the surface electrode method, it is difficult to control the detailed movements of the finger joint.

2   Related Works

Tamaki et al. [6] developed a device that applies electrical stimulus to muscles located on the forearm involved in fingers and wrist joint movements by the surface electrode method. By using the device, 11 joints can be moved with other joints, and 5 joints that can be moved independently. However, it could not control the finger joint to an arbitrary angle.

Watanabe et al. [7] constructed PID control (Proportional-Integral-Differential Controller) that regard electrical stimulus intensity to four muscles involved in wrist joint movements as input, and regard joint angles of two degrees of freedom (palm, dorsiflexion/radius, ulnar flexion) as output. By this method, they could control the wrist joint angle with high accuracy. However, could not apply the finger joints.

There are roughly two factors that make it difficult to control the detailed movements of the finger joints by FES. One is that the moment of inertia of the finger is extremely small, and the other is that the finger joint angles in no electrical stimulus given to the fingers are not uniquely determined.

The smaller the moment of inertia of the object is, the higher the rotational angular velocity with respect to the torque acting on the object becomes. Since the moment of inertia of the finger is very small compared to other body parts, the joint angular velocity is faster even if the muscle contraction generated by electrical stimulus is very small. In PID control, the input-output relationship must be linear, but the relationship between the electrical stimulus intensity applied to a single muscle and the joint angle is discrete (Fig. 1). Therefore, if the input is the electrical stimulus intensity and the output is the joint angle, control becomes difficult.

Watanabe et al. [7] adopted the CHR method (Chien-Hrones-Reswick Tuning Method) as a PID control to adjust the parameters. The CHR method is a method to determine the PID control parameters based on the degree of joint angle change when a ramp stimulus is given to target muscle alone, the time constant and time delay when a step stimulus is given to each stimulus target muscle alone, and the sampling period of

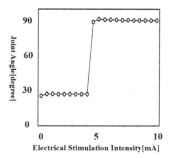

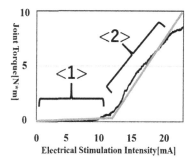

Fig. 1. Relationship between electrical stimulus intensity and finger joint angle (vertical axis: joint angle [degree], horizontal axis: electrical stimulus intensity [mA])

Fig. 2. Relationship between electrical stimulus intensity and middle finger MP joint torque and two-piece linear regression model (vertical axis: joint torque [N * m], horizontal axis: electrical stimulus intensity [mA], black solid line: measured joint torque, gray solid line: two-piece linear regression model, <1>: Joint torque minute band, <2>: Joint torque increase band)

the control system. In ramp stimulation method mentioned above, the electrical stimulus intensity increases over time, and, on the other hand, the step stimulus method is the one to give electrical stimulus suddenly with an electrical stimulus intensity that causes sufficient joint angle change from the state where no electrical stimulus is applied to muscle. However, the degree of joint angle changes when ramp stimulus is applied and the time constant when step stimulus is applied vary greatly depending on the situation, because the joint angle of finger in no electrical stimulus vary greatly depending on the situation. Therefore, it is necessary to develop a new PID control parameter adjustment method other than the CHR method.

3   The Purpose of This Study

The purpose of this paper is establishing a new method to control the middle finger MP joint (Metacarpophalangeal joint) to the static target joint angle by FES using the surface electrode method with the flexor digitorum muscle and extensor digitorum muscle as stimulus target muscles. If high accuracy control of the middle finger MP joint becomes possible, it should be possible to extend to other joints and other fingers and control the detailed movements of the entire finger.

4   Feedback Control Experiment for the Static Target Joint Angle

4.1   Modeling the Relationship Between Electrical Stimulus Intensity and Joint Torque

In this paper, we propose a method to control the joint angle and to accurately adjust the middle finger MP joint torque generated by electrical stimulus by modeling the relationship between electrical stimulus intensity and joint torque. As described in Sect. 2, the relationship between the electrical stimulus intensity applied to a single muscle and the finger joint angle is discrete. However, we found the relationship between the electrical stimulus intensity applied to a single muscle and the joint torque can be able to approximate to linear functions in each of the regions where joint torque is not generated (Fig. 2<1>) and joint torque is generated (Fig. 2<2>). Since the joint angle is determined by the ratio of the flexion torque and the extension torque acting on the joint, it is considered that the joint angle can be controlled if the joint torque can be adjusted accurately.

Our modeling method is as follows. First, the arm is fixed to the device to measure joint torque (Fig. 3), and the joint torque is measured when ramp stimulus is applied to each muscle alone. Then, two-piece linear regression modeling is performed by the obtained data. In the two-piece linear regression model, the region where the electrical stimulus intensity is smaller than the break point is called the joint torque minute band (Fig. 2<1>), and the region where the electrical stimulus intensity is larger than the break point is called the joint torque increase band (Fig. 2<2>). As, by modeling by such way, the relationship between the electrical stimulus intensity to each muscle and the joint torque can be explicitly treated, it is thought that the ratio of the flexion torque and the extension torque at the middle finger MP joint can be accurately adjusted.

4.2   PID Control Using Two-Piece Liner Regression Model

In this paper, we introduce two concepts [8] of muscle antagonistic sum and muscle antagonistic ratio, and construct a PID controller that inputs the muscle antagonistic ratio and outputs the joint angle under the constraint of constant muscle antagonistic sum. Muscle antagonistic sum is the total torque generated in the middle finger MP joint by electrical stimulus, and muscle antagonistic ratio is the ratio of flexion torque to muscle antagonistic sum. Human voluntary joint movement is performed by two mechanisms, reciprocal innervation and co-contraction. Reciprocal innervation is a mechanism in which causes joint movement by contracting the muscle that leads joint movement (hereinafter, agonist) and relaxing the muscle located on the opposite side of the bone (hereinafter, antagonist) [9]. Co-contraction is a mechanism in which contracting not only the agonist but also the antagonist to apply appropriate braking to high-speed joint movement and enable detailed movements [10]. Therefore, it can be said that the method of controlling the joint angle by adjusting the muscle antagonist ratio imitates reciprocal

Fig. 3. Joint torque measuring device

innovation, and the constraint that keeping constant muscle antagonist sum imitates co-contraction.

The method of defining the muscle antagonist ratio and muscle antagonist sum is described below. The maximum flexion torque measured by the method described in Sect. 4.1 is described by $T_{f,max}$[N * m], and the maximum extension torque is done by $T_{e,max}$ [N * m]. The electrical stimulus intensity that generates joint torque value $\min(T_{f,max}, T_{e,max})$ are set to the maximum electrical stimulus intensity. Then, $\min(T_{f,max}, T_{e,max})$ is given by the normalized joint torque 1.0 [dimensionless], and the normalized flexion torque corresponding to the electrical stimulus intensity applied to the flexor digitorum muscle at the two-piece linear regression model is described by T_f^*[dimensionless, range = [0.0, 1.0]], and the normalized extension torque corresponding to the electrical stimulus intensity given to the extensor digitorum muscle at the two-piece linear regression model is done by T_e^* [dimensionless, range = [0.0, 1.0]]. The muscle antagonist ratio r is defined as in Eq. (1), and the muscle antagonist sum a is defined as in Eq. (2).

$$r = \frac{T_f^*}{T_f^* + T_e^*} \tag{1}$$

$$a = T_f^* + T_e^* \tag{2}$$

Furthermore, the control system that inputs the muscle antagonist ratio and outputs the joint angle has a role of simplifying the control system. In a control method that calculates the electrical stimulus intensity to each muscle separately, the control method becomes complicated because the combination of inputs that generate the same joint torque are not uniquely determined. In the case of a single-input single-output system as in this study, it is possible to uniquely determine the input value that generates the same joint torque.

4.3 Determination of PID Control Parameters Using the Ziegler-Nichols Ultimate Sensitivity Method

The Ziegler-Nichols ultimate sensitivity method is one of the theoretical PID control parameter adjustment methods, and it is also an effective for control systems such as finger joints that the output value of which is not uniquely determined when no input is given to the control system.

In the Ziegler-Nichols ultimate sensitivity method, PID control parameters are adjusted only by proportional way. Equation (3) shows the proportional controller used in this paper.

$$r = K_c * e_t + b \tag{3}$$

In Eq. (3), r is the muscle antagonist ratio, K_c is the proportional parameter, e_t is the error between the target joint angle and the measured joint angle at time t, and b is the bias. The proportional parameter (Kc) is increased until occurring the continuous oscillation around the target angle. Then, the PID control parameter is calculated from the proportional parameter (ultimate gain) and the oscillation period (ultimate period T_c) when the continuous oscillation to the target angle begin to occur according to Table 1 [11].

In this paper, the Ziegler-Nichols ultimate sensitivity method was performed for three target joint angles of 10°, 30°, and 50°. Then, the relationships between the joint angle and Kc, and the joint angle and Tc were obtained by the linear interpolation on the obtained Kc and Tc (Fig. 4 and Fig. 5). Therefore, it is possible to set appropriate PID control parameters according to the measured joint angle during joint angle control. The reason for adopting such a method is that the moment arm length of the flexor tendon and extensor tendon located at the middle finger MP joint changes depending on the joint angle, and it cause the change of the relationship between the electrical stimulus intensity change and joint angle change.

Table 1. PID control parameter adjustment by ultimate sensitivity method

Proportional parameter	Integral parameter	Differential parameter
$0.6 * K_c$	$1.2 * K_c/T_c$	$0.075 * K_c * T_c$

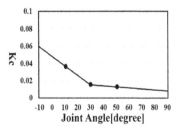

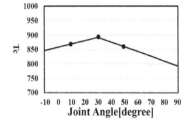

Fig. 4. A graph obtained by linearly interpolating Kc obtained by the ultimate sensitivity method for each target joint angle (vertical axis: Kc, horizontal axis: joint angle [degree])

Fig. 5. A graph obtained by linearly interpolating Tc obtained by the ultimate sensitivity method for each target joint angle (vertical axis: Kc, horizontal axis: joint angle [degree])

4.4 Experimental Devices

Electrical Stimulus Generator
We built the electrical stimulus generator that does not cause interference between the surface electrodes placed on each muscle and can continuously change the electrical stimulus intensity. The electrical stimulus was a rectangular pulse with a stimulus frequency of 40 Hz and a pulse width of 0.2 ms. In this generator, the electrical stimulus intensity are controlled using the AM (Amplitude Modulation) method in which the

height of the electrical stimulus pulse is changed. They are controlled by the microcomputer Raspberry Pi 3B, and, not to cause the interference between the surface electrodes attached on each muscle, the electrical stimulus was switched by Arduino UNO.

Joint Angle Measuring Device

Two 6-axis inertial sensor MPU-6050 is used to measure the joint angle. The roll angles of each sensor (the sensor placed on the metacarpal bone and the sensor placed on the phalanx proximalis) are calculated by the Kalman filter based on the acceleration and gyro measured by each sensor (Fig. 6) [12]. Then, the middle finger MP joint angle is calculated from the difference between the roll angles obtained by each of the two sensors.

Wrist/Arm Fixation Device

To fix the arm on this device during joint angle control, we made the device shown in Fig. 7. Using this device, the effects of gravity on the fingers can be eliminated and wrist joint angle can be fixed during finger joint angle control. As described in Sect. 2, the moment of inertia of the finger is extremely small, so the direction of gravity applied to the phalanx proximalis affects the movements of the MP joint. In addition, flexor digitorum muscle and extensor digitorum muscle are involved not only in fingers joints but also in wrist joint movements. Therefore, unless the wrist joint angle is fixed, the muscle contraction force due to electrical stimulus contributes to wrist joint torque. When the arm is fixed to this device, the angle between the straight line connecting the forearm-metacarpal bone and the ground is kept at 45°, and, so, the above effects can be eliminated.

   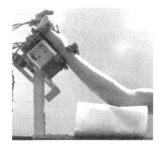

Fig. 6. Joint angle measuring device   **Fig. 7.** Wrist/arm fixation device

Flexion and Extension Torque Measuring Device

In order to measure the joint torque when ramp stimulus is applied to each muscle alone, we created the device as shown in Fig. 3. By fixing the angle of the middle finger MP joint to 45° and placing an S-shaped load cell on the back of the phalanx proximalis of the middle finger, it becomes possible to measure the flexion and extension torque when each muscle is applied the ramp stimulus.

4.5   Experimental Procedure

The experimental procedure is shown in Fig. 8.

We obtained informed consent based on the ethical guidelines for ergonomics research [13] from the participants after the explanations on the experiments. In the phase of surface electrodes position search, the position of the surface electrode were determined by trial and error until sufficient flexion and extension torque occurs at the middle finger MP joint. In the phase of middle finger MP joint torque measurement, two-piece linear regression model about the relationship between the electrical stimulus intensity and joint torque was constructed by the method described in Sect. 4.1. Then, the slope of the joint torque increase band of the two-piece linear regression model was corrected by trial and error, so that the middle finger MP joint angle became between 30 and 50° in applying electrical stimulus of the muscle antagonist ratio 0.5. In the phase of ultimate sensitivity method, K_c and T_c corresponding three target joint angles were obtained by the method described in Sect. 4.3. In the joint angle control experiment, 30°, 45°, and 60° were set as target joint angles, and the control was performed for 20 s for each.

4.6 Participants

The participants were 12 adult men who had no history of arm surgery or heart disease and did not use a pacemaker.

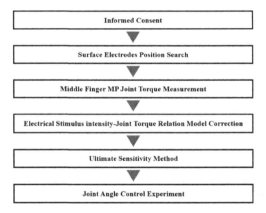

Fig. 8. Experimental procedure

4.7 Evaluation Method

We evaluate the control model by using the root mean square error (RMSE [degree]) between the target joint angle and the measured joint angle. The data used for the RMSE calculation is for 15 s, from 5 s just after the start to the end, because the RMSE immediately after the start of the control is affected by the magnitude of the error between the target joint angle and the measured joint angle before the control. Eq. (4) shows the calculation formula of RMSE.

$$\text{RMSE} = \sqrt{\frac{\sum_{i=1}^{N}(\theta_d - \theta_i)^2}{N}} \tag{4}$$

In Eq. (4), θ_d is the target joint angle, θ_I is the measured joint angle at time i, and N is the number of measured joint angle samples. In this paper, the main purpose is to suppress large continuous oscillation with respect to the target joint angle. Therefore, if the RMSE is less than 3°, we regarded that the control can be performed successfully with high accuracy.

5 Results

88.89% of all experiment trials had RMSE less than 3°. Since the large sustained oscillation to the target joint angle did not converge until the end of the control, the data of one participant was excluded from the analysis. The average values of the RMSE of the 11 participants were 1.657° at the target joint angle of 30°, 1.068° at the target joint angle of 45°, and 0.802° at the target joint angle of 60°. Figure 9 shows a typical example of the control results. In order to confirm whether the control ability differs depending on the target joint angle, a one-way analysis of variance with replication was performed. A factor was the target joint angle (3 levels: 30°/45°/60°). A p value less than 0.05 was considered statistically significant. Table 2 shows the average value and variance of the control results for each target joint angle, and Table 3 shows the results of the analysis of variance. Result of analysis of variance showed no main effect on the target joint angle factor (F (2,32) = 0.9547, p = 0.4018). Therefore, it can be said that the control method proposed in this paper have the control ability with high accuracy regardless of the target joint angle.

Table 2. Mean and variance

Level	Mean	Variance
Target joint angle 30°	1.657	4.278
Target joint angle 45°	1.068	2.567
Target joint angle 60°	0.802	0.645

Table 3. Analysis of variance table

Factor	Sum of square	Degree of freedom	Mean square	F ratio	P value
Target joint angle	4.2185	2	2.1092	0.9547	0.4018
Overall	86.6049	32	2.7064		

6 Problems of Modeling Method

6.1 Model Correction Required

As there was the strong nonlinearity between the joint angle and the muscle antagonist ratio that defined based on the two-piece linear regression model, the slope of the joint torque increase band in the two-piece linear regression model had to be corrected by trial and error. Considering the practical application of a finger joint control system using FES, it is desirable that all steps up to finger joint control can be routinely performed.

One reason why the model correction is necessary is the problem about the joint torque measurement. In this experiment, the joint torque was measured with the middle finger MP joint fixed. However, the flexor digitorum muscle and extensor digitorum muscle are polyarticular muscles and they stop at the base of middle phalanx and are involved in the movements of wrist, MP joint, and PIP joint (Proximal interphalangeal Joint). Therefore, when the muscle contraction is performed with the wrist joint and the MP joint fixed, a strong torque is generated at the PIP joint. On the other hand, the MP joint is not fixed during joint angle control, and a strong torque is also generated at the MP joint due to muscle contraction of each muscle. Because it cause the significant differences between the two-piece linear regression model and the electrical stimulus intensity-joint torque relation during the joint angle control, the two-piece linear regression model must be corrected.

6.2 Setting of Bias Value for Proportional Control in the Ziegler-Nichols Ultimate Sensitivity Method

In the ultimate sensitivity method, the ultimate gain and the ultimate period greatly differ depending on the bias setting of the proportional controller. In proportional control, if there is no error between the target value and the measured value, the input to the control system is only the bias value. Therefore, in being inputted only the bias value to the control system, the ultimate gain becomes the minimum when the measured joint angle and the target joint angle are same, and it becomes larger as the joint angle error grows. In this experiment, the relationship between the muscle antagonism ratio and the joint angle was not determined, so the appropriate bias value could not be determined. It is considered, therefore, the low control accuracy of the participant 7 (RMSE at the target joint angle of $30°:24.110°$, RMSE at the target joint angle of $45°:22.049°$) was caused because the value of proportional control parameter and integral control parameter were set larger than the optimal value.

6.3 Model Correction Failed

In this experiment, the model was corrected based on the joint angle when electrical stimulus intensity corresponding muscle antagonist ratio 0.5 was given. However, it was sometimes observed that the model correction failed because the entire input/output relationship was not taken into account. Looking at the control results of participant 6 (Fig. 10), sustained oscillation of high-frequency was generated. The joint angle of the participant 6 was much less than $30°$ when the muscle antagonist ratio was 0.5. So, we corrected the slope of the joint torque increase band in the extensor digitorum muscle model sharply. However, as the slope of the joint torque increase band becomes steeper, the electrical stimulus intensity changes like binary during the joint angle control. The reason is as follows. As shown in the Fig. 11, the electrical stimulus intensity applied to the extensor digitorum muscle is 0 mA when the muscle antagonist ratio is 1.0. On the other hand, since the slope of the joint torque minute band is gentle, when the muscle antagonist ratio is slightly lower than 1.0, the electrical stimulus intensity to the extensor digitorum muscle moves just around the break point. The steeper the slope of the joint torque increase band is, the closer the electrical stimulus intensity at the break point and the electrical stimulus intensity when the muscle antagonist ratio is 0.0 (Fig. 11<1>). Therefore, the electrical stimulus intensity changes like binary and the sustained oscillation of high-frequency was occurred when the muscle antagonist ratio changes around 1.0.

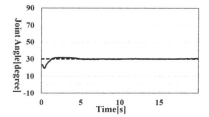

Fig. 9. Control result of participant 1 (vertical axis: joint angle [degree], horizontal axis: time [s], solid black line: measured joint angle, black broken line: target joint angle)

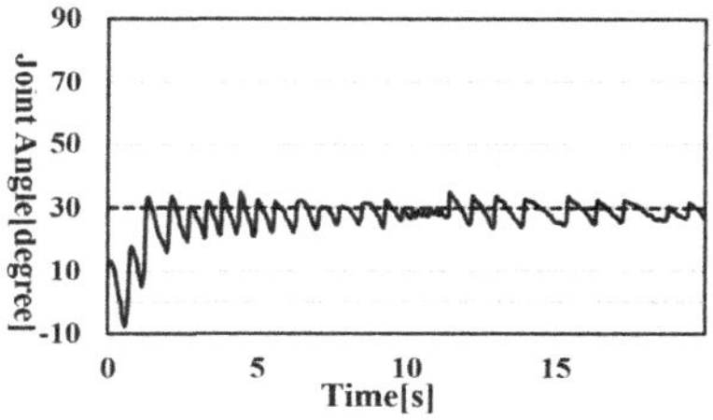

Fig. 10. Control result of participant 6 (vertical axis: joint angle [degree], horizontal axis: time [s], solid black line: measured joint angle, black broken line: target joint angle)

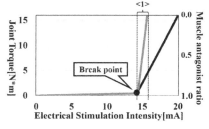

Fig. 11. Result of extensor digitorum muscle model correction for experiment participant 6 (Left vertical axis: joint torque [N * m], right vertical axis: muscle antagonist ratio, horizontal axis: electrical stimulus intensity [mA], black solid line: the model before correction, gray solid line: the model after correction)

7 Improvement of Modeling Method of Electrical Stimulus Intensity-Joint Torque Relation

Based on the problem of the modeling method described in Sect. 6, we suggest a new modeling method. This modeling method has two advantages. One is this model can be performed model correction routinely without trial and error, and the other is this model behaves taking the entire input/output relation into account.

7.1 Eliminates the Need for Trial and Error Model Correction

To eliminate the trial and error operations in the model correction, a model was constructed from the joint angle when both muscles were simultaneously stimulated.

In the two-piece linear regression model in the previous experiment, it was necessary to correct the slope of the joint torque increase band by trial and error. In modeling based on the static joint torque, it is necessary to correct the model, because the relationship between electrical stimulus intensity and the joint torque in the case of fixing the joint angle is greatly different from the one in not fixed it. Therefore, we built the electrical stimulus intensity-joint torque relation model based on the middle finger MP joint angle when both muscles were simultaneously stimulated. There are three reasons for constructing such model. The first is that the electrical stimulus intensity-joint angle relationship approaches linear with simultaneous stimulation of both muscles. In Sect. 2, it is stated that the electrical stimulus intensity-joint angle relationship is discrete when electrical stimulus applies single muscle. However, simultaneous stimulus of both muscles cause the muscle coordination, and the relationships between the electrical stimulus intensity and the joint angle can be made close to linear. The second is that it is not necessary to correct the model. This method can model the input/output relationship in the state during joint angle control where the middle finger MP joint is not fixed. The third, since the joint angle is determined by the ratio of flexion torque to extension torque, an electrical stimulus intensity-joint torque relationship model can be constructed from the electrical stimulus intensity-joint angle relationship.

7.2 Modeling Considering the Entire Input/Output Relationships

By being based on joint angles when various values of electrical stimulus intensities are applied to each muscle, this model can take into account the entire input/output relationship. Because, in the previous experiment, the relationship the electrical stimulus intensity-joint torque was corrected only based on one point of the input/output relationship, the model correction sometimes failed like participant 6. If the model that takes the entire input/output relationship into account can be constructed, it can be considered that modeling will not fail.

Furthermore, by considering the entire input/output relationship, it is possible to set the appropriate bias value of the proportional controller in the ultimate sensitivity method. Because, in this model, the relationship between the electrical stimulus intensity and the joint angle is associated with each other, the electrical stimulus intensity corresponding to the target joint angle in the ultimate sensitivity method can set as a bias value of the proportional controller. Therefore, we can obtain appropriate values of the ultimate gain (K_c) and the ultimate period (T_c).

7.3 Modeling

The modeling method described in Sects. 7.1 and 7.2 was performed in the following procedure.

First, the minimum and maximum electrical stimulus intensity given to each muscle during joint angle control are defined. The ramp stimulus is applied to each muscle alone, and the electrical stimulus intensity are measured as follows: (1) the electrical stimulus intensity at which the joint angle starts to change (S_{start}), (2) the electrical stimulus intensity at which the joint angle saturates ($S_{saturation}$). (3) the electrical stimulus intensity at which pain is felt (S_{pain}). Then, the minimum electrical stimulus intensity (S_{min}) and the maximum electrical stimulus intensity (S_{max}) are defined according to Eqs. (5) and (6), respectively.

$$S_{min} = \frac{S_{start}}{2} \tag{5}$$

$$S_{max} = \frac{S_{saturation} + S_{pain}}{2} \tag{6}$$

By applying the above method to both muscles, the minimum and maximum electrical stimulus intensity to each muscle are defined. $S_{f,min}$ and $S_{f,max}$ show the minimum and maximum value to the flexor digitorum muscle, and $S_{e,min}$ and $S_{e,max}$ show the minimum and maximum value to the extensor digitorum muscle. Then, to investigate the input/output relationship of the control system, the provisional muscle antagonist ratio is defined as in Eq. (8) under the following constraints Eq. (7).

$$a_p = \frac{S_f}{S_{f,max}} + \frac{S_e}{S_{e,max}} \tag{7}$$

$$r_p = \frac{\dfrac{S_f}{S_{f,max}}}{\dfrac{S_f}{S_{f,max}} + \dfrac{S_e}{S_{e,max}}} \tag{8}$$

a_p is the provisional muscle antagonist sum, r_p is the provisional muscle antagonist ratio, S_f is the electrical stimulus intensity to the flexor digitorum muscle, and S_e is the electrical stimulus intensity to the extensor digitorum muscle. By setting a constraint of provisional muscle antagonist sum 1.0, when the provisional muscle antagonist ratio is determined, the electrical stimulus intensity to each muscle can be uniquely determined. This makes it possible to imitate joint movements due to reciprocal innervation while keeping muscle stiffness constant by co-contraction. Figure 12 shows a conceptual diagram of the electrical stimulus intensity and the provisional muscle antagonist ratio.

Using the provisional muscle antagonist ratio, the input/output relationship is obtained in the following flow. First, the provisional muscle antagonist ratio divide into 0.2 steps from 0.0 to 1.0. Then, the electrical stimulus intensity corresponding to the divided provisional muscle antagonist ratio is applied to each muscle by step stimulus randomly. By doing so, the relationship between the provisional muscle antagonist ratio and the joint angle can be determined. After completed the above procedure, the measured joint angles are sorted in ascending order. If there is a section with a difference of 3° or more from the before section, the provisional muscle antagonist ratio of that section is further divided into smaller sections and applied to each muscle to measure the joint angle. If the situation described below occurs, the measurement is terminated. (1) The case where the joint angle difference in that section is less than 30°, and (2) the case where the joint angle difference in that section is not less than 30° even if the provisional muscle antagonist ratio divided into less than 0.01. The provisional muscle antagonist ratio-joint angle relationship can be obtained by the above method. By obtaining above relationship, it is possible to build the electrical stimulus intensity-joint torque relationship model. That is because the provisional muscle antagonist ratio and the electrical stimulus intensity are correspond, and the joint angle and joint torque are correspond. Figure 13 shows a conceptual diagram of the relationship between the provisional muscle antagonist ratio and the joint angle. Figure 14 shows a model of the relationship between the electrical stimulus intensity and the joint torque. With this method, the model can be uniquely determined from the relationship between the provisional muscle antagonist ratio and the joint angle.

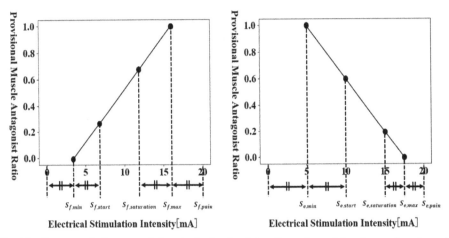

Fig. 12. Conceptual diagram of electrical stimulus intensity and provisional muscle antagonist ratio (vertical axis: provisional muscle antagonist ratio [dimensionless], horizontal axis: electrical stimulus intensity [mA], left figure: electrical stimulus intensity-provisional muscle antagonist ratio relationship in flexor digitorum muscle, right figure: Relationship between electrical stimulus intensity-provisional muscle antagonist ratio in extensor digitorum muscle)

8   Feedback Control Experiment for the Static Target Joint Angle Using Improved Model

Using the improved model, the experiments on feedback control to the static target joint angle were conducted. The experimental procedure about informed consent and surface electrode position search were the same as the experimental procedure described in Sect. 4.5. In the following phase, modeling was performed using the method described in Sect. 7.3. Three target angles in the ultimate sensitivity method ($\theta_{d,min}$, $\theta_{d,mid}$, $\theta_{d,max}$) were set according to Eq. (7), (8), and (9).

$$\theta_{d,min} = (\theta_{max} - \theta_{min}) * \frac{1}{3} \tag{9}$$

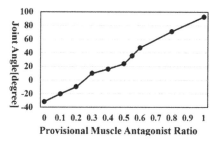

Fig. 13. Provisional muscle antagonist ratio-joint angle relationship (vertical axis: joint angle [degree], horizontal axis: provisional muscle antagonist ratio)

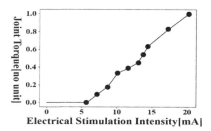

Fig. 14. Electrical stimulus intensity-joint torque related model (vertical axis: joint torque [dimensionless], horizontal axis: electrical stimulus intensity [mA])

$$\theta_{d,mid} = (\theta_{max} - \theta_{min}) * \frac{1}{2} \tag{10}$$

$$\theta_{d,max} = (\theta_{max} - \theta_{min}) * \frac{2}{3} \tag{11}$$

θ_{max} and θ_{min} are the maximum and minimum joint angle that each participant can achieve by electrical stimulus. The target joint angle in the experiment was defined as the joint angle ($\theta_{d,mid}$). $\theta_{d,mid}$ is the midpoint between the maximum joint angle and the minimum joint angle that each participant can achieve by electrical stimulus.

The participants were 9 adult men who had no history of arm surgery or heart disease and did not use a pacemaker. The evaluation method was the same as described in Sect. 4.7.

9   Results

8 of the 9 participants did not generate large oscillations to the target joint angle. Mean of root mean square error RMSE about 8 participants were 1.09°. Figure 15 shows a typical example of the control results. In order to investigate whether there is a difference in the joint angle control ability between the model used in the previous experiment and the model used in this experiment, unequal variances two sample t test about RMSE was conducted. A p value less than 0.05 was considered statistically significant. Table 4 shows the mean and variance of RMSE for each model, and Table 5 shows the results of the t-test.

As the result of the t test, no significant difference was found in the RMSE between the control method in the previous experiment and the current experiment (two-sided test, $p = 0.8434$). Table 4 also shows that the variance of the RMSE is smaller when the model in current experiment is used than the model in the previous experiment is used. Therefore, it can be said that, by using the model in current experiment, it was possible to control to static target joint angle with high accuracy and to reduce individual differences.

Table 4. Mean, variance and number of samples

Variable	Mean	Variance	Number of samples
Model of previous experiment	1.1754	2.7064	33
Model of current experiment	1.0919	0.7395	8

Table 5. Result of t test

Degree of freedom	T value	P value (two-sided test)
21	−0.2000	0.8434

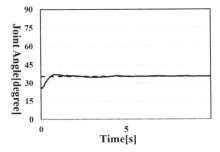

Fig. 15. Control result of participant 3 (vertical axis: joint angle [degree], horizontal axis: time [s], black solid line: measured joint angle, black dashed line: target joint angle)

10 Discussion

By using the electrical stimulus intensity-joint torque relationship model in current experiment, it was possible to control to static target joint angle with high accuracy and reduce individual differences. In the new proposed model, each parameter can be obtained routinely without trial and error, and the bias of the proportional controller in the ultimate sensitivity method can be set to an appropriate value. These contribute positive effects on the entire process from modeling to PID control parameter adjustment. In addition, using the model in the previous experiment, participant 6 could not controlled with high accuracy (the average RMSE of the control error for the three static target joint angles was 3.911°) because of the failure of the model correction. On the other hand, using the model in the current experiment, the RMSE was 1.846°, and highly accurate control was possible. From this, it can be said that using the model in current experiment also has the effect of reducing the probability of model correction failure.

11 Conclusion

In this paper, we proposed a method of controlling finger joint angle using FES, which has been considered difficult so far. To overcome the difficulty, in this study, we propose two models. In the first model, we propose the two-piece linear regression model to model the relationship between the electrical stimulus intensity and the joint torque. We also proposed a method to control the finger joint angle by adjusting the ratio of flexion torque to extension torque by PID control, where the PID control parameters are adjusted by the ultimate sensitivity method. As the result of the feedback control experiments to static target joint angle, we succeed to control to static target joint angle with less than RMSE 3° set as a goal.

However, it was necessary to correct the model by trial and error. Therefore, a new modeling method was proposed to uniquely determine the electrical stimulus intensity-joint torque relationship. This model based on the relationship between the electrical stimulus intensity on both muscles and the joint angle. By using newly model, control experiments to static joint angle were conducted. As a result, it was possible to control to static target joint angle with less than RMSE 3°. Furthermore, using this model, individual differences were reduced, and the modeling failure probability was reduced.

12 Future Work

In this paper, controlling to static target joint angle was possible with less than RMSE 3°. In the future, we are going to investigate a control method that can perform high accurate control to dynamic target joint angle that changes with time.

Acknowledgments. This work has been supported by Shotoku Science Foundation.

References

1. Nakagomi, S., Yamamoto, Y., Ito, T.: Sports Psychology Contact Point Between Body and Movement and Mind. Baifukan Co., Ltd., Tokyo (2008)
2. Fujita, K.: Biological interface using electrical stimulation. J. Hum. Interface Soc. Hum. Interface **6**(1), 39–42 (2004)
3. Pedro, L., Alexandra, I., Willi, M., Daniel, H., Patrick, J., Patrick, B.: Proprioceptive interaction. In: CHI 2015 Proceedings of the 33rd Annual ACM Conference on Human Factors in Computing Systems, pp. 939–948 (2015)
4. Tatsuno, S., Hayakawa, T., Ishikawa, M.: Sports skill acquisition system based on electrical stimulation through balling task. Virtual Reality Soc. Jpn. **22**(4), 447–455 (2017)
5. Handa, Y., Hoshimiya, N.: Restoration of upper extremity function by electrical neuromuscular stimulation. Soc. Biomech. Jpn. **9**, 75–82 (1988)
6. Tamaki, E., Miyaki, T., Rekimoto, J., Sasabe, T.: PossessedHand: techniques for controlling human hands using electrical muscles stimuli. In: CHI 2011 Proceedings of the SIGCHI Conference on Human Factors in Computing Systems, pp. 543–552 (2011)
7. Watanabe, T., Iibuchi, K., Kurosawa, K., Hoshimiya, N.: A method of multichannel PID control of 2-degree-of-freedom wrist joint movements by functional electrical stimulation. IEICE Trans. Inf. Syst. (Jpn. Ed.) **34**(5), 25–36 (2002)

8. Atsuumi, K., Nagai, M., Taniguchi, K., Matsui, K., Nishikawa, A.: Test of human finger-joint movement model using functional electrical stimulation based on equilibrium point hypothesis under an isometric condition. Trans. Jpn. Soc. Med. Bio. Eng. **56**(5), 198–208 (2018)

9. Komiyama, T., Kasai, T.: Effects of varying ankle dorsiflexion force onto the agonist facilitation and the antagonist inhibition in man. Jpn. Soc. Phys. Educ. **33**(2), 135–144 (1988)

10. Smith, A.M.: The coactivation of antagonist muscles. Can. J. Physiol. Pharmacol. **59**(7), 733–747 (1981)

11. Ziegler, J.G., Nichols, N.B.: Optimum settings for automatic controllers. Trans. ASME **64**(8), 759–768 (1942)

12. Hirose, K., Kondo, A.: Special issues no. 3: measurement technique for ergonomics, section 1–2: measurement of body motion – motion measurements by inertial sensors. Jpn. Hum. Factors Ergon. Soc. **50**(4), 182–190 (2014)

13. Japan Human Factors and Ergonomics Society: The ethical guidelines for ergonomics research (2009)

Augmented Reality Fashion Show Using Personalized 3D Human Models

Shihui Xu[1]([⊠]) [iD], Jingyi Yuan[1] [iD], Xitong Sun[1] [iD], Yuhan Liu[1] [iD], Yuzhao Liu[1] [iD], Kelvin Cheng[2] [iD], Soh Masuko[2] [iD], and Jiro Tanaka[1] [iD]

[1] Waseda University, Kitakyushu, Japan
{shxu,jingyyuan}@toki.waseda.jp, {sunxitong,liuyuhan-op,
liuyuzhao131}@akane.waseda.jp, jiro@aoni.waseda.jp
[2] Rakuten Institute of Technology, Rakuten, Inc., Tokyo, Japan
{kelvin.cheng,so.masuko}@rakuten.com

Abstract. When purchasing clothes online, consumers usually have to imagine what they might look like when wearing them in real life surroundings. This can hinder their ability to make appropriate purchasing decisions. In order to alleviate this uncertainty, we propose using augmenting fashion show, a new immersive experience to enable consumers to create personalized 3D models of themselves and have them fitted with a variety of purchasable clothing using Augmented Reality. Furthermore, their models are enhanced with animations (walking and a variety of poses) depending on the real environment. In this way, consumers can see a representation of themselves wearing a variety of clothes, and get a sense of what they would look like in real life surroundings. A prototype of our system was demonstrated, and a preliminary evaluation was conducted to verify our system. We have received positive feedback in terms of effectiveness, assistance and potential application.

Keywords: Augmented Reality · Virtual fashion show · Personalized human model

1 Introduction

A fashion show is an event to showcase the new and upcoming clothing and accessories designs, usually organized by fashion designers each season during a period known as Fashion Week [1]. Typically, there is a runway with light and special effects decorated, where models dressed in clothes designed by designers can walk the catwalk. With the widespread adoption of ready-to-wear collections [2], ready-to-wear fashion shows are becoming more and more diversified, with examples being held in street and supermarket scenes [3], and promote the retail of fashion industry to a certain extent [2].

Despite the popularity of ready-to-wear fashion shows, consumers may still have difficulty knowing whether the clothes are suitable for themselves or not. Clothes are perfectly tailored at fashion shows, and appear at their best on the models. However, they may not be suitable for consumers themselves, because of the differences in body

© Springer Nature Switzerland AG 2020
S. Yamamoto and H. Mori (Eds.): HCII 2020, LNCS 12184, pp. 435–450, 2020.
https://doi.org/10.1007/978-3-030-50020-7_31

shapes. In addition, it may be difficult for customers to imagine wearing these clothes in their daily life. Some of the current fashion shows are not limited to the runway or stage, instead the models are static, standing or sitting in an artificially constructed environment. But the constructed environment is still far from customers' everyday lives.

Considering the above, we present an AR fashion show system in this paper, using augmented and mixed reality. Our system enables users to have their own 3D models which are customized for users and can reflect the appearance of the users (i.e. body shapes and facial appearance). Virtual fitting room is provided for users, where users can select the purchasable clothes virtually, and try them on their 3D human model. With dressed 3D models, users can join in fashion show conducted in real-world environment. Fashion show can be adaptively augmented to the daily life scenes where the users are. In other words, according to real environment's scene type (e.g. an office scene, a street scene and a home scene) and spatial layout (e.g. size and shape of floor plane, number and distribution of wall plane), the form of fashion show can vary, e.g. with different postures or walking route.

In this way, we intend to offer ordinary customers immersive experience of attending a ready-to-wear fashion show by themselves (Fig. 1). By using AR fashion show, we provide customers with a preview of themselves wearing those fashion items in their daily lives, which in turn can help them in their decision-making process when purchasing fashion items. In addition, we have conducted a preliminary evaluation to validates our system and received positive feedback in terms of effectiveness, assistance and potential application.

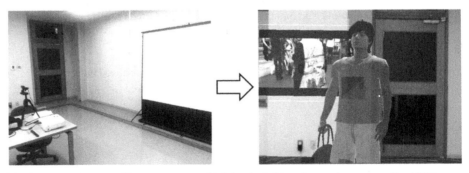

Fig. 1. Our system provides users a way of joining in fashion show using personalized 3D human models of themselves, making the real-world environment (left) an AR fashion show (right).

2   Related Works

We considered related works from three aspects, *fashion show, personalized avatar* and *virtual clothes try-on* .

2.1 Fashion Show

With the development of AR technology, many designers have thought about taking AR into fashion show. For example, the autumn/winter 2014 fashion show by Goelia had used AR technology to decorate runway [4]; Xenium Digital and Magnum enabled virtual animals like tiger, panther and cheetah to walk together with models on runway using AR [5]; Three launched mixed reality show where models are companied with special effects during catwalk [6].

In this paper, we consider how to leverage advances in AR and MR to make it possible for ordinary customers to imagine themselves wearing the clothes that they are considering purchasing in the form of a fashion show. In this vein, previous systems in human-computer interaction and computer graphics, such as the motion capture system of Ryuzo Okada et al. [7] and the virtual fashion system of Stephen Gray [8], developed virtual fashion show system that renders a computer graphics clothes to a 3D virtual model. But these works lack of information of real world. In their works, fashion show is isolated to real world, which means users have no ideas about the fashion show in daily life scenes.

2.2 Personalized Avatar

In the field of computer vision, a personalized avatar is a graphical representation of a user. Human avatar needs to be as realistic as possible.

There are several previous works explored generating personalized avatars for users. Earlier work on personalized avatar were mostly based on parameter-driven modelling from images. Generally, 3D body modelling consists two parts: the representation of body joints or skeleton structures, the body shape of the model. Gavrila [9] consider human body can be built using a 22-DOF model and the class of tapered super-quadrics [10]. Pascal Fua [11] proposed a framework which can form accurate body shape description by a small number of parameters and have an effective use of stereo and silhouette data.

In recent years, 3D scanning technique are used to acquire the shape and pose of a human body. Hasler [12] described an accurately model muscle deformations as a function of pose. Silvia Zuff [13] proposed stitched puppet model which has the realism of 3D body models and the graphical structure of the graphical body model. The body part can be described by low-dimensional state space and the whole parts will be connected by pairwise potentials. Skinned Multi-Person Linear model (SMPL) [14] is a learned model of accurate human shape and pose. Based on SMPL, Federica Bogo proposed SMPLify [15], a way of automatic estimation of 3D human pose and shape from an image.

For our system, we employ the method of Alldieck [16] called video avatar which is based on the parametric body model. Video avatar can infer highly accurate 3D model shapes requiring only an RGB camera. To generate a 3D face model from a single facial image, we use 68 feature key-points used the Dlib library.

2.3 Virtual Clothes Try-on

With the development of computer graphics, virtual clothes models are becoming more realistic. Earlier work on virtual try-on, mostly conducted in computer graphics [17–19]. Anna Hilsmann retextured garment overlay for real-time visualization of garments in a virtual mirror environment [20]. Yamada et al. proposed a method of reshaping the garment image based on human body shapes to make fitting more realistic [21]. However, like many other retexturing approaches they operate only in 2D without using 3D information in any way, which lacked the ability for users to view their virtual self from arbitrary viewpoints.

In recent years, some interactive 3D virtual try-on solutions have been reported. M Yuan et al. presented a mixed reality system for 3D virtual clothes try-on that enables a user to see herself wearing virtual clothes while looking at a mirror display [22]. Whereas, these kinds of system still do not allow users to see the textured garment from arbitrary viewing angles.

Other virtual try-on system based on virtual avatar have been proposed, which enables users to view the virtual garment from different angles. However, most virtual try-on systems provide virtual fitting experiences on a default virtual avatar, rather than one generated from user's own body [23–25]. And some virtual try-on systems provide virtual fitting experiences on a virtual avatar with user's face [22] without personalized user body. The absence of "true fit" may disappoint customers when shopping online.

For our system, we propose to create virtual personalized models for each user, which can reflect their body shape and facial appearance, making the 3D virtual try-on experience for users. Allowing user to view their virtual self with garment model from different viewpoints.

3 AR Fashion Show

Different from typical fashion shows, our purpose is to make a daily life fashion show using users' life-size 3D human models, which means it could adapt to the scenes where users are physically located. As shown in Fig. 1, our system aims to make the real-world environment where the user virtual self become part of the fashion show using AR. Our AR fashion show consists of three parts: scene preprocessing, immersive show and user interaction, which will be introduced in detail below.

3.1 Scene Preprocessing

Scene means the real-world environment where the user is standing. To make a daily life fashion show, we need to do some preprocessing to the daily life scene, including recognition of scene and awareness of spatial layout (Fig. 2).

Recognition of Scene. Currently, scene information is seldom used as input in clothes try-on system. While previous works had shown that the scene type has had a crucial influence on outfits of customers [26, 27]. We propose to recognize the scene where users are and make it an input to AR fashion show system. For example, the scene type could be office, street, supermarket and so on. With different scene as input, AR fashion show is given different theme and form.

Fig. 2. Scene preprocessing: recognition of scene type (left) and awareness of spatial layout (right).

Awareness of Spatial Layouts. To align virtual items to the real-world, spatial awareness system is needed. Our system scans the real environment through depth cameras and understands the planes in real-world, and then decides the position of users' models in real-world according to the spatial layouts of real-world.

With scene preprocessing, AR fashion show can adapt to multiple scenes in real life, which can facilitate users to have previews of wearing clothes in different daily scenes.

3.2 Immersive Show

Immersive show is provided for users in which users can see a 3D model of themselves wearing the fashion items in AR and get some sense about taking a show. Generally, most people watch fashion shows online or on TV, but few have the chance to watch fashion show in person or take part in a fashion show. We therefore propose immersive show, making the life scene a fashion show. With the personalized 3D human models of users, users can get a sense of taking a show. At the same time, they can also watch the immersive show from various points of view.

The styles of immersive show contain dynamic walking and animated pose.

Dynamic Walking. During the immersive show, 3D human models can dynamically walk in AR environment, giving users a dynamic view of wearing fashion items on their own body models while moving around.

The 3D models will find ways and walk around the real-world space. The walking route is as the dotted line in Fig. 3. Wayfinding of model is based on the result of scene preprocessing, so the ways may vary according to the scene change. From the result of scene preprocessing, the max floor plane (green plane in Fig. 3) is found as the plane where fashion show is superimposed. Next, to get the route, our system will assign four points on the floor plane as the vertexes of rectangle, based on the position and size of floor plane. The points are the quarter points of max floor's length or width. The four sides of defined rectangle will be the route of dynamic walking.

The postures of models' dynamic walking are diversified and associated with the type of scene. Usually, people walk differently in different occasions. To make the virtual 3D human models walk naturally in various real-world scenes and give users a realistic feeling, we construct a library of walking animations for every user model. Every animation has its suitable application scenes. The walking animations contain catwalk, walking with bag, happy walking, texting while walking etc. According to scene type we get from scene recognition, 3D models will be triggered to walk in different forms. Figure 4 shows some examples of walking postures in an office scene. Figure 5 shows the examples of walking postures in a street scene. In this case, users can better understand what they will look like walking in those daily life scenes.

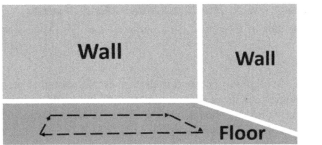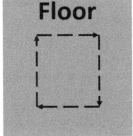

Fig. 3. The route of dynamic walking is illustrated using dotted line with arrows. Route of dynamic walking is defined by four points on the floor plane. (Color figure online)

Fig. 4. Dynamic walking: female catwalk walking, walking with bag and male happy walking.

Animated Pose. To make the fashion show more diverse and varied, we enable 3D human model to make pose during the show. Animated pose is performed in the middle of dynamic walking, i.e. the second vertex of route rectangle, which is called the pose point. When 3D human model walks to the pose point, it will stop to make an animated pose. As the dynamic walking, a library of pose animations is also prepared for each 3D human model. Models poses according to the current scene. For example, as the Fig. 6

Fig. 5. Text while walking

shows, the animated pose ranges from looking around pose, female stand pose, waving pose, saying hello pose and so on, which is relevant to our daily activities. The scene shown in Fig. 6 is an office scene, so models will do the animated pose related to the office environment. This is designed for achieving a simulation of users' daily actions so that the AR fashion show is more relevant to people's daily life.

3.3   User Interaction

Interactions are available to enhance the engagement of users, including the interactions among multiple users and the interactions with environments.

Show Partner. Show partner is a multi-user interaction. AR fashion show system enables users to invite another user as the partner of show. Show partner is designed to give users some outfit inspirations about how to look good as a couple. Matching styles for couples have been popular in recent fashion industry. Users could be families, friends or lovers, and want to select clothes for matching with each other. But currently, users could not know how they and their partners will look like wearing matching styles clothes. In light of this, show partner is provided for users to let them have a broad understanding of the looks as a couple. Once a user is invited as a partner of another user, the pair of users' models will be assigned as show partners. Show partners will walk together and make paired poses, as shown in Fig. 7.

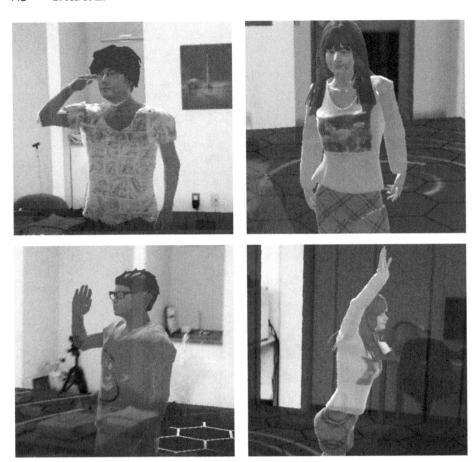

Fig. 6. Animated pose

Fig. 7. A pair of show partners.

Interactions with Models. Interaction with models directly is also made possible in our system. Users can give a "like" to any model by clicking the "like" button beside the models. The number of likes received will be shown on the left of every model's like button, as shown in Fig. 8. Users can use hand gestures to interact with their own model as well, including moving or rotating it.

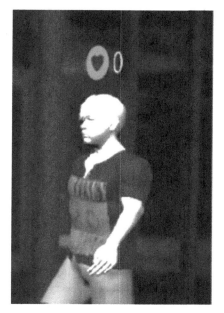

Fig. 8. Like a model

4   Personalized 3D Human Model

Personalized 3D human model is generated for every user so that they can virtually try on clothes and take part in AR fashion show using their own model. The generation of personalized 3D human model consists of the generation of 3D body shape model and 3D face model. As the Fig. 9 shows, we generated the 3D body shape model of user using Alldieck et al's method [16], and generated the 3D face model of users using Deng et al's method [28]. The two parts are then combined to get the complete user's personalized 3D human model.

4.1   3D Body Shape Model

3D body shape model of user is generated from a 2D video in which user rotates 360 degrees in front of a camera. To realize this, we use video from user as the input of the whole system. To get the body model, we followed the method of Thiemo Alldieck [16].

We see human body modeling as part of preprocessing. After getting the video from user, the system will split the video into a series of frames. These frames can be used as

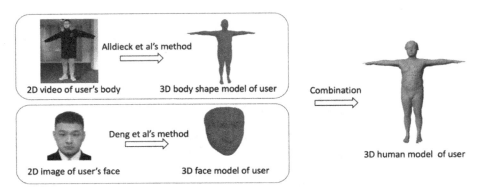

Fig. 9. Process of personalized 3D human model generation

input of preprocessing. Each frame will generate a corresponding mask using a method called OSVOS [29]. This method can tackle the problem of semi-supervised video object segmentation using a fully-convolutional neural network architecture.

Then we need to detect body joints data (such as human body, hand, foot key points) using OpenPose [30]. Pose can be represented by many formats. We choose COCO as pose output format which uses 18 key points to represent body joints. This information will be stored into the json file. And each frame will generate a corresponding json file.

After getting the whole masks and key points files, we can use Alldieck' work to generate 3D human body model by SMPL model. Every SMPL model has two kinds of parameters: pose and shape. We only care about the shape parameter because the system will set every model to T-pose to rig the model. Alldieck's work will calculate shape parameter. Afterwards, the system will generate user's body model as the output.

4.2   3D Human Face Modeling

In this part, we need to generate a 3D face model from a single facial image as the face of the 3D avatar of the user. To realize this, we first need a face image of the user. After that, the facial feature points of the image are required for modeling. To extract the feature points, here we used the Dlib library to get the 68 feature points of the user's face. From these points, we select the 5 points, the left eye, the right eye, the nose, the left mouth corner and the right mouth corner and got their pixel coordinates for the latter use. After getting these 5 points' information, we followed Yu Deng's work to generate the 3D face model of the user. In the process, we used the points information and the face image as the input, and we could get the 3D face model.obj file as the output. In this way, we can generate the 3D human face model of the user.

We also need a hair model which is suitable for the user's hair in order to make our 3D avatar more realistic. We collected many hair models, and collected them as a library. From this library, the most similar hair model compared to the user's haircut will be chosen to generate the 3D avatar.

After having both the 3D body shape model and the 3D face model, we used Blender to combine them together. Finally, the 3D user model will be served as the user's avatar.

5   Virtual Fitting

For virtual fitting, users can select clothes in the form of 2D images from shopping website such as H&M. Then corresponding virtual clothes will be fitted on user's personalized 3D human model. They can select the garments fitting in a real-life scene and view the virtual garment from various angles. The overall architecture of our system for virtual try-on are shown in Fig. 10.

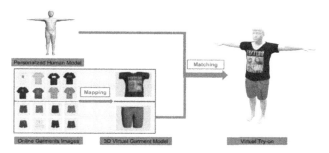

Fig. 10. The overall architecture of the virtual try-on

We gather various clothing design and information from websites, and map 2D Garment images to generated 3D virtual garment templates, then match the clothes to personalized body model of users.

5.1   Garment Model Generation

Our approach collects garment image information from existing shopping websites (e.g. H&M [31], Zara [32]) to create a virtual garment library. Textures are extracted from the online garment image and mapped onto the 3D garment model in 3Ds Max.

Cloth weaver [33] is a blender garment template library which is used as the basis for creating various garment models. We used Cloth Weaver to build several 3D garment model templates for personalized human models. Some 3D clothing templates provided to users are shown in Fig. 11. Such as short T-shirts, pants, skirts and long sleeves.

Fig. 11. Some 3D garment templates provided for users

We collect garment images on existing shopping websites such as H&M [31], ZARA [32] …) and mapped these garment images onto the generated 3D garment model templates in 3Ds Max. Some textured garment models are shown in Fig. 12 below.

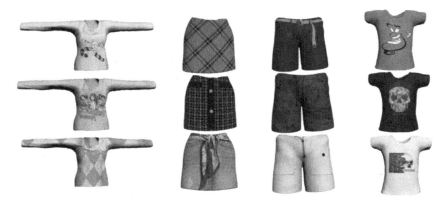

Fig. 12. Textured garment models

5.2 Virtual Fitting Room

In virtual fitting, users can select clothes in the form of 2D images from shopping website such as H&M. The corresponding virtual clothes will be fitted on user's personalized model. The users' personalized models wearing the virtual clothing will appear standing on the floor in front of them.

The animation of human body enables users to view the dressed human model in a dynamic and interactive way, from various perspectives. Therefore, users can have a better understanding of whether the garment is suitable or not, while they move. Most of the previous work focused on fitting on a static body model [19, 25]. So far, there is a lack of research exploring virtual try-on with motion. Therefore, we provide dynamic interaction with the virtual human model in virtual fitting room.

6 Implementation

AR fashion show is developed using Unity 3D. We implemented our system on a see-through type head-mounted display, Microsoft HoloLens, with Intel 32-bit CPU, 2 GB RAM, and a $120° \times 120°$ depth camera.

6.1 Scene Type and Spatial Layout

We used the Mixed Reality Capture API [35] provided by Microsoft to capture the photo of real environment. Then the captured photo is processed by using Google cloud vision API [36] to get the labels of photo. The labels usually contain objects such as table, road, room and so on. The depth camera embedded in HoloLens is used to calculate the spatial layout of the real environment.

6.2 Libraries of Animations

To build the libraries of dynamic walking animations and animated pose animations, we have used Maximo [37] from Adobe, which enables to empower various animations with 3D characters. We classify the animations from Maximo into several sets according to scene usage. In another word, we added the information of the scene to the animations we get from Maximo to ensure the animations will be triggered correctly in different scenes.

7   Preliminary Evaluation

We have conducted a user study to evaluate our system. The evaluation is conducted from the aspects of effectiveness, assistance and potential application.

7.1   Participant

Ten participants were recruited for this evaluation, including 7 males and 3 females aged from 21 to 25. All of the participants have a background in human-computer interaction with a basic knowledge of AR technology.

7.2   Task and Procedure

Each participant was asked to virtually try on clothes by the personalized 3D human model which is generated by our system. Then using the dressed 3D models of themselves, participants can take part in an AR fashion show. During the show, they can watch their models and interact with them.

The study was conducted in an office which was about 10 by 10 m.

After the show, participants were asked to complete a questionnaire to evaluate our system using 5-point Likert scale (1: strongly disagree to 5: strongly agree).

7.3   Results

We have asked 5 questions which covers the effectiveness, assistance and potential application of our system. The results from our questionnaire reveals positive feedback from our users. Table 1 shows the 5 questions and their average scores.

Effectiveness. Questions 1, 2 and 3 are designed to evaluate the effectiveness of our system. The effectiveness testing includes the effectiveness of personalized 3D human model, the effectiveness of augmenting fashion show to real-world scenes and the effectiveness of user interaction.

For question 1, we intend to know whether users can get a better understanding of how the clothes would look on their body by using a virtual avatar. We see an average score of 4, indicating that the personalized 3D human model of our system can reflects the personality of the user. We have gotten feedbacks about the photorealism of personalized 3D human model from participants. Most participants feel that body model part is more similar to the real person than the face model. We thought it might be because people are more familiar with their face than their body shape, so that they could recognize quite small differences between face models and real faces. But participants also referred that similarity of body shape model is more important than face model during the selecting of clothes, so there is no problem if the face model has a few differences with real face.

Table 1. Questions and corresponding scores

	Question	Average score
1	I could get feelings about wearing clothes on my own virtual body by using this system	4
2	I could get feelings about wearing clothes in real life scene by using this system	3.5
3	I feel the user interactions are interesting and make me engage with the show	4
4	I could make better purchasing decisions when buying clothes using this system	4.5
5	I would like to use the system when purchasing clothes in the future	4.5

From question 2, we intend to know whether users can get a better understanding of how the clothes would look like in a real-life scene. The average score for question 2 is higher than neutral value, suggesting that augmenting a fashion show to the real environment is effective for users to imagine the look in their daily life.

Question 3's result shows that the user interaction can increase the amusement and engagement of AR fashion show experience.

Assistance. Question 4 is to evaluate whether our system can benefit customers, leading to better decisions on the purchase of fashion items like clothes. The result is between agree and strongly agree, indicating that our system do indeed help users in general.

Potential Application. Question 5 explored the application prospect of our system. Result shows that our system has a lot of potential.

In general, the average scores of all questions were higher than 3 (neutral), which implies that our system was generally viewed as positive in all aspects. This might verify that our system designs are reasonable and practical.

8   Conclusion and Future Work

In this paper, we present an AR fashion show system which uses personalized 3D human models of users. Our system enables ordinary customers an immersive fashion show experience within their real environment. A preliminary evaluation was conducted to validate our system. It demonstrated that our system is effective and can help customers make better decisions on the purchase of clothes, having potential applications in future.

Since the fashion industry has the features of diversity and is rapidly changing, we need to supplement or change the clothes models in time. In future, we hope to improve the quality and quantity of clothes model in order to increase the universality of our system.

References

1. Fashion show. https://en.wikipedia.org/wiki/Fashion_show. Accessed 30 Jan 2020
2. Ready-to-wear. https://en.wikipedia.org/wiki/Ready-to-wear. Accessed 30 Jan 2020
3. Chanel ready-to-wear collection. https://en.wikipedia.org/wiki/Chanel_ready-to-wear_coll ection. Accessed 30 Jan 2020
4. https://www.youtube.com/watch?v=YMGnLDcx-mA. Accessed 30 Jan 2020
5. https://www.youtube.com/watch?v=4r73e2MjaB4. Accessed 30 Jan 2020
6. http://www.threemediacentre.co.uk/news/2019/three-launch-worlds-first-5g-mixed-reality-catwalk-at-london-fashion-week-featuring-lennon-gallagher.aspx. Accessed 30 Jan 2020
7. Okada, R., Stenger, B., Ike, T., Kondoh, N.: Virtual fashion show using real-time markerless motion capture. In: Narayanan, P.J., Nayar, Shree K., Shum, H.-Y. (eds.) ACCV 2006. LNCS, vol. 3852, pp. 801–810. Springer, Heidelberg (2006). https://doi.org/10.1007/11612704_80
8. Gray, S.: In virtual fashion. IEEE Spectr. **35**(2), 18–25 (1998)
9. Gavrila, D.M., Davis, L.S.: 3-D model-based tracking of humans in action: a multi-view approach. In: Proceedings of CVPR IEEE Computer Society Conference on Computer Vision and Pattern Recognition, pp. 73–80. IEEE (1996)
10. Metaxas, D., Terzopoulos, D.: Shape and nonrigid motion estimation through physics-based synthesis. IEEE Trans. Pattern Anal. Mach. Intell. **15**(6), 580–591 (1993)
11. Plankers, R., Fua, P.: Articulated soft objects for video-based body modeling. In: Proceedings Eighth IEEE International Conference on Computer Vision, ICCV 2001, vol. 1, pp. 394–401. IEEE (2001)
12. Hasler, N., Stoll, C., Sunkel, M., Rosenhahn, B., Seidel, H.P.: A statistical model of human pose and body shape. In: Computer Graphics Forum, vol. 28, no. 2, pp. 337–346. Blackwell Publishing Ltd., Oxford (2009)
13. Zuffi, S., Black, M.J.: The stitched puppet: a graphical model of 3D human shape and pose. In: Proceedings of the IEEE Conference on Computer Vision and Pattern Recognition, pp. 3537–3546. IEEE (2015)
14. Loper, M., Mahmood, N., Romero, J., Pons-Moll, G., Black, M.J.: SMPL: a skinned multi-person linear model. ACM Trans. Graph. (TOG) **34**(6), 1–16 (2015)
15. Bogo, F., Kanazawa, A., Lassner, C., Gehler, P., Romero, J., Black, M.J.: Keep it SMPL: automatic estimation of 3D human pose and shape from a single image. In: Leibe, B., Matas, J., Sebe, N., Welling, M. (eds.) ECCV 2016. LNCS, vol. 9909, pp. 561–578. Springer, Cham (2016). https://doi.org/10.1007/978-3-319-46454-1_34
16. Alldieck, T., Magnor, M., Xu, W., Theobalt, C., Pons-Moll, G.: Video based reconstruction of 3D people models. In: Proceedings of the IEEE Conference on Computer Vision and Pattern Recognition, pp. 8387–8397. IEEE (2018)
17. Han, X., Wu, Z., Wu, Z., Yu, R., Davis, L.S.: VITON: an image-based virtual try-on network. In: Proceedings of the IEEE Conference on Computer Vision and Pattern Recognition, pp. 7543–7552. IEEE (2018)
18. Sekine, M., Sugita, K., Perbet, F., Stenger, B., Nishiyama, M.: Virtual fitting by single-shot body shape estimation. In: Proceedings of International Conference on 3D Body Scanning Technologies, pp. 406–413. Citeseer (2014)
19. Decaudin, P., Julius, D., Wither, J., Boissieux, L., Sheffer, A., Cani, M.P.: Virtual garments: a fully geometric approach for clothing design. In: Proceedings of Computer Graphics Forum, vol. 25, no. 3, pp. 625–634. Blackwell Publishing, Inc., Oxford (2006)
20. Hilsmann, A., Eisert, P.: Tracking and retexturing cloth for real-time virtual clothing applications. In: Gagalowicz, A., Philips, W. (eds.) MIRAGE 2009. LNCS, vol. 5496, pp. 94–105. Springer, Heidelberg (2009). https://doi.org/10.1007/978-3-642-01811-4_9

21. Yamada, H., Hirose, M., Kanamori, Y., Mitani, J., Fukui, Y.: Image-based virtual fitting system with garment image reshaping. In: Proceedings of 2014 International Conference on Cyberworlds, pp. 47–54. IEEE (2014)
22. Yuan, M., Khan, I.R., Farbiz, F., Yao, S., Niswar, A., Foo, M.H.: A mixed reality virtual clothes try-on system. IEEE Trans. Multimed. **15**(8), 1958–1968 (2013)
23. Meng, Y., Mok, P.Y., Jin, X.: Interactive virtual try-on clothing design systems. Comput. Aided Des. **42**(4), 310–321 (2010)
24. Li, R., Zou, K., Xu, X., Li, Y., Li, Z.: Research of interactive 3D virtual fitting room on web environment. In: Proceedings of 2011 Fourth International Symposium on Computational Intelligence and Design, vol. 1, pp. 32–35. IEEE (2011)
25. Warehouse. https://www.warehouselondon.com/row/homepage. Accessed 30 Jan 2020
26. Yu, L.F., Yeung, S.K., Terzopoulos, D., Chan, T.F.: DressUp!: outfit synthesis through automatic optimization. ACM Trans. Graph. **31**(6), 1–134 (2012)
27. How to dress to make the right first impression in 7 scenarios. https://www.mentalfloss.com/article/79760/how-dress-make-right-first-impression-7-scenarios. Accessed 30 Jan 2020
28. Deng, Y., Yang, J., Xu, S., Chen, D., Jia, Y., Tong, X.: Accurate 3D face reconstruction with weakly-supervised learning: from single image to image set. In: Proceedings of the IEEE Conference on Computer Vision and Pattern Recognition Workshops. IEEE (2019)
29. Caelles, S., Maninis, K.K., Pont-Tuset, J., Leal-Taixé, L., Cremers, D., Van Gool, L.: One-shot video object segmentation. In: Proceedings of the IEEE Conference on Computer Vision and Pattern Recognition, pp. 221–230. IEEE (2017)
30. Cao, Z., Simon, T., Wei, S.E., Sheikh, Y.: Realtime multi-person 2D pose estimation using part affinity fields. In: Proceedings of the IEEE Conference on Computer Vision and Pattern Recognition, pp. 7291–7299. IEEE (2017)
31. Wang, L., Villamil, R., Samarasekera, S., Kumar, R.: Magic mirror: a virtual handbag shopping system. In: Proceedings of 2012 IEEE Computer Society Conference on Computer Vision and Pattern Recognition Workshops, pp. 19–24. IEEE (2012)
32. H&M. https://www.hm.com. Accessed 30 Jan 2020
33. ZARA. https://www.zara.com. Accessed 30 Jan 2020
34. Cloth-weaver. https://clothweaver.com. Accessed 30 Jan 2020
35. Mixed reality capture for developers. https://docs.microsoft.com/en-us/windows/mixed-reality/mixed-reality-capture-for-developers. Accessed 30 Jan 2020
36. Cloud Vision documentation. https://cloud.google.com/vision/docs/?hl=en. Accessed 30 Jan 2020
37. Maximo. https://www.mixamo.com. Accessed 30 Jan 2020

Author Index

Adnani, Veda I-85
Ainoya, Takeo I-290
Akakura, Takako I-350
Akimori, Yuna II-175
Amemiya, Tomohiro I-331
Anvari, Sam I-23
Anzalone, Robert II-96
Aoyagi, Saizo II-131
Aoyama, Kazuma I-341
Asahi, Yumi I-201, I-222, I-236
Ayedoun, Emmanuel II-145
Ayvazyan, Aram I-23

Baba, Takumi I-350
Babaian, Tamara I-183
Bai, Xiaolu I-23
Bannai, Yuichi II-231
Bao, Qian-yu II-365
Barbosa, Simone Diniz Junqueira I-104
Bonacin, Rodrigo II-3
Bowes, Jeremy I-85
Braune, Annerose I-377
Brauner, Philipp II-111
Bredholt, Mathias I-156, II-447
Brenger, Bela II-324
Brillowski, Florian II-111
Butterfield, Joseph II-305

Casement, Alf II-305
Catini, Rita de Cássia II-3
Chen, Ting II-385
Chen, Xiang II-385
Chen, Yuhong II-385
Chen, Zhijiang I-250
Cheng, Kelvin I-363, I-435
Choh, Ikuro I-301
Côrtes Vieira Lopes, Hélio I-104

Daraseneeyakul, Paporn II-433
de Almeida, Rodrigo B. I-104
de Macedo, Paulo Cesar II-3
de Sousa, Alysson Gomes I-104
Desai, Prasad II-96

Diamond, Sara I-85
dos Reis, Julio Cesar II-3
Du, Yin-lan II-365

Feng, Jinjuan Heidi I-250
Ferguson, Robin Stuart II-305
Frisson, Christian I-156
Fujimoto, Yuki II-245
Fujisawa, Satoshi I-407
Fukuda, Ken I-265
Fukuda, Takuto II-375
Fukumori, Satoshi II-131
Fürhoff, Loïc I-3

Gibson, Zara II-305
Gosho, Kakiha II-529
Gotoda, Naka II-164, II-469
Guan, Kathleen I-125

Hamasaki, Ryodai II-491
Hancock, Gabriella M. I-23
Hara, Kenta I-201
Hara, Naoyuki II-506
Hashiyama, Tomonori II-350
Hayashi, Toshihiro II-164
Hayashi, Yuki II-145, II-206, II-264
Herdel, Viviane I-39
Herrmann, Thomas I-72
Hikawa, Naoto II-469
Hofeditz, Lennart II-324
Hsu, Su-Chu II-479
Hsu, Yen I-170, II-278, II-418
Huang, Fanwei II-529
Huang, Yu-Hsiung II-479
Huang, Zhentao II-65

Iizuka, Shigeyoshi I-212
Ikei, Yasushi I-407
Izumi, Tomoko II-289

Jansen, Bernard J. I-125
Jelonek, Markus I-58, I-72
Jung, Soon-gyo I-125

Kacmaz, Ufuk   I-72
Kaida, Keita   II-338
Kano, Toru   I-350
Kasamatsu, Keiko   I-290
Kato, Hiroshi   II-55
Kato, Yoshiharu   II-350
Kawaguchi, Kaito   II-433
Kewalramani, Iman   I-85
Kinoe, Yosuke   II-175
Kirkegaard, Mathias   II-447
Kitajima, Eiki   II-194
Kitamura, Takayoshi   II-289
Kitazaki, Michiteru   I-407
Kodaka, Asuka   I-212
Kojima, Hisashi   II-457
Kojiri, Tomoko   II-22
Kometani, Yusuke   II-164, II-469
Kondo, Masaru   I-222
Kondo, Nobuhiko   II-55
Kubota, Ryoji   II-219
Kunieda, Takayuki   II-469
Kuniwa, Tomoki   II-433
Kuzuoka, Hideaki   II-407

Lanezki, Mathias   I-39
Lee, Yu-Chi   II-395
Li, Zhinan   I-363
Liang, Zhipeng   II-506
Lin, Feng Cheng   II-519
Lin, Yixiong   II-385
Liu, Boyang   I-363
Liu, Jun-jie   II-365
Liu, Shih-Ta   II-479
Liu, Yuhan   I-435
Liu, Yuzhao   I-435
López, Ania   II-324
Lotfalian Saremi, Mostaan   II-96
Lu, Pei Wen   II-519
Lüdtke, Andreas   I-39

Ma, Ruichen   I-363
Maekawa, Yoshimiki   II-194
Maeshiro, Midori   II-39
Maeshiro, Tetsuya   II-39
Mariano, Greice C.   I-85
Martin, Christopher   I-377
Masuko, Soh   I-363, I-435
Mather, Gregory P.   I-23
Matsuda, Takeshi   II-55

Matsuyama, Yoshio   I-236
Matthews, Theresa   I-250
McBride, Amanda S.   I-23
McCoy, Kelsey M.   I-23
Meneses, Eduardo A. L.   II-375
Meng, Jian   II-385
Mok, Nicole B.   I-23
Morales, Natalia   I-23
Mori, Hirohiko   I-279, I-417, II-338
Muramatsu, Shoki   I-145
Muroya, Daiki   II-206

Nagaoka, Keizo   II-219
Nakamura, Keisuke   II-491
Nakashima, Yusuke   II-231
Nakatani, Yoshio   II-289
Nakayama, Koichi   II-457, II-491
Nakazawa, Hiro   I-212
Nare, Matthew T.   I-23
Nielsen, Lene   I-125
Nihei, Yasunori   II-506
Niida, Sumaru   I-312
Nishii, Shozo   I-212
Nishimura, Hiromitsu   II-433
Nishimura, Satoshi   I-265

Obuchi, Kohei   I-363
Ohta, Eiji   II-433
Oka, Makoto   I-279, I-417, II-338
Okubo, Masashi   II-245
Oota, Yuichi   I-265
Oshima, Chika   II-457, II-491
Otsuki, Mai   II-407
Oura, Fuko   I-290
Ozawa, Yuri   II-39

Pan, Jiemao   II-385
Peng, Xiangjun   II-65, II-78

Rafferty, Karen   II-305
Rehwald, Stephanie   II-324
Ribeiro, Dalai S.   I-104
Roorda, Matthew J.   I-85
Ross, Björn   II-324
Rother, Marius   II-324
Rudolph, Dominik   II-324

Saga, Ryosuke   II-506
Sagawa, Yuji   I-393

Salminen, Joni   I-125
Saremi, Razieh   II-96
Sato, Yuji   II-407
Schaar, Anne Kathrin   II-111
Schemmer, Thomas   II-111
Seta, Kazuhisa   II-145, II-206, II-264
Shen, Yang Ting   II-519
Shibata, Yuri   I-393
Shigeta, Katsusuke   II-55
Shimohara, Katsunori   I-145, II-254, II-529
Shioya, Ryo   I-145
Shiozu, Yurika   I-145
Song, Zilin   II-65
Sugikami, Akio   II-22
Sugimoto, Aoi   II-264
Sun, Xitong   I-435
Sun, Xu   II-65, II-78
Suzuki, Yusuke   II-407

Takadama, Keiki   II-194
Takahara, Madoka   II-529
Takahashi, Kyosuke   II-469
Takebe, Takanori   I-212
Takenouchi, Kaname   I-301
Takesue, Naoyuki   II-539
Tanaka, Hiroshi   II-433
Tanaka, Jiro   I-363, I-435
Tanaka, Mizuki   I-145
Tanaka, Toshimitsu   I-393
Tanev, Ivan   II-529
Tang, Bin   II-385
Tanimoto, Eriko   I-212
Tano, Shun'ichi   II-350
Terui, Chiharu   I-279
Thompson Furtado, Pedro Henrique   I-104
Tokunaga, Toru   I-350
Tsukatsune, Kenta   I-312

Ueda, Sachiyo   I-407
Uwano, Fumito   II-194

Veerakiatikit, Phaphimon   II-433
Vogl, Raimund   II-324

Wanderley, Marcelo M.   I-156, II-375, II-447
Wang, Bo   I-85
Wang, Huabin   II-395
Wang, Jian   I-170
Wang, Qingfeng   II-78
Wang, Rui   I-183
Wang, Shuolei   II-78
Wang, Tzu-Yang   II-407
Wang, Xinyan   II-278
Wang, Zhizhong   II-433
Watanabe, Kyosuke   I-417
Watanabe, Yuki   II-55
Wilms, Konstantin   II-324
Wortelen, Bertram   I-39

Xiao, Chao   II-385
Xu, Baoping   II-395
Xu, Rui   II-418
Xu, Shihui   I-435

Yaegashi, Rihito   II-164, II-469
Yamamoto, Michiya   II-131
Yamamoto, Sakae   I-279
Yang, Chen   II-65
Yang, Junbiao   II-385
Yasui, Tomonori   II-289
Yokota, Taiga   II-539
Yonemaru, Koichiro   II-469
Yonezaki, Katsuhiko   I-145
Yoshida, Haruka   I-312
Yu, Wai   II-305
Yuan, Jingyi   I-435

Zhang, Hongzhi   II-78
Zhang, Rui-rui   II-365
Zheng, Ying   I-250
Zhou, Xiaosong   II-78
Ziefle, Martina   II-111